Rethinking the Case Study in International Business and Management Research

Rethinking the Case Study in International Business and Management Research

Edited by

Rebecca Piekkari

Aalto University, School of Economics, Finland

Catherine Welch

University of Sydney, Australia

Edward Elgar

Cheltenham, UK • Northampton, MA, USA

Published by
Edward Elgar Publishing Limited
The Lypiatts
15 Lansdown Road
Cheltenham
Glos GL50 2JA
UK

Edward Elgar Publishing, Inc.
William Pratt House
9 Dewey Court
Northampton
Massachusetts 01060
USA

A catalogue record for this book
is available from the British Library

Library of Congress Control Number: 2011922865

MIX
Paper from
responsible sources
FSC® C018575
www.fsc.org

ISBN 978 1 84844 184 2 (cased)

Typeset by Servis Filmsetting Ltd, Stockport, Cheshire
Printed and bound by MPG Books Group, UK

Contents

PART V TAKING ACCOUNT OF DIVERSE CONTEXTS

Contributors

Yair Aharoni, Professor Emeritus, Faculty of Management, Tel Aviv University, Israel.

Pasi Ahonen, Research Fellow, Bristol Centre for Leadership and Organizational Ethics, University of the West of England, UK.

Phil Almond, Reader in International and Comparative HRM, De Montfort University, UK.

Poul Houman Andersen, Professor, Aarhus School of Business and Social Sciences, Aarhus University, Denmark.

Susanne Blazejewski, Professor of Management and Organisation, Alanus University, Germany.

Mary Yoko Brannen, Visiting Professor of Strategy and Management, INSEAD, France and Spansion Chair of Multicultural Integration, Lucas Graduate School of Business, San Jose State University, USA.

Trevor Buck, Professor Emeritus of International Business, Loughborough University, UK.

Ed Clark, Professor of Organisation Studies, Royal Holloway, University of London, UK.

Trevor Colling, Senior Lecturer in Industrial Relations, Warwick Business School, University of Warwick, UK.

Philippe d'Iribarne, Director of Research, CNRS, France.

Tony Edwards, Reader in Comparative HRM, King's College, UK.

Margaret Fletcher, Lecturer in International Business and Marketing, University of Glasgow, UK.

Jean Helms Mills, Professor of Management, Sobey School of Business, Saint Mary's University, Canada.

Leila Hurmerinta, Professor of Marketing, Turku School of Economics, University of Turku, Finland.

Robert J. Jensen, Assistant Professor of Strategy and International Business, Brigham Young University, USA.

Martin Johanson, Professor of Business Administration, Department of Business Studies, Uppsala University, Sweden.

Hanne Kragh, Associate Professor, Aarhus School of Business and Social Sciences, Aarhus University, Denmark.

Jon Erland B. Lervik, Associate Professor, Department of Leadership and Organizational Management, Norwegian School of Management BI, Norway.

Albert J. Mills, Director, PhD Business Administration (Management), Sobey School of Business, Saint Mary's University, Canada.

Raza Mir, Professor of Marketing and Management Sciences, William Paterson University, USA.

Fiona Moore, Lecturer in International Human Resource Management, Royal Holloway, University of London, UK.

Ricardo Morais, Professor of Management and Strategy, Catholic University of Portugal, Portugal.

Matti Nojonen, Programme Director, Transformation of the World Order Research Programme, Finnish Institute of International Affairs, Finland.

Niina Nummela, Professor of International Business, Turku School of Economics, University of Turku, Finland.

Rebecca Piekkari, Professor of International Business, School of Economics, Aalto University (formerly Helsinki School of Economics), Finland.

Emmanuella Plakoyiannaki, Assistant Professor of Marketing, Aristotle's University of Thessaloniki, Greece.

Ayse Saka-Helmhout, Reader in International Management, University of Surrey, UK.

Asta Salmi, Professor of International Business, School of Economics, Aalto University (formerly Helsinki School of Economics), Finland.

Anna Soulsby, Associate Professor of Organisational Behaviour, Nottingham University Business School, University of Nottingham, UK.

Gabriel Szulanski, Professor of Strategy, INSEAD, Singapore.

Hui Tan, Reader in Strategy, Royal Holloway, University of London, UK.

Janne Tienari, Professor, Organizations and Management, School of Economics, Aalto University (formerly Helsinki School of Economics), Finland.

Eero Vaara, Professor of Management, Hanken School of Economics and Business Administration, Helsinki.

Catherine Welch, Senior Lecturer, University of Sydney, Australia.

April Wright, Senior Lecturer in Strategy, UQ Business School, University of Queensland, Australia.

Foreword

In my childhood there was only one variety of sports shoe, whose sole was made of rubber and the upper part of cloth, either white or dark blue. This was used for all sports, from football to handball, both indoor and outdoor. Product development has led to differentiation so that there are now numerous varieties of shoes for – to take an example – jogging, depending on the track or the floor, the weight of the individual and the jogging style. Ultimately, a person can have individualized shoes adjusted to his or her specific needs. We are moving in a similar direction with regard to case study methodology, which is differentiated to fit the objective and the context of the research. When I started to do research, there was only one way of doing case studies and the only acceptable motivation for doing them was to 'dig up' issues on which to focus 'serious' research.

This attitude, I believe, was based on a little-brother complex *vis-à-vis* the sciences – such as physics and chemistry – where large-scale data collection under strictly controlled circumstances allowed statistical analyses. That was research! We tried to imitate. Over time I think we have gradually dropped bits of that inferiority complex, realizing that the objects of study in business and management are quite different from those of the sciences, based as the latter are on 'eternal laws'. However, I think we, as the collective of researchers in international business and management, still have some distance to travel before we are able to think completely independently about what constitutes high-quality research in our areas. This book adds to the knowledge of the repertoire we have. That is a great contribution.

'Pluralism', the first word of the title to the introductory chapter, sets a wonderful tone to this book. It signals an openness towards new ideas while acknowledging that some older thinking on case study methodology has merit, and that quality levels must be upheld. I believe we must be generous to each other in judging the case methodologies that we apply. While there is a delicate balance between these two criteria, in my mind, we should err in the direction of generosity. I have attended conferences, not in international business I am eager to point out, where discussions have been destroyed by proponents for different methodologies accusing each other of 'not sticking to the true faith'. So, sectarianism should not be mistaken for quality.

A number of years back, there was an evaluation made by American business and industry concerning activities performed by business school professors. It turned out that those in business, when responding to the survey, were pleased with the quality of the educational programmes offered. They were, on the other hand, very critical towards the relevance of the research produced at those schools. In my mind, there is something to that view and I believe that doing case study research will create an improved understanding of and interest in research into the realities of management, and stimulate more of us to think about relevance to practitioners. And the realities of management are exciting indeed!

At the annual meeting of the Academy of Management in 2004 I was asked to take part in a session to honour the memory of Sumantra Ghoshal by talking about how to produce pathbreaking research. Those of us who spoke were surprisingly united in suggesting that some of the secrets were: inductive case studies, working in a group of people rather than as individuals and staying with the research theme for a relatively long time. I take the opportunity to pass on this prescription, echoed in the objective of this book. Working inductively by no means implies that the researcher should be a-theoretical. On the contrary, in my opinion, the researcher should be well versed in the theory of the firm, and perhaps in some more specific theories, but staying open when interpreting what has been discovered.

This volume indeed brings insight into the large and complex area of case study methodologies. There will no doubt be numerous references to it, and it will raise the quality not only of the 'methodological chapter' of dissertations and reports but also of the research itself. Hopefully, that will be true also for articles in journals, which we must ensure publish case study research.

I would like to congratulate the editors as they have been able to find and enlist so many skilled authors to produce insightful chapters on various aspects of case study methodology.

Jan-Erik Vahlne
Gothenburg, November 2010

Acknowledgements

Early career researchers are often advised not to waste their time on book chapters, not to mention editing or writing entire books. Given that books or chapters in books do not count in academic career progression, they are often regarded as activities that simply distract our attention from what we should be focusing on, namely getting published in top-tier refereed journals. We have already challenged this view once by editing the *Handbook of Qualitative Research for International Business*, published in 2004. Now we are following it up with what is not a second edition of the *Handbook*, but rather a more focused volume devoted solely to the most popular qualitative research strategy in international business (IB), namely the case study.

In retrospect, what have we gained from the two book projects? We believe that the two books have opened up a new debate about the (mis) use of qualitative methods in IB and international management (IM) research. We are very pleased to see that this debate continues and gains prominence at international conferences and in special issues of journals. This would not have been possible without the support of contributors to both the previous and present volumes. They did not just write their individual chapters, but also, in the case of many, attended panel sessions at various conferences. We would also like to thank the conference audiences who provided us with feedback along the way, as well as those who were involved in the conference sessions as participants or conference chairs.

Specifically, in 2006, at the annual conference of the European International Business Academy (EIBA) in Fribourg, Switzerland, Stephen Young chaired a session in which we presented the initial idea of the case study as a disciplinary convention. Emmanuella Plakoyiannaki, one of Stephen's collaborators, was in the audience and this encounter marked the beginning of our very fruitful research partnership with her. We are extremely grateful to Stephen for connecting us with Emmanuella and for his support and encouragement in our efforts to raise the profile of qualitative methods in IB in general and case research in particular. In 2009, Stephen organized and co-hosted the annual conference of the Academy of International Business (AIB) UK and Ireland Chapter at the University of Glasgow in Scotland. Thanks to Stephen, we were allocated an entire track devoted to case study methodology together with Emmanuella, and in our sessions several book contributors presented their work: Margaret Fletcher, Leila Hurmerinta, Fiona Moore, Niina Nummela and Ayse Saka-Helmhout.

In a Professional Development Workshop of the Academy of Management (AOM) in Philadelphia in 2007, Raza Mir presented an early version of his chapter. We would like to thank Stuart Macdonald for coming up with a catchy title for this workshop, namely 'Making case study research count: best practices and future directions'. Later in the same year the EIBA conference was organized in Catania, Italy; Ricardo Morais as well as Asta Salmi took part in our special session on case studies. At the following year's EIBA conference in Tallinn, it was the turn of Ed Clark, Margaret Fletcher, Emmanuella Plakoyiannaki and Anna Soulsby to present their work.

In 2008 the annual conference of the AIB was organized in Europe, this time in Milan, Italy. Our panel – entitled 'How to theorize from field-work?' – turned out to be an important theme for our book, for teaching and for later publications. As well as Mary Yoko Brannen and Gabriel Szulanski presenting their chapters, Lorraine Eden, then Editor-in-Chief of the *Journal of International Business Studies*, shared her experiences and observations about publishing qualitative research, particularly case studies. In this session, she announced that *JIBS* would have a special issue devoted to 'Qualitative Research in International Business', for which Mary Yoko Brannen became one of the guest editors. Yves Doz acted as discussant of the panel and reflected upon the panellists' contributions in the light of his career as a prominent case researcher.

The AOM held its annual meeting in Chicago in 2009 and, in response to an initiative from Jane Salk, we co-organized a panel entitled 'Making the case: rhetoric, rigor and "getting it right" with case study research'. We would like to thank her for her passionate presentation on how much the case study has lost during the process of making itself 'legitimate' as a scientific research strategy. We would also like to thank her for the opportunity to develop, in the panel proposal, many of the ideas that we later fleshed out in our introductory chapter to this book.

The last session associated with the present book took place at the EIBA annual conference in Porto, Portugal 2010. Our special thanks are due to Ana Tavares-Lehmann, the EIBA President, who accepted our panel proposal out of the many that she received from the IB community. We would also like to thank our book contributors who were willing to present the final versions of their work at EIBA 2010: Susanne Blazejewski, Ed Clark, Margaret Fletcher, Martin Johanson, Jon Erland Lervik, Emmanuella Plakoyiannaki and Anna Soulsby.

We were very fortunate that both our home institutions, Aalto University, School of Economics (formerly Helsinki School of Economics), and the University of Sydney are academic members of the Global Alliance in Management Education (CEMS). This alliance provided financial support to our PhD courses in Finland and brought some additional students from other CEMS partners into the classroom. Our course, entitled 'CEMS Doctoral Course on Case Studies in Management and Business Research', was an excellent forum for refining our ideas for the book. It soon became very obvious to us that these bright students were not just a passive audience on whom we could test our emerging ideas. On the contrary, they kept challenging us during the critical 'product development process' and helped us communicate in an accessible way the more complex themes of the book, such as the practical relevance of different philosophical assumptions for the case researcher. As most students were very receptive to our emerging ideas, we found them a source of inspiration and energy. We were also able to give seminars on the case study to PhD students at the University of Leeds. We owe this opportunity to our colleagues at the Centre for International Business at the University of Leeds: Peter Buckley, Malcolm Chapman, Jeremy Clegg and Hanna Gajewska-De Mattos. We wish to express our gratitude to them for making this possible and for being such generous hosts.

We very much appreciate that Jan-Erik Vahlne accepted without hesitation our invitation to write a foreword. In a book that is looking to the future of case research, we are grateful that he – along with Christopher Bartlett and Yair Aharoni – could ground this vision in the achievements of the past. We would also like to thank Malcolm Cunningham, another researcher who recognized the potential of case studies early on, for his kind encouragement.

During the editing process, we have been assisted by others. Julian Birkinshaw facilitated the interview with Christopher Bartlett. We would like to thank Geoff Easton, Joel Hietanen and Kalle Pajunen for their expertise on critical realism and their helpful comments on Ricardo Morais's chapter. Mika Skippari, a specialist in historical longitudinal research, provided us with insightful views on Susanne Blazejewski's chapter. We are indebted to Fanny Salignac for her expertise in translating Philippe d'Iribarne's chapter from French to English, and to Martin Fougère for turning the French references of this chapter into English at very short notice. Fanny's assistance was instrumental in overcoming the language barrier that would have prevented us from fully appreciating the contribution of d'Iribarne's chapter.

The two books that we have edited have both been published by Edward Elgar. We have very much enjoyed working with the Edward Elgar team and we would like to extend our thanks to Edward Elgar himself who has during his regular trips to Sydney always taken the time to visit Catherine and express his support for our endeavour. We have been blessed to have had as our editor Francine O'Sullivan, whose professionalism and extensive knowledge of IB as a field have been an important resource for us.

In 2007 Catherine spent a one-year sabbatical in Finland at the Hanken School of Economics and Business Administration. We would like to thank Ingmar Björkman for inviting her to the Department of Management and Organization and for his generosity and support towards this project. We also gave a seminar to the PhD students of the Nordic Research School of International Business (NORD-IB) programme, of which Ingmar is a founding member. Catherine's sabbatical enabled us to have regular meetings with Eriikka Paavilainen-Mäntymäki, with whom we have collaborated for several years. We would like to thank Eriikka for sharing our journey through the case study literature.

Rebecca came to Sydney to work on the book for a month during Christmas and New Year in 2008–09. We very much appreciate the financial support granted by the following foundations: Helsingin kauppakorkeakoulun Tukisäätiö, Ella and Georg Ehrnroothin säätiö, Liikesivistysrahasto, Marcus Wallenbergin säätiö and Jenny and Antti Wihurin rahasto. The confidence that they expressed in our work enabled us to be physically co-located for at least part of the editorial process.

We would also like to thank Galina Velikodnaia, who provided meticulous assistance in formatting the 25 book chapters under a tight schedule. Bea Alanko also became involved in the book project when we needed her excellent computer skills to handle the lay-out and visualization of complex figures in the chapters.

Ben Aveling, Catherine's husband, has been an irreplaceable resource during our two book projects. This time he played the roles of technical support and graphical designer, among others. Lauri Piekkari, Rebecca's husband, has been very patient and understanding during the long project. However, what has puzzled him as a business practitioner is the strong motivation that has kept us going for so long without foreseeable monetary rewards. The answer lies in the pleasure of working closely with a great colleague and friend, and of making discoveries, even small ones, along the way. That is what we have gained from embarking on book projects.

PART I

Past, present and future of case studies in international business and international management research

1. Pluralism in international business and international management research: making the case

Rebecca Piekkari and Catherine Welch

INTRODUCTION

The purpose of the present volume is to bring together a variety of perspectives on the case study and enrich case study practices in international business (IB) and international management (IM) research. The case study is a key research strategy in the field but to date only a fairly narrow selection of possible case study approaches have been used (Piekkari et al. 2009). Researchers in IB and IM typically rely on a case study approach that could be characterized as 'qualitative positivism' (Prasad 2005, p. 4), and which is loosely derived from the guidelines set out by Eisenhardt (1989) or Yin (2009). This approach to the case study has become a 'disciplinary convention' that prevails even in situations when there would have been another, more appropriate way of 'getting the case study right'. In this book, we position this convention in relation to its alternatives, offering a range of viable options for practising case researchers as well as guidance for those who evaluate case studies.

The dominance of qualitative positivism is not a surprise, given the history of the case study in business and management research. A key milestone for the legitimization of the case study within business and management was the publication of Yin's seminal text in 1984. Platt (1992) has observed that this legitimization occurred at the expense of some of the long-established assumptions, practices and aims associated with this research strategy. In particular, she notes that as a result of Yin's influence, the case study is no longer synonymous with participant observation. She characterizes Yin as 'not especially concerned with time-span and historical depth, with richness of data, or with access to personal meaning, and [he] shows no interest in emphasizing data in people's own words' (Platt 1992, pp. 45–6).

This trend was further reinforced by Eisenhardt's (1989) guide to building theories from case studies, which very much followed Yin's path.

Eisenhardt explicitly noted that her approach to the case study was a positivist one. Such an approach advocates multiple over single case designs, because 'replication' is seen to enable more robust theories. This tradition favours a 'design' logic, in which fieldwork only commences once a detailed 'blueprint' (Yin, 2009) has been specified. Multiple data sources are encouraged as a form of triangulation, which allows the research to converge on a single account. Positivist authors regard case studies as the exploratory stage in the scientific quest to arrive at generalizable laws that specify the relationship between variables regardless of context. Authors working within this tradition take a variable-oriented approach: in other words, cases are decomposed into variables, with each independent variable assumed to have an autonomous influence over variation in the dependent variable (Ragin 1987, 2008). In Eisenhardt's (1989) version of the case study, the end point is the generation of propositions, which form the basis for follow-up large-scale empirical testing (see Figure 1.1, below). This is reflected in the way in which the case study is written up and reported. The body of the text consists of propositions, supported by evidence from each of the cases, with the propositions then linked together in a model (Eisenhardt and Graebner 2007; for an example from research practice, see Gilbert 2005).

Yet within the case approach, diverse schools of thought can be identified, which are very different from one another, as well as from the dominant tradition of 'qualitative positivism'. These alternative perspectives on the case study can be found in the methodological and management literature, even though they may not have had the same prominence in IB research. These schools of thought often originate from other fields (such as ethnography and history), identify themselves with interpretivist or critical realist philosophies and challenge the tenets of positivist case research. In this book we adopt the position that this plurality of case study approaches has been obscured by the popularity of Yin's and Eisenhardt's models. The legitimacy of the case study has been achieved at the expense of narrowing the diverse options available to case researchers.

Recently, there have been signs of a renewed interest in exploring alternative approaches to the case study. While we were preparing the current volume, two landmark publications were released that bring together new methodological developments on the case study. The first is the *Encyclopedia of Case Study Research* (Mills et al. 2010). This two-volume collection seeks to reflect the 'breadth of disciplines, philosophical paradigms, and geographical situatedness' of case study traditions (p. xxxiv). The second publication, *The Sage Handbook of Case-based Methods*, is the most recent in a string of innovations in case research by Charles Ragin and collaborators (Byrne and Ragin 2009). In this volume, they provide an alternative to the nomothetic view of cases as 'sites for observing and measuring variables' (Byrne 2009, p. 2). Criticisms of the nomothetic project are not new; the idiographic alternative, which advocates rich description and the study of the particular, is well established in much of the social sciences, even if it is still rare in IB. The contribution of Ragin and his colleagues is rather that they suggest a third way that 'gets beyond the dichotomies of quantitative/qualitative–explanation/interpretation' (Byrne 2009, p. 2). They argue that once social scientists recognize that the search for universal laws is fictional, case studies enable them 'both to elucidate causation *and* to specify the range of applicability of our account of causal mechanisms' (Byrne 2009, p. 2; original italics). Ragin's work and the possibility of a 'third way' has been a profound influence on us as editors (see also Welch et al. 2011), as it has broadened the possibilities for pluralism in case research.

As well as these developments in the broader methodological literature, the case study also appears to be back on the agenda in business and management disciplines. In 2010, *Industrial Marketing Management* published a special issue on the quality of case research in the study of industrial marketing (see also Piekkari et al. 2010). In the IB field, separate conference sessions and even entire tracks devoted to contemporary methodological issues, including qualitative methods, have become common practice in annual meetings of the Academy of International Business and the European International Business Academy. Interestingly, the special issue of the *Journal of International Business Studies* (2011) on qualitative research attracted the highest number of submissions of any special issue in the entire history of the journal: more than 115 manuscripts.

Twenty-five years following the publication of the first book on the case study (Yin 1984), we argue that it is time pluralism is no longer regarded as a threat to the legitimacy of the case study. The purpose of this volume is to confront the prevailing positivist stereotypes and rhetoric about the case study and open up space for alternative ways of conceiving and using this research strategy. The stereotypes regarding the case study do not just originate from the 'quantitative' camp, but are also held by case researchers themselves. Therefore, our ambition for this volume is to confront them in an explicit and transparent way.

OUR OWN JOURNEY TOWARDS GREATER PLURALISM

Our conviction that the present volume would be useful was formed while conducting an analysis into the articles published in four key IB journals over the 1995–2005 period, as well as one journal from 1975 to 1994 (Piekkari et al. 2009). The starting point for our analysis was to categorize every empirical article published within this period as quantitative, qualitative or case based. For this purpose, we defined the case study as 'a research strategy that examines, through the use of a variety of data sources, a phenomenon in its naturalistic context, with the purpose of "confronting" theory with the empirical world' (Piekkari et al. 2009, p. 569). The definition was the result of our attempt to synthesize the dimensions of the case study commonly mentioned in the methodological literature. First, the case study is usually described as a research strategy rather than a method or methodology (for example, Eisenhardt 1989; Mills et al. 2010). It can be used in conjunction with an array of different methods (for example, interviews, ethnography, content analysis) and methodologies (for example, phenomenology, postmodernism, hermeneutics). Second, it typically combines a range of data sources (for example, Creswell 1994). Third, its focus is on a single entity, event, instance or phenomenon (Creswell 1994; Stake 1995). Fourth, this phenomenon or event is placed in its context (for example, Yin 2009). Finally, the purpose of the case study is to 'generate theory and/or contribute to extant theory' (Mills et al. 2010, p. xxxii).

While case studies were, unsurprisingly, far behind quantitative approaches in popularity, they formed the majority of qualitative articles in our dataset. Based on our review, we realized that understanding qualitative research in IB means coming to terms with the case study. It is also important to note that, while the case study is typically combined with qualitative methods, this does not preclude the use of quantitative methods: 'case study is not synonymous with qualitative methods' (Simons 2009, p. 19). Our review uncovered mixed-method case studies and even a few quantitative case studies (Piekkari et al. 2009). Hurmerinta-Peltomäki and Nummela (2006) argue that mixed methods are under-represented in IB research, so it was not a surprise that mixed-method case studies formed a small part of our dataset. Interestingly, of the 20 case studies published in *JIBS* in the 1995–2005 period, 10 used mixed methods, two were quantitative and eight qualitative.

In the next stage of our investigation, we undertook a qualitative content analysis of each case-based article, making notes on the study's design (for example, the number of cases), data sources and methods of analysis, underlying philosophical assumptions and how the study had been reported. A central finding from this content analysis was that the case studies tended to show similar traits. The 'disciplinary convention' in IB research was exploratory, interview-based multiple case studies, drawing on positivist assumptions and cross-sectional designs. By 'exploratory' we mean, following Yin (2009, p. 9), that the objective is to 'develop pertinent hypotheses and propositions for further inquiry'. However, in the published case study articles we analysed, the term 'exploratory' was often used in a very broad sense, as a synonym for qualitative research in general.

It might be argued that the prevalence of a disciplinary convention is necessary, in that it provides an initial roadmap for case researchers, as well as a template for reviewers when assessing the quality of a case study. As Pratt (2009) has observed, qualitative research generally suffers from the lack of a template or 'boilerplate'. However, a contention underlying this book is that ultimately, a disciplinary convention can be counterproductive – particularly if it is seen as the only way in which case studies should be conducted. In such situations, the disciplinary convention turns into a disciplinary cage, limiting reflexive and innovative applications of the case study.

Our reasons for seeking to go beyond the current disciplinary convention are manifold. First, the very strength of the case study lies in its diversity and flexibility. As a research strategy, the case study is responsive to different research questions, divergent philosophical assumptions and to variations in context. The case study has a rich and varied history that has been traced back to the Chicago School in the US, Bronislaw Malinowski's ethnographies and Frédéric Le Play's fieldwork in nineteenth-century France (Hamel 1993). Some of this original richness was undoubtedly lost in recent years when Eisenhardt and Yin codified the case study as a 'scientific' approach but in the process distanced themselves from what Dyer and Wilkins (1991) label the 'classic' in-depth case study.

Second, the current disciplinary convention in IB contains numerous weaknesses and internal contradictions. Perhaps most seriously, it inclines towards sacrificing depth for breadth: not only are multiple case studies the norm, but one-third of the multiple case studies were what we termed 'large-N cases' in that they contained more than the 4–10 cases recommended by Eisenhardt (1989). Inevitably, this meant that as the number of cases increased, the number of informants per case fell and the rich contextual insights were lost (Piekkari et al. 2009). Therefore, we concur with the judgement of Dubois and Gadde (2002, p. 558) that '[i]t is difficult to comprehend how a little depth and a little width could contribute to the analysis of any problem'.

Third, as suggested above, the role of the case study tends to be limited to early, exploratory stages of theory building and development rather than theory testing. As Figure 1.1 illustrates, positivists (most notably Eisenhardt 1989) regard the case study as an instrument to develop hypotheses that can subsequently be tested in large-scale surveys through

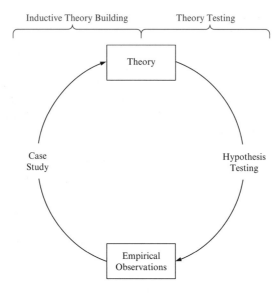

Figure 1.1   Eisenhardt's positivist circle

statistical analyses. Put more strongly, the case study *per se* is not valuable, rather it is viewed only as an intermediary step in the quest for generalizable laws and context-free explanations. However, case researchers subscribing to interpretivism or critical realism, for example, grant a much broader role to the case study in theorizing (Welch et al. 2011).

Fourth, one of the tensions and internal contradictions in the current disciplinary convention stems from Eisenhardt's (1989) original work. Eisenhardt associates her approach of building theory from case studies with induction (see Figure 1.1). On the one hand, she warns against the use of pre-existing theory before entering the field by stating that '[t]heory-building research is begun as close as possible to the ideal of no theory under consideration and no hypotheses to test' (p. 536). On the other hand, Eisenhardt (p. 536) advises case researchers, upon getting started, to engage in 'a priori specification of constructs' as it can also 'help to shape the initial design of the theory-building research' and 'permits researchers to measure constructs more accurately'. Her use of the term 'induction' reflects underlying positivist assumptions that case researchers citing her may not be aware of and do not share. As PhD students ourselves in the 1990s we were definitely not aware of these underlying philosophical assumptions and found it challenging to follow Eisenhardt's seemingly straightforward steps in building theory. Moreover, Eisenhardt's (p. 546) theory-building 'process is alive with tension between divergence into new ways of understanding the data and convergence onto a single theoretical framework'. Perhaps it does not come as a surprise that Eisenhardt's theory-building approach has often been misinterpreted and wrongly applied in research practice (Piekkari et al. 2009).

In our investigation of the case study in IB research, we analysed the final version of the case studies as they appeared in print, so we were not able to trace their journey to publication. We can therefore only speculate about the reasons why the disciplinary convention has taken hold. However, as we are ourselves case study researchers who submit to IB journals, we are all too familiar with the pressures to conform to quantitative standards and positivist assumptions – even if these prescriptions are misguided or even wrong when applied to the case study. To take a recent example of a case study that one of us submitted to the *Journal of World Business*, the following comment was received from a reviewer, and then repeated by the relevant senior editor as a major reason for rejecting the paper:

> You have an N of just five for the research – a very small sample, despite the number of people you interviewed . . . Given your research question, it would have been more effective – even within a qualitative study – to conduct interviews within a larger sample of companies. Eisenhardt recommends a larger sample than five companies . . .

This comment does not just constitute a misreading of Eisenhardt, who, as we have mentioned, famously – and controversially – advocates between four and 10 cases. It also reveals the lingering influence of quantitative surveys, in which the larger the sample size, the more credible the results. This reviewer's comment seems to encapsulate the hidden pressures that drive IB scholars towards the large-N case study. When queried about these misconceptions, the *JWB* co-editor did not intervene to ensure that the case study was judged according to appropriate standards – and was not even prepared to acknowledge that the reviewer had misquoted Eisenhardt. We are sure that readers of this book will have their own war stories to tell of the vagaries of the review process. Our own sense is that in IB/IM as a field, knowledge about how to recognize a quality case study is still not widespread enough to ensure that a case-based article is assessed on its merits. We believe that the chapters in this volume will be instrumental in educating editors and reviewers about the case study as a research strategy and will provide case researchers with authoritative references. This would transform the tone of methodological sections in published case studies from the overly defensive to the confident and accessible.

For the above reasons, this volume seeks to go beyond the 'disciplinary convention' and encourage greater pluralism in IB and IM case research. We argue that increased awareness of prevailing disciplinary conventions

– and their limitations – increases the potential for methodological innovation in case research. It also encourages an open debate about how, as
a scholarly community, we can judge the quality of case research. In the
next section, we discuss how the chapters in this book contribute to a more
pluralist future.

STRUCTURE OF THIS BOOK AND OVERVIEW OF ITS CONTRIBUTIONS

This collection of chapters aims to be an eye-opener for those who have
little experience and training in qualitative methods, as well as seasoned
researchers with preconceived notions about the case study. It consists of
25 chapters that are organized under five broad themes: (i) past, present
and future of case studies in international business and management
research, (ii) multiple paradigms for theorizing, (iii) alternative case study
designs, (iv) the potential of multiple data sources and analytical methods
and (v) taking account of diverse contexts. Thus we hope to enrich case
study practices in a number of ways: in terms of philosophical approaches,
conceptions of theorizing, case study design, data sources and analytical methods used, temporal and spatial boundaries, levels and units of
analysis as well as the range of research contexts in which case studies are
undertaken.

Unlike many methodological texts and guidebooks that introduce the
case study as a research strategy, this book takes an additional step by
also incorporating the use of the case study in theorizing. We show how a
discussion of the philosophical foundations of the case study can be very
practical for conducting and evaluating case research. We also devote
particular attention to rethinking the theorizing potential of the case
study. Throughout the book we keep the research context of IB and IM at
centre stage. The choice of topics for this book is an outcome of teaching
case-based research for PhD students in several countries, which allowed
extensive 'product development and testing' over the years.

The contributors to this volume examine case study traditions in depth,
and seek to question well-established assumptions about how and why
case studies should be conducted. They challenge persistent myths associated with case research, each chapter offering alternatives to the dominant
convention, based on the authors' own experiences (as case researchers
but also as editorial board members and reviewers) and on their insights
into case methodology. By bringing together a diverse group of scholars
using case studies – diverse in their educational, disciplinary and cultural
backgrounds – we want to stimulate and explore pluralism. We are not

advocating pluralism at the expense of rigour; rather, we would argue that 'getting the case study right' requires an awareness of the different traditions and uses of the case study.

Part I: Past, Present and Future of Case Studies in International Business and Management Research

In Chapter 2, an interview with Professor Emeritus Christopher Bartlett from Harvard Business School provides a 'behind the scenes' insight into his landmark case-based studies. By revealing the methodological underpinnings of his work, Bartlett shows how his case studies were planned and conducted, and also how they were facilitated by, and in turn reinforced, synergies with his classroom teaching and industry engagement.

The interview with Bartlett is followed (in Chapter 3) by the reflections of another influential scholar who also received his doctoral degree from Harvard Business School, Yair Aharoni. In his case-based doctorate, Aharoni used the insights he gained from extensive fieldwork to challenge the economic assumptions about firm behaviour that prevailed at the time. In his chapter, Aharoni weaves together his own experiences of conducting case studies with a defence of studying the singular and the rare.

We then move to the editorial office of the *International Business Review* and have a conversation with Professor Pervez Ghauri, the Editor-in-Chief, about the history and editorial policy of the journal, which has emerged as an important source of greater pluralism in IB (Chapter 4). The understanding and appreciation of the case study as a research strategy in the scientific community of IB and IM not only requires high-quality authors who demonstrate professionalism and in-depth knowledge of the case study and its potential, but is equally dependent on high-quality reviewers and editors who may need to be educated to evaluate the case study on its merits. Ghauri's track record as editor shows how journals can successfully provide leadership in publishing high-quality qualitative work.

Part II: Multiple Paradigms for Theorizing

In this part, we seek to demonstrate that there are multiple paradigms for theorizing from case studies and that paradigmatic assumptions matter. The prevailing convention in IB confines the case study to what Eisenhardt (1989, p. 536) terms 'inductive theory building': in other words, to enter the field as close as possible to the 'ideal of a clean theoretical slate', and from the rich empirical data collected in the field, to generate propositions about the relationships between constructs that hold across all cases (see Figure 1.1).

In this book we adopt the critical position that the dominance of the inductive method of theorizing is limiting. There has been little consideration in the IB field of the case study's potential to test theory, generate causal explanations and challenge existing conceptualizations. It also means that the products of this quest for generalizability – IB theories themselves – are abstracted away from context and run the risk of being oversimplified. Brannen and Doz (2010, p. 237) describe mainstream IB theories as being 'too distant from the phenomena they purport to explain', and instead urge researchers to view the phenomena they study 'up close and personal' (p. 245).

Paradigmatic assumptions also determine how the quality of case studies is judged. Our review of IB journals certainly suggests that positivist and quantitative criteria dominated the decade we studied (Piekkari et al. 2009). This could be seen in the way that case researchers defended their studies: reduction of bias and accuracy of reporting were a recurring concern, while the small-N nature of the study was noted as a limitation. For example, Brouthers and Bamossy (1997) were concerned to outline how they had ensured the 'objectivity' of their study, and Galperin and Lituchy (1999, p. 332) assert that 'standardization of the instrument [i.e. interview guide] was required'. Tsang (2001) apologizes for the fact that his study contained 'only' 18 cases. Traditional, positivist notions of validity and reliability were the most widely used (see Gibbert et al. 2008 for similar findings from their review of the *Strategic Management Journal*). Quality criteria are typically presented as self-evident facts, but we would argue that they are highly value laden and ultimately contestable (see Johnson et al. 2006 for a similar argument).

The contributors to this part offer alternatives to Eisenhardt's (1989) assertion that case studies are best suited to inductive theory building. These alternatives fall into two categories. The first, more radical alternative is to reject the paradigmatic basis for Eisenhardt's claim, and to seek other, postpositivist paradigms[1] to illuminate the case study (see the chapters by Morais and Ahonen, Tienari and Vaara). The paradigms canvassed in this part are critical realism, critical discourse analysis and postmodernism. The second alternative is to accept the goal of generalizability, as does Eisenhardt, but propose innovative approaches to theorize from case studies and use the unexploited potential of this research strategy (see the chapters by Szulanski and Jensen, and Brannen).

In the first category, Ricardo Morais (Chapter 5) shows how critical realism can be used to strengthen and enrich explanatory case studies in IB research. Morais conducts a review of critical realism and adopts the position that this approach is well suited to case research. He focuses on the nature of causation, explanation and generalization, and argues that as a field IB would benefit from reassessing the explanatory value of the case study. Case studies can in fact provide a more powerful explanation than statistical studies: the former can identify the causal combinations of conditions that lead to an outcome, whereas the latter are limited to measuring quantifiable changes.

Pasi Ahonen, Janne Tienari and Eero Vaara (Chapter 6) introduce a critical perspective to case studies in IB. They conduct a critical discourse analysis of media texts about a major industrial closure in Finland. They position themselves firmly against the positivist tradition in IB research and introduce critical management perspectives as an alternative. The case study which they reflect on in their chapter is highly unusual in the IB context in a number of ways: first, by selecting critical discourse analysis as the methodological approach to the study of the case; second, turning to media texts as the dominant source of data; and third, by making the perspective of company management take a back seat, and instead focusing on the voices that are typically silenced: workers, community representatives, politicians and trade unionists.

In their 'confessional tale' (Van Maanen 1988), Gabriel Szulanski and Robert J. Jensen (Chapter 7) explain how they responded to the challenge posed by Sumantra Ghoshal to test a theory with a single case and have it published in a top-tier journal. To do so, they use the repeated measures quasi-experimental design, which they discovered is an established tradition in health economics. Szulanski and Jensen's account honours the unexploited potential of the case study to test theory and gives credit to the richness of a single case. This chapter, as well as the one by Brannen, belong to the second category of articles, which takes a reconciliatory approach to the positivist tradition of conducting case studies.

Mary Yoko Brannen (Chapter 8), in turn, develops her own design to overcome the trade-off between deep, contextual insights provided by ethnography and the urge to build generalizable theory that is applicable beyond the ethnographic field site. She rejects this trade-off by conducting multiple follow-up case studies to test deductively the constructs and frameworks induced from the 'focal ethnography'. Her contribution blurs the boundaries, currently upheld by the disciplinary tradition, between theory building and theory testing.

The final chapter in this part, by Poul Houman Andersen and Hanne Kragh (Chapter 9), offers a critique of Eisenhardt's positivist approach to inductive theory building. The authors provide two alternatives to theory building from case research which they label *in vivo* and *ex ante*. The first approach, *in vivo*, is associated with critical realist assumptions and also known by the name of 'systematic combining' (Dubois and Gadde 2002). It builds on abduction, an iterative process in which 'the original framework is successively modified, partly as a result of unanticipated empirical findings, but also of theoretical insights gained during the process' (Dubois and Gadde 2002, p. 559). The *ex ante* approach is in turn associated with postmodernist assumptions. The two alternative approaches to theory building are illustrated with Andersen and Kragh's own fieldwork.

Part III: Alternative Case Study Designs

We have argued that philosophical assumptions and dominant disciplinary conventions shape the choices that case researchers make. This can also be seen when it comes to the attitudes and preferences towards case study designs found among IB case researchers. As already discussed, we found a clear preference for multiple case designs in our analysis of IB case studies (Piekkari et al. 2009). Case researchers also conformed to the dominant paradigm when representing the design of their research processes. Articles were typically written up to mimic the fixed designs and deductive logic of quantitative articles. In other words, the literature review and research questions were presented upfront (and propositions and hypotheses were even formulated), and the changes and redirections that typically occur during a case study (Dubois and Gadde 2002) were smoothed away. In this part, contributors confront widespread myths and misconceptions regarding the design of case studies, discuss alternative case study designs and acknowledge the emergent nature of case research. A particular focus is longitudinal and mixed-method case study designs, both of which are routinely called for in IB research, but which are still rarely found (Piekkari et al. 2009).

This part starts with Margaret Fletcher and Emmanuella Plakoyiannaki's chapter on key decisions in case selection (Chapter 10). They argue that case selection is a dynamic process spanning multiple levels rather than a single decision preceding data collection. They problematize case selection by outlining eight misconceptions regarding the key questions that are involved, namely: what cases to select? How to select them? When to select them? How to select? Fletcher and Plakoyiannaki make a call for more informed decisions about case sampling in order to strengthen the theorizing potential of case studies.

Trevor Buck's chapter (Chapter 11) is an immediate response to Fletcher and Plakoyiannaki's call. Based on his own experiences of qualitative, in particular historical, and quantitative case studies, Buck speaks for case selection that is informed by theory. He argues that the perceived limitation of case studies – the 'bias' in selecting a small number of cases – can actually become a strength if cases are carefully selected to match the theoretical purpose. He introduces an innovative approach to selecting cases, namely the matched-pair case design, which he has extensively and successfully used in his own work.

Buck's use of both quantitative and qualitative data in case research leads us to Chapter 12 by Leila Hurmerinta and Niina Nummela, who bridge the methodological literature on case studies with that on mixed methods. They make the point that methodological guides recommend that the case researcher draw on multiple data sources which are qualitative only. Hurmerinta and Nummela also argue for collecting quantitative data and propose two strategies – 'compartmentalized' and 'aggregated' – as innovative approaches to mixing methods in case studies. The former refers to studies in which the case or cases form a separate, independent part of the research – in a way, a study inside a study. The latter strategy is defined as a case study within which both quantitative and qualitative data are collected and analysed. When mixed methods are applied within the case context, the case(s) act as a platform for their use. They term this an 'aggregated strategy'.

In Chapter 13, Jon Erland Lervik shows how three different research designs – the single-N, small-N and large-N designs – can be used to capture the same phenomenon, namely the multinational corporation (MNC). In this way he powerfully challenges the widespread assumption that the 'case' always equals the firm. Lervik contributes to the diversity of available research designs for case researchers by outlining the three established alternatives. Moreover, he introduces an additional design that bridges mixed methods and the single-N case design. His discussion exemplifies Hurmerinta and Nummela's aggregated strategy. Lervik shows how an exploratory pre-study and a quantitative main study can be successfully combined in one MNC. The mixed-method approach allowed Lervik to simultaneously build and test theory within the boundaries of a single study.

In Chapter 14, Susanne Blazejewski critically reviews existing longitudinal studies in IB and provides different temporal design options for researchers undertaking longitudinal case studies. She identifies four temporal dimensions along which longitudinal case studies vary: case time (the period under analysis), research time (the period during which data are gathered), temporal research perspective (whether the research process is simultaneous or *ex post*) and temporal data perspective (whether the data are real time or retrospective). Blazejewski's careful delineation of different designs represents a major contribution given the current lack of guidance on this issue in IB.

Anna Soulsby and Ed Clark (Chapter 15) introduce an innovative temporal design which they label 'the punctuated longitudinal case study' (PLCS). The PLCS is based on qualitative data, generated through a repeat-pattern of research visits and revisits to the same organizational settings. The temporal period, starting with the first field visit, is punctuated by regular but much shorter field revisits. This design is drawn from the authors' own almost 20 years' experience of conducting fieldwork within a transition economy. As a temporal design, it reconciles the tension between conducting real-time or retrospective research in a methodologically sound yet practical way.

Part IV: The Potential of Multiple Data Sources and Analytical Methods

According to many definitions, the case study is characterized by its use of multiple data sources, which in turn can be analysed with multiple methods. However, our review of IB case studies found that overwhelmingly, case researchers relied on interviews as their primary data source (Piekkari et al. 2009). Contributors in this part (Mir, Moore, Mills and Mills, and Wright) redress this imbalance, and consider the unexploited potential of other data sources such as ethnography, documents and archives. In Part II, the chapter by Ahonen et al., which presents a case study drawing on media texts as an unusual data source in IB and IM research, echoes similar concerns. These authors draw on their own studies, which made extensive use of non-interview data. Noticeably, they are reflexive about their own paradigmatic assumptions, and consider explicitly how these assumptions affected the way in which they approached their fieldwork, and how they interpreted and used their data sources. Mills and Mills, and Wright, in particular, invite case researchers to fundamentally reconsider how they analyse data.

Raza Mir (Chapter 16) debates the possibility of combining ethnography with case research. Mir's 'hybrid' approach allows him to collect rich data through ethnography while writing up the study with the help of case analytic techniques. In this way, constructivism, which underlies ethnography, can coexist with the more positivist epistemology that Mir associates with the case study. Thus, like Brannen, and Hurmerinta and Nummela, he questions existing dichotomies and distinctions between methodological approaches. Instead he advocates the richness of a more pragmatic stance that recognizes synergies between approaches that are usually regarded as distinct or even opposing.

Following Mir's path, Fiona Moore (Chapter 17) uses ethnographic techniques to gain a more holistic perspective on her case company and argues for the advantages of so-called 'ethnographic case studies'. The richness and depth of her single-case analysis challenges the current disciplinary convention, which is characterized by shallow multiple case studies. She counters the common conception that ethnographic methods can only be used for understanding the micro processes of small groups; rather, they can provide insight into whole organizations.

In Chapter 18, Albert J. Mills and Jean H. Mills introduce another uncommon data source, namely archives, and an even less common approach in IB, postpositivism, to analyse them. They contrast and compare the positivist with the postpositivist approaches to working with archives and analysing them. They use their own case study on the gendering of airline cultures over time as a source of insights and inspiration. They voice serious concerns about the uncritical and non-reflexive nature of mainstream IB and IM theories.

In Chapter 19, April Wright continues the discussion on analytical techniques. As a starting point she notes that in IB case studies, documents such as minutes of meetings, agendas, letters of correspondence, strategic plans, and public and internal reports are undervalued and rarely used. She argues that documents do not merely 'say' things – they are produced and used by actors with an interest in 'doing' things. In this way, she redirects scholarly attention in case analysis towards the role of documents as agents in organizations. She shows how analysis can go beyond treating documents as content, to understanding how they stand in relation to each other hierarchically and sequentially (genre analysis). She also provides insight into how researchers can 'enfold' existing theory into the analysis. Such an approach deepens the analysis and enriches the theoretical insights gained from the case study.

Data analysis is also the focus for Ayse Saka-Helmhout (Chapter 20), who reflects the growing interest that can be found among social scientists in how to develop 'case-oriented' rather than 'variable-oriented' explanations. According to Ragin (1987), the distinguishing feature of a case-oriented explanation is that it treats the case holistically, rather than breaking it down into variables. At the basis of this holistic view is the recognition that causes of social events are 'conjunctural' or combinatorial in nature. In other words, combinations of factors produce an outcome. Moreover, different combinations of factors can produce the same outcome. As a result, case-oriented explanations are focused on understanding the combinations of causal conditions that produced a particular outcome. Saka-Helmhout introduces comparative historical analysis as a useful technique for providing causally complex yet rigorous theories in international management research.

Part V: Taking Account of Diverse Contexts

Understanding the phenomenon in its natural context is one of the hallmarks of the case study. However, the contributors to this part show that there is a diversity of contexts to be considered, including national, cultural, institutional, political, organizational and team contexts. For example, how can researchers capture the complexities of the multicultural, multilingual and geographically dispersed MNC? How can they reach an understanding of different cultures and national conditions, which affect not just the case itself, but also the way in which the case is studied? Case studies on the MNC exist (see especially Bélanger et al. 1999; Kristensen and Zeitlin 2005, and the studies reviewed by Lervik, Ch. 13 in this volume). Moreover, some case studies have been conducted in 'forgotten' locations (for example, Marschan-Piekkari and Welch 2004). However, there has been little discussion in the methodological literature about the implications of such contexts for designing, conducting and theorizing from case studies. We would argue that the IB field can benefit from a debate about how to conduct case studies in foreign settings and multiple countries, and about how context should best be folded into the process of theorizing from case studies. In this part, authors contribute to such a debate by reflecting on their own experiences of crossing national borders when conducting case research.

In Chapter 21, Tony Edwards, Phil Almond and Trevor Colling focus on the MNC as an organizational context as well as a context for conducting collaborative research in teams. The authors discuss the challenges associated with comparative research on MNCs or MNC units located in different countries. When matching cases across borders, researchers may be faced with a situation of comparing the incomparable. Building on Perlmutter's (1969) classic article, Edwards et al. contrast three ways of organizing collaborative research on MNCs, namely the ethnocentric, polycentric and geocentric designs. They use the analogy of the researcher operating like 'a flea on the back of the elephant' when trying to understand the inner workings of giant MNCs. Edwards et al. discuss the difficulties of organizing collaborative research as a truly geocentric research project which is internally well integrated and coherent.

Asta Salmi (Chapter 22) elaborates on collaborative research and argues for having an international team as collective analysts of case data as opposed to a single investigator. The diversified resources of an international team are commonly used only to reach different international contexts. Salmi introduces the concept of 'collective case studies' which invites culturally and contextually sensitive joint case analysis. Salmi rejects Yin's (2009) relatively linear case study process and opts for an abductive logic which has become popular in case research on industrial business networks (Dubois and Gadde 2002). The examples from her own research suggest that joint analysis is easier to achieve when conducting a single, shared case. Such a research design offers a platform for joint analysis and reflection which has parallels with the geocentric research design advocated by Edwards et al.

In Chapter 23, Philippe d'Iribarne takes us beyond organizational and team contexts to national and cultural contexts which are commonly acknowledged in IB and IM research. However, as d'Iribarne points out, the analysis of national cultures is mostly left to quantitative research. Based on his extensive experiences of conducting cultural research within modern societies, he argues that the case study is well suited to decipher what represents national culture and what is uniquely local. He answers the fundamental question of how observations made in a specific case can be transformed into evidence of the society's culture as a whole. As editors, we had first-hand experience of the French cultural context when editing the original French text and trying to do it justice.

Hui Tan and Matti Nojonen (Chapter 24) focus on China as a national, cultural, political and institutional context and provide two contrasting perspectives on engaging in case research. Tan approaches the challenge of case research from his position as a 'boundary' spanner between the Chinese and Western worlds. He was born in China but educated and trained in the UK, which explains his experiences of balancing two competing sets of rules. He compares case research in foreign-owned firms with state-owned enterprises and notes that the former are far more receptive to academic research requests. Nojonen, in turn, discusses case research in China from the perspective of a Western researcher but he focuses on state-owned enterprises. In his confessional tale, Nojonen argues that the regulatory structure for controlling fieldwork conducted by foreigners in China has become tighter since the 1990s. What Nojonen brings to the fore is not only the hostile regulatory environment and the culture of fear in China, which he personally experienced during his own non-official fieldwork in the 1990s, but also the increasing self-censorship practised by foreign scholars. He provocatively argues that we are in danger of voluntarily sacrificing our academic integrity and independent critical thinking for personal gain.

Finally, in Chapter 25 Martin Johanson offers another confessional story about the difficulties of conducting a processual case study in a transition economy such as Russia. The aim of the study was to follow the change process of an inter-firm network. However, the long search for a suitable case company was characterized by many frustrations, failures, and poor interviews with Russian informants. Johanson describes how the Russian interviewees were not used to being interviewed, and were often unwilling to participate. He struggled to ensure repeated access to the local case company which was a prerequisite for the processual study. During the course of the study, Johanson took on the roles of a consultant, researcher and cultural interpreter which secured him access to the required information. His chapter illustrates the practical challenges of identifying a suitable case in Russia. In the end, as Johanson puts it, the case company found him. This chapter echoes many of the issues raised in Part III in terms of longitudinal case designs (Blazejewski, and Soulsby and Clark) and applicable criteria for case selection (Fletcher and Plakoyiannaki).

The chapters in this volume are united by several common themes. To various degrees all chapters are critical about the current status quo and raise, in a multivocal way, a number of central methodological questions. The authors are reflexive in their approach and analyse their own experiences (see, for example, Brannen, Houman Andersen, d'Iribarne, Mir, Morais, and Wright). While many authors emphasize the role of context in the case study (see, for example, Johanson, d'Iribarne, Nojonen and Tan), others bring to the fore the possibility of producing contingent generalizations from case research (see, for example, Brannen, Buck, Lervik, Mir, and Moore). The challenge of demonstrating causality through case research was also picked up by, for example, Saka-Helmhout, Szulanski and Jensen, and Mills and Mills. Finally, we consider the processual nature of case research to be a recurrent theme throughout the book (see, for example, Blazejewski, Johanson, Soulsby and Clark).

CONCLUDING REMARKS

This book has opened up a debate on the case study and showed the various possibilities of using this flexible research strategy. The individual chapters draw on the multidisciplinary methodological literature on the case study and the authors' rich personal experiences from conducting fieldwork. In doing so, several key research projects in the field by, for example, Aharoni, Bartlett and Ghoshal, Buck, Edwards et al., and Szulanski and Jensen are examined from a methodological perspective. While their theoretical merits have been widely recognized, the methodological contributions of these studies are seldom acknowledged. For example, the case studies by Bartlett and Ghoshal were based on unique access to large multinationals, resulting in hundreds of personal interviews with top managers, and supplemented by some survey data (see Piekkari and Welch, Ch. 2 this volume). Not surprisingly, their research has been described by Van Maanen and Westney (2010) as a unique view from the executive suite. Edwards et al. designed their rich case studies as an international collaborative effort in which four national teams in Germany, Ireland, Spain and the UK conducted case studies on the same

US-owned MNCs with operations in these four European countries. Each national team took on the responsibility for the fieldwork in their own country, ensuring that the significance of local institutions and practices was appreciated. Szulanski and Jensen in turn developed a rare research design by testing a theory with a single case study and managing to get it published in a top-tier journal. Buck offers an innovative approach to studying corporate governance through dyadic, matched cases. This book draws attention to the methodological contributions that these established authors have made to the field.

While the present collection of book chapters opens up a methodological debate, we wish to see it as a broader contribution to the development of IB theories. Brannen and Doz (2010) have recently criticized the field for generating decontextualized theories that remain detached and distant from the research phenomenon under study. We would argue that methodological reflexivity and rigour should not be an end in itself; rather the impact of our book, we hope, is that future IB theorizing will be enriched.

Our firm belief is that the debate on the case study has only begun. We hope that future IB and IM research will witness greater methodological pluralism and more informed discussions among authors, reviewers and editors about the case study as a research strategy. We hope that case researchers, whether junior or senior, will find their 'own' perspective with which they can identify among the many views introduced in the book. In this way, the book may offer reassurance to case authors and an authoritative methodological reference point when subjecting the case study to evaluation. As active case researchers ourselves, we are excited about the future potential of the case study and trust that the following pages will convey our and our contributors' confidence and enthusiasm about the case study and its future in our field.

NOTE

1. Postpositivist authors have been described by Prasad (2005, p. 9) as 'tend[ing] to approach questions of social reality and knowledge production from a more problematized vantage point, emphasizing the constructed nature of social reality, the constitutive role of language, and the value of research as a critique'.

REFERENCES

Bélanger, J., C. Berggren, T. Björkman and C. Köhler (eds) (1999), *Being Local Worldwide: ABB and the Challenge of Global Management*, Ithaca, NY: Cornell University Press.

Brannen, M.Y. and Y.L. Doz (2010), 'From a distance and detached to up close and personal: bridging strategic and cross-cultural perspectives in international management research and practice', *Scandinavian Journal of Management*, **26** (3), 236–47.

Brouthers, K.D. and G.J. Bamossy (1997), 'The role of key stakeholders in international joint venture negotiations: case studies from Eastern Europe', *Journal of International Business Studies*, **28** (2), 285–308.

Byrne, D. (2009), 'Case-based methods: why we need them, what they are, how to do them', in Byrne and Ragin (eds), pp. 2–10.

Byrne, D. and C.C. Ragin (eds) (2009), *The Sage Handbook of Case-based Methods*, London: Sage.

Creswell, J.W. (1994), *Research Design: Qualitative and Quantitative Approaches*, Thousand Oaks, CA: Sage.

Dubois, A. and L.-E. Gadde (2002), 'Systematic combining: an abductive approach to case research', *Journal of Business Research*, **55** (7), 553–60.

Dyer, W.G. and A.L. Wilkins (1991), 'Better stories, not better constructs, to generate better theory: a rejoinder to Eisenhardt', *Academy of Management Review*, **16** (3), 613–19.

Eisenhardt, K.M. (1989), 'Building theories from case study research', *Academy of Management Review*, **14** (4), 532–50.

Eisenhardt, K.M. and M.E. Graebner (2007), 'Theory building from cases: opportunities and challenges', *Academy of Management Journal*, **50** (1), 25–32.

Galperin, B.L. and T.R. Lituchy (1999), 'The implementation of total quality management in Canada and Mexico: a case study', *International Business Review*, **8** (3), 323–49.

Gibbert, M., W. Ruigrok and B. Wicki (2008), 'What passes as a rigorous case study?', *Strategic Management Journal*, **29** (13), 1465–74.

Gilbert, C.G. (2005), 'Unbundling the structure of inertia: resource versus routine rigidity', *Academy of Management Journal*, **48** (5), 741–63.

Hamel, J. with S. Dufour and D. Fortin (1993), *Case Study Methods*, Newbury Park, CA: Sage.

Hurmerinta-Peltomäki, L. and N. Nummela (2006), 'Mixed methods in international business research: a value added perspective', *Management International Review*, **46** (4), 439–59.

Johnson, P., A. Buehring, C. Cassell and G. Symon (2006), 'Evaluating qualitative research: towards a contingent criteriology', *International Journal of Management Reviews*, **8** (3), 131–56.

Kristensen, P.H. and J. Zeitlin (2005), *Local Players in Global Games: The Strategic Constitution of a Multinational Corporation*, Oxford: Oxford University Press.

Marschan-Piekkari, R. and C. Welch (eds) (2004), *Handbook of Qualitative Research Methods for International Business*, Cheltenham, UK and Northampton, MA, USA: Edward Elgar.

Mills, A.J., G. Durepos and E. Wiebe (eds) (2010), *Encyclopedia of Case Study Research*, 2 vols, Thousand Oaks, CA: Sage.

Perlmutter, H. (1969), 'The tortuous evolution of the multinational corporation', *Columbia Journal of World Business*, **4** (1), 9–18.

Piekkari, R., E. Plakoyiannaki and C. Welch (2010), '"Good" case research in industrial marketing: insights from research practice', *Industrial Marketing Management*, **39** (1), 109–17.

Piekkari, R., C. Welch and E. Paavilainen (2009), 'The case study as disciplinary convention: evidence from international business journals', *Organizational Research Methods*, **12** (3), 567–89.

Platt, J. (1992), '"Case study" in American methodological thought', *Current Sociology*, **40** (1), 14–48.

Prasad, P. (2005), *Crafting Qualitative Research: Working in the Postpositivist Traditions*, Armonk, NY: M.E. Sharpe.

Pratt, M. (2009), 'For the lack of a boilerplate: tips on writing up (and reviewing) qualitative research', *Academy of Management Journal*, **52** (5), 856–62.

Ragin, C.C. (1987), *The Comparative Method: Moving beyond Qualitative and Quantitative Strategies*, Berkeley, CA: University of California Press.

Ragin, C.C. (2008), *Redesigning Social Inquiry: Fuzzy Sets and Beyond*, Chicago, IL: University of Chicago Press.

Simons, H. (2009), *Case Study Research in Practice*, London: Sage.

Stake, R.E. (1995), *The Art of Case Study Research*, Thousand Oaks, CA: Sage.

Tsang, E.W.K. (2001), 'Managerial learning in foreign-invested enterprises of China', *Management International Review*, **41** (1), 29–51.

Van Maanen, J. (1988), *Tales of the Field: On Writing Ethnography*, Chicago, IL: University of Chicago Press.

Van Maanen, J. and E. Westney (2010), 'The casual ethnography of the executive suite', AIB/AOM Joint Symposium on Qualitative Research in International Business, Academy of Management Annual Meeting, Montreal, 6–10 August.

Welch, C., R. Piekkari, E. Plakoyiannaki and E. Paavilainen-Mäntymäki (2011), 'Theorising from case studies: towards a pluralist future for international business research', *Journal of International Business Studies*, forthcoming, doi: 10.1057/jibs.2010.55.

Yin, R.K. (2009), *Case Study Research: Design and Methods*, 4th edn, Thousand Oaks, CA: Sage, first published 1984.

2. The career of a case researcher: an interview with Christopher Bartlett

Rebecca Piekkari and Catherine Welch

R.P. Why did you decide to take a case-based approach to your PhD rather than a survey?

C.B. I used to work for an honest living before I became an academic, so I came as a practitioner. I had worked first in Australia for Alcoa as a product manager. Then, after I got my MBA, I worked for McKinsey for a while and then I ran the French subsidiary of Baxter, the international healthcare company. So I'd been in and seen the practical issues in management, and that's what really fascinated me and was part of my motivation in coming back and wanting to teach. So coming as a practitioner myself, I really saw practitioners as being a very legitimate and important audience that I wanted to talk to. It also gave me a level of comfort dealing with those problems in their messiness. I guess in going through the doctoral programme, I just found a lot of the survey-based research narrow or remote or shallow and didn't really capture the world that I knew as a practitioner.

The other motivation, as I entered an academic career, was to become a teacher. It seemed to me, particularly having done an MBA at Harvard, that the richness came from bringing case materials into the classroom – where you deal with the messy, unstructured and interesting kinds of problems that managers deal with. Students struggle through the data, turning that into an analysis and generating options and making decisions, then turning decisions into action, and then coming into a classroom and defending their points of view and adapting and adjusting them. All those things are the reality, that's the bloodstream of business and it's what I wanted to do as a teacher as well.

Frankly, if practitioners and students were the two audiences I had in the forefront of my mind, the third audience was the academic audience, and at that stage in my life, I thought, well, they'll respect whatever comes out. As long as I'm teaching to the people whose behaviour we're trying to influence, then hopefully the academic audience will understand and respect and value that. I think my view of the academic audience, and what their expectations were, changed as I got into an academic career and the views of at least some of the academic profession were not as open as I believed at that time.

If we're talking about the general framing of my research, it was based on the stages model, which John Stopford had done before I came to Harvard. I didn't ever meet John in the doctoral programme, but he'd framed the stages theory of multinational structure [Stopford 1968]. I respected the stages model and I could see where it really did become prescriptive, but it was very structural and it essentially equated organization with structure. I knew that that wasn't the case; that structure is the organization's anatomy, but organizations also have a physiology and psychology. The physiology is the flows through the organization, the processes, the systems, the communication, the relationships; and the psychology is the culture, the values, the way people think and act. Managers shape organization through anatomy and physiology and psychology. The constraint, I think, of survey-based work is you can capture hard-edged things like organizational structure, but you can't capture process and culture and communications nearly as well. My dissertation [Bartlett 1979] was really to add some flesh and blood, if you like, to a framework that Stopford had put together and, in doing so, really challenged some of its prescriptive power.

R.P.   How did you choose your case companies for your doctoral dissertation?

C.B.   Well, Stopford had said there was this stages model – and, to be fair to John, it was descriptive. In the end he became tentatively prescriptive but I think it was the interpretation and other work subsequently that made that into a prescriptive model. But I'd lived and worked in organizations, both in Alcoa and then in Baxter, where I'd worked in an international division in stages of development that were way beyond what Stopford's model would have predicted. So that was the practitioner in me saying, wait a minute, why aren't those companies behaving this way? It became the tool to say, well, if these are outliers, why are they outliers and how are they making the adaptation? Are they misfits or are there other ways in which you can adapt to growing complexity to be more globally integrated and/or more nationally responsive?

The other thing that was very interesting to me was that, like a lot of stages models, this was a 'one size fits all' model and that didn't seem right to me. I'd only been in two industries – healthcare and aluminium – but I knew that the strategic imperatives in those industries were vastly different. So I took a sample of companies from the food and from the pharmaceutical industries and said, look, the tasks are different and, therefore, if the strategic imperatives are different then the organizational responses are likely to be different. That was the doctoral dissertation: let's look at companies that are managing in these very different task environments, and yet with what looks like similar organizational structures. But dig below the surface and you started to see some of these interesting differences that I could tease out a little bit.

C.W.   Now, in doing so, did you see yourself as following in the footsteps of previous Harvard Business School scholars? Did you see yourself as very much fitting into that tradition?

C.B.   Well, I guess we select ourselves into situations that fit our own interests. I mean, as I came back to an academic career I was unlikely to apply to Chicago. I felt comfortable at Harvard. In fact, it was a big motivation for me in wanting to have an academic career. When I came to the MBA programme I saw a huge difference. I'd done an economics degree in Australia – and there, you know, some crusty old lecturer would get up and dust off last year's lecture notes and draw the demand and supply curves crossing up on a blackboard and we'd all copy down the demand and supply curves and that's how you set price. Yet, I'd go home in the evening and my dad was in business and I knew he didn't sit around drawing demand and supply curves to set price. It was, I thought, unconnected to reality – although it was interesting and it was a good discipline to have. But when I got to Harvard we started dealing with management issues that were real and live, and we'd discuss and engage and debate, and good teaching would shape your learning through that process. I was engaged. I saw the difference between teaching and learning, and I was very interested in creating a learning-based environment. So when I came back wanting to be a teacher, there was no question that I fitted into that Harvard tradition. I believed this was a very powerful means, firstly, of allowing students to learn and, secondly, of allowing you as a researcher to learn. In the end, unless we learn, how do we help managers to improve practice? So, I very much subscribe to that Harvard philosophy and fit in with its tradition, both in teaching and research.

C.W.   At this point we'll ask a question which is very speculative. If you were embarking on the same or a similar doctoral dissertation today, would you make the same decision about doing case research?

C.B.   I almost certainly would – in fact, let me take out the 'almost' – I certainly would. I think it's driven from inside, and I think any doctoral student making choices has got to be motivated first by what really fascinates and interests, engages and excites them. For me, that's the most exciting thing. I love getting out into the field because I learn and I also love the challenge of capturing that complexity and teasing it out. Because for me, even in the doctoral days, I started working at the same time as a research associate developing classroom material, so I was learning a craft that would support me as a teacher as well as a researcher. That internal motivation was powerful and, even though today I'm emeritus, right now I have four cases that I'm working on because I love doing what I'm doing. There's also pride involved. My cases have sold over three million copies, which is more than anyone else ever has through Harvard. It's probably a silly thing, but I love that and I love the fact that what I'm creating is not only something that I use for my own teaching but that students and teachers around the world can be using. So it's incredibly powerful from that point of view. But there's a pyramid for me. Typically I bring material into the classroom first where students engage with it and we both learn; as we take that for a test drive and pull it apart, there's an enormous amount of learning. Now, obviously, the material that I've got back in my files is much richer. I have to create something that I can bring into the classroom. But then you start seeing some concepts and frameworks and hypotheses developing and that allows me then to write an article. As you then work across a broader sample or different cuts across the same sample, you develop multiple articles and those multiple articles eventually, if they're connected, can result in a book. It's a very inductive process that grows from the learning that takes place in the field, that's leveraged in the classroom, that grows as one begins to think about it. In my relationship and partnership with Sumantra Ghoshal, he and I would bang around ideas and butt up against each other and those ideas would get developed and they'd become the articles and books. Would I do it again today? I love the process, so, yes I would.

C.W.   Do you advise others to follow suit?

C.B.   If they've got that same passion that I have, that's the internal drive. The external constraint that I think you're probably implying in this is, so how do you get it published? For the mainstream is that you publish more typical survey-based research but I think that gets set up as more of a bogeyman than it is. Certainly Sumantra and I went through our career publishing the kind of work that we were doing and we wanted it to be academically acceptable and managerially relevant. So we would always try to publish in the *Journal of International Business Studies* or *Strategic Management Journal* or *Academy of Management Journal* or *Academy of*

Management Review or whatever was the appropriate journal, and we'd also try to publish in *Harvard Business Review* or *Sloan Management Review* or whatever, and we'd bring it into the classroom and really use the research to drive three audiences [i.e., students, practitioners and academics].

R.P. You mentioned earlier on that the academic audience wasn't as open as you had initially thought. Do you have some examples of that?

C.B. I think it's pretty clear in the reviews that come back from some submissions to the more academic journals that some reviewers don't understand what case-based research can do. Case-based research is designed to be hypothesis generating. Most of what is done in survey-based research is hypothesis testing, but to create the frameworks and the concepts and the big models, case-based research is an incredibly powerful tool. That's what's always fascinated me – to go out and see if we could describe the big questions. Now, *Managing Across Borders* [Bartlett and Ghoshal 2002] has a sample of nine companies in three industries in three countries. It's designed so that there's some logic that's framing the tension between those companies, but you can't prove anything. You can create some very clear hypotheses – it developed some very rich hypotheses out of that fine-grained information and data that you have – and then, as has happened, lots of researchers will then take pieces and challenge and question and elaborate and test and refine, so it generates a lot of research work. People can do and did that follow-up research – and we did some – but, to be honest, what fascinated me much more was to go out and generate the hypotheses.

C.W. You've mentioned the *Managing Across Borders* project, so this might be a good time to turn to that. It seemed to us, when we were comparing your PhD dissertation with *Managing Across Borders*, that one big difference was that *Managing Across Borders* was quite an ambitious multicountry study, so you had firms from multiple countries included. What were the challenges in terms of jumping from your doctoral research to a multicountry, multimethod study?

C.B. Well, again, the motivation was I'd come from a career where I'd grown up in Australia and that's where I'd begun my work, but I'd lived and worked in London with McKinsey, I'd run a subsidiary in France with Baxter. So there was an interest there, as well as a background that gave me some experience and comfort. Also, my field was international business so I didn't want to deal just with US-based multinationals when teaching, it just seemed to me to be such an ethnocentric view of the world. Yes, you're right that the doctoral dissertation had been on US-based multinationals in which I'd pushed the hypothesis that was there's not a one size fits all, that industry matters – that pharmaceuticals had a very different set of demands, and therefore organizational requirements, than the food-based industry. But I was also very aware that country mattered and culture mattered, so this really allowed the research to go to another level and say, it's not only the external demands of your industry characteristics but it's the cultural differences and the historical differences that come from your country of origin. That was something that was, I guess, a hypothesis – although I didn't think of it in those terms – but I believed that and I wanted to put my arms around that in research. The challenges that come with that, I guess, are that I needed more money to be able to travel and I needed more time to be able to do the research – in the doctoral programme, as you know, the clock is ticking and you're trying to get out of there so the last thing you need is a multicountry study. The third thing, frankly, was access. As an Assistant Professor I had more access than I did as a doctoral student, and there's no question that coming from Harvard Business School was a huge asset that allowed you to open doors.

So I wanted to keep the dimension of industry difference, and in fact even elaborate it, across three industries this time, and I wanted to keep the geographic dimension, so that led to the design of three countries and three companies. Now, obviously, you can't bet that everyone is going to say yes, so I did initially approach a number of different industries – I can't recall now what they were – but I think I approached companies in probably five industries. I do remember I kept going with pharmaceuticals and maybe food as well – chemicals, I think, was another one of them. Anyhow, in the end, because I needed three leading companies who were fairly advanced in their international strategy to agree in each of the industries, that's where we ended up. But it was a challenge and it's a huge task to do that. We ended up doing 236 interviews across those countries and not just in the country of origin, in all cases we did them in subsidiaries around the world; so it wasn't just Japan and Europe and the USA, we were also in Brazil, Korea, Australia and other countries around the world to gather data.

C.W. Who's the 'we' here? Did you have local collaborators as well on the team? How large was the team behind the scenes?

C.B. Well, it was a team of one to start with. This was my project. Then in the process – in fact, I was probably a year into the research and the data gathering and, like most of us, presenting in seminars at various places and particularly at Harvard Business School in a doctoral research seminar – a young guy from across the river came, who was actually just finishing up his PhD at Sloan, and that was Sumantra. Sumantra came in and after the seminar, in his usual very intense way, said, 'I think this is fascinating and I'd love to be a part of it'. I said, 'But Sumantra, you've just done your PhD over at MIT'. He said, 'I know, but I want to start again'. So he engaged and, by that stage, things were pretty far along but a third dimension was emerging in this research. One of the great things about doing clinical field-based research, and the most powerful thing about it, is you follow the data, you see where it takes you. So, the initial framing of the design around the two dimensions of global integration and national responsiveness gave birth to this third dimension that became an important component of *Managing Across Borders*. Companies had to be globally integrated, nationally responsive and able to develop and diffuse knowledge and innovation worldwide – that third dimension emerged and it was neither global efficiency nor national responsiveness. So I said to Sumantra, 'Well, this is the piece that's emerging now and you're at the early stages of it so if you wanted to grab that then I could introduce you to the sites and we could carve you out a piece of it'. So the 'we' involved Sumantra at a later stage.

Also, when I did the interviewing in Japan, obviously there's a huge cultural barrier there – not least of which is the language, but it's also getting the entrée and the trust and the relationship. I had a very good friend in Japan, Tadeo Kagono, who was helpful but he was also pretty busy on his own research, so he introduced me to a guy called Hideki Yoshihara who really became a kind of collaborator. He put it down to learning, he wanted to go and get involved in field-based research. He would come with me to all these interviews and often act as translator, although the companies often supplied translators, but he was there to help me and then arrange for me to come and be a visiting faculty member at Kobe University, which allowed me to do some in-depth research over there. Anyhow, that's the long answer to your question.

C.W. So, did your life at that stage consist of jumping on planes and spending weeks or months in various parts around the world?

C.B. Well, I also had a wife and the beginnings of a young family, so you know, you have to keep a balance in your life. Yes, I was travelling a lot but I was very conscious of wanting to spend time at home. So, with the exception of the intensive time in Japan – that was a two-month period as I recall, and Barbara came over at the back end of it – I'd typically be away for a week or 10 days at a time but I tried to make it not longer than that.

But it was a lot of living on a plane and that was the days before frequent flyer miles, so I didn't even benefit from it.

R.P.   In terms of the challenges associated with running such an international project, were there any specific ones in addition to language, culture and negotiating access?

C.B.   Well, the logistics, as always; so getting airlines bookings and hotel bookings and rental cars and passports and visas. Being as casual and laid back as I am, at one stage I forgot to renew my visa to Japan, and they're supposed to check it at the airport in the US, but I got literally to Tokyo Airport and these guys said, 'no visa'. They escorted me into a dark room where, I remember, there was a leak in the roof and they had a bucket underneath it. Next to me, there was a family from the Philippines who was being put back on a plane – I thought, I can't do this, I had all these interviews set up. So this was where my friend Yoshihara Sensei came in very helpful. I called him and he called some pretty high-up person who then intervened and, anyhow, they got me in. So all that went on as well. Mostly it was me just doing it and, you know, Sumantra was a doctoral student so he didn't have the resources but he was very engaged. We'd travel together and we developed, at that stage, the beginnings of that 20-plus years' relationship of banging ideas back and forth and arguing and carrying on, so that was a very helpful part of the process.

C.W.   So how long did the project take?

C.B.   It was probably five years from the beginning to when the book was done.

C.W.   So, of these 236 interviews, how many did you do?

C.B.   I was in all of them because Sumantra was still learning, but he would accompany me. So we carved out for him NEC, Matsushita and Philips, I think, so for several months he would come along. But I, literally, was in all of them.

C.W.   You usually assume that the assistants do the interviews for Harvard professors!

C.B.   No, no, I didn't have an assistant – even now, if I have a Research Associate [RA], it's largely an apprenticeship process, really. Because being a good clinical field researcher is not easy; I know that it took me a long time up a ramp to get there. What I do – and still do with RAs who come out in the field – is go through and outline it together and frame it together, and typically I'll take the lead on that at the beginning. Then after a while I'll say to them, 'Why don't you outline how we should do this?' But I'll lead the interviews for quite a few times and then I'll say to them, 'Why don't you lead? Then I'll fill in gaps if I see them, or inject a follow-on question if it looks like it's appropriate'. But the training wheels are on for quite a while.

R.P.   Now, returning to *Managing Across Borders* and your description of data collection in Japan, you mentioned that Yoshihara acted some-times as a translator and that you also had company translators. Could you tell us a little bit about the language challenge in interviewing, because you said that you were present in all of these 236 interviews you did in subsidiaries and headquarters?

C.B.   Well, it is a barrier, there is no question, and it's not just in lan-guages that one doesn't speak. Even in Australia, where English is the first language, you have to have cultural sensitivity to know when the laconic Australian is rubbishing or is straightforward. The American coming in will not get the nuance and often won't understand what is being said, even in countries divided by the same language. Certainly if you are speaking English as a second language, often there's nuance and interpretation. So it does take an ear to hear that and then to ask ques-tions in different ways to make sure you understand. The biggest barrier with the Japanese was a formality that you had to get past and past the canned answer, so you develop techniques. Often the biggest challenge is to get them away from the generality and get them onto specifics, so very quickly I'd try to get them to describe a project or a programme rather than a philosophy or a value because the philosophies and values could go right back to the company's booklets and slogans. I wanted them to describe their world.

C.W.   So, what are some of the other lessons that you try to instil into your research associates and doctoral students?

C.B.   Well, I think, before you leap into the field be very clear about what is the question that you're trying to deal with. It's not just, maybe if I stumble around out there I'll come across something interesting; you're going to exhaust people and you won't know what you're looking for. I guess, if you don't know where you're going any road will take you there and so you'll end up with something that doesn't mean very much.

So clarity of the question and then select the sites well; firstly, that they give you some insight into the question. For example, with my doctoral research it was companies that were managing through an international division that had grown well beyond that stage in Stopford's sense, so let's find companies that do that. Also, companies that are going to be open, and I mean that in a couple of senses: that they welcome you; that they're interested in the issue as well – they've got to see some benefit for them, that they're going to learn out of this as well; and not a great deal of intrusion. You don't want a situation where you're going to have to run everything through the public relations department; being escorted around by either the public relations or legal department are, for me, warning flags and I'm very clear to companies that this is not a public relations exercise and we don't want to be so defensive that everything we say is bland. Let's understand that you deal in a complex, difficult world and let's capture that. Sometimes with cases that you bring into public, if there are delicate issues you may have to disguise some of the competitive data or you may even have to disguise some of the names or, in the extreme, disguise the company to bring it into a classroom. So select the sites well. And when you come in you've got to have clarity, show you're professional and that you're not going to waste managers' time and that you will give them some kind of feedback at the end: you'll hold a mirror up to the organization and share your findings and spend time with them and nurture the relationship.

I think the other point I'd say is what we were talking about: let the data lead you because it will always lead you somewhere you didn't expect to go and stories will often get you there, and if you're listening well you can follow that. You know, I was talking about how knowledge transfer became a third dimension of *Managing Across Borders* and almost every time I go into the field I'll end up at a different place than I expected to. Speak to enough people that you can build a fine-grained understanding of the site. In other words, people who think that they are doing field research and go out and interview two people in a company – or worse still, just do a telephone interview with the chief strategy officer or something – they don't understand the company. I think of it as building a mosaic and each of the interviews is one of the tiles in the mosaic that you're building. Each one of the tiles may have a different colouring and shape and sheen and form and, individually, you think you've got the picture but when you stand back from the wall of tiles, that's when you really see the picture and you do need multiple perspectives on any question. All you see is a strategic intent at the beginning or a strategic outcome, but you don't understand how they got there until you get inside and understand that richness that comes from the managerial stew inside any company. So that would be a handful of things that I'd say to people. Oh, and really become a good listener in the field – listen very hard and follow where they're taking you and that's letting the data lead you.

R.P.   You've been primarily referring to interview data and I was wondering to what extent have you used documents or archives alongside interviewing key players in organizations?

C.B.   Always. Before I go to a company I'll do extensive research on it, everything from their annual reports to analysts' reports to articles in the newspapers and magazines, to other research that's been written about the company – I will go there very well prepared, so that's critical. Then in the interviews with companies I'll ask them for the documents that led to the analysis or the presentation that they made to management to get this investment agreed to, or whatever. Yes, they're very important support for the interviews.

C.W.   To what extent did you then apply the lessons learned, and the experience and so on, to your subsequent projects? We're thinking in particular of the linkages and the similarities and differences between *Managing Across Borders* and *The Individualized Corporation* [Ghoshal and Bartlett 1997].

C.B.   Well, all of this is very internally driven. For me, my internal motivation didn't change. I loved dealing with interesting, challenging questions that fascinated me personally. I guess the traditional academic career would have dictated I stayed with international business – but what you could really see in the early 1990s was that companies were going through this downsizing, delayering, restructuring, re-engineering, outsourcing, empowerment, organizational learning. All those things were going on and it seemed to me that the international part was built into it. I just looked at companies – most of them were global, multinational or transnational or whatever, but they were operating globally – so I was more interested in what looked like a change going on in the management model as profound as any I'd seen in my business life in this intense period of time. Sumantra was equally engaged and interested and he was a very curious, high energy kind of guy. The two of us got excited about this. So, one, it was driven by what we were excited about.

The second piece, the methodology, never was in question. I guess that we always knew that we'd go out into the field to learn because this was so unformed and unclear that we had to grab hold of it and just jump into the mess and see if we could make some sense of it. In saying that, I guess by this stage the partnership between Sumantra and me and our way of working together and the joy of that – of bouncing ideas and challenging and questioning and pushing each other – meant we needed something that both of us were interested in and excited about, both of us could engage in, that we could go out and grab the data. I guess the motivation, the research agenda, the methodology, the partnership – all of that was what we brought. The methodology was part of it, but equally part of it was our sense of the audience; that we wanted to do something that we could (a) bring into the classroom and drive our teaching; (b) translate into value-added contributions to the practical world that we operated in, not just as researchers but also consultants and board members – the roles we had outside where we were in touch with business; and (c) hopefully to have the academic community see value in it. I don't mean to put the academic community third but, certainly, we didn't feel like we had to make this fit some preconceived ideas that academia thought was the way we should do it. What we thought was, you know, we're professors of business administration, our field of interest and expertise is in management. So what we want to do is to teach young people how to be more effective managers – responsible, ethical, good managers – and we want to be able to help managers be more effective in running organizations and make some contribution there; in doing that, we hope that the academic community sees value in both those dimensions. That's the philosophy and the methodology that carried over to all of the subsequent work.

C.W. So you didn't sit down and say, well, if we include 20 companies this time round it'll be easier to get through the review process?

C.B. No, no. It's just that the problem was messier. Also, I guess, we were further down the learning curve and had a greater capacity. Both of us, by this stage, had research associates – I mean, a series of them who had worked with us – and doctoral students, so you had more leverage. But the motivation of a larger sample size was not driven at all by what's publishable.

R.P. Are there some companies you have studied for a long time?

C.B. If there's one company that sort of cuts across all of this research and I've spent my whole career in touch with and learning from, it's GE. If you look at the company that really transcends all the projects – and, in fact, right now I am working on a case called GE's Imagination Breakthroughs: The Evo Project [Bartlett et al. 2008]. But of all the companies that I've done research in, I learn more at GE – it's not a perfect company by any means but it's an incredibly well-managed company and I learn a lot from it every time I jump inside.

C.W. Another difference between *Managing Across Borders* and *The Individualized Corporation* was not just the sample size, but in *Managing Across Borders* you had a multimethod study, which you didn't then use next time round.

C.B. Right.

C.W. So why did you go from a multimethod approach for *Managing Across Borders* and then not for *The Individualized Corporation*?

C.B. Well, frankly, go back to the history of what I explained. Sumantra came in when the project was well along its way and he worked with me at some of the clinical sites. Then because of his MIT training, I think, and also because of his interests, he wanted to do this follow-up question-naire research, both with the three companies that he was working with and then a larger sample survey. I said to him 'that would really differ-entiate your doctoral dissertation', so he did that and he drove that – I was an adviser on it but that was very much his. To be honest, not a lot of that gets into *Managing Across Borders*. What it did was go from the hypothesis generation to the hypothesis-testing stage. It focused primarily on the innovation and learning. We'd developed these models about the difference between local and global and transnational innovation; and that managing those processes required the use of a different mix of the tools that we called centralization, formalization and socialization, and we hypothesized how they worked and what the tools were you needed. Centralization was obviously structurally driven, just pulling the roles and responsibilities and the decision making to the centre; formalization was largely embedding it in systems; and socialization was in building it in culture. So those were the hypotheses. Now, that's what Sumantra tested and, in fact, the tests came out pretty much confirming the hypotheses. It refined and said strong and medium amounts, but it was a refinement. *Managing Across Borders* was taking too big a view to get much of that into one part of one chapter and so it got into articles, subsequently, and then Sumantra wrote, with Nitin Nohria, a book called *The Differentiated Network* [Ghoshal and Nohria 1997] that largely explored and used that data.

My interests had always been much more in hypothesis generating and doing the clinical fieldwork. I would work with doctoral students and encourage them to do the survey work but it was something that didn't drive me, so I was interested in it but not willing to invest in it – that took time away from what, really, I loved, which was getting out into the field. By the time we did *The Individualized Corporation*, I think Sumantra's interest had equally moved onto doing the hypothesis generating, and then lots of people did the testing and did wonderful instruments that they went out and tested bits and pieces and that was terrific. You know, I think you add where your interests and your abilities are and that was what was driving us, I think.

C.W.   So what you're saying is that initially, when you designed *Managing Across Borders*, it was purely a case design?

C.B.   Yes, it was. In fact, if you read the book, the surveys are put in the appendix. Basically, the surveys confirmed the hypotheses that we've got in this book but the book doesn't use any of those data; there are no beta coefficients in the book, there's no fine-grained kind of calibration of how much centralization and formalization – it is written as a managerially accessible book but if you look in the appendix it says, you can have some confidence and this is where we've done some tests and it seems to hold up.

R.P.   Now, out of curiosity, you use the term 'clinical fieldwork' or 'clinical research' a lot. Where does that come from?

C.B.   The language is that of sociologists and anthropologists, which, I think, is much more where we operate. I think part of our field has been dominated by economists, and although I am an economist if I go back far enough in my history, I think that's just one discipline that can be very helpful. But no one asked Margaret Mead to send out a questionnaire – you've got to get out into the population to understand it.

C.W.   One of the questions we have is, is there a Chris Bartlett style of doing case research, and I think you've basically answered it. Tell me if I've got this right: the Chris Bartlett way is to go out into the field, bring back something which you then present in class. Your ideas and concepts then emerge from that experience of teaching, thinking about the data, collecting more data and generating research but also teaching material along the way. Is that how you see yourself working?

C.B.   Yes, I think that it's undergirded by a philosophy of personal learning, and that learning and insight really starts in the field. It's amplified when you take part of that field research and package it for a classroom, and that leverages it because it forces you, in preparing this, to think about it more deeply. But the research case is a lot richer than what you bring into the classroom; it's the file of 30-odd interviews that you've done in each of the companies and then written up in much more detail than you could ever bring into the classroom. That's leveraged not only by your own insight but, if you were fortunate enough to have a really good partnership, a big part of the learning was in the back and forth between Sumantra and me, so there's another way in which the data gets processed. Then the discipline of developing that into articles and then pulling articles together into a book. It's the freedom of following the data and then the discipline of interpreting the data and framing it, developing the hypotheses. Yes, I guess that's a philosophy, if there is one, or a style.

R.P.   It seemed to me that in terms of publication strategy, you talked about articles. But the real outcome of the project seems to be a book. Is that right?

C.B.   Well, the book puts it all together but the articles were a way of communicating to different audiences and in more fine-grained pieces. Lots of managers don't read books but they will read an article, so the *Sloan Management Review* or the *Harvard Business Review* or the *California Management Review* articles got to a lot of people and influenced practice. The same thing with academics; a lot of academics won't read books, and particularly books that are managerially relevant as well as hopefully academically respectable, but they will read their journals. It also allows you to dig in more depth around a particular issue – around innovation, for example, or around certain processes in an organization. So, yes, they serve different purposes: one is to help refine and develop one's own thoughts and, secondly, to communicate to different audiences. But the first time that I articulated the transnational concept was a chapter that I wrote for Mike Porter [Bartlett 1986], who edited a book called *Competition in Global Industries* back in 1986. That was one of the first articulations of the framing, and that's the sort of thing that, I think, forces your thinking and then becomes part of the outcome in the book.

C.W.   Getting back to the issue of getting published, you said on the one hand that the academic community was perhaps a little more narrow-minded than you originally anticipated coming into this new world but, on the other hand, you did get these pieces published, and in top journals. What, in your experience, are the main reservations that reviewers have about case-based research?

C.B.   Well, I think the bias is that it's not a large sample and so therefore you can't prove anything. But I think that's only part of it. The other part of it is often, if we're really brutally honest, a lot of case-based, field-based research is not well done – either the research isn't well done or it isn't well presented and so there's not the richness. Sometimes people do the field research and then they get driven back into writing it up in a format that really is designed for, or used by or accepted by people in presenting essentially survey research. So that by the time they go through all the literature review and tipping their hat at everyone and then the research design and whatever, out of all this rich research they present about a fifth of the paper trying to show what they've come up with and it just doesn't resonate, or at least it doesn't capture what they've gone through. So, I think there's a supply side and a demand side to the problem and that is something that we, as an academic community, have to deal with. There's a huge amount of criticism of academic research by the business community saying, look, we don't see the value in this, and yet we're turning to them for the funding of our institutions and they are employing the people whom we educate – there's got to be some credibility, that they believe that we're in touch with their world and that we can contribute to it.

C.W.   So, do you remember any ways in which you would convince the reviewers that, despite the fact that you didn't have statistics, or despite the fact that you only had a sample of nine – or even a sample of 20 – companies, nevertheless this was research that was 'scientific'?

C.B.   Well, yes. You don't get an opportunity to convince the reviewers apart from the document that you send them, so it's the quality of the work that will convince them. I think there is a bias in our journals and in our review system that reflects our business school academic community that's economics dominated. That's fine when you're dealing with macro issues of industry structure or competitive dynamics, often you can do that with databases that are more quantitative. But psychology and sociology and anthropology are legitimate disciplines that undergird the understanding of business. All I can say is, if we keep acknowledging only the economists then if you live by that market you'll die by that market. Or we see our legitimate contributors to this field as being other disciplines, and also that there's an importance attached to the application of those disciplines – in other words, the world in which we live, the business world which we influence. I guess if it's well done and the journals chosen are not the extreme – you probably wouldn't want to go into something that was an economics-driven journal – then you've probably got a chance.

REFERENCES

Bartlett, C.A. (1979), 'Multinational structural evolution: the changing decision environment in international divisions', DBA thesis, Graduate School of Business Administration, Harvard University.

Bartlett, C.A. (1986), 'Building and managing the transnational: the new organizational challenge', in M. Porter (ed.), *Competition in Global Industries: A Conceptual Framework*, Boston, MA: Harvard Business School Press, pp. 367–401.

Bartlett, C.A., N. Bennett and B.J. Hall (2008), 'GE's imagination breakthroughs: the Evo project', Harvard Business School, 9-907-048.

Bartlett, C.A. and S. Ghoshal (2002), *Managing Across Borders: The Transnational Solution*, 2nd edn, Boston, MA: Harvard Business School Press.

Ghoshal, S. and C.A. Bartlett (1997), *The Individualized Corporation: A Fundamentally New Approach to Management*, New York: HarperBusiness.

Ghoshal, S. and N. Nohria (1997), *The Differentiated Network: Organizing the Multinational Corporation for Value Creation*, San Francisco, CA: Jossey-Bass.

Stopford, J. (1968), 'Growth and organizational change in the multinational firm', DBA thesis, Graduate School of Business Administration, Harvard University.

3. Fifty years of case research in international business: the power of outliers and black swans

Yair Aharoni

INTRODUCTION

I started my acquaintance with case studies at Harvard Business School: as part and parcel of the requirements of my doctoral research I wrote several dozen cases on firms considering investments in Israel. Since then, and additionally, I have written more than 150 cases. The home countries of the case firms were the United States, Europe and Israel. I have also used case research methods in numerous studies, for example on subsidiaries of multinationals and their relationships with headquarters. I am deeply convinced that – at least in some of my studies – I would not have understood many business phenomena, or the way decisions are made, had I used any other method. Case study enables the researcher to gain a holistic view of a certain phenomenon or series of events, such as cultural systems of action (Feagin et al. 1991) – the latter referring to sets of interrelated activities engaged in by the actors in a social situation. Of course, in other studies I used other research methods that were more appropriate. Thus, in a study of all MBA graduates or of all Israeli managers, I used a carefully designed questionnaire.

When I was a doctoral student at Harvard Business School, MBA students took three classes a day and for each one of these classes they had to read a case study and prepare themselves for a heated discussion in class. Harvard strongly believed that generalizations reached from studies of individual cases are the best way to distil pearls of knowledge about the management of organizations. I understand that when the Harvard Business School started its operations, there were no textbooks suitable to a graduate programme in business. They therefore interviewed leading practitioners of business and wrote detailed accounts of what these managers were doing. I later learned that the case study method was used by researchers across a variety of disciplines. Sociology researchers in Chicago relied on case study research. In the 1930s, however, a movement within sociology attempted to make it more scientific. This movement called for applying quantitative measurements to research design and analysis. Columbia University sociology professors were the champions of a more rigorous scientific method. In 1935, they won a public debate between them and the supporters of the Chicago School. In medicine, prospective doctors learned to diagnose diseases by examining individual patients and learning to look for symptoms. Law students, too, are being trained by using case studies.

At the same time, case studies have been criticized by many researchers as lacking scientific rigour and reliability. I am not going to repeat the different allegations against case study research, nor do I try to answer these allegations or enumerate the many benefits researchers can gain by using case studies, which others have done. Instead, I shall reflect on my experience in the last five decades of researching through case studies and teaching cases. The reader may perhaps see this chapter as a case study on case studies. I believe this case demonstrates why I think case studies are essential to the understanding of organizations and to the development of plausible hypotheses. I shall also reflect on why case studies lost their attractiveness as a research tool, discussing the changes in the perceptions of the case study over the years in international business (IB) research.

THE FOREIGN INVESTMENT DECISION PROCESS

My doctoral research was aimed at finding how US firms decide to invest in foreign markets. I was distressed by the apparent failure of less-developed countries (LDCs) to attract manufacturing investments from the United States. Specifically, foreign direct investment (FDI) into Israel, despite the fervent attempts by the Israeli government to encourage it by enacting the Law for Encouragement of Capital Investments, did not in fact materialize. Therefore, I resolved to study the way foreign investment decisions are made by US manufacturing firms. I hoped that by finding out the considerations business persons took into account in making FDI decisions, I could unearth ways and means to increase FDI in LDCs. Based on my training in economics, I assumed that since tax incentives permit a higher rate of return, such incentives can make otherwise unpromising investments attractive. I therefore believed that the conferral of tax benefits would induce foreign investors to initiate projects which they would not otherwise have undertaken. The problem seemed to be straightforward: how large should the incentives be?

I made a list of firms that had considered an investment in Israel. I wrote about 40 case studies on the history of the decisions, both by interviewing managers and by reading files of correspondence and other documents related to the decision. I soon found out that tax incentives did not play the decisive role I had expected them to play. Moreover, the picture emerging from my field research seemed to be one of utterly irrational behaviour and a complete lack of economic logic. The decision process had very little in common with the classical economic theory of capital investments. It was necessary to look at the system as a whole, recognizing that decisions are made under uncertainty within an organization and a social system. Once I changed the lens what seemed irrational made sense. I could then offer a behavioural theory that explained how and why decisions are made and how and why commitments accumulate.

I started my research with a set of preconceived notions, dictated by my previous studies. Again, I was sure that firms could be attracted by offering a tax holiday. The only question was how much? I could have designed a questionnaire, asking a carefully chosen sample of managers to rank the size of the tax holiday they would require in order to make a foreign investment, and add some other questions on related topics. I am sure I would have received answers that could have been tabulated and regressed against other variables. I am also sure the answers would have indicated that tax holidays are desirable – which managers would say they would not want these holidays? I am also convinced that in the decision-making process – as it unfolded according to my research – considerations of tax subsidies come late in the process. First and foremost, a powerful force should operate that will make the firm decide to even look abroad. Based on the strength of this force the firm starts a long process of investigation. The decision to invest is a result of a long process dependent on many variables that will not be repeated here. My field study convinced me that in order for a country to attract a foreign investment, it is crucial to trigger a decision to look at the country in question. In other words, I learned that countries have to be actively marketed – and at that early but crucial stage tax holidays are not an important variable. I published a paper on that idea (see Aharoni 1966). Finally, and most importantly, had I followed my preconceived idea and chosen to study foreign investments through a questionnaire – however carefully designed – I would never have been exposed to the rich saga of the real foreign investment decision process and to the way real managers in real firms make decisions.

BUSINESS STRATEGY IN DOMESTIC AND IN INTERNATIONAL MARKETS

For many years, I taught business strategy to MBA students. When I was a doctoral candidate, there was no such course – the nearest equivalent was called Business Policy. In the tradition of the Harvard Business School we learned and attempted to reach generalizations from case studies describing specific situations. In Israel, no such case studies existed – and I had to write many of them. Thus I was exposed to many specific – often fascinating – problems of business strategy in a small country. At the time Israel protected its local firms employing so-called import substitution policies. In many cases, the strategy of the firm concentrated on getting benefits from the government rather than on achieving competitive advantage in the marketplace. In subsequent years, the government changed its policies, exposing the firms to foreign competition. Many of those relying only on government protection as a competitive advantage could not continue operations. Others developed competitive advantages in a market now dominated by giant foreign firms.

My case research has shown that the successful firms did not attempt to compete head on against the foreign giants. Instead, they identified a particular market niche in which they were basically a monopoly – being the only firm that supplied a certain unique product or service. Strategy, I realized, was not about *gaining competitive advantage in an industry* but about *creating a monopoly in a well-defined niche.* In other words, strategy is about being unique, different from others – not about being part of the herd. I also learned that if the niche remains small, the firm does too. Alternatively, the firm grows by diversification – entering several distinct niches. At the same time, if the niche grows very large, it may attract large firms who can make life difficult for the small competitors. Often a large firm acquires the small firm to get access to the accumulated knowledge. This observation was even more relevant to international operations: Israeli firms cannot even hope to compete head on in the global market against the giant multinational firms. They can, however, be very successful when they define a small niche that is either ignored (often because of its size) or is unknown to the large firms in the industry. As one example, Netafim, an Israeli multinational firm, invented drip irrigation. It is able to sell to those who are willing to pay more to save water – in areas in which water is a scarce commodity. Of course, markets for new products develop simultaneously around the world. A growth-oriented firm must rapidly develop an international network in the business. Further, since product life cycles are growing shorter the firm must constantly develop new products or processes. It must also develop the intensive customer interaction necessary for good product development and market adaptation. Being small, many successful Israeli firms concentrate on niches in which the number of customers is small.

Michael Porter (1980, 1981, 1985) revolutionized the field of strategy by adapting ideas and concepts developed by Bain (1968) to the field of industrial organization. For Porter, the main analytical tool was identifying the forces of competition in an industry. He made examination of industry structure a cornerstone in the strategic analysis of the firm. Strategy has been assumed to be generic, largely determined by environmental forces. His work, as we all know, had an enormous impact on the field. Many young researchers flocked into the field, studying different industries. They paid more attention to industry characteristics than to unique means of achieving competitive advantage. A large flow of statistically based research efforts attempted to connect industry structure with strategy, with performance or with other variables. Their research turned out to be easier to publish. Referees seem to like a large table with many results from regression analysis. This research output allowed important insights but also ignored or left unanswered many issues. The firm was taken as a 'black box'. The theoretical constructs and the data led to a concern for the explanation of a Marshallian 'representative firm'. In an attempt to achieve scientific rigour, strategy research abandoned its major *raison d'être* – the search for the unique. To some extent the same phenomenon could be seen in the advance of the population ecology field in sociology. When one looks at all competitors in an industry, one fails to identify great strategies designed by an outlier that is operating by different ideas, achieving success by being unique in a certain specific, well-identified, niche in which this firm does not compete – it controls.

One of the many examples I liked to use is familiar to many – unlike some very specific examples from Israel. This is the story of Perrier. The firm was very successful in selling water in easy to recognize bottles. Now if Perrier had perceived itself as part of the mineral water industry it should have concluded that shipping heavy bottles from France to the United States in which water is abundant is not a viable strategy. Perrier, however, did not sell water. It sold prestigious beverages – and was very successful in doing so. Much later, two INSEAD professors coined the term 'value innovation' for such a policy (Kim and Mauborgne 2005). They illustrate through 150 cases the high growth and profits an organization can generate by creating new demand in an uncontested market space, or a 'blue ocean', as opposed to competing head to head with other suppliers for known customers in an existing industry. Their book became a bestseller – perhaps because they did not compete in the general industry of books or even that of strategy books, but offered something unique and created new demand. I am sure that insights like the ones offered on the blue ocean, or those I had offered my students, cannot be distilled from a statistical study of a large population of firms in an industry. Such insights are only the result of a careful study of specific cases. The case study method enabled me to understand better the complex real-life activities of firms. Case studies also allowed learning more about real-life decisions as opposed to what managers would like you to think or the preconceived notions the researcher has because of clinging to economic theory.

Parenthetically, researchers may study a large population and reach wrong conclusions because the choice of the population studied was not a representative sample. Thus, many of the conclusions reached by Porter (1990) are the result of studying mainly US-based corporations. Many Israeli firms (and for that matter, Canadian ones) did not grow first in their home market. In fact, the Israeli high-technology industry exports more than 90 per cent of its output. In several cases, the firm does not sell in Israel at all. Again, these ideas, and others, could not have been unearthed without deeply penetrating the ways firms actually behave.

BUSINESS AND GOVERNMENT

In 1970, I spent a sabbatical teaching at IMEDE in Lausanne, Switzerland. The school started as a place for educating managers. When I joined its faculty, a decision was made to start an MBA programme. I argued forcefully that unlike in the United States, European firms are very much affected by the government and other environmental forces. In most European countries at that time, the government owned firms. It also had an enormous impact on private firms. My view was accepted. The faculty decided to include an innovative course in environmental analysis coined OIE (Organization and Its Environment) and I was asked to teach it. No suitable material could be found for such a course. Casebooks prepared in the United States dealt exclusively with the American environment, which did not seem appropriate for a student body that was largely European in composition and whose members were anticipating careers in international management. With the help of an able research assistant, I embarked on a two-year case research effort, collecting and creating materials and teaching the new course. Later, environmental analysis seemed increasingly to find a place in the IB curriculum and we decided to publish the core of these cases (Aharoni with Baden 1977). The cases underlined the fact that understanding the environment is a universal need. It was also obvious that there is no simple formula for analysing problems in the environment – no break-even formula, no decision tree, and no income statement. Yet one can – and should – identify the relevant actors in each situation and evaluate their relative positions, and the importance of the problem to them. One can then evaluate the total system and find out how the different actors might interact. Situations may seem innocuous at first sight but often involve a large number of actors. A regular environmental analysis helps managers to understand trends, foresee potential problems, evaluate alternative courses of action and avoid conflict situations. More importantly, it may reveal new opportunities in the environment.

When I came back to Israel I continued this line of research, writing cases on business–government relations, or on a quarry perceived by the Society for Protection of Nature as detrimental to clean air and a safe environment. All these cases allowed me to penetrate issues in business–government relations. Note that one of the characteristics of a democratic society is that power is diffused throughout the society. The spectrum of interest groups is wide. These groups may hinder the manager from achieving certain objectives. Business itself is one of the most powerful organized interest groups. Managers should be able to identify different actors and assess their strengths both in their home as well as in the host country.

SERVICES

In the mid-1980s I began to study the globalization of services, such as management consulting, accounting, lawyers, educational institutions, health services and several other industries. These studies reminded me of the falsification rule, proposed by Karl Popper (1959). Falsification is one of the most rigorous tests to which a scientific proposition can be subjected: if just one observation does not fit with the proposition it is considered not valid generally and must therefore be either revised or rejected. Popper himself used the now famous example of 'All swans are white', and proposed that just one observation of a single black swan would falsify this proposition and in this way have general significance and stimulate further investigations and theory building. The case study is well suited for identifying 'black swans' because of its in-depth approach: what appears to be 'white' often turns out on closer examination to be 'black'.

Indeed, services provided many 'black swans'. Thus, IB theory attempted to explain why firms invest abroad rather than export despite the additional costs as a result of so-called 'liability of foreignness'. The explanation was that firms possess an exploitable factor that creates an oligopolistic advantage. John Dunning's eclectic theory referred to 'ownership advantages' (Dunning 1980). Based on this line of reasoning one may assume that firms would invest abroad when they possess a clear ownership advantage. However, world famous universities did not create subsidiaries abroad, despite their clear advantage. Harvard Business School attempted to offer executive education in Switzerland but failed. Further, received IB theory assumed that firms seek to control their subsidiaries and therefore want full ownership to protect their intellectual property. Only because government, having the advantage of bargaining obsolescence, demands joint ventures, does the firm use this route. Many researchers cited IBM as a firm that, because of its ownership advantage in the form of a never-ending pipeline of new patents, could force, for example, the Indian government to allow it full ownership of its subsidiaries. Yet hotel chain management seems to prefer joint ventures and use this form even when the government allows full ownership.

As to industries, according to Porter, when competition in each nation is essentially independent the industry is multidomestic, for example banks and life insurance firms. In contrast, in global industries firms are compelled to compete internationally in order to achieve or sustain competitive advantage. Firms compete on global market share. 'But choosing a domestic focus in a global industry is perilous, no matter what the firm's home nation' (Porter 1990, p. 54). Yet in many professional services such as management consultants, accountants, engineers or lawyers one encounters many domestic firms and also a few multinationals. Is the theory wrong or the definition of industry erroneous? Further, according to Porter (1990) and many others, experience in a (large) home country is essential to gain ownership advantages and then invest abroad. However, consider the case of ISS. Its home country is Denmark and it works all over the world offering cleaning services – although its home market is small.

One reason for the differences is that the world is changing. If there is any theme that can surely characterize the IB world of the last quarter of the twentieth century it is change, but change that is taking place at an unprecedented rate. Technological changes and new innovations alter the way business is done, the macroeconomic situation is very different from what it was, confrontations are more violent and 'irrational' than ever before, older populations grow with extended life expectancy and there are relatively fewer young persons so deficits in pension plans grow exponentially. The multinational enterprises (MNEs) of several dozens of years ago extracted rents from existing resources and knowledge developed at home. Today they are learning and developing new capabilities in a globally coordinated network. In this network, knowledge can be developed in any subsidiary and then transferred to the whole network. Indeed, the MNEs are transforming themselves. They learn and adapt themselves to the changing environment. Clearly, theory should adapt too. Indeed, IB theory does not have the ability to predict the future or to anticipate many of these changes. To a large extent, the theory is very much context dependent. It does not necessarily apply to different environments and diverse contexts nor is it independent of these factors. The case study method is very well suited to produce this context-dependent knowledge. Donald Campbell explains:

> After all, man is, in his ordinary way, a very competent knower, and qualitative common-sense knowing is not replaced by quantitative knowing. . . . This is not to say that such common-sense naturalistic observation is objective, dependable, or unbiased. But it is all that we have. It is the only route to knowledge – noisy, fallible, and biased though it be. (Campbell 1975, p. 179)

Despite these facts, case research lost its appeal to researchers of international business. It is intriguing to speculate why so many researchers plead against the use of case studies as a research method. Why is it that so many strategy researchers study industries rather than firms and ignore the issue of distinctive competence? The next section of this chapter speculates on this issue.

WHY DID CASE RESEARCH LOSE ITS ATTRACTIVENESS?

Social scientists are trained to avoid studying actions seen as purely random or idiosyncratic. They study the behaviour of groups of firms, not that of any particular one. The pioneers of scientific management attempted to discover general rules of behaviour, such as number of hierarchical levels or span of control, assumed to be pertinent to all organizations. Only decades later were contingent variables introduced – again explaining the behaviour of a population. In sociology, the population ecology school emphasized evaluation of the population of organizations, seeing survival as based on natural selection and luck in achieving a fit with a changing environment (for example, Hannan and Freeman 1977). Economists stressed that scientific interpretation must be based on solid analysis of a large enough number of observations to allow statistical testing of the significance of the results. Economists also tended to look down at researchers not using the toolkit that the economists believed in. Caves (1980, p. 88), in a survey of strategy contributions, argued that strategy researchers 'lacked the tools to follow [their] blueprints' and proposed that 'errors and omissions' can be avoided by using economic models. He declared 'professional modesty' but concluded that 'well-trained professional economists could have carried out many of the research projects cited in this paper more proficiently than did the authors, who were less effectively equipped by their own disciplines' (Caves 1980, p. 88). Porter (1981) also recommended the application of economic reasoning to business strategy issues.

Of course, international economists refused to even mention or recognize the existence of the MNE in their textbooks, concentrating only on international trade. Free trade in these textbooks was based on assumptions of a frictionless world and homogeneous products. Yet after the work of Hymer (1976) and other pioneers, and based on the path-blazing ideas of Ronald Coase (1937), they moved to an analysis of the MNE. When transaction costs are recognized, the need to internalize firm-specific advantages will lead to FDI by multinational firms. These firms operate in oligopolistic industries and must have firm-specific advantages in intangible assets that they can internalize to compensate for the additional costs of foreign operations. Yet, an attempt was made to look for generic ownership advantages – not to unique means of achieving such an advantage. Specifically, IB researchers learned to look at the firm as a black box and ignored any study of top management teams or behaviour of executives. Later it was understood that successful MNEs also learn very quickly; they can transfer any good ideas emanating in one country to all other countries in the network. Environments were treated most of the time as objective facts, independent of the firms. The ability to generate oligopoly rents by political action or through collusion is almost always ignored. The ability to change the environment by innovation of new products that alter the structure of the market was recognized only recently.

In my view, these discrepancies are largely a result of clinging onto principles of economic theory, ignoring signals from the real world of real firms that could have been discovered through case study research. One major exception for the total reliance on economic models has been the area of culture. Geert Hofstede's (1980) great contribution was to offer future researchers a toolkit to study large populations based on his codification of different cultural dimensions. He himself had the advantage of a huge databank of surveys of IBM employees between 1967 and 1973 in 40 countries. His groundbreaking contribution was the development of a set of cultural dimensions that can be measured through survey instruments.

One possibility for the decline of case research is the seductive appeal of the availability of large databases. I personally contributed some observations to the large databank developed by Raymond Vernon on US-based multinationals. One result of the existence of this source was several excellent and thought-provoking PhD theses that took advantage of the databank. In fact for quite some time the term 'multinationals' became synonymous with giant US multinationals. Vernon's databank purposely ignored firms that were not listed in the Fortune 500. He and his followers thus did not have to explain how a firm like International Flavors and Fragrances became a multinational. Further, multinationals whose home country was, say, Switzerland or Sweden, were not considered. The ease of access to a rich database has certainly been a reason for studies based on this source.

Indeed, another and related reason is the long time it takes the researcher to conduct a case study. It is much easier to design a questionnaire, mail it to a defined population, and employ different methods of statistical analysis, hoping to get a high level of significance. To be sure, the probability of acceptance for a paper based on a statistical analysis of a population is several degrees greater than for a paper claiming results distilled by the author – with no statistical proof – from a few or even dozens of case studies. Here, incidentally, there is also a sort of a cultural bias. Medical doctors can analyse one case of a disease and get the paper published. Reviewers of IB papers would reject such a paper outright as not scientific enough. It may also be that case research necessitates much more experience and expertise. A young scholar is surely much more equipped to use statistical analysis of a large population than to interpret and fine tune the evidence unearthed in a case research. Parenthetically, in the 1950s and 1960s teachers of strategy tended to be old and experienced. When teaching strategy and conducting research on it researchers came to rely on clear and rigid rules stemming from large aggregates of firms that textbooks offered. These 'eternal truths' were based on, for example, PIMS or Compustat; long experience ceased to be a prerequisite for research or teaching.

I believe that the major reason why case research is considered inferior to quantitative analysis is the urge of IB scholars to be as scientific as the natural sciences. Many of these researchers were trained as economists – and economists prefer econometric methods to what is perceived as descriptive case study research. The quest and temptation of additional rigour called for a solid analysis of a large number of observations. The scientist adopts the position of an objective researcher who collects facts about the social world and then builds up an explanation of social life by arranging such facts in a chain of causality. Unfortunately, to achieve rigour the researchers find themselves very distant from reality – which is socially constructed rather than objectively determined. The task of IB researchers should not be to gather facts and measure how often certain patterns occur, but to appreciate the different constructions and meanings that people place upon their experience. Human behaviour is very complex. Executives do not always maximize profits. They are also family members, belong to different clubs and interest groups and are citizens of a nation – and all of these affiliations impact on our behaviour.

As one example, assume we want to understand the meaning of MNE home country for strategy and other variables. Theoretically, one can argue that this is a totally irrelevant fact. The top management team should make decisions that will maximize the value of the firm to its shareholders. Thus, the MNE should split the value chain and outsource activities to where they could be done in the cheapest possible manner. At least in some cases I researched, the nationality of the home country did make a difference. In the case of the largest Israeli-based multinational Teva, the by-laws by which it is governed specifically require that its CEO will reside in Israel. Despite Milton Friedman's dictum, the social responsibility of the firm is not only to maximize profits. Here lies the advantage of case study research. It allows an understanding of a complex issue. Case studies emphasize detailed contextual analysis of a limited number of events or conditions and their relationships. It is the best means to investigate a contemporary phenomenon within its real-life context (see Yin 2009) using a qualitative approach. Denzin and Lincoln (1994) explain that 'qualitative' implies an emphasis on processes and meanings that are not rigorously examined, or measured (if measured at all) in terms of quantity, amount, intensity, or frequency. Researchers should be interested in insight, discovery and interpretation rather than hypothesis testing.

A frequent criticism of case study methodology is that since it is based on a single case or a small number of cases it cannot establish reliability or generality of findings. However, the seminal contribution of Chandler (1962) to strategy is based on a painstaking analysis of four cases. As Flyvbjerg (2006) points out, Galileo Galilei's falsification of Aristotle's law of gravity was not based upon observations 'across a wide range', or 'carried out in some numbers'. The rejection consisted primarily of a conceptual experiment and later of a single practical experiment; that is, a case study (Flyvbjerg 2006). It consisted of trials of objects – not even selected by random sampling – falling from a wide range of randomly selected heights under varying wind conditions. The Aristotelian view was not finally rejected until half a century later, with the invention of the air pump. The air pump made it possible to conduct the ultimate experiment whereby a coin or a piece of lead inside a vacuum tube falls with the same speed as a feather. After this experiment, Aristotle's view could be maintained no longer. What is especially worth noting, however, is that the matter was settled by an individual case due to the clever choice of the extremes of metal and feather (Flyvbjerg 2006). I would emphasize that the case study method was used in refuting a theory in the natural sciences!

CONCLUSION

IB research has prematurely settled on a rather narrow scope of problems to be studied, ignoring managerial behaviour, processes, politics and, to a large extent, dynamics and technological change. In an ever-shifting turbulent environment, IB research failed to cope with changing reality in the global arena. Far too much attention – from Raymond Vernon to Alan Rugman – has been devoted to the giant firms of the Fortune 500 list and on statistical analysis. Many new innovations in the operations of firms may have been explained after they happened – but were not predicted by researchers. Researchers may find it rewarding to look at the unique, the different and the outlier rather than search for central tendencies in a population of MNEs. The outlier changes the rules of the game and may achieve immutable and sustainable high profits. Careful case studies may unearth rules for identification of successful breakthroughs, means of achieving firm-specific advantages, a better understanding of the behaviour of top management teams as well as the interaction of international business and governments. As I pointed out in a recent paper (Aharoni 2010), the success of MNEs is at least as much a function of management ability and behaviour as it is of industry characteristics or environmental factors. MNE managers, like all managers, display human limitations, such as overconfidence, that affect judgement. Yet IB researchers still tend to ignore management in their research, treating the firm as a black box. To the extent that the top management team is considered, rational behaviour in the classical economic sense is assumed, yet, clearly, managers behave according to different rules from those assumed in much of the IB literature. Further, managers are not part of a herd, but unique. The result of such a lacuna is that theory fails to predict actual behaviour and does not allow the best guidance for policy options (Aharoni 2010). A return to case research is one means to correct this problem.

REFERENCES

Aharoni, Y. (1966), 'How to market a country', *Columbia Journal of World Business*, **1** (2), 41–9.

Aharoni, Y. (2010), 'Behavioral elements in foreign direct investments', *Advances in International Management*, **23**, 73–112.

Aharoni, Y. with C. Baden (1977), *Business in the International Environment: A Casebook*, London: Macmillan.

Bain, J.S. (1968), *Industrial Organization*, 2nd edn, New York: Wiley.

Campbell, D.T. (1975), 'Degrees of freedom and the case study', *Comparative Political Studies*, **8** (1), 178–93.

Caves, R.E. (1980), 'Industrial organization, corporate strategy and structure', *Journal of Economic Literature*, **18** (March), 64–92.

Caves R.E. (1984), 'Economic analysis and the quest for competitive advantage', *American Economic Review*, **74** (May), 127–36.

Chandler, A.D. (1962), *Strategy and Structure: Chapters in the History of the Industrial Enterprise*, Cambridge, MA: MIT Press.

Coase, R. (1937), 'The nature of the firm', *Economica*, **4** (3), 386–405.

Denzin, N. and Y. Lincoln (1994), *Handbook of Qualitative Research*, Thousand Oaks, CA: Sage.

Dunning, J.H. (1980), 'Towards an eclectic theory of international production: some empirical tests', *Journal of International Business Studies*, **11** (1), 9–31.

Feagin, J., A. Orum and G. Sjoberg (eds) (1991), *A Case for Case Study*, Chapel Hill, NC: Unversity of North Carolina Press.

Flyvbjerg, B. (2006), 'Five misunderstandings about case study research', *Qualitative Inquiry*, **12** (2), 219–45.

Hannan, M.T. and J. Freeman (1977), 'The population ecology of organizations', *American Journal of Sociology*, **82**, 929–64.

Hofstede, G. (1980), *Culture's Consequences: International Differences in Work-related Values*, Newbury Park, CA: Sage.

Hymer, S.H. (1976), *The International Operations of National Firms: A Study of Direct Foreign Investment*, Cambridge, MA: MIT Press.

Kim, W.C. and R. Mauborgne (2005), *Blue Ocean Strategy: How to Create Uncontested Market Space and Make the Competition Irrelevant*, Boston, MA: Harvard Business School Press.

Popper, K. (1959), *The Logic of Scientific Discovery*, New York: Basic Books.

Porter, M.E. (1980), *Competitive Strategy: Techniques for Analyzing Industries and Competition*, New York: Free Press.

Porter, M.E. (1981), 'The contributions of industrial organization to strategic management', *Academy of Management Review*, **6** (4), 609–20.

Porter, M.E. (1985), *Competitive Advantage*, New York: Free Press.

Porter, M.E. (1990), *The Competitive Advantage of Nations*, New York: Free Press.

Yin, R. (2009), *Case Study Research: Design and Methods*, 4th edn, Beverly Hills, CA: Sage.

4. The view from the editorial office: an interview with Pervez Ghauri

Rebecca Piekkari and Catherine Welch

International Business Review (*IBR*) was founded in 1991 and the first volume came out in 1992. Its original name was *Scandinavian International Business Review* but in 1993 the journal underwent a name change in order to overcome the perceived liability of being associated with research on Scandinavia or from scholars affiliated with institutions from the region. In 2003 *IBR* became the official journal of the European International Business Academy, which reflected its growing influence and standing in the field. The journal was accepted into the Social Sciences Citation Index (ISI) in 2005 and the first impact factor (1.200) came out in 2008. In 2008, the acceptance rate was 14 per cent. The founding editor, Pervez N. Ghauri, has remained at the helm of the journal since 1992.

R.P.   As Editor-in-Chief of *IBR*, could you tell us why the journal was established back in the early 1990s?

P.G.   The primary motivation to establish a new journal stemmed from European scholars' frustration with the parochialism and methodological biases that characterized US journals at that time. While they favoured quantitative techniques, Europe had a longstanding tradition of qualitative research. For example, the classical article by Jan Johanson and Jan-Erik Vahlne, published in the *Journal of International Business Studies* (*JIBS*) in 1977, was based on qualitative case research. Many scholars, including Jan and Jan-Erik themselves, speculate that had this paper been submitted 10 years later the Uppsala model, which has become so well cited and acknowledged in our field, might never have been accepted for publication in *JIBS*.

   IBR was therefore to be a journal without any methodological or geographical preferences. This was reflected in the composition of our editorial review board, as well as the reviewer form of the journal. For example, reviewers are explicitly asked whether they believe that the data analysis technique (quantitative or qualitative) is appropriate for the particular research question. In other words, we do not assume a particular methodology is the best or only one.

I work a lot with qualitative methods myself. In the early 1990s, I felt very strongly about starting a new journal in the field of international business, and so did several colleagues of mine based in Europe and Scandinavia. At that time there were not many journals around, and even fewer that would have accepted qualitative research. In retrospect, this decision was perhaps naive and even daring but the timing of this venture proved to be right. From the start, we had enough submissions as the scope of the journal was quite broad. *IBR* did not only cover international business and marketing but also other areas of the field. The new journal received support from well-established publishers and scholars such as Peter Buckley, Tamer Cavusgil, Jan Johanson, Philip Kotler, Jagdish Sheth and Jan-Erik Vahlne.

The first issue of *IBR* was commissioned and consisted of papers from well-established scholars in the field. However, this has been the only issue with invited papers. Looking back at the history of the journal, I would argue that not many European journals have made it in this competitive game of publishing. However, I would never have thought how much work it is to be an editor!

C.W.   Do you take methodological biases into account when selecting reviewers?

P.G.   As editors we have an important role to play in matching the right reviewer with the right paper. I would not send a qualitative paper to a quantitative researcher or vice versa. That would kill the paper for sure. *IBR* has never been short of qualitative reviewers. On the contrary, in the beginning there was a lack of quantitative researchers in Europe! Also, 50 per cent of the editorial board is European and many of them are qualitative researchers themselves. Since *IBR* was established to address the methodological bias of US journals, and I have personally struggled as a qualitative researcher to get published, my approach to methodological issues as editor is different.

Perhaps it is a common belief that editors do not accept qualitative papers. I would argue, however, that in at least 50 per cent of the cases it is the researcher's fault, not the reviewer's or editor's, that a paper is rejected. First of all, authors should be more specific about their methodological choices and decisions. Many researchers do not bother to explain and convince the reader. I would say that much of the methodological reporting is descriptive: what has been done. When reading manuscripts an editor or a reviewer is looking for arguments that explain why the authors use a particular research strategy or technique. What we look for is whether the use of a particular method or technique is appropriate for the research question at hand. It is the author's responsibility to argue strongly for the methodological choices and convince the reader about their suitability. Frankly speaking, few of them do this job properly.

Based on my long experience as editor I have come across five common problems that authors should avoid when writing and submitting qualitative papers:

1. *Problem of positioning* The author should be able to position his/her work in relation to previous contributions and the current state of theorizing in the field. For example, if the manuscript is positioned as a theory-testing piece the qualitative approach is not easy to justify. Thus, already the positioning, both theoretically and methodologically, should provide a solid justification for the chosen approach.
2. *Problem of argumentation* As mentioned earlier, the author should argue for the best possible fit between the research question and the method. While qualitative papers often lack strong argumentation, the reader is still expected to pick up the hidden message.
3. *Problem of estimation* Qualitative research is often criticized for being very subjective. For example, if the author develops a model or propositions he/she proposes relationships between constructs. They may take the form of rank order, level of intensity, frequency or importance, for example. The question arises: how does the author estimate the influence of different aspects on the phenomenon he/she is studying? This becomes even more problematic in cross-cultural (international) research because the author needs to convince the reader of the equivalence between datasets.
4. *Problem of analysis* A critical step in any qualitative study is data analysis. How does the author make sense of a large amount of textual, verbal or observational data? How is the data reduced from thousands of pages of interview transcripts to an abstract model or a set of propositions? The reader should not be wondering: what have you done with all these data you have collected? What is the connection between the descriptive data and the conclusions? Too few researchers discuss the analytical process and if they do, they should be much more argumentative and not simply recount what they have done. This stage should be as transparent as possible and it should be conducted systematically.
5. *Problem of trustworthiness* It is the author's responsibility to establish the trustworthiness of qualitative results and convince the reader of this. This can be done by ensuring that the research is conducted in a somewhat formalized and systematic manner.

C.W. During your editorship since 1992, have there been some changes in terms of qualitative manuscripts submitted to *IBR*?

P.G. I would say that there has definitely been a change in the attitude among US colleagues and journals. They are now more receptive to qualitative research and its value. Overall, it is now much more competitive to get published than previously.

C.W. Could you tell us what is the share of submissions to *IBR* in terms of qualitative and quantitative manuscripts?

P.W. I would say that about 50 per cent of manuscripts are qualitative. I desk reject a paper if the authors have not positioned their papers properly, the research question or contribution is not clear, or the paper is not methodologically sound. About 30 per cent of the papers these days are desk rejected. I believe desk rejections are necessary because I should not waste my reviewers' time. Moreover, it is good for the authors that they receive an answer soon as to whether their paper is suitable for the journal or not. As editor, I tend to take a developmental approach and suggest certain changes to the paper if appropriate. Thereafter, I sometimes even allow the authors to resubmit.

The share of qualitative and quantitative manuscripts in special issues may vary a lot. Normally we do one special issue per year. The special issues of the journal represent special themes and in *IBR* I have purposefully not allowed too many of them per year. I don't have control over special issues and therefore the credibility of guest editors is essential.

C.W. Could you tell us what happens if one reviewer is very negative and the other more favourable?

P.G. There are three options. The paper is rejected or, if I think that the comments are encouraging and the changes are doable, the authors will be given an opportunity to revise and resubmit. The paper will then be sent back to the original reviewers. Alternatively, I consult a third reviewer and make my editorial decision based on the three reviews.

R.P. What do you think are the key characteristics of a good reviewer of a qualitative paper?

P.G. I strongly believe that the reviewers should review a paper above all on the basis of its internal consistency. Is the paper properly positioned? Does it deliver what it promises in a systematic manner? The reviewers should look at the research questions and see whether the methods used are appropriate and properly argued for. If this is the case, they can be more constructive and developmental in their suggestions and recommendations. I do believe that most reviewers are constructive and do a great job in helping authors to improve their papers. But if a paper lacks these fundamental issues, it is the reviewer's responsibility to be honest and let the authors know. This is a learning experience.

C.W.   What advice could you give to other IB journals in terms of handling qualitative manuscripts?

P.G.   I think editors have a responsibility to match the reviewers to the papers in terms of methodological expertise as well as area of specialization. If this is done the authors will get good comments, regardless of whether the paper is accepted or not. I believe that we have come a long way and most journals, especially IB journals, are now very open and receptive to qualitative research, if it is conducted and presented properly.

R.P.   How do you see the future of *IBR* and the role of qualitative research in IB?

P.G.   I am quite optimistic about the future of *IBR*. We have experienced and survived many hurdles and are now reaching the same level as other top international journals. I hope our colleagues will now use *IBR* more and more as an outlet for their future research so that we can achieve a better impact factor, which is our collective responsibility!

The future of qualitative research is getting brighter every day. As I said earlier, most journals are now accepting qualitative papers. However, we should not look at IB as a battlefield between qualitative and quantitative methods or research. Both traditions serve their own purpose and in the end it is the research question that determines the type of the research method, not the researcher!

REFERENCE

Johanson, J. and J.E. Vahlne (1977), 'The internationalization process of the firm: a model of knowledge development and increasing foreign market commitments', *Journal of International Business Studies*, **8** (1), 23–32.

PART II

Multiple paradigms for theorizing

5. Critical realism and case studies in international business research

Ricardo Morais*

INTRODUCTION

What is the appropriate role for qualitative research and case studies? In the field of international business (IB), qualitative studies are thought to be especially appropriate 'to discover new relationships or situations not previously conceived' (Daniels and Cannice 2004, p. 186). Such an emphasis on uncovering new relationships may, however, reflect the underlying philosophical paradigm which the researcher has adopted – consciously or unconsciously. A positivist paradigm, for instance, assumes reality as objective and knowledge as independent of our values; science is accordingly the collection of facts. From such a perspective, the aim of research is to discover natural laws which determine human behaviour. This paradigm, which permeates the IB field, implies that qualitative studies should be restricted to exploratory research, because small samples are not suited to uncovering general laws. In Zalan and Lewis's (2004, p. 522) words, 'there has been a tendency within the positivist paradigm to confine idiographic research to the initial stages of scientific inquiry, stemming from a lack of familiarity with the ontological, epistemological and methodological principles of qualitative methods'. The dominance of positivism in IB research therefore restricts case studies to a subordinate role, and questions their ability to contribute to scientific explanation.

In contrast, other paradigms such as constructivism and critical theory (for example, Lincoln and Guba 2000) assume that reality is subjective and knowledge is value dependent. The aim of such paradigms, therefore, is to research values rather than facts. In addition, alternative paradigms to positivism may legitimize qualitative studies with explanatory aims, whose purpose is the exploration of facts. Conventional realism, for instance, is a paradigm which focuses on facts instead of values, as it shares positivist assumptions that reality is objective and knowledge independent of our values. Yet conventional realists consider case studies appropriate for both exploratory and explanatory research. Thus, they seek qualitative generation and development of theory, whereas positivism seeks quantitative testing of theory. Ontological, epistemological and methodological assumptions are thus crucial to assessing the appropriateness of qualitative research in general and case studies in particular.

Central to such a debate about the role of the case study is the claim that realism has a greater focus on context, given that positivism relies on fewer analytical variables (Ragin 1987), and in its pursuit of generalizable laws seeks to abstract away from context. A hypothesis, for instance, includes two analytical variables only. Therefore, it can be regarded as an undercontextualized simplification of reality. Conventional realist models, by contrast, tend to include more analytical variables in order to prevent undercontextualization. Such a dilemma between greater or fewer variables (see McGrath 1982) was present in my own doctoral research (Madureira 2004). In my thesis, I investigated foreign subsidiary managers (FSMs) of Finnish Multinational Corporations (MNCs). Although the research strategy I used was a multiple case study, adding variables to the analysis turned out to be insufficient in explaining the context and process of personal contacts. In other words, a variable-centred approach did not appear to capture the systemic and dynamic features of personal contacts in MNCs. My subsequent research has thus focused on scientific method in general (for example, Morais 2010), and critical realism in particular, in a quest for what I shall term in this chapter 'mechanism-centred' instead of 'variable-centred' theorizing.

As I shall discuss below, mechanism-centred theorizing reflects a critical realist approach to case study research whereas variable-centred theorizing is typical of conventional realist and positivist research. My initial interest in these topics was influenced by Andrew Sayer (for example, Sayer 2000) and Geoff Easton (for example, Easton 2010), two authors with whom I discussed critical realism during my PhD studies and whose influence carries over into this chapter. The application of critical realism to IB research was further encouraged by Mats Forsgren (for example, Forsgren 2008) who acted as an examiner of my doctoral research.

Over the last 30 years, critical realism has gained prominence as a philosophical stance (Blundel 2007). Harré (1972) and Bhaskar (1975) established the basis of 'transcendental realism' as an ontological and epistemological stance in the natural sciences which challenges conventional realist ontology by proposing that reality is stratified into three domains (Bhaskar 1975, p. 56), not all of which are observable. Such a stance was then extended into the social sciences as 'critical naturalism' (Bhaskar 1979), but with the acknowledgement of differences between natural and social phenomena. Specifically, 'critical naturalism' proposed a unity of method between the natural and social sciences while acknowledging that social phenomena are characterized by non-natural features such as the intentionality of human action, the emergence of autonomous and inherently meaningful social structures, and the interplay between social structure and human agency (Blundel 2007, p. 54). The term 'critical realism' is thus a synthesis of 'transcendental realism' and 'critical naturalism'. In Elger's words (2010, p. 256), critical realism 'opposes the traditional dichotomies of positivist and constructionist epistemologies and the associated polarization of quantitative and qualitative methods'. In that sense, it can be said to focus on facts (objectivist ontology) as well as values (subjectivist epistemology). It should not, however, be confused with critical theory (for example, Poutanen and Kovalainen 2010), which focuses exclusively on values (Morais 2010).

Critical realism has received increasing, albeit still modest, attention in business and management studies (for example, Ackroyd and Fleetwood 2000; Fleetwood and Ackroyd 2004; Blundel 2007). Easton (2010, p. 119) reports that in a search of the ISI Web of Science database, he found that critical realism was included in the title or abstract of as many as 334 papers, of which only 42 were in the field of management or organization studies. Critical realism has been applied, adapted and refined in various business-related fields, including economic geography, economics and organization studies, resulting in many different perspectives and emphases (Blundel 2007). Despite this diversity, these perspectives share a common concern with the interplay between social structure and human agency. In IB research, however, critical realism has largely been overlooked, with the notable exception of Sharpe (2005) and, more generally, Romani's (2008) attempt to conduct a 'multi-paradigmatic' study.

The present chapter thus focuses on the possibility of generating critical realist explanations through case studies. In pursuit of this purpose, the chapter reviews key assumptions of critical realism and their implications for case studies in IB, namely in terms of causation, explanation and generalization. In particular, I shall argue that critical realism provides a different view on case studies, according to which they can be explanatory and not just exploratory; that is, suited to seeking causal mechanisms. Critical realism represents, therefore, a fundamental challenge to the positivist assumption that case studies are an inferior research strategy for developing scientific explanations. Above all, my goal in this chapter is for readers to think differently about the possibilities for and applications of case studies. This means reconsidering the versatility of case study research, since case studies are compatible with alternative ontological and epistemological assumptions (Morais 2010). The re-evaluation of case study research I am advocating requires a fundamental questioning of taken-for-granted assumptions in the IB field.

I proceed by discussing the critical realist view of explanation in the next (and second) section. Such a stance goes beyond the positivist assumption that knowledge is only gained from sensory observation by distinguishing three domains of reality. Given this ontological claim, critical realism has a very different view to positivism on causation, inference and generalization. In the third section, I show how this mechanism-centred model of explanation escapes the dilemmas associated with traditional research based on analytical variables. The fourth section examines the implications of critical realism for case studies in general, and IB research in particular. The fifth section provides an example of how an IB case study can be reinterpreted in the light of critical realist assumptions. The sixth section concludes the chapter by summarizing its key arguments, and emphasizing how critical realism provides a coherent argument for the explanatory power of case studies.

CRITICAL REALIST EXPLANATION

Views on Causation

In order to discuss causation, philosophers of science (Humphreys 1981; Salmon 1989) have provided the example cited in George and Bennett (2005, pp. 145–6):

> a car went off a road at a curve because of excessive speed and the presence of sand on the road despite clear visibility and an alert driver. He [Salmon 1989] notes that the addition of another mechanism or contextual factor can change a contributing cause to a counteracting one, or vice versa: sand decreases traction on a dry road, but increases traction when there is ice on a road.

In the example above, 'sand' and 'traction' illustrate a cause–effect relationship which considers only two analytical variables ('sand' as independent variable and 'traction' as dependent variable). This variable-centred approach to research regards analytical variables as causes *per se* (for example, 'sand' as independent variable). Yet in this example, the same independent variable can lead to a very different, even contradictory, outcome (that is, increased versus decreased traction), depending on how it is combined with other factors in a particular situation.

In recognition of this, mechanism-centred approaches to research – found in critical realism – focus on causes as combinations of entities (for example, 'sand' and 'ice') rather than analytical variables *per se*. A mechanism-centred approach to research is thus focused on the ways in which structures of necessarily related objects or entities cause events to occur. When two objects or entities are necessarily related and thus have their identity mutually constituted (for example, a manager and a subordinate who can only be defined in relation to the other), they form a structure (Sayer 1992). Conversely, objects are externally or contingently related if either object can exist without the other (Sayer 1992). In the example above, 'sand' and 'traction' are two objects or entities which are contingently rather than necessarily related. Ultimately, what is necessary or contingent can come down to one's viewpoint, since 'the theoretical framework chosen governs the difference between necessary and contingent' (Easton 2010, p. 121).

A causal mechanism is, therefore, the process by which a structure is activated. A structure of objects or entities has causal powers to generate events – as Sayer puts it, 'capacities to behave in particular ways' – or causal liabilities, 'that is, specific susceptibilities to certain kinds of change' (Sayer 2000, p. 11). These causal powers and liabilities, however, may or may not be activated, and their precise effect may vary, depending on the external context (for example, Ackroyd 2009). This is highlighted by George and Bennett (2005, p. 137), who define causal mechanisms 'as ultimately unobservable physical, social, or psychological *processes* through which agents with causal capacities operate, *but only in specific contexts or conditions*, to transfer energy, information, or matter to other entities' (my italics). In the above example, 'sand' and 'ice' are objects or entities which together may generate 'traction'. The mere presence of 'sand', however, is insufficient to explain 'traction' since the effect of 'sand' is altered by other objects such as 'ice'. As Easton (2010, p. 120) points out, the concept of 'entities' with causal powers whose effects depend on contingent relationships is fundamentally opposed to variables, and offers a more powerful explanation since 'variables can only register (quantifiable) change, not its cause' (Sayer 1992, p. 180).

Although positivist and critical realist ontologies (for example, Morgan and Smircich 1980) share the assumption that 'the world exists independently of our knowledge of it' (Sayer 1992, p. 5), they differ in that critical realists believe, as do constructivists, that knowledge can only be produced in terms of available descriptions or discourses (Sayer 2000). In other words, scientific theories and discourse are transitive, but the world they address is intransitive. A critical realist perspective thus views social phenomena as dependent on the social meaning ascribed to them and the production of knowledge as a social practice, which influences its content (Sayer 1992). This is not to say that social phenomena exist exclusively as interpretations of researchers or that knowledge is exclusively linguistic, but rather that such influences must be accounted for in the evaluation of scientific knowledge. In particular, social scientists need to engage in

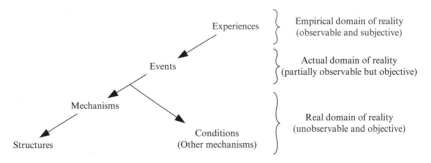

Source: Adapted from Sayer (2000, p. 15, Figure 1.2).

Figure 5.1   Three domains of reality and retroduction logic

a so-called 'double hermeneutic'; that is, interpret the theories of their
own scientific community, as well as that of 'knowing' social phenomena
(Blundel 2007, p. 54). In Blundel's (2007, p. 54) words, 'realists have been
unwilling to stop their search at the level of meaning, but prefer to see its
interpretation as merely the *starting point* for the pursuit of deeper causal
explanations' (original italics).

These assumptions are derived from the critical realist conception of
the world as consisting of more than events and our experience of them.
In particular, critical realists posit a stratified world that comprises a real,
an actual and an empirical domain (Harré and Secord 1972; Harré and
Madden 1975; Bhaskar 1979; Outhwaite 1987). As depicted in Figure
5.1, the 'real' domain consists of causal mechanisms; that is, processes by
which structured objects or entities with causal powers and liabilities act
and generate events in the actual domain. Thus, the real is 'the realm of
objects, their structures and powers' (Sayer 2000, p. 11). The real domain
is unobservable but objective since critical realist ontology assumes reality
to be independent of our knowledge of it. The actual domain, on the
other hand, consists of equally objective but partially observable events,
since scientific means such as the microscope and statistical treatment of
data may allow events that are unobservable to human senses to become
observable. The empirical domain, by contrast, consists of subjective but
observable experiences. Events are, therefore, only observable by human
senses as experiences in the empirical domain, and may be out of synch
with the causal mechanisms that create them.

Whether a causal power is activated or not depends on intrinsic conditions, which preserve the nature of the object, and on extrinsic conditions,
which are external to the object (Sayer 1992). A regular generation of

events is achieved when both intrinsic and extrinsic conditions are met, but such control of all interfering variables is only possible in closed systems (Harré and Madden 1975; Bhaskar 1979), such as laboratory-style experiments. In the social sciences (and indeed, much of the natural sciences) such conditions of closure are virtually unattainable due to: (a) individual capacity for learning and self-change, which violates intrinsic conditions, and (b) modification of social systems by human action, which violates extrinsic conditions (Sayer 1992).

It follows that 'neither objects nor their relations are given to us transparently' (Sayer 1992, p. 209). Indeed, 'it is almost impossible to attain complete knowledge of all these relations, and in addition many of them change rapidly' (Danermark et al. 2002, p. 187). In Easton's words (2010, p. 123) 'we see the tip of an iceberg but that doesn't mean that the invisible three-quarters is not there or is unconnected to what we see'. A key feature of a critical realist approach is, therefore, that 'we can use causal language to describe the world' (Easton 2010, p. 199) and ultimately choose the explanation which is more convincing in the light of existing theory and data. In particular, postulated mechanisms may be linguistic and metaphorical, rather than 'linear additive as required by statistical models or logico-rational as in box and arrow diagrams' (Easton 2010, p. 122). The critical realist stance clearly contrasts with positivist ontology, which assumes reality to consist of determinate relationships between constituent parts whose behaviour is an objective and observable phenomenon (Morgan and Smircich 1980). Positivism thus makes no distinction between the actual and the real domains of reality, assuming that objects of knowledge are atomistic events, whose regular co-occurrence may be equated with the causal laws underlying them.

Critical realism assumes instead that 'a cause is whatever is responsible for producing change' (Sayer 2000, p. 94), which can also include unique and irregular events. Critical realists are thus primarily descriptive and explanatory in their goals; they argue that 'explanation and prediction are only symmetrical under conditions of closure' (Tsoukas 1989, p. 552) – and therefore not feasible in the social world. While this may seem as though critical realists are rejecting the notion that scientific explanation is at all possible, in fact a considerable body of literature, to which I now turn, has amassed on how an understanding of open social systems is possible.

Retroduction and Transfactual Generalization

Given the impossibility of constructing closed systems in the social sciences, the positivist concern with deterministic or stochastic associations of patterns of events can, at best, support the identification of events in the empirical domain. For that reason, Figure 5.1 depicts 'events' in the actual domain of reality as partially observable. A constant conjunction of events is, however, neither a necessary nor a sufficient condition for a causal law. Causal explanation requires, instead, 'finding or imagining plausible generative mechanisms for the patterns amongst events' (Harré 1972, p. 125), leading to 'the postulation of a possible mechanism, the attempt to collect evidence for or against its existence, and the elimination of possible alternatives' (Outhwaite 1987, p. 58). According to Elger (2010, p. 254), a critical realist explanation requires a theoretically guided analysis of relationships among mechanisms (processes by which entities with particular causal powers cause events), contexts (other entities which may trigger, mediate, or contradict those powers), and outcomes (caused effects or events). Explanation does not proceed through either induction or deduction, since both remain at the level of partially observable events (that is, the actual domain). Rather, in order to understand how mechanisms and structures impact on observable phenomena, critical realist scholars have suggested a mode of inference they have termed 'retroduction'. Retroduction refers to the move from the observable experience in the empirical domain of an event in the actual domain to its causal mechanisms in the real domain (Blundel 2007).[1] In Figure 5.1, such a theorizing effort can be visualized as a movement downwards, crossing the three domains of reality.

Retroduction addresses an important question regarding the feasibility of critical realist explanation: if causal mechanisms are unobservable, how can they be accessible to social scientists? According to critical realists, an explanatory effort starts with actors' own accounts of what has caused the phenomenon (Danermark et al. 2002). Retroduction thus implies a retrospective inference of unobservable causal mechanisms in the real domain of reality from actors' accounts (that is, stated reasons) of observable experiences in the empirical domain of reality. Researchers take the descriptive accounts of actors and 'redescribe' them using available theoretical perspectives and the causal language to which Easton (2010, p. 119) refers. In order to achieve retroduction to the real domain, the researcher then has to ask: what entities and structures are necessary for this event or phenomenon to come about? In order to answer this question, the researcher applies, compares and moves beyond existing theory (Danermark et al. 2002). Accordingly, Sayer (1992, p. 107) has defined retroduction as a 'mode of inference in which events are explained by postulating (and identifying) mechanisms that are capable of producing them'.

Critical realists regard retroduction logic (see Sayer 1992, pp. 169–74) as being fundamentally different from deductive sampling logic and inductive/abductive replication logic. It is not the case that 'mechanisms are postulated then data collected', or that mechanisms are 'induced' from data (Easton 2010, p. 124). While induction and deduction are variable-centred approaches which circumscribe explanation to the actual domain of reality, critical realism focuses on mechanism-centred theorizing which extends explanation to the real domain of reality. In Lawson's (1997, p. 236) words, critical realism entails:

> a different form of inference to the more common induction and deduction. Whereas the latter are concerned with movements at the level of events from the particular to the general and vice versa, retroduction involves moving from a conception of some phenomenon of interest to a conception of a different kind of thing (power, mechanism) that could have generated the given phenomenon.

Lawson's phrase – 'that could have generated the given phenomenon' – alerts us to the provisional and contested nature of any postulated mechanism (see also Easton 2010). In particular, it is assumed that there should and will always be competing explanations, thanks to different interpretations of data, competing theoretical lenses and normal processes of academic peer review.

In line with its alternative view of causation and explanation, critical realism offers a fresh conceptualization of generalization: transfactual generalization. The term 'transfactual' implies that only transcendental, that is to say unobservable, causal mechanisms in the real domain of reality can be generalized (Tsoukas 1989, p. 552), given the near impossibility of closure in the social sciences (Sayer 1992). More specifically, Easton (2010, p. 121) relates the issue of critical realist generalization to that of necessary and contingent relations between objects or entities since 'if all relations were contingent then each explanation would be unique and incapable of contributing towards anything by way of generalization'. As a result, 'researchers do not postulate ironclad laws, but tendencies, which may or may not manifest themselves in the empirical domain' (Tsoukas 1989, p. 558). In Blundel's (2007, pp. 55–6) words:

> retroduction involves a type of scientific generalization that is concerned with the isolation of fundamental structures whose powers can be said to act 'transfactually' (i.e. continuing to exist, even though their operations may not be manifested at the level of events or observations).

Transfactual generalization (see also Danermark et al. 2002, p. 77) is regarded as an alternative to statistical and analytical generalization (for example, Bonoma 1985; Brewer and Hunt 1989), since causal mechanisms may be generalized in the real domain of reality despite not exhibiting

		Analytical generalization based on replication logic	
		Few analytical variables	Many analytical variables
Statistical generalization based on sampling logic	Many sampling units	Quantitative research: statistical 'data integrity' due to many sampling units (Bonoma 1985, p. 200) but analytical 'measurement error' due to few analytical variables (Brewer and Hunt 1989, p. 100)	Prohibitive research: 'not possible, in principle' (McGrath 1982, p. 70) due to lack of resources to study many sampling units and many analytical variables simultaneously
	Few sampling units	Critical realist research: few mechanisms (instead of analytical variables) and few sampling units since 'transfactual' generalization follows retroduction logic and focuses on 'causal powers of particular social mechanisms and their complex interaction in specific contexts' (Elger 2010, p. 256)	Qualitative research: analytical 'currency' due to many analytical variables (Bonoma 1985, pp. 200–201) but statistical 'sampling error' due to few sampling units (Brewer and Hunt 1989, p. 100)

Figure 5.2   Research dilemmas

statistical or analytical external validity in the actual domain. The distinction between mechanism-centred and variable-centred generalization is further developed in the following section.

BEYOND VARIABLE-CENTRED DILEMMAS

According to McGrath (1982, p. 70) 'all research strategies and methods are seriously flawed, often with their very strengths in regard to one desideratum functioning as serious weaknesses in regard to other, equally important, goals'. McGrath (p. 70) even goes so far as expressing scepticism about the possibility of doing '"good" (that is, methodologically sound) research'. Figure 5.2 attempts to synthesize such dilemmas in terms of two dimensions: sampling units (that is, cases) and analytical variables (Ragin 1987). In particular, Figure 5.2 suggests, following McGrath (1982), that it is prohibitive for any given study to maximize both statistical and analytical generalization due to the resources that such a research design would demand.

Figure 5.2 depicts the traditional association of quantitative research with statistical generalization and qualitative research with analytical generalization. A sampling logic assumes that sampling units represent a larger population. In order to make inferences about the latter, researchers choose between available formulae for determining the confidence with which statistical generalizations can be made. The degree of statistical confidence, in turn, depends on the size and internal variation within the universe and sample. A large number of sampling units is thus required by statistical generalization.

In contrast, replication logic, on which analytical generalization is built, assumes that a sampling logic prevents many phenomena from being empirically researched (Yin 2009). This is because there might be an absence of sufficiently large numbers of sampling units, or the topic of interest is better researched without clear boundaries delimiting the phenomenon from its context. Analytical generalization thus requires many analytical variables whereas statistical generalization requires many sampling units. Since analytical variables capture change at the actual domain of reality and not the causes of such change at the real domain of reality, replication logic is followed by conventional realist research but not critical realist research.

McGrath's (1982) view of research dilemmas, as shown in Figure 5.2, encapsulates the inability of any research strategy to simultaneously minimize threats to statistical 'data integrity' – in other words, absence of error and bias due to many sampling units – and analytical 'currency'; that is, generalization of research results due to many analytical variables (Campbell and Stanley 1963). This is due to the fact that statistical generalization requires many sampling units to the detriment of analytical variables, whereas analytical generalization requires many analytical variables to the detriment of sampling units. A high degree of data integrity, in Bonoma's (1985, p. 200) words, necessitates 'a precise operationalization of the research variables, a relatively large sample size and quantitative data for statistical power, and the ability to exercise control over persons, settings, and other factors to prevent causal contamination'. Bonoma continues (pp. 200–201):

> high [analytical] currency typically demands situationally unconstrained operationalizations of variables to allow cross-setting generalization, and observations within natural, ecologically valid settings – 'noisy' settings – where large samples, quantitative measures, and control are more difficult to achieve.

Brewer and Hunt (1989) point out that analytical currency comes at the expense of increased statistical sampling error, while statistical data integrity comes at the expense of increased analytical measurement error. By studying a few selected units rather than the whole universe, one may put additional resources into sharpening analytical measurement by acquiring more accurate data about fewer units. However, reducing analytical measurement error may increase statistical sampling error. Figure 5.2 thus synthesizes the three research dilemmas that McGrath (1982) referred to whenever research is focused on analytical variables: increased statistical sampling error (qualitative research), increased analytical measurement error (quantitative research) or prohibitive research (simultaneously qualitative and quantitative research).

Crucially, Figure 5.2 presents critical realist research as focusing on mechanisms instead of analytical variables; allowing for transfactual generalization in the real domain of reality; and following retroduction logic instead of replication or sampling logic. Transfactual generalization does not require many sampling units and, in contrast to conventional realist research, does not require analytical variables at all, since it focuses on mechanisms instead. Critical realist research is not concerned, therefore, with statistical sampling or analytical measurement errors, or with statistical data integrity or analytical currency, since these are associated with variable-centred concerns of measuring change, not determining its causes. Critical realism follows retroduction logic instead of sampling or replication logic because it focuses on causal mechanisms in the real domain of reality instead of the regular conjunction of events in the actual domain and detailed, lived experiences in the empirical domain. Figure 5.2 therefore pinpoints how critical realism offers a way out of the dilemmas of a variable-centred approach. Once a variable-centred approach is replaced by a mechanism-centred one, the trade-off between number of sampling units and number of analytical variables is no longer relevant.

CRITICAL REALIST CASE STUDIES AND THEIR APPLICATION TO IB

Now that the components of critical realist explanation have been introduced – causal mechanisms, retroduction logic and transfactual generalization – I shall turn to the more pragmatic questions of what this philosophical stance implies for case study research, and how practising researchers can adopt a critical realist approach in their case studies. These questions remain unresolved, however, since social scientists are only now beginning to think through the practical implications of critical realism in empirical research. Critical realism is primarily ontological and epistemological, not methodological. A strong bridge between the philosophical and the applied is yet to be forged, and there are very few examples of critical realist case studies to be found (for a useful discussion, see Ackroyd 2009).

There is no doubt, however, that case study research is regarded as essential to generating causal explanations in the critical realist tradition.

Sayer (1992) argues that both 'intensive' and 'extensive' forms of research are necessary to understand the social world. Extensive research – typically, although not necessarily associated with large-scale surveys – uncovers relationships of 'similarity, dissimilarity, correlation and the like' (Sayer 1992, p. 246). Extensive research is the most commonly employed research strategy, although it has weaker explanatory power since it involves understanding the common patterns of features across a population. Intensive research, by contrast, is seen as the stronger form of explanatory research because it seeks to understand 'how some causal process works out in a particular case or limited number of cases' (Sayer 1992, p. 242). As a qualitative research strategy, the case study is suited to an intensive research strategy – although Ackroyd (2009) argues that case studies can also be used extensively.

Given the diversity of case study research, the question remains as to what sort of case study design is consistent with a critical realist approach. In general, case studies may be objectivist or subjectivist depending on whether they address facts or values, respectively. Stake (2000), for instance, distinguishes between 'instrumental' and 'intrinsic' case studies. In 'instrumental' case studies the case (sampling unit) is of secondary interest, but it facilitates the understanding of a phenomenon (p. 437), whereas in 'intrinsic' case studies 'the purpose is not to come to understand some abstract construct or generic phenomenon', but the particular features of the case (sampling unit). In other words, instrumental case studies address facts whereas intrinsic case studies address values. Critical realist case studies are thus instrumental rather than intrinsic (Stake 2000), since their ultimate goal is the postulation of objective causal mechanisms in spite of taking subjective accounts of experiences as the point of departure for an iterative and retroductive explanatory effort (Danermark et al. 2002, pp. 109–11). Critical realist case studies can therefore be distinguished from case studies within constructivism (Maréchal 2010) and critical theory (Poutanen and Kovalainen 2010).

The literature does provide some suggestions as to how to design a critical realist case study, even though such studies remain rare in practice. Danermark et al. (2002, pp. 103–5), for instance, recommend the selection of 'extreme' or 'pathological' cases as well as comparative cases for the purpose of identifying causal mechanisms. Ackroyd (2009) suggests four different case study research designs, along two dimensions: causal mechanisms and contexts. Intensive single case studies allow the understanding of a specific causal mechanism in one context, whereas intensive multiple case studies allow the understanding of that specific causal mechanism in various contexts. On the other hand, extensive single case studies allow the understanding of interacting causal mechanisms in one context, whereas extensive multiple case studies allow the understanding of those interacting causal mechanisms in various contexts.

More generally, Easton (2010, pp. 123–4) proposes six steps in order to conduct a critical realist case study. First, the phenomenon to be studied should be complex, dynamic and relatively clearly bounded. Second, the research question should be of the form 'what caused the events associated with the phenomenon to occur?'. Third, the objects or entities which characterize the phenomenon should be identified, taking into account necessary as well as contingent relations among them. Fourth, data should be collected through several collection techniques, with a particular focus on plausible causal mechanisms. Fifth, data should be interpreted through retroductive logic and taking into account the double hermeneutic (interpreting knowledge in the scientific community as well as in the phenomenon under study). Finally, alternative explanations should be compared through 'judgemental rationality' (reasoned, provisional and public discussion of alternative judgements about reality).

According to Elger (2010, p. 256), however, the implications of critical realism 'for a distinctively critical realist conception of case study research remain underdeveloped and are only now being discussed'. The practical application of critical realism to case research is therefore a project for the future, and something to which IB scholars can potentially make a contribution. In the particular case of IB research, the scope for critical realist case studies is promising. On the one hand, case studies are the most popular qualitative research strategy in IB studies (Andersen and Skaates 2004; Piekkari et al. 2009). In addition, the field is well suited to debates on the philosophy of science (for example, Jacobs 2010) to the extent that 'the methodological background of IB research lies in other sciences, particularly in the social sciences' (Hurmerinta-Peltomäki and Nummela 2004, p. 163). On the other hand, however, IB researchers tend to avoid risky methodological choices given their psychic distance towards research subjects (Hurmerinta-Peltomäki and Nummela 2004). In addition, the rate of publication of qualitative research in IB journals (for example, Pauwels and Matthyssens 2004) may equally dissuade the adoption of case studies in general and of a critical realist stance in particular.

Possible topics for critical realist case studies in IB research may be assessed along Weisfelder's (2001) review, in which IB theories are categorized as follows: (i) industrial-organization theory, (ii) internalization theory, (iii) the eclectic theory of international production, (iv) transaction cost theory, and (v) the internationalization model and network theory of Nordic research. Among such theories, the internationalization model and business network theory of Nordic research appear to have the highest potential for the application of critical realist case studies. The internationalization model invokes dynamics that are inherent in critical realism's notion of 'mechanisms'. Ironically, the Uppsala model of internationalization (Johanson and Vahlne 1977) originally mentions an 'internationalization mechanism' but the assumptions of the model suggest that such a mechanism takes place at the empirical domain of reality and not at the real domain of reality, since it is based on international experiences at the individual and firm level of analysis which are subjective and observable. The network model, on the other hand, focuses on 'structures' of international interorganizational networks (for example, Johanson and Mattsson 1988) which are also subjective and observable, thus occurring in the empirical domain of reality and not in the real domain. The challenge for researchers interested in these models is, therefore, to move retroductively from actors' accounts of experiences in the empirical domain of reality to the postulation of plausible structures of entities and respective causal mechanisms in the real domain.

In a similar fashion, Ghauri (2004) gives examples of topics for case study research which seem to fit internationalization and network models. In particular, IB negotiations, international joint ventures, market entry processes and headquarters–subsidiary relationships are topics which can be researched in terms of both process and network relationships. From a critical realist perspective, however, process refers to causal mechanisms, and networks to structures of entities with causal powers and liabilities. Having said this, if a researcher follows a paradigm consistently, any research topic will be viewed through that paradigm.

Similarly to Weisfelder (2001), Forsgren (2008, preface) distinguishes between 'six perspectives, or theories, of the multinational firm that have dominated the research in international business during the last forty years'. In Forsgren's words (preface), 'I have called the perspectives "tales", not because they are fictitious, but because they emphasize certain elements at the expense of others'. This notion of 'tales' resembles Easton's (2010, p. 122) emphasis on linguistic and metaphorical postulated mechanisms as well as critical realism's emphasis on subjective accounts of experiences as a starting point for retroducting objective causal mechanisms. A critical realist perspective would therefore, I suggest, have broad applicability.

EXAMPLE OF A CRITICAL REALIST INTERPRETATION

Since my doctoral research was based on a network theory of the multinational corporation (Madureira 2004), it could be reinterpreted in order to

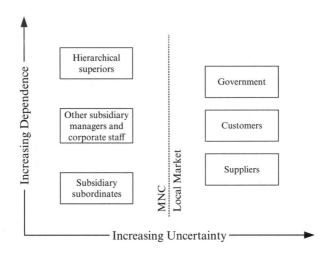

Source: Madureira (2004, p. 84, Figure 7).

Figure 5.3   Interpersonal context of FSMs in industrial MNCs

illustrate the implications of critical realism for IB research. As mentioned
in the introductory section, my doctoral research was a multiple case study
of foreign subsidiary managers (FSMs) in MNCs. The study was designed
to maximize analytical generalization based on replication logic, being
variable rather than mechanism centred. In order to describe the context
of FSMs' personal contacts two main variables were identified: 'dependence' and 'uncertainty' (Figure 5.3).

The two variables (Figure 5.3) were associated, in turn, with 36 contextual factors and 22 contents of FSMs' personal contacts (Madureira
2004, p. 142). In other words, dependence and uncertainty were associated with 58 other variables, thus illustrating the proliferation of analytical variables which may occur in conventional qualitative research
(Figure 5.3). In addition to context and content, the study was able to
describe the dynamics of FSMs' personal contacts in terms of channels,
direction, frequency and paths (Madureira 2004, p. 143). In particular,
FSMs were found to manage a formal and an informal network within
the MNC, as well as a business and a private network in the local market
(Figure 5.3). Moreover, two paths were found: a *snowballing path*
through which FSMs increase the scope of their informal and business
networks, as well as a *selecting path* through which the formal network is
used to reduce the intensity of personal contacts within the informal and
business networks.

Such findings may be reinterpreted in the light of critical realism. In particular, FSMs may be regarded as objects or entities which are necessarily related with other objects, including hierarchical superiors and subordinates within the MNC, as well as stakeholder representatives in the local market (Figure 5.3). Taken together, FSMs and such entities form structures in the real domain of reality since their identity can only be defined in relation to each other (Sayer 1992). Such structures of FSMs and necessarily related counterparts have causal powers to generate personal contacts as events in the actual domain of reality (Figure 5.1). The two interrelated causal mechanisms by which FSMs and necessarily related entities generate personal contacts are the snowballing and selecting paths. The generation of personal contacts in the actual domain of reality thus depends on other causal mechanisms (Figure 5.1) which activate FSMs' snowballing and selecting paths. Such conditions may vary in different contexts (Ackroyd 2009), thus requiring further research. Alternative conditions may be retroducted from actors' accounts of experiences in the empirical domain, such as FSMs' perception of dependence and uncertainty (Madureira 2004, p. 84).

From a critical realist perspective, the data collected in my doctoral research could be reinterpreted in order to theorize and generalize causal mechanisms in the real domain of reality rather than variable-centred cause–effect relationships in the actual domain. In particular, personal contacts and related variables in the actual domain – such as dependence and uncertainty – are no longer regarded as causes but simply events generated by causal mechanisms in the real domain of reality. Since events in the actual domain may be out of synch with the causal mechanisms that cause them in the real domain, it is important to theorize mechanisms dynamically. In fact, causal mechanisms are processes by definition (George and Bennett 2005, p. 137), since they are ways in which structures of entities cause events to occur. That also means that, in my doctoral research, only the dynamics of FSMs' personal contacts could be reinterpreted as causal mechanisms (Madureira 2004, p. 143). In particular, the two paths – snowballing and selecting – constitute causal mechanisms which can be generalized in the real domain and critically evaluated against alternative interpretations of existing data and theory. Critical realism has allowed us, therefore, to move away from variable-centred theorizing towards 'causal powers of particular social mechanisms and their complex interaction in specific contexts' (Elger 2010, p. 256).

In sum, retroductive logic stretches the interpretation of case study data in three fundamental ways. First, it requires process thinking, given that causal mechanisms are inherently dynamic and potentially out of synch with the events they generate. Second, it calls for systemic theorizing since the three domains of reality transcend traditional development of propositions and testing of hypotheses. Finally, it implies critical evaluation of theories since causal mechanisms are not observable. Critical realism may thus shed light on IB research which adopts qualitative research in general and case study research in particular. Especially prone to critical realist explanations are IB phenomena which are dynamic, systemic and multidisciplinary.

CONCLUSION

IB can be regarded as a research tradition which encompasses competing theories and alternative methods. In terms of methods, qualitative research has gained increasing recognition since it enables the study of multidisciplinary and complex phenomena. Although the term 'qualitative research' lacks a consensual definition, several qualitative research strategies can be identified. Case study research is a qualitative strategy whose appropriateness for generating causal explanations depends on the philosophical stance adopted by researchers. On the one hand, case studies may focus on facts or values depending on whether they are objectivist or subjectivist. On the other hand, they may be variable or mechanism centred depending on whether they seek analytical and statistical generalization or critical realist transfactual generalization.

The present chapter has focused on the possibility of generating critical realist explanations from case study research. For that purpose, I have reviewed the key assumptions of critical realism as a realist stance and assessed its implications for case studies in IB. While critical realism is fundamentally a philosophical movement and is not in itself a methodology, there now exists a body of literature discussing how it can be applied to empirical research. Similarly, I have argued in this chapter that critical realism can be used by practising researchers, and that case research is well suited to the critical realist project of mechanism-centred explanations.

The novelty of a critical realist stance comes from an alternative view of reality, causation, explanation and generalization. To recapitulate, reality is regarded by critical realists as stratified into a real domain of objective but unobservable structures with causal powers and liabilities which act and cause events through causal mechanisms; an actual domain of objective and partially observable events; and an empirical domain of subjective but observable experiences. This ontological view is important because it implies, in turn, an alternative view of causation. In particular, stochastic association of patterns of events in the actual domain is regarded as allowing their identification in the empirical domain, but not their explanation or prediction in the real domain. In other words, causation concerns regular as well as unique and irregular events which may be out of synch with the causal mechanisms that generate them.

From such a view of reality and causation, it follows that explanation is based on retroduction logic rather than sampling or replication logic. Retroduction logic is mechanism instead of variable centred and takes actors' accounts of subjective but observable experiences in the empirical domain as a starting point to retrospectively infer unobservable but objective mechanisms in the real domain. The corollary of such a view of explanation is an alternative view of generalization. In particular, critical realism suggests transfactual generalization as an alternative to statistical and analytical generalization since causal mechanisms (unobservable and thus transcendental) are regarded as externally valid in the real domain in spite of not manifesting themselves synchronically in the actual and empirical domains.

In sum, critical realism offers alternative ontological, epistemological and methodological assumptions which reconsider causation, explanation and generalization in the social sciences. As a result, case studies may provide explanatory insights, especially when phenomena are dynamic, systemic and multidisciplinary. IB research concerned with internationalization processes and international networks is thus especially prone to critical realist interpretations of case study research. But most importantly, no matter the specific topic, IB research generally would benefit from a reassessment of the explanatory value of case studies. In this chapter, I have argued that critical realism is a powerful means for undertaking this re-evaluation.

NOTES

*   The author gratefully acknowledges the editors' extremely valuable comments on previous versions of this chapter.
1.   Retroduction is not to be confused with retrodiction, another critical realist term. Elger (2010, pp. 254–5) distinguishes the two terms as follows: 'when the theoretically guided engagement works from outcomes and contexts to develop an account of possible mechanisms, critical realists characterize this as *retroduction*; when it works from posited mechanisms through contexts to explain specific outcomes, it is termed *retrodiction*' (original italics).

REFERENCES

Ackroyd, S. (2009), 'Research designs for realist research', in D. Buchanan and A. Bryman (eds), *The Handbook of Organizational Research Methods*, London: Sage, pp. 532–48.

Ackroyd, S. and S. Fleetwood (2000), *Realist Perspectives on Management and Organisations*, London: Routledge.

Andersen, P. and M. Skaates (2004), 'Ensuring validity in qualitative IB research', in R. Marschan-Piekkari and C. Welch (eds), *Handbook of Qualitative Research Methods for International Business*, Cheltenham, UK and Northampton, MA, USA: Edward Elgar, pp. 464–85.

Bhaskar, R. (1975), *A Realist Theory of Science*, Brighton: Harvester Press.

Bhaskar, R. (1979), *The Possibility of Naturalism*, Brighton: Harvester Press.

Blundel, R. (2007), 'Critical realism: a suitable vehicle for entrepreneurship research?', in H. Neergaard and J.P. Ulhoi (eds), *Handbook of Qualitative Research Methods in Entrepreneurship*, Cheltenham, UK and Northampton, MA, USA: Edward Elgar, pp. 49–74.

Bonoma, T. (1985), 'Case research in marketing: opportunities, problems, and a process', *Journal of Marketing Research*, **22** (2), 199–208.

Brewer, J. and A. Hunt (1989), *Multimethod Research: A Synthesis of Styles*, Newbury Park, CA: Sage.

Campbell, D. and J. Stanley (1963), *Experimental and Quasi-experimental Designs for Research*, Chicago, IL: Rand-McNally.

Danermark, B., M. Ekström, L. Jakobsen and J. Karlsson (2002), *Explaining Society: Critical Realism in the Social Sciences*, London: Routledge.

Daniels, J. and M. Cannice (2004), 'Interview studies in IB research', in R. Marschan-Piekkari and C. Welch (eds), *Handbook of Qualitative Research Methods for International Business*, Cheltenham, UK and Northampton, MA, USA: Edward Elgar, pp. 185–206.

Easton, G. (2010), 'Critical realism in case study research', *Industrial Marketing Management*, **39** (1), 118–28.

Elger, T. (2010), 'Critical realism', in A. Mills, G. Durepos and E. Wiebe (eds), *Encyclopedia of Case Study Research*, Vol. 1, Thousand Oaks, CA: Sage, pp. 253–7.

Fleetwood, S. and S. Ackroyd (2004), *Critical Realist Applications in Organisation and Management Studies*, London: Routledge.

Forsgren, M. (2008), *Theories of the Multinational Firm: A Multinational Creature in the Global Economy*, Cheltenham, UK and Northampton, MA, USA: Edward Elgar.

George, A. and A. Bennett (2005), *Case Studies and Theory Development in the Social Sciences*, Cambridge, MA: MIT Press.

Ghauri, P. (2004), 'Designing and conducting case studies in IB research', in R. Marschan-Piekkari and C. Welch (eds), *Handbook of Qualitative Research Methods for International Business*, Cheltenham, UK and Northampton, MA, USA: Edward Elgar, pp. 109–24.

Harré, R. (1972), *The Philosophies of Science*, Oxford: Oxford University Press.

Harré, R. and E. Madden (1975), *Causal Powers*, Oxford: Blackwell.

Harré, R. and P. Secord (1972), *The Explanation of Social Behaviour*, Oxford: Blackwell.

Humphreys, P. (1981), 'Aleatory theory of explanation', *Synthese*, **48** (2), 225–32.

Hurmerinta-Peltomäki, L. and N. Nummela (2004), 'First the sugar, then the eggs . . . Or the other way round? Mixing methods in IB research', in R. Marschan-Piekkari and C. Welch (eds), *Handbook of Qualitative Research Methods for International Business*, Cheltenham, UK and Northampton, MA, USA: Edward Elgar, pp. 162–80.

Jacobs, D. (2010), 'Philosophy of science', in A. Mills, G. Durepos and E. Wiebe (eds), *Encyclopedia of Case Study Research*, Vol. 2, Thousand Oaks, CA: Sage, pp. 677–82.

Johanson, J. and L.-G. Mattsson (1988), 'Internationalization in industrial systems: a network approach', in N. Hood and J.-E. Vahlne (eds), *Strategies in Global Competition*, London: Croom Helm, pp. 287–314.

Johanson, J. and J.-E. Vahlne (1977), 'The internationalization process of the firm: a model of knowledge development and increasing foreign market commitments', *Journal of International Business Studies*, **8** (1), 23–32.

Lawson, T. (1997), *Economics and Reality*, London: Routledge.

Lincoln, Y. and E. Guba (2000), 'Paradigmatic controversies, contradictions, and emerging confluences', in N. Denzin and Y. Lincoln (eds), *The Handbook of Qualitative Research*, 2nd edn, Thousand Oaks, CA: Sage Publications, pp. 163–88.

Madureira, R. (2004), 'The role of personal contacts of foreign subsidiary managers in the coordination of industrial multinationals: the case of Finnish subsidiaries in Portugal', PhD thesis, University of Jyväskylä.

Maréchal, G. (2010), 'Constructivism', in A. Mills, G. Durepos and E. Wiebe (eds), *Encyclopedia of Case Study Research*, Vol. 1, Thousand Oaks, CA: Sage, pp. 220–25.

McGrath, J. (1982), 'Dilemmatics: the study of research choices and dilemmas', in J. McGrath, J. Martin and R. Kulka (eds), *Judgement Calls for Research*, Beverly Hills, CA: Sage, pp. 69–102.

Morais, R. (2010), 'Scientific method', in A. Mills, G. Durepos and E. Wiebe (eds), *Encyclopedia of Case Study Research*, Vol. 2, Thousand Oaks, CA: Sage, pp. 840–42.

Morgan, G. and L. Smircich (1980), 'The case for qualitative research', *Academy of Management Review*, **5** (4), 491–500.

Outhwaite, W. (1987), *New Philosophies of Social Science: Realism, Hermeneutics and Critical Theory*, London: Macmillan.

Pauwels, P. and P. Matthyssens (2004), 'The architecture of multiple case study research in IB', in R. Marschan-Piekkari and C. Welch (eds), *Handbook of Qualitative Research Methods for International Business*, Cheltenham, UK and Northampton, MA, USA: Edward Elgar, pp. 125–43.

Piekkari, R., C. Welch and E. Paavilainen (2009), 'The case study as disciplinary convention: evidence from international business journals', *Organizational Research Methods*, **12** (3), 567–89.

Poutanen, S. and A. Kovalainen (2010), 'Critical theory', in A. Mills, G. Durepos and E. Wiebe (eds.), *Encyclopedia of Case Study Research*, Vol. 1, Thousand Oaks, CA: Sage, pp. 260–64.

Ragin, C. (1987), *The Comparative Method: Moving Beyond Qualitative and Quantitative Strategies*, Berkeley, CA: University of California Press.

Romani, L. (2008), 'Relating to the other: paradigm interplay for cross-cultural management research', PhD thesis, Institute for International Business, Stockholm School of Economics.

Salmon, W. (1989), *Four Decades of Scientific Explanation*, Minneapolis, MN: University of Minnesota Press.

Sayer, A. (1992), *Method in Social Science: A Realist Approach*, London: Routledge.

Sayer, A. (2000), *Realism and Social Science*, Thousand Oaks, CA: Sage.

Sharpe, D. (2005), 'Contributions of critical realist ethnography in researching the multinational organisation', proceedings of the 4th International Critical Management Studies Conference, Cambridge, UK, 4–6 July.

Stake, R. (2000), 'Case studies', in N. Denzin and Y. Lincoln (eds), *The Handbook of Qualitative Research*, 2nd edn, Thousand Oaks, CA: Sage, pp. 435–54.

Tsoukas, H. (1989), 'The validity of idiographic research explanations', *Academy of Management Review*, **15** (4), 551–61.

Weisfelder, C. (2001), 'Internationalization and the multinational enterprise: development of a research tradition', *Advances in International Marketing*, **11**, 13–46.

Yin, R. (2009), *Case Study Research: Design and Methods*, 4th edn, Thousand Oaks, CA: Sage.

Zalan, T. and G. Lewis (2004), 'Writing about methods in qualitative research: towards a more transparent approach', in R. Marschan-Piekkari and C. Welch (eds), *Handbook of Qualitative Research Methods for International Business*, Cheltenham, UK and Northampton, MA, USA: Edward Elgar, pp. 507–28.

6. 'There is no alternative' – or is there? A critical case study approach for international business research

Pasi Ahonen, Janne Tienari and Eero Vaara

INTRODUCTION

Case study conventions in international business (IB) research reflect the functionalist emphases and positivist research traditions of the discipline. While this tradition has its merits, it runs the risk of sustaining simplified models of explanation that are inadequate in a complex global business landscape. To capture the economic, cultural and political complexities of the IB setting, case study research in IB needs to expand its horizons beyond current mainstream methodologies. We propose that one possible avenue for such an expansion is the adoption of critical perspectives in IB case study research.

Critical perspectives are fundamentally interdisciplinary in nature. They draw from social theory and radical research traditions, complement and challenge mainstream insights, and offer important new avenues for IB studies. By questioning the normalized assumptions and axioms, critical approaches provide alternative ways to understand internationalization and globalization and their causes and consequences. We argue that this is especially the case when making sense of controversial corporate actions related to global industrial restructuring: downsizing, layoffs, offshoring and shutdowns.

In this chapter, we present a critical alternative for case study research in IB. We illustrate the ways in which the adoption of critical perspectives both enriches and challenges mainstream IB research. We draw from critical discourse analysis (CDA) to present an approach that assists understanding of the discursive construction of globalization. We illustrate our approach by analysing a recent industrial shutdown case in Finland. In March 2006, UPM-Kymmene (UPM), one of the world's largest multinational pulp and paper corporations, announced the shutdown of a paper mill in the town of Kuusankoski in south-eastern Finland, with the warning that there could be 'no alternative' to this decision. In this chapter, we show how CDA can be used to uncover how this case was discursively constructed in the media. In particular, we show that global, local and national discourses provide very different ways to make sense of, establish legitimacy for, or even challenge such controversial actions.

CRITIQUE IN INTERNATIONAL BUSINESS STUDIES

What Does It Mean to Be Critical?

Being critical means being attentive to, and suspicious of, taken-for-granted assumptions and the ways in which those invested with power and authority construct particular viewpoints and decisions as self-evident. It means contextual awareness, that is, sensitivity to particularities in human social interaction. It also means reasoned reflexivity on the part of the researcher *vis-à-vis* the subject of study and on the claims made to knowledge. Being critical always takes place under the watchful eye of mainstream theorists who are gatekeepers in journals and who often subscribe to another set of norms in research. Thus, critical researchers need to be particularly careful in establishing a coherent chain of argumentation in their work.

In international business and management, critical analyses have been relatively scarce. There are, however, notable recent examples. In their introduction to a special topic forum on critical approaches to international management, published in the *Academy of Management Review*, Jack et al. (2008) argue that, as a management subfield, international management research has been particularly resistant to adopting metatheoretical reflexivity about the knowledge that it has produced. Jack et al. claim that the major impediment to doing new theory therein is the extraordinary investment and the enormous baggage that this subfield carries in the form of functionalist positivism. A hegemonic epistemological structure has been thus created, selectively reporting on 'context' and 'generalizability' while systematically neglecting issues of power and ideology in its treatment of social interaction and concepts such as culture.

In brief, Jack et al. (p. 881) claim that international business and management remain paradoxically parochial: 'expectation of universal or, more modestly, generalizable knowledge is, after all, a very local position, and a historical accident of business schools, mostly in the United States'. They argue that other knowledges and others' knowledges need to be brought in to revitalize the discussions. This includes taking seriously the constitutive effects of language. We agree with Jack et al., and this chapter is a modest attempt to follow their advice.

In contrast to the positivist hegemony, critical research approaches tend to be qualitative. In the IB field, qualitative research has remained a marginalized pursuit, although its necessity is acknowledged at regular intervals (Marschan-Piekkari and Welch 2004). In the best-known IB journals, qualitative case studies are few and far between. What we would call critical case studies are – not surprisingly – even more scarce. Nevertheless, critical inquiry in IB has in recent years emerged in specialized journals such as *Critical Perspectives on International Business* and, particularly, in organization and management studies journals such as *Organization Studies* and *Organization* where established IB research traditions have been challenged and actions of multinational corporations have been scrutinized. Many such attempts have been linked to the so-called critical management studies movement.

Critical Management Studies

Critical analyses of management, managers, organizing and organizations incorporate a wide and fragmented field. As a scholarly movement, critical management studies (CMS) have, since the early 1990s in particular, provided new and alternative perspectives to studying organizations and organizing, and especially the role of managing and managers. Scholars have drawn on critical theory: for example, Theodor W. Adorno, Max Horkheimer, Herbert Marcuse and Jürgen Habermas. They have also been influenced by postmodern and poststructuralist theories; in particular by Michel Foucault's work on power, discipline and subjectivity (Alvesson and Willmott 1996; McKinlay and Starkey 1998; Alvesson and Deetz 2000).

In this tradition, management is understood as a concept and category; a historically constituted social construction with particular political dynamics and underlying ideology (Alvesson and Willmott 1996; Grey and Willmott 2005). Consequently, what management is and what managers do cannot be answered well in the abstract; there are both historical and organizational variations and the concept itself is a social resource with many differing practical applications. However, CMS does not assume the primacy of a fundamental contradiction between capital and worker interests. Instead, what is important is a feeling for organizational context, the nature of managerial work, and a careful investigation of how social processes reproduce suboptimal performance and social harms (Alvesson and Deetz 2000).

Simultaneously, it is necessary to appreciate how managerial action is embedded in wider, politico-economic institutional arrangements that operate to steer and constrain, as well as enable, managerial action

(McKinlay and Starkey 1998; Alvesson and Willmott 2003). The CMS framework emphasizes that practices and discourses that comprise organizations are never politically neutral, and challenges the centrality and the necessity of elite domination defining social reality. Importantly, managers are studied as human beings who interact with other human beings within particular social settings and have specific discursive resources at their disposal at any given time.

Critical Discourse Analysis

Like critical management studies, CDA is influenced by critical theory and Foucauldian poststructuralism (Wodak and Meyer 2001). It has, however, been developed by sociolinguists with particular interest in social inequalities and change (Fairclough 1992; van Dijk 1998; Wodak and Meyer 2001). CDA is one approach used in CMS, although it must be noted that management studies and sociolinguistics do not necessarily share the same research interests.

In particular, CDA is a theoretical framework that allows scholars to consider the constitutive role that discourses play in contemporary society. CDA covers a wide spectrum of perspectives and has in recent years become an interdisciplinary endeavour, for example, in critical studies of business and management. The approach developed by Norman Fairclough focuses on three elements in texts: textual (micro-level textual elements), discursive practices (the production and interpretation of texts) and social practice (the situational and institutional context) (Fairclough 1992). Our analysis draws from this approach, but in this chapter we shall focus on the discursive level rather than providing an example of micro-level textual analysis (for such examples, see Vaara and Tienari 2004, 2008). We propose a particular version of CDA that we suggest is applicable to the field of IB.

HOW TO APPLY CDA TO IB

Points of Departure

For the purposes of our critical discursive approach to case study research, three issues are essential. These should be carefully considered at the outset of the case study process. First, CDA focuses on the role played by language in the construction of power relationships and reproduction of domination in social and societal life. CDA attempts to make visible taken-for-granted assumptions, reproduced in and through discourse, that easily pass unnoticed in more traditional analyses. Thus, the primary objective of CDA is to distinguish discourses through which social and organizational reality is constructed.

In addressing social interaction, then, the researcher needs to be ready to confront issues related to power and ideology. Power is viewed here to reside in social relations and practices (including discursive ones). Ideologies, in turn, often work subtly through persuasion rather than coercion. In addressing questions of power, the researcher needs to be prepared to tackle issues that are potentially sensitive to those invested with decision-making authority in particular. However, CDA studies focus on texts, discourses and discursive practices, not individual managers and their traits and actions or non-actions.

Second, contextuality is a crucial issue in CDA. Consequently, the ability to place specific texts in their contexts is a key question. This means taking the social, cultural and institutional settings of the studied phenomena seriously, an approach which is exemplified by the different levels of social practice in Fairclough's models (see, for example, Fairclough 1992). Historicity is important in CDA as one cannot understand specific texts and discourses without considering the historical processes that have led to the current situation. Ruth Wodak (2001), for example, argues for a historico-discursive methodology where texts and discourses are viewed as parts of broader historical developments, and their analysis therefore must consider broader socio-cultural elements and their diachronic nature.

Third, intertextuality and interdiscursivity – linkages, slippages and borrowings between different texts and discourses – form another key issue in CDA. One cannot fully understand specific texts or discursive acts without linking them to other texts and discursive acts (at the first and second levels of Fairclough's framework). This means that the researcher needs to be prepared to account for the particular data that he/she chooses to study, as well as for the particular questions he/she sets out to answer.

From an Idea to a Case

Defining a case is an analytical exercise that the researcher can embark upon once he/she has an initial idea of what to study. Ideas, in turn, can emerge from several sources. Often, bafflement over a mundane everyday practice is a good source of inspiration, and unpacking taken-for-granted practices that constantly lead to questionable outcomes is always a worthy endeavour. Surprise is another source of ideas, whether it is surprise over a practice or an outcome. However, the contrary can sometimes also hold: researchers with some experience may anticipate and recognize an interesting idea and case when they come across one. This is what happened to us with the Voikkaa shutdown.

On 8 March 2006, when UPM announced a large-scale rationalization programme to improve its profitability, we were not surprised. The pulp and paper industry as a whole had, for some time, been singled out by investors, analysts, consultants and journalists as one in dire need of restructuring. UPM is a multinational forest industry company headquartered in Helsinki, Finland. While it used to be fully owned by wealthy Finnish families and institutions, in the latter part of the 1990s the ownership internationalized. By March 2006, some two-thirds of UPM's ownership resided outside Finland, mainly in the hands of US institutional investors. As owners, investors are well-known for short-term thinking, preferring immediate profits over long-term development, so changes in the corporate strategy could be expected.

The fact that UPM's rationalization programme included shutting down the Voikkaa paper mill in the Finnish town of Kuusankoski caught our particular attention. At the time, Pasi lived in Kuusankoski, and he experienced the local turmoil first hand. Janne and Eero, in turn, had been engaged for a number of years in a longitudinal study on the strategic decisions of the three major Finnish-based forest companies, UPM being one of them. This research made Janne and Eero anticipate that forest companies were heading for downsizing in their production in the European and US markets, shutting down production units. They had also been interested in industrial shutdowns as a relevant and timely research topic, and had already begun to study such cases in other industries. In brief, the idea now was to study in depth what happened in Voikkaa after the shutdown announcement.

What makes a 'case' is a classic question. The leap from idea to case is a make-or-break moment in the research endeavour. In Finland, it is not difficult to persuade people to agree that the Voikkaa shutdown is a significant case worthy of in-depth scrutiny in its own right. What happened in Voikkaa was groundbreaking. The shutdown was part of a larger rationalization programme that would cut some 3,000 jobs in Finland and 600 abroad, amounting to 11 per cent of the personnel then employed by UPM. The most dramatic single measure was shutting down the Voikkaa paper mill and dismissing its over 600 workers. Voikkaa was a pioneering case, as UPM's decision paved the way for its competitors to come out with similar plans. It marked the beginning of a new phase of international restructuring in the Nordic pulp and paper industry as a whole.

A traditional case study in international business would perhaps approach the UPM-Kymmene case by concentrating on the corporation itself, evaluating the various strategic options the corporate decision makers had at their disposal given market conditions and then assessing, probably using quantitative measures, the success or failure of UPM's profitability programme. However, for critical IB researchers, we suggest that the Voikkaa mill shutdown (rather than the corporation) offers a uniquely illuminating case of the interplay and tensions between global, national and local aspects of international restructuring involving MNCs. UPM's decision to shut the Voikkaa mill down was – or rather, it turned out to be – a much more complex matter than a mere reduction of production capacity and a measure to rationalize the company's operations. A sole focus on the strategic actions of the corporate decision makers would have missed out on a unique opportunity to analyse this complexity.

Initial Questions

Once the researcher has an idea of what to study, and the case is initially defined, it is important to define specific, preliminary research questions before plunging into textual material. In doing so, specifying the context of the case is crucial. Researchers need to take history into account, both in the sense of change over time and in the sense of the recalled past and its meaning(s). In relation to Voikkaa, as pointed out above, it is justifiable to consider the global restructuring of the industry, carried out by companies that had recently turned into multinationals, as the context of this case, where a struggle over meanings by protagonists and antagonists was anticipated.

Initial research questions serve the purpose of directing the data (text) production and analyses. In the Voikkaa case, at least the following questions seemed to be relevant. What were the ways in which UPM – through its senior executives and communications experts – sought to legitimize the rationalization programme and shutting down the Voikkaa paper mill? How did others – employees, politicians, journalists and the public as a whole – then react, resist or comply, and legitimize their own viewpoints?

Data

As a theoretical framework and perspective, CDA allows for the use of different kinds of methods (Wodak and Meyer 2001). Any kind of textual material (for example, media texts, archival material, interview and observation transcriptions) is open to critical inquiry. However, this kind of research demands the ability to make sense of the linkages between specific textual characteristics and particular discourses, on the one hand, and between the discourses and the relevant socio-cultural practices and historical developments, on the other. This means that CDA case study research tends to favour in-depth scrutiny and reflection upon specific sets of texts rather than, for example, content analysis relying on quantitative measures.

A crucial question in CDA is the selection of the textual material. This selection should be guided by the initial research questions. Although this has not usually been the case in CDA, we argue that it is important to initially cover a sufficiently wide range of material to be able to understand which themes and discursive practices are typical for the case and which are exceptions (Vaara and Tienari 2004). In the Voikkaa shutdown case, we decided to focus on two sources of data – company documents and media texts – and the case was specified as being the public debate over the Voikkaa shutdown. The former set of data is the most relevant source for an understanding of UPM's legitimation strategies. Corporate stock exchange releases, press releases and newsletters are examples of this data, presenting the 'official' view that the corporate decision makers want to communicate to their various stakeholder groups, most importantly, investors, analysts and journalists. Media texts, in turn, are a useful data source for understanding the national level and local discourses and discursive practices *vis-à-vis* the case at hand (at the same time, of course, it enables us to follow how the company's messages are treated by journalists in various media).

In our media data, we decided to include two global business newspapers (*The Financial Times* and *The Wall Street Journal*), which only briefly covered UPM's rationalization programme. The Finnish national media data include *Helsingin Sanomat*, the leading nationwide daily newspaper, and *Kauppalehti* and *Taloussanomat*, the two leading business dailies. The two regional daily newspapers are *Kouvolan Sanomat* (Kouvola region, of which the town of Kuusankoski is part) and *Etelä-Saimaa* (South Karelia, a nearby forest industry region). The local outlets in the data are free-delivery newspapers: *Kuusankosken Seutu* is published once a week, and *Pohjois-Kymenlaakso* and *Kaupunkilehti Seiska* twice a week.

With this in mind, setting the timeframe for the case study was a key decision for us. We decided to focus on a period of 10 months starting from 1 March 2006, because it was initially communicated by UPM that the Voikkaa mill was to cease to exist at year-end 2006. In the spirit of CDA, however, we also considered the history of the Voikkaa paper mill and the lead-up to the shutdown decision, in terms of both the industry as a whole and UPM (and its changing business portfolio) in particular.

Iterative Analyses

First, the entire initial textual material needs to be read and re-read. Although methods may vary, one option is to structure this analytical stage thematically. In analysing the textual material, the researcher seeks to answer three questions: what, who and how? 'What' means identifying recurring issues in the texts. 'Who' means locating prevailing voices (actors). 'How' means focusing on particular recurring expressions in the ways in which issues and voices are represented. In our view, this overall textual analysis could best be described as an attempt to grasp the totality of the chosen textual material. This is necessarily an iterative process.

The analysis of intertextuality (linkages, borrowings and slippages between texts) and interdiscursivity (linkages, borrowings and slippages between discourses) are of central interest in CDA. This means that we must be sensitive to recurring elements in the texts, as pointed out above. In addition to identifying recurring issues, voices and expressions, a set of exemplary texts needs to be selected for in-depth scrutiny. The close reading of specific texts is creative work, which aims at further specifying discursive practices and socio-cultural practices in the data. At the same time, we must be on the lookout for exceptions. Further, what is missing is also relevant. This means that the researcher needs to be conscious of issues, voices and expressions that for some reason or another do not appear in the data (or are marginalized therein), although their inclusion could be justified in the light of the researchers' contextual knowledge and theoretical understanding.

According to the principles of discourse–historical CDA, the analyses must take the historicity of texts and discourses seriously. Discourses have specific histories, texts are produced and used in particular historical settings, and the meanings they convey are diachronic in nature. What is important in this analysis is the ability to identify and describe distinctive ways of making sense of the world that are linked with textual representations, specific socio-cultural practices and particular ideologies. Historicity – the diachronic nature of the social – needs to be incorporated in the research. Some researchers refer to this as longitudinal research, others as exploring historical processes.

Overall, the CDA case study approach is characterized by a process of iteration; a continuous interplay between theory and different kinds of empirical work (Wodak 2001). In its discourse–historical formulation, CDA is a problem-oriented interdisciplinary approach in which 'the theory as well as methodology is eclectic; that is theories and methods are integrated which are helpful in understanding and explaining the object under investigation' (Wodak 2001, p. 69). The CDA research process is characterized by constant oscillation between (refining) the theoretical framework and (re-analysing) the empirical data: theorizing informs the ways in which the empirical data are approached and processed, while at the same time the empirical data cause adjustments in the theorizing (Wodak 2001).

Judging the Quality of the Case Study

In our view, critical perspectives in general, and CDA in particular, offer IB case analyses a source of originality, innovation and constructive scepticism of taken-for-granted understandings of the world. CDA offers a way forward in avoiding one-sided analyses of complex social and societal phenomena. The demands on the researcher are manifold. In deploying CDA, IB scholars must take heed of the basic advice given to qualitative inquiry in general (Ghauri 2004). First, multiple sources of data are a must. After all, why embark upon a qualitative case study based on a single source of evidence – interviews, for example – especially if one is interested in power relationships? Second, the research needs to be systematic in so far as it is based on accountable criteria for why particular data are chosen for inquiry and why they are analysed in particular ways throughout the iterative research process.

More so than in conventional IB analyses, CDA continuously forces the analyst to openly reflect upon his/her stand on issues and on the making of the research subject. However, this should not be misinterpreted as a licence to produce any kind of critical comment based on one's convictions or general observations. On the contrary, precisely because the researcher is dealing with complex issues that express multiple and contradictory points of view, it is necessary to make sure that one's own interpretations are backed up by textual evidence and logical chains of argumentation in producing and analysing data, as well as in reporting the research findings. Structuring one's analysis into steps, as suggested above, is likely to help in this difficult endeavour. At the same time, however, it is important to acknowledge that while all three levels of analysis – that is, textual, discursive and socio-cultural – are important in CDA, all three levels do not have to be – and, on many occasions, cannot be – the focus in a single CDA study (Vaara and Tienari 2004). In the study outlined in this chapter, the emphasis is on the last two levels of analysis.

Finally, and significantly, there is no escaping the need to account for the choice of 'case'. The classic question – what is it a case of? – needs to be precisely elaborated. For the purposes of this chapter, we offer the public debate over the Voikkaa paper mill shutdown as a revealing case of the interplay and tensions between global, national and local aspects of international restructuring involving multinational corporations. Next, to illustrate the CDA approach, we highlight some of our findings of the Voikkaa shutdown case. With this short illustration we attempt to show how a critical perspective affects the theoretical framings and methodological choices for scholars.

THE VOIKKAA SHUTDOWN CASE: THREE ALTERNATIVE DISCOURSES

The Voikkaa shutdown case exemplifies in a poignant way a key dynamic in contemporary international business: the interplay between the global, the local and the national. Accordingly, we distinguished three discourses that provided alternative ways of making sense of the shutdown case. For corporate management, the shutdown represents the need for a global balancing act (Bartlett and Ghoshal 1992) between production, raw material supply and key growth markets. For local people, in turn, the shutdown represents not only a potential economic disaster but also disappearance of a traditional way of making a living. Many of the dismissed employees in Voikkaa were third- or fourth-generation paper mill workers. The shutdown showed how, due to developments far removed from their immediate surroundings, people were suddenly and dramatically affected by the global economy. The employees' own input and performance had little to do with the shutdown decision. For a national economy that has historically been dependent on, and still heavily relies on, the profitability of forest firms as a key export industry, the Voikkaa case is a reminder that shifts in global business dynamics can have significant effects on the decline of industries, in turn implying changes to the labour market and society.

Global Discourse: There is No Alternative

UPM's initial justification for the profitability programme was explained in their press release. The argument was that the company faced a 'new business environment'. This environment had specific characteristics: (i) 'structural overcapacity' in Europe, (ii) 'dramatic' increase in 'the cost of production inputs' and (iii) new competition in the market from Asia and South America. Importantly, UPM stressed that the Profitability Programme involved 'all divisions and functions' and the aim of the programme was to 'achieve major improvement' in efficiency 'worldwide' (UPM 2006).

These goals were to be achieved, according to CEO Jussi Pesonen, by employing a 'new kind of thinking and more drastic measures than before' to achieve 'sustainable profitability improvements'. The planned closures and 'heavy restructuring' were 'necessary' for the company 'to remain a strong and active player' in the new environment. The 'least competitive paper capacity' was to be axed, since it had 'remained unprofitable in the competitive environment'. The profitability programme was not just cuts and downsizing; major investments were also planned to turn UPM's 'best units even more competitive'. The biggest investment, totalling some €325 million, was to be made at the Kymi paper mill in Kuusankoski, close to the Voikkaa mill that, as an example of the 'drastic measures', was to be shut down (UPM 2006).

The grand scale of UPM's measures escaped no one. Jyrki Ovaska, President of UPM Magazine Paper Division, explained in *Kouvolan Sanomat* that 'overcapacity' in Europe was the key challenge, and since market growth in Europe had ceased, the 'problem would not disappear through market growth as it did in the 1980s and 1990s' (Rönkkö 2006a, p. 12). A new approach was required. In their report on UPM's need for a profitability programme, *Helsingin Sanomat* quoted Pesonen as stating that 'past success cannot create the means to succeed in the future unless you yourself develop your operations' (Iivonen 2006). Something radical was needed in the new operating environment, and old approaches were outdated.

The key argument in the justification of UPM's profitability programme focused on the unavoidable economic imperative to take drastic action that necessitated the abandonment of earlier management practices and the adoption of new ones. The media played an important role in attempts to explain the significance of UPM's profitability programme (that is, to place the UPM decision in its context). The national business newspapers in particular saw a clear logic to UPM's actions. A *Kauppalehti* editorial commenting on the profitability programme saw the action as a reflection of shifts in global markets: 'demand is growing . . . in Asia and Latin America. The paper industry in particular has to be close to the client to adjust itself to the local markets' (*Kauppalehti* 2006b, p. 6).

The economic imperative of the globalization narrative was also prominent in papers that primarily concentrated on the community's reaction to the profitability programme and its effects at the local level. On 26 March 2006, the leading regional daily newpaper *Kouvolan Sanomat* published a feature article explaining the apparently iron-clad logic of the UPM programme. Prominently featured on the editorial page and titled 'It is impossible to swim against the currents of the economy', the article sought to explain how 'market forces' functioned. Reflecting the community's concerns over the effects of the plans on the employees, the article asked whether a company that recognized its social responsibility should safeguard jobs and seek only moderate profit. To answer the self-imposed question, two specialists in finance and economics – dubbed 'gurus' in the article – were interviewed. According to them, the 'most ethical' course of action is 'to strive continually to be as efficient as possible'. For a corporation, efficiency is the key virtue. 'As long as the world is open – corporations, people, goods and capital can move freely – the logic of the situation does not change very much . . . The laws of economics', the experts concluded, 'cannot be beaten. One just has to adjust' (Rönkkö 2006b, p. 3).

The initial UPM press release unmistakably sought to align UPM's measures to restore profitability with the dominant discourse of globalization by emphasizing the 'worldwide' reach of the programme (and the corporation itself). By specifically drawing attention to international competition, the ways in which the decision was contextualized in the numerous commentaries and explanations was also significant. They emphasized the explanatory power of globalization as a key element in the decision and thus reified it as a fact. Globalization was not merely a fact, but also had particular attributes, such as its economic imperative and its irrefutability. In effect, it left no room for alternatives.

Local Discourse: Paternalism and Patriotism

From the viewpoint of the town of Kuusankoski and its inhabitants, UPM-Kymmene's announcement of the planned cuts was shocking: about 1,000 people would lose their jobs. In a town of some 20,000 inhabitants, such job losses were a serious threat to the local community and economy. The proposed shutdown of the Voikkaa mill was also historically symbolic. The mill was situated in the heartland of the forest industry cluster in south-eastern Finland, the largest such concentration in Europe with a total of 16 pulp and paper mills. Established in 1897, the Voikkaa mill had a long history. It was one of the three founding mills that in 1904 formed the Kymi Corporation, which in 1996 merged with UPM to form UPM-Kymmene.

The Voikkaa mill was, it seemed to its workers, part of the very soul of the company. The news of the UPM rationalization programme, particularly its scale and the harshness of the measures proposed, took the employees, the city officials and the people in the community by surprise. The reports of the first reactions to the news were heart wrenching. 'Voikkaa's heart stops' was the headline of the regional daily *Kouvolan Sanomat* (2006, p. 1) the day following the announcement.

The irrefutability of the economic logic had seemingly equally irrefutable local consequences. 'Pesonen [CEO of UPM] killed the town', reported *Helsingin Sanomat*, quoting the chief shop steward of the Voikkaa mill, Mr Kari Haaraoja (Kallionpää 2006). The consequences of the shutdown in the community were readily available: 'I can only imagine that alcohol problems and divorces will increase. Somebody's situation might even lead to suicide', speculated one Kuusankoski inhabitant in an interview (Lehtosaari 2006, p. 13). 'Now house prices will definitely plummet, and we'll see whether even the bus bothers to stop at Voikkaa in the future', commented Mr Ari Wahlberg, the chief shop steward of the neighbouring Kymi paper mill (Kärki 2006, p. 9). The effects of the shutdown, it seemed, would follow their own inevitable logic.

Behind the alarm and despair, reported in detail, was the mill workers' deep sense of betrayal. The Voikkaa paper mill had been under pressure to improve profitability for some time before the shutdown announcement. The workers had been told earlier that they had until the end of 2006 to find measures to improve the performance of the mill. The workers felt they had done everything in their power to meet the demands. 'We had the word of the managers that we would have this year [to make the necessary changes]', the Voikkaa chief shop steward reminded readers (Kärki 2006, p. 8). The management had eaten their words. This apparent breach of the code of honour maintained within the industry was a major issue in the local reaction to the UPM profitability programme (see *Kouvolan Sanomat*, 9–25 March 2006).

To underline the sense of betrayal and loss of tradition, the paternalistic owner–managers of olden times were recollected with deep nostalgia. The apparent *noblesse oblige* of the old paper mill barons, their sense of local responsibility and duty, their good works for the community and their participation in community life had a central role in the local discourse (*Kouvolan Sanomat*, 15 March – 20 June 2006; Juntunen 2006; *Kuusankosken Seutu* 2006, p. 5; Nyberg 2006b, p. 3).

Mr Jukka Nyberg, a prominent Social Democrat Kuusankoski politician as well as the national Vice-Chair of the Union of Salaried Employees, linked the reimaginations of benevolent paternalism with fierce patriotism in his letter to the editor of *Kouvolan Sanomat*. In Nyberg's view, it was perverse that Kuusankoski, and Voikkaa in particular, was targeted in the profitability programme:

> It is curious that [the mill shutdown] was done at UPM's home ground in Kuusankoski, where paper production was begun by the father of Marshal Mannerheim already slightly before the founding of the Voikkaa mill [in 1897]. No longer does the adage hold – as it did when Finnish independence was saved with the leadership of Mannerheim – that you do not leave your brother behind. Now brothers, sisters and whole families were left behind. (Nyberg 2006a, p. 2)

The text is pregnant with nationalist historical symbolism. It also draws attention to the long history of the industry and the company in the region. Simultaneously, the text references the name of Field Marshal Mannerheim, the man who led Finnish troops in the wars against the Soviet Union during the Second World War and whose image lends itself to represent strong and capable leadership and the ability to unify the

Finnish nation in the face of an overwhelming external threat. In the face of such an external threat, cooperation is the answer, Nyberg argues, since the threat is a threat to all, companies, their employees, the nation and all Finns. Therefore, UPM's profitability measures not only break the tradition of cooperation for the national good but in fact damage the Finnish nation, exposing it to external threats. The UPM profitability programme was fundamentally unpatriotic.

Paternalism and patriotic local capitalism were the key elements of the local discourse that drew heavily on historical imagery and selective recollections of the past. Reimagined history was the counternarrative to the narrative of the inevitability of globalization. Media texts also conveyed the sense that the kind of harsh measures that UPM had chosen to carry out would not have been possible in the olden days. Back then, so the sentiment went, there was a sense of common purpose, of joint effort. Not only had the company and its employees – under the supposedly benign guidance of paternalistic paper mill barons – worked together to improve the workers' lives and the community at large, but also they had worked together for the Finnish nation and the national common good. The unfeeling ruthlessness that UPM exhibited with its restructuring plans destroyed all that. The old culture of working together for the good of the nation was sacrificed for the new management culture of global capitalism (see *Kouvolan Sanomat*, 12 March – 14 April 2006).

National Discourse: Nationalism and the (New) Role of the Nation

The global and local discourses and explanatory frameworks clashed in their conceptualization of 'the nation'. Despite – or rather as an intimate part of – the UPM profitability programme being framed as one more step in the progress of globalization, the media debate focused strongly on what the proposed measures meant to the Finnish nation and national economy. Intimately linked with the local discourse, thick with historical references, remembrances and reminders of UPM's long and seemingly glorious history as one of the key elements in the building of the prosperity of the nation, the opponents and critics of the UPM profitability programme outlined their counterarguments along nationalistic lines.

Unlike the experience in some other contexts (Martin and Oshagan 1997), attempts to influence corporate decisions were generally treated with sympathy in the media. The union and the employees in particular seized upon the potentially powerful discourses of nationalism. This, as such, was nothing new. Nationalist rhetoric and 'nation-talk' have been quite commonplace in Finland in cases where corporate restructuring has had implications of seemingly national proportions (Tienari et al. 2003; Kuronen et al. 2005), as well as in anti-globalization rhetoric (Rupert 2000; Cameron and Palan 2004). In addition, national interests have been the key element in decisions that have had fundamental effects on the pulp and paper industry in Finland in the past (Häggman 2006; Aunesluoma 2007; Jensen-Eriksen 2007; Kuisma 2008). Nationalist discourses have the potential for being effectively deployed in the media to force corporations to rethink their business strategies (Downey and Fenton 2007).

The opponents, then, had good reasons to rely on nationalist imagery and arguments – the good of the nation had long been the ostensible basis upon which important decisions had been made. Furthermore, those decisions had been made collaboratively between the captains of industry, the government and the labour unions. Drawing and relying on nationalist discourses and the long history of cooperation seemed the natural choice to build political support to resist the 'drastic measures' proposed by UPM.

The Paper Union chairperson Mr Jouko Ahonen, the voice of the union in the media, built his counterargument to UPM's measures on the long history of cooperation within the industry for the national economic good and on finding solutions to external economic challenges through negotiation and incremental changes. These, Ahonen argued, were the company's values and in keeping with the longstanding 'Spirit of the Winter War'.[1] UPM's failure to act according to its values, as well as according to the well-established models of restructuring through incremental, 'soft' measures, amounted to shirking its corporate social responsibility, Ahonen argued. The corporation should carry its responsibility towards not only its employees but also the nation by ensuring that employment is protected. After all, Ahonen reminded the public, UPM was a wealthy company (Width 2006).

In the weeks that followed, the national-level debate on the UPM profitability programme focused on the notion of corporate social responsibility (*Helsingin Sanomat*, 9 March – 20 May 2006). What, indeed, was a company's responsibility towards a nation that had made its growth and success possible? While the measures of UPM's profitability programme were the target of critique drawing heavily on nationalistic discourses, UPM received important support for its profitability programme that also built on the notion of the nation.

The CEO of the Finnish Forest Industry Federation, and former leading economist and globalization specialist at the Ministry of Finance, Ms Anne Brunila, was actively involved in presenting the UPM case in and to the media. 'These kinds of decisions have to be made if we are to stay competitive . . . The operating environment has permanently changed', is how Brunila explained the logic of the UPM profitability programme (*Kauppalehti* 2006a, p. 8). The pulp and paper industry, referred to by the indefinite 'we',[2] was facing the same challenges as UPM. It was likely that such restructuring measures would be necessary in the industry at large. The implication was that UPM's actions were, therefore, in 'our' interest, whoever the 'we' included.

As debate on the meaning of corporate social responsibility raged in the media in the weeks that followed the UPM announcement, centre-right Prime Minister Matti Vanhanen intervened. In his statement on the impact of the UPM profitability programme on the national economy, he linked Brunila's earlier argument regarding the importance of ensuring competiveness (and her indefinite 'we' in referring to it) with the needs and the good of the nation. Safeguarding jobs, Vanhanen argued, was not the primary form of corporate social responsibility, since 'the industry has the responsibility of ensuring that production in Finland remains competitive' (Törnudd 2006, p. 3). The interests of the nation, he suggested, were similar (if not identical) to those of Brunila's indefinite 'we' (presumably comprising the forest industry), which in turn (in accordance with Brunila's earlier argumentation) were remarkably close to those of UPM.

In a rather ironic twist of discursive logic, Vanhanen's comment both varied and renewed the alignment of the economic interests of the nation, the forest industry and UPM. Although UPM was no longer in any significant way a Finnish-owned company (two-thirds of its stock resided outside Finland), and although it explicitly argued for a global business logic in which Finland was only one location among many, its interests still emerged as crucial to the Finnish nation that was now conceptualized, from an equally globalist perspective, as a 'competitive' nation in the global economy.

FOOD FOR THOUGHT

In this chapter we have called for critical approaches to case study research in international business. To illustrate this, we have outlined a CDA perspective that can help scholars to understand better the social construction of globalization and its implications. By drawing on our research on global industrial restructuring, we have illustrated some important questions that need to be asked in such research and provided guidelines as to how to proceed with such analysis.

We have presented some outcomes of our analysis, which suggest that global, local and national discourses provide very different ways for making sense of the shutdown case under study and its legitimacy. The discourses can be used strategically by protagonists or antagonists alike to legitimate or resist specific actions or interpretations. Mainstream IB research would typically only focus on the global discourse, but as our case shows, it is paramount that we also acknowledge the local and national discourses to develop a fuller understanding of globalization and its implications.

Although critical case study research can, and should, be conducted in ways that best fit with the phenomenon, research questions and the case at hand, we wish to conclude by emphasizing three central requirements for successful CDA in such endeavours. First, the critical perspectives must be taken seriously, which should be shown throughout the analysis from the initial research questions to the final conclusions in the published research report. Second, because CDA is interpretative in nature, it is paramount that the analysis is based on systematic analysis of texts. Third, analysis must be context specific in nature. That is, the specific features of the case have to form an essential part of the discursive analysis, and the conclusions drawn from the analysis must be based on analytical generalizations that build on careful case-specific research.

It is also important to note that CDA is by no means the only alternative for critical IB research. For example, postcolonial theory and transnational feminism are useful alternatives. Postcolonial theory, originating from literary studies (Said 1979), challenges Western conceptualizations and forms of knowledge by questioning the ways in which that knowledge is produced, who produces it, what their interests are, what kind of structural conditions are involved in the knowledge production, and so forth (Banerjee and Prasad 2008). Transnational feminism (Mohanty 2004), in turn, is a critical perspective in feminist theorization that has been developed to critique and counter the Western conceptualizations and forms of knowledge about gender and power relations that do not apply or cannot simply be exported to non-Western settings and situations. The complex ways in which race and class intersect with gender in different structures of domination are at the core of these types of analyses.

Finally, we join Jack et al. (2008) and others who argue that mainstream approaches in IB are under pressure to respond to a plethora of challenges. In recent years, the global economy has also revealed its darker side to those who were earlier convinced of its inevitable success. There are calls worldwide to question neo-liberal notions of global business and to restrict and reregulate the global manoeuvring of capital and speculation. In our view, IB scholars need to take part in this movement, and broaden their research horizons. In this way, they would join a larger project of reassessing the ways in which academic knowledge is produced and how it is used in the world. We are convinced that it would do IB scholars a whole lot of good to be more open to critical approaches to study complex and sensitive phenomena.

NOTES

1. In the Finnish context, the statement was heavy with historical, economic and political meanings. The expression stood for a shared sense of cooperation transcending class, political and other divisions; the strong sense of unity of a nation that stands united against a common enemy. In 1939, the Finnish nation overcame the divisions over politics and history, stemming largely from a bloody Civil War and its aftermath in 1918, and joined forces to fight the Soviet invasion. In January 1940 employers' associations recognized labour unions as representatives of employees and thus paved the way for broad sectoral, and even national level, collective agreements. The 'Spirit of the Winter War', then, is a complex notion in which collaboration between different social and political groups, as well as between employers and employees, together produce benefits to the nation as a whole (see Kujala 2006; Aunesluoma 2007).
2. It is unclear whether the 'we' in Brunila's comment refers to the industry (after all, she was the industry association spokesperson at the time), the Finnish nation as an economy (thus making the issue of economic necessity) or the Finnish nation as a people (and in effect drawing on nationalist discourse and implying that the restructuring efforts of UPM are in the interest of all people of Finland). The indefiniteness of the 'we' potentially carries all those meanings.

REFERENCES

Alvesson, M. and S. Deetz (2000), *Doing Critical Management Research*, London: Sage.

Alvesson, M. and H. Willmott (1996), *Making Sense of Management: A Critical Introduction*, London: Sage.

Alvesson, M. and H. Willmott (2003), 'Introduction', in M. Alvesson and H. Willmott (eds), *Studying Management Critically*, London: Sage, pp. 1–22.

Aunesluoma, J. (2007), *Paperipatruunat: Metsäteollisuus Sodassa ja Jälleenrakentamisessa, 1939–1950* [Paper Barons: Forest Industry in War and in Reconstruction, 1939–1950], Helsinki: Suomalaisen Kirjallisuuden Seura.

Banerjee, S.B. and A. Prasad (2008), 'Introduction to the special issue on "Critical reflections on management and organizations: a postcolonial perspective"', *Critical Perspectives on International Business*, **4** (2–3), 90–98.

Bartlett, C.A. and S. Ghoshal (1992), *Transnational Management: Text, Cases, and Readings in Cross-Border Management*, Boston, MA: McGraw-Hill.

Cameron, A. and R. Palan (2004), *The Imagined Economies of Globalization*, London and Thousand Oaks, CA: Sage.

Downey, J. and N. Fenton (2007), 'Global capital, local resistance? Trade unions, national newspapers and the symbolic contestation of "offshoring" in the UK', *Current Sociology*, **55** (5), 651–73.

Fairclough, N. (1992), *Discourse and Social Change*, Cambridge: Polity.

Ghauri, P. (2004), 'Designing and conducting case studies in international business research', in R. Piekkari and C. Welch (eds), *Handbook of Qualitative Research Methods for International Business*, Cheltenham, UK and Northampton, MA, USA: Edward Elgar, pp. 109–24.

Grey, C. and H. Willmott (eds) (2005), *Critical Management Studies: A Reader*, Oxford: Oxford University Press.

Häggman, K. (2006), *Metsän Tasavalta: Suomalainen Metsäteollisuus Politiikan ja Markkinoiden Ristiaallokossa, 1920–1939* [Republic of Forest: Finnish Forest Industry in the Cross-currents of Politics and Markets, 1920–1939], Helsinki: Suomalaisen Kirjallisuuden Seura.

Jack, G.A., M.B. Calás, S. Nkomo and T. Peltonen (2008), 'Critique and international management: an uneasy relationship?', *Academy of Management Review*, **33** (4), 870–84.

Jensen-Eriksen, N. (2007), *Läpimurto: Metsäteollisuus Kasvun, Integraation ja Kylmän Sodan Euroopassa, 1950–1973* [Breakthrough: Forest Industry in the Europe of Growth, Integration and the Cold War, 1950–1973], Helsinki: Suomalaisen Kirjallisuuden Seura.

Kuisma, M. (ed.) (2008), *Kriisi ja Kumous: Metsäteollisuus ja Maailmantalouden Murros 1973–2008* [Crisis and Transformation: Forest Industry and Change in the Global Economy], Helsinki: SKS.

Kujala, A. (2006), *Paperiliiton Historia 1906–2005: Paperiteollisuuden Työmarkkinasuhteet ja Suomalainen Yhteiskunta* [History of the Paper Union, 1906–2005: Industrial Relations in the Paper Industry and Finnish Society], Vammala: Paperiliitto r.y.

Kuronen, M.-L., J. Tienari and E. Vaara (2005), 'The merger storm recognizes no borders: an analysis of media rhetoric on a business manoeuvre', *Organization*, **12** (2), 247–73.

Marschan-Piekkari, R. and C. Welch (2004), 'Qualitative research methods in international business: the state of the art', in R. Piekkari and C. Welch (eds), *Handbook of Qualitative Research Methods for International Business*, Cheltenham, UK and Northampton, MA, USA: Edward Elgar, pp. 5–24.

Martin, C.R. and H. Oshagan (1997), 'Disciplining the workforce: the news media frame a General Motors plant closing', *Communication Research*, **24** (6), 669–97.

McKinlay, A. and K. Starkey (eds) (1998), *Foucault, Management and Organization Theory: From Panopticon to Technologies of Self*, London and Thousand Oaks, CA: Sage.

Mohanty, C.T. (2004), *Feminism Without Borders: Decolonizing Theory, Practicing Solidarity*, Durham, NC and London: Duke University Press.

Rupert, M. (2000), *Ideologies of Globalization: Contending Visions of a New World Order*, Cambridge: Cambridge University Press.

Said, E. (1979), *Orientalism*, London: Vintage.

Tienari, J., E. Vaara and I. Björkman (2003), 'Global capitalism meets national spirit: discourses in media texts on a cross-border acquisition', *Journal of Management Inquiry*, **12** (4), 377–93.

Vaara, E. and J. Tienari (2004), 'Critical discourse analysis as a methodology for international business studies', in R. Piekkari and C. Welch (eds), *Handbook of Qualitative Research Methods for International Business*, Cheltenham, UK and Northampton, MA, USA: Edward Elgar, pp. 342–59.

Vaara, E. and J. Tienari (2008), 'A discursive perspective on legitimation strategies in MNCs', *Academy of Management Review*, **33** (4), 985–93.
van Dijk, T. (1998), *Ideology: A Multidisciplinary Approach*, London: Sage.
Wodak, R. (2001), 'The discourse–historical approach', in Wodak and Meyer (eds), pp. 63–94.
Wodak, R. and M. Meyer (eds) (2001), *Methods of Critical Discourse Analysis*, London and Thousand Oaks, CA: Sage.

Newspaper Articles

Iivonen, J. (2006), 'UPM aloittaa rajun saneerauksen' ['UPM begins drastic reorganization'], *Helsingin Sanomat*, 9 March, available at: http://www.hs.fi/arkisto/artikkeli/UPM+aloittaa+rajun+saneerauksen/HS20060309SI2TA01lp4.
Juntunen, K. (2006), 'Missä on tehtaanjohtajien omatunto?' ['Where is the mill bosses' conscience?'], *Helsingin Sanomat*, 17 March, available at: http://www.hs.fi/arkisto/artikkeli/Miss%C3%A4+on+tehtaanjohtajien+omatunto/HS20060317SI1MP02nye.
Kallionpää, K. (2006), 'Pesonen tappoi kaupungin' ['Pesonen killed the town'], *Helsingin Sanomat*, 9 March, available at: http://www.hs.fi/arkisto/artikkeli/Pesonen+tappoi+kaupungin/HS20060309SI2TA01lor.
Kärki, J. (2006), 'Voikkaan väki pettyi UPM:n johtoon' ['Voikkaa crew disappointed with UPM management'], *Kauppalehti*, 9 March, pp. 8–9.
Kauppalehti (2006a), 'Anne Brunila: Rakennejärjestelyjä tulee lisää' ['Anne Brunila: There will be more restructurings'], 9 March, p. 8.
Kauppalehti (2006b), 'Virheet kertautuvat' ['Mistakes compound'], 9 March, p. 6.
Kouvolan Sanomat (2006), 'Voikkaan sydän pysähtyy' ['Voikkaa's heart stops'], 9 March, p. 1.
Kuusankosken Seutu (2006), 'Kuusankosken paperiosasto 19 juhli satavuotista toimintaansa: voikkaan tehtaan lopettaminen ja paperialan tulevaisuus puhuttivat paperiväkeä satavuotisjuhlassa' ['The paper department no 19 of Kuusankoski celebrated its 100th anniversary: the shutdown of the Voikkaa factory and the future of the paper industry were discussed at the anniversary celebration'], 9 August, p. 5.
Lehtosaari, P. (2006), 'Voikkaalaiset šokissa' ['Voikkaa in shock'], *Kouvolan Sanomat*, 9 March, p. 13.
Nyberg, J. (2006a), 'Kuusankoskella raha puhuu' ['Money talks in Kuusankoski'], *Kouvolan Sanomat*, 15 March, p. 2.
Nyberg, J. (2006b), 'Uskotaan itseemme ja tehdään töitä isänmaan hyväksi' ['Let us believe in ourselves and work for the good of the Fatherland'], *Kuusankosken Seutu*, 5 December, p. 3.
Rönkkö, J. (2006a), 'Kuolinisku Voikkaalle' ['Deathblow to Voikkaa'], *Kouvolan Sanomat*, 9 March, p. 12.
Rönkkö, J. (2006b), 'Talouden vastavirtaan ei uida' ['It's impossible to swim against the currents of economy'], *Kouvolan Sanomat*, 26 March, p. 3.
Törnudd, N. (2006), 'Vanhanen ei usko kuntaliitoksen ratkaisevan Kuusankosken kriisiä' ['Vanhanen does not believe municipal amalgamation would solve the crisis'], *Kouvolan Sanomat*, 9 April, p. 3.
UPM (UPM-Kymmene Group) (2006), 'UPM to start an extensive programme to restore its profitability: efficiency improvement will involve all divisions and

functions', *8 March*, available at: http://w3.upm-kymmene.com/upm/internet/
cms/upmcms.nsf/$all/7cfd46f7e3d7c1a9c225712b002288ed?OpenDocument
&qm=menu,5,1,0&select=2006 (accessed 26 January 2007).
Width, T. (2006), 'Paperiliitto vaatii "aitoja" neuvotteluja' ['Paper Union
demands "genuine" negotiations'], *Helsingin Sanomat*, 10 March, available
at: http://www.hs.fi/arkisto/artikkeli/Paperiliitto+vaatii+aitoja+neuvotteluja/
HS20060310SI1TA02q85.

7. Sumantra's challenge: publish a theory-testing case study in a top journal

Gabriel Szulanski and Robert J. Jensen*

INTRODUCTION

This chapter reports the highlights of a 15-year journey during which we tested a theory with a single case study ($N = 1$) and published the ensuing report in the *Strategic Management Journal* (*SMJ*). It was a worthy and, we want to believe, path-finding journey.

It all began in 1990, during the exciting early days of the INSEAD PhD programme, in a doctoral seminar on Advanced Research Methods. In the opening session, Professor Sumantra Ghoshal, the course head, promised to spare no effort to expose us to the then state of the art in advanced qualitative methods for management research. To fully satisfy the requirements of this seminar we had to find ways to test a theory using a single case study, and – here is the hard part – publish our report in a top journal of our field, such as the *SMJ*, *Administrative Science Quarterly*, the *Academy of Management Journal*, or *Management Science*. That was the beginning of what would become an exciting journey. We gradually discovered the many facets of this non-trivial challenge and acquired the tools to address it. Our resolve in this journey was repeatedly tested by bemused and often sceptical audiences.

Finally, we found a way to test theory with a single case study . . . and we published it in Volume 27 of *SMJ* in 2006. After a four-year review process, Will Mitchell, an incisive, demanding, and constructive editor, accepted the paper based on the advice of two dedicated and eventually also enthusiastic reviewers. Soon after that paper was in print, we published in *Management Science* the results of a second study conducted in a different setting that relied on the same research design (Jensen and Szulanski 2007). The typical *Management Science* reader, we reasoned, would rank among the most difficult to convince when it comes to testing theory with a single case study.

So this chapter is about the road that started in Fontainebleau, during Sumantra's research methods seminar, and resulted in an *SMJ* publication. While I – Gabriel – have started this road alone I have reached the destination together with Robb Jensen, my co-author. I cannot remember exactly when Robb became a full partner. What I do know is that his empathy, enthusiasm and perseverance were crucial to this journey, as were the interest, critique, support and encouragement offered by many other colleagues, mentors, referees and editors – notably Sidney Winter, who wore all those hats and more.

We had several setbacks and moments of hesitation. The mountain we were climbing kept growing higher and higher so we began to wonder whether we should continue climbing or just give up and return to base. Thankfully we did not quit. We kept going one obstacle at a time and each moment of frustration was more than compensated by the joy of conquering the obstacles that appeared on the way to publication, a joy that only those who have some familiarity with this at times possibly irrational journey could understand. And we have learned a lot: about what it means to be a scholar, about our own academic values, and especially about what it takes to test theory with a case study. So here is our attempt to share the story and some of what we have learned.

1990, RESEARCH SEMINAR, FONTAINEBLEAU

In the spring of 1990, during my (Gabriel's) first year of doctoral studies at INSEAD, I took a seminar on Advanced Research Methods. This was the first time that such a course would be offered at INSEAD. We were the first cohort of students in that brand new PhD programme.

We knew from its description that the course would be coordinated by Professor Sumantra Ghoshal, who had earned a PhD from MIT *and* a DBA from Harvard in only three years, and who was, at the time, a fifth-year untenured Associate Professor. We had a vague notion that this seminar would be about the 'other' methodologies, the mostly soft and 'small sample' ones that included anthropology, ethnography and comparative case study research. These methods complemented the more traditional econometric and multivariate approaches that we had covered during the previous semester in a remarkable research methods class headed by Professors Spyros Makridakis and Lydia Price.

We expected that the Advanced Methods seminar would be ambitious, much like most of our previous courses. We were not to be disappointed. A skeletal course outline turned into an impressive sequence of modules taught by leading researchers that included, among others, John Van

Maanen on ethnography, Yves Doz on comparative case study research, and Jerry Zaltman on theory building. The scheduled 40 hours of class time ballooned to 72 hours. Many additional sessions were scheduled into the summer break after the semester officially ended to accommodate the availability of some of our distinguished guests. Such was the passion and the dedication of everyone involved in the programme. Moreover, each guest lecturer seemed to treat his/her session as if it were a full course on their particular subject. We read hundreds of articles and books. And this was just one of the five courses that we were taking that semester.

For example, I will never forget the disbelief we all felt when we entered the classroom where John Van Maanen, together with Sumantra, were waiting for us to begin the first session of his week-long module on Ethnography. There were articles and books neatly arranged in five identical piles along the three-metre length of a table, a tall pile earmarked for each one of the students who took that course. Amused by our distressed reaction, John smiled and said, 'Don't worry, I do not expect you to finish reading it all during this week'.

Nothing, however, captured the outsized ambition of that seminar like its final assignment. Sumantra asked us to find ways to test a theory using a single case study, the proverbial '$N = 1$', in a scholarly way. He was convinced that in-depth case studies could potentially compare to large-N datasets of numbers in their power to reject hypotheses. Sumantra wanted us to do that because, together with a formidable cast of other clinical (read 'managerial') researchers, he was finding it increasingly difficult to publish case-based research in mainstream academic journals. The number of strategy researchers who published mostly theory-testing articles based on econometrics and (relatively) large sample datasets was rapidly rising while there was a dwindling number of researchers, often labelled 'managerial', who favoured case research and whose claims to validity relied heavily on the fact that they had exclusive access to boards and CEOs. Strategy research that relied on econometric techniques was welcome in top journals and admired at academic conferences while clinical research pursued by so-called managerial researchers was becoming increasingly difficult to publish in scholarly journals. Managerial researchers increasingly felt that their conclusions could be, and often were, as valid – if not more so – than many that were reached through the exclusive application of econometric techniques.

So, Sumantra continued, we should try to publish our report in a major journal of our field, such as the *SMJ* would be for an aspiring strategy scholar. He could not show us concretely how to do it, at least not in a way that would be acceptable to a wider 'positivistic' community of organizational researchers, nor could he point to specific examples of someone who had done it already in our field.

At the time, research methods to study organizations were a burgeoning topic. We saw the publication of seminal contributions, such as a new edition of Yin's (2009) widely cited book on case study research, Kathy Eisenhardt's (1989) well-known article on theory building from case studies, and Glaser and Strauss's (1968) influential treatise on grounded theorizing. The notions of theory building with case studies and of grounded theorizing were beginning to gain wider scholarly acceptance.

Theory testing with case studies, however, was an entirely different matter. Even adventurous strategy case-based researchers such as Robert Burgelman, whose career benefited from a close acquaintance with Intel, the empirical setting of many of his publications, would publish mostly theory-building papers and cautiously allude to the possibility that cases could eventually also be used to test theory.

An important source of inspiration for us was Donald Campbell's (1975) treatise on 'degrees of freedom and the case study' where this respected methodological pioneer explains why he thawed to the idea of testing theory with qualitative case evidence, which he had forcefully berated in the past. We knew, however, of no specific concrete attempt to do theory testing with a single case study in our field. All we found were written intimations that it was doable.

As befits the novices we all were, I remember wondering naively why Sumantra made such a big deal of this assignment. I remember that my initial reaction was to think that it was easily doable. To fuel our naivety, Sumantra had a way to persuade and inspire that made most things appear within one's reach.

Moreover, at a very deep and visceral level I resonated with his challenge. As an empiricist at heart I also resonated with Herbert Simon's (1986) exhortation to economists: that they choose a lower level of analysis for data collection, rather than continue to speculate at relatively abstract levels of analysis where data were noisy but easily available. I thought that the GIGO principle – garbage in garbage out – pervaded empirical scholarly inquiry in our field and weakened many conclusions.

Yet, I also witnessed first hand how difficult it could be for a case researcher to defend claims in front of a sceptical scholarly audience. Often, they had no other option but to invoke exclusive access to the phenomena or resort to prodigious data dumps to support their claims. Invariably, these efforts would prove idiosyncratic, time-consuming and rarely convincing responses regardless of whether they were delivered verbally or on paper. There seemed to be no established methodology that would bridge efficiently this communication gulf.

Hence Sumantra's challenge. Our solution took the form of a repeated-measures quasi-experiment. And it was published in the *SMJ*.

2006, THE *SMJ* ARTICLE

To the naked eye, the *SMJ* article looks like a conventional hypothesis testing article. Its structure and its length, roughly 20 pages, is reminiscent of a medium-length empirical *SMJ* article. Yet there are distinctive differences, especially in the second part of the paper. A brief introduction, a Theory and Hypotheses section that links presumptive adaptation (our independent variable) to knowledge transfer effectiveness, is followed by a Methods section that describes the setting: international franchising, and more specifically, Mail Boxes Etc. in Israel.

The paper then becomes less conventional as we begin to explain how we have operationalized presumptive adaptation as the intentional departure from a standard franchising method. This required us to provide some elaboration and additional qualitative information. Yet network growth, our dependent measure of performance, was operationalized quite conventionally using a widely accepted metric for early-stage franchise growth: growth in the number of outlets.

Then we outline the naturally occurring repeated measures quasi-experiment (Cook and Campbell 1979; Cook et al. 1990), probably unfamiliar to most readers of a strategy journal for whom this was a relatively overlooked method. The experiment we outlined in three steps. First we identified three distinct phases in the growth of the Israel MBE franchise network. These phases were characterized by either stark presence (phases I and III) or virtually complete absence (phase II) of presumptive adaptation. These phases were demarcated by clearly identifiable transition events.

Next we focused on the relationship between presumptive adaptation and network growth. Indeed, during the two phases in which presumptive adaptation was salient the network had zero growth while in the phase when there was no presumptive adaptation, MBE Israel was the second-fastest-growing network in MBE history. This we believed suggested that presumptive adaptation and network growth were strongly and negatively related.

To establish causality, and hence complete the test of the hypothesis, we first summarily established time precedence, that is, we showed that the presumptive adaptation decisions were made before their consequences for network growth were known. Next, in a section labelled 'Threats to Validity', we examined the relative strength of our explanation by evaluating it against seven alternative explanations, relying when appropriate on the discriminating power of our research design. In the Discussion and Conclusion section we elaborated on the academic and practical value of providing a rigorous counterexample, and then we discussed how far we could sensibly generalize our conclusions beyond the specific setting of Mail Boxes Etc. in Israel. We concluded by exploring implications for future research.

In our view, the section where the paper differs most from a conventional theory testing article that uses statistics is the section called 'Threats to Validity'. While other sections reflect to some extent the unusual nature of the paper, this particular section took the longest to craft when single paragraphs could often require several weeks of additional data collection and analysis. Such a section, it turns out, is not always present in traditional theory-testing papers. Articulating and ruling out alternative explanations turned out to be our key effort, our own personal rediscovery of the abstract scientific notion of 'standard of proof' for case study-based theory testing. But of course there was more – much more – than just searching for alternative explanations in our 15-year journey.

FROM FONTAINEBLEAU TO *SMJ* IN THREE LONG STEPS

The winding way from Fontainebleau to *SMJ* started with a great replication story which we had the good fortune to board at the proverbial 'ground floor'. The next big step was realizing, towards the end of the story, that a quasi-experiment had unfolded naturally in front of us. The third and final step consisted of convincing the reviewers about the validity and reliability of our interpretations and conclusions.

Step 1: The Replication Story Lived Forward

I first encountered the idea of replication of routines in Nelson and Winter's (1982) pathbreaking treatment of economic growth. Their work in general, and especially this idea, was pivotal for my dissertation research on the transfer of best practice inside the firm. The evidence that I had collected during my dissertation's fieldwork, in particular the 'Banc One' (Szulanski 2000) and the 'Rank Xerox' (Deutsch 2000) cases, provided grist for Sid Winter's theory-building mill and galvanized his determination to develop more fully a replication perspective (Winter and Szulanski 2001b). I was fortunate to be a part of that effort, which Robb would join in due course. It did not take us long to discover, after we began searching for the ideal empirical setting to study replication, that franchise organizations, especially in the international context, came very close to the fruit flies equivalent for the study of replication. That was because such organizations performed dozens, if not hundreds, of replications every year, which could be thought of as naturally occurring experiments.

It is around that time that Albert Alhadef, a serial entrepreneur whom I knew very well, had purchased the Master Licence for Mail Boxes Etc. (MBE) in Israel. He helped us gain access to the MBE corporate office so that we could systematically research the international expansion, and later the domestic expansion of the network. In addition, Albert invited us to study in depth the growth of the Israeli network. This sounded too good to be true and as a research project it ended up surpassing our expectations. Not only did we gain a detailed understanding of the international expansion of MBE but we could also follow the establishment and growth of the Israeli network. We knew from the dramatic accounts of Dorothy Leonard-Barton (1990) and Brian Golden (1992) how valuable it could be to witness events as they unfolded as opposed to having to reconstruct them from participants' erratic recollections.

We chose to focus this study on the international franchising aspect of the network, which was particularly interesting to us because the franchise governance framework gave the national Master Licensees (MLs) substantial latitude for how to respond to national pressures for local adaptation, sometimes at the cost of looser conformity to global franchise standards. Especially in the case of the MLs, who purchase the right to develop a franchise network for an exclusive geographic territory, such as Israel, global franchise agreements are difficult to terminate prior to their expiration. The corporate office of the franchise network had a relatively weak ability to enforce standard practices in the short term, thus increasing the likelihood that substantial adaptations would be pursued in different countries in response to idiosyncratic local pressures. We believed this to be an ideal setting for our study of replication because it was likely to have a high degree of variation in adaptation decisions.

The specific setting of our study is the MBE franchise system in Israel. MBE, the largest non-food franchisor in the world, was launched in 1980 in San Diego, California, in an effort to fill a need for postal services. MBE specializes primarily in services for the small office and home office environments, including photocopying, colour copying, packing and shipping, parcel and express courier, complete mailbox service, internet access, and office and packing supplies. In 1986, when it went public, MBE had grown to 250 franchise outlets. Four years later, in 1990, it had grown to over 1,000 centres, and by 1999 had quadrupled again to nearly 4,000. After securing a strong foothold in the United States and building a strong foundation of experience, MBE decided, in 1989, to sell master franchise licences abroad. By 1999 MBE was operating or had licensing agreements in nearly 60 countries with over 700 international outlets.

MBE sold the rights to build the MBE network in Israel to Albert in August 1995. Eleven months later Albert opened his first store in Tel Aviv. The corporate office of MBE taught him how to develop an MBE network. We chose to focus exclusively on the task of building an MBE network rather than that of creating specific MBE stores. The investigation covered the period from August 1995, when the MBE franchise network in Israel was established, until July 2001.

In the first phase, Albert replaced MBE corporate guidelines for the first 52 weeks of operation with his own plan based on what he believed were the real key success factors in Israel. Within the first two years of operation he implemented only 60 of the 330 directives in the corporate plan, choosing mostly those that had to do with the establishment of a pilot store. The rest were intentionally neglected.

According to expectations set by the MBE guidelines, and also according to the experience of other international MLs, Albert should have sold nearly 14 franchises and had over seven stores already in operation by the end of the first year, that is, by December 1997. Instead, he had not sold a single franchise and was still struggling to make the pilot store profitable.

From December 1997 onwards, Albert decided, together with his top management team, to start the process over and this time follow closely the steps outlined in the 52-week corporate plan. The remaining 262 steps of the plan were briskly implemented within the year. Over the next two years the Israeli network grew from a single pilot store and no franchised stores to a network that had two pilot stores and 15 franchise outlets. As a consequence of the decision to follow closely corporate guidelines for building a network, Israel's became the fastest-growing young MBE network at the time.

Once network growth took off, Albert began to have minor problems with late royalty payments. In the second half of 1999, he shifted his attention to a new internet business he was developing. As a consequence, he gradually turned operations over to Eitan, his COO, promoting him to CEO soon after in December of that year. Upon becoming CEO, Eitan confronted the franchisees and rapidly resolved the problem of late royalty payments, at a cost. His dramatic approach soured the relationship with existing franchisees, many of whom became disenchanted enough to advise prospective franchisees against joining the network. As a result, the sale of new franchises plummeted. In response, Eitan shifted his attention from selling new franchises to increasing the revenues of existing franchisees, hoping that this would help to win them back. If he managed to increase existing store sales, he reasoned, franchisees would once again give positive referrals to prospective franchisees, reigniting growth. Part of Eitan's effort at franchisee support meant direct involvement in their day-to-day operations. Mistrust deepened further despite – or possibly because of – Eitan's initiative. By the end of 2000, the situation had deteriorated to such an extent that Eitan resigned and Albert had to bring in another CEO. Soon after, Albert sold his interests in the franchise and we learned that the MBE master franchise in Israel is again available.

By the time the story got this far, we had become familiar with the entire MBE corporation, its domestic expansion, its international expansion, knew well most of the senior management team, the country MLs, and franchisees from many countries.

Step 2: The Replication Story Understood Backwards

By this time Robb had become a full partner in this journey. In his first year at the Wharton PhD programme, Robb enrolled in my doctoral seminar on Research Methods. Students in that seminar were asked to pretend to be experts on a research method of their choice with the intent of helping them realize the magnitude of the methodological challenge that lay ahead for their dissertation research. Independently, and for different reasons, both Robb and another student in that seminar chose to focus on the repeated measures quasi-experimental design. Distinguishing features of this method included a single population (no control group) and the impossibility of administering the treatment randomly. Even though the researcher did not have control over the administration of the treatment, it was possible however to determine exactly when the treatment was occurring. Robb traced the application of this design in sociology (Cook and Campbell 1979; Cook et al. 1990). The other student traced its use in health economics (for example, Kessler and McClellan 1996).

Their write-ups and their presentations to the class revealed many interesting facts. They discovered two completely independent streams of literature, with little cross-citation, that were each dealing with the same methodological problems in isolation of each other and inevitably reinventing some of the solutions. We thought that health economists were dealing with some of the issues that had already been addressed thoroughly in Cook and Campbell's (1979) elaborated treatment of the quasi-experimental design. Moreover, it was clear that under certain conditions the repeated measures quasi-experimental design could be epistemologically superior to the comparative method, a much more popular choice by management researchers. This suggested to us that the repeated measures quasi-experiment was possibly underutilized in management research and that there was a latent opportunity to redress this fact. As if to confirm our intuition we discovered that a new edition of the 'bible' of quasi-experimental design was imminent (Shadish et al. 2002). I remember that soon after reading their class essays I started thinking that perhaps the repeated methods quasi-experimental design could possibly hold the key to answer Sumantra's challenge.

At this point, we had not yet seen the connection of this method to the MBE story which was still unfolding. The part that had unfolded, we had published in *Management International Review* (Szulanski et al. 2003). That was the turnaround story, the success story, consisting of the first two stages: failure followed by success, no growth followed by rapid growth. When the growth of the Israeli network took off once they changed their policy we decided to publish an interim report. The third stage had yet to unfold. When it did, when the growth of the Israel network stalled again under Eitan, we realized that we had found an interesting outcome pattern that fit the ideal pattern of observations of a repeated measures design. But what explained that pattern?

The hypothesis came from our efforts to refine the conceptualization of replication. We gradually understood that one of the distinguishing features of replication was that it stressed causal ambiguity of the practice. That meant that in addition to deficiencies of the recipient or of the 'channel' that all other perspectives also highlighted, replication difficulties could arise from the deficiencies of the source. This realization had important implications for the international transfer of practices because it suggested a conservative approach to adaptation since even the source might have limited understanding of the practice. Indeed, it would be dramatically more difficult to use the original working example of a practice (which we called 'the template') to diagnose a malfunctioning replica through comparison, if that replica differed substantially from the original.

Thus, we hypothesized, the right approach to replication must proceed fairly conservatively when it comes to adaptation; at least before there was enough evidence gathered that the practice could work in the host environment. Inspired by the reasoning in evolutionary economics (Nelson and Winter 1982), the right approach, we thought, required cautious modifications to the referent value of the original example. According to this logic, the observation of substantial adaptations made to a practice before its transfer would suggest the presumption that any ramp-up problem that might emerge in the new environment will be resolved *without* reference to the original, a presumption that mounting evidence suggested to be quite optimistic, if not downright unrealistic. Hence, the idea of presumptive adaptation was born.

This inspired our hypothesis that changes in adaptation policies between the three stages could explain the pattern of outcomes. Upon re-examining

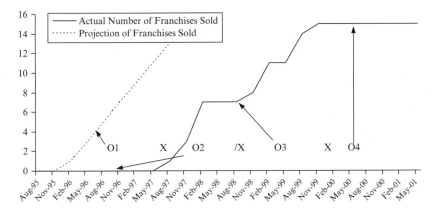

Source: Adapted from Szulanski and Jensen (2006, p. 948).

Figure 7.1 Growth of the MBE Israel network

the story we found that, clearly, MBE Israel neglected the value of the original US practices before its replica in Israel was operative. Then we saw a clear and concerted effort to follow the MBE system precisely during the second stage. And finally we saw that Eitan strikingly departed from basic principles of franchise management during the third stage of operations by overspending in support infrastructure and trying to centrally micromanage the operations of the individual franchise stores. Thus, there seemed to be three different regimes of adaptation. The second phase was characterized by a concerted effort to follow the US system precisely. The first and third phases, however, were characterized by marked departures from the established franchise systems and principles, departures that rendered the original working example useless as a referent for diagnosis.

This is when we first considered the possibility that a quasi-experiment had naturally unfolded. Indeed, there was a strikingly clear outcome pattern (Figure 7.1). Observation 1 (O1) was the expectation of growth based on corporate guidelines. O2 was the actual growth of the network during the first phase (no growth). O3 was the growth observed during the second phase. O4 was zero growth during the third and final phase of the story. And there seem to be a strong candidate for the 'treatment': presumptive adaptation. The treatment X meant presumptive adaptation. Removal of the treatment (/X) meant no adaptation, that is, follow exactly.

Looking backwards at the MBE story we saw the contours of a naturally occurring repeated measures quasi-experiment. There was a clear match between the repeated measures quasi-experimental pattern and the

Table 7.1   Addressing validity concerns

Validity criterion	Key question	How we addressed it
Conclusion validity	Is there a relationship?	Stark results
Construct validity	Is your construct what you say it is?	Being there from the beginning
		The power of richness: good access to the phenomenon
Internal validity	Is there a causal relationship?	Temporal precedence
		No plausible alternative explanations
External validity	Applies to whom else?	Proximal similarity
		Good theory and competing hypotheses: the power of the counterexample

MBE Israel story. The challenge now was to flesh it out and convince the editor and the reviewers of the *SMJ*. This took another four years.

Step 3: Convincing the Reviewers

We had a remarkable review process with *SMJ*. The timely responses from the editor also included very helpful comments from two exacting, knowledgeable and constructive reviewers. The third and final step of our journey consisted of convincing these reviewers that our conclusions were valid, that our interpretations were sound, and our contribution was suitable. Table 7.1 summarizes the main points we shall cover in this subsection.

We assumed from the start that we had to convince the reviewers *relying exclusively on traditional criteria for evaluating research*. Resorting to alternative criteria to assess qualitative validity (Guba and Lincoln 1989), we believed, would have dramatically lowered the appeal to an audience that was composed mainly of researchers practising statistically backed research. Most members of those audiences would not be easily swayed by alternative criteria, with which they were not very familiar.

In general, both reviewers readily accepted that there was a relationship between the two variables, presumptive adaptation and network growth, based on the Israel story. The results were so stark and dramatic that there was little question that there would be a correlation between the action of the ML and the outcome. After all, franchises had to be sold for the network to grow.

However, right at the outset, they asked us to relate the Israel story to that of the other countries in the MBE network so that they had a broader canvas to evaluate our findings. We had collected that information as part of our broad investigation of MBE and again could readily report it (see also Szulanski and Jensen 2008).

Reviewers also focused on construct validity, especially of the independent variable or treatment. Here the richness of our information was crucial to respond convincingly to their questions about construct validity. For example, to demonstrate presumptive adaptation during the first phase of the transfer we used quotes such as, 'We don't go back to the US. We have our own knowledge here' or 'Ask the US for help? It might be the proper way, but we have created our own experience'.

Once we were able to establish construct validity, the discussion turned to causality (internal validity). This was the dimension of validity on which we spent the most time and effort. Here we had to surface alternative explanations of our own and address the ones that the reviewers themselves suggested. Often we would not have the data to answer all the questions that they asked so we would have to go back to the company and collect more information to develop a specific argument. Gradually, the section of the paper containing alternative explanations expanded to the point that it became the most distinguishing feature of our paper when compared to a typical empirical paper in *SMJ*.

Finally, once we established the existence of conclusion, construct and internal validity, and the reviewers accepted that our findings applied to MBE in Israel, they inquired about the broader implications of these findings. We responded using two arguments. First, citing Campbell's notion of proximate similarity (Campbell 1986), we illustrated how well our findings did apply to settings that were similar to MBE Israel, such as, for example, in other countries where MBE had operations. This we addressed in our discussion section. We also invoked the notion of the counterexample to generalize our findings. Much as the exact sciences progress by reconciling laws or theorems with disconfirming evidence, we argued that established beliefs and policies should be reconciled with contradictory evidence such as that we unearthed in our research. Specifically, we asked that accepted wisdom about the desirability of *ex ante* adaptation in international transfers of knowledge be reconsidered, with potentially broad general implications for the conduct of transfers.

LOOKING BACK AT THE JOURNEY

We have shared our story with a variety of audiences along the way, seeking to understand better what particular aspects of our journey were of sufficient interest to warrant further elaboration. These audiences gave us useful suggestions and in addition asked thought-provoking, insightful questions. So we conclude this chapter by reflecting on some of those questions. The intent is to develop the issues for discussion rather than reach any particular form of closure about any of them. We simply hope to stimulate further reflection on our journey and what it could contribute to the research quests of others.

We would like to begin by noting that we only claim the modest contribution of having rediscovered a methodology, the repeated measures quasi-experiment, which is possibly underutilized in management research. This seemingly neglected design gave us a stronger epistemological base to assess and rank potential alternative explanations of our findings, through pattern matching of cause and effect. This was a key aspect of our quest which, we realized, was essentially about standard of proof.

Related to this issue, someone asked whether the occurrence of actual failure during the first and third phases of the story was essential. Failure we thought was not essential. What was essential was to have sufficient difference or variance between the observations to convince audiences that the treatment had had an effect.

Much like in Horace Walpole's famous tale of Serendipity, we did find other benefits that we did not anticipate. First, this methodology gave us an efficient way to communicate qualitative research findings. Indeed, presented as a quasi-experiment, we were able to motivate and explain our research to a variety of audiences in 15–20 minutes, much like 'quantitative' researchers do, leaving substantial time to discuss and debate our findings and elaborate their implications. This level of efficiency we thought was quite striking when compared to the not uncommon situations where a 'qualitative' researcher needs all the time at his/her disposal to merely explain and detail what has been done, leaving little room for anything else.

Furthermore, we began to realize that this research design, which hinges on a sequence of comparisons of observations of the same setting across time, could provide in some situations a much stronger standard of proof than the comparative case method. Indeed, in complex settings, such as those involving country comparisons, the 'apples to apples' assumption that is the cornerstone of the comparative method can only be stretched so far if it is to remain credible.

Finally, the experimental design inspired us to defend the validity of our findings using traditional criteria. We knew that we could competently invoke alternative criteria. However, we feared that doing so would distract our audiences from the standard of proof issue for our particular story, as it would perhaps trigger a discussion on the relative merits of different criteria to evaluate qualitative research. We felt comfortable enough to focus on traditional criteria, because we operated within the widely accepted experimental framework.

Of course, almost all audiences were stunned by the duration of our journey. Even by fieldwork standards, 15 years is a very long time. Did it have to take this long, they asked. Clearly not, we answered. The method does not have to be rediscovered again. Moreover, our work can be invoked as precedent and used as shorthand to explain what has been done. Stories must still be lived forward. However, they can be understood backwards faster. Furthermore, in many cases datasets which tell the story may already exist, together with the concepts and constructs that are necessary to define the experiment. So searching for naturally occurring quasi-experimental patterns in existing datasets should not necessarily take longer than an average traditional research project.

Questions were also raised as to why we selected the MBE Israel story. Why, they asked, was this story a good one to test this particular theory? Given the magnitude of our investment, we were naturally expected to go to extreme lengths to justify our choice. We answered that, in all our research on replication we have not yet encountered a better story. This would not in and of itself make the MBE story a good one. We could, however, point to the fact that the phenomenon of interest was transparently observable, that the pattern stood out because of the dramatic outcome reversals, and that the unparalleled access to the setting gave us the ability to return to it and collect additional information to evaluate the validity of alternative explanations to our findings.

Others probed on the separation between theory building and theory testing. As George and Bennett (2005, pp. 111–12) put it:

> [R]esearchers are frequently advised not to develop a theory from evidence and then test it against the same evidence; facts cannot test or contradict a theory that is constructed around them. In addition using the same evidence to create and test a theory also exacerbates risks of confirmation bias, a cognitive bias toward affirming one's own theories . . .

We had a clean answer to this question. First, we did report our story as it developed, greatly assuaging any concerns of confirmatory biases. Selective exposition of the findings was not an option for us because the story had already been made public in real time before its conclusion was known and before we had begun our analysis. Moreover, we had developed the theory almost completely independently from the MBE Israel context. Indeed, it had emerged from prior theoretical work and observations in other settings, mostly Banc One and Rank Xerox. This was also in the public domain (Winter and Szulanski 2001a, 2001b).

Finally, we were asked about our choice of outlet for the reports. In some sense these were obvious choices as explained above. However, there was more to it. The *SMJ* represented a knowledgeable and interested research community that we knew would appreciate knowing about the repeated measures quasi-experimental design, as a way to rigorously report qualitative strategy research, and as it turned out, also efficiently. We have found that many hitherto sceptical audiences became much more receptive once they found out that our story had been published by a top journal.

EPILOGUE: I WISH SUMANTRA HAD SEEN IT

Sumantra lived long enough to know that the *SMJ* article would eventually be published. I can imagine him listening to this story with his signature reflective pose, gleaming green eyes focused far away, and a big enigmatic smile. I can imagine that maybe he is proud that his challenge bore fruit. Or maybe he is incredulous that we stuck to it for so long, praising our dogged persistence, and also seriously wondering about our sanity. Maybe he is thinking that he should tone down future exhortations. For him the fun was always in the provocation, in generating the argument. That was his way to stimulate deep thought by relying on 'stretch' goals to generate debate. For him, the technical answer to the challenge was often the least exciting aspect, especially once he understood the outline of the solution, and how fast he understood! Perhaps we disappointed him by taking this long. Unfortunately 15 years turned out to be longer than he had left to live, so we shall never know how he would have reacted. I wish Sumantra was here to tell us. I wish I knew what would be his next challenge. He is sorely missed.

NOTE

*   The authors would like to thank the editors Rebecca Piekkari and Catherine Welch and audiences at AIB/Cornell, Wharton, University of Ca' Foscari, Sid Winter, and participants in the 2009 AOM session Making the Case for encouragements and valuable comments.

REFERENCES

Campbell, D.T. (1975), 'Degrees of freedom and the case study', *Comparative Political Studies*, **8** (1), 178–91.
Campbell, D.T. (1986), 'Relabeling internal and external validity for applied social scientists', *New Directions for Program Evaluation*, **31**, 67–77.
Cook, T.D. and D.T. Campbell (1979), *Quasi-Experimentation: Design and Analysis Issues for Field Settings*, Boston, MA: Houghton Mifflin.

Cook, T.D., D.T. Campbell and L. Peracchio (1990), 'Quasi experimentation', in M.D. Dunette and L.M. Hough (eds), *Handbook of Industrial and Organizational Psychology*, Palo Alto, CA: Consulting Psychologists Press, pp. 491–576.

Deutsch, G.M. (2000), *Rank Xerox Team C: Global Transfer of Best Practices*, Philadelphia, PA: Wharton.

Eisenhardt, K.M. (1989), 'Building theories from case study research', *Academy of Management Review*, **14** (4), 532–50.

George, A.L. and A. Bennett (2005), *Case Studies and Theory Development in the Social Sciences*, Cambridge, MA: MIT Press.

Glaser, B.L. and A.L. Strauss (1968), *The Discovery of Grounded Theory: Strategies for Qualitative Research*, Chicago, IL: Aldine.

Golden, B.R. (1992), 'The past is the past – or is it? The use of retrospective accounts as indicators of past strategy', *Academy of Management Journal*, **35** (4), 848–60.

Guba, E.G. and Y.S. Lincoln (1989), *Fourth Generation Evaluation*, Newbury Park, CA: Sage.

Jensen, R.J. and G. Szulanski (2007), 'Template use and the effectiveness of knowledge transfer', *Management Science*, **53** (11), 1716–30.

Kessler, D. and M. McClellan (1996), 'Do doctors practice defensive medicine?', *Quarterly Journal of Economics*, **111** (2), 353–90.

Leonard-Barton, D. (1990), 'A dual methodology for case studies: synergistic use of a longitudinal single site with replicated multiple sites', *Organization Science*, **1** (3), 248–66.

Nelson, R. and S. Winter (1982), *An Evolutionary Theory of Economic Change*, Cambridge, MA: Belknap Press.

Shadish, W.R., T.D. Cook and D.T. Campbell (2002), *Experimental and Quasi-Experimental Designs for Generalized Causal Inference*, Boston: Houghton Mifflin.

Simon, H.A. (1986), 'Rationality in psychology and economics', *Journal of Business*, **59** (4), 209–24.

Szulanski, G. (2000), 'Appropriability and the challenge of scope: Banc One routinizes replication', in R. Dosi, R. Nelson and S. Winter (eds), *The Nature and Dynamics of Organizational Capabilities*, Oxford: Oxford University Press, pp. 69–98.

Szulanski, G. and R.J. Jensen (2006), 'Presumptive adaptation and the effectiveness of knowledge transfer', *Strategic Management Journal*, **27** (10), 937–57.

Szulanski, G. and R.J. Jensen (2008), 'Growing through copying: the negative consequences of innovation on franchise network growth', *Research Policy*, **37** (10), 1732–41.

Szulanski, G., R.J. Jensen and T. Lee (2003), 'Adaptation of franchising know-how for cross- border transfer', *Management International Review*, **43** (3), 131–50.

Winter, S.G. and G. Szulanski (2001a), 'Replication of organizational routines: conceptualizing the exploitation of knowledge assets', in N. Bontis and C.W Choo (eds), *The Strategic Management of Intellectual Capital and Organizational Knowledge: A Collection of Readings*, New York: Oxford University Press, pp. 207–21.

Winter, S.G. and G. Szulanski (2001b), 'Replication as strategy', *Organization Science*, **12** (6), 730–43.

Yin, R.K. (2009), *Case Study Research: Design and Methods*, 4th edn, Thousand Oaks, CA: Sage.

8. Using multiple case studies to generalize from ethnographic research

Mary Yoko Brannen

INTRODUCTION

Ethnographic method has been praised for its utility in inducing theory. Noted for its high level of external validity,[1] this is at once the key methodological strength and weakness of ethnography. On the one hand, there is no question (provided the ethnographer is well trained and disciplined in the methodology) that the research has verisimilitude with the research site. On the other, it is unclear whether what has been learned is generalizable to other sites. In this chapter, as an organizational theorist trained as an ethnographer, I reflect upon my own research trajectory to show how I naturally fell into a way out of this methodological conundrum. Over time, fuelled by intellectual curiosity not only to describe interesting organizational phenomena but also to build theory, I developed a methodology of using multiple follow-up case studies to deductively test constructs and frameworks induced from what I term a 'focal ethnography'.

In addition to providing advice for choosing and using case studies as a supplement to ethnographic method in international business research, this chapter provides an in-depth illustrative research example that led to the development and refinement of the construct of recontextualization: how transferred firm offerings take on new meanings in distinct organizational contexts. I first review what ethnography is – method and intent, strengths and limitations – and what I see as its potential contribution to international business research, showing several ways in which researchers have strived to generalize from ethnography. I then formalize the method of 'focal ethnography with multi-case study triangulation' by means of a framework, while firmly establishing the distinction between ethnography and case study research, and provide an in-depth example of the use of this method around the induction and testing of the construct of 'recontextualization'.

ETHNOGRAPHY

As Fiona Moore points out in Chapter 17, ethnography is a research method specifically developed for describing cultural phenomena. If we go back to the Greek roots of the word 'ethnography', we can break it down into two parts: (i) 'ethnos' (ἔθνος) meaning people (generally of the same race or nationality) who share a culture; and (ii) 'graphein' (γράφειν), meaning writing. In other words, ethnography is writing about culture; and, as Van Maanen and Barley (1984) have argued, although culture is a group-level phenomenon, it is enacted and sustained at the individual level by ongoing interactions between people in a specific organizational context. Ethnography then is the method of choice when seeking to illuminate holistic accounts of people's cultures.

Anthropologists originated and honed this method predominantly for the sake of description alone – the method reaching its descriptive peak within the field of interpretative anthropology with Clifford Geertz's (1973) coining of the term 'thick description'. Ethnographies written by anthropologists generally read as heavily textured narrative accounts (at best) or rather dry catalogues (at worst) of the behaviours, values and norms of a given group of people. Perhaps the most unique aspect of ethnography with respect to other research methodologies is that the researcher, as participant observer – deeply ensconced in the field site – is in and of him-/herself the primary research tool. As such, special care is taken in the field of anthropology to explicate methodological issues concerning the ethnographer's own effect on the research site. In fact, the criticality of the role of the researcher in ethnographic method spurred what became known as the 'crisis of anthropology' in the late 1980s, and continues to be debated in epistemological writings on 'ethnographic authority' and 'reflexivity' (for example, Abu-Lughod 1986; Clifford and Marcus 1986; Marcus and Fischer 1999).

Validity and, to a lesser extent, replicability (or 'restudy reliability' as it is often called in anthropology; see Kirk and Miller 1986) of the ethnographic findings matter in order for the research to contribute to an authentic body of knowledge regarding specific cultures and to our understanding of world cultures in general. Perhaps the most public case of the subjective variability of ethnographers on research is Derek Freeman's (1983) critique of Margaret Mead's classic, *Coming of Age in Samoa* (1926). Generalizability of ethnographic findings, however, has not been a key concern of ethnographic inquiry. In fact, given that ethnographic method was developed with the intent to illuminate specific cultural contexts, the generalization of ethnographic findings would seem to contradict this original intent, if not the core epistemelogical foundations of the interpretative research paradigm whence it arose.

Ethnography and International Business Research

In international business, we generally want to know about culture in order to understand how culture might affect foreign direct investment (FDI), mergers and acquisitions, market entry, transfer of technology, organizational processes, norms and the like. Despite the fact that the term 'culture' is more often than not used synonymously with national culture in the field of international business, it is decidedly a multifaceted and complex construct involving the coming together of various spheres of culture – including national, regional, institutional, organizational, functional and so on – that people negotiate on an ongoing basis (Brannen and Salk 2000). Moreover, research settings in international business are rife with multilevel cultural interactions due to diverging cultural assumptions brought together in real time by the merging (often virtually) of individuals across distance and differentiated contexts (Brannen 2009). Consequently, traditional positivist approaches to understanding culture fall short in adequately capturing the complexity of cultural phenomena in international organizations (see Lincoln and Guba 1985; Bhagat et al. 2002). Ethnography with its two essential elements – fieldwork, including its central methodological building block of participant observation, and a focus on culture – is, as many have argued, perhaps the most effective method for gaining insights into micro-level embedded cultural phenomena (Van Maanen 1988).

Another equally important aspect of ethnographic methodology that is particularly useful to international business research is that it is one of the most effective methods to utilize when the organizational phenomenon under study is relatively new. In an otherwise heated debate on the strengths and weaknesses of single versus multiple case study methodology taken up by Dyer and Wilkins (1991) and Kathleen Eisenhardt in the *Academy of Management Review* (1991), there is agreement that in-depth, single case studies are particularly useful for inductive theory building in the early stages of a field of research. The strength of in-depth, ethnographic studies, such as those of Whyte (1943), Gouldner (1954) and Dalton (1959) – classics in the field of sociology – and Van Maanen (1975), Weick (1993), Perlow (1997) and Kunda (2006) in the field of organizational studies, are in their generation of strong constructs that advance theory and may in fact serve as the basis for deductive theory testing. As these examples illustrate, ethnographic methodology has ventured outside the realm of anthropology to induce relevant and cutting-edge theory in organizational settings. However, rarely has ethnography been used in international business research. This is due in part to the difficulty of conducting ethnographic research in one's home culture, let alone a foreign one, and to the time commitment involved. These barriers are, of course, exacerbated by the bias towards positivist, large-scale quantitative deductive studies in management research in general.

Nascent and evolving contexts such as changing geographical boundaries, emerging markets, countries with economies in transition, new workplace demographics such as people with mixed cultural origins (for example, biculturals, multiculturals and global cosmopolitans) are the *sine qua non* of international business. As such, ethnographic method has much to offer international business research. In sum, it is particularly useful under the following conditions: (i) when the research agenda involves understanding micro-level cultural phenomena and (ii) when the organizational phenomenon is relatively new and there is very little research on which to base one's theoretical orientation.

Generalizing from Ethnography

Anthropologists have never denied that the observations of the ethnographer as participant observer are limited, subjective and often speculative. The discussion cited above on ethnographic authority and the importance given to reflexivity as a way of contextualizing the role of the ethnographer makes this quite clear. As research becomes less about description and more about theory development, there is an increased risk that ethnographic observations will become even more limited (Naroll and Cohen 1973). The crisis of anthropology precipitated researchers to shy away from simply presenting thick descriptions of cultural phenomena and to begin augmenting such studies by using the observations to generate ideas and constructs that might apply outside of any specific culture. This new aim for ethnography is in keeping with the need in international business research to find a way of linking the understandings gleaned from ethnography to the multiplicity of cultural contexts in international businesses.

In order to extract general theory from empirical ethnographic observations, some type of comparative analysis must be utilized. Doing so calls for a comparative approach between extant theory and practice where the researcher looks for the repeating categories, thinks about relationships among them and then begins to ask why such relationships exist. This involves a new orientation to ethnographic and also qualitative research in general because it implies a shift from the 'idiographic', in which the researcher strives to offer a thick description of the research site, to the 'nomothetic', where the researcher searches for constants and regularities in the data (see Burrell and Morgan 1979). The shift towards nomothetic research then pulls the researcher into making inferences and validating interpretations, practices that have been refined by quantitative researchers (Preview and Fielding-Barnsley 1990).

An obvious way of spanning the breadth of this shift would be to utilize a multimethod approach involving qualitative/quantitative between-method triangulation. An example of this would be a 'T' design where the horizontal part of the 'T' would be an ethnography or an in-depth qualitative study. This would serve to induce constructs and perhaps scale items that could then be deductively tested at the site by means of a question-naire (for example, Brannen and Peterson 2009) and then expanded into a large-scale cross-sectional study – the vertical aspect of the 'T' – that would serve to generalize the findings to a larger population.

Brannen and Peterson used this type of between-method design to induce and test the construct of alienation in bicultural work contexts. A between-method triangulation was performed at the ethnographic site to (i) test whether the construct was prevalent and (ii) build the scale items to complement previous alienation scales. The scale items can then be used in a cross-sectional study of a population of cross-border merger and acquisi-tion sites to deductively test the generalizability of the construct. Thus, the 'T'-design can be used to generalize to the whole of an organization or to a larger population (such as all Japanese-owned companies/FDI). This type of a between-method design is the most challenging for an ethnographer to execute as a single researcher because it calls for an epistemological schizo-phrenia of sorts and it may be the best choice to do such a method in a pairing up of a qualitative and quantitative methodologist (Romani 2008).

Distinction between Ethnography and Case Studies

It is important to underscore here the distinction between ethnography and case study. For an anthropologist, there is a significant difference between them, but for the average organizational researcher the focal ethnography described above may seem nothing more than an in-depth case study. In other words, it seems that the distinction between the two methods is generally seen by organizational researchers as a difference in degree rather than kind. Some noted qualitative researchers in the field of strategy have even coined a new methodological term, as it were, by refer-ring to their own work as 'mini-ethnographies' (a term that would be an obvious oxymoron to anthropologists).

In fact, the distinction between the two methods is a matter of both degree and kind. In kind, ethnographies and case studies differ with regard to subject matter, research intent, methodology and research outcome. If a researcher conducts a case study, it means that there is a specific research site and the methodology of choice is to interview key players at the site with regard to the research question. Case studies are designed to elicit accounts of specific incidents, events or decisions and offer an academic interpretation of one instance or event that is the object of research. As such, case studies are generally retrospective. Although the intent of case studies is usually to build theory, case study methodology may also be used to test theory, as is often done in multiple case study research where structured or semi-structured interview schedules are employed in order to replicate and deduce the generalizability of research findings.

Ethnographic study is decidedly more restricted in focus as it is a method designed specifically for the study of groups of individuals (cultures) with the intent to describe and understand how they function – their norms and patterns of behaviour, values and basic assumptions. The research intent of ethnography is also more restrictive than the case study eliciting either thick description in and of itself, or induced theoretical constructs, models and frameworks around cultural phenomena that are new and undiscovered, and/or emergent and evolving. Although it is possible to conduct a historical ethnography using secondary data and narrative accounts of experienced cultural phenomena, ethnographies are generally conducted in the present moment and are focused on understanding ongoing cultural phenomena. The research outcomes of ethnography are detailed narrative accounts of cultural phenomena told as much as possible from the native's point of view.

Both approaches involve field study (in other words, research conducted *in situ* as opposed to in an 'ivory tower' as is the norm for survey research, lab experiments, simulations and so on). However, because the intent of ethnography is to gain a close and intimate familiarity with a given group of individuals and their practices, capturing as much as possible the native point of view, participant observation is a key aspect of the methodology. The method originated in fieldwork of social anthropologists, especially Bronistaw Malinowski and his students in Britain, the students of Franz Boas in the United States, and in the urban research of the Chicago School of sociology. A key principle of the method is that one may not merely observe, but must also find a role within the group under observation from which to participate in some manner, even if only as 'outside observer'. Participant observation, therefore, is limited to contexts where the community under study understands and permits it.

The discussion of participant observation brings up a final and important distinction between case studies and ethnography that is perhaps more in the order of a difference in degree rather than kind. Both case study researchers and ethnographers want to elicit an understanding of phenomena from the field site. However, the amount of time spent in the field and the methodological approach to collecting the data vary significantly by degree between the approaches. Since the ethnographer's aim is to understand predominantly tacit, complex, contextually embedded, existential phenomena, the amount of time spent in the field must be substantial – to an anthropologist this means at least one year, though this to most would still seem too brief especially if the site involves learning or perfecting a new language on the part of the researcher. Case studies vary largely with regard to length of time at the site, from a handful of on-site meetings to spending a year at a production plant.

Further, depending on whether the case study is designed to build or test theory, the data collection methods and, in particular, the care given to making as sure as it is possible to elicit the native's point of view rather than impose a priori theorizing varies significantly between the two methods. Anthropologists undergo strict and intensive training in order to hone the skill of participant observation at practice research sites prior to going into the field. This is undertaken in order to train the ethnographer in how to maintain the important balance between being both an outsider and an insider, while intensively interacting with people in their natural environment over an extended period. Reaching and maintaining this balance is not easy, but it is critical from the research perspective of an ethnographer. Since the bulk of cultural phenomena is tacit, deeply socialized, implicit knowledge and as such, invisible, as it were, to insiders, the ethnographer's outside point of view is integral to being able to surface the interlocking, taken-for-granted aspects of the culture under study. In other words, ethnographers must get close enough to the context to look at it from the native point of view, but not so close that they lose the advantage of their outside perspective.

Finally, it is important to note the distinction between action research (a variant of case study research) and ethnography. Again, this may also be a variance in degree as opposed to kind. Action research refers to a method established in the field of social psychology (Lewin 1946) wherein the researcher acts as a change agent for the field site. In this method, the researcher goes into the field site with the clear intention of having an impact on the organization much as a hired consultant would. The difference between action research and consultancy is that action researchers aim to research the effect of change efforts on organizations. Accordingly, they pay close attention to the effect they have on the research site by employing pre- and post-measures regarding the object of the research, attributing a large part of the difference to the effect of the outside agent (themselves). With ethnography, the researcher is at pains to try not to affect the research phenomenon while knowing full well that being at a site intensively for extended periods of time will have an effect on it. This is a significant operational conundrum for ethnographers and as such has led to the formalization of the practice of reflexive inquiry wherein the ethnographer goes to great lengths to document his/her effect on the research site (see Dwyer 1982; Abu-Lughod 1986 as exemplars of this method).

FOCAL ETHNOGRAPHY WITH MULTI-CASE STUDY TRIANGULATION

Another type of between-method approach that is more in keeping with the epistemological orientation of ethnography is to follow up a focal ethnography with multiple case studies to expand and test the theory so that it can be generalized to other industries and organizational contexts. This is an especially useful approach when not much is known about the research question. Since this is a methodological approach that has not been documented previously, the rest of this chapter offers a detailed description of the method illustrated both graphically (Figure 8.1), as well as by means of a detailed example of this methodology used in my own research around the building and deductive extensions of the construct of recontextualization. While the use of multiple case studies (see Figure 8.1) needs no further explanation than previously discussed herein and in this volume, I shall now briefly discuss the less familiar elements of this research design – the focal ethnography and optional comparative ethnography – before explicating this design with my own research examples.

The Focal Ethnography

The focal ethnography is the starting point from which general understanding and the inklings of new constructs are induced. In order to induce theory, several within-method triangulations are used to check for internal validity (see focal ethnography ellipse in Figure 8.1). These ethnographic strategies for validation included the following: (i) the use of multiple data collection methods for primary and secondary data; (ii) the documentation of different perspectives on the phenomenon under study by means of conducting formal and informal ongoing interviews with key informants from differing functional, hierarchical, departmental and national groups; and (iii) the repetition of data collection over time for each method employed. This third strategy is frequently operationalized by conducting prolonged participant observation at a field site and by interviewing the same informants at different time periods throughout a course of study. The following are examples from my own work using focal ethnographies to induce theory: (i) a model of issue-driven, contextually *negotiated culture* for understanding organizational culture evolution over time in cross-border mergers and acquisitions (Brannen 1994; Brannen and Salk 2000); (ii) the construct of *bicultural alienation* as a variation on work alienation in complex cultural arenas (Brannen and Peterson 2009); (iii) the construct of *recontextualization* – how firm offerings take on new meanings in new contexts (Brannen 2004); and (iv) understanding *biculturalism* as the new

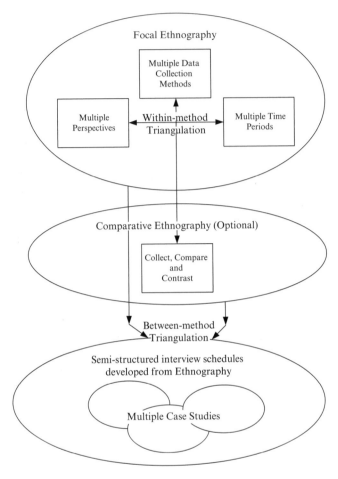

Figure 8.1   Focal ethnography multiple case study triangulation

workplace demographic and as a hidden yet critical strategic human resource (Brannen et al. 2009).

Optional Comparative Ethnography

A comparative ethnography is often helpful (see Figure 8.1). This can be conceived of in two ways: as part of the original research design, done simultaneously (for example, Barley 1996; Brannen et al. 1999), or *post hoc* as a follow-up to the original ethnography (see Brannen and Salk 2000; Brannen 2004; O'Mahony and Bechky 2006). Comparative ethnographies in the field of anthropology are generally conducted in order to collect, compare and contrast diverse ethnographic data that can be used in cross-cultural analyses of human culture and behaviour. Each ethnography is a 'stand-alone' study that is then compared with other ethnographies on specific cultural content areas such as kinship relations, coming of age rituals, eating habits and so on. The Ethnographic Database Project (EDP) is a web-based interface for the collection and standardization of such comparative ethnographic data. Founded by the Societé Internationale d'Ethnologie et de Folklore (SIEF) established in Athens in 1968, the EDP enables anthropologists to enter information about their field research using a set of standard codes developed for cross-cultural application. The codes relate to a society's organization, kinship and marriage practices, subsistence economy, and pattern of sexual division of labour.

In organizational studies in general, and international business research especially, comparative ethnographies are useful in order to further generate theory by comparing and contrasting two like pairs of field data that vary just slightly, for example, across distance or differentiated contexts (national cultural, organizational, institutional, technological and so on). A comparative ethnography in this sense is another type of within-method triangulation where a whole ethnographic study is mirrored or replicated as the case may be. This might also be seen as an ethnographic extension of the constant comparative method (see Glaser and Strauss 1967) to uncover further aspects of a construct that might not have been gleaned by studying a single field site. It is often the situation that one can uncover more about the nature of what something is by learning more deeply of what it is not within the confines of multifaceted similitude.

A CASE ILLUSTRATION OF THEORY DEVELOPMENT AROUND THE CONSTRUCT OF *RECONTEXTUALIZATION*

The Initial Focal Ethnography

Recontextualization is the transformation of the meaning of firm offerings (technologies, work practices, products and so on) as they are uprooted from one cultural environment and transplanted to another. The original ideas around this construct were developed from an initial descriptive ethnography of Tokyo Disneyland that I conducted from a radical humanist perspective (Burrell and Morgan 1979) as a graduate student in cultural anthropology, in which the main thesis induced in the study was that a quintessentially American cultural artefact was appropriated by the Oriental Land Company and used to advance a sense of Japanese cultural hegemony in the Pacific Rim. To quote from the original study, I surmised the following:

> What is significant about this recontextualization of Disneyland is that it complicates the usual way we understand cross-cultural hegemony. In the Western imperialist model of hegemony, imported cultural artifacts are either imposed intact onto the Other's culture or are domesticated by the Other; in either case the move is to make the exotic familiar. But, in the case of Tokyo Disneyland, the owners have insisted upon constructing an exact copy of the original and thereby keeping the exotic exotic to the point of effectively denying that they have familiarized it. My explanation for this difference in the way that Disney cultural artifacts are imported is that it represents a specific Japanese form of cultural imperialism. The process of assimilation of the West, the recontextualization of Western simulacra, demonstrates not that the Japanese are being dominated by Western ideologies, but that they differentiate their identity from the West in a way that reinforces their sense of their own cultural superiority, or what we might call Japanese hegemony. (Brannen 1992, pp. 220–21)

The Follow-up Comparative Ethnography

After I had started my first academic assignment in a business school and needed to focus my research more directly on management-related outcomes, I conducted a follow-up comparative ethnography of Tokyo Disneyland and Disneyland Paris to further develop theory around the central question of how cultural contexts affect internationalization (Brannen and Wilson 1996). This secondary study was motivated in large part by the fact that the empirical evidence did not support extant theory on internationalization. Specifically, whereas Prahalad and Doz's (1987) global integration versus local responsiveness framework suggests that Disney should have favoured a global integration strategy in both cases due to Disney's globally recognized brandname and inimitable core competencies, this strategy when employed in Japan was met with extreme success but when employed in France was met with unanticipated failure. To exacerbate matters, cultural similarity theory would have predicted that Disney would have been more successful in the cultural context it was most similar to (France as opposed to Japan) – yet the opposite was found. Finally, FDI theory suggests that foreignness should be a liability, but Disney's first attempt at internationalization into Japan – a country with high cultural distance from the USA – proved more successful than Disney's wildest dreams and continues to be so despite Japan's ongoing recession. In any case, many unexpected outcomes, both positive and negative, emerged. Thus, I decided to conduct a comparative analysis

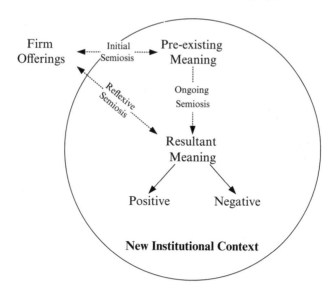

Figure 8.2   The process of recontextualization of firm offerings

of ethnographic data from Tokyo Disneyland and Disneyland Paris to explore the factors that led to these unexpected results.

The data were collected over a period of five years combining repeated site visits, archival research at the Disney Archives in Burbank and at the Anaheim Public Library in California, and in-depth interviews with Disney executives, ride operators, and theme park customers in the US, Tokyo and Paris. My aim was to uncover how the unexpected outcomes came about so as to unbundle what otherwise might be attributed to good or bad luck in the internationalization process by developing a more sophisticated understanding of the issues of global integration and local responsiveness that goes beyond strategic fit. From this comparative ethnography, using semiotic analytic tools from linguistic anthropology, the construct of recontextualization and the recipient host environment's role in transforming firm offerings (see Figure 8.2, initially presented in Brannen et al. 1999 and fully expanded in Brannen 2004) were induced.

In brief, this comparative ethnography expanded my understanding of recontextualization beyond observing its occurrence and the active role the recipient culture has in cross-national transfer to being able to more clearly articulate the process of recontextualization including the identification of three distinct instances of semiosis (skidding of semantic fit). Every cultural environment is embedded with its own system of organizational signification involving distinct work-related assumptions, behaviours and practices. Given this, misalignments easily occur between what is sent from abroad and how it is perceived locally. The comparative ethnographies showed that recontextualization involves both how firm offerings are initially understood as well as how meanings evolve in a new environment. By comparing and contrasting the two ethnographies, I was able to illuminate how transferred offerings go through a preliminary round of recipient cultural sensemaking in which they are assimilated into pre-existing meanings, then, as they are implemented, acted on, and interacted with, they continue to undergo recontextualization. As depicted in Figure 8.2, I was further able to capture the important observation that recontextualization can have both negative and positive effects on a firm's internationalization, thus turning on its head, as it were, the notion of 'liability of foreignness' (LOF) in international business. Successful recontextualization, if the process is properly understood, can become a source of organizational learning and, in turn, become a competitive advantage. Unsuccessful recontextualization, on the other hand, in line with and extending what we know of LOF, will result in lost opportunities for site-specific learning and strategic realignment, and may seriously hinder transfer efforts in the most severe cases.

Yet, the comparative ethnography also revealed that planning for and monitoring recontextualization are not simple matters. In most cases managers are initially unaware of all but the most obvious aspects of recontextualization, such as differences in company language, organizational structure, shop-floor layout, and industrial and supplier relations. Much of recontextualization happens *in situ* and in real time; as such, it cannot be planned for. At best, managers become aware of recontextualization as they are confronted with organizational barriers to implementing technology transfer. What they are aware of is only a small part of what is. So, how might my work help reduce some of the uncertainty around recontextualization and offer guidance to individuals in multinational organizations on how to monitor and manage this inevitable process?

The Multiple Case Study Triangulation

In terms of theory building, even though recontextualization was an integral part of the internationalization story for a highly people-dependent industry like theme parks, it was unclear whether the construct would be critical in harder industries such as automobiles or paper, or in high-technology industries such as semiconductors and the like. In order to find out whether the construct was generalizable outside of people-dependent industries, I designed a between-method triangulation research agenda conducting multiple case studies guided by structured interview schedules developed from focal ethnographies to deductively test and extend the construct of recontextualization. Although I have subsequently extended the domain of theory building around the construct of recontextualization to other industries, including high-technology industries, for illustrative purposes in this chapter, I have chosen to highlight the multiple case study triangulation in the manufacture of ball-bearings because it is one of the most dissimilar industries to theme parks, in that it involves hard technology that is significantly less people dependent.

Generalizability of Recontextualization to a Contrasting Industry

NSK, Nippon Seiko Kooji, is the world's second largest manufacturer of ball-bearings after AB SKF of Sweden, with a 14 per cent share in the global market. Following the general research design described in Figure 8.1, the study commenced with a focal ethnography at NSK's main parent plant in Ishibe, Japan, followed by a series of five comparative case studies in the US, the UK, China and Brazil. These plants, seven in all – three in the US, two in the UK, and one each in China and Brazil – were differentiated by context, geographically as well as by history and organizational structure: some were unionized, some were greenfields and others were acquisitions.

The research team for the focal ethnographies in the US and Japan comprised three members: a professor of engineering and specialist in total quality control, a Japanese business historian fluent in Japanese, and myself (also bilingual). The subsequent case study triangulations were performed by myself – the lead ethnographer of the study. Data were collected predominantly in English and Japanese, using interpreters in China and Brazil, and were mostly qualitative in nature, relying heavily on observation, semi-structured interviews, organizational documents and other secondary data. We utilized a structured interview schedule because the intent was to deductively test by means of the case studies whether or not the construct of recontextualization was applicable to hard technology industries (the polar opposite of entertainment) and if so, whether further theory could be elaborated with regard to what kinds of firm offerings are more or less vulnerable to recontextualization by comparing and contrasting the findings from the two industries. The interview schedule was greatly facilitated by the fact that due to its long history of internationalization, NSK had a clearly articulated strategy that included explicit notions of what they wanted to transfer intact to their various subsidiaries.

Fitting with its lead position in the industry, NSK has many excellent manufacturing practices characteristic of top Japanese manufacturers. NSK's plants, both in Japan and abroad, proudly display awards granted by industry such as the ISO/QS 9000 certification, and customers such as

Toyota, Nissan, Chrysler and Ford have given NSK awards for excellence in delivery, performance and quality. Mr Ueno, the plant manager of NSK's Ishibe plant – the designated parent plant to each of the overseas facilities in the multiple case study – explained that these practices are integral parts of NSK's 'bearing culture' that must be transferred to make high-quality products efficiently. 'Bearing culture' is the way things are done within NSK to make high-quality bearings, he intoned; 'bearing culture', he explained, 'can be transferred and used universally throughout NSK's global enterprise'.

These sentiments were echoed by the vice president of corporate planning, as well as engineers and managers in the overseas project division both at Ishibe and at the Tokyo headquarters. NSK believes very strongly in its engineering standards as essential to high-quality operations. High precision is what drives bearing culture. Tolerances of plus or minus three microns are common. At this level of precision even a speck of dirt can throw off a bearing's functioning. Follow-up interviews with Mr Ueno and members of the internationalization division at headquarters suggested that the formal standardized processes, techniques and procedures that have evolved within NSK over decades is what they meant by 'culture' – in keeping with what Schein refers to as the artefact and norm levels of culture (Schein 1985). This was what they wanted to transfer one to one.

Having such a clearly articulated transfer strategy around tangible artefacts greatly helped the research agenda, in that it was quite clear what to look for and ask about in the pursuit of recontextualization at the subsidiary plants. However, what NSK meant as 'culture' and what an anthropologist generally includes in the scope of the term is quite distinct. Most notably, missing from NSK's view are the assumption-level aspects of culture that are implicit and harder to surface and track. Indeed, there were certainly human resource requirements that the successful transfer of NSK's 'ball-bearing culture' were predicated upon that NSK did not take into consideration. For example, machine operators need to be flexible, oriented towards problem-solving, and capable of maintaining the discipline needed to produce high-quality bearings with a minimum of waste. This, in turn, assumes a shared work culture among employees. However, NSK's teams that were sent overseas were not charged with transferring their work culture. Rather, in essence, their job was to set up production equipment and machinery and to teach standard operating procedures (SOPs) to supervisors and operators.

The 'hard side' of NSK's production system (what NSK calls 'hardware') – the equipment, technical process flow (such as heat treat and machining), automation and flexible assembly – generally is transferred intact from Japan to its various country subsidiaries. NSK's general approach to overseas transfer of production technology is to design and build equipment in Japan, set it up and debug it in a Japanese parent facility, bring representatives of the overseas operation to Japan for training on the equipment, and then disassemble and ship it to the overseas facility. It arrives with a complement of Japanese production engineers who help with the local installation and debugging. The 'soft side' of NSK's production system (what NSK calls the 'software') has many common features associated with Japanese manufacturing: a strong system of quality assurance, now known as total quality management, a clean and orderly workplace, very well-maintained equipment with thorough preventive maintenance programmes, continuous flow production wherever possible, flexible lines to reduce set-up times, and extensive inventory control.

Results: Evidence of Recontextualization

Initially, the research team was fearful that recontextualization would be all but nil at the overseas subsidiaries due to how NSK understood their 'ball-bearing culture' as predominantly 'hard' technological systems. However, early on in the comparative case study process, preliminary interviews with the plant manager and his Japanese assistant plant manager in one of the US plants in Ann Arbor, Michigan, uncovered significant disparities in what they wanted to transfer and in what was actually transferred with regard to the set of core practices and technologies included in their definition of a 'ball-bearing culture'. Whereas many of NSK's standards and technical processes were transferred relatively unaltered, other processes differed significantly between the plants, especially those that were people dependent and therefore predicated on the existence of complementary human systems in the subsidiary locales that were taken for granted and therefore overlooked by the Japanese parent plant managers.

For example, although NSK's Ann Arbor plant has turned out to be something of a success story, success has by no means been realized in a linear fashion, as the story of quality improvement in Ann Arbor will attest. Over a one-year period from 1984 to 1985, Ann Arbor cut scrap from 5 to 2.5 per cent. This was remarkable but it should be said that quality had not improved in the 30 years prior to this time. With further efforts, the scrap rate was reduced by a factor of five – to just under 0.5 per cent. In other words, the scrap rate moved from 1 out of 20 parts to 1 out of 200 parts during a 10-year period. Compared to NSK's plants in Japan, which run at 0.09 per cent scrap, Ann Arbor is still generating over five times the scrap rate of its Japanese counterparts.

Preliminary interviews with local plant managers and their Japanese counterparts at the parent plant in Ishibe, coupled with ongoing observation by the team of researchers on the shop-floor, uncovered numerous disparities with regard to how core practices and technologies were operationalized *in situ* at the transfer locations. We immediately noted incongruence in what NSK intended to transfer and in what was actually transferred. Most notably, the structure and meaning of workteams and teamwork differed significantly between plants, particularly in the case of NSK's Ann Arbor plant, which was fully unionized and a brownfield acquisition.

In interviews with the NSK's Japanese transfer managers, they explained that while they felt that it is necessary to provide technical assistance, particularly in the early stages of overseas operations, to get equipment running in accordance with NSK's SOPs, it was not their business to interfere in overseas personnel management issues, or what they called the 'people side' of management. It was as if technical standards and SOPs were independent of the more social and cultural aspects of their system.

However, technology is always coupled with social and cultural systems and if these linkages are left unmanaged, unexpected outcomes occur, frustrating successful transfer. Japanese managers may say they do not wish to change personnel management practices in America, yet there is a great deal of cultural information being communicated to American plants through Japanese expatriates and by regular visits of American plant members to Japan, as the following quote shows: 'We tell our American managers that who is at fault is not important. If you criticize workers they may feel embarrassed' (Assistant to Plant Manager, Ann Arbor plant, 14 June 1995). While this statement is consistent with Japanese norms with regard to work responsibility and social sanctions, an emphasis on 'face-saving' is not the rule in the United States where blaming individuals is more common.

In order to better understand why some aspects of NSK's production system were transferred fairly intact, while others met significant barriers to implementation, we found it useful to sort the technologies. We first sorted processes by whether they were 'hard' or 'soft' technologies. The sorting was motivated by NSK's own custom of distinguishing between 'hardware' and 'software' when referring to transferred processes. However, in line with the constant comparative method (Glaser and Strauss 1967), we found that this distinction was supported by theory in research on technology transfer that distinguishes between physical and social technologies (Tornatzky and Fleischer 1990). Our informants at NSK did not really elaborate what they meant by either term, but it was clear that they were using 'software' as a shorthand for technologies that were heavily people dependent. In analysing 'hard' and 'soft' technologies and processes, the distinction is clearly based on the extent to which technologies and processes rely on accompanying organizational contexts. We therefore named this dimension 'contextual embeddedness' and defined it as the degree to which technologies and processes were more or less tightly integrated with other technical and social contexts.

Tornatzky and Fleischer (p. 10) defined technology as 'tools or tool systems by which we transform parts of our environment, derived from human knowledge, to be used for human purposes'. Using this broad definition, a second categorical dimension became evident – the knowledge base associated with the technology. By knowledge base we mean something akin to what Kogut and Zander (1993) call 'know-how' associated with implementing and operating technology. 'Know-how' was well articulated and codifiable in some cases, but not in others.

This led us to think about technologies in terms of the distinction between their explicit and tacit knowledge base (Polanyi 1966; Nonaka and Takeuchi 1995; Doz 1996). Whereas the former type of knowledge is relatively easy to articulate and document, the latter is not. Rather, tacit knowledge is the taken-for-granted understandings associated with techniques and processes that are learned over time through socialization (interacting within an organization and with society at large). Tacit knowledge is deeply embedded in a member's consciousness and is therefore difficult to access. These dimensions, induced by case data and supported by theory, gave way to a recontextualization framework (Figure 8.3) for understanding the vulnerability of firm offerings (both hard and soft) to recontextualization in new user environments.

After identifying the two salient dimensions for categorization, we mapped transferred technologies and processes on a grid with the x-axis as the degree of contextual embeddedness (context free versus context bound) and the y-axis as the degree of implicit or explicit knowledge base (see Figure 8.3). This mapping indicated that some technologies and processes were recontextualized to a greater extent than others. Processes with high embeddedness and a large tacit knowledge base were recontextualized to a greater extent than those with low contextual embeddedness and high explicit knowledge. We therefore introduced a third axis (the z-axis) to represent the degree of recontextualization as a function of contextual embeddedness and implicit versus explicit knowledge. This grid can also be helpful to a managerial audience both for diagnosing where recontextualizations are more or less likely to be expected, and for planning appropriate transfer strategies.

CONCLUSION

In order to extract general theory from empirical ethnographic observations, some type of comparative analysis must be utilized. Doing so calls

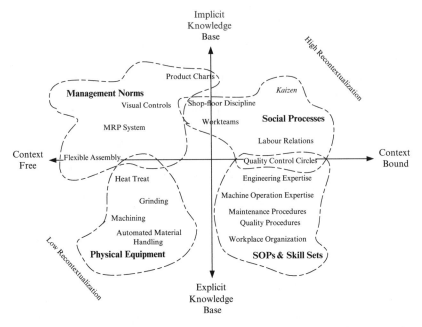

Figure 8.3   Framework for understanding NSK's recontextualizations of firm offerings

for a comparative approach between extant theory and practice where the researcher looks for repeating categories, thinks about relationships among them and then begins to ask why such relationships exist. This involves a new orientation to ethnographic and also qualitative research in general because it implies a shift from the 'idiographic', in which the researcher strives to offer a thick description of the research site, to the 'nomothetic', where the researcher searches for constants and regularities in the data (Burrell and Morgan 1979).

In the example of theory building around the construct of recontextualization, the multi-case study triangulation of the ethnographic findings served both as deductive tests of the recontextualization construct as well as an ongoing inductive theory-building opportunity. Further, the multiple case studies served not only to test the construct in a disparate industry but also to extend it by means of further induction. To point, we were able to induce a framework for understanding what types of firm offerings are more or less affected by recontextualization in cross-national transfer. Although the direction and amount of recontextualization cannot be gauged in advance, our framework can help managers anticipate initial misalignments, monitor ongoing adjustments, and take advantage of positive recontextualizations as sustainable firm advantages in the future. In such a way, the multi-case study triangulation enabled us to refine, extend and ultimately to generalize our findings from the focal ethnographies into a framework that can be used in multiple and diverse organizational contexts.

NOTE

1. Here I am not using 'external validity' in the quantitatively established sense of generalizability to a larger population. Rather, it refers to the fact that although ethnographies are decidedly idiosyncratic as co-created outcomes between researcher and researched, the theoretical inductions resulting from the studies can indeed be generalizable understandings (for further discussion, see Golafshani 2003).

REFERENCES

Abu-Lughod, L. (1986), *Veiled Sentiments: Honor and Poetry in a Bedouin Society*, New York: Oxford University Press.

Barley, S.R. (1996), 'Technicians in the workplace: ethnographic evidence for bringing work into organization studies', *Administrative Science Quarterly*, **41**, 404–41.

Bhagat, R.S., B.L. Kedia, P.D. Harveston and H.C. Triandis (2002), 'Cultural variations in the cross-border transfer of organizational knowledge: an integrative framework', *Academy of Management Review*, **27** (2), 204–21.

Brannen, M.Y. (1992), 'Bwana Mickey: constructing cultural consumption at Tokyo Disneyland', in J. Tobin (ed.), *Remade in Japan: Consumer Tastes in a Changing Japan*, New Haven, CT: Yale University Press, pp. 216–64.

Brannen, M.Y. (1994), 'Your next boss is Japanese: negotiating cultural change at a Western Massachusetts paper plant', Doctoral Dissertation, University of Massachusetts, Amherst, MA.

Brannen, M.Y. (2004), 'When Mickey loses face: recontextualization, semantic fit, and the semiotics of foreignness', *Academy of Management Review*, **29** (4), 593–616.

Brannen, M.Y. (2009), 'Culture in context: new theorizing for today's complex cultural organizations', in C. Nakata (ed.), *Beyond Hofstede: Culture Frameworks for Global Marketing and Management*, Chicago, IL: Macmillan, pp. 81–100.

Brannen, M.Y., J.K. Liker and M.W. Fruin (1999), 'Recontextualization and factory-to-factory knowledge transfer from Japan to the U.S.: the case of NSK', in W.M. Fruin, J.F. Liker and P.S. Adler (eds), *Remade in America: Transplanting and Transforming Japanese Production Systems*, New York: Oxford University Press, pp. 117–54.

Brannen, M.Y. and M.P. Peterson (2009), 'Merging without alienating: interventions promoting cross-cultural organizational integration and their limitations', *Journal of International Business Studies*, **40** (3), 468–89.

Brannen, M.Y. and J. Salk (2000), 'Partnering across borders: negotiating organizational culture in a German–Japanese joint venture', *Human Relations*, **53** (4), 451–87.

Brannen, M.Y., D.C. Thomas and D. Garcia (2009), 'Biculturals as natural bridges for intercultural communication and collaboration', *International Workshop on Intercultural Communications (IWIC) Proceedings*, Stanford University.

Brannen, M.Y. and J.M. Wilson (1996), 'Recontextualization and internationalization: lessons in transcultural materialism from the Walt Disney Company', *CEMS (Community of European Management Schools) Business Review*, **1** (1), 97–110.

Burrell, G. and G. Morgan (1979), *Sociological Paradigms and Organizational Analysis: Elements of the Sociology of Corporate Life*, London: Heinemann.

Clifford, J. and G. Marcus (1986), *Writing Culture: The Poetics and Politics of Ethnography*, Berkeley, CA: University of California Press.

Dalton, M. (1959), *Men Who Manage*, New York: Wiley.

Doz, Y.L. (1996), 'The evolution of cooperation in strategic alliances: initial conditions or learning', *Strategic Management Journal*, **17**, 55–83.

Dwyer, K. (1982), *Moroccan Dialogues: Anthropology in Question*, Baltimore, MD: Johns Hopkins University Press.

Dyer Jr, W. and A. Wilkins (1991), 'Better stories, not better constructs, to generate better theory: a rejoinder to Eisenhardt', *Academy of Management Review*, **16** (3), 613–19.

Eisenhardt, K. (1991), 'Better stories and better constructs: the case for rigor and comparative logic', *Academy of Management Review*, **16** (3), 620–27.

Freeman, D. (1983), *Margaret Mead and Samoa: The Making and Unmaking of an Anthropological Myth*, New York: Penguin.

Geertz, C. (1973, reprinted 2000), *The Interpretation of Cultures*, New York: Basic Books.

Glaser, B. and A. Strauss (1967), *The Discovery of Grounded Theory*, Chicago, IL: Aldine.

Golafshani, N. (2003), 'Understanding reliability and validity in qualitative research', *The Qualitative Report*, **8** (4), 597–607.

Gouldner, A.W. (1954), *Patterns of Industrial Bureaucracy*, Glencoe, IL: Free Press.

Kirk, J. and M. Miller (1986), *Reliability and Validity in Qualitative Research*, Newbury Park, CA: Sage.

Kogut, B. and U. Zander (1993), 'Knowledge of the firm and the evolutionary theory of the multinational corporation', *Journal of International Business Studies*, **24** (4), 625–46.

Kunda, G. (2006), *Engineering Culture: Control and Commitment in a High-Tech Corporation*, Philadelphia, PA: Temple University Press.

Lewin, K. (1946), 'Action research and minority problems', *Journal of Social Issues*, **2** (4), 34–46.

Lincoln, Y. and L. Guba (1985), *Naturalistic Inquiry*, Newbury Park, CA: Sage.

Marcus, G.E. and M.J. Fischer (1999), *Anthropology as Cultural Critique: An Experimental Moment in the Human Sciences*, Chicago, IL: University of Chicago Press.

Mead, M. (1926), *Coming of Age in Samoa: A Psychological Study of Primitive Youth for Civilization,* New York: American Museum of Natural History.

Naroll, R. and R. Cohen (1973), *Handbook of Method in Cultural Anthropology*, New York: Columbia University Press.

Nonaka, I. and H. Takeuchi (1995), *The Knowledge Creating Company*, New York: Oxford University Press.

O'Mahony, S. and B.A. Bechky (2006), 'Stretchwork: managing the career progression paradox in external labor markets', *Academy of Management Journal*, **49** (5), 918–41.

Perlow, L. (1997), *Finding Time: How Corporations, Individuals and Families Can Benefit from New Work Practices*, Ithaca, NY: Cornell University Press.

Polanyi, M. (1966), *The Tacit Dimension*, Garden City, NY: Doubleday.

Prahalad, C.K. and Y.L. Doz (1987), *The Multinational Mission*, New York: Free Press.

Preview, B. and R. Fielding-Barnsley (1990), 'Acquiring the alphabetical principle: a case for teaching recognition of phoneme identity', *Journal of Educational Psychology*, **82** (4), 805–12.

Romani, L. (2008), 'Relating to the other: paradigm interplay for cross-cultural management research', Doctoral Dissertation, Stockholm School of Economics, Institute for International Business, Stockholm.

Schein, E. (1985), *Organizational Culture and Leadership*, San Francisco, CA: Jossey-Bass.

Tornatzky, L.G. and M. Fleischer (1990), *The Processes of Technological Innovation*, Lexington, MA: Lexington Books.

Van Maanen, J. (1975), 'Police socialization: a longitudinal examination of job attitudes in an urban police department', *Administrative Science Quarterly*, **20** (2), 207–28.

Van Maanen, J. (1988), *Tales of the Field: On Writing Ethnography*, Chicago, IL: University of Chicago Press.

Van Maanen, J. and S.R. Barley (1984), 'Occupational communities: culture and control in organizations', in B.M. Staw and L.L. Cummings (eds), *Research in Organizational Behavior*, Vol. 6, Greenwich, CT: JAI Press, pp. 287–365.

Weick, K. (1993), 'The collapse of sensemaking in organizations: the *Mann Gulch* disaster', *Administrative Science Quarterly*, **38**, 628–52.

Whyte, W.F. (1943), *Street Corner Society*, Chicago, IL: University of Chicago Press.

9. Beyond the inductive myth: new approaches to the role of existing theory in case research

Poul Houman Andersen and Hanne Kragh

INTRODUCTION

The international business (IB) field has seen growing interest in case research and other qualitative approaches as powerful means for investigating complex social phenomena. This interest is not surprising given the multidisciplinary nature of phenomena in IB that lend themselves to qualitative approaches for theory building (Marschan-Piekkari and Welch 2004). However, the IB field is not particularly innovative with respect to using and reflecting upon case research, at least when compared to other disciplines such as, for instance, marketing or management. Whereas both of these disciplines have been supplying theoretical concepts and even research questions to IB (Tsui 2007), advances in case-based research methodologies in these fields have not been adopted within IB. A recent study concluded that a convention of exploratory and positivistic approaches to case studies dominates the research published in dedicated IB journals (Piekkari et al. 2009).

One particular area where more diversity could advance theoretical development in IB is the use of pre-existing theoretical knowledge. The assumption in IB is that case studies are based on inductive reasoning. Reflecting its positivist origins, induction is concerned with the process of inference from the known to the unknown, basing the steps towards generalization on observable facts through the use of logic (Mill 1974). An inductive research process is not concerned with the role and use of existing theory, but sees the logic applied to empirical observation as a way to reach knowledge. Researchers are often advised to proceed with caution. Literature warns us against being too theoretically predetermined when conducting inductively oriented qualitative research, because it may prematurely lock our analytical focus (Mills 1959; Glaser and Strauss 1967; Weick 1989; Maxwell 1996). We concur that keeping an open mind and avoiding premature conclusions or being guided strongly by one's expectations will enhance the quality of research. However, one result of the inductive influences on qualitative research is a lack of satisfactory guidelines on how to use existing theoretical frameworks in case research.

In contrast to the assumptions of the inductive model, researchers do not enter a field without some theory-driven specifications and expectations (Burrell and Morgan 1979). Rather than refraining from theoretical predispositions, we would argue that qualitative researchers should embrace and understand how theory and data interact in their sensemaking efforts during theory building. This 'sensemaking' view of theorizing is distinct from the conventional inductive approach. Given this alternative perspective, the purpose of this chapter is to broaden the possibilities for combining theory and case evidence in IB research. In order to do so, we present what we have argued to be two emerging approaches to the use of theory in theory-building qualitative research – *in vivo* and *ex ante* (Andersen and Kragh 2010) – which have not yet been discussed in any depth in the IB literature. Following a short discussion on theory and theory development in qualitative research, the remainder of the chapter will introduce the two approaches, as well as demonstrate how they can be used in IB case research.

THEORY BUILDING AND SENSEMAKING

As we have discussed elsewhere (Andersen and Kragh 2010), *theory* is an abstract notion which tends to be used unreflectively and is often confused with other concepts such as models and propositions (Sutton and Staw 1995). Most definitions agree that theories express a logical linking of concepts, such as causes and effects or co-occurrences of phenomena, in this sense representing an explanation of the occurrence of specific phenomena (Jary and Jary 1985; Keringer 1986). We suggest that theory may be conceptualized as 'an ordered set of assertions about a generic behavior or structure assumed to hold throughout a significantly broad range of specific instances' (Sutherland 1975, p. 9).

A relevant issue in this context is to make a distinction between scientific and non-scientific theory. Whereas theories and theorizing are an integral part of logical human reasoning (Weick 1979), the notion of scientific theory is often reserved for more systematized sets of interrelated concepts and principles that explain a specific set of phenomena across a variety of circumstances (Kourany 1997). This idea of generalizability of theoretical insights, however, has been challenged, particularly in social science research. Theories aiming to reach a high degree of generalizability do this at the expense of other aims of research such as accuracy and simplicity (Weick 1995). Thus, the definition of theory that one subscribes to is also related to one's philosophy of science – in particular to conceptions of the nature of knowledge. Social scientists have addressed the issue of generalizability in terms of theoretical range and argued that social researchers should refrain from building grand theory in the image of the natural sciences. Instead, theory building should take a bottom-up approach and focus on theorizing and developing minor working hypotheses and mid-range theories closer to the social reality which they address (Merton 1957). For instance, the development of theories which address the internationalization of small and medium-sized enterprises, rather than all firms, is seen as a more valid approach. This is also in keeping with other insights from qualitative social scientists, suggesting that social contexts are unstable over time and do not square easily with mechanical conceptions of social reality, such as those underpinning strongly positivist approaches to social science.

As social contexts may unfold in unpredicted ways, pre-existing scientific theory may not provide an ample source of inspiration in theorizing efforts. Moreover, because theories may not be applicable as grand concepts explaining all incidents of phenomena, there is also room for simultaneously using more theories to encourage imaginative thinking, even if such theories are conflicting. The role of theory in case research is to support the researchers' ability to focus and to help sort and structure data in an informative manner in the situation of data overload that is characteristic for qualitative research (Miles 1979). However, too strong a focus on pre-existing theoretical concepts may also blind researchers in their quest for establishing new insights and therefore hinder theory development (Weick 1989). Therefore, in theory-building qualitative research, pre-existing theory should be seen as a means for 'imaginative' theorizing, a resourced form of musing, allowing for the free-flowing interplay of observation and multirelational reflection (Locke et al. 2008).

For our purposes, 'theory building' is defined as 'the process through which researchers seek to make sense of the observable world by conceptualizing, categorizing and ordering relationships among observed elements' (Andersen and Kragh 2010, p. 50). This definition builds on Astley (1985) and Weick (1989), both of whom also focus on theory building as a sensemaking process characterized by the interplay of observation and multirelational reflections. In this process, authoring – that is, explicitly and knowingly applying a theoretical perspective when interpreting 'what is going on' – plays a central role in the generation of new theory.

ALTERNATIVE APPROACHES TO USING THEORY IN CASE RESEARCH

Table 9.1 summarizes the underlying assumptions and key elements of the received inductive view, as well as two emerging approaches to using theory in case research. In this section we compare and contrast the three approaches. We are explicitly concerned with theory building from qualitative case studies. We seek to show how the use of existing theory can be extended beyond the conventional approach in IB.

The Role of Theory in Case Studies: The Inductive View

The inductive approach dominates qualitative approaches in IB research (Piekkari et al. 2009). As Table 9.1 shows, it is associated with the work of Eisenhardt (1989), Eisenhardt and Graebner (2007) and Yin (2009), which are among the most cited approaches in the literature on theory building from case studies. Notably, Eisenhardt (1989) recommends an inductive approach, which consists of 'the emergence of theoretical categories solely from evidence' (p. 534) and 'most importantly . . . is begun as close as possible to the ideal of no theory under consideration and no hypotheses to test' (p. 536). Although Eisenhardt also admits that researchers cannot have a clean theoretical slate, preordained theory is seen as a source of contamination. Theory is supposed to enter the researcher's mind at a much later stage, when emergent concepts are to be compared with the extant literature. This process, labelled 'enfolding' by Eisenhardt, adds to the existing corpus of knowledge by extending findings and theories into novel areas, or by refuting and thus limiting prior theoretical generalizations.

The use of the inductive approach reflects the positivist myth that a researcher is required to enter the field without any theoretical ballast. At the same time, however, researchers are expected to deliver a priori specification of constructs, and should follow the same procedure for defining research questions as that of hypothesis testing research, in order to measure constructs more precisely (Eisenhardt 1989). This is confusing, as researchers are expected to (a) develop theory-free questions (b) about social phenomena existing independently of theoretical framings and (c) stick to their measures and constructs without being distracted by the context in which their studies unfold. This inductive myth is frequent in IB research literature. Inductive studies are contrasted to deductive studies based on their 'tightness' to existing theory (Eisenhardt and Graebner 2007, p. 26). Whereas deductive studies are seen as scoped within an existing theory, inductive approaches, such as the case-based approach, are driven by the phenomenon studied.

*Table 9.1   Comparing three approaches to the use of theory in case
              research*

Dimension	Inductive	*In vivo*	*Ex ante*
Ontological assumptions about the nature of knowledge	Associated with positivist assumptions	Associated with critical realist assumptions	Associated with postmodernist assumptions
Role of existing theory in theory building	Seen as limiting researchers' ability to see new phenomena objectively	Seen as inspirational sources used to frame research projects and understand developments in the empirical data	Seen as language games which the researcher must learn in order to use them individually and to exploit their contradictions 'playfully'
Theory-building approach	Theory building as construction and saturation of new un-contaminated ideas generated from empirical evidence	Theory building as interpolation – complementary theories are used continuously to refine and adjust a pre-existing theoretical framework	Theory building as extrapolation – deconstruction and reconstruction of theories in order to challenge and possibly change boundaries separating existing theoretical discourses
Stage and mode of theory involvement	Late in the 'enfolding' process, when engaging in conversation with established theories	Single-perspective use of theory in the preparation and early data collection stages, which may later be extended and refined	Broad, multiparadigmatic use of theory from the outset
Examples of authoritative literature	Eisenhardt (1989) Eisenhardt and Graebner (2007), Yin (2009)	Orton (1997), Dubois and Gadde (2002)	Poole and Van de Ven (1989), Morgan (1997), Lewis and Grimes (1999)

The inductive perspective followed by Eisenhardt and others is often ascribed to grounded theory, however erroneously (Suddaby 2006). Whereas induction never transcends the collection and aggregation of observations for generalizing, grounded theory is not simply an inductive procedure of data coding. As pointed out by Glaser and Strauss (1967, p. 253): 'No sociologist can possibly erase from his mind all the theory he knows before he begins his research. Indeed the trick is to line up what one takes as theoretically possible . . . with what one is finding in the field . . . a combination of both is definitely desirable'. But no researcher is a *tabula rasa* upon which reality is imprinted; the positivist ideal of induction is neither realistic, nor sound, as it will act more as a source of confusion, than of clarification. As suggested by Glaser and Strauss, we enter the field as subjects, preconditioned by formal training or from experience, and our mental ballast will interact with our observations in framing reality for us. Delaying the inclusion of existing theoretical frameworks will only lead to unstructured research that rediscovers what is already known (Suddaby 2006). In that light, acknowledging our ballasts and biases may help us in challenging preconditioned beliefs.

The *In Vivo* Approach to Theory-building Case Research

The *in vivo* approach, as we have labelled it (Andersen and Kragh 2010), seeks to tackle the challenge of balancing theoretical focus with theoretical detachment by taking its departure from a single overarching theoretical framework, but continuing to scan, select and discard theoretical perspectives as this framework meets empirical data (see Table 9.1). Throughout this process, researchers extend and/or combine received theory with empirical findings and other theoretical perspectives in order to build new theory. This approach goes by different names, such as 'systematic combining' (Dubois and Gadde 2002) and 'iterative grounded theory' (Orton 1997). These labels indicate that the *in vivo* approach relies on constant iterations between theory and data. Accordingly, researchers make sense of theoretical ideas by linking theorizing to empirical evidence and, at the same time, transforming sensory data obtained in case studies into results through the use of theory and ideas (Ragin 1992). Case researchers outside the field of IB have applied this approach, for instance, in the area of strategy (for example, Zander and Zander 2005), knowledge management (Orlikowski 2002) and industrial marketing (for example, Anderson et al. 1994; Brennan and Turnbull 1999).

We argue that the *in vivo* process can be viewed as interpolation (Andersen and Kragh 2010); in other words, a gradual deepening of knowledge of key concepts. As it aims at generating plausible propositions from data which perhaps do not make sense when viewed in the light of an initial theoretical framework, it is often understood in terms of abduction (Dubois and Gadde 2002; Reichertz 2004; Locke et al. 2008). It urges the researcher not only to anchor theory building in empirical data, but simultaneously to use puzzlement and questions arising from these data to confront original theoretical ideas and expectations with new ideas from other theoretical perspectives. In this sense, the theoretically preconditioned pre-understandings of a researcher play an active role throughout the research process rather than at the very end of it, as is suggested in the inductive approach. This process is aimed at systematically discovering an order that fits surprising empirical facts. Such discovery is a mental process which depends on individual creativity and intellectual effort (Reichertz 2004).

In vivo theorizing also differs from traditional inductive approaches as it relies on a tightly articulated theoretical pre-understanding, which serves as the point of departure for initial data collection and preliminary analysis. Hence, pre-existing theory plays an important role as a source for inspiration in framing a research question and building theory. The theoretical framework is typically rooted in a single 'grand' perspective and focuses on a limited number of concepts, which is then gradually extended, changed or refined as it is confronted with the empirical world (Andersen et al. 1992). In this process, complementary theoretical perspectives may be applied, providing they do not violate the underlying assumptions of the dominant perspective. An example of this process in the IB literature can be found in the work of John Dunning (1988), which combines economic theories on international trade and neo-institutional theory on market imperfections in order to develop an 'eclectic' framework for understanding foreign direct investment.

Such paradigmatic anchoring is in line with Burrell and Morgan (1979, p. 25), who argued for paradigmatic closure and explained that paradigms 'are contradictory, being based upon at least one set of opposing meta-theoretical assumptions . . . one cannot operate in more than one paradigm at any given point in time, since accepting the assumptions of one, we defy the assumptions of all the others'. The need for additional theoretical insights is created as the research process progresses and is a result of learning from empirical data. In other words, theory building is an outcome of 'exposing' existing theory to reality in order to understand theoretical concepts and the 'empirical referent' (Lewis and Grimes 1999) at a deeper level.

In this way, the *in vivo* approach assumes the existence of an independent and given social reality, along similar lines as articulated within critical realism (Fleetwood 2005). The empirical world is viewed as existing independently of our knowledge of it and instead of 'revealing' itself through subjective construction, reality to a larger extent 'controls' or guides the research process. Although reality may not be directly accessible and perfect knowledge about it not attainable, it is nevertheless possible for the researcher to confront his/her theoretical pre-understanding with the empirical world as such and to use this confrontation to uncover further aspects of reality. In other words, reality is perceived as being ready for discovery by researchers.

In the research process, theories serve as input to, as well as outputs from, data collection and analysis, and one ambition is to achieve the best possible 'fit' between data and theory. This fit is reflected in the case study, which is a means of reaching closure in the relationship between theory and data (Ragin 1992), preferably in such a way that 'when the case is finally turned into a "product", there should be no confusing pieces left' (Dubois and Gadde 2002, p. 558). Consequently, the *in vivo* approach is predisposed towards the evolving theoretical framework as a mechanism for understanding empirical data. This identification of fits and misfits between emergent concepts and existing theories is also found in the process of 'enfolding literature' suggested by Eisenhardt (1989) as a means of enhancing the internal validity of an emergent theory. The process underlying the *in vivo* approach, however, is of a more iterative nature than that suggested by Eisenhardt.

The *Ex Ante* Approach to Theory-building Case Research

The ex ante approach, as we have labelled it (Andersen and Kragh 2010), advocates that researchers should look for paradoxes in the form of theoretical tensions or oppositions and use them to develop theory (Poole and Van de Ven 1989). It embraces the idea of a multiparadigmatic, paradoxical or dialectical approach to developing truly novel insights (Poole and Van de Ven 1989; Weick 1989; Elsbach et al. 1999). The general purpose is to use differences in theoretical perspectives as a starting point for creating new insights and for challenging taken-for-granted assumptions as they typically unfold within a specific research paradigm (Table 9.1); that is, to 'use theory and imagination to critically open up alternative ways of framing empirical material' (Alvesson and Kärreman 2007, p. 1267). All theories provide specific focus areas with persuasive but partial lenses. In this sense, the *ex ante* approach is in alignment with the inductive approach. However, rather than seeking to remain objective, the *ex ante* approach tries to avoid theoretical closure by seeing theories as 'language games', each with a specific set of rules that the researcher can experiment with and apply – similarly to children standing in front of a large mirror by the dresser, trying to fit their facial expressions with their parents' hats.

In this way, theory building in the *ex ante* approach is understood as extrapolation (Weick 1989). Extrapolation refers to a process whereby concepts and theories are developed and modified by subjecting them to alternative theoretical perspectives with different explanatory abilities. It is characterized by deliberate theoretical leaps among schools of thought which may hold axiomatically different conceptualizations of core concepts and therefore may propose radically diverging explanations, and even different framings of what is to be focused upon analytically in a research inquiry. However, the postmodernist-inspired approach to paradoxical thinking sees theories not only as lenses, but also as giving the reader/researcher authorship. According to postmodernism, reality is dynamic and paradoxical and therefore many things at once, which allows the researcher to see and use multiple or even schismatic theoretical perspectives simultaneously (Morgan 1993).

The inability to detach object from subject, or theory from reality, is probably what inductivists find most confusing with postmodernist approaches as they meddle with a root belief in positivist ontology. Theories, accordingly, are not regarded as projections of underlying generalized patterns, but rather as instruments that can help the researcher illuminate, understand and, not least, problematize the phenomenon studied (Alvesson and Kärreman 2007). Moreover, reality reveals itself according to the theoretical lenses applied (Morgan 1997). It is, however, important to use these theoretical perspectives respectfully, that is on their own terms and respecting their rationales and corresponding logics. Imaginative processes involving the sensitive use of multiple theoretical vantage points call for both academic discipline and reflexivity. There is a strong possibility for inconsistency, since the processes of variation, selection and retention of ideas are carried out by the same person or group of persons (Weick 1989). Although challenging, this does not make the process impossible, but calls for a consistent procedure to ensure a strong degree of openness in the initial data collection process, as well as in the process of reverting back to the empirical field for following up on both strong and weak leads.

DIFFERENT WAYS OF WORKING WITH PRE-EXISTING THEORY: ILLUSTRATIVE EXAMPLES

In order to elucidate further the two approaches presented above, we now provide an account of how they can be applied in a case study. The same case is used to illustrate both approaches. The purpose of the two examples is to illustrate the use of existing theory rather than discuss the substance of emerging theoretical conclusions. The case was part of a research project addressing the impact of internet-enabled information and communication technology (ICT) on international marketing systems. The case is the export marketing system of a software company, Comlog A/S. Comlog (www.comlog.com) is a small Danish provider of telematics solutions for the transport and logistics industry. As part of an increased focus on internationalization, Comlog has introduced an internet-based solution which has provided a number of opportunities for reconfiguring and relocating activities within the export marketing system.

The research topic does not unambiguously lend itself to one particular theoretical perspective. Over time, the organization of market exchange, in general, and export intermediation activities, in particular, have been studied within a number of fields and from a number of different theoretical perspectives. Theoretical diversity has only increased with the emerging interest in how to use internet-enabled ICT to support the organization of market exchange. Therefore, some initial classification of the existing literature is appropriate, regardless of the choice of approach. The differences between the two approaches become evident in the different ways this classification is subsequently applied and elaborated upon.

We use Astley and Van de Ven's (1983) seminal framework to classify existing, relevant literature as a means to study the organization of market exchange. The framework categorizes schools of thought according to two fundamental analytical dimensions in the social sciences: the level of analysis on the one hand, and the relative emphasis placed on deterministic versus voluntaristic assumptions about human nature on the other (Burrell and Morgan 1979). The former dimension, ranging from micro to macro levels of analysis, refers to whether the focus of a theoretical perspective is on single organizations or on populations or networks of organizations. The latter is concerned with the level of free will vested in human beings and its importance for understanding the organization of human activities (Astley and Van de Ven 1983). As illustrated in Figure 9.1, combining the two dimensions results in four different perspectives, each with a distinct focus on the issue of how internet-enabled ICT affects the organization of activities within export marketing systems. In the following subsections, first the *in vivo* approach, and thereafter the *ex ante* approach, are applied to the Comlog case.

Applying the *In Vivo* Approach to the Comlog Case

The *in vivo* approach is characterized by its dependence on a pre-existing theoretical framework to direct and redirect data collection, case construction and theory development. In the Comlog example, the theoretical

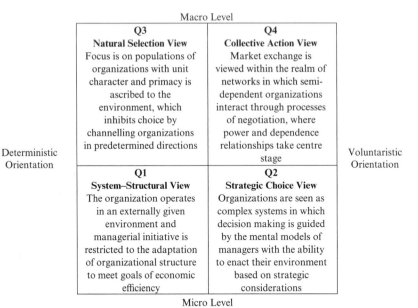

Figure 9.1   *Fundamental views on the organization of market exchange*

framework is rooted in the industrial network approach (Håkansson 1982; Axelsson and Easton 1992; Anderson et al. 1994; Håkansson and Snehota 1995), which is based on underlying assumptions from the collective action view (see Q4 in Figure 9.1). To a large extent, this preliminary framework focuses on actors as embedded in networks, and on the way the use of the internet changes these structures.

We label the first step in the development of the theoretical framework 'reorientation' (Figure 9.2). This stage is initiated when the researcher becomes aware of divergences between the initial framework and empirical data, and is similar to what Dubois and Gadde (2002) refer to as 'label-matching'. Reorientation, in this sense, includes 'the search for useful theories, complementary to the general framework . . . guided by the fact [that] the empirical observations and the current theoretical framework [do] not match' (p. 556). In the Comlog example, it became clear during the early stages of data collection that the entrepreneurial organizing of activities by single actors within a network was an important part of the project studied; however, such entrepreneurial activity was not given much leeway in the industrial network approach. These findings led us to undertake an active search for theoretical frameworks that could address

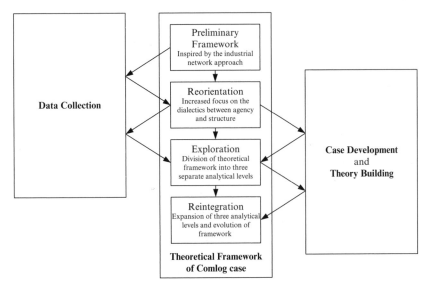

Figure 9.2   Development of the theoretical framework in the Comlog case

the role of managerial discretion in addition to system-level explanations. This in turn raised our awareness of two analytical levels within the research topic: the first level entailed how the export intermediation activities performed by individual actors were organized, while the second involved the export marketing system within which intermediation activities are performed. There is an inherent dialectical relationship between the two levels. On the one hand, the export marketing system is viewed as a negotiated setting, reflecting the vested interests of its constituent actors and constraining individual agency within the system. On the other hand, the actions of individual actors represent attempts to change existing structures, as reflected in exporters' introduction of internet-enabled ICT into their marketing systems. The two levels reflect an ongoing debate within the social sciences concerning the relative emphasis placed on the constraining properties of institutional structures on individual action versus the actors' ability to change these structures (Giddens 1984). This debate proved to be insufficiently incorporated into the initial research question and, hence, into the initial theoretical framework.

This burgeoning interest in the relevance of different analytical levels has two immediate consequences. First, the research question is reformulated to simultaneously address the two levels, as follows: *how does the use of internet-enabled ICT affect the organization of export intermediation*

activities, and how do export marketing systems change accordingly?
Second, it sets off the next stage in developing the theoretical framework,
which we have labelled 'exploration' in Figure 9.2. This is a process characterized by open-minded discovery of new theoretical perspectives, rather
than the predetermined search for specific theories, yet maintaining a tight
link between the evolving framework and the original empirical referent.
In our Comlog example, it became gradually clear that the changes taking
place displayed traits of an underlying digitalization at the network level
which affected both relationship activities and individual mindsets, but
which also acted independently on these. As part of the analytical process,
the theoretical framework is altered to address three analytical levels, that
is, an organizational level, a dyadic level and a network level. As discussed
by Easton (1992), some applying the industrial network approach start
at the level of individual firms, whereas others are preoccupied with the
relationship or the network levels. As such, it is possible to operate at
three different levels simultaneously, without violating the fundamental
assumptions of the industrial network approach, but hopefully contributing to the further development of its concepts.

After the decision to continue with a three-level theoretical framework,
each level has to be further elaborated, which takes place during a process
we referred to in Figure 9.2 as 'reintegration'. At this stage, those theoretical perspectives believed to contribute important insights into the case
under study are rewoven into the theoretical framework, a process which
may entail singling out certain concepts from the selected perspectives for
elaboration and disregarding others. In this way, the original framework
is expanded and detailed by using different complementary theories to
the industrial network approach in order to substantiate emerging theory
as well as develop the evolving case. The following provides examples of
reintegration in the Comlog case.

At the organizational level of the theoretical framework, the focus is
on Comlog's general attempts to manage their marketing system, and in
particular, on how they introduce internet-enabled ICT into this system,
and in doing so, try to change the practices and structures of that system.
Theory building at this level is inspired by literature on sensemaking and
strategic choice (see Q2 in Figure 9.1). In a similar way, at the dyadic level,
development of the theoretical framework is also inspired by complementary theory lying outside the realm of the industrial network approach.
We believe this discussion at the dyadic level is enhanced by introducing
the notion of 'routines' as traditionally discussed within the parts of evolutionary economics associated with the work of Nelson and Winter (1982)
(see Q3 in Figure 9.1). Finally, discussions at the network level are mainly
concerned with understanding the structural characteristics of a network.

These characteristics are viewed as having a formative effect on actors and, hence, represent structural contingencies to which actors conform. A major part of the literature on networks and the internet has so far been concerned with structural changes in the roles and positions of actors in a network.

Applying the *Ex Ante* Approach to the Comlog Case

Reverting to the theoretical framework in Figure 9.1, the underlying theories play a fundamentally different role when applying the *ex ante* approach as compared with the *in vivo* approach. As we have described above, the type of research process underlying the *ex ante* approach aims for a richer, more comprehensive and holistic purview stemming from the exploration of different, and sometimes conflicting, theoretical perspectives (Gioia and Pitre 1990; Lewis and Grimes 1999). We shall illustrate the application of the *ex ante* approach by subjecting the Comlog case to a process labelled 'metatriangulation', consisting of three stages: groundwork, data analysis and theory building (Lewis and Grimes 1999).

The most notable characteristic of the groundwork phase is an extensive review and systemization of literature relevant to the topic studied. Such literature reviews are not aimed at identifying certain theoretical perspectives or streams of literature as being more relevant than others, but have the explicit purpose of defining a number of lenses with differing underlying assumptions that may be used to focus the research question. In accordance with this approach, the phenomenon studied – or as Lewis and Grimes describe it, the 'common empirical referent' – is defined broadly as the effect of internet-enabled ICT on export intermediation activities.

In order to scrutinize relevant lenses, existing literature was bracketed using the framework described by Astley and Van de Ven (1983). Since the different foci may overlap as well as conflict, the aim of singling out the different perspectives in the way illustrated in Figure 9.1 is to prepare for making active use of these differences in subsequent case analysis and theory building rather than selecting one over the others, as was done in the *in vivo* example. By acknowledging, and even systemizing, differences stemming from different paradigmatic points of departure, the research process starts by opening up the empirical referent rather than prematurely closing in on a limited range of potential explanations. Hence, a wide number of different and sometimes conflicting explanations are constructed with which case data may be contrasted.

Data collection provides a particular challenge when applying the *ex ante* approach. The approach requires a dataset to be broad and detailed enough to accommodate the various theoretical perspectives. This poses a number of practical challenges with regard to the number and nature of topics covered and questions asked. Since a theoretical perspective affects and shapes data (Irvine and Deo 2006), the question arises as to how to collect a so-called metatheoretical sample that is capable of simultaneously embracing the different explanations provided by various perspectives. This problem has led Gioia and Pitre (1990), for example, to suggest that any meta-perspective should be rooted in a specific paradigm developed on the researcher's ground assumptions. The various practical problems involved in collecting a metatheoretical sample have remained almost unexamined in the literature, probably because the majority of the still limited number of exemplars applying an *ex ante* approach are based on secondary data (for example, Lewis and Grimes 1999; Saunders et al. 2003; Adriaanse and Voordijk 2005; Irvine and Deo 2006). Those collecting primary data with an *ex ante* approach either seem to accommodate the challenges by collecting multiple, separate datasets targeted at the different theoretical perspectives involved (Hassard 1991), or – to the extent that they use a single dataset – do not address the challenges of doing so (Bradshaw-Camball and Murray 1991).

In the present project, data collection was anchored in a descriptive framework constructed around the common empirical referent in question rather than around any one theoretical perspective. Accordingly, interview guides were rooted in the preliminary literature review and a descriptive framework, rather than being constructed based on the assumptions or constructs of a specific theory. Using such general interview guides, which inherently synthesize several theoretical perspectives, it becomes possible to analyse data using various theoretical 'thought trials' (Weick 1989). The drawback of such interview guides is that they may occasionally miss information pertaining to more specific issues within single perspectives. This, then, may require returning to some of the informants to collect additional information or, in some cases, accepting the lack of analytical detail.

In order to ensure rigour and reflexivity in the subsequent data analysis stage, Lewis and Grimes (1999) suggest the use of a 'paradigm itinerary', which serves as a map for navigating the different perspectives when analysing case data. In the present project, the collective action view is used as a starting point because it hosts the descriptive framework and, as such, constitutes the 'home paradigm' with which the researcher is most familiar (Gioia and Pitre 1990; Lewis and Grimes 1999; Irvine and Deo 2006).

Data analysis in metatriangulation is a matter of trying out the potential insights provided by different theoretical perspectives and deciding which ones to retain – in part or in full – for further analysis. Submitting the data from the Comlog case to what Morgan (1997) has labelled 'diagnostic reading', during which each of the four theoretical perspectives are applied to the case data, produces four different versions of the case. The strength of the diagnostic reading lies in its ability to force the researcher to see a case through different lenses without prematurely locking in on the intuitively most appealing view, or the view with which the researcher is most familiar. On the contrary, constantly shifting the analytical lens, pulling the focus in and out of different versions of the same story, and deliberately attempting to see issues discovered from opposite angles, permits making theoretical leaps in knowledge that would not be so easily attainable had analysis progressed more incrementally.

In order to develop the storyline in the Comlog case, we work systematically with the underlying differences among the four theoretical perspectives, and their differing explanatory power and relevance. The manner in which this storyline is developed resembles the strategy for working with the paradox outlined above, labelled 'opposition' (Poole and Van de Ven 1989), and includes the systematic juxtaposition of the four theoretical perspectives outlined in Figure 9.1. The idea behind this approach is that focusing on the points of divergence among views may allow us to better understand the issues on which they differ and, hence, to better appreciate their potential contribution.

In the Comlog case, a number of interesting paradoxes among the theoretical perspectives emerge. Among the different discourses or metaphors outlined in Figure 9.1, the strategic choice view stands out strongly in the Comlog case. The reshuffling of export activities taking place in Comlog's export marketing system is viewed mainly as a result of an entrepreneurial initiative taken by Comlog. The 'managerial agency' storyline is preferred because there are only limited factors in the environment that suggest the need to reshuffle activities on the scale undertaken by Comlog. Using Hamel's (1996) terminology, Comlog is better characterized as a rule-maker than a rule-follower, as it is looking for ways to renew existing and generate new ways of value creation (see Q2 in Figure 9.1).

Having ascribed much explanatory power to the strategic choice view, the tension between it and the collective action view generates particularly interesting discussions. In the case of ICT implementation, some actors positioned outside the export marketing systems may be regarded as having a fundamental influence on the organization of the marketing system. Hence, rather than having full discretion with regard to how to organize its activities, Comlog is subject to the strategic moves and positive response of, for instance, developers of back-office systems for the fleet management industry with which Comlog's system must be compatible (see Q2 versus Q4 in Figure 9.1). Furthermore, as implementation of the web-based solution progresses, the role of other actors becomes apparent, and Comlog's initial entrepreneurial vision is increasingly subjected to interorganizational negotiation. The development of the most insightful storyline for a case will always reflect the perspectives and interests that the researcher brings to the diagnostic reading of data. Nevertheless, a critical evaluation of the range of insights generated from bringing multiple theoretical lenses to the analysis is crucial if the application of the *ex ante* approach is to be more than an end in itself (Morgan 1997). When developed properly, the storyline represents the identification and prioritization of the most meaningful insights from the case analysis; and when developed into a coherent pattern, it represents the outcome of the theory-building process.

DISCUSSION

This chapter has presented two approaches to the role of existing theory in case research. Both approaches represent alternatives to the inductive perspective, which dominates qualitative research within the IB field. The illustrative examples of how each approach can be used to build theory from case studies draw attention to a number of challenges involved in their practical application. The following sets out some of the challenges we encountered.

As we have argued elsewhere (Andersen and Kragh 2010), the underlying idea of the *ex ante* approach is that the researcher should strive to break free from the constraints associated with taking a single paradigmatic stance. While it offers an intriguing way of thinking about theory development, its actual application to case construction is difficult. This is not so much because very few guidelines for such an application exist, but more because of the elaborate theoretical work that is required up front (Andersen and Kragh 2010). In our own research, much time was spent discussing and determining which theories to include under each of the four theoretical views, and even more time had to be devoted to studying these perspectives and subsequently attempting to author the case material in the light of each particular theoretical framing. Sometimes our efforts proved fruitful, whereas in others, they proved aimless or forced and, essentially, did not contribute to an improved understanding of the case. However, if successful, this strategy is also the one most likely to lead to insights that may seriously challenge taken-for-granted assumptions within a particular field of research.

Data collection in the *ex ante* approach poses another particular challenge, in that it requires a metatheoretical sample (Lewis and Grimes 1999). As already discussed, collection of such data is a cumbersome task and, faced with it, researchers have resorted to the use of secondary data. Even though we attempted to collect data for the Comlog case based on a broad interview guide, from time to time, these data were not sufficient for a very detailed reading of the case through the lens of a particular theoretical perspective to make perfect sense, leaving us with the choice between engaging in further data collection or accepting that some of the case readings could only take place at an aggregated level.

As we have explained elsewhere (Andersen and Kragh 2010), the *in vivo* approach starts out with a framework anchored in a single theoretical perspective, hence providing a tighter 'theoretical control', giving the researcher more sense of direction in data collection as well as in the search for complementary theory. Young researchers embarking on learning the craft of research may find this research approach to be the most rewarding and the least troublesome. The more controlled theoretical framework underlying the *in vivo* approach provides the researcher with a focus that may be used to guide and direct data collection to ensure that it covers the concepts of the theoretical framework. At the same time, this focus may hinder the researcher from trying to think creatively, and be properly aware of the existence of complementary theory, leading to a restricted view. Another problem pertaining to this approach is that there are no articulated guidelines on how to manage the process in order to avoid such restriction. Researchers depart from a chosen theoretical perspective and apply insights from other perspectives on an ongoing basis, also as a result of changes in the empirical terrain which they study. Sudden changes in the case context (for instance, a merger or a sudden unavailability of key decision makers) may prompt researchers to redirect their research efforts.

We would argue that the *ex ante* approach provides the opportunity to gain a comprehensive understanding of the underlying conflicts between theoretical perspectives and, hence, how their explanatory power differs according to context and circumstances. As discussed above, engaging these conflicting views with empirical data may be a fruitful way to gain novel insights. Due to the metatheoretical nature of extrapolation, however, the insights will often be superficial in nature. The *in vivo* approach, on the contrary, focuses more on the imperfections or blind spots of a single theory and, by combining this theory with complementary theories, a deeper-level understanding of the empirical referent becomes possible.

We would speculate that the relative success of new approaches to using existing theory is contingent on the maturity of the field. In a young research field, theoretical approaches tend to be quite diverse, reflecting pioneering efforts and theoretical plurality, but often also bewilderment and a constant inflow of reconceptualizations. As the field matures, certain approaches become dominant because they are supported by researchers who build their career around the promotion of specific ideas (and suppression of others). Consequently, research approaches become more sophisticated and honed, but perhaps also less pluralistic. Specific scientific puzzles and questions start defining the field and new contributions are criticized for adding to the confusion rather than to the clarity of the field. Within the IB field, such a tendency can be observed in the *Journal of International Business Studies*, which from its early issues up to the present has become less diversified with respect to both epistemology and methodology. As pointed out by Buckley (2002), IB studies used to be more agile in adapting and applying theories and metaphors from other research fields.

CONCLUSION

The arguments made throughout this chapter point to limitations of the inductive approach taken in much qualitative research within the IB field. In particular, we are concerned with the lack of attention to the role and use of existing theoretical frameworks in the early stages of research. Existing literature essentially refrains from discussing different approaches to the use of theory in case research, since the premature use of existing theory may prevent the researcher making new discoveries. Associating the use of existing theory with hypothesis testing rather than theory building means glossing over any discussion of how existing knowledge in the shape of theoretical frameworks is best put to use. In this chapter, we have attempted to challenge this 'inductive myth' that a researcher is better off entering a field of study without any theoretical ballast. On the contrary, we believe that missing out on the advantages from developing and refining more sophisticated approaches to using theory in qualitative research ultimately means running the risk of ending up with research that, under the pretence of being exploratory, ends up repeating studies already undertaken – or is simply unreflective.

We have presented and applied two approaches that can help advance IB researchers' reflections on how and when to use existing theory. Although very different in their underlying arguments, both approaches represent attempts to break away from the 'linear storyline constraint' associated with pure inductive research, which is often perceived as progressing through data collection, analysis and theory building, without much iteration between the individual stages (Orton 1997). Both approaches accordingly dismiss the idea of the 'empty-handed' researcher and instead advocate engaging his/her theoretical predispositions. The two approaches also argue for an active, extensive use of theory from the earliest stages of research and lasting throughout the research process (Orton 1997; Lewis and Grimes 1999; Meinefeld 2004; Irvine and Deo 2006). We hope the two approaches will help IB researchers embarking on theory building through case study research, and encourage further critical reflection about IB research.

REFERENCES

Adriaanse, A. and H. Voordijk (2005), 'Interorganizational communication and ICT in construction projects: a review using metatriangulation', *Construction Innovation*, **5** (3), 159–78.

Alvesson, M. and D. Kärreman (2007), 'Constructing mystery: empirical matters in theory development', *Academy of Management Review*, **32** (4), 1265–81.

Andersen, I., F. Borum, P.H. Kristensten and P. Karnøe (1992), *Om Kunsten at Bedrive Feltstudier: En Erfaringsbaseret Forskningsmetodik* [The Art of Conducting Field Studies: An Experience-based Research Methodology], Frederiksberg: Samfundslitteratur.

Andersen, P.H. and H. Kragh (2010), 'Sense and sensibility: two approaches for using existing theory in theory building qualitative research', *Industrial Marketing Management*, **39** (1), 49–55.

Anderson, J.C., H. Håkansson and J. Johanson (1994), 'Dyadic business relationships within a business network context', *Journal of Marketing*, **58** (4), 1–15.

Astley, W.G. (1985), 'Administrative science as socially constructed truth', *Administrative Science Quarterly*, **30** (4), 497–514.

Astley, W.G. and A.H. Van de Ven (1983), 'Central perspectives and debates in organization theory', *Administrative Science Quarterly*, **28** (2), 245–73.

Axelsson, B. and G. Easton (eds) (1992), *Industrial Networks: A New View of Reality*, London: Routledge.

Bradshaw-Camball, P. and V. Murray (1991), 'Illusions and other games: a trifocal view of organizational politics', *Organization Science*, **2** (4), 379–98.

Brennan, R. and P.W. Turnbull (1999), 'Adaptive behavior in buyer-supplier relationships', *Industrial Marketing Management*, **28** (5), 481–95.

Buckley, P. (2002), 'Is the international business research agenda running out of steam?', *Journal of International Business Studies*, **33** (2), 365–73.

Burrell, G. and G. Morgan (1979), *Sociological Paradigms and Organisational Analysis*, Aldershot: Ashgate.

Dubois, A. and L.-E. Gadde (2002), 'Systematic combining: an abductive approach to case research', *Journal of Business Research*, **55** (7), 553–60.

Dunning, J.H. (1988), 'The eclectic paradigm of international production: a restatement and some possible extensions', *Journal of International Business Studies*, **19** (1), 1–31.

Easton, G. (1992), 'Industrial networks: a review', in Axelsson and Easton (eds), pp. 1–27.

Eisenhardt, K.M. (1989), 'Building theories from case study research', *Academy of Management Review*, **14** (4), 532–50.

Eisenhardt, K.M. and M.E. Graebner (2007), 'Theory building from cases: opportunities and challenges', *Academy of Management Journal*, **50** (1), 25–32.

Elsbach, K.D., R.I. Sutton and D.A. Whetten (1999), 'Introduction: perspectives on developing management theory, circa 1999: moving from shrill monologues to (relatively) tame dialogues', *Academy of Management Review*, **24** (4), 627–33.

Fleetwood, S. (2005), 'Ontology in organization and management studies: a critical realist perspective', *Organization*, **12** (2), 197–222.

Giddens, A. (1984), *The Constitution of Society*, Cambridge: Polity.

Gioia, D.A. and E. Pitre (1990), 'Multiparadigm perspectives on theory building', *Academy of Management Review*, **15** (4), 584–602.

Glaser, B.G. and A. Strauss (1967), *The Discovery of Grounded Theory: Strategies for Qualitative Research*, New York: Aldine.

Håkansson, H. (ed.) (1982), *International Marketing and Purchasing of Industrial Goods: An Interaction Approach*, Chichester: John Wiley.

Håkansson, H. and I. Snehota (1995), *Developing Relationships in Business Networks*, London: Routledge.

Hamel, G. (1996), 'Strategy as revolution', *Harvard Business Review*, **74** (4), 69–82.

Hassard, J. (1991), 'Multiple paradigms and organizational analysis: a case study', *Organization Studies*, **12** (2), 275–300.

Irvine, H. and H. Deo (2006), 'The power of the lens: a comparative analysis of two views of the Fiji Development Bank', *Accounting, Auditing and Accountability Journal*, **19** (2), 205–27.

Jary, D. and J. Jary (1985), *Collins Dictionary of Sociology*, New York: Harper Collins.

Keringer, F.N. (1986), *Foundations of Behavioral Research*, Fort Worth, TX: Holt, Rinehart & Winston.

Kourany, J. (1997), *Scientific Knowledge: Basic Issues in the Philosophy of Science*, Belmont, CA: Wadsworth.

Lewis, M.W. and A.J. Grimes (1999), 'Metatriangulation: building theory from multiple paradigms', *Academy of Management Review*, **24** (4), 672–90.

Locke, K., K. Golden-Biddle and M.S. Feldman (2008), 'Making doubt generative: rethinking the role of doubt in the research process', *Organization Science*, **19** (6), 907–18.

Marschan-Piekkari, R. and C. Welch (2004), 'Qualitative research methods in international business: the state of the art', in R. Marschan-Piekkari and C. Welch (eds), *Handbook of Qualitative Research Methods for International Business*, Cheltenham, UK and Northampton, MA, USA: Edward Elgar, pp. 5–24.

Maxwell, J.A. (1996), *Qualitative Research Design: An Interactive Approach*, Thousand Oaks, CA: Sage.

Meinefeld, W. (2004), 'Hypotheses and prior knowledge in qualitative research', in U. Flick, E. von Kardorff and I. Steinke (eds), *A Companion to Qualitative Research*, London: Sage, pp. 153–8.

Merton, R.K. (1957), *Social Theory and Social Structure*, Glencoe, IL: Free Press.

Miles, M.B. (1979), 'Qualitative data as an attractive nuisance: the problem of analysis', *Administrative Science Quarterly*, **24** (4), 590–601.

Mill, J.S. (1974), 'System of logic, ratiocinative and inductive: being a connected view of the principles of evidence and the methods of scientific investigation', in J.M. Robson (ed.), *Collected Works of John Stuart Mill*, vol. 8, Toronto: University of Toronto Press, pp. 639–1251.

Mills, C.W. (1959), *The Sociological Imagination*, New York: Penguin Books.

Morgan, G. (1993), *Imaginization: The Art of Creative Management*, Newbury Park, CA: Sage.

Morgan, G. (1997), *Images of Organization*, Thousand Oaks, CA: Sage.

Nelson, R.R., and S.G. Winter (1982), *An Evolutionary Theory of Economic Change*, Cambridge, MA: Belknap Press.

Orlikowski, W.J. (2002), 'Knowing in practice: enacting a collective capability in distributed organizing', *Organization Science*, **13** (3), 249–73.

Orton, J.D. (1997), 'From inductive to iterative grounded theory: zipping the gap between process theory and process data', *Scandinavian Journal of Management*, **13** (4), 419–38.

Piekkari, R., C. Welch and E. Paavilainen (2009), 'The case study as disciplinary convention: evidence from international business journals', *Organizational Research Methods*, **12** (3), 567–89.

Poole, M.S. and A.H. Van de Ven (1989), 'Using paradox to build management and organization theories', *Academy of Management Review*, **14** (4), 562–78.

Ragin, C.C. (1992), '"Casing" and the process of social inquiry', in Ragin and H.S. Becker (eds), *What is a Case? Exploring the Foundations of Social Inquiry*, Cambridge: Cambridge University Press, pp. 217–26.

Reichertz, J. (2004), 'Abduction, deduction and induction in qualitative research', in U. Flick, E. von Kardorff and I. Steinke (eds), *A Companion to Qualitative Research*, London: Sage, pp. 159–64.

Saunders, C.S., T.A. Carte, J. Jasperson and B.S. Butler (2003), 'Lessons learned from the trenches of metatriangulation research', *Communications of the Association for Information Systems*, **11**, 245–70.

Suddaby, R. (2006), 'From the editors: what grounded theory is not', *Academy of Management Journal*, **49** (4), 633–42.

Sutherland, J.W. (1975), *Systems Analysis, Administration and Architecture*, New York: Van Nostrand Reinhold.

Sutton, R.I. and B.M. Staw (1995), 'What theory is not', *Administrative Science Quarterly*, **40** (3), 371–84.

Tsui, A.S. (2007), 'From homogenization to pluralism: international management research in the academy and beyond', *Academy of Management Journal*, **50** (6), 1353–64.

Weick, K.E. (1979), *The Social Psychology of Organizing*, Reading, MA: Addison-Wesley.

Weick, K.E. (1989), 'Theory construction as disciplined imagination', *Academy of Management Review*, **14** (4), 516–31.

Weick, K.E. (1995), *Sensemaking in Organizations*, Berkeley, CA: Sage.

Yin, R.K. (2009), *Case Study Research*, 4th edn, Thousand Oaks, CA: Sage.

Zander, I. and U. Zander (2005), 'The inside track: on the important (but neglected) role of customers in the resource-based view of strategy and firm growth', *Journal of Management Studies*, **42** (8), 1519–48.

PART III

Alternative case study designs

10. Case selection in international business: key issues and common misconceptions

Margaret Fletcher and Emmanuella Plakoyiannaki

INTRODUCTION

The case study[1] method has frequently been used in international business (IB) research (Piekkari et al. 2009). The widespread adoption of case studies among qualitative IB researchers has been justified on the grounds that they offer in-depth contextual insights by taking into consideration 'environment characteristics, resource constraints, and cultural traits' (Thomas 1996, p. 497). In other words, case research allows IB scholars to reach a deeper cross-cultural understanding of investigated phenomena. This minimizes cultural bias and ethnocentric assumptions compared to the practice of using survey instruments. As a result, this method has been used to investigate numerous topics in IB, including the internationalization process of the firm (Johanson and Vahlne 1977), international strategy (Porter 1990), international growth (Penrose 1960), entry modes in international markets such as exporting activities (Ellis and Pecotich 2001), international new ventures (INVs) (Coviello 2006) and multinational corporations (MNCs) (Bartlett and Ghoshal 1987); as well as comparative and cross-cultural phenomena.

The process of sampling[2] is central to building or testing theory through case research. This is evident in the statement by Hakim (1987, p. 61) that 'case studies take as their subject one or more selected examples of a social entity', rendering issues of sampling and sample size inherent to case research. Scholars (for example, Eisenhardt 1989; Dyer and Wilkins 1991; Easton 1995; Siggelkow 2007) argue that case selection is strongly associated with the process of theorizing from case research. Depending on the viewpoint that a researcher espouses (consciously or unconsciously), the case study method may be of an interpretivist or positivist nature (Hyde 2000), offering variety in terms of the justification of sampling choices, the number of cases and sampling techniques.

Despite the frequent application of the case study approach in the IB context, insights from research practice reveal a lack of understanding about the selection of cases. Indeed, Malhotra et al. (1996) point out that IB case researchers encounter difficulties in accounting for their sampling strategies in sufficient detail, which makes interpretation of findings difficult and affects the replication of the study. In a similar vein, Piekkari et al. (2009, 2010) point out the complexity of case selection associated with the diversity of sampling decisions that researchers undertake in a case study project.

The complexity of case selection was evident in our own experience of case research. For example, in Margaret's study into the internationalization process of small and medium-sized enterprises (SMEs) (Fletcher 2007), access was gained to firms participating in an internationalization programme, which offered information-rich cases. The case study approach provided flexibility: as the study progressed, further sampling decisions emerged as to whether cases should be dropped; for example, when ownership changed or firms de-internationalized. Similarly, an investigation into learning modes in multinational subsidiaries (Dimitratos et al., work in progress) posed the following dilemma to Emmanuella and her colleagues: should the study of learning modes generate thick descriptions (better stories) linked to a single case study design or comparable evidence relying on multiple case study design (better constructs)? In both examples, the authors made sampling decisions based on their accumulated knowledge and research experience to deal with the associated challenges.

This chapter aims to present key issues and counter common misconceptions with respect to the selection of case studies in IB research. In fact, one common misconception is that case selection is solely about deciding whether to conduct a single or a multiple case study. As this chapter progresses, we shall demonstrate that case selection involves an array of decisions in addition to that of whether to follow a single or multiple case study design. In doing so, we seek to enhance understanding about case selection in the IB field and increase the potential for innovation and pluralism in case research. The chapter uses examples from marketing and IB research, as well as the authors' own case research experiences, to illustrate the theoretical and practical challenges of case selection faced by researchers.

The chapter is structured as follows. After the introduction, the second section discusses common misconceptions and issues relevant to 'what cases to select', notably selection and equivalence of the unit of analysis. The third section discusses misconceptions linked to 'how cases are selected': sampling strategies; purposeful, selective and theoretical sampling; purposeful versus random sampling; and selection bias. The fourth section discusses 'when to select' and considers misconceptions and issues of emergent or prespecified selection. The fifth section elaborates on the number of case studies and raises the issue of single versus multiple case study design. The chapter concludes with the assertion that case research accommodates a wide range of sampling practices, which may facilitate qualitative researchers to unveil the dynamism of IB phenomena.

WHAT TO SELECT

The definition of the unit of analysis is the fundamental answer to the question 'what to select'. It is a key element of case research since a 'case study is not a methodological choice but a choice of what is to be studied' (Stake 2005, p. 443); a statement that in effect equates the case with the unit of analysis. Similarly, Patton (2002) indicates that when selecting and making decisions about the appropriate unit of analysis, a key consideration is to determine what unit it is that the researcher wants to be able to say something about at the end of the research. He argues that 'each unit of analysis implies a different kind of data collection, a different focus of analysis of the data, and a different level at which statements about findings and conclusions would be made' (p. 228). For example, in Margaret's study mentioned above, an initial decision involved whether to select the internationalization programme, the individual firm or the business owner as the unit of analysis (Fletcher 2007).

We propose that the unit of analysis may be classified into four overlapping categories:

1. social units may be an individual or individuals, a role, a group, an organization, a community or social interactions (for example, dyadic relationships);
2. temporal units may be an episode or encounter, an event or a period of time;
3. geographical units may be countries, towns or states; and
4. artefacts may be books, photos, newspapers or technological objects.

Misconception 1: The Empirical Unit Is the Unit of Analysis

The unit of analysis is the major entity analysed in the study. It is the 'what' or 'whom' that is studied. This is not to be confused with the empirical unit of observation, that is, the unit(s) from which the researcher collects data (Ragin 1992). The unit of analysis is a context-specific choice that depends on the research questions, research propositions and research setting of the study (that is, firm, nation, culture and so on). For instance, the purpose of Coviello's (2006, p. 714) article – 'to assess network dynamics in INVs' – is reflected in the unit of analysis, namely the network from the perspective of INVs; and the units of observation, that is, managers, owners and founders directly involved in the new venture's relationships and the evolution of the firm.

A case study may involve the examination of a single unit of analysis (holistic case study) or more than one unit of analysis (embedded case study) (Yin 1984 [2009]). A holistic design is used when a single case study examines only the global nature of an organization, for example; however, when subunits are analysed in a single setting, an embedded single case study approach is used (Dubois and Gadde 2002). To illustrate the latter, even though a case study might be about a single organization, data collection and analysis, as well as the presentation of findings, can occur at multiple levels, including the individual, subgroups of individuals and/or strategic business units. The use of embedded units of analysis suggests that an equal emphasis should be placed on both the subunits of the study and the case as a whole (Yin 1984 [2009]).

Misconception 2: The Unit of Analysis Is Clear-cut

Yin (1984 [2009]) considers the selection of the unit of analysis as a relatively straightforward task that usually takes place at the early phases of the case study process; that is, once the researcher has accurately specified the research questions of the study. This assertion is distinctively evident in his early work (Yin 1984), in which he implied that the unit of analysis and the boundaries of the case study are clearly distinguished and remain seemingly stable as the case study investigation progresses. In his recent writings, Yin (1984 [2009]) appears to revisit his position by acknowledging the open-ended nature of the case study process. He posits that the researcher's choice of the unit of analysis may be more confusing and dynamic in nature than originally discussed in earlier case study literature (Yin 1984 [2009]).

In practice, case researchers in the IB area encounter difficulties in identifying and selecting interlinked concepts that may serve as units of analysis in a case study project. For example, the study of autonomy in subsidiaries of MNCs also entails the investigation of various related concepts such as a subsidiary's unique resources, empowerment of the subsidiary, subsidiary initiative, innovativeness of the subsidiary and its entrepreneurial output (see, for example, Young and Tavares 2004; Birkinshaw et al. 2005). This may require an embedded case study design in which researchers progressively discover the unit of analysis and its relevance to other concepts embedded in the context of the case study.

The embedded case study design is also evident in the article by Ellis and Pecotich (2001, p. 120), who concentrate on the role of social dynamics in export initiation by exploring 'the proposed relationship between antecedent social ties and the perception of export opportunities' through the means of an embedded *ex post* case study. In order to address the purpose of the study, the authors defined the case as the SME and collected data within and across cases at multiple levels (individual and firm level). Although there were eight exporting firms in the sample, 31 export initiations were observed, each of which constituted an embedded unit of analysis within the investigated firms. In accordance with relevant studies, the authors equated the SME with the case and incorporated subunits for observation and discussion, where each export initiation is defined as a product-market entry. The multiple levels of analysis were manifested in the attempt of the authors to discuss their findings both at the firm and the export initiation levels.

Misconception 3: The Unit of Analysis Is the Same Across Cultures

Sampling issues for IB researchers include decisions about selecting the company and informant and, in cross-national research, the country. There have been calls for more cross-national approaches to IB and international marketing research (Cavusgil and Das 1997; Sin et al. 1999; Fillis 2001; Leonidou 2004). In conducting case research in a cross-national setting, care must be taken to ensure cross-cultural equivalence of investigated concepts and units of analysis. Sin et al. (1999) highlight the problem of investigating concepts in another country and the need for equivalence of the unit of analysis. For instance, the concept of the entrepreneur is deeply embedded in a temporal context and adheres to cultural, political and economic factors permeating different countries (Peng 2001). Therefore, researchers embarking on a case study project in an IB context should be open to the possibility that the unit of analysis can hold different meanings in different cultures, countries or regions and/or changes over time.

Relevant literature on quantitative as well as qualitative cross-cultural research offers recommendations for enhancing equivalence of investigated concepts across cultures. First, selecting conceptually (or culturally) equivalent definitions of the unit of analysis is promoted as a solution to address context specificity. However, the development of widely accepted definitions for most concepts seems to be an elusive task (for a relevant discussion, see Lim and Firkola 2000), which leaves researchers with a dilemma when seeking to adopt widely applicable definitions for the needs of their study.

Second, Sinkovics et al. (2005) state the importance of comparability between selected locations in terms of culture, economic, social and political circumstances, and technological developments. Sin et al. (1999) refer to sampling equivalence, whereby the sample for each country is comparable to the extent that the cross-cultural differences could not be attributable to dissimilar sample characteristics. This calls for a selection framework (Cavusgil and Das 1997) that can recommend matched samples across cultures, and the description of the sample characteristics in detail, with reference to those factors which may impact on the interpretation of results.

It may be inferred from the above that complexities associated with the definition of the unit of analysis in IB affect, in turn, the identification of case study boundaries. Viewed in this cross-cultural light, the study of IB phenomena occurs within blurred boundaries (for a discussion on the dynamic nature of organizational boundaries, see Santos and Eisenhardt 2005). In particular, practices and concepts can become transfused among cultures and countries to a degree that differentiating the idiographic (which describes phenomena unique to a country or/and culture) from the nomothetic (which describes universal cultural aspects) becomes difficult and questionable.

HOW TO SELECT CASES

Sampling is a complex issue in case research as there are many variations of sampling strategies described in relevant literature, and much confusion about what each technique entails and how it can be employed in case study practice. For instance, in an attempt to explore the concept of the 'global small firm' and how these firms achieve a presence in international markets, Emmanuella and her colleagues faced a challenge in selecting cases for investigation (Dimitratos et al. 2010). To illustrate, it was very difficult to identify 'typical' or 'instrumental' cases because there was no consensus regarding the definition and characteristics of global small firms in relevant literature, and their attributes varied across industry sectors. In order to deal with this deficiency, the authors employed criterion sampling that allowed for case selection based on experience in the international market, size and industry sector characteristics. The selection of the sampling technique was in itself a learning process that included iterations between theory and the researchers' viewpoint, as well as discussions with industry experts.

Different perspectives on case sampling have been presented in relevant literature; however, those of Yin (1984 [2009]), Patton (2002) and Stake

(2005) appear to play a key role in case study practice (Coyne 1997). Patton (2002) provides a detailed account of 18 different types of sampling – two forms of random purposeful sampling and 16 forms of purposeful sampling – that may be employed in case research, recommending that the selection of cases involve purposeful not random selection. Yin (1984 [2009]) and Stake (2005) elaborate on the rationale of single versus multiple case studies rather than discussing sampling techniques for case researchers. Despite this limitation, their approach to case sampling uncovers the complexity that such a decision entails: choice of the unit of analysis; number of case studies; sampling techniques; and application of replication logic. In this section, we focus on two of the strategies about which we would argue there is most confusion: theoretical and purposeful sampling.

Misconception 4: Theoretical and Purposeful Sampling Are the Same

The distinction between purposeful and theoretical sampling often lacks clarity in the literature. As a result, these terms are viewed as synonymous and used interchangeably, even though they are defined differently (Coyne 1997). Purposeful sampling can be seen as an 'umbrella concept' that embraces different sampling strategies – including that of theoretical sampling. It is a generic term that highlights the selection of information-rich cases for in-depth study, from which the researcher can learn a great deal about the purpose of the study and the phenomena under investigation (Patton 2002). Therefore, purposeful sampling is concerned with appropriateness, purpose and access to good information, rather than representative and random/probability statistical sampling as in quantitative studies (Coyne 1997; Hillebrand et al. 2001). Purposeful sampling serves to illustrate differences between qualitative and quantitative traditions. Evidence generated from purposeful sampling can be transferable to other empirical cases and is generalizable to theoretical propositions, not across populations as with quantitative research (Yin 1984 [2009]; Miles and Huberman 1994; Easton 1998).

Table 10.1 provides a synthesis of purposeful sampling techniques that can be employed within or across case study projects – including, perhaps surprisingly, the strategy of random purposeful sampling. Patton (2002, p. 241) argues that in some case study projects (for example, evaluation studies) 'the credibility of systematic and randomly selected case examples is considerably greater than personal, ad-hoc selection of cases'. However, he highlights that purposeful random sampling is used to enhance credibility by minimizing investigator bias in case selection; it is not a representative random sample for generalizations.

Theoretical sampling is a subcategory of purposeful sampling. It pertains to 'sampling on the basis of the emerging concepts with the aim being to explore the dimensional range or varied conditions along which the properties of concepts vary' (Strauss and Corbin 1998, p. 73). Theoretical sampling is often linked to grounded theory and the constant comparative method of analysis, which involves systematically examining and refining variations in emergent and grounded concepts. Patton (2002) also discusses variations of theoretical sampling, namely theory-based and operational construct sampling (see Table 10.1).

For instance, excellent access to firms participating in an internationalization programme enabled Margaret to carry out longitudinal multiple case research into learning processes of internationalizing SMEs, a complex and dynamic phenomenon (Fletcher 2007, 2009). Access was gained to the firms, support agency and policy makers' expertise and archival records, and consultants' reports. The firms were committed to internationalizing, and were thus appropriate to the research aims which were to explore firms' internationalization issues and ways of addressing them. The selection of these firms suited the purpose of the research (that is, application of purposeful sampling): to observe firm learning behaviour in the process of internationalizing over time. The insights gained from fieldwork facilitated Margaret's generation of a set of propositions for further investigation of the international learning phenomenon. In a similar way, Wagner and Johnson (2004) employ theoretical sampling in order to investigate the development of strategic supplier portfolios. According to the authors, 'an attempt was made to select varied cases to gain a deeper understanding of the study's concepts and to assess contingent factors' (p. 720). The authors argue in favour of theoretical sampling since it enables the identification and investigation of emerging concepts in the literature; enhances the quality of the case study evidence; and facilitates the applicability of findings to other industry contexts.

Misconception 5: Sampling Is a Single Decision

It is a common misconception that case researchers employ a single sampling strategy within a case study project. However, the selection of case studies is not a single decision; and within a case study investigation, researchers may end up using more than one sampling strategy. We propose that case researchers in IB employ a 'multilevel approach' to case sampling (see Figure 10.1). This approach suggests that (i) case sampling is a process that spans multiple levels; (ii) case researchers make informed decisions about case sampling, which range from the country, industry and/or organizational levels (for example, selection of the case), to the

Table 10.1   Purposeful sampling strategies in case research

Strategy	Description	Key reference(s)
Theoretical sampling (theory-based sampling and operational construct sampling)	Sampling on the basis of emerging concepts in order to explore the dimensional range or conditions along which the properties of concepts vary. The rationale of theoretical sampling is to select cases that are likely to replicate or extend the emergent theory, or to fill theoretical categories. Variations of theoretical sampling include theory-based and operational construct sampling. Theory-based sampling aims to find manifestations of a theoretical construct of interest so as to elaborate and examine the construct and its variations, and supports the constant comparative method of analysis. Operational construct sampling involves the study of real-world examples of constructs that are of interest	Eisenhardt (1989); Coyne (1997); Strauss and Corbin (1998); Patton (2002)
Critical case sampling, Extreme deviant or outlier sampling	Focuses on the selection of cases that are rich in information because they are unusual, special or make a point quite dramatically. The logic of this sampling strategy lies in lessons learned about unusual conditions or extreme outcomes manifested in the case	Yin (1984 [2009]); Miles and Huberman (1994); Patton (2002)
Maximum variation sampling	Aims to select cases demonstrating diversity in terms of the dependent variable or predicted outcomes linked to the case. It documents diverse variations and identifies common patterns encountered in the case. Maximum variation sampling has also been linked to the deliberate study of negative cases	Guba and Lincoln (1989); Patton (2002); Mahoney and Goertz (2004)
Homogeneous sampling	Concentrates on picking homogeneous cases or studying in-depth subgroups with homogeneous characteristics	Patton (2002)
Typical cases sampling	Consists of the selection of typical cases. These cases can be helpful particularly in early stages of a case project and can be selected with the cooperation of key informants	Yin (1984 [2009]); Patton (2002)

Table 10.1 (continued)

Strategy	Description	Key reference(s)
Selective sampling	Refers to decisions made prior to the study to sample subjects according to a preconceived but reasonable initial set of criteria	Sandelowski (1995)
Criterion sampling	Concentrates on selecting cases that meet a set of predetermined criteria important to the study. This sampling strategy has also been labelled selective sampling in that it refers to selecting cases or respondents based on an initial set of criteria	Sandelowski (1995); Patton (2002)
Sampling of confirmatory and disconfirmatory cases	Confirmatory cases fit to already emergent patterns; by confirming and elaborating on previous findings and/or theories they add richness, depth and credibility. Disconfirmatory cases question or alter findings and/or theories, leading to alternative interpretations of emerging empirical evidence	Perry (1998); Patton (2002)
Convenience sampling	Concentrates on the selection of cases which are easily accessible. This saves resources but often at the expense of information and credibility	Miles and Huberman (1994); Patton (2002)
Opportunistic sampling	Involves taking on-the-spot decisions or taking advantage of new opportunities during the data collection process regarding the selection of information-rich settings	Patton (2002)
Intensity sampling	Concentrates on selecting case studies that manifest the investigated phenomenon in intensive ways	Miles and Huberman (1994); Patton (2002)
Stratified purposeful sampling	Facilitates the selection of different subgroups for investigation or levels of analysis with a case study project or across different cases	Kuzel (1992); Miles and Huberman (1994); Patton (2002)
Snowball or chain sampling	Usually applied to within-case sampling. Aims at locating information-rich informants within a case or critical cases. It identifies cases of interest from people who know people who know which cases are information rich	Miles and Huberman (1994); Patton (2002)

Table 10.1   (continued)

Strategy	Description	Key reference(s)
Key informant sampling	Includes the selection of subjects with special expertise. May be applied within a case or across cases	Marshall (1996)
Random purposeful sampling	Includes the selection of case studies in a probabilistic manner and may facilitate confirmation of theories through case research. The rationale for random selection of cases is not the development of a representative sample as in survey research. Rather, it aims to minimize the investigator's bias often at the expense of selecting information-rich cases	Patton (2002); Lieberman (2005)
Combination/ mixed-purpose sampling	Blends purposeful with random purposeful sampling. For example, when an extreme group or maximum heterogeneity approach may yield an initial potential sample size that is still larger than the study can handle. The final selection then may be made randomly – a combination approach	Patton (2002)

level within the case (for example, the selection of sources of evidence); (iii) selection of the unit of analysis in IB research may occur at levels 1–4; and (iv) different strategies of purposeful sampling may be applied at different levels/decisions in the sampling process.

A multilevel approach to case sampling may be of use to case researchers who investigate embedded international phenomena such as business networks or MNCs and their subsidiaries. Figure 10.1 illustrates a multilevel approach to case sampling that could be used in a study on subsidiary autonomy. The multilevel approach allows case researchers to consider case sampling as an open-ended, incremental process based on informed decisions; notably, sampling decisions are based on insights gained from previous choices and/or fieldwork. It is a way of organizing the sampling process in a case study investigation by narrowing down sampling choices without dismissing their complexity. This multilevel approach to case sampling requires that researchers explain sampling decisions at different levels of the case study process rather than approach sampling as a single decision taken in the early stages of the case study project.

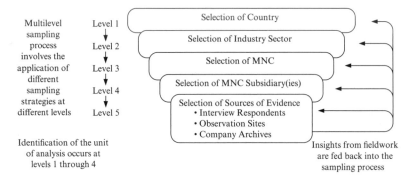

Multilevel sampling process involves the application of different sampling strategies at different levels

Level 1
↓
Level 2
↓
Level 3
↓
Level 4
↓
Level 5

Selection of Country

Selection of Industry Sector

Selection of MNC

Selection of MNC Subsidiary(ies)

Selection of Sources of Evidence
• Interview Respondents
• Observation Sites
• Company Archives

Identification of the unit
of analysis occurs at
levels 1 through 4

Insights from fieldwork
are fed back into the
sampling process

Figure 10.1   A multilevel approach to case study sampling: an illustration

WHEN TO SELECT

By characterizing sampling as a process rather than a single decision, we have already implied that the question of 'when to select cases' is one that the case researcher has to revisit during the course of the study. Choosing when to select is also related to other sampling decisions, such as determining the unit of analysis: case selection can only be tentative if the unit of analysis has not been resolved. Even more fundamentally, attitudes towards the timing of case selection are, it has been argued, linked to an author's epistemological stance; thus Piekkari et al. (2009) found that positivist researchers are much more likely to insist on early case selection – an assumption to which we now turn.

Misconception 6: An Early Decision on Sampling Is Best

According to Yin (1984 [2009]), case selection entails identification and screening of potential case study sites prior to data collection. Prespecification of the case(s) ensures that there is the required fit between research questions and empirical evidence. Viewed in this light, case sampling is completed before entering the field. This option may not be viable in the study of dynamic phenomena deeply nested in the case study milieu. In such instances, the researcher's experience in the field is vital for initial selection of the case, its context and unit of analysis, as well as within-case sampling in terms of choosing respondents, observation sites and archival documents for further investigation. For example, although the business owners/chief executive officers were initially identified as the decision makers and key informants in Margaret's research (Fletcher 2007), it became apparent from extensive fieldwork that other senior managers or company directors within some firms were important informants. This may present researchers with challenges in securing additional access.

There are case researchers who acknowledge this emergent nature of the case study process and highlight the difficulty in identifying the unit of analysis and boundaries of the case study (Piekkari et al. 2009). The open-ended nature of the case is also encapsulated in the concept of 'casing', or in other words the evolving case (Ragin 1992, p. 218). This concept acknowledges the iterative theoretical and empirical choices that the researcher makes in the course of the case study project, which may include the reconsideration of the focus of the study, the unit of analysis and, hence, the case study boundaries.

One important aspect of the process of casing can be found in Welch (1994), who employs the case study approach in international human resource management (IHRM). The author notes: 'while the initial focus of the investigation was on IHRM activities, the use of an exploratory qualitative methodological approach allowed the examination of the process of expatriate management' (p. 139). It may be inferred that neither the phenomenon under investigation nor its context is necessarily known prior to starting the research. Instead, they are brought to light gradually in the investigation, often constituting the most important findings emerging from the case study project (Ragin 1992).

HOW MANY CASES TO INCLUDE

Compared to the other questions, the question of 'how many cases to include' is the best known and most discussed in relevant literature. Given that this is familiar ground, we shall not elaborate in depth the contrasting features of single and multiple case study designs discussed by various case study scholars. Instead, we shall present two common misconceptions associated with the 'adequacy' of the sample size in case research.

Misconception 7: A Single or Multicase Approach Is an Either/Or Decision

According to Dubois and Gadde (2002), sample size in case research is relative and dependent on the purpose of the study. This statement, albeit true, is often viewed through the lens of the 'depth versus breadth' dilemma, whereby case researchers have to choose between multiple or single case study designs. For example, when the case researcher is mainly concentrating on the use of contrasting or differing observations for the advancement of propositions and replication of findings in various settings, a multicase approach appears to be appropriate (see Eisenhardt

1989; Miles and Huberman 1994). Alternatively, if the case researcher is concerned with the development of idiographic explanations and deep contextualization of case study evidence, a single case study approach may be adopted (see Dyer and Wilkins 1991; Ragin and Becker 1992; Easton 1995; Halinen and Törnroos 2005; Siggelkow 2007).

A typical illustration of a multicase approach is manifested in the study by Coviello (2006), which investigates network dynamics in INVs. Following the arguments of Yin (1984 [2009]) and Eisenhardt (1989), the author demonstrates the replication power of case research by collecting data from three organizations (INVs), and performing within- and cross-case study analysis with the purpose of developing a set of propositions for future research. A single case study design is used by Alajoutsijärvi et al. (2001) to investigate the importance of customer relationship strategies in smoothing business cycles in a global sector. The authors draw empirical evidence 'through intensive research work and long term professional experience' (p. 489). Their findings, which are largely idiosyncratic to the single case, encapsulate the emic perspective, as they explicitly state: 'we have written the case study description as it would have been related by managers themselves' (p. 489).

Inevitably, case researchers end up structuring their arguments for explaining the number of selected case studies according to Table 10.2, which incorporates the features of multiple and single case study designs. But it may be of benefit to case researchers to view the 'how many' dilemma from a different angle. Instead of choosing between a multiple or single case study design, one might consider integrating these two research modes into a single case study investigation. For example, Leonard-Barton (1990) applies a 'dual methodology' to case research in order to investigate organizational innovativeness through the process of transferring new technologies from their developers into the hands of their users. In doing so, she combines a real-time longitudinal case study with nine retrospective case studies that demonstrate the phenomenon under investigation. Her methodological choice defies the 'depth versus breadth' dilemma by reconciling the process-based single case study design with multiple snapshot comparative case studies.

In a similar vein, Pettigrew (1990) discusses the notion of the 'longitudinal comparative case method' that incorporates features of single and multiple case study designs. It is an intensive case study design that involves the investigation of multiple cases over a long period. The longitudinal comparative case method may allow researchers to examine dynamic strategic processes, such as the internationalization process of the firm, in their changing contexts (see Pettigrew 1990). Such an approach may simultaneously generate contextualized findings and 'thick'

Table 10.2   Single and multiple case selection

Single case design	Multiple case design
Deep insights: greater depth	Replication logic: greater breadth
Emphasis on thick descriptions – better stories	Emphasis on comparison – better constructs
Can be highly context specific, focus on the uniqueness of the case	Greater opportunity for generalizability and external validity
Emphasis on within-case analysis	Emphasis on cross-case analysis
High level of flexibility	Less flexibility
More likely to be interpretivist approach, using inductive, iterative processes	More likely to adopt positivist approach to some aspects e.g., following a structured process and seeking for construct validation
Theorizing concentrates on developing an understanding of the empirical setting and/or tracing causal processes in specific context	May be concerned with development of testable hypothesis and generalizable theory across settings
More opportunity to use theoretical, conceptually-driven sequential and constant comparative methods of sampling	More likely to use purposeful sampling strategies where cases and informants are predetermined
Less resources are required but requires extensive access to single case evidence	Highly resource intensive
Risk of case study selected not representing phenomenon	May need to modify design where the parallel cases selected may turn out not to provide replication

Dual mode case design
Integration of single and multiple case study designs e.g., combination of a single longitudinal case study with multiple (retrospective or snapshot) case studies

descriptions; and enhance the potential for transferability of case study evidence through the search for cross-case patterns in different investigated sites and cultures.

Case study methodologies that seek synergies between single and multiple case study designs may require extensive resources, expertise and time. Although they may consequently represent a remote scenario for some case researchers, their advantages can outweigh their costs. As case research integrates art and science, we need novelty and pluralism in case study designs so that we can enrich our insights into the investigated phenomenon.

Misconception 8: The More Cases, the Better

Researchers following a positivistic logic (Yin 1984 [2009]; Eisenhardt 1989; Miles and Huberman 1994; Sutton 1997) argue that multiple cases are preferable to single case designs since 'good theory is fundamentally the result of rigorous methodology and comparative multi-case logic' (Eisenhardt 1991, p. 627). Yin (1984 [2009, p. 53]) states that 'even if you can study only a "two-case" case study, your chances of doing a good case design will be better than doing a single case and the external generalizations of the findings will be increased' (see also Perry 1998). Similarly, Johnston et al. (2000) support the argument that evidence from multiple case designs is thought to be more compelling and credible, making the overall study more robust.

Despite the popular view that the 'more the better', there are authors who recognize the importance of a single case study design and argue that the benefits of a single case study far outweigh its drawbacks. For example, Dyer and Wilkins (1991) and Siggelkow (2007) propose that the purpose of case research is to generate deep contextualized insights into the investigated phenomena. According to their view, this purpose is best served by a single case study design which constitutes the optimum form of case research.

Various scholars point out that one case is enough to generalize, not to a population, but analytical generalization to theoretical propositions, based on real-world discovery, and offer an explanation for the relationship between investigated concepts (Platt 1988; Easton 1998; Hillebrand et al. 2001). McKeown (1999) highlights that where a phenomenon is in question only a single case is required to show that it does exist. A single case can offer alternative accounts of causation, clarify obscure theoretical relationships in a particular setting, and enable theory construction. In some circumstances, such as research on culture or business networks, the application of a single case study design is favoured due to context specificity and historical background, which make it difficult to compare cases (Halinen and Törnroos 2005).

Emmanuella's research with her colleagues on customer relationship management activities of a multinational firm used a single case study design in order to provide contextual insights into the deeply rooted process of relationship management and its interaction with the company's context. The single case study design promoted the development of thick descriptions and, in turn, the identification and explanation of associations between key concepts of the study (Plakoyiannaki et al. 2008). The in-depth investigation of the case study firm enabled the researchers to reveal a mosaic of different views in the organization, which contributed to future testing of the case study propositions.

However, when choosing a single case, access may be needed to more informants and data within the company. This may create difficulties since many organizational members will be involved and considerable resources will be committed. Furthermore, the selection of interviewees is often dependent on whether a gatekeeper (key informant) allows the case researcher to tap into his/her network of personal contacts and, via snowballing sampling, recruit interview respondents. Yin (1984 [2009]) advocates caution in the selection of a single case design, with careful consideration of the potential case in order to minimize the chances of misrepresentation, where the case selected does not represent the phenomenon being investigated.

CONCLUDING REMARKS

The case study is well suited to IB research since it can capture the complexity of cross-border and -cultural settings and contribute to the examination of emerging areas of research, such as early and rapid firm internationalization. The purpose of this chapter was to discuss common misconceptions and salient issues related to case selection in the IB research context. In particular, we presented common misconceptions relevant to the definition and equivalence of the unit of analysis; sampling strategies; purposeful and random purposeful sampling; emergent or pre-specified sampling; and single and multiple case study design. But most importantly, this chapter demonstrates that case selection is not a single decision, but rather a dynamic process incorporating multiple decisions that pose challenges for case researchers in IB.

The authors have presented alternative sampling strategies that challenge the current trend in IB case research, which favours large number multicase design (Piekkari et al. 2009). Many studies seem to be based on positivist assumptions, according to which case selection is mainly driven by the logic of quasi-statistical sampling. We argue that IB researchers should be aware of the wide range of case study approaches available which increases the potential for innovation and pluralism in case research. Both single and multiple case approaches have their merits. 'Fewer' cases should not be viewed as 'less', but provide the opportunity for 'greater' depth and richness, and case-oriented explanations. Furthermore, we argue that a single case can be enough for analytical generalization, give alternative accounts of causation, clarify relationships, and build and test theory. Multiple case research, on the other hand, noted for its merit in providing replication and theoretical generalization (as opposed to statistical generalization), can use extreme cases to observe contrasting patterns of data, qualify findings and specify variation in the main patterns.

We also suggest that cross-national and internationally comparative case studies may facilitate thorough analysis of dynamic social phenomena, such as the international behaviour of firms and individuals (Lijphart 1975). This requires the development of cross-cultural collaboration among researchers, the use of pre-existing knowledge of countries and good research networks within them when selecting case studies (Loane et al. 2006). Each researcher presents his or her own perspective that may be different from other researchers. These different subjective perspectives can be combined through joint efforts to provide a comprehensive and focused examination of IB phenomena.

In summary, we have presented important issues and misconceptions linked to case selection and attempted to offer valuable insights on how to approach these challenges once embarking on a case study project. We posit that case research directed towards generating theory and persuasive arguments can only be advanced through careful consideration of the process of case sampling, its dynamic nature and multiple levels. Indeed, theoretical contributions of a case study and the potential to theorize from case studies lie on the thoroughness and explicitness of case sampling. Case researchers may carefully consider the process of case sampling, which is the *sine qua non* of this methodology.

NOTES

1. We use the term 'case study' to refer to a qualitative case study that is characterized by 'researchers spending extended time on site, personally in contact with activities and operations of the case, reflecting and revising descriptions and meanings of what is going on' (Stake 2005, p. 450).
2. We use the terms 'case selection' and 'case sampling' interchangeably. Even though the term 'sampling' may be associated with statistical methods, it is widely used by case study researchers to describe the continuous process of case selection, whereby decisions concerning selecting cases, units of analysis and sources are taken (for example, Dubois and Gadde 2002).

REFERENCES

Alajoutsijärvi, K., M.B. Klint and H. Tikkanen (2001), 'Customer relationship strategies and the smoothing of industry-specific business cycles: the case of the global fine paper industry', *Industrial Marketing Management*, **30** (6), 487–97.

Bartlett, C. and S. Ghoshal (1987), 'Managing across borders: new strategic requirements', *Sloan Management Review*, **29** (Summer), 1–17.

Birkinshaw, J., N. Hood and S. Young (2005), 'Subsidiary entrepreneurship, internal and external competitive forces and subsidiary performance', *International Business Review*, **14** (2), 227–48.

Cavusgil, T.S. and A. Das (1997), 'Methodological issues in empirical cross-cultural research: a survey of management literature and a framework', *Management International Review*, **37** (1), 71–96.

Coviello, N. (2006), 'The network dynamics of international new ventures', *Journal of International Business Studies*, **37** (5), 713–31.

Coyne, I.T. (1997), 'Sampling in qualitative research: purposeful and theoretical sampling; merging or clear boundaries?' *Journal of Advanced Nursing*, **26** (3), 623–30.

Dimitratos, P., E. Plakoyiannaki and C. Förbom (work in progress), 'Managerial and entrepreneurial learning in multinational subsidiaries', University of Strathclyde, Glasgow.

Dimitratos, P., E. Plakoyiannaki, A. Pitsoulaki and H. Tüselmann (2010), 'The global small firm in international business', *International Business Review*, **19**(6), 589–606.

Dubois, A. and L.-E. Gadde (2002), 'Systematic combining: an abductive approach to case research', *Journal of Business Research*, **55** (7), 553–60.

Dyer, W.G. Jr and A.L. Wilkins (1991), 'Better stories, not better constructs, to generate better theory: a rejoinder to Eisenhardt', *Academy of Management Review*, **16** (3), 613–19.

Easton, G. (1995), 'Methodology and industrial networks', in K. Möller and D. Wilson (eds), *Business Marketing: An Interaction and Network Perspective*, Boston, MA: Kluwer, pp. 1–36.

Easton, G. (1998), 'Case study research as a methodology for industrial networks: a realist apologia', in P. Naudé and P. Turnbull (eds), *Network Dynamics in International Marketing*, Oxford: Pergamon, pp. 73–87.

Eisenhardt, K.M. (1989), 'Building theories from case study research', *Academy of Management Review*, **14** (4), 532–50.

Eisenhardt, K.M. (1991), 'Better stories and better constructs: the case of rigor and comparative logic', *Academy of Management Review*, **16**(3), 620–27.

Ellis, P. and T. Pecotich (2001), 'Social factors influencing export initiation in small and medium-sized enterprises', *Journal of Marketing Research*, **38** (1), 119–30.

Fillis, I. (2001), 'Small firm internationalisation: an investigative survey and future research directions', *Management Decisions*, **39** (9), 767–83.

Fletcher, M. (2007), 'Internationalising small and medium sized enterprises (SMEs): a learning approach', Unpublished PhD, University of Glasgow, Glasgow.

Fletcher, M. (2009), 'Learning processes in the development of absorptive capacity of internationalising SMEs', in M.V. Jones, P. Dimitratos, M. Fletcher and S. Young (eds), *Internationalization, Entrepreneurship and the Smaller Firm: Evidence from Around the World*, Cheltenham, UK and Northampton, MA, USA: Edward Elgar, pp. 73–90.

Guba, E.G. and Y.S Lincoln (1989), *Fourth Generation Evaluation*, Newbury Park, CA: Sage.

Hakim, C. (1987), *Research Design: Strategies and Choices in the Design of Social Research*, London: Allen & Unwin.

Halinen, A. and J.-A. Törnroos (2005), 'Using case methods in the study of contemporary business networks', *Journal of Business Research*, **58** (9), 1285–97.

Hillebrand, B., R.A.W. Kok and W.G. Biemans (2001), 'Theory testing using case studies: a comment on Johnston, Leach and Liu', *Industrial Marketing Management*, **30** (8), 651–7.

Hyde, K.F. (2000), 'Recognising deductive process in qualitative research', *Qualitative Research Methods: An International Journal*, **3** (2), 82–9.

Johanson, J. and J.-E. Vahlne (1977), 'The internationalization process of the firm: a model of knowledge development and increasing foreign market commitment', *Journal of International Business Studies*, **8** (Spring/Summer), 23–32.

Johnston, W.J., M.P. Leach and A.H. Liu (2000), 'Using case studies for theory testing in business-to-business research: the development of a more rigorous case study methodology', *Advances in Business Marketing and Purchasing*, **9** (1), 215–41.

Kuzel, A. (1992), 'Sampling in qualitative enquiry', in B.F. Crabtree and W.L. Miller (eds), *Doing Qualitative Research*, Newbury Park, CA: Sage, pp. 31–44.

Leonard-Barton, D. (1990), 'A dual methodology for case studies: synergistic use of a longitudinal single site with replicated multiple sites', *Organization Science*, **1** (3), 248–66.

Leonidou, L.C. (2004), 'An analysis of the barriers hindering small business export development', *Journal of Small Business Management*, **42** (3), 279–302.

Lieberman, E.S. (2005), 'Nested analysis as a mixed-method strategy for comparative research', *American Political Science Review*, **99** (3), 435–52.

Lijphart, A. (1975), 'The comparable-cases strategy in comparative research', *Comparative Political Studies*, **8** (2), 158–77.

Lim, L. and P. Firkola (2000), 'Methodological issues in cross-cultural management research: problems, solutions and proposals', *Asian Pacific Journal of Management*, **17** (1), 133–54.

Loane, S., J. Bell and R. McNaughton (2006), 'Employing information communication technologies (ICT) to enhance qualitative international marketing enquiry', *International Marketing Review*, **23** (4), 438–55.

Mahoney, J. and G. Goertz (2004), 'The possibility principle: choosing negative cases in comparative research', *American Political Science Review*, **98** (4), 653–69.

Malhotra, N.K., J. Agarwal and M. Peterson (1996), 'Methodological issues in cross-cultural marketing research: a state-of-the-art review', *International Marketing Review*, **13** (5), 7–43.

Marshall, M.N. (1996), 'Sampling for qualitative research', *Family Practice*, **13** (6), 522–5.

McKeown, T.J. (1999), 'Case studies and the statistical worldview: review of King, Keohane and Verba's *Designing Social Inquiry: Scientific Inference in Qualitative Research*', *International Organization*, **53** (1), 161–90.

Miles, M.B. and M.A. Huberman (1994), *Qualitative Data Analysis*, Thousand Oaks, CA: Sage.

Patton, M.Q. (2002), *Qualitative Research and Evaluation Methods*, 3rd edn, Thousand Oaks, CA and London: Sage.

Peng, M.W. (2001), 'How entrepreneurs create wealth in transition economies', *Academy of Management Executive*, **15** (1), 95–108.

Penrose, E. (1960), 'The growth of the firm. A case study: the Hercules Powder Company', *Business History Review*, **34** (1), 1–23.

Perry, C. (1998), 'Processes of a case study methodology for postgraduate research in marketing', *European Journal of Marketing*, **32** (9/10), 785–802.

Pettigrew, A. (1990), 'Longitudinal field research on change: theory and practice', *Organization Science*, **1** (3), 267–92.

Piekkari R., E. Plakoyiannaki and C. Welch (2010), '"Good" case study research in industrial marketing: insights from research practice', *Industrial Marketing Management*, **39** (1), 109–17.

Piekkari, R., C. Welch and E. Paavilainen (2009), 'The case study as disciplinary convention: evidence from international business journals', *Organizational Research Methods*, **12** (3), 567–89.

Plakoyiannaki, E., N. Tzokas, P. Dimitratos and M. Saren (2008), 'How critical is employee orientation for customer relationship management (CRM): insights from a case study', *Journal of Management Studies*, **45** (2), 268–93.

Platt, J. (1988), 'What case studies can do', in R.C. Burgess (ed.), *Studies in Qualitative Methodology*, London: Tai Press, pp. 1–23.

Porter, M.E. (1990), *The Competitive Advantage of Nations*, New York: Free Press.

Ragin, C.C. (1992), '"Casing" and the process of social inquiry?' in Ragin and Becker (eds), pp. 217–26.

Ragin, C.C. and H.S. Becker (1992), *What is a Case? Exploring the Foundations of Social Inquiry*, Cambridge and New York: Cambridge University Press.

Sandelowski, M. (1995), 'Focus on qualitative methods sample size in qualitative research', *Research in Nursing and Health*, **18** (6), 179–83.

Santos, F.M and K.M. Eisenhardt (2005), 'Organizational boundaries and theories of organizations', *Organization Science*, **16** (5), 491–508.

Siggelkow, N. (2007), 'Persuasion with case studies', *Academy of Management Journal*, **50** (1), 20–24.

Sin, L.Y.M., G.W.H. Cheung and R. Lee (1999), 'Methodology in cross-cultural consumer research: a review and critical assessment', *Journal of International Consumer Marketing*, **11** (4), 75–96.

Sinkovics, R.R., E. Penz and P.N. Ghauri (2005), 'Analysing textual data in international marketing research', *Qualitative Marketing Research: An International Journal*, **8** (1), 9–38.

Stake, R.E. (2005), 'Qualitative case studies', in N.K. Denzin and Y.S. Lincoln (eds), *Handbook of Qualitative Research*, Thousand Oaks, CA: Sage, pp. 443–66.

Strauss, A. and J. Corbin (1998), *Basics of Qualitative Research: Techniques and Procedures of Developing Grounded Techniques*, 2nd edn, Thousand Oaks, CA: Sage.

Sutton, R.J. (1997), 'The virtues of closet qualitative research', *Organization Science*, **8** (1), 97–106.

Thomas, A.S. (1996), 'A call for research in forgotten locations', in B.J. Punnett and O. Shenkar (eds), *Handbook for International Management Research*, Cambridge, MA: Blackwell, pp. 485–505.

Wagner, S.M. and L. Johnson (2004), 'Configuring and managing strategic supplier portfolios', *Industrial Marketing Management*, **33** (8), 717–30.

Welch, D. (1994), 'Determinants of international human resource management approaches and activities: a suggested framework', *Journal of Management Studies*, **31** (2), 139–64.

Yin, R.K. (1984), *Case Study Research: Design and Methods*, London: Sage (4th edn, 2009).

Young, S. and A. Tavares (2004), 'Centralization and autonomy: back to the future', *International Business Review*, **13** (2), 215–37.

11. Case selection informed by theory

Trevor Buck

INTRODUCTION

- A recently graduated MBA with business experience wished to progress to a PhD. The student wanted to base her thesis on the firm ABC Inc., with which she has excellent contacts.
- Having chosen the case study method, another PhD student proceeded quickly to the data collection stage of the work, encouraged to make vital field contacts as quickly as possible.
- A young researcher planned to conduct a postal questionnaire survey of over 500 firms. If fewer than 100 usable responses were obtained, she would resort to a case study methodology.

These three situations, or rather predicaments, perhaps illustrate why the case study methodology is not accepted more widely in the international business (IB) literature: cases are often based on 'convenience' samples, case selection may be hurried or careless, or case studies may be a methodology of last resort. However, while faulty case analysis and interpretation may be remedied, if case study selection is flawed, there is little that can be done to rescue the situation: if the examiners for a PhD thesis, or journal reviewers, challenge case selection fundamentally, this probably means scrapping the whole project and starting again. Careless case study selection may in the past have contributed to the devaluation of the methodology as a valuable part of the battery of techniques available to IB researchers.

It can be seen, therefore, that case study selection is the most crucial stage of the chosen methodology, but it is not intended that this chapter be yet another methodological review. It has been asserted with some justification that if there were as many good journal articles using case studies as there are about case study methodology, questionnaire surveys and databases would be obsolete by now! Rather, the emphasis here is on examples of different case selection strategies that this researcher has found useful as a means to getting published in journals of a decent quality. The research reviewed here is explicitly positivist, with a clear emphasis on pseudo-scientific theorizing, with few elements of critical theory involving the role of the observer or reification, though one paper does employ translation theory.

Ideally, case selection should be informed by theory and not convenience, with carefully selected cases focusing on certain variables, thus exposing theories to the possibility of refutation, or unambiguously suggesting new propositions. After a short review of the potential functions of the case study in IB research and the selection of cases using theory in general, the chapter goes on to review matched pairs of cases in recent publications by the author.

This review begins with an inductive study of an 'extreme' pair of Chinese multinational enterprises (MNEs), then a deductive study of a pair of Russian and Chinese firms that uses mainly qualitative information, followed by another deductive study of a pair of countries (Germany and Japan) subjected to military occupation that adds the feature of employing archival/historical sources, and finally a deductive study of a pair of countries (Germany and the USA) that, in addition, uses the somewhat novel features of a third intermediate case (the UK) plus the use of contemporary, quantitative data. The chapter ends with some conclusions.

FUNCTIONS OF CASE STUDY

At the outset, the case study methodology must be distinguished from the use of cases in teaching. The latter usually involve the description of a company's situation, often with a chronological perspective. As a research methodology, only the weakest applications are merely descriptive, and the best are often rich in analysis, tables and appendices (Eisenhardt and Graebner 2007).

Cases may perform two theoretical functions. First, they may be used inductively in the early stages of theorizing as an exploratory means of obtaining particular empirical data that may suggest causal generalizations or hypotheses. One example of the inductive process is 'grounded' theory (Yin 2009, p. 35). Cases may inductively suggest new propositions, hypotheses, the addition of new variables to established theories, or (what amounts to the same thing) the synthesis of different theories (Eisenhardt and Graebner 2007). Such generalizations may then be exposed to wider empirical testing.

Second, cases may be used for tests on theories previously derived inductively or deductively. In this context, a general theory attributing causation may be compared with empirical reality, and 'a previously developed theory is used as a template with which to compare the empirical results of the case study' (Yin 2009, p. 38). Of course, single or multiple cases can never provide definitive tests on an existing theory, though a strict application of Karl Popper's scientific logic would insist that a single case demonstrating an empirical contradiction of theory must require the theory's total refutation and redesign. For example, one may observe that the sun comes up every day and inductively predict that it will come up every day, but if it fails to appear on one occasion, this theory collapses (Hawking 2000, p. 11). Thus, empirical cases may produce results that are consistent with deductive theory, permitting theory to survive. Alternatively, cases may contradict theory, suggesting refutation.

In practice, however, cases are mainly used for theory building and theory testing. Full empirical tests usually involve large databases and statistical methods. These methods may controversially involve the elimination of 'outlier' observations, although if these outliers were chosen as case studies, they could imply the total refutation of theories. In addition, statistical methods often involve hypotheses being accepted with different levels of confidence. For example, with 95 per cent confidence, a hypothesis may still be accepted, despite the fact that 5 per cent of results are inconsistent with the hypothesis. Again, cases taken from this aberrant 5 per cent would suggest theoretical refutation. Indeed, this observation dispels the notion of case studies being a 'soft' methodology compared with statistical analysis.

Whether used inductively or deductively, it is clear that cases may perform an important theoretical role, and the best case study methodologies involve a careful consideration of relevant theory before cases are selected.

CASE SELECTION INFORMED BY THEORY

With deductive and inductive theories, Eisenhardt (1991) was an early advocate of what she called 'theoretical sampling'; that is, the careful selection of cases according to the extent to which they may be expected to support or contradict extant theory. She supported the use of 'deviant' or extreme cases that may be used as 'individual experiments' to develop theory inductively (Eisenhardt and Graebner 2007), and that is their role in this review.

Single cases may be selected 'straightforwardly' (Eisenhardt and Graebner 2007, p. 27) because they are (i) critical in testing an already formulated theory, (ii) extreme or unique, (iii) average or commonplace,

(iv) revelatory, where researchers are offered unusual research access or (v) longitudinal (Yin 2009, pp. 47–50). It must be conceded, however, that category (iv) comes close to the advocacy of the 'convenience' cases, much derided in our introduction. Where a case is truly revelatory, this may however be permitted in circumstances where even case description may advance our knowledge. For example, Derong and Faure (1995) gained unprecedented access to negotiations between a Chinese company operating the 'contract responsibility' system in the 1990s. These negotiations included the intervention of the central Communist Party in the most delicate of situations. Otherwise, however, theory should inform case selection.

Under category (ii) Ghauri (2004, p. 114) notes that extreme cases in practice may comprise firms that are outstanding successes or notable failures in performance terms. Although by definition such cases can never be statistically representative (Eisenhardt and Graebner 2007), this lack of representativeness may be exploited. For example, an investigator may select typical and atypical cases (Pauwels and Mattyssens 2004), or cases that deliberately skew the circumstances to maximize the possibility of refuting established theory. If a theory survives this empirical onslaught of extreme cases, it may be allowed to continue in a research process that echoes Karl Popper's emphasis on the falsification rather than the justification of theories.

Of course, multiple cases provide a stronger case for theory building. Here the emphasis is on replication, extension of theory, contrary replication and elimination of contrary explanations. However, case selection is more complicated than with single cases (Eisenhardt and Graebner 2007, p. 27). As an extension of (ii), above, 'polar' cases, taken from either extreme of a spectrum, may offer contrasting patterns. If the nature and direction of a case's 'unrepresentativeness' is known, this may provide the basis for inductive theorizing including propositions. For example, with polar or 'deviant' cases (Eisenhardt 1991), bias may be introduced deliberately and allowed for in the generation of propositions.

Of course, where cases are used inductively in the early stages of theorizing, there are often no deductive theories available to guide case selection. However, even here a researcher may include questions that probe gaps in the extant literature, or that tentatively introduce new variables into the survey instrument, for subsequent theory building.

In the examples that follow, of case study methodologies used inductively and deductively by the author, the emphasis is on dual cases, or matched pairs of cases, emphasizing the similarities and differences between them (Eisenhardt 1989, p. 540). Two cases of course fall uncomfortably somewhere between the single and multiple cases advocated by

Eisenhardt. It is proposed, however, that duplicate cases may rule out the possibility of genuine outliers being selected. In addition, matched pairs are proposed here as a case study methodology inspired by the matched pairs used in statistical *t*-tests that attempt to hold particular variables constant.

For example, if otherwise indistinguishable cases are encountered in two different locations (for example, countries) then matched cases may yield hypotheses concerning the role of location. In addition, if firm size and industrial affiliation are theoretically expected to have an influence on some dependent variable, these may be factored out by a matching process that compares establishments of the same size in the same industry, but in different countries. Of course, more than two matching establishments may be found (for example, McDonald's fast-food outlets in hundreds of countries), but for entire firms, more than two matches would represent an enormous coincidence.

It is therefore proposed here that matched pairs may offer fruitful theoretical development in the flexible context of case studies.

THEORY-DRIVEN SELECTION OF 'EXTREME' CASES

Few studies based on conventional OLI-based IB theories (consisting of ownership, location and internalization advantages) on the 'why' of outward foreign domestic investment (OFDI) have focused on so-called 'latecomer' MNEs from newly industrialized economies (NIEs). OFDI by Chinese MNEs has received little attention, particularly their expansion into developed countries (Deng 2004). Similarly, research on entry mode selection, namely the 'how' of internationalization, has so far focused exclusively on the internationalization of Western MNEs. It is important, therefore, to consider whether conventional theories of OFDI and internationalization also apply to newly emerging, 'critical instance' Chinese firms. In this sense, the generalizability of established theories is scrutinized.

Traditional, OLI-based theories on the motives behind OFDI, and entry mode theory on the form of OFDI, may be expected to work best where well-developed product and factor markets prevail. Thus, domestic ownership advantages offer opportunities for profits overseas, and proximity to markets or low-cost materials or labour offer similar opportunities as locational advantages. Such opportunities require that MNEs select appropriate entry modes for internationalization, and a traditional literature of stages or incrementalism (see Chang and Rosenzweig 2001) emphasizes that firms may initially choose low-commitment entry modes such as direct exporting and franchising, gradually evolving into joint ventures or foreign subsidiaries. In competition with incrementalism, the entrepreneurial literature on smaller, 'born-global' firms addresses the tendency for fairly small firms to leap-frog these incremental stages (Wright et al. 2005).

Therefore, China represents a significant challenge to orthodox, deductive theory. China's 'new MNEs' (Bonaglia et al. 2007) have moved very quickly through the entry mode stages, but markets in China are still not highly developed, and the state still exercises considerable levels of control over privatized, listed firms that are effectively 'carve-outs' of the best parts of former state-owned enterprises (SOEs). In this sense, the selection of any Chinese MNE case is likely to be extreme and critical in theoretical terms, but 'born-global' firms are unlikely.

The selection (explained below) of large Chinese MNEs corresponds with traditional theories, themselves founded on the analysis of large MNEs in developed economies. Most Chinese MNEs have to date relied on a strategy of low-cost production, and, again, this favours traditional, MNE-based theories, especially OLI theory in relation to locational advantages. Furthermore, listed 'carve-outs' from large SOEs are incapable of being 'born global' by definition, again favouring traditional theory.

However, Chinese case studies are chosen from a cultural and institutional environment characterized by state control, networks and relational contracting in the context of the largest overseas diaspora (Peng 2002). Lenovo and Beijing Orient Electronics Technology (BOE) each confirmed the continuing role of the Chinese state as a 'helping hand' (Shleifer and Vishny 1998). Each firm is typically a 'carve-out' of assets from a state-owned institution through partial privatization (Liu and Sun 2005). They differ from Western MNEs in the sense that they are located in a NIE that has undergone market reforms, but has still not been afforded full 'market economy' status by the EU. The senior managers of each firm have close relations with city and national politicians. Together, these networking elements in the context of strong state influence may bias the analysis away from traditional cost and revenue variables towards network explanations of OFDI and internationalization strategies.

This theoretical positioning of the cases should be remembered when the question is addressed: can conventional theories be stretched to embrace this pair of extreme, revelatory cases from the cutting edge of world business? In this sense, the paper discussed below constitutes inductive theorizing, since it proposes the synthesis of different deductive theories (Eisenhardt and Graebner 2007).

Liu and Buck (2009) decided to try to gain access to top-level managers in what was essentially the population of large Chinese MNEs with significant levels of production-oriented (that is, not minerals extraction, and so on) OFDI at the end of 2005: Lenovo and BOE. This access was facilitated by the authors' existing research partnership with the Greatwall Research Institute in Beijing which had already yielded two IB papers (Buck et al. 2008; Filatotchev et al. 2009). Greatwall offered access to Lenovo and BOE. While the selection of these two cases came close to the 'convenience' sample derided in the introduction to this chapter, it did comprise the population of large Chinese MNEs with significant levels of productive OFDI, and the authors (Liu and Buck 2009) could also claim to have collected revelatory and 'unusual access' cases. The choice of two cases again defended the methodology against the possibility of selecting a single, totally atypical outlier.

In relation to OFDI, triangulated responses from top-level executives in Lenovo and BOE (Liu and Buck 2009) reported motives for OFDI that would be familiar to any advocate of OLI theory: the main ownership advantage was derived from economies of scale through domination of a large Chinese market, and market-seeking motives were the main localization consideration, as BOE and Lenovo tried to expand into the markets of developed countries. However, the main emphasis was on motives not represented in traditional OLI theory: technology seeking and network building.

As latecomer MNEs, Lenovo and BOE both decided to produce and sell their own products as brands on the international market rather than being a manufacturer for other MNEs through original equipment manufacturing (OEM). However, they could see that Japanese firms in the 1960s took over 20 years to develop their brands, and Taiwanese and Korean firms had found it difficult to escape from OEM. Lenovo and BOE needed to shorten the process of internationalization and catch up with technological leaders by adopting a 'buy-in' strategy under which they would acquire existing networks. It was conceded that this would bring long-term growth rather than short-term profit.

This brings us to entry mode choice. Lenovo acquired IBM's PC division in 2005, giving it access to IBM's patents, networks and distribution channels across 160 countries, with over 10,000 employees. This enabled Lenovo to become a global player in a very short time, and senior managers estimated that the acquisition shortened the process of internationalization by at least five years.

BOE used a variety of entry modes for its liquid crystal display (LCD) business. It formed strategic alliances and OEM supply arrangements with Dell, Hewlett-Packard and Samsung at the same time as it opened sales and research subsidiaries in many countries, including the USA and Taiwan. Most importantly, in 2002 it predated Lenovo's acquisition of part of IBM by acquiring a substantial part of the Korean LCD maker (Hynix) and in 2004 a Hong Kong company, TPV Technology, which at that time was Number 2 global supplier in LCDs. Again, the motivation was rapid internationalization and network building in an industry where competition is between networks of multiple, interlinked firms (Mathews 2002).

These case study observations have implications for IB theory. These implications were derived inductively from the cases, and the authors had no prior hypotheses from deductive theories. Traditionally, OFDI has been analysed with reference to locational production advantages, and incremental entry, advancing gradually from markets to hierarchies. However, China seems to be establishing a new model in relation to latecomer internationalization that is consistent with network and knowledge-based theory (Chen 2003). Similarly, market-like entry modes (for example, exporting, licensing) have conventionally been associated with the fastest, low-commitment foreign market entry. Now, high-commitment/control entry vehicles, such as acquisitions, are achieving rapid market entry. Chinese firms do not seek low costs internationally, but network developments that may secure long-term profitability. Taken together, although based on only two cases, these conclusions support future directions for IB research based on network theory, or more likely an inductive synthesis (Eisenhardt and Graebner 2007) of networks and conventional OLI and stages theories.

It should always be remembered, however, that case selection from China biased conclusions in favour of networks, though other aspects of the case selection favoured conventional theories, namely the focus on large MNEs. This is an example of bias in case selection being used deliberately, so long as qualifications are entered appropriately at the conclusions stage of an article.

THEORY-DRIVEN SELECTION OF QUALITATIVE CASES

A case study methodology can involve a quantitative approach (Ghauri 2004), see below, but a qualitative approach is more common. This section reviews a mainly qualitative study of a matched pair of Russian and Chinese vehicle manufacturers (Buck et al. 2000). This pair was chosen carefully but owes its selection to the comprehensive knowledge of China and Russia possessed by two of the authors (Nolan and Filatotchev). They simply identified the serendipity of a cloned Russian car plant established in China in 1950 (explained below), which was followed up by extensive desk research and site visits to Beijing and Nizhny Novgorod to complete the chronological history of the cases.

This study confirms that a limited number of case studies can never be representative, but it may be possible to control for some important variables suggested by theory. Theories and policies of economic transition derived from the political economy discipline have produced different patterns of institutional reform, and these have been reflected in actual reforms adopted by communist regimes. The purpose of the cases was to expose these deductive theories to empirical reality and possibly refutation.

For example, reforms in the former Soviet Union mainly relied upon 'shock therapy' (for example, Sachs 1994; Anders et al. 1996) and mass privatization programmes kept SOEs intact as entities. In contrast, China adopted a 'gradualist' approach (Henning and Lu 2000) whereby SOEs were encouraged to 'carve out' portions of their operations (Liu and Sun 2005) and float them on capital markets. Critics of mass privatization predicted that foreign investors would not find entire former SOEs attractive investment targets, and inward FDI would be insignificant. On the other hand, 'carve-outs' could attract foreign investments (often in joint ventures) and thus the attainment of global product standards and high levels of export success. Mass privatization, on the other hand, would enable enterprise insiders to obstruct joint ventures and foreign investment that they identified as 'cherry-picking' involving job losses. Insiders insisted that investors take a share of all of a firm's social liabilities as well as its assets.

In order to expose these rival deductive theories to empirical reality, it would be easy to pick cases that favoured a particular pattern of reform. However, the chosen study (Buck et al. 2000) consciously selected a Chinese example of an SOE that spawned an unsuccessful joint venture, and a Russian case of an entire SOE that was able to restructure its operations and attract a lot of interest from foreign investors. At the same time, a curious twist of history made it possible to observe Russian and Chinese cases that were identical in their initial resource endowment, since the Gorky Automobile Plant (GAZ) in 1950 was cloned in China in the form of the Beijing United Automobile and Motor-cycle Manufacturing Company (BUAMM). Upon foundation, GAZ and BUAMM, though thousands of miles apart in the different national environments of Russia and China, exhibited the same product ranges, the same technologies, the same staffing levels and even the same senior managers, since Russians were seconded to work in BUAMM. Case selection effectively controlled for all these variables that could in theory affect post-reform firm performance.

As predicted by gradualists, in 1984 BUAMM was able to form a joint venture employing around 4,000 employees called the Beijing Jeep

Company (BJC) with the American Motor Company (AMC, which became Chrysler in 1995 and DaimlerChrysler after 1998). In return for an American stake in BJC that was raised to 49 per cent in 1985, BUAMM was able to obtain modern technologies that enabled it to produce and export Jeep Cherokees, mainly to the rest of Asia and to the former Soviet Union.

In contrast, GAZ (with 106,000 employees in 1999) was unable to attract significant levels of foreign investment. This was mainly because of its privatization as an entity, with massive social liabilities that included over one thousand tower blocks of apartments for employees, educational facilities for employees' children, polyclinics for healthcare and so on. Although GAZ's output mix was restructured, with less reliance on large cars such as the Volga in favour of small Gazelle vans, these products did not prove to be competitive on global export markets.

To summarize, even though cases were chosen from China and the Soviet Union to bias findings in the opposite direction, they still produced results that corresponded with theories of economic transition, which survive unrefuted. Mass privatization is predicted to bring stability in employment and social provision but little restructuring. Gradualist reforms attract foreign investments that lead to globally competitive products, but they also produce uncertainties in the form of job losses and threats to social provisions.

THEORY-DRIVEN SELECTION OF ARCHIVAL/ HISTORICAL CASES

It has been suggested that carefully selected case studies may be a realistic avenue to publication in good journals. The same can be said of archival research, a much underexploited vehicle for good IB papers. Audia et al. (2000), Buck (2003) and Toms and Filatotchev (2004) provide examples of papers offering theoretical progress using archival data. In addition to these mainstream journals, business history journals are highly rated by the business school research community, and are prominent in the many journal quality lists that have been produced as part of research assessment exercises (for example, Harzing 2008).

In this section, a business history paper using mostly qualitative, archival data for a pair of matched case studies is reviewed (Buck and Tull 2000). This paper addressed possible changes in international corporate governance, a fairly new strand in the IB literature. Corporate governance systems may be identified as belonging to an Anglo-American world of exit-based, 'stock market' or 'shareholder' capitalism or to European/

Asian style, voice-based 'welfare state' or 'stakeholder' capitalism (Dore 2000). In relation to these two broad types of corporate governance system, two schools of thought may be identified: those who predict the convergence of national corporate governance systems, either on the American model or some hybrid (Ugeux 2004), and those who foresee their continued divergence (Jackson and Strange 2008).

Advocates of continued divergence emphasize the embeddedness of corporate governance structures as part of national institutions in general (Granovetter 1985) and the persistence of national cultures that may co-evolve with institutions (Lewin and Kim 2004; Lane 2005). Deeply rooted institutions may produce inertia and path dependency (North 1990), and even when institutions appear to have been reformed, deeper examination may reveal mere ceremonial or cosmetic changes and the 'translation' of reforms to suit local institutions and culture (Czarniawska and Sevón 1996). However, although path dependency may inhibit change and thus convergence, one version of traditional institutional theory predicts that inertia may dissolve into radical change, but only in the fairly rare event of 'conquest or revolution' (North 1990, p. 89).

On the other hand, neo-institutional theory (Greenwood and Hinings 1996) identifies less dramatic circumstances in which institutional change may be expected, with its emphasis on isomorphism, or 'convergence'. As an extreme variation of this convergence phenomenon, Hansmann and Kraakman (2001) assert that the rapid adoption of American-style corporate governance practices around the world have ended the debate, with the 'end of history' for corporate law.

How could case studies illuminate this debate, at least at a national level, in the sense of exposing these deductive theories to empirical realities? The distinctive character of corporate governance in Germany and Japan, together with North's (1990) reference to conquest, raised an interesting question and suggested two archival cases. By coincidence, after the Second World War the most important representatives of stakeholder capitalism (Japan and Germany) were each occupied and administered (mainly) by an American military government intent on establishing US-style shareholder capitalism. This suggested two case studies derived from US military archives from Japan and Germany, with one case providing a check on the other.

Allied victories in 1945 were followed by the American military occupation of Japan and the former West Germany, although control in Germany was nominally shared with the French and British armies, initially at least. A major objective of these occupations was to reform corporate governance and destroy the voice-based stakeholder capitalism of Japan and Germany (featuring, particularly, cross-shareholdings, family and bank control) that was seen to have aided fascism. In these circumstances, considered by North's institutional theory to be the most propitious for institutional change, did convergence on the American model occur? Alternatively, did divergence persist, despite conquest and attempts to Americanize corporate governance by occupation forces? With a bias in favour of institutional change deliberately introduced by archival case selection, did continued institutional inertia contradict North's exception to path dependency and convergence? By implication, did the case studies contradict the neo-institutional prediction of convergence, despite case selection that favoured change and thus convergence?

The outcome of the two archival cases covering the American occupation of what was loosely called West Germany (1945–49) and Japan (1945–52) was complex. Certainly the US military government tried to introduce many of the features of shareholder capitalism. For example, in Germany, family shareholdings were sequestered, 'cartel-busting' was a major plank of American policy, and in 1947 national banks were broken up into regional banks on the American model. Trade unions had been victimized under Nazism and under American military rule, and employees were now given new stakeholder powers under co-determination legislation and supervisory boards.

However, divergence persisted in post-war West Germany. Banks continued to hold shares in industrial firms and vote the bearer stocks deposited with them, in the time-old pattern, and co-determination was actually a return to the stakeholder control exercised by employees in the nineteenth and early twentieth centuries. By the 1970s, Krupp, Thyssen and Klöckner had re-emerged as dynastic firms, and German industry generally refused to be exposed to the short-term uncertainties of shareholder capitalism. Low levels of share liquidity continued to obstruct the takeover mechanism.

In Japan, the US military government again attempted to break up Japan's industrial dynasties (the *zaibatsu*), particularly the 'big four' family holding companies (Yasuda, Mitsui, Mitsubishi and Sumitomo). In 1948, the USA tried to introduce much of the legal infrastructure of stock market capitalism (including a commercial code based on Illinois and a Securities Exchange Commission, or SEC). Family holdings of shares were disposed of on capital markets, where individual shareholders were favoured categories of buyer. To break up the old holding companies that reinforced the powers of families, industrial corporations were forbidden to hold industrial shares, and financial institutions such as banks were limited to 5 per cent of a firm's stock.

Only three months after American withdrawal and the restoration of Japanese sovereignty in May 1952, however, the SEC was abolished, and rules promoting the power of dispersed shareholders (for example, at AGMs) were withdrawn. After revisions in 1953 to the Anti-Trust Act, industrial firms were again allowed to buy stock in other firms, banks could acquire up to 10 per cent of any firm's shares, and cross-holdings re-emerged. The familiar modern *keiretsu*, based on the holding of shares by financial institutions and trading companies, developed. Three of the old family groups (Mitsui, Mitsubishi and Sumitomo) re-emerged as *keiretsu*, and Yasuda changed its name to Fuji. Again, significant path dependence may be observed in the Japanese case.

Conclusions from these archival German and Japanese cases seem clear. At a national level, institutional inertia and path dependence seem to dominate corporate governance, even when cases are chosen from episodes when a conquering power succeeded in imposing change on a defeated, submissive country. Gradually corporate governance in Germany and Japan diverged again from US-style reforms. North's (1990) suggestion that military defeat would produce exceptions to the prediction of inertia in traditional institutional theory is refuted by the two cases. Two cases cannot 'confirm' traditional institutional theory, but they may justify investments in its wider testing.

Of course neo-institutional theory and its analysis of changes in corporate governance at a firm level may still have explanatory power, and developments of this perspective have started to emerge (for example, Buck and Chizema 2006). This theme is also addressed in the next section.

THEORY-DRIVEN SELECTION OF QUANTITATIVE CASES

Although many cases are descriptive or qualitative (in the sense of using words rather than numbers), the rigorous collection of quantitative, interval scale data from cases is also legitimate. It was mentioned in the previous section that the apparent convergence of corporate governance systems explained by neo-institutional theory may be merely cosmetic. For example, hostile takeovers under welfare state capitalism (for example, in France, Germany or Japan) may in fact be friendly mergers, concealing employment guarantees and so on.

This apparent convergence and executive pay were the dimensions of corporate governance that provided the focus for Buck and Shahrim (2005). Under stock market capitalism, share price is usually the basis for the most important performance indicators, for example, for the calculation of annual bonus and, particularly, the value of share awards and executive share options (ESOs). However, ESOs bring uncertainties as well as potential value for executives and other stakeholders. Shareholders do not know in advance the cost of ESOs, for example, ESOs that are 'under water' cost nothing. Executives also bear the uncertainty of not knowing their incomes until the end of the financial year, and employees must work in firms where executives are motivated by incentives that are based on share price, possibly raising the risk of fluctuations in employment levels, as executives pursue shareholder value in every way, including labour cost-cutting.

Under stakeholder capitalism, executives and other employees are uncomfortable with these uncertainties. In the language of Hofstede's (2008) cross-cultural psychology, Germany exhibits a high national level of uncertainty avoidance. Thus, the institutional inertia noted at a national level in the archival cases of the previous section may be reinforced by resistance to change within firms. Even corporate governance change that is evident may be 'translated' (Czarniawska and Sevón 1996) by actors within firms to resemble change (for example, Americanization), under institutional pressure from stakeholders such as employees, banks and even executives themselves.

To expose the prediction of convergence and translation theory to empirical reality, the USA and Germany were chosen as a pair of countries from each end of the shareholder/stakeholder capitalist spectrum, supplemented by the UK, in between, sharing many features of shareholder capitalism with the USA, plus a proximity to the culture and institutions of mainland Europe. Case selection at a company level also proceeded subsequently, see below.

It has been observed that, admittedly after decades of resistance, most large German firms have evidently adopted the American corporate governance innovation of ESOs (Sanders and Tuschke 2007). However, German ESOs may be quite different from their American comparators, and Buck and Shahrim (2005) chose cases to examine this apparent convergence, predicted by traditional institutional theory and its path dependence, explained in the previous section.

Since the presumption is that ESO adoption constitutes convergence on an American template, it was decided to expose deductive institutional and translation theories to empirical realities by deliberately selecting cases that were most favourable to the convergence thesis. For example, only DAX100 firms were reviewed – that is, Germany's largest firms – and core industrial firms with the greatest exposure to international trade and with the resources needed to adopt a costly innovation such as ESOs. In addition, German firms were reviewed only if they provided detailed information on ESOs as a result of an American depository receipt or the adoption of the USA's accounting conventions (US GAAP).

Thus, DAX100 firms were reduced to only 14 who disclosed details of their ESO schemes. These 14 were then reduced to the seven German firms for which comparable UK and US firms (matched in terms of industrial affiliation and firm size) could be found, producing 21 cases in total. The seven German cases arguably comprised Germany's most Americanized firms (with ESOs and American-style information disclosure) that were most likely to exhibit convergence. Thus, the sample was deliberately biased in favour of the convergence thesis that German corporate governance would adopt the American ESO innovation.

However, based on knowledge of Germany's national culture and institutions reflecting that culture, it was hypothesized that German ESOs would be more employee-serving and less executive-serving. In other words, ESOs would be 'typically German', rather than clones of the American ESO template. Thus, ESOs in Germany were predicted to extend further down the managerial hierarchy than in the USA, would cover a smaller proportion of the firm's shares, would have quantitatively more performance conditions attached, and qualitatively more demanding performance conditions.

Although the seven matched pairs of German/US/UK quantitative cases were of course quite incapable of testing hypotheses rigorously, they did suggest that the convergence thesis must be seriously questioned, if not refuted: German ESOs were clearly 'translated' and bore little resemblance to the American template. For example, Deutsche Bank's ESO scheme extended down to 2,498 managers, while its American 'twin' (JP Morgan Chase) had an ESO enjoyed by only its top five executives. Similarly, German ESOs generally had stricter and more numerous performance conditions attached. The cases therefore suggested that a distinctly German form of corporate governance still prevailed, and hence divergence has persisted, despite the cosmetic adoption of ESOs. The divergence predicted by translation theory and by traditional institutional theory was found to be consistent with the case evidence, and may be allowed to survive until further, more comprehensive tests are applied.

CONCLUSIONS

Returning to the examples of misguided case study methodologies provided at the start of this chapter, this review of four papers demonstrates that, wherever possible, case studies should not be selected on grounds of accessibility alone, cases should not be selected before theoretical analysis and the identification of research gaps, and cases should emphatically not be the methodology of last resort.

An emphasis on dyadic, matched cases in this review both complements and mediates the methodological suggestions of Eisenhardt (1991) and Yin (2009) in relation to single and multiple cases. Pairs of cases may fulfil a role as extreme examples, or may avoid some of the pitfalls of single cases, while still offering theoretical benefits by holding certain independent variables constant and isolating the estimated impact of focal variables.

A case study methodology can fulfil two roles, and neither precludes publication in refereed IB journals of a decent quality. First, cases may be used imaginatively in building an inductive foundation for new theories, and in this creative process at the base of the social scientific method, there can be no rules, only warnings, and benefits identified from previous experience. Only one of the studies reviewed above was used inductively, and the Lenovo/BOE cases illustrated the possible benefits of using a pair of cases; in this case a pair that amounted to the population of large Chinese MNEs with substantial OFDI.

Second, cases may be used for tests on deductive or inductive theories, but with the emphasis on refutation or looking for evidence that is consistent with theories rather than confirming them. In two of the papers reviewed, cases corresponded with theoretical expectations, but the executive pay study contradicted the convergence predicted by neo-institutional theory, producing evidence consistent with translation and conventional institutional theory.

Whatever the theoretical function of cases, it is suggested that time and imagination must be devoted to the selection of extreme, archival, quantitative or qualitative cases before embarking on fieldwork. There is nothing wrong with practitioner journals, but access to good academic journals is likely to be attained only after a careful consideration of existing deductive theory or of theoretical gaps that may be filled by inductive enquiries.

REFERENCES

Anders, A., P.P. Boone and S. Johnson (1996), 'How to stabilise: lessons from post-communist countries', *Brooking Papers on Economic Activity*, **1**, 217–91.

Audia, P.G., E.A. Locke and K.G. Smith (2000), 'The paradox of success: an archival and a laboratory study of strategic persistence following radical environmental change', *Academy of Management Journal*, **43** (5), 837–53.

Bonaglia, F., A. Goldstein and J.A. Mathews (2007), 'Accelerated internationalization by emerging markets' multinationals: the case of the white goods sector', *Journal of World Business*, **42** (4), 369–83.

Buck, T. (2003), 'Modern Russian corporate governance: convergent forces or product of Russian history?', *Journal of World Business*, **38** (4), 299–313.

Buck, T. and A. Chizema (2006), 'Neo-institutional theory and institutional change: towards empirical tests on the "Americanisation" of German executive pay', *International Business Review*, **15** (5), 488–504.

Buck, T., I. Filatotchev, M. Wright and P. Nolan (2000), 'Different paths to economic reform in Russia and China: causes and consequences', *Journal of World Business*, **35** (4), 379–400.

Buck, T., X. Liu and R. Skovoroda (2008), 'Top executive pay and firm performance in China', *Journal of International Business Studies*, **39** (5), 833–50.

Buck, T. and A. Shahrim (2005), 'The translation of corporate governance changes across national cultures: the case of Germany', *Journal of International Business Studies*, **36** (1), 42–61.

Buck, T. and M. Tull (2000), 'Anglo-American contributions to Japanese and German corporate governance after World War II', *Business History*, **42** (2), 119–40.

Chang, S. and P. Rosenzweig (2001), 'The choice of entry mode in sequential foreign direct investment', *Strategic Management Journal*, **22** (8), 747–76.

Chen, T-J. (2003), 'Network resources for internationalisation: the case of Taiwan's electronics firms', *Journal of Management Studies*, **40** (5), 1107–30.

Czarniawska, B. and B. Sevón (1996), *Translating Organizational Change*, Berlin: de Gruyter.

Deng, P. (2004), 'Outward investment by Chinese MNCs: motivations and implications', *Business Horizons*, **47** (3), 8–16.

Derong, C. and G.F. Faure (1995), 'When Chinese companies negotiate with their government', *Organization Studies*, **16** (1), 27–54.

Dore, R. (2000), *Stock Market Capitalism: Welfare Capitalism: Japan and Germany versus the Anglo-Saxons*, Oxford: Oxford University Press.

Eisenhardt, K.M. (1989), 'Building theories from case study research', *Academy of Management Review*, **14** (4), 532–50.

Eisenhardt, K.M. (1991), 'Better stories and better constructs: the case for rigor and comparative logic', *Academy of Management Review*, **16** (3), 620–27.

Eisenhardt, K.M. and M.E. Graebner (2007), 'Theory building from cases: opportunities and challenges', *Academy of Management Review*, **50** (1), 25–32.

Filatotchev, I., X. Liu, T. Buck and M. Wright (2009), 'The export orientation and export performance of high-technology SMEs in emerging markets: the effects of knowledge transfer by returnee entrepreneurs', *Journal of International Business Studies*, **40** (6), 1005–21.

Ghauri, P. (2004), 'Designing and conducting case studies in international business research', in R. Marschan-Piekkari and C. Welch (eds), *Handbook of Qualitative Research Methods for International Business*, Cheltenham, UK and Northampton, MA, USA: Edward Elgar, pp. 109–24.

Granovetter, M. (1985), 'Economic action and social structure: the problem of embeddedness', *American Journal of Sociology*, **91** (3), 481–510.

Greenwood, R. and C.R. Hinings (1996), 'Understanding radical organizational change: bringing together the old and the new institutionalism', *Academy of Management Review*, **21** (4), 1022–54.

Hansmann, H. and R. Kraakman (2001), 'The end of history for corporate law', *Georgetown Law Journal*, **89** (1), 439–68.

Harzing, A.-W. (2008), 'Journal quality list', available at: http://www.harzing.com/resources.htm#/jql.htm (accessed 14 March 2008).

Hawking, S.W. (2000), *A Brief History of Time*, London: Bantam Press.

Henning, C. and X. Lu (2000), 'The political foundation of Chinese style gradualism: a paradox of too strong private interests?', *Journal of Institutional and Theoretical Economics*, **156** (1), 35–63.

Hofstede, G. (2008), www.geert-hofstede.com (accessed 14 March 2008).

Jackson, G. and R. Strange (2008), 'Why does corporate governance matter for international business?', in R. Strange and G. Jackson (eds), *Corporate Governance and International Business*, Basingstoke: Palgrave Macmillan, pp. 1–14.

Lane, C. (2005), 'Institutional transformation and system change: changes in the corporate governance of German corporations', in G. Morgan, R. Whitley and E. Moen (eds), *Changing Capitalisms? Complementarities, Contradictions and Capability Development in an International Context*, Oxford: Oxford University Press, pp. 78–109.

Lewin, A.Y. and J. Kim (2004), 'The nation-state and culture as influences on organizational change and innovation', in M.S. Poole and A. Van de Ven (eds), *The Nation-state and Culture as Influences and Organizational Change and Innovation*, Oxford: Oxford University Press, pp. 324–53.

Liu, G.S. and P. Sun (2005), 'China's public firms: how much privatization?', in S. Green and G.S. Liu (eds), *Exit the Dragon? Privatization and State Control in China*, Oxford: Blackwell, pp. 111–24.

Liu, X. and T. Buck (2009), 'The internationalisation strategies of Chinese firms: Lenovo and BOE', *Journal of Chinese Economics and Business Studies*, **7** (2), 167–81.

Mathews, J. (2002), *Dragon Multinational: A New Model for Global Growth*, Oxford: Oxford University Press.

North, D.C. (1990), *Institutions, Institutional Change and Economic Performance*, Cambridge: Cambridge University Press.

Pauwels, P. and P. Mattyssens (2004), 'The architecture of multiple case study research in international business', in R. Marschan-Piekkari and C. Welch (eds), *Handbook of Qualitative Research Methods for International Business*, Cheltenham, UK and Northampton, MA, USA: Edward Elgar, pp. 125–43.

Peng, M.W. (2002), 'Cultures, institutions, and strategic choices: toward an institutional perspective on business strategy', in M. Gannon and K.L. Newman (eds), *The Blackwell Handbook of Cross-Cultural Management*, Oxford: Blackwell, pp. 52–66.

Sachs, J. (1994), *Poland's Jump to the Market Economy*, Boston, MA: MIT Press.

Sanders, W.M.G. and A. Tuschke (2007), 'The adoption of institutionally contested organizational practices: the emergence of stock option pay in Germany', *Academy of Management Journal*, **50** (1), 33–56.

Shleifer, A. and R.W. Vishny (1998), *The Grabbing Hand: Government Pathologies and their Cures*, Boston, MA: Harvard University Press.

Toms, S. and I. Filatotchev (2004), 'Corporate governance, business strategy and the dynamics of networks: a theoretical model and application to the British cotton industry, 1830–1980', *Organization Studies*, **25** (4), 449–72.

Ugeux, G. (2004), 'Towards global convergence in corporate governance: an assessment of the current situation', *International Journal of Disclosure and Governance*, **1** (4), 339–54.

Wright, M., I. Filatotchev, R. Hoskisson and M. Peng (2005), 'Strategy research in emerging economies: challenging the conventional wisdom', *Journal of Management Studies*, **42** (1), 1–34.

Yin, R.K. (2009), *Case Study Research: Design and Methods*, 4th edn, London: Sage.

12. Mixed-method case studies in international business research

Leila Hurmerinta and Niina Nummela

INTRODUCTION

International business (IB) is a multifaceted field of research, crossing national, cultural and organizational boundaries, and inspiring quite complicated research questions. Lately, the nature of research questions has evolved; it seems that simple research problems have already been solved, and now the more complex ones remain. Additionally, as a relatively new field of research, IB still offers numerous avenues for exploration for which traditional research methods are inadequate, and researchers may need to apply several methods in order to stay on firm ground and to arrive safely at their destination. We assume that this will also gradually lead to combinations of diverse methods and thereby to more complex research designs.

However, to date the IB field has been clearly dominated by single-method studies (for reviews of the field see, for example, Clark et al. 1999; Peterson 2004; Hurmerinta-Peltomäki and Nummela 2006), although some exceptions do exist (for example, Brannen 1996). This is quite surprising, given that mixed-method research designs represent one of the fastest-growing areas in research methodology today (Bergman 2008). Another area attracting greater interest is the case study, as this book indicates. Yet so far, the two streams of methodological literature – on case studies, on the one hand, and mixed methods, on the other – seem to have remained largely disconnected.

In this chapter, we therefore seek to redress the neglect of mixed-method case studies in IB by looking specifically at how mixed methods can and have been used in the course of a case study. The use of mixed-method terminology is often quite ambiguous (Hurmerinta-Peltomäki and Nummela 2004), but in this chapter we treat 'mixed methods' and 'multiple methods' as synonymous terms, since both refer to the combination of qualitative and quantitative methods in the course of one study.

As a research approach that can encompass the use of mixed methods, the case study in IB has considerable potential, although we have not yet seen them widely published in top journals (Ghauri 2004; Piekkari et al. 2009). However, the majority of researchers using the case study approach seem to follow a similar pattern, namely the one described by Yin (1994), which largely assumes that the case researcher will be combining qualitative sources of evidence. Although the potential for mixing methods has since been acknowledged, including by Yin (1994 [2009]), the review of IB journals that we share in this chapter suggests that the mixed-method case study design has not been utilized in full.

It is evident that inquiring more deeply into how mixed methods could be incorporated in case studies would offer quite interesting research avenues, and therefore they deserve our attention. The purpose of this chapter, then, is to critically evaluate how mixed methods have been used in case studies published in IB journals. This analysis will allow us to identify and assess alternative strategies for combining qualitative and quantitative research in a case study. Accordingly, in this chapter we begin with a discussion on the nature and definition of a case, then continue by making explicit the main assumptions underlying this study. This is followed by an analysis of multimethod case studies that have been published in IB journals, in which we identify alternative strategies for combining multiple methods in a case study. Two strategies emerged from the dataset: compartmentalized and aggregated. The strategies differ in many ways, and therefore also the appropriate use of them is quite diverse. The analysis also revealed that the extent to which mixed methods are used varies considerably, and in many studies the qualitative data in particular were underutilized. Some authors seemed to share the illusion that increasing the number of cases would help them to avoid some of the challenges related to case studies in general (for a discussion, see Piekkari et al. 2009). The concluding section of our chapter discusses the implications of our analysis.

TOWARDS A BROADER VIEW OF THE CASE STUDY

In addition to clarifying the concept of mixed methods, our inquiry raises the question of how to define a case. Despite its popularity in the social sciences, the conceptual foundations of a case study are unclear. What is a case and who determines it? And which are the appropriate ways to conduct scientific research within this context? The term 'case' is used across many disciplines for various purposes. In colloquial language it usually refers to an interesting example or something that is under examination (*OALD* 1989). In the academic context we also distinguish between teaching and research cases, because they serve different objectives.

Teaching cases are created to set up a framework for discussion among students, whereas in research the aim is to increase our understanding of the investigated phenomenon (for example, Eisenhardt 1989).

In a research context, cases or case studies often refer to a particular type of research strategy: namely, 'an empirical inquiry that investigates a contemporary phenomenon within its real-life context when the boundaries between phenomenon and context are not clearly evident; and in which multiple sources of evidence are used' (Yin 1994, p. 23). This definition by Yin – which was presented in his earlier publications as well and has been modified only slightly in his later work (see Yin 1994 [2009], p. 18) – has become the mainstream understanding of those researchers who have followed him.

From the viewpoint of our focus on mixed methods, it is interesting that the definition presented above – as well as the majority of others to be found in the methodological literature – highlights the use of several data sources. This kind of data triangulation (for the different types of triangulation, see Denzin 1978) seems to be a prerequisite for a study to be considered a case study. However, in keeping with Yin's (1994) recommendation, triangulation is typically confined to the collection and analysis of data within qualitative research traditions (that is, within-method triangulation), instead of crossing boundaries or mixing methods (that is, between-method triangulation). Additionally, although Yin later touches on the possibility of multimethod research, this discussion is a very small section even in the most recent version of his book (Yin 1994 [2009]), and he does not elaborate on how such a case study could be conducted. The dominance of Yin as a methodological authority in IB (Piekkari et al. 2009) is perhaps one reason why alternative research designs incorporating multiple methods are still quite rare.

For the purpose of our current inquiry, given that mixed-method studies vary a great deal (for a discussion, see Hurmerinta-Peltomäki and Nummela 2006), in our opinion, a broader definition of a case would reveal a greater range of alternative research paths and thus be more illuminating. Therefore, here 'case' refers to the object to be studied – in other words, the analytic unit of the study (for example, Stake 1995; Ghauri 2004; Eisenhardt and Graebner 2007) – and we adopt a more general definition of the term 'case study'. From our viewpoint, a study can be considered a case study if it investigates the phenomenon and its dynamics in its natural settings (Eisenhardt 1989). It may also confront theory with the empirical world and apply data from multiple sources, but this is not necessary (see Piekkari et al. 2009). In order to make sure that our definition was used in a consistent manner, we did the classification of case studies ourselves – in other words, it was not necessary for the author to label his/

her study as a case study. This kind of approach allows us best to take into account the fact that cases can be used for different purposes (Eisenhardt 1989; Yin 1994; Stake 1995).

BACKGROUND ASSUMPTIONS OF OUR STUDY

IB researchers – as well as researchers in many other fields – can be roughly divided into two schools of thought: 'the purists' and 'the pragmatists' (Creswell 1994; Tashakkori and Teddlie 1998). Both of them have clearly distinct viewpoints concerning the use of mixed methods (for more details, see Hurmerinta-Peltomäki and Nummela 2004). Most researchers using the case study approach seem to be purists, as they strictly follow one paradigm by employing qualitative research methods to obtain deeper understanding (Piekkari et al. 2009).

However, the logic of pragmatists – researchers who use both paradigms effectively in order to increase their understanding of the phenomenon (Creswell 1994) – would, we believe, offer a more fertile standpoint for future studies. The benefits of mixed methods – such as capturing a holistic picture of the subject matter and allowing for the possibility of uncovering surprising features (Jick 1979) – overlap quite nicely with the potential advantages of case studies. Additionally, it has been argued that the use of different methods increases the validity of the findings (Denzin 1978; Jick 1979; Lincoln and Guba 1985; Eisenhardt 1989; Patton 1990; Bryman 1992; Hammersley 2008). As validity has often been criticized in case studies, this too constitutes a great advantage of mixed methods.

Given the benefits described above, one might question why single-method studies dominate the IB field. We would argue that the main reason is that mixing methods is by no means easy (Hurmerinta-Peltomäki and Nummela 2004). First, this strategy should only be used if it helps in solving the research problem. This requires the researcher to have sufficient conceptual and theoretical knowledge of the phenomenon in question (Jick 1979), as well as methodological competence in multiple methods (Bryman 2007; Creswell et al. 2008). Second, several researchers have pointed out that intertwining findings from multiple methods is a complicated process (for example, Jick 1979; Bryman 1992, 2007; Creswell 1994, 2008). One of the problems is that the results obtained from different methods may not necessarily converge. In the best mixed-method studies, the discrepancy of findings generated during the research process acts as a trigger for a more profound use of multiple methods (for example, Brannen 1996). However, no general guidelines exist on how different types of findings should be combined. Furthermore, the use of mixed methods is often limited by practical considerations, such as limited resources (both time and money), access to suitable units of observation, and disciplinary and political contexts (Denzin 1978; Jick 1979; Patton 1990; Brannen 1992; Hammersley 2008). We believe that methodological pluralism places extra demands on researchers' capabilities and resources.

Additionally, from the viewpoint of the research process, conducting research with multiple methods is different, at least in degree, from that of a single-method study. The process itself may be full of surprises; for example, when you start you may not even know all the purposes for which the data or method will be used. Denzin (1978) wrote about the demands for researcher flexibility and readiness to alter the course of action, change methods, reconceptualize problems and even start over if necessary. Sometimes the research question itself needs to be amended, or in extreme cases abandoned altogether. Researchers must continually evaluate their methods, assess the quality of incoming data and note the relevance of their data to theory. Methodological pluralism and methodo-logical flexibility are fundamental requirements of a mixed-method study. In other words, the initial research design is only a guide which changes along the way (Hurmerinta-Peltomäki and Nummela 2004). Thus, a flex-ible approach to the research design is required.

As a research field, IB poses additional challenges for the use of mixed methods. First, individual IB researchers often operate internationally. The study objects may be spread worldwide and the phenomenon under scrutiny may cross all kinds of boundaries, particularly geographical ones. Second, IB research typically involves cross-country comparison and cooperation with international research teams. In practice, therefore, research in this field is very resource intensive, and the related financial costs are considerable. However, we argue that the use of mixed methods may facilitate researchers to overcome some of the dilemmas that IB as research context inherently contains.

'HUNTING' FOR MULTIMETHOD CASE STUDIES

In the present study our interest lay in case studies in which a multimethod strategy had been applied. What kind of case studies are they? Here they are defined as case studies which involve the collection and/or analysis of both quantitative and/or qualitative data in a single study in which the data are collected concurrently or sequentially and are combined at one or more stages in the research process (Hurmerinta-Peltomäki and Nummela 2006, p. 441). In practice, identifying such a case study is not straight-forward. First, we need to decide whether the study in question is a case study (according to our definition), and then, we need to evaluate the use of mixed methods in the study. It should also be kept in mind that the use of mixed methods is not usually an either–or situation, but studies can be placed on a continuum according to whether they use mixed methods in an extensive or a limited way.

In order to find such studies we took a recent review of mixed-method studies in IB (Hurmerinta-Peltomäki and Nummela 2006) as the basis of our analysis. That review included a total of 68 mixed-method studies collected from four leading IB journals from the period from 2000 to 2003.[1] For the purposes of the current study, the 68 mixed-method articles were further analysed by the researchers in order to find those studies in which the case study approach had been used. That scanning revealed that among mixed-method studies in IB, a case study approach is quite rare. Only 13 articles among the 68 mixed-method studies had applied the case approach; that is, less than 20 per cent. Additionally, the existence of studies available for this chapter was not only limited in terms of number, but was also concentrated in only two of the journals, namely *International Business Review* (*IBR*) and the *Journal of International Business Studies* (*JIBS*). In contrast, only one mixed-method case study was found in *Management International Review* (*MIR*) and none at all in the *Journal of World Business* (*JWB*) (see Table 12.1).

The mixed-method case studies we identified were spread across many areas of research interest and no single topic could be identified as attracting a mixed-method approach. However, most of the studies were exploratory in nature, and one could argue that the topic was often outside the 'mainstream' of IB research, such as strategy-related beliefs in organizations (Markóczy 2000), exchange rate effects on firms (Bradley and Moles 2001), or the supplier perspective on learning and performance in buyer–supplier relationships (Nobeoka et al. 2002), just to mention a few examples. The number of cases varied considerably, from a single case to 36 cases (Table 12.1). The majority of studies had multiple cases; only three studies had a single-case design.

The order and nature of different types of data varied among the studies (Table 12.1). However, in all but three of the studies the quantitative data dominated and the qualitative data were supportive. The studies were dominated by one type of research design, in which both quantitative and qualitative data have been collected then analysed within their respective traditions: in other words, the qualitative data analysed qualitatively and the quantitative data analysed quantitatively. One exception was the study of Markóczy (2000): it included only qualitative data, which had then been analysed both quantitatively and qualitatively. In terms of research design, mixed-method case studies did not seem to deviate from

Table 12.1 Mixed-method case studies

Author(s)	Year	Journal[1]	Use of mixed methods[2]	No. of cases	Dominant method	Motive for using mixed methods	Role of cases
Bradley and Moles	2001	*IBR*	QN => QL	6	QN	Validity, knowledge	Compartmentalized
Chetty and Wilson	2003	*IBR*	QN => QL	1	QN	Validity, knowledge	Compartmentalized
Clark and Pugh	2001	*IBR*	QN + QL	19	QN	Knowledge	Aggregated
Fahy et al.	2000	*JIBS*	QL => QN	34	QN	Validity	Compartmentalized
Fenwick et al.	2003	*IBR*	QN + QL	20	QL	Knowledge	Aggregated
Gassel and Pascha	2000	*IBR*	QN => QL + QN	17	QN	Knowledge	Compartmentalized
Glaister et al.	2003	*IBR*	QN + QL	20	QL	Knowledge	Aggregated
Lye and Hamilton	2001	*IBR*	QN + QL	36	QN	Knowledge	Aggregated
Manev and Stevenson	2001	*JIBS*	QL => QN	1	QN	Facilitation, validity	Aggregated
Markóczy	2000	*JIBS*	QL => QN	5	QN	Knowledge	Aggregated
Nobeoka et al.	2002	*JIBS*	QL => QN	2	QN	Facilitation, validity, knowledge	Compartmentalized
Petersen and Welch	2000	*IBR*	QN => QL	2	Equal	Facilitation, knowledge	Compartmentalized
Testa et al.	2003	*MIR*	QN + QL	1	QN	Facilitation, knowledge	Aggregated

Notes:
1. *IBR* = International Business Review, *JIBS* = Journal of International Business Studies, *MIR* = Management International Review.
2. QN = Quantitative Methods, QL = Qualitative Methods.
   '=>' indicates methods used sequentially, '+' indicates methods used concurrently.

our broader sample of mixed-method studies (see Hurmerinta-Peltomäki and Nummela 2006). However, one should keep in mind that they are only illustrative examples of this kind of research strategy, and they do not necessarily reflect the best practices one should follow in IB research.

We also analysed the motive(s) for using mixed methods in the selected studies (Table 12.1). Generally, the motives can be classified into three types (Hurmerinta-Peltomäki and Nummela 2006). First, the other method may have only an instrumental or facilitating role: in other words, the use of a qualitative method facilitates the quantitative part of the study, or vice versa (for example, Bryman 1992). Second, it is possible that researchers use mixed methods in order to improve the validity of their research (for example, Jick 1979; Patton 1990; Bryman 1992; Hammersley 2008). Third, the use of mixed methods may also be based on the assumption that researchers will acquire a deeper understanding of the research subject (for example, Jick 1979; Hammersley 2008). By mixing methods to achieve knowledge creation, the researcher assumes that the analysis of complex issues, such as IB, requires methodological variety in order to mirror the phenomenon as completely as possible and thus to add to the existing knowledge base (Hurmerinta-Peltomäki and Nummela 2006). Interestingly, it seems that in our dataset of mixed-method case studies, mixed methods are not motivated by a single reason only, but are often used in order to achieve multiple purposes (Table 12.1). The ability to create new, additional knowledge was mentioned in all but two of the case studies. This deviates from the general distribution of the three purposes in the total dataset of 68 mixed-method studies, where validity was typically the main concern and the justification for a multimethod strategy (Hurmerinta-Peltomäki and Nummela 2006).

TWO STRATEGIES FOR MIXING METHODS IN CASE RESEARCH

In terms of research design, two alternative strategies for using mixed methods in case studies emerged from the dataset. First, in a number of studies the researcher(s) had decided to collect both quantitative and qualitative data for the study, with the qualitative data taking the form of case studies. Here the case or cases formed a separate, independent part of the study – in a way, a study inside a study (see Table 12.1). We call this a 'compartmentalized strategy'. The second strategy could be found in those articles in which the researcher(s) had decided to conduct a case study within which both quantitative and qualitative data were collected and analysed. In the latter strategy, mixed methods are applied within the case context, and the case(s) acted as a platform for their use. This is called here an 'aggregated strategy'. In the case studies we analysed, both strategies were equally represented.

These strategies are similar to the two 'nested arrangements' that Yin (1994 [2009], p. 63) outlines in his latest edition: 'case study within a survey' and 'survey within a case study'. However, we would argue that our labels are more informative and invite a broader array of quantitative methods to be utilized in case research. The nature and use of our two strategies are discussed in the following subsections.

Compartmentalized Strategy

Our dataset included six articles which had used case studies as an individual part of a larger study. The number of cases varied considerably between the studies, from a single case to a total of 34 cases. In all of these studies the methods were not actually mixed, but both quantitative and qualitative data were analysed within their own tradition, with rather traditional methods as well. With the exception of the study of Petersen and Welch (2000), in which both methods were equally represented, the studies were predominantly quantitative in nature. In other words, they were reported like quantitative studies, and the cases formed a supportive, but separate part of the study. However, in each of the studies the use of mixed methods brought added value, which we shall now describe with a few typical examples.

Nobeoka et al. (2002) aimed at studying whether Japanese suppliers are better off with more, or less, exclusive ties to customers, and why. They argued that a broader customer scope strategy should result in superior performance. To pursue their research question they conducted exploratory interviews among 11 suppliers to gain insight into the underlying issues. They used two of these interviews as illustrative cases. Exploratory interviews further informed the theory and stimulated hypothesis creation. This was followed by a more rigorous statistical analysis (correlation and regression analyses to test the hypotheses) based on a database that originally contained data on 348 major automotive component suppliers in Japan; a total of 125 suppliers were used for this study.

This study provides a typical example of a two-phase mixed-method strategy where the qualitative case study has an individual role with its own conclusions and inputs for the next, quantitative part of the research. First, the case study was used to gather information about the object (the structure and function of supplier–automaker relationships) and subject (the motives for serving multiple automotive customers) for the purpose of pre-understanding, and to inform the theory for hypothesis creation.

Second, the case study provided illustrative examples and more detailed knowledge to support the results of the quantitative part and explain them. Thus, the various methods – although having individual roles – were integrated and interpreted together in the later phases of the research process. Particularly because of this integration and joint interpretation, the 'value added' from the use of mixed methods increased considerably. Would the research outcome have been different, if only one part of the research project had been conducted? Definitely, mixing the two together – the qualitative case study and quantitative study – enabled this kind of research in the first place as the case study formed the basis for hypothesis creation by verifying the existence and relevance of the research phenomenon. It also increased the validity of the whole study and created knowledge that was confirmed by statistical analysis and explained by illustrative cases.

On the other hand, in Bradley and Moles's study (2001) the research process proceeded in a different order – the quantitative study preceded the qualitative case study. The purpose of their research was to examine the effects of direct and indirect economic currency exposure on a group of publicly listed, non-financial UK firms. The quantitative part of the research was based on two mail surveys (51%/629 companies at the first round) and the data were analysed by the use of statistical methods. Six firms from the original survey respondents were interviewed further (follow-up cases) in order to obtain further insights of the subject and validate the results. Although the data were collected sequentially and for different purposes (proposition testing and results validation), in the later phases of the research process the results were interpreted together. Structurally, this study resembles the one by Chetty and Wilson (2003), in which they followed up a quantitative study (mail survey to 300 CEOs to test hypotheses) with a single case to illustrate and deepen the results of the quantitative survey.

The first example we have described (Nobeoka et al. 2002) illustrates the traditional mixed-method research design, in which the case study acts as a pilot for the quantitative research phase; whereas the second (Bradley and Moles 2001), by using a case study as follow-up, breaks this conventional role for qualitative research as forming the initial exploratory phase. There are, however, other ways of combining methods. Petersen and Welch (2000) studied the Danish clothing and footwear industry to obtain a broad overview of the pattern of international development in companies and especially of the actual process of movement into international retail franchising. For the first objective, secondary data were analysed and after that a subgroup of nine companies with international franchising operations was selected to be sent a questionnaire by mail. Next, to complement the broad picture of the internationalization paths, representatives of two case companies were interviewed to obtain more in-depth information about the unique paths of these individual companies. In this study, the phases of the research process were built on each other, that is, the previous research stage was clearly needed for the next one. In the later phases of the research process the findings of both parts were analysed together. Here the secondary data sources, including different kinds of data, acted as a basis for the analysis and served as pre-understanding of the research subject, while interviews provided a more in-depth description of it.

Gassel and Pascha (2000) also made use of secondary data sources. They studied research alliances as a strategy in the Japanese biotechnology industry, with the aim of understanding whether cooperation meant 'milking partners' or a more interactive 'give-and-take process'. The study had a two-phase research design: in the first stage, a database containing worldwide alliances in biotechnology was explored. In the second stage, 17 case studies were carried out by conducting semi-structured interviews and employing standardized questionnaires. Thus, the study began with a quantitative approach followed by case studies employing both quantitative and qualitative methods. The cases provided greater depth of information concerning the motives and intensity of cooperative agreements. In this study the first research stage was not a prerequisite for the next one, but it provided a broader context against which the case results were analysed in later research phases.

Although the case(s) may seem to have a very independent role in a mixed-method study, the findings can converge in later phases, where the results are integrated and interpreted, and the independent role of the case disappears. Additionally, the isolation of the case may be reduced by setting a common research problem for the study as a whole; in other words, even if the case has its own research objectives, they may be strongly intertwined with the other parts of the study. However, this does not always hold. For example, in the study of Fahy et al. (2000) the linkage between the case study (34 cases in three countries for exploring the understanding of marketing terminology) and the quantitative part of the research project (1,619 responses in surveys) was very thin, as the only motive for using mixed methods was to validate the questionnaire.

These few examples indicate that two types of knowledge can emerge from case studies employing a compartmentalized strategy: knowledge which is crucial for the research process in question (for example, information about how to operationalize the key constructs) or knowledge which also has value in other contexts. In other words, this kind of strategy is appropriate, for example, in an exploratory study in which the population of interest is unknown or the theoretical constructs are either underdeveloped or applied in a novel empirical context. However, this could mean that mixed methods are not utilized to their full extent. In order to produce knowledge with a novel theoretical contribution beyond the scope of the inquiry in question – which is the broadest use of mixed methods – the case study needs to have objectives of its own and its findings should be integrated with the other parts of the study. The latter is very important, because separate research questions for the different parts of the study may also discourage the integration of findings (see Bryman 2007).

Aggregated Strategy

A researcher can also decide to apply mixed methods within a case or multiple cases. In these studies, the case provides a platform for the whole study. Our dataset included seven such studies. In line with the compartmentalized strategy described above, these studies also exhibited great variation in the number of cases, ranging from one to 36. Additionally, in these studies the quantitative methods assumed the dominant role and consequently the qualitative evidence could be thin and not reported in full when discussing the findings. However, compared to the compartmentalized strategy, the major difference is that in most of the aggregated case studies, different methods were intertwined with each other and a sequential order could be identified only in two studies. This strategy also seemed to offer greater versatility when it came to the research design, as the following examples demonstrate.

In the study of Fenwick et al. (2003), the objective was to ascertain whether psychic distance was an important factor in determining the locational choice of the firms and, if so, whether the British environment had proved to be as familiar to Australian companies as would be expected. Based on a literature review, a proposition was developed and tested with cases. Twenty case companies were selected and the CEO of each company was interviewed. The interviews were structured and based on a questionnaire with closed bivariate and rank-order questions. Additionally, some open questions were included in order to allow unexpected answers and perspectives to emerge. Due to the exploratory nature of the study, CEOs were encouraged to elaborate and exemplify their answers. The data were analysed in depth by looking for keywords and themes. Both types of data, whether quantitative or qualitative, were analysed qualitatively. In terms of research design, this study resembled the one by Glaister et al. (2003); both undertook parallel data collection and integrated findings. In order to test their propositions, Glaister et al. analysed international joint ventures with data from interviews, questionnaires and annual reports, among others.

However, parallel data collection and analysis are not necessary for this strategy, either. If the case is used as a platform for testing hypotheses, one may be able to identify sequential stages in the process. For example, Manev and Stevenson (2001) studied networks in a multinational enterprise and their study consisted of a two-stage research design. First, qualitative data were gathered through a review of archival data, interviews with key informants and observation. This stage concluded in a description of the formal structure and networks of the company, thus facilitating the later stages. Second, a questionnaire was administered to managers for collecting data on interactions within networks. Data were integrated and interpreted together in order to increase the validity of the results.

A similar type of sequential research design, with a very large dataset, can be found in the study of Testa et al. (2003). They tested their literature-based hypotheses in a large US-headquartered cruise line with over 10,000 employees from 90 countries in 14 large passenger ships. The hypotheses were related to the relationship between national culture, organizational culture and job satisfaction. In this study a single-case design was chosen in order to minimize the impact of intervening variables, but this also provided in-depth understanding of the phenomenon in its natural setting and allowed for cross-cultural sampling. In other words, the requirement for both case study and mixed-method approaches was built into the problem setting of the study. First, in line with a typical qualitative case study, data triangulation was used in multiple ways: evaluation of the organization's culture was undertaken through participant observation, a qualitative analysis of the organization structure, and interviews with employees at different levels of the organization's hierarchy. The qualitative data and analysis were done in order to verify the suitability of the case for hypothesis testing and the results were only briefly referred to in methodology section. Second, a total of 900 questionnaires were administered to non-managers, leading to 744 usable responses, and 700 questionnaires to managers, leading to 624 usable responses. This quantitative dataset was analysed with quantitative methods. Both stages in the research process served the same research problem, although each of the stages had subproblems of their own. However, it should be noted that our analysis of this study was particularly challenging because of the very concise reporting of the qualitative part.

Our dataset also included studies with less typical uses of mixed methods, such as studies combining rather exceptional types of data. For example, the study of Clark and Pugh (2001) combined archival data with interviews. They developed an 'international priority index' and examined factors affecting the sequence of foreign-country choices in a firm's internationalization process (Uppsala model). In deriving the priority index they gathered quantitative data from country-related databases.

Furthermore, they conducted interviews and collected archival information in 19 firms in order to understand their internationalization process and country choices. The result was the integration of the two types of data, producing new knowledge in the form of an index, and also more exact information regarding the model.

While Clark and Pugh diverge from the data sources most commonly used in aggregated mixed-method studies, we also found some alternatives to the typical unit of analysis or case. In the majority of studies we analysed the case was a company, but there were a few exceptions to this trend. In Lye and Hamilton (2001), the focus of the study was on 36 exporter–importer dyads. The purpose of their study was to contrast the perceptions of the importer and the exporter within the same international exchange relationship. Data were collected by semi-structured personal interviews that were supplemented by financial data, customer information, and export promotion materials, and different types of data were integrated and interpreted together.

To sum up, case studies with an aggregated strategy vary a great deal in terms of research design. However, it seems that this aggregated strategy may allow researchers to gain deeper understanding of the phenomenon under investigation, particularly when a single-case design is applied. Improved knowledge creation is mainly due to the integration of different types of data and joint interpretation of the findings. Usually this also provides the kind of theoretical contribution which extends beyond the specific research context or process. In other words, this kind of strategy is particularly appropriate for studies in nascent research fields where prior research on most of the phenomena is limited, or in more mature fields when a completely new perspective is needed to challenge the already institutionalized thinking of researchers.

DISCUSSION AND CONCLUSIONS

Mixed methods have been used for versatile purposes, such as to explore, describe and explain a phenomenon, and these are also valid aims for studies taking a case study approach. Among mixed-method studies in international business, we found that the case study approach has been applied in two alternative ways. Both strategies, compartmentalized and aggregated, share some similarities, such as the fact that the majority of them seem to follow the mainstream research process of mixing methods in IB: both types of data being analysed within their own methodological approach. However, there are also some differences, which make the challenges and the potential of both strategies somewhat dissimilar.

In studies based on a compartmentalized strategy, a sequential order of methods is used, by definition. In these studies the separation of the use of different methods seems to create a considerable challenge, as the two (or more) phases often also remain separate throughout the study. A good exception to this rule is the study of Petersen and Welch (2000), which nicely brings the different phases of the process together. Nevertheless, the division between the different phases of the study often results in underutilization of the cases, particularly if they are conducted prior to the quantitative part of the study. In the latter design, case studies are typically only utilized for improving validity and pre-understanding of the research context or the phenomenon in question. This leads to a vicious circle because when the value of cases is not recognized, they are not reported in full either. In many of the studies we analysed, they are reported only in a few pages and the methodological choices related to them are not reported at all (for an exception to the rule, see Glaister et al. 2003). In other words, although it might look favourable for cases to have an independent role in the process, it is not always beneficial in terms of their overall contribution. At best, when cases are conducted as a separate part of the study, they are utilized throughout the process, although their role may change during the process and in the end they will converge with the other parts of the study.

On the other hand, while many of the studies with an aggregated strategy also struggled to make full use of their qualitative findings it would seem that this strategy could potentially be more coherent than the compartmentalized strategy. Because of the parallel data collection and analysis processes, the different data and methods could intertwine rather seamlessly. Such a case study, incorporating a quantitative component, comes close to the traditional qualitative case study which blends multiple sources of evidence. For those researchers wanting to use such a strategy there are institutionalized procedures and 'rules' to follow which may contribute to a clear structure and better reporting of the case study methodology.

However, although these studies seem to have greater potential for creating novel knowledge, they also face some slightly different challenges. The tightly intertwined phases of the research process make it very difficult and lengthy to report. Additionally, when the results do not converge, as in the study of Gassel and Pascha (2000), researchers need to find a way to explain it. In their study, for example, explanations were found in validity-related issues, such as the up-to-dateness of the database used, rather than searching for insights emerging from a comparison of the qualitative and quantitative data. The number of cases also requires attention here: researchers should pay more attention to the level of saturation. Raising the number of cases, and thus broadening the scope of the study, is often done at the cost of depth of the findings. The threat is that the researcher achieves the advantages of neither qualitative nor quantitative research but remains somewhere in-between, providing less of a contribution than might have been possible with a single-method study.

In terms of ontology, the two strategies are not necessarily distinct. Although researchers using a compartmentalized strategy in a case study at first glance may seem to be 'purists', and those using an aggregated strategy pragmatists, this is not necessarily the case. Both strategies allow 'purist' and 'pragmatist' approaches, and either limited or broad use of mixed methods. In both strategies it is possible that the major impact of mixed methods is reflected either mainly in the research process (facilitation, validity check, that is, limited use) or also in the findings of the study (new knowledge creation, that is, broad use). In our opinion, both types of contribution are valuable and may be decisive for the success of the study. Therefore, they should also be given the credit they deserve and reported in full.

Actually, in the context of case studies, tight separation between qualitative and quantitative data and/or methods is sometimes not meaningful (see also Bergman 2008), what matters is the integration of types of data and analysis throughout the research process. In our opinion, at its best, the use of mixed methods will increase the weight put on conceptual development and interpretation of empirical findings. In line with Bryman (2007), we argue that a mixed-method study is successful when the end result is more than the sum of the individual quantitative and qualitative parts.

Mixed-method approaches seem to be a very trendy topic at the moment, but they are not always the optimal solution and the key to solving all research problems. On the contrary, in many studies it is much more appropriate to apply a single method in a rigorous manner. However, compared to other social sciences, discussion on mixed methods in business disciplines is much more recent and best practices on how to apply them are yet to be developed. At the same time, we have rather well-established techniques for conducting quantitative studies in international business, and even on the qualitative side – while still not as popular and accepted as quantitative IB research – research practices are under constant development, as this book indicates. Therefore, combining this knowledge with viewpoints from the literature on mixed methods would offer not only interesting insights, but also concrete tools for applying them. And as there still seems to be a divide between the quantitative and qualitative, mixed methods could at least partly act as a bridge between the two paradigms.

The increasing complexity of research problems in IB research, with both researchers and their research objects operating more and more on a worldwide basis, poses a challenge to research methods. The complexity of the research problems also became evident in the case studies in our dataset. As a methodological approach, mixed methods are in many ways an answer to this call by offering a means of improving research effectiveness.

Our investigation raises the question of what can be achieved by combining a case study approach with the use of mixed methods. The fact that we looked with an open mind and rather loose definitions at a set of studies opens attractive new avenues for researchers interested in methods. Although mixed methods, and especially case studies, have long been recognized as relevant methodological approaches, combining them has been rare. Recently, methodological textbooks have started to acknowledge mixed-method designs, but without going into depth into this discussion. This chapter has taken one step further by identifying two alternatives – compartmentalized and aggregated strategies – and has provided an in-depth view on the potential use, value and challenges of each of them. Examples of case studies illustrate this potential. However, the analysis in this chapter is based on a small number of case studies and therefore conclusions should be drawn very carefully. Nevertheless, we believe that increasing the number of studies would not change our conclusions significantly. Ultimately, our purpose in this chapter has been to indicate pathways which we hope others will now follow.

NOTE

1. For a detailed description of how the review was conducted, see Hurmerinta-Peltomäki and Nummela (2006).

REFERENCES

Bergman, M.M. (2008), 'The straw men of the qualitative–quantitative divide and their influence on mixed method research', in M.M. Bergman (ed.), *Advances in Mixed Methods Research*, Los Angeles, CA: Sage, pp. 11–21.

Bradley, K. and P. Moles (2001), 'The effects of exchange rate movements on non-financial UK firms', *International Business Review*, **10** (1), 51–69.

Brannen, J. (1992), 'Combining qualitative and quantitative approaches: an overview', in J. Brannen (ed.), *Mixing Methods: Qualitative and Quantitative Research*, Aldershot: Avebury, pp. 3–37.

Brannen, M.Y. (1996), 'Ethnographic international management research', in B.J. Punnett and O. Shenker (eds), *Handbook of International Management Research*, Cambridge, MA: Blackwell, pp. 115–43.

Bryman, A. (1992), 'Quantitative and qualitative research: further reflections on their integration', in J. Brannen (ed.), *Mixing Methods: Qualitative and Quantitative Research*, Aldershot: Avebury, pp. 57–78.

Bryman, A. (2007), 'Barriers to integrating quantitative and qualitative research', *Journal of Mixed Method Research*, **1** (1), 8–22.

Chetty, S. and H. Wilson (2003), 'Collaborating with competitors to acquire resources', *International Business Review*, **12** (1), 61–81.

Clark, T., H. Gospel and J. Montgomery (1999), 'Running on the spot? A review of twenty years of research on the management of human resources in comparative and international perspective', *International Journal of Human Resource Management*, **10** (3), 520–44.

Clark, T. and D.S. Pugh (2001), 'Foreign country priorities in the internationalization process: a measure and an exploratory test on British firms', *International Business Review*, **10** (3), 285–303.

Creswell, J.W. (1994), *Research Design: Qualitative and Quantitative Approaches*, Thousand Oaks, CA: Sage.

Creswell, J.W. (2008), *Educational Research: Planning, Conducting and Evaluating Quantitative and Qualitative Research*, 3rd edn, Upper Saddle Creek, NJ: Pearson Education.

Creswell, J.W., V.L. Plano Clark and A.L. Garrett (2008), 'Methodological issues in conducting mixed method research designs', in M.M. Bergman (ed.), *Advances in Mixed Methods Research*, Los Angeles, CA: Sage, pp. 66–83.

Denzin, N.K. (1978), *The Research Act: A Theoretical Introduction to Sociological Methods*, New York: McGraw-Hill.

Eisenhardt, K.M. (1989), 'Building theories from case study research', *Academy of Management Review*, **14** (4), 532–50.

Eisenhardt, K.M. and M.E. Graebner (2007), 'Theory building from cases: opportunities and challenges', *Academy of Management Journal*, **50** (1), 25–32.

Fahy, J., G. Hooley, T. Cox, J. Beracs, K. Fonfara and B. Snoj (2000), 'The development and impact of marketing capabilities in Central Europe', *Journal of International Business Studies*, **31** (1), 63–81.

Fenwick, M., R. Edwards and P.J. Buckley (2003), 'Is cultural similarity misleading? The experience of Australian manufacturers in Britain', *International Business Review*, **12** (3), 297–309.

Gassel, K. and W. Pascha (2000), 'Milking partners or symbiotic know-how enhancement? International versus national alliances in Japan's biotech industry', *International Business Review*, **9** (5), 625–40.

Ghauri, P. (2004), 'Designing and conducting case studies in international business research', in R. Marschan-Piekkari and C. Welch (eds), *Handbook of Qualitative Research Methods for International Business*, Cheltenham, UK and Northampton, MA, USA: Edward Elgar, pp. 109–24.

Glaister, K.W., R. Husan and P.J. Buckley (2003), 'Learning to manage international joint ventures', *International Business Review*, **12** (1), 83–108.

Hammersley, M. (2008), 'Troubles with triangulation', in M.M. Bergman (ed.), *Advances in Mixed Methods Research*, Los Angeles, CA: Sage, pp. 22–36.

Hurmerinta-Peltomäki, L. and N. Nummela (2004), 'First the sugar, then the eggs . . . Or the other way round? Mixing methods in international business research', in R. Marschan-Piekkari and C. Welch (eds), *Handbook of Qualitative Research Methods for International Business*, Cheltenham, UK and Northampton, MA, USA: Edward Elgar, pp. 162–80.

Hurmerinta-Peltomäki, L. and N. Nummela (2006), 'Mixed methods in international business research: a value-added perspective', *Management International Review*, **46** (4), 439–59.

Jick, T.D. (1979), 'Mixing qualitative and quantitative methods: triangulation in action', *Administrative Science Quarterly*, **24** (4), 602–11.

Lincoln, Y.S. and E.G. Guba (1985), *Naturalistic Inquiry*, Thousand Oaks, CA: Sage.

Lye, A. and R.T. Hamilton (2001), 'Importer perspectives on international exchange relationships', *International Business Review*, **10** (1), 109–28.

Manev, I.M. and W.B. Stevenson (2001), 'Nationality, cultural distance and expatriate status: effects on the managerial network in a multinational enterprise', *Journal of International Business Studies*, **32** (2), 285–303.

Markóczy, L. (2000), 'National culture and strategic change in belief formation', *Journal of International Business Studies*, **31** (3), 427–42.

Nobeoka, K., J.H. Dyer and A. Madhok (2002), 'The influence of customer scope on supplier learning and performance in the Japanese automobile industry', *Journal of International Business Studies*, **33** (4), 717–36.

Oxford Advanced Learner's Dictionary (*OALD*) (1989), Oxford: Oxford University Press.

Patton, M.Q. (1990), *Qualitative Evaluation and Research Methods*, Newbury Park, CA: Sage.

Petersen, B. and L.S. Welch (2000), 'International retailing operations: downstream entry and expansion via franchising', *International Business Review*, **9** (4), 479–96.

Peterson, R.B. (2004), 'Empirical research in international management: a critique and future agenda', in R. Marschan-Piekkari and C. Welch (eds), *Handbook of Qualitative Research Methods for International Business*, Cheltenham, UK and Northampton, MA, USA: Edward Elgar, pp. 25–55.

Piekkari, R., C. Welch and E. Paavilainen (2009), 'The case study as disciplinary convention: evidence from international business journals', *Organizational Research Methods*, **12** (3), 567–89.

Stake, R.E. (1995), *The Art of Case Study Research*, Thousand Oaks, CA: Sage.

Tashakkori, A. and C. Teddlie (1998), *Mixed Methodology: Combining Qualitative and Quantitative Approaches*, Thousand Oaks, CA: Sage.

Testa, M.R., S.L. Mueller and A.S. Thomas (2003), 'Cultural fit and job satisfaction in a global service environment', *Management International Review*, **43** (2), 129–48.

Yin, R.K. (1994), *Case Study Research: Design and Methods*, 2nd edn, Thousand Oaks, CA: Sage; 4th edn, 2009.

13. The single MNC as a research site

Jon Erland B. Lervik*

INTRODUCTION

In this chapter the options, potential and challenges of doing research in a single multinational corporation (MNC) are explored. The discussion includes research approaches that treat a single MNC as a case, studies that sample one or more cases within a single MNC, and other research designs that use a single MNC as a setting for conventional theory testing. The focus is on active research with *in situ* primary data collection, as opposed to research just based on secondary data. The objectives of this chapter are threefold. First, I examine the options by categorizing alternative research designs within a single MNC, which differ in their rationale, contributions and limitations. I distinguish single-N, small-N and large-N approaches within a single MNC. Second, a strong case is made for the potential of a combined approach that draws on both conventional theory testing and a case logic for the purpose of both developing and testing theory. I discuss advantages of a combined design, with examples from my own research, as well as that of others. Third, I discuss the challenges in collaborating closely with a single MNC. Although close involvement might 'compromise' the researcher's status as a neutral, disinterested outsider, it is rarely discussed in journal publications, where objective, distant research is espoused or assumed.

Research in international business (IB) may experience a type of liability of foreignness by doing research in foreign firms and locations. A central concern in our field is data access and quality. Whether one uses secondary panel data or engages in fieldwork, a host of challenges arises when collecting data in an international setting. The type and quality of sources and databases vary across countries, and data may be difficult to acquire from foreign settings. Doing primary data collection and fieldwork in an IB context involves the practical challenges of distance, with the time and costs involved in gaining access and gathering data. There are also differences in language, institutions and culture that require personal adjustment in doing research, and contextual sensitivity in interpreting findings (Marschan-Piekkari and Reis 2004; Noorderhaven 2004).

Focusing on a single MNC may be one strategy to minimize this liability of foreignness. A close relationship within an MNC can provide access to foreign fieldwork locations. The practical considerations of negotiating access and managing the logistics of foreign field research increase with the number of corporations involved. Also, doing research within one MNC can alleviate the hermeneutical problem of interpreting findings. In-depth knowledge of one MNC can increase sensitivity to the context and precision in interpretations.

A single MNC as a research site allows a wide variety of research designs that can contribute to developing and testing theory. We find considerable variation in methods, ranging from ethnographies to survey data, employed to examine research questions at different levels of analysis: from national context to subsidiaries, teams and individuals within MNCs. Studies thus contribute to research in various ways. Studies can highlight new or under-researched phenomena (Edwards 1998), or provide new lenses or interpretations (Kamoche 2000; Vaara et al. 2005). Focusing efforts on one MNC allows resource-demanding and complex research designs, such as longitudinal studies (Malnight 1996; Jones 2002), multilevel designs (for example, Kostova and Roth 2002) or analysis of interactions among subunits within an MNC (Hansen and Løvås 2004).

Following this introduction, the next section reviews and categorizes alternative approaches to research in a single MNC. In the third section, the case is made for a combined approach, where the context sensitivity of a case is combined with the rigour of conventional theory testing. In the fourth section I discuss the challenging balancing act that researchers face when collaborating closely with a single MNC. The final section concludes.

OPTIONS FOR USING A SINGLE MNC AS A RESEARCH SETTING

In this section current research is reviewed, and a categorization of research designs is developed. The review is somewhat coloured by my own research interests, and human resources (HR), organizational behaviour (OB) and organizational sociology are consequently over-represented. A single MNC can be the focus of a case study, or it can provide a convenient site for other types of research. The rationale, contribution and limitations of research in a single MNC vary. I here distinguish between single-N studies, small-N studies and large-N studies. Single-N case studies are useful for exploring new phenomena, and for exploring, illustrating and developing theory (Siggelkow 2007; Yin 2009). Small-N case studies balance depth and generalizability through systematic comparisons across cases (Ragin 1987) or identify patterns across cases, and can thus contribute to further rigorous theory development (Eisenhardt 1989). Large-N studies involve statistical testing of hypotheses. Large-N studies can either be framed as case studies, where the specifics and context of the MNC are incorporated in the analysis (Piekkari et al. 2009), or a single MNC is used as a convenient or suitable setting for empirical studies of phenomena at other levels of analysis (for example, Hofstede 1980).

Single-N Case Studies to Explore, Challenge, Illustrate or Develop Theory

Some case studies make a contribution by shedding new light on an important phenomenon. Edwards (1998) investigated a form of diffusion largely overlooked in the literature, namely reverse diffusion. He examined diffusion of labour practices from overseas to domestic plants in an MNC. This challenged prevailing conceptions of diffusion from the centre to the periphery, from MNC home country to host countries. Reverse diffusion can have significant implications for MNC capabilities and practices. This is an important anomaly that can nuance, for example, research on country-of-origin effects in MNCs (Noorderhaven and Harzing 2003).

Single case studies can illustrate conceptual frameworks and highlight the need for new lenses to explore phenomena. In Vaara et al.'s (2005) study of the power implications of corporate language policies, the role of the case was to illustrate a phenomenon and motivate the search for alternative lenses in order to move beyond episodic notions of power in MNCs. The virtue of the case is not its representativeness, but rather its uniqueness. The context of an international merger between a Swedish and a Finnish bank provided a unique setting where power implications of corporate language policies were highly salient.

Andrews and Chompusri (2001) provided a strong case for the influence of indigenous societal forces on corporate restructuring efforts in a foreign subsidiary. Their case study is an effective call to re-conceptualize the convergence/divergence dichotomy as a hybridization process at the 'corporate–societal interface' (Andrews and Chompusri 2001, p. 91). Again, this was an outlier case, examining corporate restructuring in a Thai subsidiary during the economic crisis in the region in 1997–98.

Siggelkow (2001) developed a new framework for analysing interdependencies within firms, using a longitudinal case of apparel maker Liz Claiborne as an empirical illustration. He examined relations between inertia in tightly coupled internal activities, from design, production and sourcing to marketing, and showed how an existing business model experienced increasingly poor external fit with environmental changes in the 1990s. One example of poor fit was how shorter planning horizons made sourcing from Asia more difficult, with its long lead and transportation times.

Malnight also investigated the evolution of single firms over time. He examined the emergence of network structure in Eli Lilly (Malnight 1995), and the European integration of Citibank's operations (Malnight 1996). His case studies contributed to process theory of MNC evolution over time through the interaction of strategic objectives, resource configurations and organizational configurations.

Single-N case studies can contribute to theory development and theory testing in various ways. Case studies can substantiate a new theory by demonstrating violations of existing theories. In studies of a single MNC it is more often about bringing in new factors or new perspectives. By describing phenomena that are new or under-researched, further theory development efforts are called for which may take the form of a new theoretical lens or theoretical framework. Single cases are especially suited to examining relations between multiple interdependent elements. Longitudinal case studies of single MNCs are clearly important in complementing variance theories developed from cross-sectional approaches.

Small-N Case Studies to Identify Patterns of Contrasts and Similarities

Goodall and Roberts (2003) examined the effort and work to maintain social networks and connectedness for international managers within an MNC. Taking three individuals within one company as case subjects, they track networks and connections. The key analytical approach here was to identify parallels and similarities across the cases.

Brannen (2004) also identified patterns and/or similarities across cases and locations in her study of Disneyland theme parks. She used a semiotic approach in analysing the transfer and re-contextualization of knowledge, artefacts and practices when Disney exported its Disneyland theme park concept to France and Japan. Examining several classes of 'transferred objects' in two host contexts, this approach allowed her to identify patterns and engage in generalized theorizing about the process of re-contextualization. Disney as a case is clearly an outlier concerning the centrality of narratives and myths in their theme parks. Brannen shows how the narratives are embedded in US myths and identities, and are thus less likely to 'travel' unimpeded.

On the other hand, Lervik and Lunnan (2004) emphasized the contrast and differences between observations in their study. Four mini-cases within one MNC show different implementation outcomes and illustrate contrasting theoretical lenses on diffusion and knowledge transfer in MNCs. They showed how a corporate management practice can be taken up in various ways, and how this corresponds with different theoretical lenses which conceptualize implementation outcomes such as conformity, transfer, translation or local modifications.

Firm boundaries that change over time create opportunities for interesting research, as Kristensen and Zeitlin (2005) found. They had previously studied autonomous firms in the dairy equipment industry that subsequently were merged into the same MNC. This spurred a book that examined the resource configurations, strategy and corporate governance of MNCs from the perspective of previously autonomous and locally embedded firms. In contrast to this example of independent companies being merged, Zeiss Germany was a single company that was split into two after the Second World War. This constituted a natural experiment on the influence of a market versus socialist economy on innovation in the two Zeiss companies. Kogut and Zander (2000) compared the innovation performance of the two Zeiss companies under socialist versus market economic regimes from 1950 to 1990. The historical circumstances of the iron curtain allowed a natural design for careful comparison.

The shared context of a single MNC influences the analytical strategies of comparative case studies. Comparative case studies typically entail sampling independent units for comparative analysis. Here, cases or occurrences have a shared context in the form of the same MNC, and the analysis benefits from both contextualizing the cases and analysing interdependencies. We find multilevel aspects in all the studies highlighted above. Kogut and Zander (2000) conducted a comparison of two companies with a shared corporate history. Brannen (2004) examined the fate of the same corporate artefacts in diverse subsidiary contexts. Lervik and Lunnan (2004) examined the same management practice in different subsidiaries. Kristensen and Zeitlin (2005) went one step further. In addition to comparing subsidiaries and subsidiary–HQ relations for each subsidiary case, they also incorporated interactions between subsidiaries and with the external context. Small-N studies within a single MNC provide an opportunity to go beyond assumed independence and pure comparison of subunit cases, to also examine relations across subunits and levels.

Large-N Studies to Test Theory

In the preceding subsection I reviewed typical or traditional case study approaches within a single MNC. In addition we find large-N studies conducted within single firms which employ quantitative and statistical approaches to test theory. These studies may be framed as case studies, or the single MNC setting may simply be a convenient or suitable research setting. Hofstede's (1980) work on national cultural dimensions is an example of the latter. His culture indices are based on survey data from 114,000 middle managers in IBM. The surveys were conducted for other purposes, and the cultural dimensions were later 'extracted' according to national differences in the surveys regarding value orientation and attitudes.

Other studies are more grounded in and sensitive to specific MNC contexts. Haas (2006b) examined the performance implications of team composition in an international aid agency. In-depth access to one MNC allowed her to examine central micro-foundations for effective knowledge sharing and knowledge transfer within MNCs (Foss and Pedersen 2004). Prior to conducting a survey, she conducted interviews and observations at several locations, and the context is presented and related to central constructs in the quantitative study.

Hansen and Løvås (2004) examined knowledge sharing between 121 software development projects in 41 different subsidiaries in eight countries. An elegant design allowed them to develop a complete matrix of knowledge sharing patterns between subunits and test hypotheses concerning the impact of distance, formal structure, informal relations and relatedness of competencies.

Kostova and Roth (2002) examined transfer of a total quality management (TQM) practice from headquarters to subsidiaries within one MNC. Close collaboration with corporate sponsors allowed in-depth access and detailed measurement of implementation and internalization of the practice in each subunit. The study also pioneered new constructs and tested new causal relationships concerning the impact of host-country institutional environments on MNC practice transfer.

Another area where studies from single multinationals have contributed to advancing new theories is intra-firm social capital. Tsai and Ghoshal (1998) examined relationships between social capital in inter-unit ties and patterns of resource exchange and product innovation within the company. Tsai (2000) included social capital theory and theories of strategic relatedness of firms' activities in order to explain the creation of new linkages between subunits within a multinational.

Comparing Approaches

In comparing the above approaches for field research in a single MNC, the following should be noted. First, there is a distinct boundary between case studies (single-*N*/small-*N*) and quantitative studies (large-*N*) not framed as case studies. The benefits derived from studying a single MNC seem to vary between the two groups. Furthermore, the logic of selecting an MNC is based on different considerations. Empirical research within one MNC encompasses major diversity. Examples shown above include both inductive and deductive approaches, aiming at developing or testing theory at various levels of analysis. In addition to 'traditional' case studies, single MNCs also provide a fertile context or empirical setting for deductive theory testing. Large-*N* studies are generally not framed as case studies. Such studies are rather framed as generalizable tests of theory, where a single MNC is chosen as a convenient or suitable context to test particular theories. Large-*N* studies focus on particular phenomena, and less on how richness of context influences focal phenomena.

The benefits derived from studying a single MNC differ between large-*N* and single-*N*/small-*N* studies. The appreciation of context and richness of data are the strengths of case studies (Yin 2009). Intimate knowledge of context provides additional lenses for interpretation. For large-*N* studies we might speculate that pragmatic considerations of research design and the logistics of data gathering are the prevalent benefits. Complex research designs involving several levels and multiple data sources may be easier to achieve with the consent and support of one corporation, as compared to working with several corporations.

The logic of sampling is also markedly different. Case studies often examine outlier companies or situations where certain attributes are augmented or especially salient (Siggelkow 2007), such as Malnight (1995) studying an 'ethnocentric' firm, Andrews and Chompusri (2001) looking at corporate restructuring in times of economic crisis or Vaara et al. (2005) examining a unique configuration of corporate and natural languages in two merging companies. MNCs in special circumstances provide an opportunity to throw light and theorize on phenomena that in other circumstances are less visible and salient. Large-*N* studies are more mixed. The orthodox argument is that a selected MNC should preferably be representative and typical of the larger population of MNCs. However, the scope of generalization can be made more explicit by acknowledging and theorizing about the unique aspects of the case. Theoretical arguments should be made only to the extent that findings are applicable to a larger population. Hansen and Haas (2001, p. 24) studied internal markets for knowledge in 'a company that had made an unusually large investment in an electronic document system'. It was thus not a typical or representative firm. However, their study examined a situation of information richness that an increasing number of organizations will be facing as more information is made available electronically. Lervik (2005) argued that his findings are applicable to other large MNCs, as there are no differences between the case company and the larger population that current literature identifies as theoretically relevant. However, findings may be less transferable to other practice domains such as finance or maintenance, as the study examined performance management, which can be said to be a 'culture-sensitive' practice.

POTENTIAL OF COMBINING CASE LOGIC WITH CONVENTIONAL THEORY TESTING

Here the merits of a combined approach are reviewed, drawing on the strengths of a case logic of small-N analysis as well as large-N approaches for testing theory. I illustrate the discussion with examples from my PhD research. The primary focus is on how qualitative fieldwork and the broader context of collaboration with one MNC can strengthen and improve a quantitative theory-testing study. This design conforms to the typical mixed-method approach in IB, in that it consists of an exploratory pre-study and a quantitative main study (Hurmerinta-Peltomäki and Nummela 2006). I acknowledge that it is only one way of doing mixed-methods research in IB (Hurmerinta-Peltomäki and Nummela 2004), but the benefits and synergies that I discuss are to a large extent transferable to other mixed-method approaches.

Mixed-method studies often involve several phases of conducting research in separate empirical settings. Case studies are often used as a pre-study to generate insights that can be tested by a subsequent quantitative approach. Zander (1991) generated theoretical insights about technology transfer from case studies in two MNCs, and propositions were tested on a large sample of technology transfers in Swedish MNCs (Kogut and Zander 1993). Kostova (1999) drew *inter alia* on interviews with subsidiary managers from many MNCs, whereas an empirical test was based on data transfer initiative in a single MNC (Kostova and Roth 2002). Haas (2006a) is an example of a combined approach within a single MNC. She conducted an interview study prior to administering a survey to project teams in a multinational aid organization.

The importance of exploratory studies for theory building is often emphasized. A combined approach within a single MNC yields added benefits, and below I discuss the following four aspects: (i) increased precision regarding the unit of analysis and relations between levels of analysis; (ii) strongly grounded theoretical concepts and well-tested measures; (iii) research design that rules out alternative explanations; and (iv) fieldwork providing a context for interpretation of results.

Increased Precision Regarding the Units of Analysis

Intra-organizational research in MNCs often examines subsidiary- or team-level phenomena. Important organizational entities within multinational enterprises are difficult to capture and define unambiguously. An emic approach based on in-depth knowledge of the research setting helps identify and capture the unit of analysis in a robust way.

International project teams or task forces are important in coordination and knowledge exchange in multinationals. Theorizing on teams requires an understanding of different types of teams, their nature, role and the effects of teams on the organization. Knowledge about what constitutes an effective cross-functional, co-located team may or may not be transferable to another type of team with a shorter life cycle, whose members are part-time or participating in multiple teams. Theorizing about teams might be based on a notion of 'generic' teams that does not exist in reality. To develop a grounded, middle-range theory may require explicit focus on a particular type of team, and data collection directed towards a particular type of team (Haas 2006a). Through a long-term presence within an MNC a researcher can develop an understanding of relevant team types. He/she can also develop background knowledge and establish networks in the organization in order to gain access and attain a suitable selection of relevant teams within that company.

Another case in point is the concept of a subsidiary. Focusing on subsidiaries as legal entities seems to be the default approach in IB research. A number of 'generalizing law' studies on intra-organizational studies in MNCs define subsidiaries as legal entities, with samples drawn from business directories (for example, Rosenzweig and Nohria 1994). However, focusing on subsidiaries as legal entities entails some weaknesses. Birkinshaw and Morrison (1996, p. 753) noted that a '"national subsidiary" is sometimes no more than a legal shell within which a variety of value-adding operations, all with different reporting lines, happen to reside'.

What is a suitable unit of analysis is contingent upon the research topic. Sampling legal subsidiaries is appropriate for studies on foreign direct investment and entry mode decisions related to ownership and risk issues (Gatignon and Anderson 1988). Subsidiaries are legal instruments used by owners to execute control and regulate their exposure to risk. However, legal entities may be less suitable units of analysis for understanding organizational issues related to work processes, value-adding activities within/across subsidiaries and coordination issues. Consider an example of a manager leading an organizational subunit encompassing several legal subsidiaries within a country, and/or daughter–daughter companies in third countries. Boundaries of managerial responsibility and legal own-ership do not always correspond closely, as illustrated with an example from my own research (Lervik 2005): a business area controller at one point spent most of his time simplifying the legal structure of operations in post-socialist countries in Europe. This was a legacy from previous acqui-sitions, and one important objective was to streamline the work processes related to consolidating the financial statements of various subsidiaries.

Sampling subsidiaries based on secondary data is restricted to captur-ing legal entities. Other approaches to get at operational entities include snowball sampling through inter-firm personal networks (for example, Björkman and Lu 2001), or using HQ informants to identify relevant sub-units for the research topic (for example, Andersson et al. 2001). Kostova (1996) examined one MNC, and her access and insight into the company facilitated a selection of units of analysis that suited the organizational structure of the company. She examined *inter alia* how subsidiary–HQ relations affected knowledge transfer, and she pointed out how national subsidiaries could contain multiple business units reporting to various divisions at HQ. Thus the concept of HQ–subsidiary relations was only meaningful at the individual business unit level, and not for the national subsidiary as a whole. This shows how conceptualizing organizational subsidiaries must be sensitive to the nature of the organization and the type of research analysis.

Lervik (2005) examined implementation of performance management practices in subsidiaries of one multinational. The practice was imple-mented in subunits at all organizational levels, from divisional level to subunits within national subunits. A central challenge was to establish a priori a list of subunits that was mutually exclusive and collectively exhaustive. This was achieved using several layers of organization charts from each division, and by checking ambiguities with HR directors in each division.

Conducting research within one MNC, where one engages in fieldwork over a longer time period, allows the researcher to develop sensitivity to issues of sampling and to identify the units of analysis. These meticulous, time-consuming tasks are more attainable, and with greater precision, when focusing efforts on one MNC.

Grounded Concepts and Tested Measures

Combined research approaches, aiming both at theory development and theory testing, can be the best of both worlds in terms of identify-ing concepts that are empirically grounded. Such an approach can throw light on important phenomena, which is then operationalized and carried into rigorous empirical tests. Specifically, when conducting research in one MNC, I shall point to three issues: (i) constructs that emerge from fieldwork; (ii) measurement instruments inspired by fieldwork; and (iii) improvement of measurement instruments in collaboration with company representatives.

First, in my own research I examined adoption of organizational practices in MNC subsidiaries, and through qualitative fieldwork identified the importance of introducing practices and routines to be embedded and to become interconnected within existing structures and systems in the subunit context (for example, Lervik and Lunnan 2004). I coined the term 'integration' and developed a theoretical model to account for variations among subsidiaries in how they adopted and integrated corporate organizational practices (Lervik 2005).

The next step is then to structure and test constructs. In my research, not only was the construct itself inspired by fieldwork observations, but many of the items were also derived from fieldwork observations. Kostova and Roth (2002) utilized secondary data from a corporate chairman's award to identify corporate criteria for successful implementation. In this way the survey instrument captured implementation in a way that was specifically relevant to the enterprise's objectives, while also comprehensible to survey recipients.

Third, fieldwork in one MNC often entails a research partnership with corporate personnel. They are insiders who can help clarify and improve interview guides and survey instruments. There are, of course, difficult issues to consider, such as avoiding too much interference in the direction of the research. On the positive side, company personnel may help to clarify ambiguous wording and avoid use of questions and terminology which do not fit the corporate context of the research. One firm used the term 'sectors' instead of 'divisions', so if we had asked survey questions about the divisions' role, their interaction with division HQ and so on, the answers might have been random or difficult to interpret.

Elimination of Alternative Explanations and Strong Tests of Theory

When examining intra-organizational phenomena, testing theory yields some benefits from the homogeneity of observations selected from one MNC. In my PhD work (Lervik 2005), I examined subsidiary-related factors that affected adoption of organizational practices. Previous research had identified that adoption patterns are influenced by type of practice (for example, whether it is an HR or a finance practice) and characteristics of the MNC (home country, global versus multi-domestic strategy). By testing the research model in one MNC that was introducing a particular organizational practice, variation in practices and company-specific factors were ruled out as an influence on the dependent variables in this study.

An empirical test within a homogeneous sample (meaning subsidiaries within one MNC) reduces residual error and improves the power of the statistical tests (Calder et al. 1982). When the purpose of a study is to test new theoretical propositions (Calder et al. 1981), it is appropriate to choose a research setting that provides a homogeneous sample and minimizes variation on non-theoretical variables. A traditional concern in statistical approaches is the use of a representative sample to ensure external validity (Lynch 1999). However, it is important to distinguish between different types of research objectives. If the objective is to generalize the effects of a particular treatment on a population, the research setting and sampling should accurately reflect the real-world phenomenon and population one seeks to generalize (so-called 'correspondence procedures', Calder et al. 1982). However, if the purpose is to test a general theory, a homogeneous sample (on non-theoretical variables) may be more important than ensuring correspondence. Drawing on methodological insights from Ilgen (1986) and Sackett and Larsen (1990, p. 435), Schulze et al. (2001, p. 106) noted:

> representativeness is less of a concern when the sample is prototypical of the relevant population and the research question concerns whether hypothesized effects can occur as opposed to determining the frequency or relative strength of the observed effects.

In a Popperian view, progress and cumulative knowledge are achieved through developing falsifiable propositions, and subjecting them to strong empirical tests where propositions are likely to be falsified. The statistical power of a test increases when tested on a homogeneous sample where random error variance is reduced. A general theoretical model on the transfer of organizational practices is expected to hold valid for any sub-sample of the specified population. In my PhD research, the selected MNC provided a setting with ample variation in subsidiary-related variables of theoretical interest in my model (national culture, organizational context and change management). At the same time, variation was reduced for other factors that are also known to affect transfer, but which were not addressed in this study. Central factors that are likely to affect the model or increase residual errors are company-related factors such as MNC home country (Rosenzweig and Nohria 1994; Child et al. 2000; Geppert et al. 2003) or the company's degree of international experience (Björkman and Lu 2001). A study of one specific organizational practice may reduce representativeness, but also reduces residual variation in practice-related factors such as knowledge characteristics. In other words, the factors influencing practice transfer are expected to be valid for the whole population of MNCs. Thus, if the setting (a single MNC) is typical of the global population of large MNCs, testing the theory in that subpopulation is a valid and useful contribution.

Fieldwork Provides a Context for Interpretation

The final observation is that a prolonged contact through fieldwork and interaction with a company provides a source of interpretations and insights that may complement statistical findings. Other studies remind us of the importance of an interpretative perspective. The central idea in the hermeneutic circle is that of the interplay between interpretation of elements and the whole. Noorderhaven (2004) reported an example where positivist theories of causal relations fall short of explaining or understanding what goes on in a foreign context. Henry (1991; cited in Noorderhaven 2004) described the introduction of a highly detailed manual to formalize work processes and decision making in the national drinking water company in Togo. Our established administrative theories suggest that extreme formalization of tasks would reduce autonomy, efficiency and motivation of employees in the organization. The formalization initiative is, however, highlighted by the World Bank as an example of 'best practice'. According to Henry, the use of manuals increases rather than decreases the employees' independence, as they can rely less on asking supervisors for advice in ambiguous situations.

Another telling example is from the early post-socialist period in Hungary, when managers adopted an 'open-door policy' in pursuit of modern management ideas intended to signify progress and change (Bye 1994). However, many employees interpreted the physical manifestation of open doors from the perspective of their historical life world and saw this as evidence of managers' intensified intent to monitor and control employees. In my own research, the findings from the quantitative study are complemented by findings and contextual understanding derived from various fieldwork methods such as interviews, document analysis and participant observation. Findings could be illustrated with qualitative examples, and unexpected results could be explored further in the qualitative field data.

In this section the case was made for a combined approach in order to exploit the potential for developing and testing theory within a single MNC. This presupposes in-depth access and close involvement with the MNC. This close involvement also entails some challenges for the researcher in order to balance roles *vis-à-vis* a case company and informants.

CHALLENGES IN COLLABORATING WITH A SINGLE MNC

Here I address the challenges and balancing acts involved when researchers become closely involved with their field of study. Most in-depth fieldwork in MNCs depends on close relations with corporate sponsors, particularly when researching a single MNC. Often the relationship takes on the character of collaboration. In formal and/or long-term collaboration the identity of the researcher changes from being an organizational outsider to something in between an insider and an outsider. This aspect of research collaboration is often glossed over in journal publications, where the 'ideal' is a disinterested and objective research approach. Collaborative research can entail practitioner involvement in setting the research agenda, initiating a joint project with shared objectives, or building a research team consisting of both insiders and outsiders (Louis and Bartunek 1992; Van de Ven and Johnson 2006). I focus here on collaborative research with the explicit purpose of generating general knowledge for the research community. I do not address action research approaches that focus primarily on improvement of a local situation (Greenwood and Levin 1998, p. 4), such as participatory rural appraisal (Chambers 1994), or Freire's liberation theology (2000).

Let me now return to my own PhD work and present the research setting in more detail, in order to use this as a sounding board for discussing the role of the researcher in collaborative research. Presenting an outlier case can often be effective in highlighting a phenomenon, even though it may not be representative or 'typical' (Siggelkow 2007). I was part of a research team working with a Fortune 100 MNC over a period of five years. The research project followed a corporate change initiative which sought to implement performance management globally in the MNC. The research project had dual objectives: to contribute to generalizable academic knowledge and to contribute to ongoing change management efforts in the firm. Research methods included participant observation, interviews, document analysis, and annual employee surveys. I was one of two PhD candidates involved in the project, the other being a previous employee of the company. Twenty-five per cent of our time was assigned to the corporate HR department, with office space at corporate HQ. This was to ensure close interaction between the researchers and the corporation, facilitate in-depth access, and enhance learning opportunities for the corporation and the researchers.

Our contribution to the ongoing change management efforts in the company involved four activities: (i) evaluating the change initiative through annual employee surveys; (ii) acting as a discussion partner for

corporate HR; (iii) providing formative feedback in all corporate learning networks; and (iv) contributing to development projects, for example,
designing new management tools and processes. The research group was
deeply involved in the field of study, and to some extent became participants in ongoing change processes. From this I derive three balancing acts
that researchers face in collaborative research: (a) balancing proximity
versus distance in the researcher's orientation to the field of study and
the worldview of insiders; (b) being an observer versus actor in the system
under study; and (c) remaining neutral versus being (perceived as) a
'headquarters' man'.

Proximity/Distance

Balancing proximity and distance is a recurring conflict in fieldwork
research (Kalleberg 1996; Hennestad 1999). Anthropologists are warned
against the Scylla and Charybdis of 'going native' or being too 'ethnocentric' (Gold 1958). The pressures for proximity – becoming part of and
buying into the worldviews of insiders in the system under study – may
be quite strong when collaborating closely with a single MNC. In-depth
access to an MNC is often based on social ties, trust and shared understanding between researchers and corporate sponsors. Moreover, sponsors have a stake in the research, and the research is often expected to be
useful or to contribute to the sponsors.

Recommendations for collaborative research include doing research
that is relevant and that produces knowledge for practitioners (Van de
Ven and Johnson 2006). Early involvement of practitioners in defining the
research agenda can increase commitment and support for research (Van
de Ven and Poole 1990). A risk is that the idiosyncrasies of one organization may guide the research questions and conceptualizations too much.
As a PhD student on the project, I sometimes identified too much with
the problems and perspectives of practitioners, and some initial research
questions in my PhD project reflected that I was too eager to make their
problems my own. Supervisors, peers or members of academic advisory
boards, who are less embedded in the field of study, may thus be important
to achieve distance and balance.

Actor/Observer

Knowledge useful to practitioners not only hinges on the relevant research
questions, but also depends on collaborative processes of knowledge
generation and dissemination. A useful model is trailing research, which
'integrates formative and summative evaluation in a planned learning

process coupled with producing knowledge for the scientific community' (Finne et al. 1995, p. 11). We furnished the company with feedback and support through several activities. One arena where the roles intertwined most clearly took place when we participated in workshops and corporate learning networks. We provided evaluation and feedback on the implementation process as input to discussions in the learning networks. This gave us a legitimate role in the workshops as participant observers. As such, there was a synergy in that acting as a consultant provided space for doing ethnography in the same setting. However, switching between the roles of observation and note taking, and simultaneously engaging in discussions, was a difficult balancing act. We experimented and assumed different roles in different networks; sometimes the consultancy role became dominant, while in other settings we were just observers.

In other participant observation activities we stressed our role as passive observers who were there in order to learn, for example, in observing the annual HR review meetings of various divisions. However, during lunch breaks and through informal interactions before and after meetings, negotiated roles were often turned around, when managers asked for our perspectives and expert opinions.

It should also be noted that data gathering itself is also intervention. Annual surveys supported HQ monitoring of the process and sent signals to employees. Asking questions in an interview can elicit cognitive and affective processes among informants. According to Lundin and Wirdenius (1990), we need to 'recognize that research is interaction and act accordingly' (p. 140).

In general, the ambiguous roles of observer versus actor required reflection on researchers' influence on the field of study. Welch et al. (2002) noted that researchers sometimes need to juggle the roles as academics and consultants in feedback processes. The feedback of intermediate research results to informants is valuable for improving accuracy and additional interpretations (Hammersley and Atkinson 1995). Feedback processes may also take on the nature of consultancy for the firm, providing fresh perspectives and recommendations on managerial processes. Feedback at the end of a research project might not be of any consequence, whereas in our project feedback and interaction were central elements throughout.

Various ways of compartmentalizing research and consulting may ensure research validity: separation in time by providing feedback after the primary research has been completed; or separation in space by acting as adviser in some parts of the organization, while collecting data in others. Our role as advisers was most prominent at headquarters, whereas the researcher role was stressed in contact with peripheral units.

Sometimes the roles of actor and observer cannot be compartmentalized. Members of our research team were actors in corporate learning networks, such networks being an important source of insights and inspiration. An empirical argument stating that 'it is so because we have observed it' is weakened when observations arise from a setting where we were actors and observers at the same time. Thus in writing and theorizing 'one needs to convince the reader that the conceptual argument is plausible' (Siggelkow 2007, p. 23), and not lean on empirical observations as 'proof'. Thus, in publications we sometimes did 'closet qualitative research' (Sutton 1997) as we did not always present and analyse the empirical sources of insights and inspiration.

Neutral Outsider/Headquarters' Man

The asymmetry in our relationship with our HQ sponsors and various other units as research sites highlights another pitfall of MNC research: being (perceived as) a headquarters' man. Welch et al. (2002) pointed out that since fieldwork is mostly done with the support of corporate sponsors, researchers are sometimes perceived as HQ spies by subsidiary managers. This is something I also experienced during interviews. One informant encouraged me to convey his strongly felt views on an unrelated topic to central decision makers, while another explicitly stated that he did not want to share his personal opinions on a sensitive issue with a messenger. What he had to say, he would communicate directly to HQ.

Our role meant we were 'headquarters' men' to some extent. We had a role in providing information to HQ about other parts of the organization. This entailed ethical considerations regarding presentation and information sharing; about how we presented ourselves in fieldwork encounters concerning our objectives, motives, obligations and loyalties. It also entailed a balancing act in sifting and concealing information to protect informants' confidentiality while at the same time providing useful information to HQ. Clarifying with HQ what we could and could not provide was also important at various stages.

This role of providing HQ with 'intelligence' was most explicit concerning annual surveys that we conducted to assess implementation of the corporate change initiative. Surveys performed several roles: (i) gathering data for researchers, (ii) monitoring for corporate HQ, and (iii) signalling to employees that corporate HQ were serious about getting this process implemented globally.

While participating in learning networks, our affiliations and obligations could be observed and questioned. By providing feedback, interpretations and recommendations, we sometimes 'took sides' on contested issues where, for example, HQ staff and divisions might have different views. We were not partisan in the sense of always supporting our sponsors. Generally we aimed to provide 'objective' research-based findings and reflections. However, some situations required that we relinquish the neutral outsider role and disclose our position on, for example, contested political issues within the organization. At the same time it required diplomacy. A maxim, from which we benefited, was that positive feedback could be given publicly, while negative feedback should be anonymized and provided in private.

CONCLUSION

A central point in this chapter is to develop a more open notion of what a case is in a single MNC as a research setting. We tend to assume that in a study of a single MNC the case is automatically the firm. The first part of the chapter sought to show the potential in a single MNC as a research site for studying also other units of analysis, for example, subsidiaries, cross-national teams, or distributed innovation projects. The MNC in its entirety can be the case but the unit of analysis (the case) can also be embedded within the MNC, or the MNC is turned into a fruitful research context. In this chapter, I have identified single-N, small-N and large-N studies with distinct approaches and contributions to international management research. Hopefully this review can raise awareness of a broader palette of research options and facilitate design choices that support various research objectives in single MNC projects.

Further, a strong case has been made for the benefits of combining the case logic with conventional quantitative tests. Conventional theory testing can be complemented with a case logic that views a phenomenon in its context. This can increase both the internal and external validity of a study. The reverse is also true: case studies of single MNCs can be followed up by theory testing, extending and validating insights from case studies. In-depth contextual knowledge can contribute to developing better theory, rigorous constructs and measures. The setting also allows a dialogue between quantitative and qualitative data in the interpretation of results.

Fieldwork in a multinational setting is difficult and resource demanding. Collaborating with a single MNC may reduce some of these barriers, but introduce issues of managing the research collaboration. I conclude this chapter by drawing attention to risks that are accentuated when doing research in or with a single MNC. Close collaboration with a single MNC might 'compromise' the researcher's status as a neutral, disinterested outsider. Close involvement with a single MNC requires careful reflection, especially about the researcher's influence on the field of study, validity of results, who benefits from the research and other issues regarding research ethics. This aspect of research collaboration is often glossed over in journal publications, where objective, distant research is espoused or assumed.

NOTE

* I would like to thank Rolv Petter Amdam, Randi Lunnan and the editors Rebecca Piekkari and Catherine Welch for helpful and thoughtful comments on earlier versions of this chapter.

REFERENCES

Andersson, U., M. Forsgren and U. Holm (2001), 'Subsidiary embeddedness and competence development in MNCs: a multilevel analysis', *Organization Studies*, **22** (6), 1013–34.

Andrews, T.G. and N. Chompusri (2001), 'Lessons in "cross-vergence": restructuring the Thai subsidiary corporation', *Journal of International Business Studies*, **32** (1), 77–93.

Birkinshaw, J. and A.J. Morrison (1996), 'Configurations of strategy and structure in subsidiaries of multinational corporations', *Journal of International Business Studies*, **26** (4), 729–53.

Björkman, I. and Y. Lu (2001), 'Institutionalization and bargaining power explanations of HRM practices in joint ventures: the case of Chinese–Western joint ventures', *Organization Studies*, **22** (3), 491–512.

Brannen, M.Y. (2004), 'When Mickey loses face: recontextualization, semantic fit, and the semiotics of foreignness', *Academy of Management Review*, **29** (4), 593–616.

Bye, R. (1994), 'Fra retribialisering til byråkratisering: en ungarsk bedriftsorganisasjon i forandring' ['From re-tribalization to bureaucratization: a changing Hungarian enterprise'], MSc thesis, Norwegian University of Science and Technology.

Calder, B.J., L.W. Phillips and A.M. Tybout (1981), 'Designing research for application', *Journal of Consumer Research*, **8** (September), 197–207.

Calder, B.J., L.W. Phillips and A.M. Tybout (1982), 'The concept of external validity', *Journal of Consumer Research*, **9** (December), 240–43.

Chambers, R. (1994), 'The origins and practice of participatory rural appraisal', *World Development*, **22** (7), 953–69.

Child, J., D. Faulkner and R. Pitkethly (2000), 'Foreign direct investment in the UK 1985–1994: the impact on domestic management practice', *Journal of Management Studies*, **37** (1), 141–66.

Edwards, T. (1998), 'Multinationals, labour management and the process of reverse diffusion: a case study', *International Journal of Human Resource Management*, **9** (4), 696–709.

Eisenhardt, K.M. (1989), 'Building theory from case study research', *Academy of Management Review*, **14** (4), 532–50.

Finne, H., M. Levin and T. Nilssen (1995), 'Trailing research: a model for useful program evaluation', *Evaluation*, **1** (1), 11–31.

Foss, N.J. and T. Pedersen (2004), 'Organizing knowledge processes in the multinational corporation: an introduction', *Journal of International Business Studies*, **35** (5), 340–49.

Freire, P. (2000), *Pedagogy of the Oppressed*, New York: Continuum.

Gatignon, H. and E. Anderson (1988), 'The multinational corporation's degree of control over foreign subsidiaries: an empirical test of a transaction cost explanation', *Journal of Law, Economics, and Organization*, **4** (2), 305–36.

Geppert, M., D. Matten and K. Williams (2003), 'Change management in MNCs: how global convergence intertwines with national diversities', *Human Relations*, **56** (7), 807–38.

Gold, R. (1958), 'Roles in sociological field observations', *Social Forces*, **36** (3), 217–23.

Goodall, K. and J. Roberts (2003), 'Repairing managerial knowledge-ability over distance', *Organization Studies*, **24** (7), 1153–75.

Greenwood, D.J. and M. Levin (1998), *Introduction to Action Research: Social Research for Social Change*, Thousand Oaks, CA: Sage.

Haas, M.R. (2006a), 'Acquiring and applying knowledge in transnational teams: the roles of cosmopolitans and locals', *Organization Science*, **17** (3), 367–84.

Haas, M.R. (2006b), 'Knowledge gathering, team capabilities, and project performance in challenging work environments', *Management Science*, **52** (8), 1170–84.

Hammersley, M. and P. Atkinson (1995), *Ethnography: Principles in Practice*, Abingdon, UK and New York: Routledge.

Hansen, M.T. and M.R. Haas (2001), 'Competing for attention in knowledge markets: electronic document dissemination in a management consulting company', *Administrative Science Quarterly*, **46** (1), 1–28.

Hansen, M.T. and B. Løvås (2004), 'How do multinational companies leverage technological competencies? Moving from single to interdependent explanations', *Strategic Management Journal*, **25** (8–9), 801–22.

Hennestad, B.W. (1999), 'Kritiske valg i forskning på organisasjonsendringer' [Critical choices in research on organizational change], in K. Friedman and J. Olaisen (eds), *Underveis til Fremtiden: Kunnskapsledelse i Teori og Praksis* [On the Way to the Future: Knowledge Management in Theory and Practice], Oslo: Fagbokforlaget, pp. 71–89.

Hofstede, G. (1980), *Culture's Consequences: International Differences in Work-related Values*, Beverly Hills, CA: Sage.

Hurmerinta-Peltomäki, L. and N. Nummela (2004), 'First the sugar, then the eggs ... Or the other way round? Mixing methods in international business research', in R. Marschan-Piekkari and C. Welch (eds), *Handbook of Qualitative Research Methods for International Business*, Cheltenham, UK and Northampton, MA, USA: Edward Elgar, pp. 162–80.

Hurmerinta-Peltomäki, L. and N. Nummela (2006), 'Mixed methods in international business research: a value-added perspective', *Management International Review*, **46** (4), 439–59.

Ilgen, D.R. (1986), 'Laboratory research: a question of when, not if', in E.A. Locke (ed.), *Generalizing from Laboratory to Field Settings*, Lexington, MA: Heath, pp. 257–67.

Jones, G. (2002), 'Control, performance, and knowledge transfers in large multinationals: unilever in the United States, 1945–1980', *Business History Review*, **76** (3), 435–78.

Kalleberg, R. (1996), 'Forord: feltmetodikk, forskningsopplegg og vitenskapsteori' [Foreword: field study methodology research design and the Theory of Science], in M. Hammersley and P. Atkinson (eds), *Feltmetodikk* [Field Study Methodology], Oslo: ad Notam, pp. 5–28.

Kamoche, K. (2000), 'Developing managers: the functional, the symbolic, the sacred and the profane', *Organization Studies*, **21** (4), 747–74.

Kogut, B. and U. Zander (1993), 'Knowledge of the firm and the evolutionary theory of the multinational corporation', *Journal of International Business Studies*, **24** (4), 625–46.

Kogut, B. and U. Zander (2000), 'Did socialism fail to innovate? A natural experiment of the two Zeiss companies', *American Sociological Review*, **65** (2), 169–90.

Kostova, T. (1996), 'Success of the transnational transfer of organizational practices within multinational companies', PhD thesis, University of Minnesota.

Kostova, T. (1999), 'Transnational transfer of strategic organizational practices: a contextual perspective', *Academy of Management Review*, **24** (2), 308–24.

Kostova, T. and K. Roth (2002), 'Adoption of an organizational practice by subsidiaries of multinational corporations: institutional and relational effects', *Academy of Management Journal*, **45** (1), 215–33.

Kristensen, P.H. and J. Zeitlin (2005), *Local Players in Global Games*, Oxford: Oxford University Press.

Lervik, J.E. and R. Lunnan (2004), 'Contrasting perspectives on the diffusion of management knowledge: performance management in a Norwegian multinational', *Management Learning*, **35** (3), 287–302.

Lervik, J.E.B. (2005), 'Managing matters: transfer of organizational practices in MNC subsidiaries', PhD thesis, Norwegian School of Management BI.

Louis, M. and J. Bartunek (1992), 'Insider/outsider research teams: collaboration across diverse perspectives', *Journal of Management Inquiry*, **1** (2), 101–10.

Lundin, R.A. and H. Wirdenius (1990), 'Interactive research', *Scandinavian Journal of Management*, **6** (2), 125–52.

Lynch, J.G.J. (1999), 'Theory and external validity', *Journal of Academy of Marketing Science*, **27** (3), 367–76.

Malnight, T.W. (1995), 'Globalization of an ethnocentric firm: an evolutionary perspective', *Strategic Management Journal*, **16** (2), 119–41.

Malnight, T.W. (1996), 'The transition from decentralized to network-based MNC structures', *Journal of International Business Studies*, **27** (1), 43–65.

Marschan-Piekkari, R. and C. Reis (2004), 'Language and languages in cross-cultural interviewing', in R. Marschan-Piekkari and C. Welch (eds), *Handbook of Qualitative Research in International Business*, Cheltenham, UK and Northampton, MA, USA: Edward Elgar, pp. 224–43.

Noorderhaven, N.G. (2004), 'Hermeneutic methodology and international business research', in R. Marschan-Piekkari and C. Welch (eds), *Handbook of Qualitative Research Methods for International Business*, Cheltenham, UK and Northampton, MA, USA: Edward Elgar, pp. 84–106.

Noorderhaven, N.G. and A.-W. Harzing (2003), 'The "country-of-origin effect" in multinational corporations: sources, mechanisms and moderating conditions', *Management International Review*, **43** (2), 47–66.

Piekkari, R., C. Welch and E. Paavilainen (2009), 'The case study as disciplinary convention: evidence from international business journals', *Organizational Research Methods*, **12** (3), 567–89.

Ragin, C.C. (1987), *The Comparative Method: Moving Beyond Qualitative and Quantitative Strategies*, Berkeley and Los Angeles, CA: University of California Press.

Rosenzweig, P.M. and N. Nohria (1994), 'Influences on human resource management practices in multinational corporations', *Journal of International Business Studies*, **25** (2), 229–51.

Sackett, P.R. and J.R.J. Larsen (1990), 'Research strategies and tactics in industrial organization psychology', in M.D. Dunnette and L.M. Hough (eds), *Handbook of Industrial and Organizational Psychology*, Vol. 1, 2nd edn, Palo Alto, CA: Consulting Pscyhologists Press, pp. 419–89.

Schulze, W.S., M.H. Lubatkin, R.N. Dino and A.K. Buchholtz (2001), 'Agency relationships in family firms: theory and evidence', *Organization Science*, **12** (2), 99–116.

Siggelkow, N. (2001), 'Change in the presence of fit: the rise, the fall, and the renaissance of Liz Claiborne', *Academy of Management Journal*, **44** (4), 838–57.

Siggelkow, N. (2007), 'Persuasion with case studies', *Academy of Management Journal*, **50** (1), 20–24.

Sutton, R.I. (1997), 'The virtues of closet qualitative research', *Organization Science*, **8** (1), 97–106.

Tsai, W. (2000), 'Social capital, strategic relatedness and the formation of intra-organizational linkages', *Strategic Management Journal*, **21** (9), 925–39.

Tsai, W. and S. Ghoshal (1998), 'Social capital and value creation: the role of intrafirm networks', *Academy of Management Journal*, **41** (4), 464–76.

Vaara, E., J. Tienari, R. Piekkari and R. Säntti (2005), 'Language and the circuits of power in a merging multinational corporation', *Journal of Management Studies*, **42** (3), 595–623.

Van de Ven, A.H. and P.E. Johnson (2006), 'Knowledge for theory and practice', *Academy of Management Review*, **31** (4), 802–21.

Van de Ven, A.H. and M.S. Poole (1990), 'Methods for studying innovation development in the Minnesota Innovation Research Program', *Organization Science*, **1** (3), 313–35.

Welch, C., R. Marschan-Piekkari, H. Penttinen and M. Tahvanainen (2002), 'Corporate elites as informants in qualitative international business research', *International Business Review*, **11** (5), 611–28.

Yin, R.K. (2009), *Case Study Research: Design and Methods*, 4th edn, Thousand Oaks, CA: Sage.

Zander, U. (1991), 'Exploiting a technological edge: voluntary and involuntary dissemination of technology', PhD thesis, Stockholm School of Economics.

14. When truth is the daughter of time: longitudinal case studies in international business research

Susanne Blazejewski

INTRODUCTION

Longitudinal case studies are still a 'minority taste' (Pettigrew 1995, p. 115) in the social sciences and even more so in the field of international business (IB) research (Piekkari et al. 2009). A quick search in a comprehensive business studies database (EBSCO) reveals only 19 entries over a 10-year period (1998–2008). A volume-by-volume analysis of the *Journal of International Business Studies* from 2003 to 2007 results in four longitudinal case studies out of a total number of 94 empirical papers. It has been argued that the limited application of the longitudinal case study approach relates to the substantial practical challenges, including publication delays, involved in conducting in-depth research over an extended period of time and across multiple countries (Leonard-Barton 1990; Pettigrew 1995; Pettigrew et al. 2001). In addition, the 'pressure for quantification' (Jones and Khanna 2006, p. 454) seems to be particularly strong in IB research, discouraging deeper engagement with historical data or long-term field projects. In my view, the lack of longitudinal approaches in IB is also due to the long-term focus of the field on questions regarding spatial (for example, cross-country comparisons) rather than temporal patterns. According to Mainela and Puhakka (2007), processual research is currently expanding in IB but dynamic models and process-oriented research methodologies are still under-represented. Therefore, the call for longitudinal and historical approaches in IB research has recently become more articulate (Jones and Khanna 2006; Morck and Yeung 2007). Certain 'truths' in IB research might be undetectable except from a longitudinal perspective.

Although limited in number, the longitudinal studies available in IB journals present a broad variety in terms of research questions, methodology and temporal design. It is a key objective of this chapter to give a structured overview of these different approaches. In order to do so, I first develop a typology of longitudinal research designs. So far, methodological literature on the longitudinal case study approach in IB research is largely missing. Authors in the IB field are usually forced to rely on references from the area of organizational behaviour (see, for example, Eisenhardt 1989; Pettigrew 1995; Jensen and Rodgers 2001; Yin 2009) which, however, do not take into account the specific challenges of research in an international context. In turn, even recent books on IB research methodologies (see, for example, Neelankavil 2007) do not discuss case studies in any way. When mentioned at all, the discussion of longitudinality in case study research is often limited to a passing remark (see, for example, Ghauri 2004; Bryman and Bell 2007; Siggelkow 2007; Dul and Halk 2008; Yin 2009). This lack of adequate literature is possibly a reason for the weak methodological sections in many longitudinal case studies which, in turn, might hinder publication in leading IB journals.

The second core interest of the chapter lies in the discussion of the relationship (fit or misfit) between current research questions in the IB field and alternative longitudinal case study designs. On the one hand, I want to show that a number of important IB topics, particularly those relating to processes and practices, provide a rich field for applying longitudinal in-depth research. On the other hand, I base a critical review on an analysis of several published longitudinal case studies with diverse temporal designs. This review is intended to demonstrate what longitudinality in case studies actually contributes to the advancement of IB theories – and where and why its contribution is limited in some instances. The penultimate section of the chapter is dedicated to practical challenges of (and some solutions to) designing and managing longitudinal case study projects in IB. The final section concludes.

A NEED FOR LONGITUDINAL CASE STUDIES IN IB RESEARCH?

There is no need to repeat the arguments in favour of case study research in general. Instead, I shall suggest a number of good reasons why longitudinal case study designs should receive more attention in IB research. In a similar vein, business historians Jones and Khanna (2006) have recently advanced important arguments in favour of historical approaches in IB research.[1] Most importantly, they maintain that historical variation (from long-term time-series data) can provide a valid alternative to the cross-sectional variation popular in the IB field. Moreover, certain issues of interest are not addressable except in the long run. These include questions of path dependency as well as, for example, long-term effects of foreign investments (Jones and Khanna 2006). Similarly, I argue that the field itself has developed into a direction where an increasing number of research questions call for a longitudinal approach – although so far the call has not been heeded by large numbers of researchers.

IB research has recently reflected two broad trends. On the one hand, there is a strong interest in 'processes'; that is, the 'sequence of events . . . unfolding over time' (Pettigrew et al. 2001, p. 700). On the other, more and more researchers focus on 'practices'; that is, contextually embedded micro-level action (in contrast to the pure formulation of policies which, for example, are rarely adopted one to one in subsidiaries of multinational corporations). In this respect, IB research follows a general trend in the social sciences in which 'process research' and the 'practice turn' have become strong and persistent research streams over the past two to three decades (Knorr Cetina et al. 2000). In my view, this development necessitates a renewed discussion of methodological issues in the IB research community. Both process- and practices-oriented research call for an increased use of longitudinal data in empirical studies.

Process research is the classic domain of longitudinal cases in organizational studies (Huber and Van de Ven 1995; Pettigrew et al. 2001). Process research can be defined as the investigation of a 'temporal sequence of events' (Huber and Van de Ven 1995, p. ix). Pettigrew et al. (2001, p. 700) maintain that process research focuses on verbs (ongoing processes) rather than nouns (inputs and outcomes). As such, it requires a methodological approach which acknowledges time itself as a crucial dimension of organizational research: 'time must be an essential part of investigation . . . if processes are to be uncovered' (Pettigrew et al. 2001, p. 697). Longitudinal case studies are one methodology that allows researchers to uncover temporal patterns (Monge 1995) and thus has the potential to contribute to the development of dynamic theories. For a long time, IB researchers have focused on spatial rather than on temporal dimensions;[2] for example, on the comparison of multinational corporation (MNC) entry strategies across countries rather than on the development of entry strategies over time. The current attention to process is thus a healthy counter-motion in the IB field which might eventually contribute to the integration of temporal and dynamic elements into established models. Longitudinal research is particularly suitable in research fields which inherently entail processual elements, evolutionary developments or path dependencies which can only be uncovered through long-term data. Potential areas of application include the development of strategic alliances or international joint ventures (JVs) over time, knowledge transfer processes in MNCs, or long-term patterns of internationalization and market entry processes. In fact, the few available longitudinal case studies in IB are concentrated in these areas. A number of them will be discussed in more detail below.

The second stream of research in IB calling for longitudinality is practices research. While the need for longitudinal case studies in process research is quite straightforward, the argument here is more intricate. Practices research is concerned with understanding and explaining actual behaviour of (micro-level) actors in organizations (Knorr Cetina et al. 2000); for example, the actual usage of human resource or leadership instruments in daily manager–employee relationships, or the enactment of strategies in decision-making situations. Practices research, however, does not position the individual (or group) actor as an independent unit of analysis as does methodological individualism. Following Giddens's (1984) duality thesis, practice and structure, action and context are inherently interrelated. Practices research in IB is therefore concerned with both micro and meso/macro phenomena, in that it seeks to understand the dual relationship between different levels of observation.

According to Pettigrew (1995), 'embeddedness', which is found in this kind of practices research, is – next to process – a second key indicator for longitudinal research designs. Why is that so? Different levels of context are usually characterized by asymmetry (Pettigrew et al. 2001). That is, they do not develop at the same pace. For example, individual firms differ regarding the rate at which they emulate a general trend in their industrial sector (for example, due to organizational inertia). Or subsidiary managers resist and thus delay an intended change in overall MNC strategy by applying local power means. Micro-level actors are able to slow down practices transfer processes within the MNC through obstruction, manipulation, misplacement or adjustment of the intended practice which, in turn, might necessitate time-consuming processes of renegotiation, hybridization or reinterpretation of the practices in question by subsidiary and MNC headquarters. Even if practices are not resisted, implementation and internalization processes in diverse national environments add a temporal dimension to practices research. When single observation designs instead of longitudinal approaches are used in studies of practices transfer, they might miss conflictual adaptation and internalization processes which occur after a seemingly unproblematic implementation. Short-term designs also run the danger of misattributing causes and effects of observed behaviour; for example, when a current change in MNC subsidiary structure is considered to be the reason for an observed practices change, whereas in fact evolutionary changes in the subsidiary's traditional local network produces the internal adjustments.

Often, longitudinal designs are required in practices research not solely because of the temporal effects of asymmetric micro/macro interdependencies but also because the identification of actual behavioural patterns – as opposed to formulated policies or desired behaviour – necessitates in-depth observation. Consequently, field studies and ethnographic methods are called for which take a longer-term view than, for instance, one-time surveys or interviews conducted at a single point in time. This is particularly true for international studies in which researchers need first of all to immerse themselves in different, often foreign cultures in order to reveal and understand actors' idiosyncratic enactments of practices in their specific contexts (see contributions by Brannen, Ch. 8 and Moore, Ch. 17 in this volume for a detailed discussion of ethnographic methods in IB research).

Regarding practices, Kostova (1999) has nicely identified and conceptualized the multiplicity of influences and levels impacting the transfer of practices in MNCs: relational, organizational, local, national and transnational. My own empirical work in this area (Blazejewski 2006) has shown how prolonged conflictual processes might flow from this heterogeneity of contexts, which one-shot survey designs would quite certainly miss. Similarly, the case study project initiated by Almond and Ferner (2006) convincingly demonstrates the impact of the firms' embeddedness in traditional long-term relationships and local identities on the adoption and adaptation of US human resources (HR) practices in European subsidiaries. Although Almond and Ferner's work is only partially longitudinal, it shows that the inclusion of the temporal embeddedness of actors is indispensable in explaining practices transfer in international contexts.

My review of selected longitudinal case studies below confirms that research on practices and micro/macro linkages almost always encompasses some process aspect as well. While there are a number of studies which focus on process only (see, for example, Steier 2001; Zander 2002; Jones and Miskell 2007; Kotabe et al. 2008), practices and network research practically always involves both aspects: processual *and* multi-level elements. This is in line with Pettigrew's (1995, p. 93) understanding of 'contextualism as a theory of method', according to which temporal and spatial (in the sense of inner and outer organizational contexts) factors simultaneously shape organizational events.

LONGITUDINALITY IN CASE STUDY RESEARCH: DEFINITIONS AND DESIGN OPTIONS

Although it is an established method in organizational studies, there is very little debate on what exactly constitutes a longitudinal case study. It is

Table 14.1   Combinations of case time and research time

Temporal dimension	Option 1: continuous	Option 2: multiple shot	Option 3: *ex post*
Case time	├———————┤	├————————┤	├————————┤
Research time	├---------┤	├-┤ ├-┤ ├-┤	├-┤
Case and research time combined	Research time and case time coincide	Research time and case time coincide but only at intervals	Research process starts only after the events under study are terminated

difficult to establish a shared understanding on the 'longitudinal' element of the longitudinal case study approach. The limited methodological literature available on such case studies from the area of organization studies and organizational change, interestingly, does not even attempt to discuss this basic question. In research practice, what is considered and labelled 'longitudinal' varies substantially. The spectrum ranges from a couple of months of ethnographic field study (Sharpe 2002) to 20+ years (including phases of real-time observation and retrospective data gathering) in the large-scale project on organizational change initiated by Pettigrew (1985).

In my view, we need to differentiate between four time-related dimensions in longitudinal case study research to allow for a systematic assessment and comparison of existing longitudinal case studies, and for an informed choice of the proper research design for a new research project. First, *case time* concerns the period of analysis: for example, the case company's development between 1987 and 1995. Second, *research time* denotes the total time used for gathering case study data; that is, the time spent in the field. Research time is closely related to the data-gathering methods applied. An ethnographic approach might require an extended period of observation whereas collecting data from secondary, published material or single (non-repeated) interviews can be feasible in a week's time. Case time and research time can be combined in different ways (Table 14.1): research time can coincide with case time (continuous), coincide but only at intervals (multiple shot), or follow case time (*ex post*).

The third dimension, *temporal research perspective*, describes the researcher's positioning *vis-à-vis* the case of interest. The research process can take place either while the events of interests are ongoing (simultaneously) or after they have come to a conclusion (*ex post*, historic). In the latter case, the researcher has no unmediated access to the events under study but needs to rely on recorded or retrospective data.

The fourth dimension – *temporal data perspective* – describes how the

		Research perspective	
		Simultaneous	Expost
Data perspective	Real-time	e.g. 'classical' ethnographic field study, participant observation, repeated interviews	e.g. recorded interviews, emails or meeting notes produced at the time of events under study
	Retrospective	e.g. documents and narratives about previous events which relate to the events under study	e.g. annual reports, historical accounts, retrospective interviewing

Figure 14.1   Combinations of temporal research and data perspectives

data sources used in the research process relate to the case investigated. Real-time data are produced at the time of events. Examples include participant observation and real-time interviewing but also board minutes or records of the ongoing email communication during the case time. In turn, retrospective data is produced at a distance from the events of interest. Past events are reported and interpreted from the point of view of the present (for example, in retrospective interviews), which is influenced by the outcomes of the events investigated (such as success or failure of a joint venture, for instance) and, consequently, by the potentially altered position of the interviewee. Retrospective data are associated with a number of limitations such as lack of recall or difficulties in determining cause and effect (Leonard-Barton 1990; Golden 1992; Van de Ven and Poole 1995). In turn, in real-time studies the involvement of interviewees in ongoing events might lead to emotional biases, misattribution, distortion or actual concealment of important facts. Many authors of longitudinal case studies therefore use a combination of real-time and retrospective perspectives, which can also help to contain the considerable time demands placed on researchers by pure real-time field studies. They often fail to acknowledge, however, that both kinds of data sources produce potentially different time-bound 'truths'. Yet the multiplicity of perspectives is frequently cited as a key defining feature of the case study approach. Feasible combinations of the four temporal dimensions are presented in Figure 14.1.

Nevertheless, the question regarding the 'proper' length of a longitudinal case study remains unanswered. For an ethnographic study of communication in a global team, a one-year real-time field study might duly be considered longitudinal. In contrast, a study of the success of a recent market entry of an MNC based on a number of interviews conducted during a two-week visit at the company in question would hardly be labelled longitudinal, although case time might actually be identical in both examples. What is judged 'longitudinal' (and whether longitudinality is actually required in a particular case study project) thus ultimately depends on the research question and the research methodology selected (Monge 1995; Yin 2009).

LONGITUDINAL CASE STUDIES IN IB RESEARCH: AN OVERVIEW

Appendix Table 14A.1 provides an overview of a number of longitudinal case studies conducted in IB between 1998 and 2008. The selection is based on a simple search in the EBSCO database using the keywords 'longitudinal case study' and 'international business'. I have added Kristensen and Zeitlin's (2005) outstanding book because of its innovative emergent research design and important results on management practices in MNCs (discussed in more detail below). The list is intended to present variety rather than completeness. Yet, as already discussed in the introduction, the total number of longitudinal case studies in IB is limited. In addition, the selected cases here are typical of the field in that they show which design options are preferred and in which research fields longitudinal designs are currently located in IB.

The analysis of the papers reveals one issue first of all: clear information on the temporal design is generally lacking. It is therefore not always easy (and sometimes impossible, indicated by '?' throughout Table 14A.1) to identify whether a study is actually real time or retrospective and whether data were gathered at one point in time or at multiple intervals. Often it was necessary to read between the lines in order to figure out what kind of data were collected when and how (see, for example, Zander 2002; Kotabe et al. 2008). Or, as in the case of Kristensen and Zeitlin's (2005) otherwise exemplary work, the rather sparse (and inconsistent) information on the temporal research strategy is relegated to small-print footnotes (pp. 28, 40, 51, 104, 135). Sometimes, the reader has to go through considerable search and calculations only to discover that a study claimed to be longitudinal is not really longitudinal at all. This is the case, for example, with the paper by Inkpen and Dinur (1998), who claim to investigate the long-term process of knowledge transfer from international JVs to the parent corporation but really only deliver a static view of types of knowledge and transfer mechanisms.

This formal inattentiveness to temporal issues seems, on the one hand, to be typical of a field in which questions of research methodology, in particular qualitative methods, are generally not as extensively discussed as, for example, in organization studies. On the other hand, the lack of information on temporal designs might be related to the case study approach as such and its common usage in business studies. Case studies are still often characterized by a lack of methodological rigour (see Eisenhardt and Graebner 2007 and Yin 2009 for a similarly critical assessment), which makes them easy prey for journal reviewers with, as is often the case in IB, a background in and preference for quantitative approaches. This risk becomes even more acute because, apart from a lack of information on the temporal design, many authors presented in Table 14A.1 refrain from thoroughly discussing their methodological choices. Often a passing reference to Yin (2009) or Eisenhardt's (1989) by now classic paper is considered sufficient, although Eisenhardt does not even mention longitudinal case studies and Yin (2009, p. 42) checks them off with one sentence.

Once the actual temporal design is (at least roughly) established, Table 14A.1 reveals a preference for two options: simultaneous/multiple-shot designs on the basis of real-time data and *ex post* perspectives. Six out of seven papers applying an *ex post* approach are concerned with truly long-term developments such as epochs of internationalization (Eckert and Mayrhofer 2005, 22 years; Jones and Miskell 2007, 35 years) or the long-term evolution of MNC networks (Zander 2002, 100 years; Welch and Wilkinson 2004, 50 years). For such extensive periods, simultaneous data collection is practically impossible. Five papers rely predominantly on archival material (company documents, news articles), which facilitates *ex post* analysis.

The second dominant design is simultaneous/multiple shot (Salmi 2000; Salk and Shenkar 2001; Steier 2001; Carr 2005; Soulsby and Clark 2006; Sippola and Smale 2007). It allows researchers to follow events while they occur through stages of real-time observation and interviewing. At the same time it keeps the research process manageable because case periods before, in-between or after observation points can be included in the analysis through archival data. In this way, a longitudinal project might become realizable despite limited resources on the researcher's side. In addition, this design enables authors to gain in two ways: they can observe the longer-term development of events in a specific case without sacrificing depth. This is particularly valuable in studies which focus on the transfer or evolution of practices in IB which, as discussed above, requires an in-depth understanding of actors' actual patterns of behaviour and interpretation (see, for example, Salmi 2000; Soulsby and Clark 2006; Sippola and Smale 2007).

A CRITICAL ASSESSMENT OF LONGITUDINAL CASE STUDIES IN IB RESEARCH

After the brief overview of longitudinal case studies in IB – what is actually out there? – this section focuses on the contribution of longitudinal designs to theory development in IB. What kind of 'truth' does 'time' actually engender? Do the results of longitudinal case studies justify the efforts a researcher has to devote by committing substantial resources to one – in terms of publication output and career advancement – rather risky project over an extended period?

In order to answer this question – is it really worth it? – I briefly recapitulate what kinds of output are generally expected from case study research. In relation to the specific interest of this chapter, the criterion for evaluation is precise: what does the longitudinality of the case study contribute to the advancement of IB theory? Based on the selected studies in the appendix, there are four different kinds of output in this respect. Please note that I discuss only the contribution of longitudinality to theory development in each of the selected studies, although many of the papers mentioned have provided important insights in a number of other respects. Also, some of the studies from Table 14A.1 are assigned to more than one category because they contribute to theory development in multiple ways.

First, a number of studies are concerned with the identification of temporal patterns in the longer-term development of the IB field. They focus on either the identification and description of stages or phases of development (Li 1998; Eckert and Mayrhofer 2005; Johanson and Johanson 2006; Jones and Miskell 2007; Kotabe et al. 2008) or on the discovery of rhythmic patterns such as recurring events or actions over time (Maznevski and Chudoba 2000). The first type of paper mainly contributes to the advancement of evolutionary or process theories of IB (based on the work by Johanson and Vahlne 1977). Johanson and Johanson's (2006) paper, for instance, produces a set of hypotheses which relate phases of internationalization to particular market entry activities and types of discoveries (operative or strategic information) acquired in each phase. The second type of paper uses longitudinality to add a temporal dimension to research on global teams. In particular, Maznevski and Chudoba (2000) demonstrate that effective global virtual teams have a strong temporal rhythm set by face-to-face meetings which provides long-term stability for the team.

A second set of studies (Salmi 2000; Salk and Shenkar 2001; Zander 2002) seeks to make a contribution to the IB field by adding a new (time-bound) variable – 'historical roots', 'traditional identities' or 'historical legacy' – to a variety of established theoretical models. Salk and Shenkar (2001), for example, are able to add to the advancement of social identity theory in at least two ways. Their case study of the long-term development of an international (British–Italian) JV reveals that (a) national or parent identity remains dominant over time even when events occurred and contexts changed in ways that were expected to foster JV identity, and (b) the formative phase of an international JV has a crucial influence on the long-term evolution of social identities. Salmi (2000) helps improve network theory by emphasizing how the historical background of business partners affects network relationships in the long run. Similarly, but again with a different theoretical background, Zander (2002) introduces the notion of historical legacies as an important variable into evolutionary theory. His case of the long-term development of Asea and Brown Boveri into ABB demonstrates how firm-specific events in the past determine current processes of integration of the merged company's innovation networks.

The third set of studies comprises research focuses on organizational practices (Maznevski and Chudoba 2000; Sharpe 2002; Kristensen and Zeitlin 2005; Soulsby and Clark 2006; Sippola and Smale 2007) or network structure and development (Salmi 2000; Welch and Wilkinson 2004; Mainela and Puhakka 2007). Although starting from different research questions and interests, both kinds of papers essentially contribute to the advancement of the same theoretical approach, that is structuration theory (Giddens 1984), and in particular its adaptation for research objectives in the field of IB. These studies make a contribution by drawing from longitudinal empirical data to substantiate their theoretical arguments (Sharpe 2004). They (a) provide in-depth analysis and conceptualization of practices and their contextual constitution, (b) identify actor-level games and strategies, and (c) trace the temporal effects of these games and strategies. Real-time longitudinal studies such as Sharpe (2002) provide in-depth insights into the contextual constitution of practices in MNCs. They thus improve our understanding of the complex relationships between actual behaviour and multiple-level contexts such as organizational structure, local, cultural and multinational environments.

Micro-level strategizing is also at the centre of the work by Kristensen and Zeitlin (2005), who focus on the identification of actors' games in MNCs. Their case study reveals, for instance, how a group of subsidiary managers from Denmark, the so-called 'Danish mafia' (Kristensen and Zeitlin 2005, p. 97), make use of their local context (local network, resources) to change the overall MNC power structure which, in turn, influences the Danish subsidiary's development over time. The example demonstrates how the duality of strategic action and structure in MNCs is a continuous recursive relationship in which planned global strategies are offset by seemingly peripheral actor groups searching for local solutions. Similarly, Mainela and Puhakka (2007) are able to advance what they call 'network action theory' by identifying five different ways of strategizing of actors in international JV networks.

The investigation of the associated time lags and delays produced by actor-level strategizing enables another group of authors (Soulsby and Clark 2006) to (re)introduce a focus on the temporal, dynamic dimension of structuration theory. Although Giddens (1984) himself emphasized time in his theoretical model, in its application in business and management research the temporal dimension of the action–structure duality has quite often been disregarded. Although not their core interest, the work by Soulsby and Clark clearly shows how the initiation of macro-level structural changes in the Czech transition context triggers micro-level action, which in turn produces a delay of the intended structural change. Their work can thus be used as a starting point for the investigation of temporal effects of the action–structure interdependency, such as time lags, acceleration or temporal rhythms, as in the work of Maznevski and Chudoba (2000).

The fourth, surprisingly large group of papers (Inkpen and Dinur 1998; Steier 2001; Roy and Wilkinson 2004; Carr 2005; Coviello 2006; Sippola and Smale 2007) is set apart from the other three already discussed less by its specific contribution to theory development but by the authors' inability to put their 'longitudinal advantage' to proper use. This does not mean that in other respects the papers' contribution is not outstanding, but only that the longitudinality of the approach does not produce any specific insights which would have been missed if a non-longitudinal design had been applied. In essence, the lack of a clear output from longitudinality can be interpreted as an indicator of a potential mismatch between the research question and the case study design chosen. Steier (2001), for example, conducts a multiple-shot real-time study over a period of eight years, but then presents a set of hypotheses relating to liabilities of smallness or geographic distance in internationalization process of new ventures. Apart from 'newness', derived from population ecology, the paper provides no theoretical conceptualization or clarification of the dynamics of new venture internationalization over time. Coviello (2006) introduces a temporal scheme (the four-stage concept of network development by Kazanjian 1988) early in her paper but her own propositions are limited to spatial and relationship variables such as network range, network centrality, and social versus economic ties in network building. Although theory building is anyway not her core intent, she essentially forgoes the chance to refine network theory by adding a temporal dimension through tying her propositions to Kazanjian's process model.

CONDUCTING LONGITUDINAL CASE STUDIES: PRACTICAL CHALLENGES AND SOME SOLUTIONS

This section is devoted to practical suggestions regarding the design and management of longitudinal case study projects. Alternative techniques for longitudinal data analysis are comprehensively discussed by Van de Ven and Poole (1995) and Langley (1999). With regard to case study design, I shall re-emphasize that the longitudinal data analysis must match the research question. There is no use in investing time and effort in a longitudinal case study if the research question does not really require a longitudinal perspective. Once you have opted for a longitudinal design, make sure that you actually make use of the longitudinality of your data for analysis, as well as concluding propositions and discussion of theoretical contributions of your study. It is a pity if, as in the articles by Steier (2001) and others discussed above, the potential return on the substantial effort of gathering longitudinal data remains unrealized.

The next important question is when to start and when to end a longitudinal case study project. What exactly is the relevant case time, for example, for a study on long-term knowledge transfer in MNCs? This is crucial because choices about the temporal design set the frame for what is actually seen in the case (Pettigrew 1995). Pettigrew (p. 102) suggests looking for 'dramas'; that is, particular events cited by interviewees or other experts in the field which bracket the process of interest.

Often it might be easier to define when a longitudinal process has started in the past (merger, establishment of a joint venture and so on) than when to end data collection. This is particularly true for real-time studies in which it is difficult for the researcher to gain sufficient distance to ongoing events to actually see and set the boundaries of processes still under way. Quite frequently, external events bring the research process to a sudden end, as in the study by Kristensen and Zeitlin (2005) in which the acquisition of the case company led to a withdrawal of access and forced the research team to conclude data collection. In such instances it might be useful at least to continue to collect secondary, published data on the case company and keep informal contact to former informants in order to ensure that decisive events and outcomes of observed processes can still be included in your case description. This will also be helpful if you want to renegotiate access at a later point in time.

Similarly, the exchange of personnel in the case company can pose a serious challenge to longitudinal research designs (Hyder and Ghauri 2000). This problem is particularly pressing in Central and Eastern Europe where high rates of personnel turnover and even bankruptcy still make it difficult to develop stable long-term relationships with informants (Michailova and Liuhto 2000). Often large parts of the workforce have been switched during transition, so that nobody among the current personnel might be able to report retrospectively on developments before the core transition phase. In my own work on Beiersdorf-Lechia in Poland (Blazejewski and Dorow 2003; Stüting et al. 2003), started in 2000, we had to contact retired employees in order to receive reliable information on the company's development before the Beiersdorf acquisition in 1997. This specific situation forces researchers to become creative in searching for relevant informants and to set aside some extra time because, for example, former personnel might not be available for interviews at the case company's premises. To facilitate interviews with new personnel entering the case company during the research phase, Hyder and Ghauri (2000) recommend the preparation of interim reports which summarize previously collected case data and can serve as a starting point for first-time interviews.

Even if the personnel situation is more stable, one has to expect problems of access and sustaining the motivation of key informants in the long run. According to Kristensen and Zeitlin (2005, p. 172), some global managers seem actually to 'despise' history and are quite unwilling to talk about the past, thereby inhibiting retrospective data gathering. In my own longitudinal case project (Blazejewski and Dorow 2003; Stüting et al. 2003) I found that even though access was unproblematic, motivation was more difficult over the long term because the key informants' interests tended to shift over time. In interviews it was thus difficult to stay focused on the original research question. Instead, we had to allow for many detours and a number of small-scale projects on the side, even when unrelated to our core interest, in order to ensure the interviewees' ongoing cooperation in the larger longitudinal study. Although this approach tied up considerable resources, mostly unpredictably, our responsiveness to their acute needs also helped to establish a strong personal relationship with key managers. As confirmed by Michailova and Liuhto (2000), strong personal relationships might, particularly in Central and Eastern European countries, be the only way to gain and maintain research access into companies of interest. Much research in the IB field would actually profit from a deeper understanding of, and closer interaction with, the people, processes and places under investigation. In fact, a strong, long-term relationship between researcher and researched, often with divergent cultural backgrounds, might provide a basis for disclosure and in-depth understanding of differing interpretations and cultural practices inherent in IB settings.

Changing personnel, forced breaks and shifting motivations over time are typical challenges of longitudinal case study research, making a complete, careful upfront planning of the research process difficult. This does not mean that you should dispense with thorough preparation; for example, a pilot study to gain insider knowledge on the case industry and facilitate the negotiation of access (Pettigrew 1995). But you should remain open to changes in the research design. In effect, close attention to chances offered by and changes in the research environment can actually open up paths to successful longitudinal research. Kristensen and Zeitlin (2005), for instance, emphasize that their longitudinal study of the APV corporation could not have been 'design[ed] . . . in advance of the opportunities and contacts that emerged during the course of the research itself' (p. xx). Similarly, our study on Beiersdorf-Lechia in Poland (Stüting et al. 2003) was not intended as a longitudinal study early on. It evolved into one, now in its eighth year, only because our strong personal relationships with key managers and an emerging set of shared interests and topics provided a reliable basis for multiple return visits and mutual trust. This is not to say that a clear 'up-front commitment' by managers to a longitudinal case study project as recommended by Leonard-Barton (1990, p. 263) is not desirable, only that in many cases it might be unattainable. Then an emergent design can be a viable alternative, at least for non-dissertation projects in which the pressure on time and definite output is less strict. Also, being open for an emergent design does not mean paying less attention to methodological rigour. On the contrary, only when the collection and documentation of data are clearly structured and comprehensive from the start, might a small-scale study eventually develop into a long-term research project.

A thorough methodology and its full documentation can also help to overcome the publication challenges attached to longitudinal case study research (Pauwels and Matthyssens 2004). Although all of the case studies reported in Table 14A.1 are published papers, some even in high-ranking journals such as the *Journal of International Business Studies*, only very few of them actually contain clear information on the temporal design of the case study, data collection and data analysis methods. As already noted above, this lack of explicit information makes it quite difficult for readers and reviewers alike to identify core elements of the research design such as case time and research time and thus to assess the quality of the methodological approach (see Mainela and Puhakka 2007, for an exception).

A second problem related to the publication output of longitudinal case study research is the fact that final research results are often only attainable after many years. This is also the reason why longitudinal case study research is often not the first choice for dissertation projects. Even faculty members are subjected to today's strenuous publication pressures and might refrain from devoting their time to a longitudinal study with unclear outcomes. There are, however, valid strategies to overcome this publication dilemma. Pettigrew (1995, p. 109) suggests different types of output (the diagnostic case, the interpretative case, the theoretical–comparative case) which can be put onto the market at different stages of the work. Some longitudinal research questions also lend themselves to division into smaller, partial subquestions which might be developed into publishable papers on the basis of interim results. If data for an international comparative project are collected sequentially across countries, single country or single subsidiary case studies might also help to overcome delays in the publication of the full comparative study and lessen the potentially detrimental effects on academic career advancement associated with longitudinal research.

Devoting only part of your resources to a longitudinal project and simultaneously working on smaller-scale empirical work or theoretical papers is a further potential strategy to avoid publication gaps. It is particularly feasible when the longitudinal project is not conducted by a single researcher but by a research team, which lessens the investment required by each team member. A research team can also be useful if your longitudinal case study project requires real-time data from different international subsidiaries. Yet, international academic teams have problems of their own (Milliman and Von Glinow 1998; see Salmi, Ch. 22 in this volume). To name only one, there is the trade-off, according to Leonard-Barton (1990), between the ability of a team to collect in-depth data in multiple geographically dispersed sites and the advantages of a single researcher who is able to obtain synergies between multiple datasets more efficiently. The use of shared software, which forces team members to collect, store and analyse data systematically and in a comparable way across sites and countries, can be helpful in this respect.

There are a number of additional challenges involved in longitudinal case studies, such as funding and case selection. Pettigrew (1995) provides a comprehensive discussion of these challenges for longitudinal case study research, although without its international dimension. In turn, Ghauri (2004) gives a number of useful suggestions for the management of case study research in IB, but only briefly refers to longitudinal designs.

CONCLUSION

The lack of methodological literature on longitudinal case studies in IB was the key motivation for this chapter. The available literature either focuses on longitudinal case studies, but without addressing the specific context of IB; or it deals with the case study approach in IB research but disregards the specific challenges of longitudinal designs. This chapter is an attempt at closing this gap. It provides an introduction to different design options for longitudinal case study research and discusses potential research questions from the IB field which call for longitudinal designs. In particular, I distinguish between four temporal dimensions of longitudinal case study designs: the case time, research time, temporal research and temporal data perspectives. The resulting framework allows researchers from the IB field to reflect systematically on and decide about the proper temporal design for their specific case project. It can also help them to corroborate their methodological sections, which have often been easy prey for journal reviewers.

A review of selected case studies has revealed typical patterns in use in the IB research community such as the *ex post* perspectives and multiple-shot designs combining real-time interviews with archival data. The analysis of the theoretical contribution of longitudinal case studies in IB has demonstrated that the added effort and resource commitment required by longitudinal designs does not always pay off. I have argued that this is often due to a mismatch between research question and study design or to a neglect of temporal dimensions when analysing the data collected. Other researchers, however, have effectively used the longitudinality of their case study to substantially contribute to the advancement of IB research. It has allowed them to refine existing models by differentiating temporal patterns or to add new time-bound dimensions to established approaches in the IB field such as evolutionary, network and structuration theory.

The selection of longitudinal case studies presented here is neither complete nor representative of the field. Nevertheless, it has revealed typical challenges of using the longitudinal method in case study research, as well as some opportunities. Regarding the practical management of longitudinal case studies in IB, a flexible, emergent approach such as the one used by Kristensen and Zeitlin (2005) provides a chance to upgrade ongoing case studies into longitudinal studies over the course of the research process even though the required access and resources are not available up-front. Such an 'emergent logic' would also provide a valuable counterweight to the dominant 'design logic' of research methodologies in the IB field (Piekkari et al. 2009). Whereas a design logic predefines strict boundaries for the case study project (for example, duration, case number, level of analysis, data sources), an emergent approach allows researchers to adjust their research focus, follow detours and integrate additional variables as the project progresses. Researchers who take their time in this way will most likely come closer to the 'truth' of their cases (even if this lies only in the discovery of multiple, irreconcilable 'truths') than those who rush to a conclusion.

NOTES

1. Both historical and longitudinal approaches emphasize the need for long-term data and evolutionary perspectives in IB research. They differ, however, in that historical

approaches focus on the 'really long term' (Jones and Khanna 2006), that is, at least several decades of case time, and on an *ex post* positioning of the researcher (see the next section for an explanation of the terms).

2. Jones and Khanna (2006) rightly point out that this was not always the case. First-generation researchers in IB in fact 'appear more engaged with historical data' (Jones and Khanna 2006, p. 454), but these early attempts remained singular and were not sustained over time.

REFERENCES

Almond, P. and A. Ferner (eds) (2006), *American Multinationals in Europe*, Oxford: Oxford University Press.

Blazejewski, S. (2006), 'Transferring value-infused organizational practices in MNCs: a conflict perspective', in M. Geppert and M. Mayer (eds), *Global, National and Local Practices in Multinational Corporations*, Basingstoke: Palgrave, pp. 63–104.

Blazejewski, S. and W. Dorow (2003), 'Managing organizational politics for radical change', *Journal of World Business*, **38** (3), 204–23.

Bryman, A. and E. Bell (2007), *Business Research Methods*, Oxford: Oxford University Press.

Carr, C. (2005), 'Are German, Japanese and Anglo-Saxon strategic decision styles still divergent in the context of globalization?', *Journal of Management Studies*, **42** (6), 1155–88.

Coviello, N.E. (2006), 'The network dynamics of international new ventures', *Journal of International Business Studies*, **37** (5), 713–31.

Dul, J. and T. Halk (2008), *Case Study Methodology in Business Research*, Oxford: Butterworth-Heinemann.

Eckert, S. and U. Mayrhofer (2005), 'Identifying and explaining epochs of internationalization: a case study', *European Management Review*, **2** (3), 212–23.

Eisenhardt, K.M. (1989), 'Building theories from case study research', *Academy of Management Review*, **14** (4), 532–50.

Eisenhardt, K.M. and M.E. Graebner (2007), 'Theory building from cases: opportunities and challenges', *Academy of Management Journal*, **50** (1), 25–32.

Ghauri, P. (2004), 'Designing and conducting case studies in international business research', in R. Marschan-Piekkari and C. Welch (eds), *Handbook of Qualitative Research Methods for International Business*, Cheltenham, UK and Northampton, MA, USA: Edward Elgar, pp. 109–24.

Giddens, A. (1984), *The Constitution of Society: Outline of the Theory of Structuration*, Cambridge: Polity.

Golden, B.R. (1992), 'The past is the past – or is it? The use of retrospective accounts as indicators of past strategy', *Academy of Management Journal*, **35** (4), 848–60.

Huber, G.P. and A.H. Van de Ven (eds) (1995), *Longitudinal Field Research*, Thousand Oaks, CA: Sage.

Hyder, A.S. and P.N. Ghauri (2000), 'Managing international joint venture relationships: a longitudinal perspective', *Industrial Marketing Management*, **29** (3), 205–18.

Inkpen, A.C. and A. Dinur (1998), 'Knowledge management processes and international joint ventures', *Organization Science*, **9** (4), 454–68.

Jensen, J.L. and R. Rodgers (2001), 'Cumulating the intellectual gold of case study research', *Public Administration Review*, **61** (2), 236–46.

Johanson, J. and J.-E. Vahlne (1977), 'The internationalization process of the firm: a model of knowledge development and increasing foreign market commitments', *Journal of International Business Studies*, **8** (1), 23–32.

Johanson, M. and J. Johanson (2006), 'Turbulence, discovery and foreign market entry: a longitudinal study of an entry into the Russian market', *Management International Review*, **46** (2), 179–205.

Jones, G. and T. Khanna (2006), 'Bringing history (back) into international business', *Journal of International Business Studies*, **37** (4), 453–68.

Jones, G. and P. Miskell (2007), 'Acquisitions and firm growth: creating Unilever's ice cream and tea business', *Business History*, **49** (1), 8–28.

Kazanjian, R.K. (1988), 'Relation of dominant problems to stages of growth in technology-based new ventures', *Academy of Management Journal*, **21** (2), 257–79.

Knorr Cetina, K., T.R. Schatzki and E. von Savigny (2000), *The Practice Turn in Contemporary Theory*, Milton Park, UK: Routledge.

Kostova, T. (1999), 'Transnational transfer of strategic organizational practices: a contextual perspective', *Academy of Management Review*, **24** (2), 308–24.

Kotabe, M., M.J. Mol and S. Ketkar (2008), 'An evolutionary stage model of outsourcing and competence destruction: a triad comparison of the consumer electronics industry', *Management International Review*, **48** (1), 1–29.

Kristensen, P. and J. Zeitlin (2005), *Local Players in Global Games*, Oxford: Oxford University Press.

Langley, A. (1999), 'Strategies for theorizing from process data', *Academy of Management Review*, **24** (4), 691–710.

Leonard-Barton, D. (1990), 'A dual methodology for case studies: synergetic use of longitudinal single site with replicated multiple sites', *Organization Science*, **1** (3), 248–66.

Li, P.P. (1998), 'The evolution of multinational firms from Asia: a longitudinal case study of Taiwan's Acer Group', *Journal of Organizational Change Management*, **11** (4), 321–37.

Mainela, T. and V. Puhakka (2007), 'Embeddedness and networking as drivers in developing an international joint venture', *Scandinavian Journal of Management*, **24** (1), 17–32.

Maznevski, M.L. and K.M. Chudoba (2000), 'Bridging space over time: global virtual team dynamics and effectiveness', *Organization Science*, **11** (5), 473–92.

Michailova, S. and K. Liuhto (2000), 'Organization and management research in transition economies: towards improved research methodologies', *Journal of East–West Business*, **6** (3), 7–46.

Milliman, J. and M.A. Von Glinow (1998), 'The academic international research team: small world after all', *Journal of Managerial Psychology*, **13** (3–4), 150–55.

Monge, P.R. (1995), 'Theoretical and analytical issues in studying organizational processes', in Huber and Van de Ven (eds), pp. 267–99.

Morck, R. and B. Yeung (2007). 'History in perspective: commentary on Jones and Khanna's article "Bringing history (back)" into international business', *Journal of International Business Studies*, **38** (2), 357–60.

Neelankavil, J.P. (2007), *International Business Research*, Armonk, NY: M.E. Sharpe.

Pauwels, P. and P. Matthyssens (2004), 'The architecture of multiple case study research in international business', in R. Marschan-Piekkari and C. Welch (eds), *Handbook of Qualitative Research Methods for International Business*, Cheltenham, UK and Northampton, MA, USA: Edward Elgar, pp. 123–43.

Pettigrew, A.M. (1985), *The Awakening Giant: Continuity and Change in ICI*, Oxford: Basil Blackwell.

Pettigrew, A.M. (1995), 'Longitudinal field research on change: theory and practice', in Huber and Van de Ven (eds), pp. 91–125.

Pettigrew, A.M., R.W. Woodman and K.S. Cameron (2001), 'Studying organizational change and development: challenges for future research', *Academy of Management Journal*, **44** (4), 697–713.

Piekkari, R., C. Welch and E. Paavilainen (2009), 'The case study as disciplinary convention: evidence from international business journals', *Organizational Research Methods*, **12** (3), 567–89.

Roy, S. and I. Wilkinson (2004), 'International long term business relationships, communities of practice and innovation: a longitudinal case study of NDDB, India and Tetra Pak, Sweden', *International Journal of Technology Transfer and Commercialisation*, **3** (4), 454–69.

Salk, J.E. and O. Shenkar (2001), 'Social identities in an international joint venture: an exploratory case study', *Organization Science*, **12** (2), 161–78.

Salmi, A. (2000), 'Entry into turbulent business networks', *European Journal of Marketing*, **34** (11–12), 1374–90.

Sharpe, D. (2002), 'Teamworking and managerial control within a Japanese manufacturing subsidiary in the UK', *Personnel Review*, **31** (3), 267–82.

Sharpe, D. (2004), 'The relevance of ethnography to international business research', in R. Marschan-Piekkari and C. Welch (eds), *Handbook of Qualitative Research Methods for International Business*, Cheltenham, UK and Northampton, MA, USA: Edward Elgar, pp. 306–23.

Siggelkow, N. (2007), 'Persuasion with case studies', *Academy of Management Journal*, **50** (1), 20–24.

Sippola, A. and A. Smale (2007), 'The global integration of diversity management: a longitudinal case study', *International Journal of Human Resource Management*, **18** (11), 1895–916.

Soulsby, A. and E. Clark (2006). 'Changing patterns of employment in post-socialist organizations in Central and Eastern Europe: management action in a transitional context', *International Journal of Human Resource Management*, **17** (8), 1396–410.

Steier, L. (2001), 'New venture firms, international expansion, and the liabilities of joint venture relationships', *Journal of High Technology Management Research*, **12** (2), 295–321.

Stüting, H.-J., W. Dorow, F. Claassen and S. Blazejewski (eds) (2003), *Change Management in Transformation Economies: Integrating Corporate Strategy, Structure, and Culture in Poland*, Basingstoke: Palgrave.

Van de Ven, A.H. and M.S. Poole (1995), 'Methods for studying innovation development in the Minnesota Innovation Research Program', in Huber and Van de Ven (eds), pp. 155–85.

Welch, C. and I. Wilkinson (2004), 'The political embeddedness of international business networks', *International Marketing Review*, **21** (2), 216–31.

Yin, R.K. (2009), *Case Study Research: Design and Methods*, 4th edn, Thousand Oaks, CA: Sage.

Zander, I. (2002), 'The formation of international innovation networks in the multinational corporation: an evolutionary perspective', *Industrial and Corporate Change*, **11** (2), 327–53.

Appendix Table 14A.1   Longitudinal case studies in international business, 1998–2008

Authors	Topic of interest	Number of cases	Temporal structure	Data sources
Carr (2005)	Changes in decision-making practices in German, UK, Japanese and US companies	Multiple: two companies (UK and Japanese car component industry) [part of a larger, non-longitudinal study with >70 cases]	Simultaneous/multiple shots Case time: 1989–2002 Research time: intervals in 1989, 1994 and 2002	Real-time interviews (retrospective in between research intervals)
Coviello (2006)	Network dynamics of international new ventures	Multiple: networks of three companies (New Zealand software industry)	*Ex post* (?) Case time: 1999–2004 Research time: not specified except that the process was 'iterative'	Data perspective combination Retrospective interviews, documents (websites, planning documents, promotional material)
Eckert and Mayrhofer (2005)	Epochs of internationalization: identification and explanation	Single: Hoechst/ Aventis	*Ex post* Case time: mid-1980s to 2002 Research time: not specified	Real-time archival documents (annual reports, CEO speeches, published interviews, news articles)
Hyder and Ghauri (2000)	Development of international JVs over time, Swedish firms in India	Multiple: two Swedish firms/JVs in India	Research perspective combination (?) Case time: 1960s to 1997 Research time: 1982–97	Real time (?) participant observation, interviews, archival documents (internal reports, annual reports, memoranda)

Study	Focus	Case design	Research perspective/time	Data perspective
Inkpen and Dinur (1998)	Knowledge management processes in international JVs, in particular mechanisms/types of knowledge transferred from JV to parent firm	Multiple: five US–Japanese JVs	*Ex post* (?) Case time: not specified Research time: May 1993–September 1994 (+ two years prior for preparatory interviews)	Retrospective (?) interviews
Johanson and Johanson (2006)	Market entry of Swedish firm in Russia, processes of 'discovery' (of knowledge) in turbulent markets	Single: Swedish firm (Karlshamns)	Research perspective combination Case time: 1987–93 Research time: 1990–96	Data perspective combination Interviews (retrospective for period before 1989, 1990–93 real time)
Jones and Miskell (2007)	Long-term firm growth through international acquisitions	Multiple: Unilever tea and ice-cream businesses	*Ex post* Case time: ca. 1960–95 Research time: not specified	Real time archival documents (board minutes, meeting memos)
Kotabe et al. (2008)	Long-term effects of outsourcing	Multiple: three companies (Emerson Radio, Sony, Philips)	*Ex post* Case time: 1954–2007 Research time: not specified	Data perspective combination (?) Retrospective interviews (?), archival documents (news articles, company documents, published reports)
Kristensen and Zeitlin (2005)	Actors' strategies within an MNC, evolution of subsidiaries from different national business systems within an MNC	Multiple: '4-in-1': single multinational with three subsidiaries plus HQ	Research perspective combination (?) Case time: early 1980s to 1997 (+ company history since 1880) Research time: ca. 1984–97	Data perspective combination (?) Archival documents (for company histories), real-time (?) and retrospective interviews (for events during core case time)

Appendix Table 14A.1 (continued)

Authors	Topic of interest	Number of cases	Temporal structure	Data sources
Li (1998)	Evolution of multinational firms from Asia	Single: Acer	*Ex post* Case time: 1976–95 Research time: not specified	Data perspective combination Archival documents (corporate brochures, annual reports, news articles, published case studies)
Mainela and Puhakka (2007)	Individual action and embeddedness as drivers of international JV development in Poland	Single: one Nordic–Polish international JV	Research perspective combination Case time: 1989–2000 Research time: 1997–2001	Data perspective combination Retrospective interviews (1997 and 2000), archival documents (yearly reports, JV agreements, published articles)
Maznevski and Chudoba (2000)	Dynamics and effectiveness of global virtual teams	Multiple: three teams in one company	Simultaneous/ continuous Case time: 21 months (+group history up to 7 years) Research time: 21 months (3 informal discussions, 9 observation, 9 discussions)	Real-time interviews and participant observation (max. 2 days of meeting), archival documents, communication logs, questionnaires

			Research perspective combination	Data perspective combination
Roy and Wilkinson (2004)	Communities of practice and innovation in long-term business relationships	Single: relationship between NDDB, Tetra Pak and its Indian JV HPCL	Case time: 1957–98 Research time: (1982–) 1997/98	Real-time participant observation by one author 1982–95 (no systematic data collection), interviews 1997–98, archival documents (company files)
Salk and Shenkar (2001)	Social identities in international JVs (British/Italian)	Single: British–Italian JV	Simultaneous/multiple shot Case time: 4 years Research time: 30 months	Real-time interviews, participant observation, archival documents (employee surveys, memos, press clippings)
Salmi (2000)	Market entry of Western firm into Estonia	Single: one company	Simultaneous/multiple shot Case time: 1991–94 Research time: five phases of data gathering in 1991, 1992, 1993, 1994, 1996	Real-time interviews
Sharpe (2002)	Contextual impact on HR (control) practices in Japanese subsidiaries in the UK	Multiple: four teams in two sites of one company	Simultaneous/ continuous Case time: not specified, min. 2 months per case + historical context of site Research time: total 15 months	Real-time participant observation

Appendix Table 14A.1 (continued)

Authors	Topic of interest	Number of cases	Temporal structure	Data sources
Sippola and Smale (2007)	Diversity management in MNC	Single: Finnish MNC subsidiary	Simultaneous/multiple shot Case time: 2003–05 Research time: 2003–05	Real-time interviews, focus group, documents
Soulsby and Clark (2006)	Employment patterns in Czech corporations	Multiple: three companies	Simultaneous/multiple shot Case time: 1992–2001 Research time: 1992–2001	Real-time interviews
Steier (2001)	Internationalization of new ventures firms through JVs: liabilities and instability	Single: Canadian/Arab international JV	Simultaneous/multiple shot Case time: 1990–98 Research time: 1990–98	Real-time participant observation (four or more times a year), interviews, archival documents (quarterly reports, copies of correspondence, JV agreements)
Welch and Wilkinson (2004)	Political embeddedness of a network of a company over time (formation, transformation, dissolution)	Single: one Australian sugar company and its international networks	*Ex post* Case time: 1951–2000 Research time: not specified	Retrospective (?) interviews, archival documents (not specified)
Zander (2002)	Long-term formation of innovation networks in an MNC	Single: ASEA/Brown Boveri/ABB, plus ABB's international subsidiaries	*Ex post* Case time: 1890–1990 Research time: not specified	Retrospective secondary sources (not specified), quantitative data on US patents

15. Theorizing process through punctuated longitudinal case study research

Anna Soulsby and Ed Clark

INTRODUCTION: PROCESS AND PROCESS RESEARCH

The last 20 years have seen increasing interest in methodological strategies to address the challenge of working with and theorizing from process materials in order to understand how and why organizations grow, adapt, fail or otherwise undergo change. This concern reflects a 'process turn' that has spread through many areas of management research. Although process research is still conducted by only a minority of management scholars, its promotion up the theoretical and methodological agenda results from not only the incessant dynamic realities of globalization and competition but also dissatisfaction with the process credentials of multivariate techniques, demographic methods and other forms of quantitative model building (Mohr 1982; Van de Ven and Huber 1990; Parkhe 1993; Lawrence 1997).

In order to understand what happens within a sequence of events as it unfolds over time, many organization and management researchers have therefore reoriented their attention towards ways of studying temporal organizational phenomena through a process lens (Pettigrew 1990; Van de Ven and Poole 1995; Langley, 1999; and Tsoukas and Chia 2002). In turn, this has begun to influence debates within the international business (IB) and international management (IM) literatures. For example, scholars have examined the internal dynamics of international strategic alliances (Yan and Gray 1994; Doz 1996; Ariño and de la Torre 1998) and the integration of acquisitions into multinational corporate frameworks (Vaara 2003; Kristensen and Zeitlin 2005; Bouquet and Birkinshaw 2008).

The primary aims of process research are to reveal the sequential order of events, examine how event sequences have unfolded over time and explain why they have evolved in a particular way towards a certain outcome or endpoint (Abbott 1990; Van de Ven and Poole 1995; Langley 1999). However, it is made difficult because of the very nature of organizational process, which has been variously described as messy, fluid, fragmented, spatially and temporally dispersed and subjectively perceived from multiple perspectives in the organization (Barley 1990; Pettigrew 1990; Langley 1999). These characteristics affect how process can be observed in the form of events, decisions and actions, and recorded as 'data'.

Given the complexity of conceptualizing process and capturing it in data, it is not surprising that direct longitudinal studies of organizational process remain relatively rare (Mintzberg 1979; Eisenhardt 1989; Pettigrew 1990; Van de Ven and Huber 1990; O'Connor et al. 2003), especially in the field of international or comparative organization (Parkhe 1993; Yan and Gray 1994; Doz 1996; Pettigrew et al. 2001; Shenkar and Yan 2002). Like these scholars, we take the main task of process research to be the devising of a methodologically sound and practical longitudinal research design, based on qualitative data collected from real organizations at multiple points in time, through which it is possible to construct a theory that explains event progression by identifying underlying generative mechanisms (see, for example, Tsoukas 1989; Van de Ven and Poole 1995).

The starting point in studying process is how to collect data that can offer a reliable foundation for process theorizing. In this respect, many longitudinal studies have tended to rely on data that derive from respondents' present-day recollections of historical events, because retrospective data minimize the problems associated with carrying out real-time study at many points over a period (Miller et al. 1997). The validity of process theorizing when inducted solely from respondents' retrospectively constructed accounts presumes their ability and willingness to recall accurately and avoid those personal, professional or political motives that, in creating nuance or distortion, may distance or detach their accounts from the reality they purport to describe (Miles 1979; Huber 1985; Leonard-Barton 1990; Golden 1992). Not only does the retrospective nature of all sensemaking (Weick 1995) introduce significant doubts about how 'accurately' *post hoc* accounts reflect what 'really' happened, but respondent accounts are also influenced by the complex social dynamics of the interview situation (Fontana and Frey 2000; Alvesson 2003). The final representation of process in retrospective qualitative data is rightly the subject of intense methodological debate.

Like many scholars who hold an ontologically realist position, we assume that 'real' processes do take place and that our task as social scientists is not just to understand how these are experienced by actors within the social situation but to explain the actual processes that led to their subjective experiences. While acknowledging the problem of recall bias, we argue that organizational process can in some way and to some degree be captured in what insiders say about their work experiences. Studying insider retrospective narratives is therefore one means through which scholars can approach the greater objective of explaining these real processes (Tsoukas 1989; Pentland 1999; Wolfram-Cox and Hassard 2007).

Given a commitment to intensive, qualitative longitudinal study of process, the problems of retrospective research might at first appear to advance the case for an ethnographic research design, since it permits on-the-spot observations that lead to real-time data collected as the process unfolds (Barley 1990; Moore 2005). However, ethnographic research is not without problems (Czarniawska 2004). Deep immersion in the field, which raises its own reflexive challenges, does not guarantee that the ethnographer can comprehend 'an event' or its location in a sequence. Organizations have a multiplicity of different internal time cycles of action which can affect actors in other parts of the organization in various subtle and complex ways that may be invisible to the researcher (Ancona and Chong 1996; Goodman 2000). The temporal embeddedness of events varies according to duration, intensity and relevance, and therefore the significance of events may take time to emerge within an organization (Glick et al. 1990; Langley 1999; Orlikowski and Yates 2002; Staudenmayer et al. 2002). By the time the 'real' meaning of events becomes understood, the ethnographer may be long gone. In short, although ethnographic studies can offer direct insight into process, they tend to be spatially and temporally constrained.

Quite apart from these methodological matters associated with real-time studies of process, there are strong practical constraints on any time-intensive pattern of longitudinal research. Full-time academics have other commitments associated with teaching and administrative roles and few have the freedom or funding to spend prolonged periods immersed in the field. These practicalities permeate all efforts to be a 'field researcher', but are likely to be exacerbated when exploring international organizational processes through intensive engagement with geographically distributed sites. The need to make practical compromises based on convenience and opportunity (Ancona et al. 2001) may tempt researchers to fall back on research designs that are likely to reduce the temporal dimension of process (Mohr 1982) and lead to processually undertheorized constructs (Abbott 1990; Mitchell and James 2001).

In short, the challenge is to develop a research design that optimizes the theoretical insights that can be drawn within these methodological and practical constraints on qualitative longitudinal case studies. The systematic approach developed in this chapter addresses some of these enduring issues associated with process research. Our arguments are framed by three general questions. First, what kinds of data provide a sound basis for understanding how events are linked through time? Second, how can we move from the level of concrete observation (process data) to the level of abstract process theory? Third, how can we minimize the methodological problems associated with process research that relies on retrospective data for its process credentials?

In answering these questions, the chapter makes four main contributions to the methodology of process research in organized settings that may be geographically dispersed. First, and most generally, we advocate a research design called the punctuated longitudinal case study (PLCS). Drawn from our own research experiences, this design may reconcile the pressures of conducting real-time and retrospective research in a methodologically sound and practical way. Second, we explore the possibilities of this research design for collecting two types of process-relevant material – synchronic and diachronic (especially narrative) data – which result in the compilation of a temporally rich qualitative database. Third, we borrow and adapt Polkinghorne's (1988, 1995) concepts of narrative inquiry in order to propose different ways of moving from synchronic and diachronic data to levels of process-theoretic explanation. Fourth, we argue that this combination of data is especially appropriate for controlling accuracy issues arising from retrospective accounts in the study of organizational process.

The next section introduces PLCS through reflections upon our own research experiences in a longitudinal study of organizational change over two decades. This leads us to consider in more detail the nature of the synchronic, diachronic and narrative data that form the empirical foundation of qualitative observations, and then explore two narrative-based approaches to the analysis of the qualitative database that give shape to the possible modes of understanding process. We then show how the data types and the typical forms of narrative inquiry in PLCS research design allow the researcher to address methodological concerns over the necessary use of retrospective materials. In concluding with observations about the usefulness of PLCS for developing process theory, we reflect on the main limitations of this research design.

OUR RESEARCH PROJECT

The research project that is the source of inspiration and illustration for the discussion in this chapter is a comparative longitudinal study of four former state-owned enterprises (SOEs) in the Czech Republic that started in 1992. Vols, Jesenické Strojírny, Montáže Jesenice and Agstroj[1] are located in the mechanical engineering and metal-working industries, and extensive details of the enterprises and the changes that they have experienced can be found elsewhere (Clark and Soulsby 1995, 1996, 1998, 1999a, 1999b, 2007; Soulsby and Clark 1996, 1998). They have experienced varying degrees of success as senior managers have tried to make adjustments to the impacts of globalization and the requirements of a Western-style market economy.

Within the research project, our theoretical interests have followed where the empirical issues have led. We started with a variety of restructuring questions such as privatization, decentralization, divisionalization and fragmentation, but when analysis of the data revealed the explanatory importance of how the pre-1989 enterprises were differentially embedded within their communities (Clark and Soulsby 1998), we resolved to examine the social and historical contexts of the enterprises more closely (Yin 2009). Since about 2000, when foreign companies began to acquire the whole or parts of the enterprises, our research project has encompassed more IB and IM concerns about forms and styles of foreign management.

Adopting a case study approach allowed us to examine in detail how these enterprises changed under the post-socialist conditions of societal transience. Our aim was to build fine-grained, qualitatively rich case studies of the enterprises (Geertz 1973) in order to trace the key events in the change processes and thereby to understand the role of strategic choice in the adoption and institutionalization of new structures and practices (Child 1972; Hambrick 1981). This intensive qualitative approach not only reflected a methodological rationale but also shared personal preferences about conducting hands-on, in-depth research within a small number of organizations (Glick et al. 1990; Leonard-Barton 1990; McPhee 1990; Monge 1990).

Drawing on local contacts well connected to the Czech mechanical engineering industry, we arranged field visits to the four enterprises in 1992, 1993 and 1994, while they were awaiting privatization. At the centre of each two-week visit were the traditional research methods for qualitative case studies: semi-structured interviews, supplemented with daily informal field notes, the recording of emergent themes and the systematic noting of reflexive impressions (Eisenhardt 1989; Yin 2009). We conducted the semi-structured interviews with the assistance of informed translators, who acted as oral mediators in meetings with managers, as cultural interpreters of those aspects of the Czech organizational context that were alien to us and as collaborators in making sense of the bigger picture that emerged from what respondents said (Soulsby 2004). Interviews on average lasted about two hours and were conducted with senior and middle managers across levels and business functions. In these interviews, we collected a lot of information about the current state of the enterprise, but also many fascinating stories about the enterprise, its history and traditions, its 'heroes' and 'villains', and how it came to be where it was. We also gathered extensive secondary materials about each of the organizations.

At the time of our initial field visits, it was not possible to anticipate the project's potential for longitudinal work. It soon became clear, however, that our work had generated enough goodwill within each enterprise to allow us to return. Thus, we resolved to consolidate the project around a pattern of revisits, each lasting one to two days and involving very long interviews with a few senior and well-informed respondents. Thereafter, the research process has continued through a programme of revisits that take place broadly every two years. Through these revisits, we have collected interview, observational and documentary data about the ongoing processes of change – the events that had taken place in the intervening period and insiders' views about why they had taken this temporal form.

The resultant 'punctuated longitudinal case study' research design is characterized as an approach that intentionally collects qualitative data through a repeat pattern of research visits and revisits to the same organizational settings (see Foster et al. 1979; Leonard-Barton 1990; Burawoy 2003). Although we have used historical and retrospective methods to collect material about the state socialist history of these enterprises, the real-time temporal period of each case study starts with the first field visit. This temporal period – and the event sequences that fill it out as process – has been punctuated by regular but much shorter field revisits. The endpoint of the study is of course moving, since each revisit extends the period of study, giving a new point of closure that can be characterized by process 'outcomes'.

We have not enjoyed complete success with this design strategy. While we have assembled comprehensive sets of interview, observational and documentary data for Vols, Jesenické Strojírny and Montáže Jesenice, our later research contacts with Agstroj have been at best sporadic. For Vols, for example, we have visited the plant nine times from 1992 to 2007. However, Agstroj has been such a politically sensitive object of inquiry that it has been difficult to arrange revisits. As a result, we often had to interview our respondents off site and our communications eventually broke down after 2003. Despite this, the PLCS approach has yielded interviews with over 200 directors and managers, some of whom have been re-interviewed on consecutive occasions.

In this chapter, we focus our attention on the temporal design characteristics of PLCS. By combining varied sources (interviews, documents, observations, archival materials) of different types of qualitative data (historical, real time, retrospective) located at multiple historical points dispersed across time, it offers a practical approach to studying process, with a number of methodologically important advantages.

FROM PROCESS DATA TO PROCESS THEORIZING

The visit–revisit pattern permits the accumulation within one database of two broad types of process-relevant data. Each contributes in different ways to understanding temporal sequences of events by providing the evidential basis for different modes of process theory, the possibility of tracing the development of events and sequences, and mechanisms for evaluating retrospective data. The iterative process of collecting diachronic and synchronic data as part of every field visit creates an extensive and complex archive of real-time and retrospective materials, including the original interviews, field notes, internal and external documents, reflexive notes and descriptive case studies (see also Barley 1990). Together, these data types form the basis from which the process researcher can identify patterns and sequences of events and develop process theory.

This section focuses on the analytical and interpretive questions of how to move from these complex, messy and fragmentary process-relevant data to the construction of explanatory theory. We tackle this challenge by building on Polkinghorne's (1988, 1995) different modes of 'narrative inquiry'. Narrative inquiry is at the root of qualitative longitudinal case study research, because narratives are legitimate forms of both data and theory. In this section, we turn first to diachronic data and suggest the use of narrative analysis to make sense of diachronic data as first-order narratives. Thereafter, we introduce synchronic data and outline narrative construction[2] as a technique for making sense of synchronic data and building process explanation in the form of second-order narratives. We conclude this section by showing how these two forms of process data and analysis can be combined to generate process explanations.

From Diachronic Data to First-order Narrative Analysis

Diachronic data convey information about temporal events and how (possibly why) they unfolded in a particular sequence; that is, they contain 'time'. As in corporate documents and histories, diachronic data can take a simple chronological form with list-like qualities (Polkinghorne 1995; Czarniawska 2004). However, mostly when people write or talk about 'how we got to the current state of affairs', they tend to imbue an event sequence with a plot that gives it a narrative form with its own meaningful internal ordering.

As with other scholars, we use the term 'narrative' to describe a storied form of discourse, recognizing that it is not just a type of explanation but an appropriate form for representing temporal sequence in organizations (Van Maanen 1988; Czarniawska-Joerges 1995; Brown 1998). As diachronic data collected from interviewees, narratives are first-order retrospective accounts, which, in the mind of the respondent at least, have their own internal logic or plot located within their own experiences of context (Bruner 1990). These accounts provide a powerful insight into process for a number of reasons. First, they are representations of how past events unravelled to the present day; second, they show the event sequence from the respondent's moral viewpoint, offer an attitude towards the events and assess the actions of the main social actors (Linde 2001); third, they are methodologically significant because they are inherently processual accounts and explanations that have close connection to and motivational potency in the field. As Pentland (1999, p. 712) reminds us, actors 'not only make sense of their world in narrative terms . . . but proactively plan and enact narratives that are consistent with their expectations and values'.

First-order narratives, which are constructed and emplotted by respondents, form the basis of narrative analysis. The aim of the researcher in narrative analysis is to interrogate these diachronic data and search for patterns in the sequencing of the events and in how insiders have made sense of them. This mode of narrative inquiry accepts that organizational reality will generate multiple first-order narratives that reflect the differing perspectives inherent in organizational life. The analysis can take one of two forms. As a deductive process, the researcher can apply analytical criteria drawn from the existing literature in order to find evidence of theoretical constructs or propositions within and across cases, for example, using pattern matching (Yin 2009). Inductively, the researcher can proceed by identifying abstract themes and constructs in the narratives that constitute the database, using, for example, data reduction methods (Miles and Huberman 1984). Either way, the theoretical outcome is a framework of constructs and propositions about conceptual relationships that holds as generalizable characteristics of the first-order accounts (Polkinghorne 1995). In Bruner's (1986) terminology, this search for common themes or conceptual manifestations across the stories constitutes a paradigmatic understanding of the empirical data.

We have tended to adopt narrative analytical logic in the academic reporting of our research. In examining why employment rates in Vols held up so much better than in Jesenické Strojírny during the 1990s, for example, we could examine the diachronic explanations of employment policy and practices given by various respondents in the two enterprises. The stories that we were told alerted us to the different ways in which the two organizations related to – were embedded in – their local communities. Vols's senior managers wove their narratives of change around the taken-for-granted truth that 'Volna is Vols'; that is, the community is totally dependent on the enterprise. Thus, Vols's Metallurgy Director in 1992 spoke passionately about how his decision making on employment was affected by the fact that he lived alongside employees' families and had seen their children grow up. In Jesenické Strojírny, on the other hand, senior management narratives of restructuring were predicated on business-related themes of decentralization and management efficiency; that is, with little sense of external social burdens. Data reduction analyses of the senior managers' narratives led us to identify enterprise embeddedness as a common factor that could explain their different approaches to employment over time (Clark and Soulsby 1998; Soulsby and Clark 2006).

Narrative analysis comprises more conventional ways of moving from qualitative storied data to theoretical explanation based on the abstraction of concepts and propositions of a more formal nature. Such theoretical models – which are invariably more acceptable to international journals – use more standard paradigmatic reasoning about how antecedents, processes and consequences are linked through an unfolding stream of time. Insider plots, with their descriptively rich emic qualities, are turned into conceptually abstract propositions that lose the original detail in favour of a more tightly constructed etic theory of process (Abbott 1990; Monge 1990).

From Synchronic Data to Second-order Narrative Construction

Synchronic data comprise both qualitative and quantitative data that describe aspects of the current state of organizational affairs. Within the interviews, questions in the form 'what have been the main changes since the last visit?' prompted respondents to offer here-and-now descriptions of the 'current' situation and very recent events (see Leonard-Barton 1990). These real-time probes concerned issues such as strategy, structure, employment numbers, top management team membership, technology and products; the resultant synchronic data enabled us to put together a picture of the organization at a particular point in the event sequence. While synchronic data in principle lack a sense of historical development (Polkinghorne 1995), in practice, they tend to be 'lifted' from the end of more elaborate storied accounts about 'how we got here'. These synchronic data can be checked against other data sources using conventional triangulation techniques.

Narrative construction starts from the temporal layers of synchronic data, which record contemporary judgements of recent or here-and-now events as revealed in interviews or documents written at the time. The researcher arranges these events within a temporal order to constitute the components of a processual sequence. Drawing on contextual and other information (including diachronic materials), the researcher uses interpretive and synthesizing skills to 'fill the gaps' and construct an explanatory story (Langley 1999). The researcher is actively involved in identifying a suitable plot that gives sense to the ways in which the component events are combined. The theoretical outcome of narrative construction is a second-order story that provides an internally coherent and plausible explanation of how purpose, actors, decisions, events and chance are connected through time, culminating in a dénouement (Van Maanen 1979; Polkinghorne 1995; Pentland 1999). Within a comparative design, researcher-constructed stories of organizational process can then be compared and contrasted with those constructed about other organizations in order to develop a meta-narrative account.

In our own research, the series of visits from 1992 to 1998 raised important empirical questions about the power, role and position of the personnel function within the four enterprises. Our good connections with personnel staff enabled us at each visit to collect synchronic data about the 'current' situation: size of the department, its level in the organization structure, the important managers and to whom they reported, what influence (they felt) they had on top decisions, relationships with other functional managers, and so on. Structurally, the data showed that the position of the personnel department – once powerful as the enterprise representative of the Communist Party – fluctuated widely during the early 1990s in all four enterprises. In 1990, it disappeared as a named department to become a small 'section' hidden under finance or administration, but by 1996–98 it had resurfaced as a senior department.

The choice of personnel manager provided important clues about what was going on. In 1990, immediately after the collapse of communism, the existing 'Cadre and Personnel' director – a trusted member of the Party – was either demoted or dismissed, to be replaced by a known non-communist; in turn, he/she was usually replaced when the department resurfaced as a senior management function, sometimes by a former communist manager. Supported by data from other sources, we constructed a plausible story about the ebbs and flows of the personnel function. Insiders generally understood the process in terms of the collapse and reinvention of managerial and organizational legitimacy. In turn, we have been able to link our overarching stories about the changing status and legitimacy of the personnel function to an interpretive sociological version of institutional theory (Soulsby and Clark 1998).

In this example, the synchronic data pointed to the existence of an

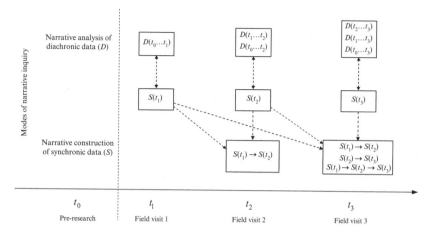

Figure 15.1   Narrative data types and modes of narrative inquiry

empirical process problem – the changing nature of the personnel function over time – to be explained. In trying to fill the temporal gaps between the events observed during different visits, we drew on the whole database to construct an overarching second-order narrative, based on the changing nature of legitimacy in a post-socialist society and reflecting a more abstractly theorized story. This narrative identified broader themes that enabled us to link it to established forms of organizational theory. The empirical problem was turned into a theoretical solution by narrative construction.

Mixed Modes of Narrative Inquiry

Over a number of visits, synchronic and diachronic materials accumulate into a qualitatively rich, temporally layered database (see Figure 15.1). First, there are diachronic narratives of the form $D(t_1 \ldots t_n)$, which is an internally emplotted account (D) of the process and its constituent events collected at the visit at time 'n' and covering the period between the first visit (t_1) and 'this' visit (t_n). During each visit, interviews produce narratives from each respondent, whose retrospective accounts may cover a variety of historical periods. On the third visit, for example, each interviewee may construct narratives covering the whole organizational history ($D(t_0 \ldots t_3)$), the period since the first visit ($D(t_1 \ldots t_3)$), and the period since the last visit ($D(t_2 \ldots t_3)$). Each first-order story has its own internal integrity and offers potential explanations (as experienced from inside the process) of the sequence of events, though it may also reflect a respondent's cognitive frailties, diverse values and interests in the organizational process (Huber 1985; Golden 1992; Miller et al. 1997).

Second, each interview produces synchronic data (*S*) that describe the state of the organization at the time of a particular visit. $S(t_n)$ thus refers to one respondent's version of the state of affairs at the time of visit *n*. Methodologically, they offer real-time accounts of 'events' in an ongoing process at different points in time. Third, when compared across time, synchronic data have the analytical potential for dynamic theorizing through the process of interpretive gap-filling. Thus, after the third visit, the three separate layers of real-time synchronic data can be meaningfully connected through the researcher's interpretive (emplotting) action to produce a second-order narrative of the form $S(t_1) \rightarrow S(t_2) \rightarrow S(t_3)$ (Langley 1999). These second-order accounts, for example in the form of case studies, add layers to the database in the same way as diachronic and synchronic data.

As Figure 15.1 demonstrates, longitudinal researchers with a combined synchronic and diachronic database can use either narrative inquiry option – narrative analysis or narrative construction – to generate process theory. In practice, however, they are likely to draw on the different types of data more expediently and move iteratively between the two modes of reasoning. We would argue that mixing modes of narrative inquiry has a lot to offer the researcher with a processually rich database. For example, first-order narratives can be a source for second-order narratives, while synchronic data can offer a legitimate foundation for paradigmatic reasoning; equally, it is important that conceptual frameworks and narrative theorizing are explored for synergies so that the explanatory power of process-theoretical outputs can be increased (Brown 1998; Langley 1999; Pentland 1999).

We consciously adopted a mixed-mode approach in developing explanations of the role of top management teams (TMTs) in strategic decision making in Vols from 1990 to 2003. By 2003, our database had become a detailed archive of synchronic materials, including information about the demographic details (age, tenure, management experience, homogeneity) of Vols's TMT at five different points in time. Comparing across these times, it was possible to identify changes in TMT demography that could be associated with various processual outcomes (such as performance). At the same time, we had a temporally layered collection of management stories about how these process outcomes had come about. By treating the time-compared synchronic data iteratively with the insider stories over the same period – that is, overlaying narrative analysis techniques with the construction of a second-order narrative – it was possible to create a more persuasive and plausible theoretical account of the process of management and its effects on organizational performance (Clark and Soulsby 2007).

Using these narrative inquiry modes independently or in combination, it is possible to develop a single, nuanced theoretical account from the empirical noise of multiple, partial, subjective, and even conflicting respondent accounts. In doing so, we can move towards the 'discovery' of underlying patterns in the sequence of events and their generative mechanisms (Tsoukas 1989; Van de Ven and Poole 1995; Pentland 1999). This approach to constructing overarching narratives serves to develop levels of analytic generalization (Yin 2009) and theoretical plausibility (Weick 1989), while sustaining close connection to the original diachronic and synchronic data.

ADDRESSING RETROSPECTIVE BIAS

The diachronic and synchronic materials assembled and generated from the PLCS visit–revisit pattern result in temporal layers of respondent and researcher accounts, which together constitute an important safeguard against the methodological limitations of longitudinal research that is wholly dependent for its temporal dimension on retrospective data.

From the perspective of a recent visit (for example, Time 3 in Figure 15.1), first-order narratives that offer plot-lines to explain a contemporary outcome (for example, $D(t_2 \ldots t_3)$) or a past ending (for example, $D(t_1 \ldots t_2)$) can be analysed alongside synchronic data ($S(t_1)$, $S(t_2)$ and $S(t_3)$) and researcher-constructed narratives inferred from synchronic data covering the same periods of time: $S(t_1) \rightarrow S(t_2)$, $S(t_2) \rightarrow S(t_3)$, and $S(t_1) \rightarrow S(t_2) \rightarrow S(t_3)$. The temporal layers of diachronic and synchronic data made available through real-time studies at multiple points in time offer different methods of checking respondents' retrospectively constructed accounts against the same or other respondents' accounts of the status quo at different points of observation.

Let us consider a respondent's retrospective account of the structural changes that took place between 1996 and 2000, as narrated in 2000 ($D_{(1996-2000)}$). We know that his/her memories of 1996 may have been affected by the lens through which he/she now interprets the past, but if we assume that the PLCS database also includes data from a visit in 1998, we can examine the methodological opportunities for checking retrospective bias. Having reread field notes taken in 1996, the researcher can interrogate respondents' contemporaneous accounts (S_{1996}) and later historically constructed accounts that provide information about 1996 ($D_{(1996-1998)}$). At the same time, the accuracy of *ex post factum* event recall and narrative emplotment can be compared directly with second-order narratives ($S_{1996} \rightarrow S_{1998}$). Since all these temporal layers in the database already exist, they are independent of the retrospective account in question.

The 'accuracy' of a respondent's narrative can therefore be tested for consistency or inconsistency (rather than affirmation or refutation) with existing materials. If the respondent's power of recall passes these tests, researchers can have increased confidence in both the recalled events and the stories, nullifying worries about his/her cognitive abilities and political motives. If retrospective stories fail these tests, the researcher knows that the diachronic data have to be evaluated more critically. Moreover, knowledge of the 'misconstruction' of past events may offer new avenues for empirical and theoretical investigation. The scope for such internal accuracy testing improves as the temporal layers in the database increase.

For example, we interviewed one senior manager in Jesenické Strojírny in both 1993 and 1996 and followed his career as he moved to become the General Director of Montáže Jesenice in the early 2000s, where we later interviewed him twice more. His stories of how Jesenické Strojírny had restructured in the mid-1990s were directly misleading in that he systematically screened out the role that he and his senior managerial colleagues had played in making decisions that turned out to be fateful for the enterprise. We could make these evaluations because of the layers of synchronic and diachronic data that covered the period in question. This conclusion not only led us to make judgements about his overall credibility as a historical witness and re-examine other respondents' accounts more carefully; it also made us consider alternative ways of interpreting his past and current motives.

CONCLUSIONS

Our aim in this chapter is to contribute to the methodology of process research by exploring strategies that allow qualitative researchers to examine organization and management through a process lens. In outlining our proposal for studying and theorizing process in organizations, we have drawn on 17 years' experience of conducting fieldwork research within transforming societies. Reflecting upon the evolution of the project, we believe that the punctuated longitudinal case study design as outlined above can inform IB and IM scholars interested in developing process research. As a research design, PLCS offers solutions to a number of pressing problems that have dogged process research.

First, we have considered the kinds of data that can provide a sound basis for understanding how events are linked through time. The generation of diachronic and synchronic materials – especially those gleaned from semi-structured interviews – is the critical empirical foundation for developing a theory of process. These types of data reflect different routes taken through the messy reality that is process. When collected over a number of temporally dispersed field visits, synchronic data, while essentially static, serve as the basis for developing an interpretive understanding of how events are connected through time. Diachronic data, especially in the form of first-order narratives, are in themselves internally theorized accounts of process, where event sequences take the form of insider-constructed plots.

Second, we have discussed different narrative inquiry approaches that allow us to move from process-relevant data to the level of process theory. The collection of diachronic and synchronic materials enables researchers to use both narrative analysis and narrative construction procedures to interrogate the database. Narrative analysis, in principle, analyses diachronic data paradigmatically in order to discover theoretically generalizable patterns and themes that can be conceptualized and formed into propositional logic. Narrative construction takes temporally dispersed synchronic data and fills the temporal gaps through interpretation and synthesis, culminating in a narrative form of theoretical understanding. In practice, we have argued that these two modes of narrative inquiry tend to be used iteratively in order to develop theory that is always directly traceable to the empirical base.

Third, we have proposed how PLCS can deal with major practical and methodological constraints on the conduct of qualitative longitudinal research. As the PLCS project unfolds, it is also possible to address the problem of recall accuracy that is implicit in longitudinal studies that are dependent on retrospective accounts. The visit–revisit pattern allows researchers to monitor the accuracy of insider stories by comparing them with previous real-time accounts of respondents. Researchers can also reflect upon and assess retrospective accuracy against their own recorded impressions of process and change over the same period.

All research designs and methods have their limitations; we highlight here four particular challenges associated with the long-term, punctuated and narrative characteristics of PLCS. First, there are complicated issues linked to keeping contact with important managers in order to organize continuing visits to research sites. Managing a longitudinal project depends on relations of mutual trust between researcher and contact, and securing access is particularly difficult over a longer period, because managers move on in their career, get demoted or retire. Second, the long-term nature of research cooperation implicit in a PLCS project places both administrative and emotional pressures on the research team, given the normal strains of academic life. Keeping a PLCS project going – even sustaining commitment to processual research – can be thoroughly tested by the needs to create enough 'organizing space' and to nurture enthusiasm as research priorities change over time. This problem can be exacerbated when colleagues work in different institutions and countries or come from different academic disciplines (Adler 1983; Easterby-Smith and Danusia 1999; Ancona et al. 2001; O'Connor et al. 2003; Birkinshaw 2004; Marschan-Piekkari and Welch 2004).

Third, the database can rapidly become a 'data beast' as its growing complexity and size conspire against its accessibility for interrogation. Beyond simple database management, however, there is also the intellectual task of remaining close to the materials (Miles 1979; Leonard-Barton 1990; Van de Ven and Huber 1990). As the number of visits increases, it takes more and more time for the researchers to reimmerse themselves in the materials in order to explore first-order accounts, identify themes and construct higher-order narratives within and across organizations (Van de Ven and Huber 1990).

Fourth, there are the more commonly discussed methodological issues associated with the collection of narrative data and the interpretive process of constructing higher-order narratives. Interpretive practices can be understood as political acts that selectively silence some voices while privileging others (White 1981; Riessman 1993; Bal 1997) as the researcher searches for a personally preferred or theoretically more coherent account (Brown 1998; Pentland 1999). As we know, writing is not an innocent practice (Denzin and Lincoln 2003), and the choice of language can conceal as much as it reveals as the researcher smoothes over the messy reality of process to project an orderly account (Spence 1982).

Given these problems, it is perhaps not surprising that there are few examples of real-time and retrospective longitudinal research sustained over a long period. Nevertheless, we contend that the PLCS design offers enormous potential benefits for studying process through qualitative case studies, because it allows the reflexive field researcher to trace not only the development of organizational process itself but also his/her contributions to the development of theorized narratives. At a personal level, the intellectual reward that comes from developing a deep understanding of organizations over time cannot be overstated. There is always genuine excitement upon going back to the research settings and discovering changes that have taken place since the last visit and profound satisfaction in being able to identify the historical origins of current events and evaluate earlier expectations of process against later occurrences (Soulsby 2004).

When researchers are willing and able to show commitment to qualitative longitudinal research with multiple observation points, they have the opportunity to capture longer-term views of process. PLCS projects not only produce a series of time-constrained case studies, each of which extracts from ongoing process discrete sequences of events that describe and explain particular change processes (such as privatization, decentralization and internationalization); they also place these 'temporal glimpses' of process and their constituent events within the broader arc of organizational history.

NOTES

1. All names have been changed in the reporting of this research in order to preserve the confidentiality and anonymity of our respondents.
2. Polkinghorne (1995) calls these narrative modes, respectively, 'narrative analysis' and 'analysis of narratives', which we believe is quite confusing, especially since the former is really a synthesizing rather than analysing procedure. Polkinghorne (p. 15) acknowledges this point and we have adopted the term 'construction' to recognize the mode of reasoning involved.

REFERENCES

Abbott, A. (1990), 'A primer on sequence methods', *Organization Science*, **1** (4), 375–92.

Adler, N.J. (1983), 'Cross-cultural management research: the ostrich and the trend', *Academy of Management Review*, **8** (2), 226–32.

Alvesson, M. (2003), 'Beyond neopositivists, romantics and localists: a reflexive approach to interviews in field research', *Academy of Management Review*, **28** (1), 1–33.

Ancona, D. and C.-L. Chong (1996), 'Entrainment: pace, cycle, and rhythm in organizational behavior', *Research in Organizational Behavior*, **18**, 251–84.

Ancona, D.G., P.S. Goodman, B.S. Lawrence and L.M. Tushman (2001), 'Time: a new research lens', *Academy of Management Review*, **26** (4), 645–63.

Ariño, A. and J. de la Torre (1998), 'Learning from failure: towards an evolutionary model of collaborative ventures', *Organization Science*, **9** (3), 306–25.

Bal, M. (1997), *Narratology: Introduction to the Theory of Narrative*, Toronto: University of Toronto Press.

Barley, S.R. (1990), 'Images of imaging: notes on doing longitudinal field work', *Organization Science*, **1** (3), 220–47.

Birkinshaw, J. (2004), 'Publishing qualitative research in international business', in R. Marschan-Piekkari and C. Welch (eds), *Handbook of Qualitative Research Methods for International Business*, Cheltenham, UK and Northampton, MA, USA: Edward Elgar, pp. 570–84.

Bouquet, C. and J.M. Birkinshaw (2008), 'Managing power in the multinational corporation: how low-power actors gain influence', *Journal of Management*, **34** (3), 477–508.

Brown, A.D. (1998), 'Narrative, politics, and legitimacy in an IT implementation', *Journal of Management Studies*, **35** (1), 35–58.

Bruner, J. (1986), *Actual Minds, Possible Worlds*, Cambridge, MA: Harvard University Press.

Bruner, J. (1990), *Acts of Meaning*, Cambridge, MA: Harvard University Press.

Burawoy, M. (2003), 'Revisits: an outline of a theory of reflexive ethnography', *American Sociological Review*, **68** (5), 645–79.

Child, J. (1972), 'Organizational structure, environment and performance: the role of strategic choice', *Sociology*, **6** (1), 1–22.

Clark, E. and A. Soulsby (1995), 'Transforming former state enterprises in the Czech Republic', *Organization Studies*, **16** (2), 215–42.

Clark, E. and A. Soulsby (1996), 'The re-formation of the managerial elite in the Czech Republic', *EuropeAsia–Studies*, **48** (2), 285–303.

Clark, E. and A. Soulsby (1998), 'Organization–community embeddedness: the social impact of enterprise restructuring in the post-communist Czech Republic', *Human Relations*, **51** (1), 25–50.

Clark, E. and A. Soulsby (1999a), 'The adoption of the multi-divisional form in large Czech enterprises: the role of economic, institutional, and strategic choice factors', *Journal of Management Studies*, **36** (4), 535–59.

Clark, E. and A. Soulsby (1999b), *Organisational Change in Post-Communist Europe: Management and Transformation in the Czech Republic*, London: Routledge.

Clark, E. and A. Soulsby (2007), 'Understanding top management and organizational change through demographic and processual analysis', *Journal of Management Studies*, **44** (6), 932–54.

Czarniawska, B. (2004), 'On time, space, and action nets', *Organization*, **11** (6), 773–91.

Czarniawska-Joerges, B. (1995), 'Narration or science? Collapsing the division in organization studies', *Organization*, **2** (1), 147–52.

Denzin, N.K. and Y.S. Lincoln (2003), 'Preface', in N.K. Denzin and Y.S. Lincoln (eds), *Strategies of Qualitative Inquiry*, 2nd edn, London: Sage, pp. vii–xi.

Doz, Y.L. (1996), 'The evolution of cooperation in strategic alliances: initial conditions or learning processes?', *Strategic Management Journal*, **17** (Summer), 55–83.

Easterby-Smith, M. and M. Danusia (1999), 'Cross-cultural collaborative research: toward reflexivity', *Academy of Management Journal*, **42** (1), 76–86.

Eisenhardt, K.M. (1989), 'Building theories from case study research', *Academy of Management Review*, **14** (4), 532–50.

Fontana, A. and J.H. Frey (2000), 'The interview: from structured questions to negotiated text', in N.K. Denzin and Y.S. Lincoln (eds), *Handbook of Qualitative Research*, 2nd edn, London: Sage, pp. 645–72.

Foster, G., T. Scudder, E. Colson and R. Kemper (1979), *Long-term Field Research in Social Anthropology*, New York: Academic Press.

Geertz, C. (1973), *The Interpretation of Culture: Selected Essays*, New York: Basic Books.

Glick, W.H., G.P. Huber, C.C. Miller, D.H. Doty and K.M. Sutcliffe (1990), 'Studying changes in organizational design and effectiveness: retrospective event histories and periodic assessments', *Organization Science*, **1** (3), 293–312.

Golden, B.R. (1992), 'The past is the past – or is it? The use of retrospective accounts as indicators of past strategy', *Academy of Management Journal*, **35** (4), 848–60.

Goodman, P.S. (2000), *Missing Organizational Linkages: Tools for Cross-level Research*, Thousand Oaks, CA: Sage.

Hambrick, D.C. (1981), 'Strategic awareness within top management teams', *Strategic Management Journal*, **2** (3), 159–74.

Huber, G.P. (1985), 'Temporal stability and response-order biases in participant descriptions of organizational decisions', *Academy of Management Journal*, **28** (4), 943–50.

Kristensen, P.H. and J. Zeitlin (2005), *Local Players in Global Games: The Strategic Constitution of a Multinational Corporation*, Oxford: Oxford University Press.

Langley, A. (1999), 'Strategies for theorizing from process data', *Academy of Management Review*, **24** (4), 691–710.

Lawrence, B.S. (1997), 'The black box of organizational demography', *Organization Science*, **8** (1), 1–22.

Leonard-Barton, D. (1990), 'A dual methodology for case studies: synergistic use of a longitudinal single site with replicated multiple sites', *Organization Science*, **1** (3), 248–66.

Linde, C. (2001), 'Narrative and social tacit knowledge', *Journal of Knowledge Management*, **5** (2), 160–70.

Marschan-Piekkari, R. and C. Welch (2004), 'Qualitative research methods in international business: the state of the art', in R. Marschan-Piekkari and C. Welch (eds), *Handbook of Qualitative Research Methods for International Business*, Cheltenham, UK and Northampton, MA, USA: Edward Elgar, pp. 5–24.

McPhee, R.D. (1990), 'Alternate approaches to integrating longitudinal case studies', *Organization Science*, **1** (4), 393–405.

Miles, M.B. (1979), 'Qualitative data as an attractive nuisance: the problem of analysis', *Administrative Science Quarterly*, **24** (4), 590–601.

Miles, M.B. and A.M. Huberman (1984), *Qualitative Data Analysis*, Newbury Park, CA: Sage.

Miller, C.C., L.B. Cardinal and W.H. Glick (1997), 'Retrospective reports in organizational research: a re-examination of recent evidence', *Academy of Management Journal*, **40** (1), 189–204.

Mintzberg, H. (1979), 'An emerging strategy of "direct" research', *Administrative Science Quarterly*, **24** (4), 580–89.

Mitchell, T.R. and L.R. James (2001), 'Building better theory: time and the specification of when things happen', *Academy of Management Review*, **26** (4), 530–47.

Mohr, L.B. (1982), *Explaining Organizational Behavior*, San Francisco, CA: Jossey-Bass.

Monge, P.R. (1990), 'Theoretical and analytical issues in studying organizational processes', *Organization Science*, **1** (4), 406–30.

Moore, F. (2005), *Transnational Business Cultures: Life and Work in a Multinational Corporation*, Aldershot: Ashgate.

O'Connor, G.C., M.P. Rice, L. Peters and R.W. Veryzer (2003), 'Managing interdisciplinary longitudinal research teams: extending grounded theory-building methodologies', *Organization Science*, **14** (4), 353–73.

Orlikowski, W.J. and J. Yates (2002), 'It's about time: temporal structuring in organizations', *Organization Science*, **13** (6), 684–700.

Parkhe, A. (1993), '"Messy" research, methodological predispositions, and theory development in international joint ventures', *Academy of Management Review*, **18** (2), 227–68.

Pentland, B. (1999), 'Building process theory with narrative: from description to explanation', *Academy of Management Review*, **24** (4), 711–24.

Pettigrew, A.M. (1990), 'Longitudinal field research on change: theory and practice', *Organization Science*, **1** (3), 267–92.

Pettigrew, A.M., R.W. Woodman and K.S. Cameron (2001), 'Studying organizational change and development: challenges for future research', *Academy of Management Journal*, **44** (4), 697–713.

Polkinghorne, D.E. (1988), *Narrative Knowing and the Human Sciences*, Albany, NY: State University of New York.

Polkinghorne, D.E. (1995), 'Narrative configuration in qualitative analysis', in J.A. Hatch and R. Wisniewski (eds), *Life History and Narrative*, London: Falmer Press, pp. 5–23.

Riessman, C.K. (1993), *Narrative Analysis*, London: Sage.

Shenkar, O. and A. Yan (2002), 'Failure as a consequence of partner politics: learning from the life and death of an international cooperative venture', *Human Relations*, **55** (5), 565–601.

Soulsby, A. (2004), 'Who is observing whom? Fieldwork roles and ambiguities in organisational case study research', in E. Clark and S. Michailova (eds), *Fieldwork in Transforming Societies: Understanding Methodology from Experience*, Basingstoke: Palgrave Macmillan, pp. 39–56.

Soulsby, A. and E. Clark (1996), 'The emergence of post-communist management in the Czech Republic', *Organization Studies*, **17** (2), 227–47.

Soulsby, A. and E. Clark (1998), 'Controlling personnel: management and motive in the transformation of the Czech enterprise', *International Journal of Human Resource Management*, **9** (1), 79–98.

Soulsby, A. and E. Clark (2006), 'Changing patterns of employment in post-socialist organizations in Central and Eastern Europe: management action in a transitional context', *International Journal of Human Resource Management*, **17** (8), 1396–410.

Spence, D.P. (1982), *Narrative Truth and Historical Truth: Meaning and Interpretation in Psychoanalysis*, New York and London: W.W. Norton.

Staudenmayer, N., M. Tyre and L. Perlow (2002), 'Time to change: temporal shifts as enablers of organizational change', *Organization Science*, **13** (5), 583–97.

Tsoukas, H. (1989), 'The validity of idiographic research explanations', *Academy of Management Review*, **14** (4), 551–61.

Tsoukas, H. and R. Chia (2002), 'On organizational becoming: rethinking organizational change', *Organization Science*, **13** (5), 567–82.

Vaara, E. (2003), 'Post-acquisition integration as sensemaking: glimpses of ambiguity, confusion, hypocrisy, and politicization', *Journal of Management Studies*, **40** (4), 859–94.

Van De Ven, A.H. and G.P. Huber (1990), 'Longitudinal field research methods for studying processes of organizational change', *Organization Science*, **1** (3), 213–19.

Van De Ven, A.H. and M.S. Poole (1995), 'Explaining development and change in organizations', *Academy of Management Review*, **20** (3), 510–40.

Van Maanen, J. (1979), 'The fact of fiction in organizational ethnography', *Administrative Science Quarterly*, **24** (4), 539–601.

Van Maanen, J. (1988), *Tales of the Field: On Writing Ethnography*, Chicago, IL: University of Chicago Press.

Weick, K. (1989), 'Theory construction as disciplined imagination', *Academy of Management Review*, **14** (4), 516–31.

Weick, K. (1995), *Sensemaking in Organizations*, Thousand Oaks, CA: Sage.

White, H. (1981), 'The value of narrativity in the representation of reality', in W.J.T. Mitchell (ed.), *On Narrative*, Chicago, IL: University of Chicago Press, pp. 1–24.

Wolfram-Cox, J. and J. Hassard (2007), 'Ties to the past in organization research: a comparative analysis of retrospective methods', *Organization*, **14** (4), 475–97.

Yan, A. and B. Gray (1994), 'Bargaining power, management control, and performance in US–China joint ventures: a comparative case study', *Academy of Management Journal*, **37** (6), 1478–517.

Yin, R.K. (2009), *Case Study Research: Design and Methods*, 4th edn, Thousand Oaks, CA: Sage.

PART IV

The potential of multiple data sources and analytical methods

16. Blurring the boundaries between case analysis and ethnography: reflections on a hybrid approach to researching multinational corporations

Raza Mir

INTRODUCTION

Qualitative researchers in the field of organizational studies have often used case studies inductively, but in a positivistic way (for example, Galunic and Eisenhardt 2001). Their research seeks to move from the specific to the general, but the emphasis is still on discovery and unearthing, as if the case will reveal underlying information on the way organizations function. On the other hand, ethnographers operating primarily in other social sciences are more constructivist in their orientation, recognizing that the researcher is implicated in the research process (Kondo 1990). Both of these approaches are often suitable for different elements of organizational research. Unfortunately, case studies in organizational studies are almost exclusively associated with pedagogical approaches, while ethnography has often been (needlessly) equated with the study of indigenous cultures, and also has an intimidating disciplinary connection with anthropology. Moreover, proponents of the case approach have consciously disavowed the ethnographic approach as analytically distinct from case studies (Yin 2009). This disconnect has prevented a fruitful discussion from emerging as to how these two approaches can be combined, what they have to teach each other, and how they can add rigour and relevance to organizational research.

In this chapter, I explore ways in which ethnographic analysis could be used to layer case analysis with greater complexity. My recent publications (Mir et al. 2008; Mir and Mir 2009) have explicitly tried to combine the two approaches, and in my research, I have found the two approaches to be not only complementary, but also mutually enriching. My ethnographic research in a multinational corporation (MNC) has led to the development of several case studies, where the context assumed greater importance to the firm than a traditional case-analytic framework would require. While the traditional case study approach prides itself on a holistic approach, my own sense was that most case studies draw specific, and often arbitrary boundaries around the area of discussion, most of which are disciplinarily determined. For example, a case study of an organization in India would not spend much time debating issues related to caste-based divisions of labour in Indian society. An ethnographic approach to the same would be able to capture not only the salience of caste in Indian professional life, but also the multiple, non-trivial ways in which it impacts on the workings of individual corporations.

Given that the other contributions in this volume have eloquently discussed the case study from multiple facets, I would like to work off those approaches, and not discuss the case study at all (initially). Rather, in the rest of the chapter, I shall launch into a discussion of ethnography as a research method, and describe a particular project in which I used an ethnographic approach, and which ended up being more similar to case analysis than I had initially budgeted. Having described the project, I shall propose a variety of ways in which these two research approaches can enter into a meaningful collaboration on the terrain of organizational research, in a manner that is mutually enriching.

ETHNOGRAPHY AS A RESEARCH METHOD

I initially opted to use the methodology of ethnography for my research. As this chapter will detail, my approach underwent a transformation over time, where my methodological approach turned into a hybrid of the ethnographic and the case study perspective. I must clarify that my understanding of the term 'methodology' is much broader than the term 'method' (Mir and Watson 2000). A method is a tool or a technique that is used in the process of inquiry. However, a methodology is a more expansive term, incorporating an 'intricate set of ontological and epistemological assumptions that a researcher brings to his or her work' (Prasad 1997, p. 2). Given the inductive nature of my research questions and my inclination towards a non-positivist epistemological position (Burrell and Morgan 1979), I chose an analytic technique that was more suited to studying processes rather than contingencies. Ethnography, with its emphasis on studying the situated nature of processes, was most suitable because it helps us 'preserve the identity of things and enfold them in larger worlds of sense at the same time' (Geertz 2000, p. xi).

Ethnography is of course not a new methodology in organizational studies, having its origin in the Hawthorne Studies experiments (Roethlisberger and Dickson 1939, which to me remains a classic early exemplar of the unstated collaboration between case-based and ethnographic approaches). Neyland (2008) provides a current and updated account of how organizational theorists have been deploying ethnography in their research. Ethnographies conducted in the organizational realm in more recent times include Gideon Kunda's examination of the culture of engineering in high-tech companies in the US (Kunda 1992), Christina Garsten's study of how a transnational corporation like Apple maintains its organizational identity despite geographical dispersion (Garsten 1994) and Stephen Barley's study of technicians' work and the way in which they make sense of their organizational roles (Barley 1996). Ethnography is a process by which the researcher is able to study the quotidian aspects of (an organization's) processes and develop an understanding of the broader social and cultural fields in which it is embedded. One ethnographic technique deployed by the anthropologist Clifford Geertz analyses a particular event in a culture and uses it to develop a 'web of meaning', whereby one can go beneath the surface of the event, and see in it the hidden complexity of the society being studied. Geertz most clearly demonstrated this aspect through a 'thick description' of a Balinese cockfight. In this celebrated work, Geertz analysed how we can understand a number of things about Balinese culture as a whole from the cockfight: it is not just about the staging of an event, but a commentary on the hierarchical ordering of Balinese society and how it is enveloped in various webs of significance (Geertz 1973). In this study, I decided to use the exemplar of the Balinese cockfight to zero in on a specific episode of knowledge transfer across international boundaries in an attempt to construct the webs of meaning that populate the organizational understanding of knowledge transfer.

I would like to conclude this discussion with a brief analysis of the philosophical approach that drove my research. Organizational scholars have been cognisant for some time of the importance of philosophical assumptions in organizational research. Much of social science research is dominated by the paradigm of logical positivism, which attempted to produce a research tradition in the social sciences that mimicked their understanding of research in the natural sciences. Positivists combined their knowledge of empiricism, or the notion that observational evidence was the primary source of knowledge, with a rationalist approach that saw rule systems as being able to define and predict the world (for a discussion of the philosophical underpinnings of organizational research, see Smircich and Stubbart 1985). Other approaches to organizational philosophy include constructivism, a philosophical school of thought arguing that research is fundamentally theory dependent. According to constructivists, the theoretical position held by researchers not only guides their basic position, but also determines what gets construed as a research problem, what theoretical procedures are used, and what constitutes observations and evidence (for an application of constructivism to organizational studies, see Mir and Watson 2000).

My approach to organizational research was explicitly constructivist. Ethnography was methodologically consistent with my philosophical position that knowledge is theory driven. This point may best be illustrated with a metaphor. While as a positivist, I might have conceived of the research process as excavation, where the terrain of phenomena could be mined for valuable nuggets of naturally occurring insight, as a constructivist ethnographer, I chose to view the process more as an act of sculpting, where the imagination (or the theory base) of the artist interacts with the medium of phenomena to create a model of reality which we call knowledge. The constructivist view is therefore premised on the belief that a researcher always approaches a problem with a preconceived notion (a default theory) about the nature of the problem, and by implication, a possible solution for it (Fosnot 1996). The theory-laden nature of observation is not to be understood as a problem *per se*, but rather as an inevitable artefact of the research process. Constructivists believe that as long as researchers are transparent about their a priori theoretical position, the process of research is not impeded. However, they oppose a 'nomothetic' approach to methodology, which assumes that researchers are essentially discoverers of 'natural' phenomena, and that adherence to systematic protocol and technique will eliminate all biases from the research process (Burrell and Morgan 1979, p. 6).

Also, as an ethnographer, I believed that the separation of the researcher (subject) and the phenomena under investigation (object) is not feasible. According to constructivists, the philosophical positions held by researchers determine their findings. This approach was popularized by the sociological treatises of Berger and Luckmann (1966), and further defined as social constructionism (Gergen 1995). Indeed, many organizational theorists have adopted this approach to suggest that organizational 'reality' (Astley 1985) – or the truth that academic disciplines avow (Canella and Paetzold 1994) – is socially constructed.

Similarly, my ethnographic approach suggested that the separation between theory and practice was equally infeasible. This contention by constructivists effectively negates the issue of whether theory drives practice or vice versa. Constructivists believe that theory and practice are fundamentally interlinked. This particular insight is especially important for applied fields like organizational studies, where events in the performative realm of organizations often move faster than the theories in the field. According to constructivists, practice exists both before and after theory. As Butts and Brown (1989) theorize, there exists a phase of pre-theoretical praxis that leads to the formalization of theory, and ultimately guides future praxis.

IN THE FIELD

Brief Description of My Project

My discussions in this chapter relate to a slice of a larger project, and I would direct the interested reader to my dissertation monograph (Mir 2001), where the discussion is presented in greater detail. In this project, I was trying to study the process of knowledge transfer between the headquarters and international subsidiaries of MNCs. My disciplinary affiliation was with strategic management, and my study was specifically focused on the manner in which knowledge transfer was presented to subsidiaries by the headquarters as a different way of thinking and doing, and the way in which these commands were internalized, assimilated, and resisted by the subsidiaries. I also wanted to study the ways in which the subsidiaries hybridized, transformed and indigenized the demands of the headquarters to carve out a space of 'local' agency within their 'globalized' environment.

Through my research, I wanted to answer questions at three levels. At the macro level, I wished to explore the reciprocal relationship between the economic policies of nations and knowledge exchange within MNCs. At the organizational level, I wished to study the ways in which the headquarters of the organization attempt to restructure the subsidiary to make it a better receptacle for centralized knowledge, while at the same time, they appropriate local knowledge for global deployment. At the suborganizational level, I wanted to see how the subsidiary responds to knowledge transfer, how formal communication channels and regimes of socialization are created, and how the process of knowledge transfer means different things to different subjectivities, and how the headquarters deploys this heterogeneity to its advantage.

While my undergraduate training had been in engineering, and I had been predisposed through my doctoral coursework to think of research primarily through a quantitative lens, I nevertheless decided that no quantitative approach would help me capture the data complexity I was seeking in this multilevel work. I therefore decided upon a qualitative approach for my project.

For the purposes of conducting a theoretically informative empirical inquiry into the process of international knowledge transfer, I felt that an inductive approach was considered most feasible (Eisenhardt 1989). I chose to focus on a setting that would be conceptually appropriate, in other words, an MNC where the unit of analysis could be a knowledge transfer transaction. Of course, it is not appropriate to generalize from the observed events of one organization to any broader setting, but my aim was to achieve conceptual coherence, for which single-firm studies are considered appropriate (Miles and Huberman 1994). Such a research project can provide an internal validity that is more important for a theory-building exercise of this nature rather than external validity that comes from large sample analyses (Jacobides 2005). Again, in hindsight, the potential for a hybrid approach was already inherent in my approach. While I did appreciate the commitment to and insistence on rigour that characterized proponents of the case study approach, my epistemological position was not constrained by the realist demands of reliability and validity that inform case studies. I therefore used the techniques of data gathering that had been suggested by case study approaches, but was more inclined to let the object of my inquiry be informed by the epistemological imperatives of ethnography. Such an approach may also have reflected my desire to publish my work in organizational journals, where reference to such techniques rendered my work more defensible to anonymous peer referees.

Site of Analysis

Based on my research questions, I needed to gain entry into an MNC where I would be granted access to the headquarters, the national subsidiary, and any other entities especially relevant to the chosen episode of knowledge transfer. I also needed to be granted relatively extensive and high-level access to various organizational meetings, personnel and documents. Given that my study could have findings that were relatively critical of organizational processes, but that the purpose of my study was not to critique any particular organization, I was prepared to sign confidentiality clauses which stipulated that I would take great care not to identify the organization in any way. Eventually, I was able to negotiate access into two different corporations, and duly signed non-disclosure agreements with them. The organization described in this chapter is code-named Chemicon, and is one of the leading manufacturers of consumer products in the world, with annual revenues in excess of $25 billion. It is based in the USA, but operates in over 100 countries, and I was granted access to its Indian subsidiary, which has been operational for over 50 years. Chemicon had first begun operations in India as an exporting house, and had eventually developed its own manufacturing plants around three decades ago. Chemicon India had been incorporated as an Indian corporation, and its shares had initially been quoted on the Indian stock exchange. However, since the mid-1990s they were no longer traded because Chemicon India was now fully owned by its parent company. Chemicon India was designated a 'fully integrated operating subsidiary', which meant that it manufactured most of the products needed for the domestic market in-house. It owned three manufacturing facilities, and also used around 20 third-party manufacturing locations in India. Outsourcing was a recent aspect of Chemicon India's business, given that only since 1992 have MNCs been allowed under Indian company law to use contract-manufacturing facilities.

Data Collection

In keeping with the ethnographic approach, my data collection relied heavily upon participant observation, as well as a number of interviews with members of the organization as well as external personnel. This was supplemented by the collection of secondary data. (Those readers who use case study will be struck by the relative similarity of data collection techniques in ethnography. The key difference is that participant observations in multiple settings over long periods is a cornerstone of ethnographic research, which usually makes it much more time intensive and context rich than regular case study research.)

Participant observation lies at the heart of ethnography. I spent over 11 months in India documenting various aspects of Chemicon's operations, during which time I attended strategy meetings and technical briefings, watched manufacturing operations, accompanied salespersons on calls, interviewed top managers as well as workers and, especially relevant to this chapter, spent a lot of time at the premises of Chemicon India's contractors. Over 1,000 pages of field notes were generated as a result of this exercise. These were supplemented with notes on several interviews (I conducted 54 interviews during the course of this project, 19 of which were directly related to the issues being discussed in this chapter), some of which were tape-recorded and transcribed (many interviews were also held without tape recordings, but detailed notes were made on those as well). Interviewees included managers at Chemicon, both of Indian and US affiliation, the CEO of Pavan Enterprises, the contractor firm, workers at Chemicon and Pavan, economists who were working on issues of legal reform in India, office-bearers of local trade federations and labour unionists. Secondary sources included a variety of documents, such as 'firewall-protected' FTP sites, public internet sites, internal memos, press releases and other public documents, and transcripts of executive speeches. I juxtaposed this data with macro data on changing corporate laws in India and communiqués from trade federations (such as the Federation of Indian Chamber of Commerce and Industry) and international regimes (such as Project LARGE, which was a United Nations Development Programme (UNDP) initiative in India for 'Legal and Administrative Reform for a Globalizing Economy'). The collected data were organized and stored under a total of 10 headings according to the data source (for example, field notes, interview notes, company correspondence) and accessibility (that is, whether it was public or confidential).

The management of data is one of the trickiest elements of ethnography. One can, if one is not careful, be submerged in it and never see any nugget of insight in the morass of data that such an intensive approach determines. It is here that the organization of primary data and scrupulously disciplined techniques of analysis become especially important. Insights in ethnography are slow to develop, and are notorious for derailing any a priori assumptions that the reader may have had. In my own case, I found that my final findings were quite off base from what I had initially thought I would uncover. Ethnography not only altered the answers, but in many cases, it fundamentally transformed the questions being asked by my research.

One area where ethnography differs substantially from other research approaches is the complicated (and often lonely) process of data collection. The solitude and loneliness of the ethnographer has been the subject of many an anthropological reflection. According to Marie Louise Pratt (1986, p. 31),

> [P]ersonal narrative is a conventional component of ethnographies. It turns up almost invariably in introductions or first chapters, where opening narratives commonly recount the writer's arrival at the field site, for instance, the initial reception by the inhabitants, the slow agonizing process of learning the language and overcoming rejection, the anguish and loss at leaving.

Pratt's observation about personal narrative in ethnography almost sounds tired, as if these declarations at the beginnings of ethnographic research have become perfunctory. However, I do feel that there is an important value in rendering transparent the fraught nature of the fieldwork process. First, it helps in circumscribing the research, rendering it less grand than an authoritative statement on the subject of study. The subjectivity of the research process is placed at the forefront of the inquiry, rather than its pretense to be a scientific process. Finally, by acknowledging the halting and tentative character of the process, the researcher is impelled to constantly evaluate the trajectory of research, incorporate newer findings, pay attention to ignored perspectives, and in general, be more circumspect in the act of data collection.

By way of an example, I shall reproduce the following section from my fieldwork diary, which I recorded barely a week into my fieldwork:

> I have been in Chemicon India for a week. Sitting alone in this empty 'office', waiting for lunchtime so that I can grab the attention of the trainees and accompany them, a strange sense of insecurity seems to near-paralyze me. My interactions with the organization thus far have been extensive. I have been meeting people at various levels of the organization and talking to them endlessly. I am already full of 'data', which I now hope to integrate into some kind of a basis for future study . . . Multiple cases, sharply edged stories brimming with potential insights into the knowledge transfer process in Chemicon, appear ready to await my research agenda.
>
> Why then this insecurity?
>
> I cannot put my finger on it, but essentially, I feel that one of the major barriers to my analysis here is going to be the totally sanitized manner in which my experiences thus far have been cast. In my idealized image of ethnography, I believed that I would be an invisible, unobtrusive presence in the organization, quietly recording the processes that unfolded around me. However, I now realize how different the case is going to be.
>
> For one, my entire being currently screams 'management'. In my interactions with people, one clear identity position that people seem almost anxious to relate to is 'US-based'. There are very specific, if unwritten dress codes in the organization, and as an invited guest of the management, I dress like them, and thus immediately alienate myself from the non-managerial staff. At the factory, I was taken to lunch to the 'executive dining room', where I drank soup with croutons, tilting the bowl away from me to scoop the bottom. A napkin on my lap shielded my trousers from food that was eaten by a fork, and fruit cut with knives. A floor below, I discreetly peeped into the 'workers' canteen', and watched them eat spicy Indian food with their hands on stainless steel plates. We appear destined never to meet; they even have different restrooms.
>
> How will I develop a shared context with people lower down in the rank and file of the organization? I need to pay more attention to this dilemma in my next visit.

The above entry details an important aspect of my research: I did not have a well-informed idea of how I would conduct my research. While I had a well-developed theoretical perspective on ethnography, having read several ethnographic accounts and theoretical treatises on the ethnographic process, my research was characterized by a great deal of tentativeness, on-field improvisations, and retrospective sensemaking with respect to my data. As a researcher who had been granted entry into the organization I was already invested with a certain legitimacy, but that legitimacy often was the cause of suspicion among people who populated the lower rungs of these organizations.

This of course served to problematize the issue of 'legitimacy' for me. I consciously attempted to avoid the trappings of top management. First, I began to dress more informally. Then I would pass up on offers by managers to 'break for lunch' when I saw that non-management workers continued to work. I began not to use the management restroom, choosing to go to the workers' facilities. The breakthroughs were slow in coming, but ultimately, I feel that I was successful in my endeavour to gain the trust of various members of these organizations. Consider for example, my experiences at Chemicon India. I believe that when I came to the office on the Deepavali festival, the information systems department finally accepted me. When I involuntarily hummed a Marathi song while watching a production run at the assembly line, I could sense the tension among the workers. And when I accompanied a salesman on a tedious trip to a remote location, I was able to have more meaningful conversations not only with him, but also with all the salespeople in Chemicon India, news of my informal attitude having spread across the grapevine.

Another side-effect of the ethnographic process relates to the inability on the part of the researcher to control the point at which fieldwork is terminated. Institutional and financial considerations determined when I would have to leave the sites of my study. And while I left with more information than I could possibly use, I still could not avoid the sense of incompleteness that I felt at the abruptness of my departure. Indeed, it helped tremendously that I was fortunate enough to be able to follow up on my fieldwork with a three-week trip back to India, but while I was in the field, I did not have a clear sense of where my data would lead me, or whether I would make sense of it all myself at the end. However, if there was one thing I was sure of, it was that my data were rich in detail, interesting, and often led to some extremely counterintuitive findings.

In hindsight, then, I went through all those stages that Pratt (1986) identifies in her description of fieldwork. It took time for me to be 'accepted' by my informants. I struggled initially with possible rejection. And while I did not learn a new language, I feel that I had to learn an entirely new and heterogeneous 'grammar' of communication at the workplace. Once learned, that grammar was what made the difference between a superficial and a meaningful organizational interaction.

THEORY DEVELOPMENT VIA DATA ANALYSIS

It was during my data analysis that my ethnographic approach benefited extensively from my understanding of the case approach. In my experience, anthropologist ethnographers rely on a variety of observation-centred analytics, which are usually opaque, and it is only through the detailed understanding of individual accounts that the reader can gauge the depth of analytics deployed. For example, when we read an account of Margaret Mead in Samoa or Bronislaw Malinowski in Kula, their rigour is measurable primarily through the extraordinary detail they bring to their observation, which is only possible through book-length expositions. Such an approach was difficult for me for three reasons. First, the choice of the organization as a unit of analysis meant that the data had to be structured so that organizational-level findings could be highlighted. Second, I felt that given the vastness of my data, the reductiveness imposed by case study analytics could be compensated by the benefits afforded by the ease of organization it allowed. Finally, and of great pragmatic importance, these analytics offered a way by which conversations about the 'reliability' and 'validity' of my findings could be initiated with institutional gatekeepers such as journal editors, and make the journey from 'story' to 'theory'. A fine balance between the reductiveness of structure and the benefits of organization played a role in my decision, and eventually enriched my findings. I made the decision, therefore, to use the same analytic techniques as the ones adopted by case researchers, at the risk of undermining my 'anthropological legitimacy'.

Data analysis was performed in three stages. I first studied the data in as much detail as possible, and identified as much of it as I felt had direct relevance to the identified episode of knowledge transfer. Then, I read this subset more carefully and identified (judgementally and on the basis of frequency of occurrence) several themes or concepts that resonated within observations, conversations and secondary data. Finally, I created a 'conceptually ordered display' (Miles and Huberman 1994, p. 127), by which I was able to link these concepts into broader organizational processes. Through an analysis of different conceptual linkages, I was able to make broad theoretical observations, which were then supported by both the data and the theories. Consistent with the guidelines for qualitative research (Yin 2009), I used external experts to validate my data at various stages in the concept generation process. These experts mainly included academics like myself, but I also used one rater who was in the corporate sector, though not a Chemicon employee. As the reader might discern, the concepts of reliability and validity derive primarily from a positivistic epistemological tradition, but in the last instance, I feel that such approaches are useful even to ethnographers and non-positivist scholars; they reflect a commitment to rigour and a formalized widening of the circle of analysts. The difference would be that the ethnographer would not necessarily see inter-rater disparities as delegitimizing to the analytical process, but rather an intriguing artefact to be probed for theoretical insight.

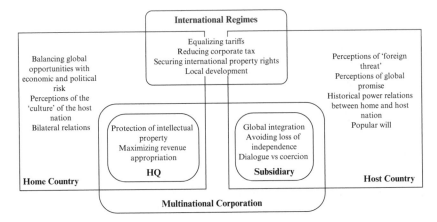

Figure 16.1   Conceptual framework: issues involved in knowledge transfer (multiple theatres of research, both in case study and in ethnography)

My conceptually ordered display was represented through 'concept cards' (Martin and Turner 1986), by which I tried to identify some of the salient and recurring themes in the data. Around 19 concept cards were developed, on themes such as 'communication systems', 'innovation in manufacture', 'intellectual property issues', 'Pavan Chemicon differences in culture', and so on. However, I found concept cards to be an inadequate device for developing an overarching framework from which I could theorize the relationship between the micro episodes of knowledge transfer I observed and macro events such as policy changes (for an ethnographic approach to the linkage between micro processes and broader social frames, see Burawoy 2000). However contingent, I felt that my research did point to some obvious linkages between micro and macro phenomena, which I could not depict satisfactorily through concept cards. I therefore created a framework wherein various episodes of knowledge transfer, various conceptual issues, and various theoretical approaches could be mapped.

Figure 16.1 deals with the conceptual issues encountered during the study of knowledge transfer. It shows that knowledge transfer can be studied at multiple levels, including the host country, home country, the MNC headquarters and subsidiary, and the international regime, all of whom have a complex say in the process of knowledge transfer. The headquarters of the organization is primarily concerned with issues of the protection of intellectual property rights as well as maximizing revenue appropriation, while the subsidiary is interested in being integrated in the

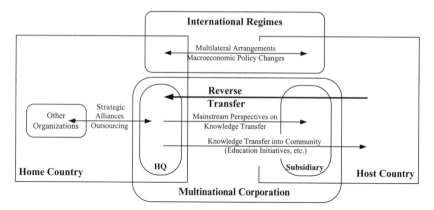

Figure 16.2   *The directionality of knowledge transfer (multiple webs characteristic of an ethnographic approach)*

global space in such a manner that its voice is dialogically heard, and its independence is not compromised. The country that exists at the subaltern level of this transaction is focused on the maintenance of its national identity and sovereignty, but at the same time, is eager to get the benefits of global investment. The home country is also concerned with developing favourable trade terms, and has the task of balancing the potential opportunities afforded by internationalization against attendant economic and political risks. Finally, international regimes are charged with transnational concerns such as the securing of intellectual property rights and the management of tax and tariffs. For example, the World Trade Organization is focused on developing platforms for multilateral discussions between corporations and countries, on issues as wide ranging as patent protection, tariff reduction and currency convertibility. In the space characterized by episodes of organizational knowledge transfer, international regimes often function more as agents of the dispersed corporation. Each entity approaches the issue of knowledge transfer with different areas of focus. The challenge for the theorist, then, is to develop a framework that uses the knowledge transfer transaction as a unit of analysis, yet is still sensitive to the enactment of all the compulsions and focus areas.

Figure 16.2 maps the different forms of knowledge transfer that I can observe in international organizational settings. I also used the same framework to ground my literature review, so that I could postulate a meaningful relationship between the empirical findings and the existing theoretical traditions in the field. As Figure 16.2 shows, the various episodes of knowledge transfer can be mapped on to this same conceptual

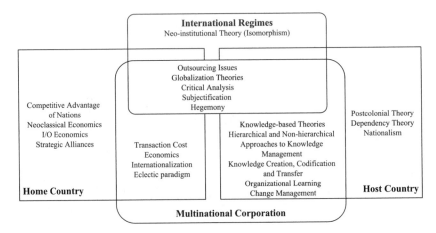

*Figure 16.3   Mapping theoretical positions on to the conceptual
framework (useful for case study as well as ethnography)*

space. Knowledge can flow between organizations through strategic alliances or outsourcing arrangements, within organizations through headquarter–subsidiary contacts of inter-subsidiary sharing, or can diffuse into the broader environment through external economies, modernization and learning effects. Studies of knowledge transfer tend to focus mostly on the transfer of knowledge between the headquarters and the subsidiary (Gupta and Govindarajan 2000), or the issue of strategic alliances (Porter et al. 2000). My focus was on the reverse directionality of knowledge transfer, from a national hinterland into the space of a corporation's headquarters, a relatively untheorized area. Figure 16.2 functions to place my study in relation to other empirical investigations of knowledge transfer.

Finally, the literature map of the framework is shown in Figure 16.3. It shows how a variety of theoretical traditions within and peripheral to organizational studies can be mapped on to the same framework that I used for the first two figures. A number of theoretical traditions can be brought to bear in the study of organizational knowledge transfer, from institutional theory, resource-based views of the firm, industrial organization (IO) economics, theories of the MNC, postcolonial theory and neoclassical economics.

The substantive arguments of my research are not the focus of my chapter (for more on this project, see Mir 2001). However, I have included these three figures, despite the sketchiness of their discussion here, to foreground the mutuality between theory development, firm-level empirics, and a broader theoretical discussion. In this chapter, I am more interested in discussing methodological issues, as a way to generate a discussion between ethnographers and case researchers. However, some substantive points are necessary to flesh out the story. In brief, I used two specific episodes of knowledge transfer to understand broader organizational phenomena. One episode involved the adoption of a complex enterprise resource planning (ERP) system from the headquarters to the subsidiary. (I have reported on this in great detail in Mir et al. 2008.) The system was replacing an indigenously developed management information system (MIS) shell at the subsidiary level, and many of the managers at the MNC subsidiary had felt that they were actually replacing a superior system with an inferior one. However, their complaints were not legitimized in the set-up, for three reasons. The first was that the headquarters was predisposed to think of the subsidiary as being relatively unqualified in matters as complex as computer systems. Second, there were global considerations involved, where the headquarters wanted to produce uniformity at the corporate level, and did not wish to grant too much autonomy to the subsidiary. Finally, there existed constituencies in the subsidiary that felt they could further their career better by saying yes to everything the headquarters demanded. This put an interesting pressure on the managers of the subsidiary who resisted such moves; they risked delegitimation even at the local level.

The second episode I studied (documented in Mir and Mir 2009) involved the informal and undocumented transfer of knowledge from a contractor of the corporation to the headquarters. Here, headquarters was forced to part with proprietary technology to a contractor at the subsidiary level. Much to their surprise, the contractor proceeded to show them that their design was flawed, and made substantial improvements in the manufacturing process. The headquarters of the MNC then proceeded to appropriate this technology as an innovation made by the firm, without acknowledging the role of the subsidiary. There was nothing illegal in what they did, because the contracts between the two firms had been drawn in that manner. The subsidiary thus becomes the enabler in the appropriation of intellectual property by the headquarters from the contractor.

Through an analysis of these two (and other) episodes, I was able to theorize that the current formulations of knowledge transfer in the organizational theory and strategic management literature were inadequate to describe what exactly went on in corporations, and develop a 'reverse directionality' of knowledge transfer that legitimized resistive practices by MNC subsidiaries and offered greater room to conceptualize why a subsidiary might resist knowledge transfer from the headquarters. I concluded that an organization with a more egalitarian (less colonial) approach to knowledge is more sensitive of dialogic issues, despite the existence of a power differential favourable to itself. When an organization achieves its ends through coercive means, it ends up a loser despite potential short-term gains.

DISCUSSION: WHAT CAN ETHNOGRAPHERS AND CASE THEORISTS TEACH EACH OTHER?

Based on my research and my interaction with several peers who use the case study, I have concluded that the similarities between these two approaches far outweigh their differences. My hybrid approach may antagonize purists from both sides, but I contend that it can also, in the best of circumstances, provide a bridge between the approaches, and blur the boundaries between them.

Based on my empirical experiences, I have distilled a few areas of commonality and a few area of differences between the case study and ethnography. Four clear similarities between these two approaches are evident:

1. *Single (or few) setting(s)*   Both approaches confine themselves to a limited number of settings. To that end, they are better set up to explore nuances of different settings and situations. Historical analyses are possible, as is an understanding of social, institutional and industrial networks in which a firm is embedded. The description is richer than can be achieved in large sample studies. There are some exceptions to this process, such as the multi-sited ethnography. Marcus (1999, p. 79) urges cultural analysts to 'move out of the single sites and local situations of conventional ethnography designs to examine the circulation of cultural objects, meanings and identities in diffuse time space'. Case study approaches could consider this. In a journalistic way, Friedman (2005, pp. 414–29) follows the supply chain of a single Dell laptop to uncover its global character. Rivoli (2005) has done the same with the analysis of a single T-shirt. Similar approaches can be tried with a pair of sneakers, a cup of coffee or a hamburger.
2. *Inductive approach*   Both these methodologies eschew deduction in favour of an approach that begins with the specific (though ethnographers are arguably more hesitant to leap into an understanding of the general, preferring to leave their study to stand on its own). This is an important counterpoint to the large sample studies pervading organizational research that provide deductive (usually theory-confirming) insight, for inductive studies are amenable to theory building, and have often been the sites where new insights into organizations have been most clearly visible.

3. *Mixing primary and secondary data*   Both case studies and ethnography provide appropriate settings where researchers can begin with the collection of some primary data, but supplement their analysis with a variety of secondary data to marshal their findings. In my own case, I started my ethnographic data collection with extensive participant observation, and moved on to more direct forms of primary data collection through interviews and recording of meetings. But my project was also fleshed out by the use of secondary data sources, such as firm-level filed documents, speech transcripts and so on. Macro public data from the internet, legal systems, data from broader institutions helped immeasurably in contextualizing my study, which will also be very useful for researchers using the case study.

4. *Narrative reporting*   One of the most important research tasks, be it for a case study writer or an ethnographer, is to 'narrativize' their account, that is, to place their different fragments of data and information into a spatial and temporal continuum so that it takes the shape of a 'story' which then lends itself to consideration as a 'theory' as well. This is a tough task, for it involves choosing which data to highlight and which data to leave behind. It is important to remember that the research presented either in a case study or an ethnography is not meant to reflect an authoritative account of the goings on at the site of the researcher's study. Rather, it represents an attempt by researchers to make sense of the sea of data collected during the research, and their political act of 'narrativizing' their experiences within the contingent and colligative bounds of a story. As the historian Sudipta Kaviraj (1992, p. 38) notes, 'the interstices of every narrative are filled with semblances rather than truth. Thus, the telling of true stories in history would not rule out the telling of other stories different from the first, which are also true'. For example, in my case, I contended that my story of knowledge transfer was as authoritative as the mainstream accounts of knowledge flows in MNCs (Zander and Kogut 1995; Zack 1999). My account simply provided an important counter-narrative. This alternative historicizing is a way of restoring the balance, and remaining true to what Gadamer (1975, pp. 267–74) has referred to as 'the principle of effective history'. This is also true of case study research.

However, there are some ways in which ethnography is a distinct research process, and I feel that case study researchers could take note of some of its distinctive features. The obvious first step is that ethnography by its very nature is a time-consuming process whereby researchers are perforce required to immerse themselves in their organizational settings for long periods. To that end, this is not a research design for someone on a tight time schedule, or who wishes to work mostly off secondary documents. On the other hand, in an ethnography it is notoriously difficult to present a dominant unit of analysis, while in a case study, it is easy to place a subject (say a firm) at the centre of the study. There are, in my opinion, four important aspects that distinguish ethnographic research from the case approach:

1. *Non-positivist epistemological focus*   While there can be such a thing as a positivist case study, the notion of a positivist ethnography is a contradiction in terms. Ethnography must necessarily subscribe to the constructivist notion that there are aspects of knowledge that are socially constructed, and that there are interpretations of reality that can compete for legitimacy. To that end, ethnographies cannot focus on the perspectives of single individuals (such as top managers of corporations). They must see reality as refracted through the cognitive and emotive lenses of multiple constituencies. In my case, my ethnographic study of organizational knowledge was consistent with Patriotta's (2003, p. 350) call for a phenomenological approach to organizational knowledge, one that relies on the 'analysis of everyday organizational discourse as instanced by the construction of narratives in the workplace'.

2. *Study of the 'quotidian'*   Much of case ethnographic research does not focus on unusual events, but rather studies the day-to-day activities and interactions in the setting. For example, in his landmark ethnography of an engineering organization, Gideon Kunda (1992) focused on day-to-day actions to demonstrate how a technologically oriented culture was produced at that firm, and how such a cultural production was 'ideological' in character (in that it represented the interests of the corporate elite as the interests of the firm). Kunda's work is a masterful exposition of how the unremarkable activities of daily organizational life can be used to reach relatively counterintuitive and nuanced observations about organizations (and make a theoretical contribution as well).

3. *The researcher needs to be 'visible'*   While it is very tempting on the part of a researcher to say that they are mere chroniclers of phenomena, and free of any researcher bias in the pursuit of organizational truth, such an approach runs counter to the spirit of ethnography. There are specific entry points into the empirical terrain that need to be made explicit. In other words, ethnographic accounts are often personal, with occasional confessional elements on the part of the researcher, either of implicit biases, or of ways in which their presence

as researchers irrevocably altered the terrain of the research (Van Maanen 1988). For example, the presence of an observer can change the tenor of a meeting, the researcher may have obtained some data by subterfuge or eavesdropping, he/she may have done something dramatic at some time in the research that fundamentally altered his/her relationship with informants or terms of access. These matters may seem trivial and unimportant to a case researcher, but the tradition of the ethnographic process demands that they be formally reported, as a way of acknowledging that researchers are neither inert nor truly objective, but become part of their concepts. In the language of ethnography, they 'go native'.

4. *Analysis of webs of meaning*   As Figure 16.1 suggests, the organization is embedded in a variety of macro institutions. There are industry-level networks (competitors, suppliers, customers, substitute firms) as well as macro networks (governments, trade institutions, policy issues, general trends in the economic, cultural, legal and political spheres). At the suborganizational level also, there are a lot of networks (departments, geographies, individuals), which interact with the organization, producing a dense ecosystem, where multiple levels of sensemaking coexist. Ethnographies demand that such networks be given their due importance in the analysis of an organization, in the tradition that Clifford Geertz refers to as 'thick description'. In his landmark book *The Interpretation of Cultures*, Geertz (1973) refers to a 'wink', a thin description of which would not be able to describe the multiple social and cultural contexts in which it could be interpreted. Similarly, in my research, when a subcontractor refused to attend a mandatory meeting at Chemicon, or when a worker was upset when a holiday was declared for Thanksgiving, my ethnographic approach served me well in providing a thick description of both events, as acts of token resistance against perceived (and geo-politically understood) oppression by the US headquarters.

While the above four approaches show ways in which ethnographic approaches stake out a claim for distinctness, I have contended that there is no real incommensurability between these four aspects and a good case study. Case studies can be non-positivist in character, and be good exemplars of combining inductive logic and constructivism (Stake 1995). Recent calls for methodological plurality in the case study literature (Piekkari et al. 2009) continue to make room for non-positivistic approaches, and legitimize its eventual linkages with ethnography. Likewise, I have found in my own research that the study of the quotidian rhythms of organizational life provide great insight into an organization's strategy, its culture and its information flow dynamics (Mir and Mir 2009). There is no problem with a case study researcher engaging in an introspective analysis of their role while researching organizations, and finally, the case study could benefit immeasurably from a thick description approach, as detailed by Dyer and Wilkins (1991) in their critique of thin case studies. Likewise, ethnographers could learn from case researchers about ways in which data can be organized and analysed in a relatively parsimonious manner.

CONCLUSION

Despite incipient incommensurabilities, the paradigms of ethnography and case study can coexist, if theorists adopt non-sectarian approaches to the problem of methodology. In my case, I was first drawn to ethnography as a research methodology because of its promise of a context-enriched research frame. This approach served me well in the field, and opened my eyes to a contextual horizon that far exceeded the brief of standard case-analytical approaches. However, once the vast amounts of data needed to be shoehorned into specific firm-level arguments, I found myself drawn back to the relative analytical parsimony of the case study. I contend therefore, that case study analysis and ethnography can coexist, if there is a sufficient and conscious attempt to balance the richness of ethnography with the focus of the case study. In many cases, an ethnographic approach has enriched case analysis (Humphreys and Brown 2002). Likewise, a focus on narrativizing ethnography as case study can make organizational literature more readable and amenable to theory building (Kunda 1992; Garsten 1994). Many case studies currently show the signs of an ethnographic influence (for example, Nguyen 2005; Sunaoshi et al. 2005). It remains to be seen whether such collaborations can be formally acknowledged; this chapter is a brief foray into this uncharted territory.

Overall, there are many ways in which these two approaches can produce a happy collaborative effect. For case study researchers, ethnography offers a way by which they can go beyond the simplistic analysis of linear trends into webs of meaning, thick descriptions and making the research process much more transparent. Likewise, organizational ethnographers would benefit from reading case studies closely to understand the different ways in which multilevel data can be narrativized into simple, readable and actionable stories. There is a lot more collaboration possible between these two streams, and this chapter has hopefully gone some way in initiating a greater dialogue between the two approaches.

REFERENCES

Astley, W.G. (1985), 'Administrative science as socially constructed truth', *Administrative Science Quarterly*, **30** (4), 497–513.

Barley, S.R. (1996), 'Technicians in the workplace: ethnographic evidence for bringing work into organization studies', *Administrative Science Quarterly*, **41** (3), 404–41.

Berger, P.L. and T. Luckmann (1966), *The Social Construction of Reality: A Treatise in the Sociology of Knowledge*, Garden City, NY: Doubleday.

Burawoy, M. (2000), *Global Ethnography: Forces, Connections, and Imaginations in a Postmodern World*, Berkeley, CA: University of California Press.

Burrell, G. and G. Morgan (1979), *Sociological Paradigms and Organisational Analysis*, London: Heinemann.

Butts, R. and J. Brown (1989), *Constructivism and Science: Essays in Recent German Philosophy*, Dordrecht: Kluwer.

Canella, A. and R. Paetzold (1994), 'Pfeffer's barriers to advance of organizational science: a rejoinder', *Academy of Management Review*, **19** (2), 331–41.

Dyer, W.G., and A.L. Wilkins (1991), 'Better stories, not better constructs, to generate better theory: a rejoinder to Eisenhardt', *Academy of Management Review*, **16** (3), 613–19.

Eisenhardt, K.M. (1989), 'Building theories from case study research', *Academy of Management Review*, **14** (4), 532–50.

Fosnot, C. (1996), *Constructivism: Theory, Perspectives, and Practice*, New York: Teachers College Press.

Friedman, T. (2005), *The World Is Flat: A Brief History of the Twenty First Century*, New York: Farrar, Strauss & Giroux.

Gadamer, H. (1975), *Truth and Method*, London: Sheed & Ward.

Galunic, D. and K. Eisenhardt (2001), 'Architectural innovation and modular corporate forms', *Academy of Management Journal*, **44** (6), 1229–49.

Garsten, C. (1994), *Apple World: Core and Periphery in a Transnational Organizational Culture*, Stockholm: Almqvist & Wiksell International.

Geertz, C. (1973), *The Interpretation of Cultures*, New York: Basic Books.

Geertz, C. (2000), *Local Knowledge: Further Essays in Interpretive Anthropology*, 3rd edn, New York: Basic Books.

Gergen, K. (1995), 'Social construction and the education process', in L.P. Steffe and J. Gale (eds), *Constructivism in Education*, Hillsdale, NJ: Erlbaum, pp. 17–40.

Gupta, A. and V. Govindarajan (2000), 'Knowledge flows within multinational corporations', *Strategic Management Journal*, **21** (4), 473–96.

Humphreys, M. and A. Brown (2002), 'Narratives of organizational identity and identification: a case study of hegemony and resistance', *Organization Studies*, **23** (3), 421–47.

Jacobides, M. (2005), 'Industry change through vertical disintegration: how and why markets emerged in mortgage banking', *Academy of Management Journal*, **48** (3), 465–98.

Kaviraj, S. (1992), 'The imaginary institution of India', in P. Chatterjee and G. Pandey (eds), *Subaltern Studies VII*, New Delhi: Oxford University Press, pp. 1–39.

Kondo, D. (1990), *Crafting Selves: Power, Discourse and Identity in a Japanese Factory*, Chicago, IL: University of Chicago Press.

Kunda, G. (1992), *Engineering Culture: Control and Commitment in a High-tech Corporation*, Philadelphia, PA: Temple University Press.

Marcus, G. (1999), *Ethnography Through Thick and Thin*, Princeton, NJ: Princeton University Press.

Martin, P. and B. Turner (1986), 'Grounded theory and organizational research', *Journal of Applied Behavioral Science*, **22** (2), 141–57.

Miles, M. and A. Huberman (1994), *Qualitative Data Analysis: An Expanded Sourcebook*, Thousand Oaks, CA: Sage.

Mir, R. (2001), 'Migrating ideas: an empirical study of intra-organizational knowledge transfer', PhD thesis, University of Massachusetts, Amherst.

Mir, R., S. Banerjee and A. Mir (2008), 'Hegemony and its discontents: a critical analysis of organizational knowledge transfer', *Critical Perspectives on International Business*, **4** (2), 203–27.

Mir, R. and A. Mir (2009), 'From the corporation to the colony: studying knowledge transfer across international boundaries', *Group and Organization Management*, **34** (1), 90–113.

Mir, R. and A. Watson (2000), 'Strategic management and the philosophy of science: imperatives for a constructivist methodology', *Strategic Management Journal*, **21** (9), 1–13.

Neyland, D. (2008), *Organizational Ethnography*, Thousand Oaks, CA: Sage.

Nguyen, T. (2005), 'Learning to trust: a study of interfirm trust dynamics in Vietnam', *Journal of World Business*, **40** (2), 203–21.

Patriotta, G. (2003), 'Sensemaking on the shop floor: narratives of knowledge in organizations', *Journal of Management Studies*, **40** (2), 349–75.

Piekkari, R., C. Welch and E. Paavilainen (2009), 'The case study as disciplinary convention: evidence from international business journals', *Organizational Research Methods*, **12** (3), 567–89.

Porter, M., H. Takeuchi and M. Sakakibara (2000), *Can Japan Compete?*, Cambridge, MA: Perseus.

Prasad, P. (1997), 'Systems of meaning: ethnography as a methodology for the study of information technologies', in A. Lee and J. Degross (eds), *Qualitative Methods and Information Research*, Boston, MA: Kluwer, pp. 1–33.

Pratt, M. (1986), 'Field work in common places', in J. Clifford and G. Marcus (eds), *Writing Culture*, Berkeley, CA: University of California Press, pp. 27–50.

Rivoli, P. (2005), *The Travels of a T-Shirt in the Global Economy: An Economist Examines the Markets, Power, and Politics of World Trade*, New York: Wiley.

Roethlisberger, F. and W. Dickson (1939), *Management and the Worker*, Cambridge, MA: Harvard University Press.

Smircich, L. and C. Stubbart (1985), 'Strategic management in an enacted world', *Academy of Management Review*, **10** (4), 724–36.

Stake, R. (1995), *The Art of Case Study Research*, Thousand Oaks, CA: Sage.

Sunaoshi, Y., M. Kotabe and J.Y. Murray (2005), 'How technology transfer really occurs on the factory floor: a case of a major Japanese automotive die manufacturer in the United States', *Journal of World Business*, **40** (1), 57–70.

Van Maanen, J. (1988), *Tales of the Field: On Writing Ethnography*, Chicago, IL: University of Chicago Press.

Yin, R. (2009), *Case Study Research: Design and Methods*, 4rd edn, Thousand Oaks, CA: Sage.

Zack, M. (1999), 'Managing codified knowledge', *Sloan Management Review*, **40** (4), 45–58.

Zander, U. and B. Kogut (1995), 'Knowledge and the speed of the transfer and imitation of organizational capabilities', *Organization Science*, **6** (1), 76–92.

17. On a clear day you can see forever: taking a holistic approach to ethnographic case studies in international business

Fiona Moore

INTRODUCTION

Although the benefits of ethnographic research have been long recognized in international business studies, for the most part it is still an underutilized technique in this discipline. One frequently cited explanation for the lack of use of this technique is that, while it is useful for obtaining an in-depth perspective on a single, small group, it is less effective at producing an image of the organization as a whole. I would argue, however, that researchers can also use ethnographic techniques to gain more holistic perspectives on the organization. Through using multiple participant-observation sessions with different groups within an Anglo-German manufacturing company, I was able to gather data showing how these groups connect with each other and with other groups and organizations in the wider community.

To begin with, I shall consider a selection of the anthropological literature on ethnography and the question of whether it can be used to gain a holistic perspective on any given organization. It is generally agreed by anthropologists that there is no hard-and-fast definition of ethnography. Fetterman (1989, p. 11) defines it as 'the art and science of describing a group or culture', adding that to do so, 'the ethnographer writes about the routine, daily lives of people'. Hammersley (1998, pp. 2, 8) defines it as studying behaviour in everyday contexts, engaging in 'unstructured' (although not unsystematic) data collection, using a small number of cases, and analysing these through interpreting the meaning of human actions; he also stipulates that it is characterized by 'naturalism', that is, understanding naturally occurring human behaviour in context as opposed to through artificial settings or structured interviews. Clifford (1986, p. 13) further notes that 'the ethnographer's personal experiences . . . are recognised as central to the research process, but they are firmly restrained by the impersonal standards of observation and "objective" distance'. In the management studies sphere, the term 'ethnography' can be loosely employed, sometimes referring simply to conducting interviews which are longer, less structured and/or more qualitative than the norm (see, for instance, Shimoni and Bergman 2006), but generally speaking tends to refer to a research process in which the researcher's own experiences, as observer and/or participant in the organization, form the core of the methodology.

While some are uneasy with considering ethnography under the heading of 'case study research', viewing this as reductive and positivist and seeing ethnography instead as a theoretical approach or a more inclusive programme of scientific study, I would argue that ethnography can be used to generate case studies. The focus on small groups and significant incidents mean that case studies can be found within ethnography and, if the researcher chooses, can be used as support or material for a case study-focused approach. For the purposes of this chapter, ethnography can be roughly defined as experiential data collection, with the researchers themselves, through their own experiences, the primary tool for gathering information, tempered with adherence to standards of observation and scientific methods. This technique therefore can, arguably, fit with the case study approach by generating case material for exploration, if this is the researcher's aim.

Ethnography is, however, subject to a dichotomy in terms of its uses as a means of generating case study material. On the one hand, it is supposed to provide a holistic image of the group under study, a sense of its lived experiences (Fetterman 1989), the integration of this group in wider society, and the complexity of human life (Kaberry 1957). At the same time, however, it tends to be characterized in practice by the focus on a single small group, to the point where it can sometimes lose track of the wider picture (Dresch 1992). The result is that while in a business context ethnography could provide a perspective for seeing organizations as a complete system, integrated into the outside world (as noted in Sharpe 2004), it often focuses instead only on a small group and considers the wider context largely from the periphery or from the group's perspective.

ETHNOGRAPHY AND THE HOLISTIC PERSPECTIVE: LITERATURE REVIEW

In line with ethnography's small-group focus, industrial anthropology tends to be characterized by a focus on workers, with little attention given to managers, possibly because it is easier to obtain access to the shop-floor

than the boardroom (Chapman et al. 2004). Castles and Kosack's (1973) study of labour migrants, *Immigrant Workers and Class Struggle in Western Europe*, ignores the elite stratum entirely and argues that to focus on ethnic identity is to legitimize the oppression of immigrants by obscuring their inferior class position. They present the workers' experience as a thoroughly distressing one for all concerned, leading Watson (1977) to mount a strong critique of their monograph on the grounds that they ignore migrants' own agency. Equally, they ignore business migrants, professionals and other labour migrants and focus instead only on the bottom stratum of the labour market. Other research on labour migrants (for instance, Grillo 1985) exhibits the same trend of considering the lower strata and lacks comparison to the wider context.

Outside the migrant literature, Willis's (1977) *Learning to Labour* focuses on white British working-class young men and how they become integrated into the social and mental patterns which both affirm class identity but also ensure that they remain in a subordinate position within the system, but again does not consider the role of other groups within this system (middle-class young men, for instance, or working-class young women), while Westwood's (1984) *All Day, Every Day* similarly focuses on working-class women, although with a more positive view of their situation and with a broader range of ethnic identities and ages. While all of these are excellent studies which give strong insights into the situations of different sorts of workers, we normally have a focus on the workers and their perspective, as opposed to considering how they integrate into a whole system of different groups, perspectives and systems.

However, the ethnographic literature on international business is still fairly rare, and is similarly focused on management to the exclusion of other perspectives. Law (1994), Czarniawska (1997), Sakai (2000), Sharpe (2001) and Moore (2005) all focus on white-collar workers of various types (research scientists in the case of Law, public sector in the case of Czarniawska, managers in the case of Sakai, Sharpe and Moore). With rare exceptions, such as Sharpe (2006), this literature does not consider others within the same company (while banks, such as those studied by Sakai and myself, do not have a blue-collar workforce, there nonetheless exists occupational stratification, with contract and temporary workers occupying a very different social world to the managers and permanent employees). Some more holistic material exists in the work–life balance literature, but the focus on workers is limited, with them being seen as victims or obstructers of management policy rather than as active agents within the organization. Thus while Lambert and Haley-Lock's (2004, p. 179) paper takes an 'organizational stratification approach' to consider how different levels in the workplace receive benefits, they seem to

focus mainly on how workers in the lower strata of the organization are excluded from work–life balance policies and programmes, rather than considering what they actually do in this regard. The ethnographic literature on workers and on managers thus provides much rich data on how each group sees the organization, but little work has been done on considering how the two perspectives combine, oppose and influence each other.

Some ethnographic studies exist, however, which indicate that it is indeed possible to integrate two or more perspectives on the same society in a single ethnography, and gain a more holistic perspective. I would here define a holistic perspective as one which combines the perspective of multiple groups within the social unit under study, and/or which takes a longitudinal approach to the subject. The single-event case study, such as Max Gluckman's *Analysis of a Social Situation in Modern Zululand* (1958), considers the perspectives of different groups within a given society on a single event, and how they come together in such situations, making the connections, divisions and interactions between the different elements clearer. While much of this sort of work may be in the line of critical incident studies, this does not mean that it cannot be expanded and developed in time and space. Mayer and Mayer's (1961) research on two sections of a single urban ethnic group in Southern Africa – the 'Red' Xhosa and 'School' Xhosa – shows them not in isolation but as part of a whole system of cultural discourses, in constant interaction over what it means to be Xhosa. There are also many long-term studies of particular groups, and studies by different anthropologists over time, which provide multiple perspectives on the culture. It is thus possible for ethnographic case studies to consider different groups in a single organization not as isolated units, but as part of a whole system which is integrated within itself and embedded in outside contexts.

A couple of examples of holistic ethnographies also exist in the anthropology of organizations and/or industry. Jeannie Lo's *Office Ladies, Factory Women* (1990) is an ethnography of two different types of female workers at the same Japanese company, comparing and contrasting the experiences and viewpoints of women working on the shop-floor with those working in the office, and how both fit in with the company as a whole. *Maids and Madams*, a 1986 ethnographic film on South Africa directed by Mira Hamermesh, interviews and follows both black maids and the white women who employ them, exposing in the process how both are differently affected by the Apartheid system then in force, while at the same time contributing to each other's views and discourses. Examples thus exist of circumstances in which different groups within a single workplace can be seen as interacting within a whole system, through the use of ethnographic study and writing techniques. I would thus argue that such techniques can be more widely applied to organizations to gain an in-depth and detailed

perspective on particular groups, which also provides a fuller picture of the organization in which they work, through using multiple ethnographic studies of different groups within the same organization.

Finally, a note about the theoretical and epistemological stance of this study. I approach the anthropology of business from the perspective of a researcher who was educated in traditional anthropology (studying small-scale societies in the developing world) at two institutions, one whose approach was predominantly Marxist, the other whose approach was structuralist, at a time when postmodernist concepts were very much in vogue. Consequently, this chapter is written from a structuralist perspective (see Levi-Strauss 1972), with some elements of postmodernism (Clifford 1986), particularly with regard to the embracing of reflexivity and the rejection of overall 'grand narratives' in favour of a case-by-case approach. I tend to take a traditional anthropological approach to the ethnography of business, aiming at drawing conclusions about human behaviour from longitudinal, participation-heavy study of a particular small group or small groups.

BACKGROUND TO THE PRESENT STUDY

This chapter is based partly on participant-observation fieldwork at an Anglo-German automobile factory, BMW MINI, partly on interviews with its employees, and partly on archival research with local historical collections. In 2003, I gained access to the company as part of a group of researchers affiliated with the Said Business School who had been asked to propose studies of the organization by the top management. I was to conduct a study of gender diversity and staff retention among the workforce, as the firm wished to recruit and retain more female shop-floor workers, yet were unable to determine, from exit questionnaire results and staff surveys, precisely why they were failing to do so. This meant that a study in which a female researcher experienced life on the line personally was required.

As part of my research, I spent three months on the line in the Final Assembly Area (more colloquially referred to as 'Assembly') of the plant, working as a temporary employee of the firm (known officially as an 'associate') with their full knowledge and permission. Two tours were also taken of the entire plant as an outsider. Subsequently, I have spent about 12 months, intermittently, working with a group of managers from the Human Resources (HR) department on two projects, one involving the development of a management education programme aimed at teaching managers how to use ethnographic techniques in their daily activities, and one aimed at assessing how the workforce feel about the plant's management style and working on ways of improving managerial practices. I was also able to briefly follow up my research in Assembly through making an exploratory visit to one of the company's German plants. Until the end of 2003, I lived in Oxford and was affiliated with the Said Business School as a postdoctoral research associate (having completed a doctorate the previous year at Oxford's Institute for Social and Cultural Anthropology), meaning that I was able to follow how the plant was portrayed in the local media and how it formed part of the wider community.

Formal interviews were conducted with 13 staff members in total. Most were in white-collar managerial and/or coordination functions, although some were shop-floor managers. Most of the interviewees were associated with the Final Assembly Area, but there were also some involved with the Paint Shop or Body in White (the area where the unpainted car is assembled) sections as well. Most formal interviews were recorded, although in a few cases in which the interviewee was not comfortable with the presence of a tape recorder, shorthand notes were taken instead. In some cases, follow-up interviews were conducted, normally over the telephone. Informal, unrecorded discussions were held with workers on the line during the period of fieldwork, as well as with the HR managers with whom I worked on the two projects mentioned above. This approach was taken because my earlier experiences of studying different social strata within an organization had strongly confirmed Briggs's (1986) findings that people in the lower strata of an organization (thus, its more vulnerable members) may find an interview a threatening situation, and prefer informal discussions as a means of imparting information. While in Germany, I also interviewed five managers, all of whom had been involved with the change in ownership of the British plant, regarding their experiences as expatriates and the differences between the plants. The comments which follow are thus from interviews in the case of managers, but from informal discussions in the case of workers.

My own role within the organization was thus a multifaceted one, as I shifted from the role of outside researcher, to worker, to consultant (a 'semi-insider' role) over a period, and was also affected by the changes within the organization over the longitudinal period of the study (I was, for instance, able to observe some of the changes which were made to management practice due to my initial report). In addition, my age (27 at the start of the study), gender (female) and ethnicity (white Anglophone Canadian) impacted upon my results. The fact that my accent did not conform to British middle- or working-class norms, for instance, meant that I was treated with more or less the same degree of acceptance/lack of acceptance by both classes, whereas a native Briton would automatically be pigeonholed by accent. I have here endeavoured to present the different voices within the organization as accurately as possible, but this will be subject to my theoretical background, identity and the opportunities which were presented to me as a fieldworker. The firm did not ask for confidentiality in publications, and, indeed, given its unique position in the market, it would be impossible to conceal its identity; however, I have opted for partial confidentiality, disguising the identities of all interviewees.

THE SETTING

The Plant: Rover/BMW MINI

The plant at which my study was conducted started out as a small domestic British car manufacturer, originally Morris Motors (later BMC, British Leyland, and finally forming part of the Rover Group), in the early 1910s (Newbigging et al. 1998), remaining more or less under the same ownership until the late 1960s. During this time, it rapidly became a focus of social activity for its workers, developing its own sports teams, bands, amateur dramatic societies, volunteer organizations and social venues (Newbigging et al. 1998). At least some of the people working at the factory at the time of fieldwork told me that they were second- or even third-generation factory workers, reminiscing about being taken to the Rover Workers' social club for Christmas parties as children (see also Bardsley and Laing 1999).

While Morris Motors initially prospered, being one of the British success stories of the immediate post-Second World War period (Whisler 1999), the company was also hit by the decline which affected industrial Britain from the early 1960s onwards. Outcompeted by foreign companies and subject to questionable senior management decisions (Whisler 1999), it was nationalized in 1968 and, when it continued to decline, was reprivatized in the 1980s, being owned variously by Honda, BAe and finally being taken over by BMW – German heavy industry having, in contrast to the British, expanded and developed in the postwar period (Greenhalgh and Kilmister 1993). Today the plant produces a single automobile model, the MINI, a small car developed from Morris's original Mini and which, like its predecessor, has a popular following around the world; the plant is consequently known as BMW MINI.

The Managers

The managers at BMW MINI, while they might at first glance seem like a unified group, were, I found as I spent time with them, tacitly divided into two subgroups: the shop-floor managers and the office managers. The latter were further subdivided into British and German (or local and expatriate, since the two ethnic groups were more or less contiguous with expatriate status in this branch). The managers tended to be physically divided in terms of where they worked (the shop-floor or the office), and, in the case of the office managers, divided in terms of who they associated with, where they worked, their national origin and their career pattern as described to me in interviews. It was thus possible for me to identify different cohorts among the managers, based on the geography of the plant and who associated with whom.

The German managers had either been brought in specifically to help with issues in the restructuring of the plant, or were part of the general management, as BMW had an 'international stream' system whereby managers were encouraged to take up expatriate positions in other branches. Most of these managers remained in their position at the branch for three years or less; all the ones of whom I was aware were white, male and in their thirties or early forties.

The British managers tended to be of a greater range of age and background; most tended to be of local origin, and most were from the town in which the factory was located. The gender ratio was roughly one-third female to two-thirds male, and most of the managers were white. They also had more of a social investment in this particular branch, with some having worked at the plant for 30 years, and all, as far as I could tell, planning on a reasonably long-term career with the branch. Some of them told me that they had worked at other branches in the group, taking advantage of exchange programmes or else arranging to join the 'international stream'. They tended to place less emphasis on academic qualifications than the expatriates when describing themselves, instead emphasizing professional qualifications and demonstrable skills.

The Workers

The unskilled and semi-skilled employees in the Final Assembly Area were known as 'associates', a term meant to imply membership and partnership in the firm as opposed to a particular position in the hierarchical chain of command, but which also implies a degree of detachment from the firm as a whole. As with the managers, what appeared at first to be a unified group proved upon further inspection to be more diverse. The associates fell into two categories: those with a permanent contract and those hired through a temporary labour agency. It was impossible to tell the difference between the two groups in terms of appearance or duties, and there were some temporary associates who had been working at the plant for longer than most contract associates. The difference was largely one of rights and benefits, but the social implications of this will be discussed below. At the time of the fieldwork, the ethnic composition of employees in Assembly was slightly over two-thirds white, with the remaining third approximately evenly divided between black/Afro-Caribbean and Asian associates. The gender ratio was slightly over 90 per cent male (statistics obtained from BMW, with permission).

The managers and workers of the plant were thus divided in terms of their social position, ethnic mix and situation within the plant's social structure, all of which, one can safely assume, gives them very different perspectives on the organization. We shall now consider the views of the managers and workers on their situation, and how these were discovered through ethnographic fieldwork.

MANAGERIAL POLYPHONY: THE DIVERSE VIEWS OF THE MANAGERIAL STRATUM

The managers' attitude to their work was, generally speaking, very brand-focused, in that they tended to take pride in the product and the company. In conversation, they were generally enthusiastic both about the MINI and the international standing of BMW; they appeared to take the company's successes as sources of personal pride, and, during my participant observation with them, reacted badly to any remark which they took as a slight on its products, even if it was not so intended. At the same time, however, there was a degree of ambivalence in that there was a feeling that this new owner was erasing the positive things about the previous owner: as one HR manager said in an interview, 'This site has a history, good and bad, and all the qualities seem to have been stripped away'. This behaviour thus indicates that managers took pride in the product, but also felt that their pride in the company's history was under threat.

There was, as a result, some friction between the expatriates sent over to change the branch's practices and the local managers, as I observed in the way in which both groups discussed, and reacted to, each other. The German owners of the company had originally intended to take a very hands-off management style, but had become increasingly hands-on in recent years, and the British managers periodically expressed to me in interviews and conversations that they sometimes found this intrusive, particularly as they had greater local knowledge than the expatriates. Cultural differences also had an impact: for instance, one HR manager told me that, whereas the British will work longer hours during the week if it means they can leave early on Fridays, the Germans view this pattern as unacceptable, meaning that both groups regarded each other, somewhat unfairly, as 'lazy', and leading to what he saw as a kind of competition between the groups as to who could work the longest and put in the most overtime. Discussions with British managers thus indicate that the managers' view of the factory was coloured by the takeover situation.

I also observed that the managers maintained particular signifiers of their class position. The managers generally stayed in the office as much as possible: those managers who did work on the shop-floor were treated less like managers and more like workers by the other managers, with there being a definite sense that the managers' place is in the office. This also fed into the above-mentioned friction with the expatriates, as Germany has no such signifier of class division and consequently the new managers set up programmes encouraging managers to spend more time on the shop-floor. However, while the local managers all spoke enthusiastically about the programme as a concept, few of them took it up in practice. While none of them explained this to me in as many words, the fact that they generally maintained a physical distance from the workers suggested that the problem had more to do with tacit feelings of inappropriateness than with any of the excuses actually given for not participating (which generally had to do with lack of time). The managers thus used their isolation from the shop-floor as a class signifier, unspoken but visible through their behaviour.

The **BMW MINI** managers' view of their relations with the workers was that there should be mutual trust between the groups, based on a programme of corporate social philanthropy in the local community. Several philanthropic programmes were in place, including sponsorship of a volunteer fire brigade, blood drives, and donations of prizes to local charities, which were featured in the plant's internal magazine as well as in local newspapers, and which I periodically encountered in other ways. Posters advertising blood drives would be put up in the staff canteen, for instance, and, while visiting a local fun-fair on my day off, I encountered a 'Win a MINI' prize draw raising funds for the local hospital trust. Two British managers spoke to me of an incident during the recession of the 1970s in which the workers of one of BMW's German plants took a temporary pay cut rather than see the company go under, evidence, so the managers said, of a strong tradition of trust between the company and its workers, which they were trying to maintain in the UK.

In sum, then, ethnographic work indicates that within the broad category of 'managers', there was a diversity of managerial identities, focusing around their different roles in the business and their perspectives on the changes being implemented, with a continuous jockeying for power between managerial groups. As will be discussed in the next section, this contrasts with the workers' concerns, which focused for the most part on obtaining full-time contracts with the company, financial concerns, and maintaining a good work–life balance.

ALONG THE LINES: DIVERSE WORKER PERSPECTIVES

Although some of the workforce joined with the intention of working for short periods (such as students working during the summer break, artists earning money to support their activities, housewives supplementing the family income to pay for Christmas or summer holiday expenses, and recent migrants to the UK who had taken a factory job as a 'stopgap' while looking for a job more to their liking), among the rest, full-time contracts were much in demand for the financial and social security they provided, as well as the implied recognition of the employee's value by the company. This led to power politics, as one shop-floor manager said to me in an interview:

> It can give me a slight advantage, because the people who haven't got a contract I can motivate towards getting a contract. The issue it gives me is that contracts are in short supply, BMW has a strict percentage as to how many are contract and how many are agency associates [i.e., hired through a temporary labour agency] . . . I've got one person who's an agency associate and he's been here for just a couple of months short of two years, so . . . he's not top of the list when it comes to assigning contracts 'cause although he does a fairly good job he could do better, and he worked twenty years at Rover before taking voluntary redundancy. And he's come back and would dearly love a BMW contract.

I also observed that workers whom I knew were hoping for a contract tended to be keen to learn new techniques and to behave in ingratiating ways with the team coordinators. The workers' desire to obtain contracts thus apparently enabled managers to have a degree of control over some, if not all, of the workforce.

Despite the managers' focus on corporate philanthropy, and although the workers acknowledged the benefits of this, all workers on the line occasionally said in conversation that they felt that the company 'doesn't care' about them. While they were not on the whole discontented with their work, the lack of formal training programmes at the time, and attempts to speed up the line, were held up as evidence that the company was only interested in the workers for their labour. The attempt by one line supervisor at a *kaizen* meeting (a meeting of workers aimed primarily at discussing means to improve the assembly process) to point out that the workers benefited from the overall success of the company was derided by the workers as 'taking the party line'. The workers and managers thus described the same workplace in different ways; moreover, power relations were not a simple equation of managers imposing their will on powerless workers, as the workers had a number of ways, of varying degrees of subtlety, of contributing to the overall identity of the branch.

The workers generally viewed the factory less as a prestigious workplace than as a community asset. Many associates described the factory as something they could 'fall back on' when they needed work. While there were a couple of associates on my team (of about 10 individuals) who said that they were aiming for long-term contracts, the rest fell into the more temporary categories described above. In contrast to their managers, the workers, while they visibly took pride in their work, praising high-quality performance and competing to learn new skills, could be very critical of the factory's product in and of itself, sometimes comparing it unfavourably to other cars.

The workers also tended to focus on money as a key aspect of their reasons for being at this factory. This is illustrated by an incident in which I turned down a request from my team coordinator to work on my day off, and a co-worker told me repeatedly that I was 'turning down big money' and that I was 'making a mistake'. At the same time, though, the workers were strongly protective of their work–life balance. The same colleague, when I explained to her that I had personal plans on my day off, did not press the issue, and nor did the team coordinator who had made the original request.

Their views on former versus current owners were also ambivalent, but in a different way from the managers. The workers spoke of the Rover regime as one that was less target focused and more relaxed, where it was easy to 'have a laugh' and the work was relatively easy to do when compared to the more technically demanding processes of BMW. However, the general attitude on the line was that people were not concerned about the ownership of the plant, so long as it continued to operate and provide jobs for locals. Older members of the workforce spoke approvingly of all the owners under which they had worked, regardless of whether the company was, at that time, financially successful. The one exception was a former owner which had sold off large portions of the company: significantly, very few workers mentioned this owner at all (even those whose employment at the factory dated from after this period of ownership) and, when pressed, they were fairly taciturn, saying simply that this owner had wanted to 'asset strip' the firm and 'didn't care' about the business.

In contrast to the managers, then, the line workers generally focused on the company as a source of income and a community asset: they valued their work–life balance and were not particularly concerned about the prestige of the company, but at the same time they were willing to put up with discomfort in order to obtain high wages and/or contracts. Like the managers, however, ethnographic research revealed a number of cohorts or subgroups, with different positions, attitudes and ideas, within the general category of 'workers'. Ethnographic research among the workers thus revealed a different, if equally complex, spectrum of attitudes to the managers, despite both working for the same company.

JUST REWARDS: CONFLICT BETWEEN MANAGERS AND WORKERS

In this section, I shall briefly consider two instances of conflict between managers and workers at BMW, and consider how a holistic perspective, which takes the views of both groups into account, casts light on the nature of the conflict and the functioning of the organization. While the literature tends to paint manager–worker relations, particularly at automobile factories, as a simple opposition, the situation between managers and workers at BMW MINI was more complex.

To turn to the first example, conflict between managers and workers took place at more of a cultural than an industrial level. While the company had a policy of engaging in non-financial reward practices, the workers described gifts of company-branded merchandise (such as mugs and fleeces) as patronising, while regarding the sponsorship of outings, such as group visits to the dog racing track, more positively. The reasons for the conflict become apparent when one considers the different approaches of the two groups to the factory. The workers, as noted, were more concerned about fun and friendships, whereas the managers were focused on pride in the product and the brand. So, whereas the managers might have viewed merchandise bearing the prestigious brand as an appropriate reward through their pride in the brand, the workers preferred dog-racing sessions as this is a fun activity which can be done with a group of friends. Considering multiple perspectives on the organization thus clarifies the reasons for the conflict.

The other example involves a display which was set up by managers in an empty display case at the main entrance to the Final Assembly Area, which provides a powerful example of how participant observation among the workers caused new meaning to be read into a manager-created artefact. This involved a diorama of mannequins dressed and posed to look like a team of workers assembling a car and a visitor observing them. From the point of view of the managers, this was an opportunity to indicate both the different uniforms in the plant and the components of correct safety dress for visitors; they seemed quite happy with the diorama, and one manager even wrote a positive article encouraging people to see it for the plant newsletter.

The associates, however, commented that all the mannequins were white, and the visitor was the only female figure in the diorama, which, to them, sent out a message that their diverse workforce was not suitable for representation to the public. I myself felt uncomfortable with the representation of the plant portrayed each time I passed it, and, at one point when I was walking in to work via the main entrance before work with a white male colleague in his late thirties, he pointed to it and referred jokingly to the all-white nature of the team versus the multiethnic reality of assembly-line work. Part of the problem may stem from the ethnic composition of the managerial stratum: posters in the German BMW plant which I visited also showed a lack of ethnic diversity in its representation of workers, and Koopmans and Statham (1999) note that discourses of ethnic diversity are less entrenched in Germany than in Britain. As for the British managers, their relative isolation from the shop-floor may have resulted in them not being aware of the strength of feeling about diversity recognition among the workforce: certainly they did often give the impression in interviews and in conversations that their default image of the workers was as white British working-class men. Thus, seen from both perspectives, what seems like a slight on the part of the managers is in fact a mistake of omission.

When both perspectives are taken into account, then, the two conflict situations discussed here are understandable. However, it requires one to consider both groups' positions within the firm to understand the reasons behind each group's actions, and how they influence each other. Had I not been able to engage in participant observation with both groups, I would not have been able to see where the conflict arose, or how the divisions within the groups affected the conflict situations.

HOLISTIC ETHNOGRAPHY: ANALYSIS AND DISCUSSION

The primary finding illustrated by this chapter is that it is both possible and fruitful to develop holistic case studies of organizations using ethnographic techniques. It has long been recognized that ethnographic techniques can provide more organic and experiential perspectives on organizations than more conventional methods for studying organizations, and can provide insight into conflicts and situations which cannot be answered through straightforward quantitative means (recall that the initial impetus for this study involved tackling a practical management issue which could not be addressed in traditional ways). In this chapter I have gone beyond this to suggest that creative use of ethnography can not only provide an individual or small-group perspective on the organization, but can also contribute insights into broader issues of organization, such as the reasons behind particular conflicts and the nature of appropriate rewards and sanctions for the workers. Ethnographic research can also illustrate the diversity of organizations, indicating the many subgroups or cohorts contained within the external categories of 'managers' and 'workers'. By obtaining perspectives from many people within an organization, ethnographers can build up a usable picture of the whole organization which is both holistic and ethnographic.

The main difficulty of this approach is that the level of detail required for a successful ethnography is fairly extensive, as is the time which would be needed to gather sufficient data, which is one reason why anthropologists have tended historically to focus on small groups. However, the fact that many anthropologists have successfully studied multiple groups (including, among others, Margaret Mead, Ruth Benedict and E.E. Evans-Pritchard), suggests that it would not be impossible to follow them. Furthermore, this approach has greater applications than simply the industrial context, but could be applied to, for instance, the fields of the anthropology of development or that of conflict management. By studying different groups and their perspective on the same organization or wider group, anthropologists can gain broader perspective.

Other issues which must be considered include the resource intensity of the technique (in terms of the personal investment of training, time and attention on the part of the researcher), issues of access (I was fortunate in having access to two quite different groups within the same organization) and opportunity (being in the 'right place at the right time'). In particular, access is a significant problem: most ethnographers are fortunate even to have detailed access to a single group in the organization, and the opportunity to do wider fieldwork is thus akin to having lightning strike twice. It is worth noting, however, that it is not impossible for such a degree of access to be attained, as, for instance, in the longitudinal research on Czech companies of Soulsby and Clark (2007).

Furthermore, the lack of formal training procedure for ethnographers may seem disconcerting to outsiders. I attended two pre-fieldwork courses at different universities in different countries, and both mainly focused on providing novices with a good grounding in the ethical issues and knowledge of the possible research tools available rather than in prescribing particular methods. My own experiences of fieldwork also suggested strongly to me that ethnographic work is sufficiently individual that it does need to be treated on a case-by-case basis rather than as a general practice. However, most guides to fieldwork note that observant researchers can almost always identify some material of interest (see, for instance, Fetterman 1989), simply through considering the issues that are relevant to one's fieldwork situation, and also note that the technique does pay off in terms of providing an in-depth image of the lived experience of working for an organization. A researcher interested in such techniques thus requires tenacity, creativity, and good observation and communication skills.

Finally, the ethnographic techniques outlined here provide us with a different view of the firm compared to the traditional monolithic image. From a holistic perspective, we see the firm as a number of distinct groups (while this chapter began with a focus on two only, the subsequent analysis indicated a number of different subgroups existing within those categories), each with different connections to one another and with the outside world. These groups show different perspectives on the organization, and link to different outside groups, and yet also come from mutually compatible standpoints which allow communication. Holistic ethnographic research thus paints a very different perspective on the firm than that obtained by quantitative methods and/or traditional small-group-focused ethnography, as a nexus of groups interacting with one another and the outside world rather than as an isolated unit with a manager-driven culture and with manager–worker conflict limited to visible cases of industrial action.

Ethnographic methods, furthermore, have particular benefits which may be useful in investigating culture and social embeddedness. Unlike the interview-based approach which remains the most common form of qualitative study in international business (Piekkari et al. 2009), participant observation allows the researcher access to aspects of working life in the firm which interviewees might not mention in interview settings for various reasons. The literature on network theory (for example, Andersson 2003) and on corporate social responsibility (Conley and Williams 2005) argues that we should view companies not in isolation, but as part of integrated social networks. However, as McSweeney (2002) notes in his critique of Hofstede, this isolated picture of organizations is at least somewhat encouraged by the use of more quantitative and/or interview-focused methods, which artificially exclude other connections aside from that being directly considered. A more realistic perspective on the firm can be provided by ethnographic case studies of the sort conducted here, which allows the consideration of multiple perspectives on the firm.

Ethnographic case studies thus have well-known benefits in terms of being able to provide a picture of the lived experience of working at a particular company (Conley and Williams 2005). Furthermore, although they are often criticized for providing a limited perspective, in that they normally focus on a small number of individuals, the BMW study indicates that it is more than possible to develop wider-reaching perspectives while still retaining the richness and depth of traditional ethnography.

CONCLUSION

In terms of further directions for research, the application of holistic ethnography to more situations in the workplace might go some way to counter the critique raised by more quantitative researchers that ethnography fails to provide a complete picture of the organization, and encourage the greater use of ethnographic case studies in conventional business research. There may also be other means of using ethnographic methods which take into account a variety of perspectives rather than being limited to a single group, beyond that of doing ethnographic fieldwork among different groups in the same organization. Furthermore, space has not permitted an exploration of the sheer variety of perspectives which can be found among managers and workers, or the experiences of shop-floor managers, who fall between the two categories. Both anthropology and business studies could thus benefit from more holistic, but still qualitative and ethnographic, perspectives, in other areas.

I conclude, first, that ethnographic techniques can provide a way of looking at members of organizations not as oppositional groups or groups in isolation, but as parts of an integrated social nexus. Second, I argue that the use of ethnographic methodology need not limit the researcher to studying a single group, or even a single organization, but that longitudinal studies of different groups within organizations, or the same sector, or the same area, can provide a variety of perspectives, building up an integrated picture and revealing the many voices within a single company. Ethnographic methodologies thus have much to offer business researchers in terms of their utility in studying organizations as embedded, diverse entities: not just as a means of exploring the lived experience of a single group in depth, but also as a means of gaining a picture of diverse groups within the organization.

REFERENCES

Andersson, U. (2003), 'Managing the transfer of capabilities within multinational corporations: the dual role of the subsidiary', *Scandinavian Journal of Management*, **19** (4), 425–42.

Bardsley, G. and S. Laing (1999), *Making Cars at Cowley: from Morris to Rover*, Stroud: British Motor Industry Heritage Trust.

Briggs, C.L. (1986), *Learning How to Ask: A Sociolinguistic Appraisal of the Role of the Interview in Social Science Research*, Cambridge: Cambridge University Press.

Castles, S. and G. Kosack (1973), *Immigrant Workers and Class Struggle in Western Europe*, Oxford: Oxford University Press.

Chapman, M., H. Gajewska-De Mattos and C. Antoniou (2004), 'The ethnographic international business researcher: misfit or trailblazer?', in R. Piekkari and C. Welch (eds), *Handbook of Qualitative Research Methods for International Business*, Cheltenham, UK and Northampton, MA, USA: Edward Elgar, pp. 287–305.

Clifford, J. (1986), 'Introduction: partial truths', in Clifford and G.E. Marcus (eds), *Writing Culture: The Poetics and Politics of Ethnography*, Berkeley, CA and London: University of California Press, pp. 1–26.

Conley, J.M. and C.A. Williams (2005), 'Engage, embed, and embellish: theory versus practice in the corporate social responsibility movement', *Journal of Corporation Law*, **31** (1), 1–38.

Czarniawska, B. (1997), *Narrating the Organization: Dramas of Institutional Identity*, Chicago, IL and London: University of Chicago Press.

Dresch, P. (1992), 'Ethnography and general theory', *Journal of the Anthropological Society of Oxford*, **23** (1), 17–36.

Fetterman, D.M. (1989), *Ethnography: Step by Step*, London: Sage.

Gluckman, M. (1958), *Analysis of a Social Situation in Modern Zululand*, Manchester: Manchester University Press.

Greenhalgh, C. and A. Kilmister (1993), 'The British economy, the state and the motor industry', in T. Hayter and D. Harvey (eds), *The Factory and the City: The Story of the Cowley Automobile Workers in Oxford*, London: Mansell, pp. 26–46.

Grillo, R.D. (1985), *Ideologies and Institutions in Urban France: The Representation of Immigrants*, Cambridge: Cambridge University Press.

Hamermesh, M. (1986), *Maids and Madams*, Channel 4 Films.

Hammersley, M. (1998), *Reading Ethnographic Research: A Critical Guide*, 2nd edn, Harlow: Addison-Wesley.

Kaberry, P. (1957), 'Malinowski's contribution to field-work methods and the writing of ethnography', in R. Firth (ed.), *Man and Culture: An Evaluation of the Work of Bronislaw Malinowski*, London: Routledge & Kegan Paul, pp. 71–92.

Koopmans, R. and P. Statham (1999), 'Challenging the liberal nation-state? Postnationalism, multiculturalism, and the collective claims making of migrants and ethnic minorities in Britain and Germany', *American Journal of Sociology*, **105** (3), 652–96.

Lambert, S.J. and A. Haley-Lock (2004), 'The organizational stratification of opportunities for work–life balance', *Community, Work and Family*, **7** (2), 179–96.

Law, J. (1994), *Organizing Modernity*, Oxford: Blackwell.

Levi-Strauss, C. (1972), *Structural Anthropology*, Harmondsworth: Penguin.

Lo, J. (1990), *Office Ladies, Factory Women: Life and Work at a Japanese Company*, London: East Gate.

Mayer, P. and I. Mayer (1961), *Townsmen or Tribesmen: Conservatism and the Process of Urbanization in a South African City*, Oxford and Cape Town: Oxford University Press.

McSweeney, B. (2002), 'Hofstede's model of national cultural differences and their consequences: a triumph of faith – a failure of analysis', *Human Relations*, **55** (1), 89–119.

Moore, F. (2005), *Transnational Business Cultures: Life and Work in a Multinational Corporation*, Aldershot: Ashgate.

Newbigging, C., S. Shatford and T. Williams (1998), *The Changing Faces of Cowley Works*, Witney: Robert Boyd Publications.

Piekkari, R., C. Welch and E. Paavilainen (2009), 'The case study as disciplinary convention: evidence from international business journals', *Organizational Research Methods*, **12** (3), 567–89.

Sakai, J. (2000), *Japanese Bankers in the City of London: Language, Culture and Identity in the Japanese Diaspora*, London: Routledge.

Sharpe, D. (2001), 'Globalization and change: an in-depth case study of processes of organizational continuity and change within a Japanese manufacturing organization in the UK', in G. Morgan, P.H. Kristensen and R. Whitley (eds), *The Multinational Firm: Organizing Across National and Institutional Divides*, Oxford: Oxford University Press, pp. 196–218.

Sharpe, D. (2004), 'The relevance of ethnography to international business research', in R. Marschan-Piekkari and C. Welch (eds), *Handbook of Qualitative Research Methods for International Business*, Cheltenham, UK and Northampton, MA, USA: Edward Elgar, pp. 305–23.

Sharpe, D. (2006), 'Shop floor practices under changing forms of managerial control: a comparative ethnographic study of micro-politics, control and resistance within a Japanese multinational', *Journal of International Management*, **12** (3), 318–39.

Shimoni, B. and H. Bergman (2006), 'Managing in a changing world: from multiculturalism to hybridization: the production of hybrid management cultures in Israel, Thailand, and Mexico', *Academy of Management Perspectives*, **20** (3), 76–89.

Soulsby, A. and E. Clark (2007), 'Organization theory and the post-socialist transformation: contributions to organizational knowledge', *Human Relations*, **60** (10), 1419–42.

Watson, J. (1977), 'Introduction: immigration, ethnicity and class in Britain', in J.L. Watson (ed.), *Between Two Cultures: Migrants and Minorities in Britain*, Oxford: Basil Blackwell, pp. 1–20.

Westwood, S. (1984), *All Day, Every Day: Factory and the Family in the Making of Women's Lives*, London: Pluto Press.

Whisler, T.R. (1999), *The British Motor Industry, 1945–94: A Study in Industrial Decline*, Oxford: Oxford University Press.

Willis, P. (1977), *Learning to Labour: How Working-class Kids Get Working-class Jobs*, Farnborough: Saxon House.

18. Digging Archaeology: postpositivist theory and archival research in case study development

Albert J. Mills and Jean Helms Mills

INTRODUCTION

In this chapter we take up the recent call of Piekkari et al. (2009, p. 567) 'for greater methodological pluralism in conducting case studies' through the development of alternative case study traditions. To that end, we discuss the fun and challenges of linking postpositivist methods (Prasad 2005) and archival research in the development of the case study. Archival research and postpositivist methods are rarely used in case study research, and even more rarely in concert. We explore these foci through our own research on the gendering of organizational culture over time in three airline companies: British Airways (BA), Air Canada (AC) and Pan American Airways (Pan Am).[1] We then draw some conclusions for postpositivism and international business research. It is not our intention to replace positivist with postpositivist approaches but rather to encourage the view that knowledge is *plural* and relies heavily on underlying ontological and epistemological assumptions (Burrell and Morgan 1979; Corman 2000; Piekkari et al. 2009). Indeed, as we shall now make clear, 'archives', 'postpositivism' and 'case study' are themselves contested terms.

Turning first to the definition of archives: the materials in archive collections were collected for a variety of reasons, ranging from the filing of documents for marketing, legal, or other business-related requirements through to the establishment of a historical record. In the former cases the collected materials do not formally constitute an archive but the term is often applied by researchers who access them for the purpose of studying a particular phenomenon, institution, group, place or person (Helms Mills 2003). It is usually once these kinds of materials are specifically collected together for the purpose of preserving a 'history' of an organization, person, or place, and are 'housed' in a distinct location that they become formally designated an 'archive'.[2]

Definitions of postpositivism vary sharply; ranging from those who respond in 'a limited way' to the critiques of positivism 'while remaining within essentially the same set of beliefs' (Guba and Lincoln 1994, p. 109), through to those who view postpositivism as a tradition that approaches 'questions of social reality and knowledge production from a more problematized vantage point, emphasizing the constructed nature of social reality, the constitutive role of language, and the value of research as critique' (Prasad 2005, p. 9).

To be clear, we are working within this latter tradition. However, as Prasad (p. 9) makes clear, this cannot be seen as a 'single invariant tradition', but rather as 'a number of diverse genres such as dramatism, hermeneutics, critical theory, semiotics, [strands of feminism] and poststructuralism – all of which are primarily united in their rejection of prominent positivist assumptions'. Our own postpositivist orientation includes an intersection of feminism, critical theory and poststructuralism, which will also be made clear in explorations of our case study research.

In our understanding of case study research, we agree with Piekkari et al.'s (2009) notion of case study as 'a research strategy' that utilizes a variety of methods (for example, interviewing, textual analysis) and sources (for example, conversations, documents) for focusing on a phenomenon in context. In so doing we regard the entire process as a sensemaking strategy (Weick 1995) for developing plausible (rather than accurate) accounts of reality and knowledge. We agree that it is important to study a phenomenon in context because it allows a richer understanding of the interrelationships between various 'actants' (that is, ongoing and embedded relationships such as cultural artefacts – Latour 2005) and the event, behaviour and/or sense of identity being explored. Nonetheless, we are acutely aware that the notion of context itself is constructed from highly selected elements (for example, we may privilege studies of gender over economic relations). In the end all we can hope to achieve is the presentation of a plausible account of a selected event, behaviour, or sense of identity (each of which is also constructed in some sense or other), that is, one that is believable due to coherence of approach and argument, and the robustness of the methods used. We would note that we believe that positivist accounts are also sensemaking strategies in their appeal to scientific and empiricist assumptions about knowledge in the form of statistical and other representational cues.

Recent studies of business research methods indicate a growing use of case study research (see for example, Madansky 2008; Serenko et al. 2008; Hartt et al. 2009). However, the picture is far from rosy for those of us who are not steeped in the positivist tradition. Piekkari et al.'s (2009) analysis of the use of case study research in international business indicates that positivism is dominant, to the extent of constituting a 'disciplinary convention', influencing not only the conduct of case studies but the legitimacy of the knowledge produced. Nonetheless, there have been attempts to broaden the field to include alternative approaches. Bryman and Bell (2007), for example, attempt to naturalize (and possibly neutralize) the paradigmatic differences in case study research by citing interpretative, feminist and critical management cases as exemplars. More consciously Mills et al. (2010) set out to 'reclaim the field of case study research' as paradigmatically rich and varied, through inclusion of a range of paradigmatic approaches in their encyclopedia of case study research. These attempts to broaden the field are still as yet limited in number and this chapter is a contribution to the argument for alternatives approaches.

ARCHIVAL RESEARCH AND CASE STUDY STRATEGIES

Positivist and postpositivist understandings of archival research differ in three different regards: (i) location, (ii) associated artefacts and (iii) mode of analysis. We shall now discuss each in turn. Most of the positivist descriptions of archival research refer to places where researchers can access certain 'documents'. These places are invariably referred to as archives. Yin (2009), for example, refers to 'the accessibility' of 'archival records' (p. 102), which include such things as 'census and other statistical data [collected by] federal, state, and local governments' as well as 'service records . . . organizational records, such as budget or personnel records; maps and charts . . . and survey data' (p. 105). Not surprisingly, Yin (p. 102) argues that these kinds of archival documents are strong sources of evidence because they are 'precise and usually quantitative'. Nonetheless, Yin (p. 106) cautions that archival documents are produced and collected for specific purposes and audiences, which need to be taken into account when accessing their 'accuracy'.

While positivists view archives as 'an empirical data corpus' (McHoul and Grace 2003, p. 30) of artefacts and documents that are more-or-less associated with a physical location, or 'archive' (Prasad 2005), Foucauldian poststructuralists have a broader sociological meaning, and that is the approach from which we are drawing. Foucault (1978) argues that 'archive' refers not to 'the mass of texts which have been collected at a given period, or chanced to have survived oblivion from this period' but rather to 'a set of rules which at a given period and for a definite society' structure the conditions in and through which knowledge is produced (quoted in McHoul and Grace 2003, p. 30). Rules in this case refer to a complex system of practices whose very form and regularities 'govern one's manner of perceiving, judging, imagining, and acting' (Flynn 1996, p. 30) but also, significantly, one's sense of identity; that is, self-knowledge is bounded by the production of knowledge *per se* (May 2006). These regularities (for example, the way that certain expectations are repeated in practice) are not 'conscious rules dictating what can be said . . . [but rather] unconscious structurings of discourse' (May 2006, pp. 38–9).

It would appear that (Foucauldian) poststructuralist accounts of archives differ significantly from those of positivist accounts. However, as we shall see below, there is a point where the activity involved in *doing* archival research is remarkably similar in appearance, and that similarity is in the use and accessing of documents and other artefacts, which have been, in the traditional sense, archived: for the sake of clarity we shall use the term 'archive' to refer to the physical location and/or collections of materials, and (the italicized) *'archive'* to refer to a complex system of embedded rules. The difference lies in the treatment of the documents. Thus, while much of Foucauldian analysis involves the use of

> meticulous and detailed textual documentation, this documentation is not, in itself what Foucault means by 'archive'. The documentation and its arrangement by the historian only exist to reveal the archive: the conditions (the 'set of rules') by which it is possible to 'know' something at a specific historical point and by which this knowledge changes. (McHoul and Grace 2003, p. 31)

Indeed, in Foucault's 'view there is, within a given archive, a stability of discursive rules that remains until a historic break' (May 2006, p. 80). The problem is that he does not say much about how this historic break comes about (May 2006, p. 39). As we shall discuss below, it is that issue – of a historic break – that is the focus of much of our case study research.

We pursued the notion of rule sets, how they are stabilized and change (or break) over time, through a focus on organizational culture, which, by the time of our initial study (namely, British Airways in 1991) had become a popular research strategy in business studies (Deal and Kennedy 1982; Schein 1985). However, the field was largely dominated by positivist accounts that drew on a variety of theories of culture (Smircich 1983; Martin 2002) and totally neglected gender in the process (Mills 1988). In developing a feminist theory of organizational culture we drew on Clegg's (1981) notion of rules; in particular, the idea that organizational control is achieved through 'rules' that 'formulate the structure underlying the apparent surface of organizational life' (Clegg 1981, p. 545). This was extended to a conceptualization of organizational culture as a 'configuration of "rules", enactment and resistance, within which gendered relationships are embedded and manifest' (Mills 1988, p. 366). Drawing on this approach, it was then argued, 'the gendered character of a specific organizational culture can be understood through analysis of the particular rule aspects (e.g., extraorganizational, strategic, etc.) that compose a certain configuration' (Mills 1988, p. 366). Although focused on specific 'organizational' rather than 'social' realities, this notion of a 'configuration of rules' can be seen as compatible with Foucault's broader idea of the *archive*.

OUR CASE STUDY ON THE GENDERING OF AIRLINE CULTURES OVER TIME

In 1991 we embarked on the first of three major case studies of international airlines, beginning with British Airways (BA) then Air Canada (AC) and Pan American Airways (Pan Am). The focus of our case studies was the gendering of organizational culture over time. We were interested to understand how discriminatory practices develop, are maintained and change over time. It was this focus that led us to archival research as a way of capturing a sense of an organization over time, a sense that was not accessible through ethnography or observational techniques, and only partially accessible through interviews.

Our theoretical starting point was Oakley's (1972) distinction between *sex* as the basic physiological differences between males and females, and *gender* as culturally specific patterns of behaviour that come to be associated with the sexes. What role, we wondered, do organizational cultures play in the social construction of gender and what are the outcomes? These questions were distinctly absent from the literature on organizational culture of the time (Mills 1988). Specifically, we were interested to 'discover' how the gendering of organizational culture develops (that is, how patterns of behaviour in organizations become regularly associated with the sexes), how gendered patterns of behaviour are maintained, and how they change. This project, we felt, would shed some light on understanding and thus redressing workplace discrimination. It can be noted here that the scope of the project lent itself to a case study given that we set out to find a way of studying a *specific* organizational culture over time.

To undertake the initial case study the following set of criteria was established, and was used in subsequent studies. The organization had to have been in existence for at least 50 years; with an accessible archive; be the subject of one or more written histories; and be socially and methodologically relevant (Mills 2002). Fifty years was chosen as a time-frame sufficient for an organization to have developed a culture and to have undergone some level of culture change over time; the existence of a company archive would allow us to track events and personnel over a relatively long space of time; existing company histories, although highly problematic, would provide important clues to selected personnel, events and critical incidents, while serving as important cultural artefacts in their own right; and, in terms of social and methodological relevance, we wanted an organization that – through name recognition and socio-economic influence – could provide an anchor for the development of a plausible, rather than a generalizable, account. We felt that the case would be more convincing if the organization was viewed as having a powerful standing within a given economy.

In the end we were quite limited in finding organizations that fit our criteria: there are relatively few companies that have been the subject of histories and who maintain an accessible archive. Nonetheless, of the organizations that we could choose from, we were drawn to airline companies because of their enduring association in popular culture with gendered imagery (for example, the iconic sexy flight attendant and heroic pilot, see Mills 1997), and their involvement in high-profile anti-discrimination legal cases (Whitelegg 2007), both of which added important new dimensions of relevancy to a case study focused on gender, culture and discriminatory practices.

Our postpositivist orientation includes an intersection of feminism, critical theory and poststructuralism (Helms Mills and Mills 2000). These epistemological strands were established long before we embarked on our case studies of airline companies but continued to be developed and refined in the process of ongoing research. They did, however, shape our approach to the study of gender and organizational culture. From a feminist perspective we were interested not in organizational outcomes (for example, efficiency) so much as the impact of organizational processes on gender and associated discriminatory practices (for example, how ideas of efficiency contribute to notions of men and women – Mills 1988). From a critical perspective we were interested in what we could learn about the impact of organizational structure and process on the potential for human liberation (Mills et al. 2006). And, from a poststructuralist perspective we were interested in how organizational discourses contribute to gendered identities over time (Mills and Helms Mills 2006). This led us to examine a range of corporate materials, histories and memoirs for dominant and recurring images of men and women and what they tell us about the potential for change. The following quote is an example of the type of imaging that turns women into 'girls', equates and reduces them to a certain form of sexuality, and values that sexuality in terms of its usefulness as emotion labour (Hochschild 1983):

Passengers checking in at the airport can't fail to have noticed the warmth of welcome from the smiling BA girls behind the desks, and the freshness of their looks, their complexions smooth, their make-up alive with colour and gloss. If – heaven forbid – there should be a delay or baggage hold-up, the girls are all smiling efficiency and sympathy. (From British Airways 'BA News', quoted in Sampson 1984, p. 221)

Identification of an appropriate organization to study, the elaboration of the epistemological grounding of our methodology (Burrell and Morgan 1979) and the amplification of key concepts (gender, culture) were only some of the methodological choices we had to make as part of our overall case study strategy. We also had to navigate the tensions between the archive and the *archive*; make sense of the interrelationship between time and change; decide appropriate methods of study; and make sense of cross-national comparisons between airlines. We now move to discussion of how we handled each of these decisions.

ARCHIVES AND *ARCHIVES*

In studying gender over time we focus on a single organization with the aim of understanding how gendered practices at work develop and change over time. We are also interested in how localized configurations of rules are constitutive of an organization (Clegg 1981) and contribute to the broader formation of *archives*. This focus and level of analysis differs from Foucault's broader sociological studies of madness (1965), sexuality (1980) and punishment (1979), which focus on society-wide construction of a particular phenomenon. To be clear, we view organizations as socially constructed aspects of broader social formations, and thus can be seen as important local spaces in which broader discourses are developed, maintained and changed.

To gain a sense of a particular organization (for example, BA) we undertook extensive analysis of the selected company's archived materials. To explore the links between organizational (namely, airline companies) and social discourse we adopted different strategies, including analyses of histories of specific airlines, the airline industry in general, and gender and popular culture for the country in which the airline was located. In this way, we were able to develop a sense of a given organization in its socio-historical context. We also followed the study of a single airline (that is, BA) with different case studies of comparative airlines in Canada (AC) and the United States (Pan Am). Arguably this overall approach enriched understanding of a given organization's cultural rules and allowed for analysis of the potential interrelationship between organizational and societal rules.

Working with Archives

Archives present the researcher with a number of general possibilities and challenges.[3] An archive can facilitate the 'tracing' of events and people back in time, highly useful for a study of change and organizational culture. Archival materials allow the study of a range of factors that are beyond, but may be complementary to, the techniques of observation and interviewing. Thus, for example, corporate minutes can provide insights into past decisions that are beyond observation, as well as the memory or 'knowledge' of informants. Similarly, in-house corporate newsletters can provide clues to the thinking and behaviour of people in the context of periods long past; contexts that may not be reproduced by informants who are asked to reflect on the past from a position in the present. Some periods, such as the early years of BA (1919), Pan Am (1927) and even AC (1937), would be virtually impossible to 'trace' through interviews.

On the other hand, archives are highly problematic. The ability to trace people and events is dependent on a combination of factors, including the type, extent and purpose of the materials developed and collected. 'Precise' and 'quantitative' materials of the type described by Yin (2009, p. 102), for example, limit the possibilities of exploring relationships and events. Airline archives, for example, include an abundance of technical manuals, innumerable photographs of aeroplanes, and data on employee numbers, job levels and pay grades. While the manuals and photographs are of limited use for studies of organizational behaviour, employee data can be useful for documenting such things as the extent and character of female employment. We were able, for example, to assess the percentage of female employees over time in BA and AC (Mills and Helms Mills 2004, 2006), and comparative pay rates between male and female employees in BA (Mills 2006). Nonetheless, a paucity of this kind of material made it almost impossible to track the changing percentages of female employees in Pan Am or to get a sense of the relative rates of pay for men and women in comparable jobs in AC and BA. To some extent we were able to overcome this problem by identifying the different male- and female-associated jobs reported throughout company documents. That way we could gain a sense not only of differences in the range of male- versus female-associated jobs but also the extent to which the respective jobs were reported in company materials.

The reasoning behind the development and collection of certain materials can affect more than 'accuracy' (Yin 2009, p. 106). Problems include the highly selective use of items to downplay certain problems and people and overemphasize others. This limits the amount of data that can be collected but can also become data in their own right. Thus, for example, our biggest challenge was in finding material on women in any of the three airlines. On the other hand, the limited nature of the imaging of women in airline materials provides important clues to the gendered character of the corporate communications, and the thinking behind it. This was particularly poignant in the following example, where BA's rules for certain positions took it for granted that they were male-only jobs. Thus, Regulation 10(c) of the *Flight Clerks Pay and Allowances, 1938* included provisions for 'the Flight Clerk's wife [when] accompanying him', and the *Radio Officer Pay and Allowances, 1938* stated that the airline 'will bear the cost of the transport of wives . . . of staff proceeding overseas or returning home on contract leave' (quoted in Mills 2006, p. 56).

Similar problems are evident in the collection of archival materials, where decisions are made as to what is collected or saved and what is discarded. The problem is best illustrated in the case of Pan Am where company Vice President John Leslie began to pull together materials for the development of a history of the airline. This collection was shaped by his desire to develop a history that focused on the positive role of the airline and its president Juan Trippe in the development of commercial aviation and the well-being of the United States (Durepos et al. 2008). Despite these partial roots of the Pan Am collection the great bulk of the material came from different sets of former employees who made sure that vast numbers of various documents and artefacts were donated to the University of Miami.

Working with *Archives*

Working through archived collections of a particular organization also provides important clues to sociological *archives* but need to be read alongside a range of other materials (for example, histories, other archived collections and materials, media reports and so on). As the following example illustrates, the process then becomes iterative as you move back and forth in analysis of organizational and socio-historical contexts.

BA archives indicate that in the pre-Second World War era there were few women employed by the airline, all in general office and secretarial duties. This was not entirely unexpected as women were absent from a large number of industries, professions, job levels and workplaces in the UK in the early to mid-1920s (Mills 2006). However, research beyond BA's archive collection provided important new 'clues' that helped to make sense not only of female employment in commercial aviation in the UK but also dominant notions of manhood and womanhood of the time, and the potential relationship between organizational practices and sociological *archives*. The 'clues' were drawn from sources that included the Women's Royal Air Force (WRAF), aviation and the development of warfare, the introduction of employment rules in 1924 that guided the development of BA for decades to come,[4] and rules developed by international airline associations that BA was a part of.

The WRAF was established in 1918, with 32,000 women, including 600 officers, passing through its ranks before it was disbanded in 1920. Members were excluded from combat roles and associated activities (that is, ground crew jobs) but a sizeable minority served in 'non-traditional jobs as drivers, aircraft repairers, welders, coppersmiths, tinsmiths, sheet-metal workers, turners, machinists, carpenters, painters and dopers, photographers, motor-cyclists, and even airplane mechanics' (Mills 2006, p. 36). Yet none of these women ended up in any form of commercial aviation work. There were several reasons for this, not least of which was the powerful influence of the First World War on the postwar revival of the domestic idyll whereby 'the home' was seen as a valued place that women nurtured and working men returned to each day (Weeks 1990).

Warfare also helped to strengthen the notion of men as warriors and women as helpmates both during and in the aftermath of the First World War (Mills 2006). The wartime association of aviation with masculinity, not withstanding the establishment of the WRAF, had at least two impacts on postwar commercial aviation in Britain. First, it served to exclude women not only from flying and other in-flight activities, but also from ground crews. Second, it provided the personnel, networks and associated camaraderie to run the fledgling airlines, complete with various symbols (for example, former air force aerodromes, ranks, uniforms and aeroplanes) that served to reproduce wartime masculine imagery.

These wartime carryovers were also an influence on the development of new recruitment rules at both the airline and international aviation levels. When the British government merged four small airlines in 1924 to create a larger, government-subsidized company it introduced rules that all pilots and 75 per cent of ground personnel, including administrative staff, had to have been members of the Royal Air Force (RAF), the Reserve, or the Auxiliary Air Force prior to joining the airline (Penrose 1980, p. 37). This effectively restricted the recruitment of women to a few general office positions. This situation was solidified when, under the leadership of BA's 'Chairman' (sic), the International Civil Aviation Organization (ICAO) voted in 1925 to exclude women from employment as pilots or other flight crew. These new rules formalized what had previously been informal practices. Through these organizational measures – of the WRAF, BA and the ICAO – women were excluded from key aviation positions and an *archive* of gendered imagery was reinforced.

METHODS OF ANALYSIS

So far we have talked about time and change – both of which presented us with some of our biggest challenges. In terms of time, our focus was on attempting to understand how historic breaks occur in people's thinking about gender. We did this through exploration of the employment and social construction of women at work in a single organization over time. Here we reviewed the various archived materials to identify distinct difference in workplace practices in regard to women. In each airline this generated different notions of women (and men) for different points of time. This then provided the starting point for analysis of the material using a heuristic that we refer to as a 'juncture'. A juncture is a heuristic 'for studying organizational change over time' and 'refers to a concurrence of events in time in which a series of images, impressions and experiences come together, giving the appearance of a coherent whole that influences how an organization is understood' (Mills 2010, p. 509). Through this approach we made detailed notes of different 'periods' and probed further to see if the different 'periods' coincided with specific contextual factors and dominant 'ways of thinking'; ways of thinking that can be seen as constituting a discourse of gendered behaviour and expectations. It should be noted, however, that our 'reading' of different periods was informed by postmodernist scepticism about the linear and progressive nature of time (Foucault 1972; Lyotard 1984). In other words, we did not assume that one period (or juncture) builds on another period in a gradually progressive way. Rather, what we have are different understandings of gender over time that need to be understood in context. Such understandings may, from one juncture, appear to be an advance on previous junctures, but in fact are more likely to reflect the contextualized thinking of people in time. Our interest lay in uncovering strategies that bring about such changed thinking.

Using this approach we generated eight 'junctures' at British Airways: J1 (1919–24) – the absence of female employees; J2 (1925–39) – the introduction and growth of female employment; J3 (1940–45) – the rapid growth and disbursement of female employment during the Second World War; J4 (1946–60) – the 'normalization' of female employment in the immediate postwar era; J5 (1961–74) – the eroticization of female labour; J6 (1975–early 1980s) – equity struggles; J7 (early 1980s to 1990) – the professionalization of female labour; and J8 (1990 onward) – the emergence and consolidation of female management and leadership (Mills 2006).

In some ways this presents a picture of ongoing progress, as airlines move from employing few women in low-level jobs through to the employment of a sizeable number of women in a range of airline jobs, including management. Certainly we would not want to disparage the idea that change can be to the betterment of women (and men) over time. However, the idea of 'betterment' has to be viewed as our specific values, understood in the context of today's discourses of gender, and, as such, not simply the result of the progressive unfolding of gender equity. For example, the percentage of women employed by BA fell from 34 per cent in 1944 to 10 per cent in 1946 and never again reached the higher percentage (Mills 2006). Similarly, BA's 'equity' focus on the hard-working character of its female staff in the late 1940s gave way to an almost exclusive and narrow focus on the erotic possibilities of women by the 1960s (Mills 1997).

Having found a series of dominant employment patterns, the next stage of the research was to review the various materials for themes, narratives and stories to see if there was evidence of discursive influences that might provide clues to the character of each juncture (namely, the construction of gendered notions of work) and clues to changes over time (Mills and Helms Mills 2006). Given the nature of the material, we were drawn to various methods of textual analysis that were consistent with our epistemological grounding. We used content analysis (Bryman and Bell 2007) to judge such things as the relative space and imaging given to women as compared to men; critical sensemaking (Mills and Helms Mills 2004) to look for clues as to how men/masculinity, women/femininity were made sense of by corporate documents but especially by writers of those documents and, rarely, those who responded to them; critical hermeneutics (Prasad and Mir 2002) to understand text through its location in specific socio-political contexts; and critical discourse analysis (Phillips and Hardy 2002). For reasons of space and clarity we shall focus on the latter.

Our approach to discourse analysis draws on the work of Foucault and his theorization of 'social reality [as] produced and made real through discourses, and social interactions [that] cannot be fully understood without reference to the discourses that give them meaning' (Phillips and Hardy 2002, p. 3). From this approach discourse is viewed as an 'interrelated set of texts, and the practices of their production, dissemination and reception, that brings an object into being' (Phillips and Hardy 2002, p. 3). However, by analysing text (for example, images of 'sexy' flight attendants), talk (for example, discussions about the relative employment value of men and women) and related practices (for example, hiring practices) our approach is *critical* in that we set out to understand how social and political domination – in particular gender discrimination – is reproduced (Fairclough 1995). Thus, we searched the archived materials for clues to dominant discourses that were demonstrably and plausibly associated with gendered relations at different points in time. Our analysis was pursued through 'texts', which refer to such things as documents but also conversations, symbols, pictures and other artefacts. The focus of the analysis was to understand how configurations of texts 'contribute to the constitution of social reality by *making* meaning' (Phillips and Hardy 2002, p. 4; original italics).

Using critical discourse analysis (van Dijk 1993; Fairclough 1995) we reviewed a multitude of archival and other materials, particularly histories of the respective airlines, as well as various social histories. We were particularly interested in discourses of gender and how they constructed dominant notions of men and women at given points of time. Following Calás and Smircich (1992), we examined the impact of organization *on* women (from a women's voice approach) but also the construction *of* women by organizational realities (from a feminist poststructuralist approach): focusing on discrimination against women, while avoiding language that pre-assumes and references essentialized notions of women. We were interested in how discursive practices construct notions of women and men and in the process create knowledge of the relative value of people.

In each of our studies, we looked for dominant imagery (text, pictures and other artefacts) that contributed to the social construction of 'men' and 'women', while also collecting comparative data (for example, employment percentages, job levels, wages and so on) on men and women. Examples of the latter include evidence that immediately prior to the Second World War women constituted less than 10 per cent of BA, AC and Pan Am employees, but in each case climbed to 33 per cent during the Second World War (Mills 2006).

In terms of imagery, AC's initial recruitment of female (1938) and male (1944) flight attendants, for example, provide interesting contrasts: women had to be young (between 21 and 25 years old), small with a trim figure (under 5 feet 5 inches and 125 pounds), unmarried, with a personable and pleasing manner, a smart appearance, a 'bright smile', no eyeglasses, nursing qualifications, and a combination of 'the comeliness of Venus with the capabilities of Florence Nightingale' (Garner no date). Male recruits, in contrast, were 'ex-servicemen', valued team members, and national icons who

> will not be a mere adjunct to the present four-man transatlantic crew, but rather an integral part of a five-man team. His work is too important to permit of any less evaluation. His activities will be coordinated with those of his fellow crew members . . . It is no exaggeration to say that on the performance of these young men will be based many an evaluation of our entire national worth. (Trans-Canada Air Lines 1945)

We were interested in both the similarities and differences between gender identities in a given organization and the broad socio-economic context in which it was located. As we saw in the BA example above, the new commercial airline industry in the UK was influenced by social attitudes to gender, reproducing and encouraging restrictive hiring practices. However, BA also influenced the association of flying and masculinity by restricting piloting and flight crews to men. Similarly, in our AC examples about female recruitment in 1938, mimetic isomorphism influenced the changed gender relations in the new airline by introducing females as flight attendants to the all-male airline. However, through a combination of rugged, individualist forms of masculinity – drawn from the bush piloting, railway and military experiences of management and employees – narrow images of womanhood were constructed as recruitment expectations and enduring images of women (Mills and Helms Mills 2006).

CONCLUSION: LESSONS FOR INTERNATIONAL BUSINESS RESEARCH

In this chapter we have discussed using an uncommon data source (archives/*archives*) and an even less common philosophical approach (postpositivism) for case study research (Hartt et al. 2009; Piekkari et al. 2009). We now draw some conclusions for the study of international business. In particular, we argue that a postpositivist focus on archives/*archives* draws attention towards those elements that are normally overlooked and/ or which are taken for granted in international business research; elements that may arguably have been perpetuated by a 'disciplinary convention' in international business research (Piekkari et al. 2009). This includes the constitutive role of language, *archives* (or rules sets), the production of knowledge, localized understandings, and the conceptualization and focus of key units of analysis (namely, organization and culture).

From a postpositivist perspective the study of international business has to be problematized at all levels, including the theoretical framework of international business itself. A focus on the constitutive role of language (Phillips and Hardy 2002), for instance, encourages a rethink of the very project of 'international business', by questioning the terms of the debate. As Piekkari et al. (2009) have argued, the study of international business has become a 'disciplinary convention', whereby preferred methods of analysis arise out of a dominant notion of international business. In turn, the use of those (positivist) methods serves to reinforce an objectivist notion of international business. This can be seen, for example, in the use of surveys and structured interviews to assess the relationship between national culture and organizational structure (Pugh and Hickson 1976; Hofstede 1980): both structure and culture are simultaneously constructed and studied as concrete entities that owe little to social construction. A postpositivist approach encourages a focus on the processes through which dominant notions of international business are developed and maintained over time, and how that dominant notion is constituted as knowledge that precedes further study. This, of course, would be a case study in its own right – a case study of international business as discourse!

By deconstructing (Derrida and Caputo 1997) international business a number of units of analysis also become problematic, including culture, structure and organization, to name but three central concepts in case study research. National culture, for example, is a useful *heuristic* for making sense of processes that influence a chosen area of study (for example, organizational structure – see Pugh and Hickson 1976; Hofstede 1980). However, the problem is then making sense of the data. From a postpositivist perspective, culture – national or organizational – is not some*thing* that countries or organizations have but rather a heuristic for making sense of selected phenomena (Smircich 1983). Nor is it a unitary phenomenon that is shared by everyone involved but rather a fragmented set of discursive practices where the *appearance* of a single culture has to be explained rather than taken as given (Martin 2002). In practice a postpositivist approach could mean such things as taking account of not only local customs and language, but also the discursive practices that they represent and the knowledge they produce. Thus, it may not be simply a case of understanding language and cultural differences. It may be more the case of understanding the heart of a different group's knowledge *archives* and where that group stands, through localized practices, in relationship to those *archives*. Through this process of analysis we would be better placed to understand not only the rules of business but also the rules of 'knowledge' across social groups. Similar arguments can be made for the problematization of structure (Giddens 1976) and organization (Weick 1979).

All this makes for a very challenging approach to case study research within and of international business. To that end, we have attempted to reveal some of our own challenges. We studied three 'international' airlines but would argue that this is not an imperative to study international differences: we did not study differences in gendering as the outcome of three different national cultures. Rather, we used the different case studies to draw attention to differences at the 'local' (or 'organizational') level (Mills 2006) – not for the purpose of comparison so much as to reveal the importance of 'localized' discursive practices (Foucault 1972). We focused on organizational culture to make sense of influences on gendered practices but make it clear that we view 'organizational culture' as a heuristic, and one that is problematic (Mills 2002; Mills and Helms Mills 2006). Our focus on organizational processes over time also raises issues about the problematic nature of 'organization' – a problem that can be exacerbated when a case study attempts to follow a single organization over time. The normally taken-for-granted notion of an organization can get in the way of making sense of socially constructed realities. The claim that BA's history can be traced back to 1919, for example, is only sustained by a corporate focus on the legal status and leadership of some of the 57 companies that were merged over time (Penrose 1980). Our resolve was to avoid engaging in the construction of a corporate history but rather to understand 'how particular social arrangements impact people's understandings of gender' (Mills 2006, p. 19). Thus, we dealt with the problem by focusing on 'a particular set of regularized social interactions and [following] them through several periods of development and change' (Mills 2006, p. 19).

Finally, postpositivist *archival*/archival case study research problematizes the idea of case study research itself. Through an iterative and reflexive process case study researchers are encouraged to question the relationship between knowledge production (for example, research findings), and the discursive practices (for example, disciplinary conventions) that precede but reinforce case study as a methodological strategy (Mills et al. 2010). We contend that the process of problematizing the method of 'case study' will – far from weakening it – open it to the 'greater methodological pluralism' called for by Piekkari et al. (2009).

NOTES

1. For the sake of clarity we have used these three airline names to refer to companies that have undergone a series of changes over time, including mergers, takeovers and various name changes.
2. For example, in the 1950s John Leslie, a Vice President of Pan Am, began to collect and save corporate materials in preparation for the development of a history of the airline. In the process he ensured that innumerable documents were saved that otherwise would have been destroyed. He also generated new materials, including taped interviews with existing and former employees that were specifically developed for a history of the airline. In 1970 the collection was formally designated the Pan American Foundation Archive. Eventually, following the collapse of the airline in 1991, the collection was donated to the Otto Richter Library at the University of Miami and has since been greatly added to from various sources.
3. All three airlines that we studied have a wealth of material in their archives, including memoranda, corporate minutes, in-house newsletters, letters and photographs. The Pan Am and AC archives included tape-recorded interviews with former employees, and the BA archive included a series of corporate films. The British Airways Archive Collection is located in London's Heathrow Airport; the Air Canada Archive is at the National Aviation Museum in Ottawa; and the Pan American Airways Collection is located at the Otto Richter Library at the University of Miami.
4. British Airways traces it roots back to 1919 through over 57 predecessors, including four airlines that were merged in 1924 to form Imperial Airways. For simplicity we use the name British Airways, even though it was not adopted until 1974 (Mills 2006). The

problem of developing a case study of an organization over time has been discussed at length elsewhere (Mills 2002).

REFERENCES

Bryman, A. and E. Bell (2007), *Business Research Methods*, Oxford: Oxford University Press.

Burrell, G. and G. Morgan (1979), *Sociological Paradigms and Organizational Analysis*, London: Heinemann.

Calás, M.B. and L. Smircich (1992), 'Using the "F" word: feminist theories and the social consequences of organizational research', in A.J. Mills and P. Tancred (eds), *Gendering Organizational Analysis*, Newbury Park, CA: Sage, pp. 222–34.

Clegg, S. (1981), 'Organization and control', *Administrative Science Quarterly*, **26** (4), 545–62.

Corman, S.R. (2000), 'The need for common ground', in Corman and M.S. Poole (eds), *Perspectives on Organizational Communication*, New York: Guilford Press, pp. 3–13.

Deal, T.E. and A.A. Kennedy (1982), *Corporate Cultures*, Reading, MA: Addison-Wesley.

Derrida, J. and J.D. Caputo (1997), *Deconstruction in a Nutshell: A Conversation with Jacques Derrida*, New York: Fordham University Press.

Durepos, G., A.J. Mills and J. Helms Mills (2008), 'Tales in the manufacture of knowledge: writing a company history of Pan American World Airways', *Management and Organizational History*, **3** (1), 63–80.

Fairclough, N. (1995), *Critical Discourse Analysis: The Critical Study of Language*, London and New York: Longman.

Flynn, T. (1996), 'Foucault's mapping of history', in G. Gutting (ed.), *The Cambridge Companion to Foucault*, Cambridge: Cambridge University Press, pp. 28–46.

Foucault, M. (1965), *Madness and Civilization: A History of Insanity in the Age of Reason*, New York: Pantheon Books.

Foucault, M. (1972), *The Archaeology of Knowledge*, London: Routledge.

Foucault, M. (1978), 'Politics and the study of discourse', *Ideology and Consciousness*, **3**, 7–26.

Foucault, M. (1979), *Discipline and Punish: The Birth of the Prison*, New York: Vintage Books.

Foucault, M. (1980), *The History of Sexuality*, Vol. 1, New York: Vintage Books.

Garner, L. (no date), Lucille Garner Files, *Air Canada Archives*, Air Canada Archives, National Aviation Museum, Ottawa.

Giddens, A. (1976), *New Rules of Sociological Method: A Positive Critique of Interpretative Sociologies*, London: Hutchinson.

Guba, E.G. and Y.S. Lincoln (1994), 'Competing paradigms in qualitative research', in N.K. Denzin and Lincoln (eds), *Handbook of Qualitative Research*, Thousand Oaks, CA: Sage, pp. 105–17.

Hartt, C., A.R. Yue, J. Helms Mills and A.J. Mills (2009), 'Method and disciplinary convention in the Administrative Sciences Association of Canada, 1978–2008: implications for teaching and research', Proceedings of the annual conference of the Atlantic Schools of Business conference, Moncton, NB, October.

Helms Mills, J. (2003), *Making Sense of Organizational Change*, London: Routledge.

Helms Mills, J. and A.J. Mills (2000), 'Rules, sensemaking, formative contexts and discourse in the gendering of organizational culture', in N.M. Ashkanasy, C.P.M. Wilderom and M.F. Peterson (eds), *Handbook of Organizational Culture and Climate*, Thousand Oaks, CA: Sage, pp. 55–70.

Hochschild, A.R. (1983), *The Managed Heart*, Berkeley, CA: University of California Press.

Hofstede, G. (1980), *Culture's Consequences: International Differences in Work Related Values*, London: Sage.

Latour, B. (2005), *Reassembling the Social*, Oxford: Oxford University Press.

Lyotard, J.-F. (1984), *The Postmodern Condition: A Report on Knowledge*, Minneapolis, MN: University of Minnesota Press.

Madansky, A. (2008), 'Teaching history in business schools: an outsider's view', *Academy of Management Learning and Education*, **7** (4), 553–62.

Martin, J. (2002), *Organizational Culture: Mapping the Terrain*, Thousand Oaks, CA: Sage.

May, T. (2006), *The Philosophy of Foucault*, Toronto: McGill-Queen's University Press.

McHoul, A. and W. Grace (2003), *A Foucault Primer: Discourse, Power and the Subject*, New York: New York University Press.

Mills, A.J. (1988), 'Organization, gender and culture', *Organization Studies*, **9** (3), 351–69.

Mills, A.J. (1997), 'Duelling discourses: desexualization versus eroticism in the corporate framing of female sexuality in the British airline industry, 1945–60', in P. Prasad, A.J. Mills, M. Elmes and A. Prasad (eds), *Managing the Organizational Melting Pot: Dilemmas of Workplace Diversity*, Newbury Park, CA: Sage, pp. 171–98.

Mills, A.J. (2002), 'History/herstory: an introduction to the problems of studying the gendering of organizational culture over time', in I. Aaltio and A.J. Mills (eds), *Gender, Identity and the Culture of Organizations*, London: Routledge, pp. 115–36.

Mills, A.J. (2006), *Sex, Strategy and the Stratosphere: The Gendering of Airline Cultures*, London: Palgrave Macmillan.

Mills, A.J. (2010), 'Juncture', in Mills et al. (eds), pp. 509–11.

Mills, A.J., G. Durepos and E. Weibe (2010), *Sage Encyclopedia of Case Study Research*, Thousand Oaks, CA: Sage.

Mills, A.J. and J. Helms Mills (2004), 'When plausibility fails: towards a critical sensemaking approach to resistance', in R. Thomas, A.J. Mills and J. Helms Mills (eds), *Identity Politics at Work: Resisting Gender and Gendered Resistance*, London: Routledge, pp. 141–59.

Mills, A.J. and J. Helms Mills (2006), 'Masculinity and the making of Trans-Canada Air Lines, 1937–1940: a feminist poststructuralist account', *Canadian Journal of Administrative Sciences*, **23** (1), 34–44.

Mills, A.J., J.C. Helms Mills, J. Bratton and C. Forshaw (2006), *Organizational Behaviour in a Global Context*, Peterborough, ON: Broadview Press.

Oakley, A. (1972), *Sex, Gender and Society*, London: Temple Smith.

Penrose, H. (1980), *Wings Across the World: An Illustrated History of British Airways*, London: Cassell.

Phillips, N. and C. Hardy (2002), *Discourse Analysis: Investigating Processes of Social Construction*, Thousand Oaks, CA: Sage.

Piekkari, R., C. Welch and E. Paavilainen (2009), 'The case study as disciplinary convention: evidence from international business journals', *Organizational Research Methods*, **12** (3), 567–89.

Prasad, A. and R. Mir (2002), 'Digging deep for meaning: a critical hermeneutic analysis of CEO letters to shareholders in the oil industry', *Journal of Business Communication*, **39** (1), 92–116.

Prasad, P. (2005), *Crafting Qualitative Research: Working in the Postpositivist Traditions*, Armonk, NY: M.E. Sharpe.

Pugh, D.S. and D.J. Hickson (1976), *Organisational Structure in its Context: The Aston Programme I*, London: Saxon House.

Sampson, A. (1984), *Empires of the Sky: The Politics, Contests and Cartels of World Airlines*, New York: Random House.

Schein, E.H. (1985), *Organizational Culture and Leadership*, San Francisco, CA: Jossey-Bass.

Serenko, A., M. Cocosila and O. Turel (2008), 'The state and evolution of information systems research in Canada: a sociometric analysis', *Canadian Journal of Administrative Science*, **25** (4), 279–94.

Smircich, L. (1983), 'Concepts of culture and organizational analysis', *Administrative Science Quarterly*, **28** (3), 339–58.

Trans-Canada Air Lines (1945), *Between Ourselves*, **32** (October).

van Dijk, T.A. (1993), 'Principles of critical discourse analysis', *Discourse and Society*, **4** (2), 249–283.

Weeks, J. (1990), *Sex, Politics and Society*, 2nd edn, London: Longman.

Weick, K.E. (1979), *The Social Psychology of Organizing*, 2nd edn, Reading, MA: Addison-Wesley.

Weick, K.E. (1995), *Sensemaking in Organizations*, London: Sage.

Whitelegg, D. (2007), *Working the Skies: The Fast-paced, Disorienting World of the Flight Attendant*, New York: New York University Press.

Yin, R.K. (2009), *Case Study Research: Design and Methods*, 4th edn, Thousand Oaks, CA: Sage.

19. Watch what I do, not what I say: new questions for documents in international business case research

April Wright

INTRODUCTION

This chapter explores the methods used to analyse documents in international business (IB) case research. Documents such as minutes of meetings, agendas, letters of correspondence, strategic plans, and public and internal reports may be made available to a researcher studying companies or subsidiaries operating internationally. However, despite the availability of documents, recent analysis of case studies published in core IB journals reveals that documents are universally underutilized and undervalued (Piekkari et al. 2009). Few authors specify the types of documents to which they gained access, and documents are subsumed in importance to interview data when reporting empirical findings (Piekkari et al. 2009). The neglect of documents is driven, in no small part, by the narrowness of methods available to analyse documents. The traditional approach to documentary analysis, which focuses on documents as records of text-based content, asks the question, 'What does this document say?' Methods of analysis consistent with this question include summarizing document content into a historical case background as a precursor to richer, multi-method data collection and analysis. It also includes content analysis of themes recorded in documents or, less frequently, discursive analyses of the languaging and meaning-making in documents such as annual reports.

This chapter proposes a new question about documents as sources of IB case data. Rather than focusing narrowly and partially on what documents say, case researchers should ask holistically, 'What does this document do?' Because organizational documents connect to other documents in sequences and hierarchies, and because organizational documents take particular and purposive genre forms, documents do not merely say things – documents are produced and used by actors with an interest in *doing* things. Agendas for meetings between head offices and subsidiaries, for example, are used to include and exclude problems and solutions from debate and managerial attention. Similarly, reports from official sources may be invoked as mandates for action or non-action in entering foreign markets. The chapter explores how case analysis can be deepened, and potential theoretical insights for IB opened up, by redirecting researcher analysis towards the role of documents as agents in organizations.

This approach to analysing documents is consistent with an interpretative view of discourse analysis. Within this view, discourses are structured collections of texts which construct social and organizational reality through language as a symbolic medium (Heracleous and Barratt 2001; Phillips et al. 2004). Meaning is socially constructed as actors produce, disseminate and interpret texts. A text is any spoken, written or other symbolic expression which, because it takes on material form, is able to be accessed by others (Taylor et al. 1996). Organizational documents are a distinctive type of written text. Max Weber's theory of bureaucracy championed, as one of the elements of rational and efficient organization, the recording of administrative acts and decisions in writing to provide organizational memory and continuity over time. Written documents increase the communicability, reproducibility and durability of patterns of thought and action (Hasselbladh and Kallinikos 2000). Because documents are a pivotal text through which organizing occurs and by which organizations are constituted, IB case researchers need to pay greater attention to empirical analysis of documents.

In the next section of this chapter, documents as sources of data are discussed and the assumptions which underpin a method for analysing what documents do – called 'documents-in-action' – are presented. In the third section, my own case study research into an international human resource practice is briefly outlined. The specific study focused on the employment of overseas players in first-class county cricket in England and involved analysis of a sample of archival documents. Cricket is a bat-and-ball sport which spread throughout the English colonies in the 1800s (Bowen 1970) and today is the most popular sport in the Asian subcontinent. Using this case study as an exemplar, I devote the remainder of the chapter to stepping through the three stages I progressed through when analysing the archival documents. The first stage of making sense of documents as chronologically ordered content gave way to a second stage of making sense of documents as genres of communication and, ultimately, to a third stage of making sense of documents as whole social agents in action. This third stage required questioning not only what documents do, but also how they are produced, used and circulated to construct a social reality about the employment of overseas players as a human resourcing practice at different moments in time. The final section offers conclusions and reflections about the utility of the documents-in-action approach for IB case researchers.

DOCUMENTS AS SOURCES OF DATA

Although written documentation is central to modern organization (Weber 1979), talk and behaviour have been privileged over writing in Western philosophical thought (Derrida 1976). The result is a qualitative methods literature offering diverse guidance for researchers seeking to collect and analyse interview data, and narrow advice to analyse documents, whether historical or contemporary, as text-based content (Prior 2003). Because of this, IB case researchers have focused on using the content of organizational documents to prepare chronological background narratives and to validate and triangulate primary sources of data such as interviews and field notes from site visits. This narrowness is disappointing because 'methodological variants . . . prevent our tools from dictating and limiting the nature of our insights' (Leonard-Barton 1990, p. 264). For IB case researchers, methodological tools that focus solely on the text contained within a document ignore an important part of the story of how organizational processes are carried out within firms competing internationally. If, as Atkinson and Coffey (2004, p. 69) argue, 'the systematic relationships between documents actively *construct* the rationality and organisation that they purport transparently to record' (emphasis in original), then the reality of an organization is socially constructed by and through its documentation. This is true whether the IB case researcher is interested in the large multinational enterprise, the foreign subsidiary or the small exporter or importer. That is:

> Documents are 'social facts', in that they are produced, shared and used in socially organised ways. They are not, however, transparent representations of organisational routines, decision making processes or professional diagnoses. They construct particular kinds of representations using their own conventions . . . [O]ur recognition of their existence as social facts (or constructions) alerts us to treat them very seriously indeed. (Atkinson and Coffey 2004, p. 58)

This chapter elaborates one approach for analysing documents as 'social facts' that are produced and used in dynamic action – what Prior (2003) labels as the 'documents-in-action' approach. As the above quote illustrates, approaching documents as products and producers of action is underpinned by structuration theory (Giddens 1979, 1984, 1990) and, more broadly, interpretivist assumptions about the nature of reality. Thus, the documents-in-action approach should be judged against the

ᵈd standards of methodological and interpretative rigour
ᵤba 2000, p. 174), instead of the more narrowly defined
. conventions of external, internal, construct and statistical con-
ᵤsion validity and measurement reliability (Cook and Campbell 1979).
No set of 'goodness criteria' is innately superior, for all criteria are mul-
tidimensional, socially constructed and value-laden (Lincoln and Guba
2000, p. 174). Moreover, scholarly research is 'inherently legitimate'
when the methods of analysis are clearly communicated, follow from
research assumptions and lead transparently to conclusions (Cannella and
Paetzold 1994, p. 336).

In the remainder of the chapter I illustrate the documents-in-action
approach using an exemplar case study of first-class county cricket in
England. The case study focuses on the importing of professional cricketers born outside of the United Kingdom by county cricket clubs. These
cricketers are officially termed 'overseas players'. In the discussion that
follows, I attempt to write with transparency and ownership about how I
condensed, manipulated and made sense of documents at different stages
of the analysis. My purpose is to provide sufficient 'footprints to allow
others to judge the utility of the work' (Miles and Huberman 2002, p. xi)
and the rigour of the data collection and analysis (Suddaby 2006). In so
doing, I hope to encourage IB case researchers who want to move beyond
analysing documents as static content to analysing them as they are
'integrated into fields of action' (Prior 2003, p. 2).

EXEMPLAR CASE STUDY: OVERSEAS PLAYERS IN ENGLISH COUNTY CRICKET

The starting point for the case study research was the observation of
an empirical phenomenon: clubs competing in professional team sports
leagues were importing foreign athletes. Sports economists analyse these
leagues as efficient cartels which produce an entertainment experience for
spectators live at matches or via broadcast media (Scully 1974; Fort and
Quirk 1995; Vrooman 1995). My research question sought to explore
why and how the phenomenon of player importation occurred in sports
leagues. I chose to investigate the research question in the case context of
first-class county cricket in England. A championship involving matches
between geographically defined county clubs was formally sanctioned in
1873 by the game's legislative authority, the Marylebone Cricket Club
(MCC) (Birley 2003). These clubs produced cricket matches for the entertainment of club members, who paid an annual subscription fee, and spectators who paid at the 'gate'. Qualification rules defined which cricketers

could play for a club based on birth or a period of residence within the county's geographic boundaries. At the end of 1967, residential qualification was removed to allow a quota of cricketers born outside the United Kingdom to play for a county without serving a residential qualification period. These cricketers were officially categorized as 'overseas players'.

The major source of data for the case study was archival documents. The MCC generously permitted access to their private archives. Documents in these archives reported the 'back-stage' (Goffman 1967) processes of county cricket governance by the MCC through the Advisory County Cricket Committee (ACCC) and its associated subcommittees. The ACCC comprised representatives from the MCC and each of the 17 counties designated as first class from 1921 (an eighteenth county was added in 1992). Much of the regular coordinating work of cricket administration was carried out on behalf of the counties by the MCC Cricket Sub-Committee and the MCC Secretariat. The back-stage documents related to the work of the web of committees forming the collaborative governance structure for county cricket. I focused on the period from 1937 to 1967, when the rules concerning instant qualification of overseas players were most contested. My dataset comprised: 354 minutes of meetings, 13 agendas, 26 reports, 50 memoranda, 195 questionnaires, 156 press clippings and 147 letters of correspondence.

I approached the analysis of the documents as 'sensemaking'. Sensemaking is 'making something sensible' or plausible by constructing meaning after the event (Weick 1995, p. 16). Researchers adopt 'sensemaking strategies' because 'a variety of "senses" or theoretical understandings may legitimately emerge from the same data' (Langley 1999, p. 694). A summary of the stages of my data analysis, as a process of fitting my documentary data to different sensemaking frames, is presented in Figure 19.1.

Stage 1: Approaching Documents as Content

My initial orientation towards the documents as data was pragmatic. My goal was to become familiar with the content of the documents at a global level and to construct an overview of the numerous organizational structures, practices, procedures, actions and issues which are relevant to the importing of overseas players. As a researcher, my sensemaking frame was underpinned by what Prior (2004) described as an assumption that documents are containers of content. Because the documents I had collected contained text and dates, I took it for granted that textual units were the most appropriate for analysis and chronology was the most appropriate rule for ordering the documents as a sample of raw data. This analytical approach is standard for documents collected within longitudinal case

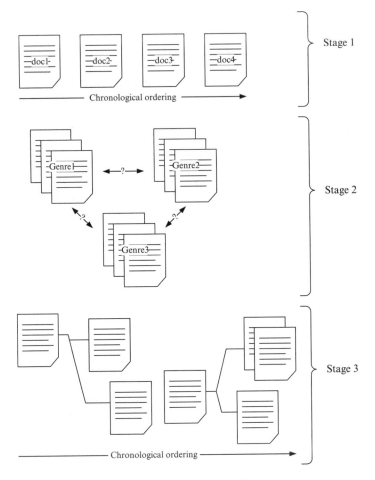

Figure 19.1   Method of analysis as a process of sensemaking

studies of organizations (for example, Leonard-Barton 1990; Pettigrew 1990).

The procedures I followed during this initial stage were influenced by Legewie's (1994) method of global analysis, as explained by Flick (2002, pp. 193–4). Used in this context, global refers to an overarching level of analysis, rather than the more typical use of the term in IB as a worldwide strategy. I began by reading the hard copies of the documents chronologically. As I read the documents in chronological sequence for a second time, I wrote summary notes about the textual content of each document, an activity that corresponds with Legewie's (1994) suggestion to produce a table of contents for each document that records central concepts and key words (as quoted in Flick 2002). Summaries for individual documents ranged from a few key words and phrases for a short letter of correspondence, to multiple categories and subcategories of key words, phrases, discussion topics, actors and decisions for the lengthy minutes of a biannual ACCC meeting. The notes were written at a low level of abstraction and were faithful to the constructions of the organizational actors who produced, and/or were referenced in, the documents. I replicated, as much as possible, the categories and languaging contained in the original source documents to capture the 'repertoire of stock phrases for recurrent actors and actions' (Atkinson and Coffey 2004, p. 65) and the types of legitimating accounts used to justify action or non-action (for example, Strang and Meyer 1993; Elsbach 1994; Suchman 1995; Strang and Soule 1998; Bacharach et al. 2000; Stryker 2000).

Thus, global analysis, as I practised it through note-writing, was a time-intensive and mechanical rather than creative activity of data reduction, which generated broad familiarization with the content of the documents in the data sample. From a pragmatic perspective, the physical output of my note-writing was an electronic database that facilitated more timely search and comparison of content across the sample of documents. As my analysis became progressively deeper at subsequent stages, the database enabled me to quickly identify relevant documents and to retrieve, for further analysis, the source documents from my hard-copy files. More importantly, I could develop an overview of the characteristics of the context in which rules for the importing of overseas players was developed. I undertook preliminary coding of data by assigning the content reported in documents to extant categories, albeit in a loosely structured procedure. My purpose at this early stage of analysis was to build not theory but an understanding, albeit at a low descriptive level, of how overseas player importing was approached as a problem solution by the administrators running English cricket, as reported in the content of the back-stage documents of collaborative governance.

Stage 2: Genre Analysis of Documents-in-action

During my initial orientation to the data, in which my sensemaking was framed by documents as content, I extracted cues from the data concerning both interrelationships between documents and the production and circulation of documents as a source of power by office bearers. Not only was I unable to incorporate these cues into a sensemaking frame which defined documents as content, I inferred that a content-only sensemaking frame had generated a one-sided description of my data sample. What concerned me was not that my approach was partial, for all explanation is partial and multiple interpretations are always possible (for example, Van Maanen 1979; Weick 1995; Czarniawska 1998; Calás and Smircich 1999; Alvesson and Deetz 2000; Lincoln and Guba 2000). Rather, I was uncomfortable with the *degree* of partiality for I was ignoring, it seemed to me, much of the theoretically salient data in the documents. I feared that by focusing on texts I was overplaying the role of document content and underplaying the physical, spatial and temporal presence of whole documents in the rule change for importing overseas players.

My response was to search the literature for a new sensemaking frame for analysis. However, methodological guidance for researchers seeking to approach documents as something other than content is sparse. I found the writing of three sets of authors, who advocated different but complementary treatments of documentary materials 'as data in their own right' (Atkinson and Coffey 2004, p. 59), to be insightful. First, Yates and Orlikowski's (1992) suggestion for conceiving of different types of organizational documents as genres of communication was consistent with my emergent understanding of the system of documentation for cricket's governance (see also Orlikowski and Yates 1994). Second, implicit in Atkinson and Coffey's (2004, p. 59) claim that documents 'often enshrine a distinctively documentary version of social reality' was the potential for actors to use documents to reconstruct reality. Finally, Lindsay Prior (2003, 2004) articulated a duality of documents grounded in the assumptions of structuration theory (Giddens 1984). Prior (2003, p. 3) argues that documents 'stand in a dual relation to fields of action', entering the field both as 'containers of content' and as agents in their own right able to be mobilized by others. In his 2003 book, Prior pioneers an approach to analysing documents as both products and producers of action. While acknowledging that no standardized procedure for conducting an analysis of documents exists because of the specialized nature of much organizational documentation, Prior (2003) explicates some of the theoretically meaningful questions that social scientists can ask of documents.

Incorporating the specific insights of Yates and Orlikowski (1992) and Atkinson and Coffey (2004) into Prior's (2003, 2004) foundational approach, I shifted from my sensemaking frame of documents-as-content to a sensemaking frame of 'documents-in-action'. This required making sense of the different types of documents as genres of communication before examining the hierarchical and sequential relationships between the documents as they were produced and used by actors. Thus the unit of analysis, as I defined it in the first instance, was the document as a whole entity and the primary ordering of the data was categorical rather than chronological. Yates and Orlikowski (1992, p. 301) define a genre of organizational communication as 'a typified communicative action invoked in response to a recurrent situation'. Genres are characterized by similarities in: (i) substance, including social motives, themes and topics expressed in the communication, (ii) form, namely the physical and linguistic features of the communication, and (iii) invoking situations (Yates and Orlikowski 1992). My genre analytical approach involved searching for similarities and differences within and across genres of documents, which is analogous to the search for cross-case patterns in a multiple case study analysis (Eisenhardt 1989). I took the following actions to make sense of the function, sequence and hierarchy of the genres within county cricket's system of documents:

First, I consolidated the limited literature on the analysis of documents as genres and as social agents into a list of questions, as presented in Box 19.1. There are four major structural questions to be asked of documents, some with sub-questions that probe more deeply. I printed the structural questions on a single sheet of paper, leaving white space to handwrite brief notes.

Second, using the information contained in the document identification codes, I differentiated categories of documents based on communication genre, as defined by form, substance and producer. I included the criterion of producer to distinguish that different genre rules may be constructed for the production of substantively and formatively similar documents. For example, while minutes are a genre of communication which record decisions taken at meetings, the minutes of different types of committee and subcommittee meetings are produced through different genre rules as shaped by the level of authority vested in the meeting. The genre categories are presented subsequently in Figure 19.2.

Third, I retrieved from my hard-copy files the documents belonging to a single genre type. I retrieved, for example, all the letters of correspondence with the public. My electronic summary notes, which listed document identification codes, guided me in locating the subsample of documents that belonged to a particular genre. However, these notes were inadequate for the tasks of genre analysis because they had been written with a focus on content.

Fourth, I read the subsample of documents representing the particular genre to gain an overview of the genre. The structural questions in Box 19.1 acted as sensitizing concepts (Strauss and Corbin 1990) that oriented my reading. I recorded my initial impressions as brief notes in pencil underneath the relevant structural question on the genre summary sheet.

Fifth, I sifted iteratively through the documents within a particular genre, asking structural and probing questions of the documents and searching for similarities in the answers across the documents. When I

BOX 19.1   STRUCTURAL AND PROBING QUESTIONS FOR DOCUMENT GENRES

1. How does the genre predominantly manufacture 'facts' as a basis for action? (adapted from Prior 2003)

    - How does the author function in the manufacture of the documents within the genre?
    - What rules of classification and ordering are used in the manufacture of facts?
    - Does the genre make 'things' visible and traceable?

2. How is the genre used predominantly to do things? (adapted from Prior 2003)

    - Is the genre used to mediate social relationships and structure social identities?
    - Is the genre used to instigate future action-at-distance?
    - Are the documents used to constitute events?
    - Are the documents recruited by other actors to legitimate a worldview?

3. How do genre rules function as instruments and outcomes of power?
    (Yates and Orlikowski 1992)

4. How is the particular genre linked to other genres to form a documentary reality? (adapted from Atkinson and Coffey 2004)

---

gained a sense of the similarities across the documents in terms of how the documents were produced, used and circulated, I added these similarities as brief notes underneath the relevant structural question on my genre summary sheet. I returned the hard-copy documents to the file folders.

Sixth, I repeated Steps 3, 4 and 5 for successive genres of documents. If I discerned a relationship between the current genre and a genre analysed previously, I added a note to this effect underneath the fourth question on both genre summary sheets. An example of a fully elaborated genre summary sheet, which analyses letters of correspondence with the public, is presented as Box 19.2.

BOX 19.2 SAMPLE GENRE SUMMARY SHEET FOR LETTERS FROM THE PUBLIC

How are Letters from the Public and MCC replies, as forms of documents, manufactured?

1. Replies to letters received from the public authored by MCC secretary. Author structures self as an expert authority (e.g., 'there is no error to correct', 'in fact') and as caretaker/guardian of the game's traditions and laws.

2. Author structures identity of letter writers as either true-cricket-loving 'students of the game' or as ill-informed change agents. Writers in Category 1 received replies that were lengthier and included technical discussion of the writer's proposal, as well as evaluations of its practical rationality. MCC secretary often made himself transparent in these letters (e.g., 'I am in agreement', 'I think', and 'my own opinion is'). Replies to writers in Category 2 were shorter in length, sometimes dismissive in tone and the authorial voice typically included the more generic 'we'.

3. MCC secretary played a role in manufacturing letters from the public (e.g., 'I am glad that my remarks to the County secretaries (meeting) this week have produced new suggestions, all of which will be considered').

How are Letters from the Public and MCC replies used to do things?

1. Gatekeeping actions by the MCC secretary: (i) advises letter writer to write to a county club directly, (ii) replies to and files letter in general correspondence without referral to a committee, (iii) refers letter to 'appropriate committee' – suggestions relevant to conduct of the game referred to general committee and suggestions relevant to a special or subcommittee's Terms of Reference referred to that committee. Scheduling of committee meetings creates a lag between receipt of letters from the public, their referral and consideration at meetings, and receipt of a reply by letter writer.

2. Gatekeeping actions of MCC secretary construct boundaries around which letters from the public can be recruited by actors in committee debates as 'evidence' to legitimate a conception of a problem and a course of action.
3. MCC reply was a 'performance of identity' – MCC's identity constructed as the guardian of the game constrained by powerful counties and captains.

How are Letters from the Public linked to other documents?

Letters from the public 'review(ed)' by MCC secretary and suggestions 'extracted', then 'consolidated analysis' is presented and minuted at meetings.

Seventh, after a genre summary sheet had been completed for every genre, I searched for similarities and differences within the genre summary sheets. The answers to different structural questions were frequently supportive of a key genre function. In addition, I searched for similarities and differences across the genre summary sheets, to gain a sense of how different genres were produced, used and circulated to do different kinds of work. I recorded these global-level insights as handwritten notes on the back of the relevant genre summary sheet along with sketches and mind-maps of how that genre related to other genres, as suggested by the answers to the fourth question.

Eighth, I combined the insights written on the back of the genre summary sheets into a table and a figure which visually mapped the function, sequence and hierarchy of the different genres of documents in first-class county cricket in England.

The outcome of my analysis, as documents-in-action, of the communication genres that reflected the governance of first-class county cricket are shown in Table 19.1 and Figure 19.2. Table 19.1 describes the function of the different genres of documents while Figure 19.2 traces the relationships between the documents produced and circulated by different producers. The solid arrows reflect the direct reporting relationships into, and out of, the ACCC, the major committee governing county cricket. The dotted arrows represent less direct relationships, with documents available for recruitment by actors associated with the ACCC and its committees as mandates for action. Figure 19.2 illustrates how the documents are hierarchically structured because of the way the documents capturing the work of different levels of committees as producers of documents feed into each other.

Table 19.1   Functions of different genres of documents of county cricket

Document genre	Function
Proposal	To mobilize other actors by requesting a change to the Laws of Cricket, Rules of County Cricket, or Championship Playing Conditions
Memorandum	To provide a justifying account in support of a proposal
Agenda	To demarcate those issues, events and observations which are included within the legitimate attention of actors and those which are excluded
Minutes	To express theorizing, as shaped by interests, about the rationality of problem solutions
	To provide an account of collective sensemaking by committee actors
	To provide a warrant for action, or inaction, that is available for recruitment by actors at future meetings of (i) the same committee/subcommittee and/or (ii) other committees/subcommittees at higher and lower levels in the organizational hierarchy
Letter of correspondence between MCC and counties	To negotiate the boundaries of the alliance between individual county interests and collective game interests
Pro formas (e.g. attendances by gate-paying spectators, match results and impact of television on attendances)	To define, classify and measure a problem (gate attendances) and its symptoms and causes
Questionnaire	To make problems, causes and symptoms visible by reducing them to aggregated statistics and to measure effectiveness of prior solutions
Letter from the public	To legitimate a particular vision of problems and solutions when recruited by actors and committees
Press report	To disseminate traditionalist cricket rhetoric to the wider public
Terms of reference of a specially formed committee	To prescribe the boundaries around the search for solutions to a specific problem(s), such as by a committee of enquiry
Report	To persuade readers that the recommendations of the committee as a collective (the presence of individual actors is masked) are rational solutions to the problem(s) defined in the terms of reference

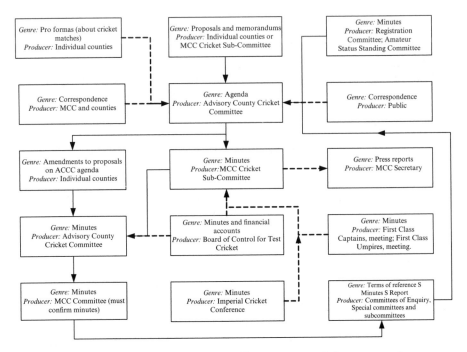

*Figure 19.2   Relationships between different genres of documents of
               county cricket*

The table and figure show that by reflectively undertaking the eight steps of
genre analysis, as I constructed them, I was able to deepen the descriptive
understanding of the documents I had developed in the first stage of sensemaking. My understanding continued to be located at a global level but
was less partial, for I was oriented toward the documents as active agents
in a social process of creating, sustaining and changing an institution (see
Prior 2003; Atkinson and Coffey 2004). At the same time, the legitimating
accounts expressed in the documents about issues, as well as action or non-
action taken by county cricket actors in response to the problem of overseas
players, now seemed to me to be plausible, rational and unsurprising. This
was an indication that my understanding had moved toward a level of
Verstehen, or interpretative understanding, such that I was beginning to
read into the documents the common-sense understanding and everyday
meanings with which the county cricket actors saw themselves.

The different levels at which *Verstehen* operates in social research has
been well articulated by Schutz (1970–71) in his writing on the life-world,
through which human subjects inherit conceptual understandings of the

world as well as the rational supports which underpin these understandings. Schutz argued that the common-sense thinking by which human subjects experience and take for granted the meaning of their life-world is a first-order construct, for which social scientists create explanations, as second-order constructs, in the form of thought-objects. Applying these ideas to ethnographic research, Van Maanen (1979, p. 540) maintained 'first-order concepts are the "facts" of an ethnographic investigation and second-order concepts are the "theories" an analyst uses to organize and explain these facts'. Lee (1991) contended that organizational researchers must be able to replicate the common-sense understanding of the observed human subjects prior to constructing theoretical explanations.

Yet if I was approaching a first-order understanding of the common-sense meanings and 'facts' of overseas players as actors, and documents had actively constructed them within a collaborative governance structure, I was doing so at a relatively global level. To craft a plausible explanation for overseas player importing at the second order of understanding, I needed to 'figure out what the devil they think they're up to' (Geertz 1983, p. 58) in terms of how actors and documents defined, theorized, prioritized and decided on specific solutions pertaining to the employment of overseas players in county cricket. This required that I undertake a deeper and more focused analysis of some of the documents-in-action. Narrowing the scope of my attention to a small number of problem solutions would, I hoped, bring the local 'into simultaneous view' with the global (Geertz 1983, p. 63). A third shift in my sensemaking frame to achieve second-order insights was occasioned as a result.

Stage 3: Developing Second-order Insights

This final stage of analysis involved delving deeper into the academic literature to refine the theoretical approach informing the study and its contribution. Eisenhardt (1989) described this as enveloping the most theoretically salient literature. During the first and second stages of my analysis, I had observed the initiation, theorization, debate, legitimation, negotiation, prioritization, acceptance, deferral and rejection of a diversity of solutions to the problem, as defined by and through documentation, of the qualification of overseas players in first-class county cricket. In this final stage, I looked to envelop institutional theory to develop second-order insights.

Institutional theory was relevant because the rules for importing overseas players into county cricket represented the rules of an institutional structure. Changes to institutional rules depend on 'latitude to get away with framing a problem and its attendant solution' (Rao and Giorgi 2006,

p. 273). The core framing tasks undertaken to facilitate agreement and to mobilize action are: diagnostic framing, in which problems are identified and causality attributed; prognostic framing, in which possible solutions to the problem are proposed; and motivational framing, in which vocabularies of motive are constructed (Benford and Snow 2000, pp. 614–18). Institutional theorists label diagnostic and prognostic framing as 'theorization', which is the 'rendering of ideas into understandable and compelling formats' (Greenwood et al. 2002, p. 75; see also Strang and Meyer 1993; Tolbert and Zucker 1996). Rhetorical strategies are used to build legitimacy for problems and solutions (Green 2004; Suddaby and Greenwood 2005). I adopted the following analytical procedures as the basis for deepening my theoretical understanding of the importing of overseas players:

1. *Identification of the relevant subsample of documents* I searched electronically and visually through my summary notes, as created in Stage 1, for records of documents containing content which referenced overseas players. Following Hill (1993), a Type I error of rejecting a true hypothesis would occur, for example, if I disregarded the historian's correct advice to read a section of microfiche or the contents of a box; if I searched a section of microfiche that the historian had correctly advised was not relevant; or if I searched a box whose finding aid indicated correctly that it would not be helpful. A Type II error of failing to reject a false hypothesis would occur, for example, if I accepted the historian's advice that a microfiche section was not relevant when in fact it was; if I assumed from the finding aid that a box contained nothing relevant when in fact it did; or if I skimmed through the folders in a box that the finding aid or historian suggested would be helpful when in fact it was not. To minimize the risk of a Type II error of excluding relevant documents, I skimmed the hard-copy documents in their file folders as a confirmatory check.

2. *Initial orientation towards the content and the genres of the documents* I read the subsample of hard-copy documents in chronological order to gain an overview of how textual content concerning competitive structures shifted over time. I recorded my observations as notes. These observations were descriptive and written at a low level of abstraction. I read the subsample of documents a second time by flipping between documents of the same genre to gain an overview of how different committees and subcommittees had produced and used documents which referenced overseas players. I added my observations to my notebook.

3. *Clustering of nested documents over time* As I continued reading and writing notes, the subsample of documents began to make sense

to me as intertemporal clusters of nested documents. 'Nested' refers here to the hierarchical relationships between documents, which was illustrated in the feeder relationships between different committees in Figure 19.2. Thus, each cluster of documents contained chronological and hierarchical relationships. At any single point in time, a group of documents constituted the current social reality of overseas players. This remained the social reality until it was challenged by a later group of documents, as manufactured by actors.

4. *Iterative questioning of documents and document clusters* I removed the first cluster of documents concerning overseas players from the file folders. As I read the individual documents chronologically at my computer desk, I further probed each document according to the questions listed in Box 19.1. My answers were a combination of scribbling on note paper and more structured typing into the computer. I returned the first cluster of documents to the file folder and repeated the procedure for the next cluster of documents. However, I found that as my attention focused on a new cluster, my insights from previous clusters gained depth and clarity. What I had tried to structure as a systematic and linear process of end-stage data analysis became, inevitably, an intuitive and organic process of sensemaking. Many times I retrieved documents I thought I had finished with and refined notes that I was convinced had said everything there was to say. This revisiting of the data is typical of, and adds rigour to, qualitative data analysis. Emergent explanations are viewed, with an attitude of scepticism, as provisional (Strauss and Corbin 1990).

5. *Second-order theoretical understanding* The process of iterative questioning created, following Schutz (1970–71), understanding located at the second order. As I sifted iteratively through the documents within a cluster, and between clusters, I moved from first-order insights about the social reality of the employment of overseas players in county cricket, as ongoingly constructed and reconstructed in the documents, to second-order insights about what this meant for IB theories of human resource practices. Alvesson and Karreman (2007, p. 1273) describe the process I followed as constructing a 'mystery' from empirical material through 'openness'. Engaging with the mystery necessitated 'enfolding literature' from institutional theory (Eisenhardt 1989, p. 544). This shifted institutional theory from my 'superficial repertoire' to my 'deep repertoire' (Alvesson and Karreman 2007, p. 1274). As I iterated between theory and empirical data, I engaged in what Weick (1995) describes as a process of sensemaking. That is, I extracted cues from the data, which struck me as paradoxical or mysterious in some way, and tried to fit these cues

to frames of extant theory. If a cue did not fit the theoretical frame, I had to 'make sense' by reconfiguring the boundaries of the theoretical frame to accommodate it. This process has also been described as 'abduction' in response to doubt (Locke et al. 2008). My abduction evolved around two core ideas. First, at any moment in time, rules governing the qualification of overseas players existed at the institutional level. Second, through the choices they made in recruiting overseas players, county administrators translated the institutional rules into human resource practices at the organizational level.

CONCLUSIONS AND REFLECTIONS

> My analogy [for documents-in-action] concerns an operatic libretto (the set of words and phrases that is sung). Taken on its own a libretto rarely adds up to much. The text as narrative is often disjointed, repetitive and lacking in depth. I cannot think of a single one that might hold a person's attention as a gripping tale. Yet, a libretto is not intended to be analysed in isolation. It demands to be analysed in action. How it is integrated into the dramatic action on stage, how it relates to the melody and the rhythm of the music, how it is called upon (recruited) and manipulated by singers, how it is performed – all of these are of primary importance. Its substance as displayed on the inert page is only of secondary importance. (Prior 2003, p. 173)

The use of documents-in-action as a sensemaking frame has several advantages for IB case researchers. First, documents-in-action as a method of analysis is both multilevel and processual (see Mohr 1982; Rousseau 1985; Dansereau et al. 1999; Kozlowski and Klein 2000) and, in turn, generates explanations that are holistic and temporally interconnected. Thus the approach can be classified as a contextualist theory of method, which Pettigrew (1990, p. 269) argues is fundamental to understanding practices within organizations. Second, inherent in the documents-in-action method is a continual questioning of documents, as data, from multiple angles and perspectives, which enhances the plausibility and interpretative rigour of the theoretical understandings ultimately generated (see Weick 1989; Strauss and Corbin 1990; Lincoln and Guba 2000), particularly when insights from the content, production and usage of documents converge (see Jick 1979; Eisenhardt 1989).

Third, the documents-in-action method, as I 'walked' through it, facilitates deep analysis of large quantities of data and leaves behind equally deep 'footprints' for other scholars to judge the trustworthiness and authenticity of the findings (see Strauss and Corbin 1990; Golden-Biddle and Locke 1993; Miles and Huberman 1994). Finally, the documents-in-action method is grounded in assumptions about the duality of structure and action (Giddens 1984). It recognizes that documents structure the current social reality of all organizations – including multinational enterprises, their foreign subsidiaries and the smallest of exporters and importers – by defining legitimate and consensual organizational and individual actions, meanings and understandings. At the same time, this stock of documents is available for recruitment and manipulation in the production of future documents by actors with access, power, and interests in promoting alternative IB strategies.

REFERENCES

Alvesson, M. and S. Deetz (2000), *Doing Critical Management Research*, London: Sage.

Alvesson, M. and D. Karreman (2007), 'Constructing mystery: empirical matters in theory development', *Academy of Management Review*, **32** (4), 1265–81.

Atkinson, P. and A. Coffey (2004), 'Analysing documentary realities', in D. Silverman (ed.), *Qualitative Research: Theory, Method and Practice*, London: Sage, pp. 56–75.

Bacharach, S.B., P. Bamberger and V. McKinney (2000), 'Boundary management tactics and logics of action: the case of peer-support providers', *Administrative Science Quarterly*, **45** (4), 704–36.

Benford, R.D. and D.A. Snow (2000), 'Framing processes and social movements: an overview and assessment', *Annual Review of Sociology*, **26**, 611–39.

Birley, D. (2003), *A Social History of English Cricket*, paperback edn, London: Aurum Press.

Bowen, R. (1970), *Cricket: A History of its Growth and Development throughout the World*, London: Eyre & Spottiswoode.

Calás, M.B. and L. Smircich (1999), 'Past postmodernism? Reflections and tentative directions', *Academy of Management Review*, **24** (4), 649–71.

Cannella, A.A.J. and R.L. Paetzold (1994), 'Pfeffer's barriers to the advance of organizational science: a rejoinder', *Academy of Management Review*, **19** (2), 331–41.

Cook, T.D. and D.T. Campbell (1979), *Quasi-experimentation: Design and Analysis Issues for Field Settings*, Boston, MA: Houghton Mifflin.

Czarniawska, B. (1998), 'Who is afraid of incommensurability?', *Organization*, **5** (2), 273–5.

Dansereau, F., F.J. Yammarino and J.C. Kohles (1999), 'Multiple levels of analysis from a longitudinal perspective: some implications for theory building', *Academy of Management Review*, **24** (2), 346–57.

Derrida, J. (1976), *Of Grammatology*, trans. G.C. Spivak, Baltimore, MD: Johns Hopkins University Press.

Eisenhardt, K.M. (1989), 'Building theories from case study research', *Academy of Management Review*, **14** (4), 532–50.

Elsbach, K.D. (1994), 'Managing organizational legitimacy in the California cattle industry: the construction and effectiveness of verbal accounts', *Administrative Science Quarterly*, **39** (1), 57–88.

Flick, U. (2002), *An Introduction to Qualitative Research*, 2nd edn, London: Sage.

Fort, R. and J. Quirk (1995), 'Cross-subsidization, incentives, and outcomes in professional team sports leagues', *Journal of Economic Literature*, **33** (3), 1265–99.

Geertz, C. (1983), *Local Knowledge: Further Essays in Interpretative Anthropology*, New York: Basic Books.

Giddens, A.G. (1979), *Central Problems in Social Theory: Action, Structure, and Contradiction in Social Analysis*, Berkeley, CA: University of California Press.

Giddens, A.G. (1984), *The Constitution of Society*, Berkeley, CA: University of California Press.

Giddens, A.G. (1990), *The Consequences of Modernity*, Cambridge: Polity.

Goffman, E. (1967), *Interaction Ritual: Essays on Face-to-Face Behavior*, Garden City, NY: Anchor Books.

Golden-Biddle, K. and K. Locke (1993), 'Appealing work: an investigation of how ethnographic texts convince', *Organization Science*, **4** (4), 595–616.

Green, S.E. (2004), 'A rhetorical theory of diffusion', *Academy of Management Review*, **29** (4), 1022–54.

Greenwood, R., R. Suddaby and C.R. Hinings (2002), 'Theorizing change: the role of professional associations in the transformation of institutionalized fields', *Academy of Management Journal*, **45** (1), 58–80.

Hasselbladh, H. and J. Kallinikos (2000), 'The project of rationalization: a critique and reappraisal of neo-institutionalism in organization studies', *Organization Studies*, **21** (4), 697–720.

Heracleous, L. and M. Barratt (2001), 'Organizational change as discourse: communicative actions and deep structures in the context of information technology management', *Academy of Management Journal*, **42** (4), 755–78.

Hill, M.R. (1993), *Archival Strategies and Techniques*, Newbury Park, CA: Sage.

Jick, T.D. (1979), 'Mixing qualitative and quantitative methods: triangulation in action', *Administrative Science Quarterly*, **24** (4), 602–11.

Kozlowski, S.W.J. and K.J. Klein (2000), 'A multilevel approach to theory and research in organizations: contextual, temporal and emergent processes', in K.J. Klein and S.W.J. Kozlowski (eds), *Multilevel Theory, Research and Methods in Organizations*, San Francisco, CA: Jossey-Bass, pp. 3–90.

Langley, A. (1999), 'Strategies for theorizing from process data', *Academy of Management Review*, **24** (4), 691–710.

Lee, A.S. (1991), 'Integrating positivist and interpretive approaches to organizational research', *Organization Science*, **2** (4), 342–65.

Legewie, H. (1994), 'Globalauswertung' [global analysis], in A. Bohm, T. Muhr and A. Mengel (eds), *Texte verstehen: Konzepte, Methoden, Werkzeuge* [Understanding Texts: Concepts, Methods, Tools], Konstanz: Universitatsverlag, pp. 100–114.

Leonard-Barton, D. (1990), 'A dual methodology for case studies: synergistic use of longitudinal single site with replicated multiple sites', *Organization Science*, **1** (3), 248–66.

Lincoln, Y.S. and E. Guba (2000), 'Paradigmatic controversies, contradictions, and emerging confluences', in N.K. Denzin and Y.S. Lincoln (eds), *Handbook of Qualitative Research*, Thousand Oaks, CA: Sage, pp. 163–88.

Locke, K., K. Golden-Biddle and M.S. Feldman (2008), 'Making doubt generative: rethinking the role of doubt in the research process', *Organization Science*, **19** (6), 907–18.

Miles, M.B. and A.M. Huberman (1994), *Qualitative Data Analysis: An Expanded Sourcebook*, London: Sage.

Miles, M.B. and A.M. Huberman (2002), *The Qualitative Researcher's Companion*, Thousand Oaks, CA: Sage.

Mohr, L.B. (1982), *Explaining Organizational Behavior*, San Francisco, CA: Jossey-Bass.

Orlikowski, W.J. and J. Yates (1994), 'Genre reporting: the structuring of communicative practices in organizations', *Administrative Science Quarterly*, **39** (4), 541–74.

Pettigrew, A.M. (1990), 'Longitudinal field research on change: theory and practice', *Organization Science*, **1** (3), 267–92.

Phillips, N., T.B. Lawrence and C. Hardy (2004), 'Discourse and institutions', *Academy of Management Review*, **29** (4), 635–52.

Piekkari, R., C. Welch and E. Paavilainen (2009), 'The case study as disciplinary convention: evidence from international business journals', *Organizational Research Methods*, **12** (3), 567–89.

Prior, L. (2003), *Using Documents in Social Research*, London: Sage.

Prior, L. (2004), 'Documents', in C. Seale, G. Gobo, J.F. Gubrium and D. Silverman (eds), *Qualitative Research Practice*, London: Sage, pp. 375–90.

Rao, H. and S. Giorgi (2006), 'Code breaking: how entrepreneurs exploit cultural logics to generate institutional change', in B.M. Staw (ed.), *Research in Organizational Behavior: An Annual Series of Analytical Essays and Critical Reviews*, **27**, Oxford: Elsevier, pp. 269–303.

Rousseau, D.M. (1985), 'Issues of level in organizational research: multi-level and cross-level perspectives', in B.M. Staw and L.L. Cummings (eds), *Research in Organizational Behavior*, Greenwich, CT: JAI Press, pp. 1–37.

Schutz, A. (1970–71), *Collected Papers* (3 vols), 3rd unchanged edn, The Hague: Martinus Nijhoff.

Scully, G.W. (1974), 'Pay and performance in major league baseball', *American Economic Review*, **64** (5), 915–30.

Strang, D. and J. Meyer (1993), 'Institutional conditions for diffusion', *Theory and Society*, **22** (4), 487–511.

Strang, D. and S.A. Soule (1998), 'Diffusion in organizations and social movements: from hybrid corn to poison pills', *Annual Review of Sociology*, **24**, 265–90.

Strauss, A. and J. Corbin (1990), *Basics of Qualitative Research: Grounded Theory Procedures and Techniques*, Newbury Park, CA: Sage.

Stryker, R. (2000), 'Legitimacy processes as institutional politics: implications for theory and research in the sociology of organizations', in B. Staw (ed.), *Research in Sociology of Organizations*, **17**, Oxford: Elsevier (JAI Press), pp. 179–223.

Suchman, M.C. (1995), 'Managing legitimacy: strategic and institutional approaches', *Academy of Management Review*, **20** (3), 571–610.

Suddaby, R. (2006), 'What grounded theory is not', *Academy of Management Journal*, **49** (4), 633–42.

Suddaby, R. and R. Greenwood (2005), 'Rhetorical strategies of legitimacy', *Administrative Science Quarterly*, **50** (1), 35–67.

Taylor, J.R., F. Cooren, N. Giroux and D. Robichaud (1996), 'The communicational basis of organization: between the conversation and the text', *Communication Theory*, **6** (1), 1–39.

Tolbert, P.S. and L.G. Zucker (1996), 'The institutionalization of institutional theory', in S.R. Clegg, C. Hardy and W. Nord (eds), *Handbook of Organization Studies*, Thousand Oaks, CA: Sage, pp. 175–90.

Van Maanen, J. (1979), 'The fact of fiction in organizational ethnography', *Administrative Science Quarterly*, **24** (4), 539–50.

Vrooman, J. (1995), 'A general theory of professional sports leagues', *Southern Economic Journal*, **61** (4), 971–91.

Weber, M. (1979), *Economy and Society*, Berkeley, CA: University of California Press.

Weick, K.E. (1989), 'Theory construction as disciplined imagination', *Academy of Management Review*, **14** (4), 516–31.

Weick, K.E. (1995), *Sensemaking in Organization*, Thousand Oaks, CA: Sage.

Yates, J. and W.J. Orlikowski (1992), 'Genres of organizational communication: a structuration approach to studying communication and media', *Academy of Management Review*, **17** (2), 299–326.

20. Comparative historical analysis in international management research

Ayse Saka-Helmhout

INTRODUCTION

The way in which cross-national studies on organizational phenomena are carried out tends to overlook complex patterns of interaction (Ragin 1987). Case studies do not lend themselves easily to coping with complexity as their numbers and levels of analyses increase. If there are literally dozens of meaningful dimensions along which case studies are different, and dozens along which they are similar, then how does one determine the causal connections between the multiplicity of causes and the variations in a given outcome? The highly interactive processes that are subject to various contextual influences, such as culture and history, pose a challenge to attaining causality in more than a handful of cases, and, in turn, to comparability and generalizability (Öz 2004). In a similar vein, in the absence of systematic methods, many qualitative researchers consider data analysis an art that is performed by the experienced researcher in a way that is hardly communicable (Miles and Huberman 1984, p. 16). This makes the analysis phase one of the least developed aspects of case study methodology (Yin 2009).

Several methods do offer guidelines for organizing data, notably pattern matching, explanation building, time-series analysis and programme-logic models (Yin 2009); data reduction, data display, and conclusion drawing and verification (Miles and Huberman 1984); and the search for within-group similarities coupled with inter-group differences (Eisenhardt 1989). But these address only some aspects of the challenges of systematically analysing findings from a multiple case study. First, they do not adopt a configurational logic, according to which different parts of the whole are understood in relation to one another and in terms of the total picture that the parts constitute. Second, they focus on the constructs developed and their measurability, and do not take into consideration the historical context of cases. For instance, Yin (2009) focuses on contemporary as opposed to historical events. In a multiple comparative case design, cases are chosen in alignment with the deductive approach, because of their theoretical relevance. Both Eisenhardt and Yin emphasize a deductive logic for comparative case studies as a means for shaping hypotheses and sharpening constructs. There is not much room for a regular dialogue between theory and empirical evidence that can serve to clarify both concepts and the empirical category to which the cases belong.

A method that meets the challenge of dealing simultaneously with capturing the complexity of interactions and attaining causality in patterns of activities for generalizability is comparative historical analysis (CHA), which is used extensively in political science and historical sociology. CHA formalizes the unique strengths of case-oriented research – the treatment of cases as whole entities and conjunctural understanding of causation (that is, several conditions might produce an outcome) – in comparative social science. It offers control over unwanted causal inferences in case comparison and enables a holistic case-oriented approach to data analysis for more comprehensive explanations. It simplifies complex data structures in a logical and holistic manner without disaggregating cases into variables prior to analysing them. For instance, many different combinations of conditions may result in social revolt, leading to different outcomes within and across nations. Although one can expect a predictable pattern or a describable order to these combinations, this pattern may not come to the fore if a variable-based approach to case analysis is assumed. By contrast, case-oriented thinking conceptualizes variables as interdependent and often complementary. 'Variables' are considered in the context of a particular case as a cluster. In other words, outcomes are examined in relation to different empirical combinations of variables. Cases serve as the basis for placing boundaries around the measurement of variables (George and Bennett 2005). By contrast, the variable-oriented approach focuses on variables or particular dimensions that constrain or impact on an outcome.

Although there are a number of significant uses of CHA in the institutional analysis of national systems in the field of management (for example, Djelic 1998; Kogut and Ragin 2006), sociology (for example, Cress and Snow 2000; Dixon et al. 2004), and political science (for example, Jonoski and Hicks 1994), the importance of the method to analysing international management (IM) phenomena is barely acknowledged. The aim of this chapter is to advocate the use of this method in the IM field to delineate patterns of causalities or regularities in microsociological phenomena embedded in historical contextual singularities across countries to improve the generalizability of cross-case comparisons.[1] A common concern raised by scholars (for example, Child 2000; Redding 2005; Jones and Khanna 2006) is the inattentiveness to the role of history, context and social meaning systems in studies on collaborations in IM settings. Specifically, Redding (2005) cautions us that the 'etics perspective', which assumes context-free rational agency and determinacy, continues to remain the dominant form of IM research. Where institutional contexts are studied, variable-based approaches to understanding contexts are adopted (Jackson and Deeg 2008). Redding (2005) proposes, instead, that greater emphasis should be paid to the 'emic perspective', which is more attentive to the role of history and agency in IM research but which is bound to increase complexity. We believe that this challenge is a methodological one that can be met by CHA, given that the latter adopts a holistic view of contexts whereby institutions, conceptualized as configurations, are compared to understand diversity. We describe below what CHA encompasses. This is followed by an illustration of the method in the context of knowledge diffusion processes in a cross-national setting, namely from Japanese multinationals to their affiliate firms in the UK. The last two sections address the challenges of applying CHA and point to the contributions of the methodology to explaining cross-national phenomena.

COMPARATIVE HISTORICAL ANALYSIS (CHA)

CHA is a research approach that dates back to John Stuart Mill's (1843 [1967]) methods of logical induction, and is used extensively in political science (comparative politics) (for example, Rueschemeyer et al. 1992) and historical sociology, such as welfare state studies (for example, Skocpol and Somers 1980). The approach combines detailed case studies with systematic comparison. Detailed accounts ensure that the context-boundedness of (the conditions underlying) a phenomenon of interest is elicited. A systematic comparison allows for a significant theoretical leverage so that generalization is made possible. For such an analysis to serve its role as a theoretical lever, the cases must be theoretically sampled and comparable. In other words, they must resemble each other in many respects except in the phenomenon of interest, so that unwanted causal inferences can be controlled (George and Bennett 2005). It is important to note here that CHA cannot assist the case researcher in managing qualitative data in the absence of systematic methods. Its aim is not to describe rich data but to seek control for comparability and generalizability.

Among the logical foundations of CHA, the 'method of agreement' and the 'method of difference' are the most important (Mill (1843 [1967]). Both methods are concerned with the systematic matching and contrasting of cases in order to establish common causal relationships by eliminating all other possibilities (Berg-Schlosser et al. 2009). The former method refers to eliminating all similarities except for one or more combinations of conditions. It is assumed that where two or more outcomes across cases are common (labelled as the 'positive comparative method'), there will be similarities in bundles of conditions that, at least in part, account for that outcome. This method is applied by initially identifying instances of the phenomenon under investigation, and then determining which conditions precede its appearance. The condition that satisfies this requirement is taken as the cause. The method of agreement works on a logic of elimination. For instance, an investigator who is interested in the causes of an institutional change may search for the possibility of a shift in the societal balance of power (see Collier and Collier 1991; Huber and Stephens 2001), the liberalization of markets (see Crouch and Keune 2005), the introduction of new technology or innovation (see Ventresca et al. 2003), or regulatory pressure (see Djelic and Quack 2003). If all of the possible causal conditions prevail in the first case, then the method of agreement would require the investigator to analyse other cases of institutional change in an effort to eliminate some of the explanatory conditions. For instance, if a case of institutional change lacking regulatory pressure were found, this condition would be eliminated. The process of elimination would continue until the investigator would reach a cause or a set of causes. If the cases agree on all of the conditions, these conditions would be taken as significant. However, there is a problem with the use of this method in isolation. It does not establish a link between cause and effect. The fact that cases of institutional change are observed in conjunction with, for instance, the liberalization of markets does not guarantee that market liberalization causes institutional change. An unidentified condition, such as a coercive mandate from a supranational entity such as the EU, may be the cause of both market liberalization and institutional change. Hence, the method of agreement is best used in combination with the method of difference to avoid the dangers of identifying 'false positives'.[2]

The method of difference establishes the absence of a common cause or effect, even if all other circumstances are identical. It compares cases with different outcomes. It requires that cases in which the phenomenon is absent also be included in the comparisons, with the expectation that the cause will be absent in those additional cases (Skocpol and Somers 1980; Ragin 1987). For example, if cases displaying both institutional change and market liberalization also display regulatory pressure, a possible explanation of institutional change, then some of the cases displaying an absence of both market liberalization and institutional change should also display regulatory pressure. This pattern of results would allow the investigator to reject regulatory pressure as a possible explanation of

Table 20.1   Methods of agreement and difference in comparative analysis

Case	Conditions present	Outcome
1	x, y, b, c	A
2	t, u, b, c	A
3	t, u, b, l	E
4	t, u, c, m	F

institutional change because institutional change is absent in the second set. In effect, the method of difference applies the method of agreement in its cross-tabulation of cause and effect, and rejects competing single-factor explanations through paired comparisons (Ragin 1987).

When the methods of agreement and difference are combined, it becomes easier to identify bundles of conditions that account for variation in outcomes. For instance, the bundle of conditions that is responsible for outcome A in Table 20.1 is confirmed through the negative cases (that is, Cases 3 and 4). The negative cases demonstrate that conditions b or c alone are not sufficient to result in outcome A. Their influence needs to be considered in combination.

Mill's methods have been extended by Charles Ragin (1987) to constitute qualitative comparative analysis (QCA). Both analytical methods serve the functions of (i) building a typology of differing cases accounting for the same phenomenon, (ii) describing the various conditions present at the occurrence or non-occurrence of a phenomenon, (iii) testing various existing theories to empirical observations, and (iv) going beyond mere observation to build middle-range theory through the use of logical cases (Yamasaki 2003). Although the logic underlying Mill's method and Ragin's QCA is the same, the former does not accommodate equifinality; that is, the possibility of different causal patterns leading to similar outcomes across cases. Different constellations of factors may lead to the same result as, for instance, different paths in democratization research (for example, Berg-Schlosser 1998; Collier 1999) or different social forces leading to the emergence of welfare states in Western Europe (for example, Esping-Andersen 1990). Equifinality challenges and undermines Mill's assumption that similar outcomes in several cases must have a common cause that remains to be discovered.

By contrast, QCA allows for the possibility of equifinality (George and Bennett 2005). It uses the Boolean technique – the conversion of data into binary values – to identify causal regularities that are parsimonious; that is, they can be expressed with the fewest possible conditions within the whole set of conditions that are considered in the analysis. However, for this analysis to be performed, there must be a minimum of five cases and the model must be specified in such a way that the number of variables is significantly lower than the number of cases (see Marx 2006). As the number of cases increases, the likelihood that a given causally relevant condition will be common to the entire set of cases decreases. The complexity is further increased when there are large numbers of causal conditions, leading to the examination of many combinations of conditions. Such complexity makes the use of QCA software essential. For instance, with eight causal conditions, there are 256 possible combinations. With a high number of relevant conditions, it is advisable to revisit theory and consider merging several variables into broader variables (Rihoux 2003), and limiting the investigation to specific types of causal factors rather than all possibly relevant causes (Ragin 1987).

By the same token, QCA presents a challenge to the calibration of conditions. It is argued that the Boolean technique results in loss of information, and that the threshold of dichotomization is set arbitrarily (Goldthorpe 1997). The challenge does not so much lie in determining the absence or the presence of a condition such as personal or public ownership as in assigning values to continuous variables, such as the release of counterpart funds in a given national system of industrial production. Rihoux (2003) advises that the threshold for positive membership can be determined inductively while performing data exploration with QCA. Using CHA based on Mill to analyse a small number of cases, it is easier to place cases relative to each other by relying on the substantive knowledge of cases. However, with a larger number of cases and where conditions are interval- and ratio-scale variables, as in QCA applications, direct[3] and indirect methods can be used to calibrate variables according to external standards (see Ragin 2008).

A key question common to both CHA based on Mill and QCA is which conditions or combinations thereof are 'necessary' or 'sufficient' to produce a given outcome. According to Rihoux and Ragin (2009), a condition is *necessary* for a given outcome if it is always present when the outcome occurs, that is, when the outcome cannot occur in its absence. A condition is *sufficient* for an outcome if the outcome occurs when the condition is present, but it can also result from other conditions. The most commonly used method for identifying necessary and sufficient causes is typological theory (George and Bennett 2005). This requires the construction of theoretical types that are systematically matched to determine whether cases follow patterns of correspondence consistent with necessary or sufficient causation (Mahoney 2004). A given type is not necessary for an outcome if the type is both present and absent among a group of cases that all exhibit the outcome of interest. Similarly, a type is not sufficient for an outcome if the type is present in both cases where the outcome is present and the cases where the outcome is absent. This method is used in the light of one's theoretical and substantive knowledge of the cases.

CHA is an inductive as much as a deductive methodology. Its deductive nature is derived from the theoretical notions that serve as guides in the search for similarities and differences across cases. At the same time, the method is inductive, for the investigator decides which of the commonalities and differences are operative by examining empirical cases (Ragin 1987). The initial theoretical ideas are enhanced through this induction. These processes encourage a regular dialogue between theory and empirical evidence (Rihoux 2003; Ragin 2005).

ILLUSTRATION OF CHA: CROSS-NATIONAL DIFFUSION OF CONTINUOUS IMPROVEMENT PRACTICES

CHA based on Mill is applied here to a study that compares the diffusion of continuous improvement practices from Japan to the UK (see Saka 2003). The purpose was to highlight the institutional influences on the extent to which foreign practices are accepted by the local workforce at three firms, namely Nissera UK, Teniki UK (both pseudonyms) and the Rover–Honda collaboration. Although, at the time of the research, there were 35 cases of Japanese foreign direct investment (FDI) in automobile and automobile parts (Invest in Britain Bureau 1995), only a small number of cases could be selected owing to the design of multiple levels of analysis in the investigation.[4] A comparison of two subsidiary firms alone would not have provided diversity in the study. According to Yin (2009), at least four cases need to be designed to pursue two different patterns of theoretical replication. As there was no case similar to the Rover–Honda collaboration in the UK automotive sector, a fourth comparable site could not be added to the sample. The aim was to strike a balance between collecting data that allowed for rigorous analysis yet avoided data overload, which leads to skewed analysis.

The choice of the home (Japan) and host (UK) contexts is based on the assumption that when practices are highly localized and acquired through engagement in specific action contexts, they can prove 'sticky' to diffuse to foreign firms (Szulanski 1996). This is especially the case in Japan, where the activities of a 'highly coordinated business system' (Whitley 1999) are generally carried out in accordance with highly implicit rules and social norms. Given that the institutional profile of Japan sharply contrasts with the compartmentalized business system of the UK, it is proposed here that the institutional differences between these two countries will hinder the diffusion of practices. As the interest is in performing a controlled comparison of historical and contextual influences (at the national and local institutional levels), as well as meanings attached by organizational members to new practices, CHA is applied to the data. Nissera UK and the Rover–Honda collaboration served as the positive cases, in which the outcome proved sufficiently similar; that is, foreign practices were institutionalized to a high degree. Teniki UK served as the negative case where practices acquired from Japan were institutionalized to a lower degree. However, this polarity in cases did not become apparent until midway through data collection. At the start of the research, all of the three cases were claimed by the gatekeepers to be good examples of firms that implemented Japanese continuous improvement schemes to make them work in the UK. Consequently, cases were selected on the basis of theoretically derived typologies rather than on instances of the outcome, namely high and low institutionalization of foreign practices.

Accordingly, affiliates of multinational corporations (MNCs) operating in highly coordinated business systems at the national level, located on a greenfield site and in a service-dominated region at the local institutional level, and with emphasis on tacit knowledge or cultural and control-related practices at the organizational level, were proposed to exhibit a high degree of institutionalization of Japanese work systems. A similar proposition was made in order to take into account the potential negative impact of less tightly-knit institutional settings and an emphasis on explicit knowledge or structural practices at the organizational level on the institutionalization of work systems (see Saka 2003). Consequently, conditions at the national and local institutional levels, and the nature of diffused practices (structural versus processual) at the organizational level, were derived from the literature. The remaining conditions were identified during the course of the fieldwork through open and axial coding (Strauss and Corbin 1998). This is elaborated in the subsection on identifying patterns of regularities. All three cases had combinations of favourable and unfavourable conditions in all typologies. Although they were all located in compartmentalized national business systems (proposed as being associated with low degree of institutionalization), one of the companies (Nissera UK) was based on a greenfield site and emphasized both explicit and tacit practices (proposed as being associated with high degree of institutionalization). In other words, there was emphasis on diversity of situations and of causal conditions beyond relative frequencies, distribution and case representativeness.

There was an attempt to match characteristics along the lines of sector and nature of diffused practices across firms for comparison. Nissera UK was similar to Teniki UK in ownership form, company size, nature of diffused practices and sector. However, in terms of company age (that is, the period from the point of initial investment to that of data collection), Nissera UK was similar to the Rover–Honda collaboration.[5] Although the Rover–Honda collaboration operated under a different form of ownership and was larger in terms of employee numbers than the two subsidiaries, it was similar to Teniki UK and Nissera UK in terms of the nature of diffused practices and the sector in which the firms operated. Rover had a local institutional context that was similar to that of Teniki UK, particularly in terms of a site location that hosted a pre-existing manufacturing culture. Rover's similarity with Nissera UK was more in terms of both companies aspiring to be successful models of diffused Japanese practices. Table 20.2 summarizes the characteristics of sampled cases.

The field study, which was carried out between 1998 and 2000, drew on 73 open-ended and semi-structured interviews and factory tours at both the Japanese and UK companies, a week-long participant observation at the UK companies, and document analysis. The broad aim was to understand the experiences of these companies in the transfer and use of 'foreign' practices. The research questions addressed the nature of the relationship and the division of responsibility between the Japanese parent and the subsidiary, the means by which continuous improvement practices were diffused, the factors that facilitated and inhibited the diffusion process, perceived cultural and managerial differences, and the learning opportunities available to both the parent and the subsidiary. Information on the extent to which practices were institutionalized was obtained from the field observations and on-the-job discussions with operators. The degree of institutionalization was categorized as 'high' (relative to the other firms) where the operators accepted new practices with little resistance, or 'infused [them] with value beyond the technical requirements of the task at hand' (Selznick 1957, p. 17).

Cross-case Analysis of Bundles of Conditions

Findings, as summarized in Table 20.3, indicate that the initiatives taken by firms to institutionalize meanings and values produce conspicuous differences in the extent to which continuous improvement practices are institutionalized across the three firms. In this subsection, findings are discussed in relation to the organizational, local institutional and national levels of analysis.

At the organizational level of analysis, the findings showed that employees could accept and approve Japanese source companies' practices where old routines were redesigned to integrate these practices through company

Table 20.2   Characteristics of sampled cases

Cases	Year of establishment	Site	Core business	Size (no. of employees in 1999)	Form of ownership	Nature of diffused practice	Sector
Teniki UK	1996	Pre-existing culture (brownfield)	Car component assembly	Medium (170)	Subsidiary	Continuous improvement schemes	Automotive manufacturing
Nissera UK	1988	New culture (greenfield)	Car component assembly	Medium (300)	Subsidiary	Continuous improvement schemes	Automotive manufacturing
Rover–Honda collaboration	1985 (when the R8/YY project commenced)	Pre-existing culture (home of Britain's traditional car manufacturing base)	Automobile design, engineering, and manufacture	Large (~39,000)	Technical collaboration	Continuous improvement schemes	Automotive manufacturing

Source: Saka (2003).

Table 20.3 Cross-case analysis

	Conditions	Teniki UK	Nissera UK	Rover–Honda R8/YY Project
National	National institutional gap	Institutional gap between the compartmentalized UK business system and the highly coordinated Japanese business system	Institutional gap between the compartmentalized UK business system and the highly coordinated Japanese business system	Institutional gap between the compartmentalized UK business system and the highly coordinated Japanese business system
Local	Location site	Brownfield	Greenfield	Brownfield
	Location area	Centre for tourism	Centre for manufacturing	Traditional home of Britain's car manufacturing base
Organizational level	Emphasis on Japanese expatriates	4 (the managing director is British)	12 (including the managing director)	Regular visits by Honda engineers (1986–89), liaison office established in 1985
	Nature of training	Hands-off	Hands-on	Hands-on
	Nature of diffused practices	Emphasis on structural practices such as shift to team structure	Emphasis on both structural and processual practices such as securing commitment to continuous improvement schemes	Emphasis on both structural and processual practices such as securing commitment to continuous improvement schemes
	Emphasis on training	Low	High	High in quality skills and car development system
	Financial orientation	Short term	Long term	Long term
Outcome	Degree of institutionalization	Low	High	High

visits and cross-functional teamwork, as at the Rover–Honda collaboration, and the active role of Japanese expatriates as boundary-spanning individuals, as found at Nissera UK. Company visits and boundary-spanning individuals encouraged socialization, allowing tacit knowledge to be acquired through experience. For example, the heavy use of expatriates who were hands-on in imparting continuous improvement practices at Nissera UK – 12 members – served to establish an organizational culture that aligned with the parent company's values.

In comparison, Teniki UK had the least number of Japanese expatriates, with only three members who made themselves available for training, and tended to be hands-off in management. Older operators, in particular, preferred the traditional British work organization of union activity and craftsmanship. This could be evidenced in a statement made by a senior operator at Teniki UK: 'We need the trade union down here to improve the work environment'.

Annual reports, operational plans and internal memos provided further evidence on the variation in the implementation of major practices across the three UK sites. For example, the pattern of authority relations at Teniki UK and Nissera UK was changed from one based on superintendents, supervisors and hourly-paid workers to one built around team leaders, team coaches and hourly-paid workers arranged in a production cell layout rather than in assembly lines. However, fluid job descriptions associated with team-based structures evident in the Japanese parent companies were not widespread in the two subsidiaries. For instance, team leaders and assistants at Nissera UK had clearly defined responsibilities and their positions were treated as managerial ones. At Rover, there was a shift from functional authority relations to a project-based structure. Within a project-based structure, engineers who were assigned to project teams could consult a central pool of expertise on technical difficulties. However, internal memos revealed that, unlike in Honda, weekly meetings with every project leader could not be held at Rover, owing to the geographical separation of Rover body engineers from interior and other engineers. Although there was a shift in work organization at all three sites towards a flatter team structure, this was not accompanied by an emphasis on continuous improvement philosophies such as the instilling of team spirit at Teniki UK.

Rover engineers identified with the continuous improvement schemes as more collaborative projects were carried out with Honda engineers: 'As the project went on, we were more and more subtly encouraged to go the Honda way on everything. In essence, we adapted our specifications to meet theirs at the end of the day' (Principal Electrical Engineer at Rover). There was willingness to invest considerable effort in sustaining Honda practices, such as the *gebba-kai* process,[6] suggesting a high level of emphasis by Honda on quality skills.

The previous (British) ownership focused on teaching skills that were related to an operator's immediate task rather than the overall integrated production process. Although job training under Japanese management was typically provided internally and included consultation with staff, in line with the practices in Japan, the training and development plan had not instilled a continuous improvement culture at Teniki UK. Japanese expatriates had a short-term outlook towards developing capabilities, owing to the financial pressure exerted on Teniki (Japanese parent company) by a major car manufacturer. This lack of consistency with Japanese practices is evidenced by the following statement:

> Teniki have pressure on them to put pressure on ourselves to make the returns faster than normal. In that case, we have had to have very stringent sort of budgetary control and cutting of budgets which would affect the long-term, that is the training budgets are not as good as they should be in my belief. (British Operations Manager at Teniki UK)

The local institutional level of analysis was able to relate practices observed among operators to the regional context in which the sample firms operated. The location of Teniki UK on a brownfield site in a centre for tourism contrasted sharply with the location of both Nissera UK on a greenfield site in a centre for manufacturing and Rover in a traditional manufacturing base (based on local development agency reports). Given space limitations, we focus our discussion below on Teniki UK's circumstances.

Teniki UK was located in a region where a large portion of the labour force (nearly 40 per cent in 1997) was employed in the public sector. Employment trends in 1997 showed that 12 per cent of the working population was employed in manufacturing (Salisbury Economic Development and Tourism Unit 1998). Although statistics relating to social class by occupation indicated that the highest percentage (18 per cent) of the population was economically active in the managerial and technical group, this skills base was concentrated in the financial services sector. The study also showed that location on a brownfield site, where preconceptions of work practices were abundant, tended to lead to practices that more closely resembled local practices, inhibiting the institutionalization of Japanese practices.

A historical analysis was carried out at the national level, where macro-institutional and cultural dynamics could play a role in the diffusion of practices. History could be discerned from evidence in the literature on cultural and normative differences between Japan and the UK (for example, Lillrank 1995; Dore and Sako 1997; Whitley 1999). The highly coordinated institutional context of Japan nurtures collectivist values and tightly-knit networks that encourage low strike activity, absenteeism and turnover. Japanese corporate values and norms, such as employment stability and strong employee identification with the company, are still seen as having positive implications for participative, hands-on management, commitment to continuous improvement activities, teamwork and on-the-job training in the manufacturing sector (Dirks et al. 2000; Morris et al. 2008).

By contrast, the institutional context of the UK discourages cooperation between business partners, including superordinates and subordinates (Whitley 1999). Management's desire for control over many key operating decisions, and arm's-length relations between actors, have reinforced a basic conflict model of the workplace in which strike activity, absenteeism and turnover have been common occurrences (Lane 1996; McMillan 1996). Limited collaboration among employers, unions and other groups tends to discourage cooperation in the management of training systems (Whitley 1999).

Consequently, it could be inferred that Japanese practices were interpreted and sustained differently by the UK workforce owing to the variation in normative and cultural frames of reference between Japan and the UK that quite often led to the appropriation or the blending of new work systems with existing ones. Teniki UK exemplified the institutional differences between Japan and the UK in the following manner: '[I]n Japan, employees are grateful for being given a project to do. However, in the UK, there is demarcation. Employees will ask "why ask me to do the project?"' (Personnel and Training Manager at Teniki UK). Employees in the UK were perceived as trying to find an alternative method of carrying out a task rather than working to a rigid process. For example, according to a senior manager in manufacturing integration, Rover lacked the self-discipline to rigorously prove a process, train people and introduce double checks to stabilize the system. This was observed in the way Rover raised project change requests (PCRs).

> Again we might not have the discipline that they adopt in terms of the PCR changes. PCRs are supposed to be all resolved and signed off at the [*gebba-kai*] event. But not everybody turns up. Sometimes it is quite difficult to judge whether you should invite all your suppliers, because some of our suppliers come a long way. So we might not have the discipline to fully do it but we still basically adopt it. (Principal Electrical Engineer at Rover)

As the analysis at the national, local institutional, and organizational levels indicates, Nissera UK and the Rover–Honda collaboration were more successful in institutionalizing meaning to alternative practices than Teniki UK.

Identifying Patterns of Regularities

The main principle of CHA is the examination of set-theoretic relationships between causal conditions and a clearly specified outcome. These relationships are then interpreted in terms of necessity and sufficiency of conditions. In this subsection, the analytical process is outlined, from initial coding to cross-case comparison.

Initially, interview transcriptions and observation notes were scanned to generate a list of tentative subcategories or conditions at the organizational level under the main categories of training and control that were identified as having an impact on employee perceptions of work organization. Open and axial coding revealed conditions – such as the emphasis on and nature of training and financial orientation of the MNC towards the subsidiary – that were associated with the degree of institutionalization of continuous improvement practices. An example can be found in the responses to the question on barriers to/facilitators of transfer of practices that focused on training. As other respondents acknowledged this, theoretical saturation was reached and 'training' was included as a category in the analysis. Subcategories were identified on the basis of a category's properties and dimensions, such as the 'nature of and emphasis on training' (Strauss and Corbin 1998). To verify the explanatory power of the codes, axial coding was carried out to relate subcategories to the outcome of the degree of institutionalization (see Table 20.4 for an illustrative list of codes and their definitions as well as the statements denoting how these are related).

A qualitative approach to threshold setting – the level that serves as a reference point to determining the full inclusion of combinations in the set of high degree of institutionalization – was followed during the course of the fieldwork (see Varone et al. 2006 for a similar approach). Two outcome variables were identified, and the cases were classified as having highly or lowly institutionalized foreign practices on the basis of workers' attitudes towards Japanese work systems. The existing conditions and their strength were examined in a case-by-case manner. The selection of conditions at the organizational level was based on an inductive approach whereby conditions were mostly selected on the basis of case knowledge and not on existing theories (Amenta and Poulsen 1996). There was not an appropriate single theory that could be called upon to explain varying degrees of institutionalization of new practices. Based on in-depth knowledge of the cases and the literature emphasizing tacit knowledge production in Japan,

Table 20.4 Illustrative list of codes

Categories related to degree of institutionalization	Subcategories	Teniki UK	Nissera UK	Rover–Honda collaboration
Training (i.e. means of imparting workers with the skills, know-how to work with continuous improvement practices)	Hands-on/ hands-off nature of training	The four Japanese advisers who are in a position to train the operators are preoccupied with start-up projects, and do not have the time to invest in training	The Japanese guy was very patient. He would tell you all you needed to know. He explained things . . . If there was a reject, it would go to the line that produced the fault for rework. Japanese look for the source of the problem. In the UK, you are just told what to do	Rover engineers were able to observe the *gebba-kai* [quality circles adopted by engineers to solve problems at the end of each build phase] process during their six to 12 months' joint engineering work with Honda engineers in Japan
	High/low emphasis on training	I believe people understand that they need to cut costs in the business. However, the adoption and the ownership of correcting the problems, they do not do. That again is partly through training and the pressure on the business, not being able to release them to train . . .	Although they had more strict rules, Japanese managers would help you work. They would go to the source of the problem. British managers make up titles and waste money	Learning from Honda was that you must go through a process of evolution and all the components that fit into the vehicle must be off-tool and off-process. One of the requirements that Honda laid down was that the more you practised, the better the product

398

Control (i.e. monitoring of operational processes and financial outcomes)	Financial orientation	Teniki [Japanese parent] have pressure on them to put pressure on ourselves to make the returns faster than normal. In that case, we have had to have very stringent sort of budgetary control . . . which would affect the long term, that is the training budgets are not as good as they should be in my belief	Sometimes we do not chase profit. Otherwise we would be money traders. We invest. Our profit is generated from the products we manufacture. We sometimes try to forget about profitability. For the first three years, we do not expect a profit. We expect a profit in the fourth, fifth year	As the project went on, we were more and more subtly encouraged to go the Honda way on everything. In essence, we adapted our specifications to meet theirs at the end of the day . . . Rover's liaison officers facilitated information flow and helped forge good working relations

eight conditions that were individually insufficient to result in low institutionalization of work systems in the UK were identified with the use of a 'crisp set'. This refers to identifying the presence or absence of conditions, or their membership or non-membership in sets of firms, that are linked to a high degree of institutionalization. For the sake of convenience, we shall define these conditions, as QCA analysts do, by binary values.

As can be seen in Tables 20.2 and 20.3, the causally relevant conditions are as follows, with presence indicated by 1 and absence by 0: (i) 'national institutional gap': the gap between the home and host institutional contexts; (ii) 'location site': whether the plant was a greenfield site; (iii) 'location area': whether the plant was located in a service-dominated geographical area; (iv) 'emphasis on expatriate managers', based on the number of Japanese HQ staff occupying strategic positions in relation to the other cases; (v) 'nature of training': whether there was hands-on training; (vi) 'nature of diffused practices': the emphasis on structural and processual practices; (vii) 'emphasis on training', in terms of the number of staff involved and the nature of their involvement in relation to other cases; and (viii) 'financial orientation': whether there was a long-term perspective.

The dependent variable – that is, the degree of institutionalization of new practices – takes the value of 1 (present, represented by an upper-case letter in the QCA terminology) if it is observed to a high degree in comparison to the other cases. By the same token, a low degree of institutionalization takes the value of 0 (absent, represented by a lower-case letter).[7] The membership scores of the three cases in the nine sets (which refer to the outcome variable and the eight causal conditions) are presented in Table 20.5.

The combination of conditions associated with high degree of institutionalization at Nissera UK is ABcDEFGH[8] (where A = Institutional gap between the UK and Japan, B = Greenfield site, C = Service-dominated area, D = High number of Japanese expatriates, E = Hands-on nature of training, F = Emphasis on both structural and processual practices, G = High emphasis on training, and H = Long-term financial orientation). Whereas the Rover–Honda collaboration, which is also high on the degree of institutionalization of Japanese work systems, offers a different combination: AbcDEFGH. Here, the conditions of 'service-dominated area' and 'greenfield location site' are absent. Although this constitutes a different pathway to the same outcome, it needs to be analysed in conjunction with the results of Teniki UK – AbCdefgh – which has the outcome of low degree of institutionalization, in order to arrive at a list of necessary and/ or sufficient conditions.

The conditions that are always present (hence necessary) when there is

Table 20.5   Truth table indicating necessary and sufficient conditions

Case Conditions	Teniki UK	Nissera UK	Rover– Honda	Implication
National institutional gap	1	1	1	–
Location site	0	1	0	Sufficient,* not necessary
Location area	1	0	0	–
No. of Japanese expatriates	0	1	1	Necessary,† sufficient
Nature of training	0	1	1	Necessary, sufficient
Diffused practice	0	1	1	Necessary, sufficient
Emphasis on training	0	1	1	Necessary, sufficient
Financial orientation	0	1	1	Necessary, sufficient
Institutionalization	0	1	1	(Outcome)

Notes:
* Sufficient means the outcome is observed when the condition is present.
† Necessary means the outcome is never observed in the absence of the condition.

high degree of institutionalization (at Nissera UK and the Rover–Honda collaboration) are the 'high emphasis on expatriate managers', 'hands-on training', 'emphasis on diffusing both structural and processual practices', 'high emphasis on training', and 'long-term financial orientation'. Location on a 'greenfield site' and in a 'service-dominated area' are not necessary conditions. As the 'national institutional gap' is present when the outcome is absent, this is also not a necessary condition. The same type of outcome should occur in the absence of that independent variable (Goertz 2006). This causal configuration indicates the existence of only one path to 'high degree of institutionalization'. In other words, a high degree of institutionalization of Japanese work systems is a product of high membership in the set of firms with a high emphasis on expatriate managers, hands-on training, emphasis on diffusing both structural and processual practices, high emphasis on training, and long-term financial orientation (see Table 20.5).

The conditions that are sufficient for high degree of institutionalization – that is, are present when the outcome always occurs but do not necessarily always lead to the outcome – are the 'location site', 'emphasis on expatriate managers', 'nature of training', 'nature of diffused practices', 'emphasis on training' and 'financial orientation'. As Table 20.5 shows, 'location site' is a condition that does not necessarily always lead to high degree of institutionalization.

The analysis demonstrates that if we were to examine the national institutional context of diffusion in the absence of the enactment process, as a number of comparative institutionalists have done (for example, Lane 1996; Djelic 1998; Whitley 1999),[9] then we could argue that the diffusion of Japanese practices to the UK is an isomorphic process. However, when we also consider lower levels of analysis, such as organizational initiatives, then we arrive at a more comprehensive understanding of how agency at the firm level can shape the institutionalization of practices. By the same token, if we were to focus on the local institutional characteristics alone, then we could simply argue that greenfield firms are better able than brownfield firms to impose their practices on local labour market conditions, as a number of scholars in the Japanization literature have argued (for example, Danford 1998; Elger and Smith 1998). Similarly, the organizational context alone would lead to the conclusion that there are barriers to institutionalizing new practices where there is, for instance, limited investment in training. However, comparing cases as wholes, as ordered and meaningful combinations of parts, in conjunction with searching for competing explanations based on a theory-testing logic, enables us to take into account the impact of national and local institutional influences on the institutionalization of new practices in combination with that of organizational features for a closer understanding of the realities of cross-national diffusion of knowledge.

CHALLENGES OF APPLYING CHA

One of the appeals of CHA is the control it offers in comparing cases. It enables researchers to make use of experimental logic to draw causal inferences as long as the cases are comparable. However, such control may be difficult to achieve in practice. It is challenging to find cases that resemble each other in a sufficient number of features, which may lead to an inadequate number of cases of various phenomena of interest. One way of addressing this 'imperfection' in controlled comparison is to combine comparative methods with 'process-tracing' (whereby intervening variables in a causal process can be identified through a detailed narrative), hypotheses, analytic explanation, or more general explanation (see George and Bennett 2005). By the same token, more often than not, cases cannot be categorized a priori. Outcomes become apparent during data collection. In such instances, including the study reported here, cases can be selected on the basis of theoretically justified causal conditions rather than the outcome. As the outcome is revealed, more negative and positive cases can be added to the sample. This is particularly encouraged in contexts where the same values on independent variables exhibit different values on the outcome variable. Instead of ignoring such contradictory cases in a mechanical application of CHA, the researcher should explore them closely to identify omitted variables (Ragin 1987). Eight strategies – ranging from probabilistic to the combination of various approaches – are identified to address this issue (see Yamasaki and Rihoux 2009).

CONCLUSION

Cross-national case studies, more often than not, use interpretative analysis at the expense of controlled examinations of cases or systematic causal analysis (for example, Ruta 2005; Barger 2007). Cheng (2007) refers to this as the descriptive nature of international management studies that lack a more analytical approach to investigating economic, legal, political and cultural systems on organizational practices. By means of filling in this gap, this paper proposes the use of CHA in international management, in particular the cross-national diffusion of practices. Although the method has its limitations, such as the complication arising from an increase in the number of cases to analyse, its contributions far outweigh its limitations. First, cases are investigated as wholes in which combinations of conditions (possibly at various levels of analysis) are compared to address causal connections among diverse experiences of organizations operating in different nations. In other words, there is an orientation towards examining historically embedded cases comprehensively. Second, the constraints of quantitative analysis do not apply, in the sense that the investigator does not assume that all the cases are drawn from the same population, and the operationalization of conditions is exactly the same across the cases. This encourages a regular dialogue between theoretical ideas and empirical data. At the same time, control is exercised over the examination of cases that can directly result in empirical generalizations while the intensiveness of data is retained.

Controlled CHA can provide both a deeper understanding of particular cases, highlighting distinctive features of particular systems, and leverage for generalization. It also addresses the weaknesses in the mainstream IM literature in the handling of history and agency, the origins of which lie in the discipline's commonly accepted methodologies and epistemological roots (Redding 2005; Cheng 2007). CHA provides a way to build more comprehensive explanations, grounded in socio-economics, in which historical interpretation can be combined with an analysis of large number of cases to enhance understanding at several levels.

NOTES

1. The use of the term 'historical' is understood here as the historically shaped national systems of industrial production or structural frameworks, that is, physical, ownership, organizational and governance structures, that influence practices of firms in a particular country. Whitley (1999) refers to these as different varieties of capitalism that have developed over the course of the twentieth century, or the dominant ways through which organizational routines, hierarchies and institutionalized expectations coordinate economic decisions and actors in various market economies.
2. 'False positives' refer to the attribution of causal significance to the conditions that seem to be associated with the variance in outcome in the first two cases when, in fact, these conditions may not be present in other cases with the same outcome (George and Bennett 2005).
3. A direct method may include the calibration of, for instance, 'high unemployment' as a 3-year moving average. Double-digit figures may correspond to full membership in the set and a full non-membership may be below 4 per cent. The double-digit and 4 per cent figures can be based on general media reporting of what is considered as high and low unemployment (see Avdagic 2010).
4. So far, in almost all CHA applications, cases and outcomes are situated at the macro or meso levels such as policy fields, collective actors, organizations, and country or regional characteristics. Only a few investigators have applied CHA to micro-level data despite the potential to do so (Rihoux et al. 2009). There is a need to broaden the range of CHA applications to incorporate micro-level analysis.
5. At the Rover–Honda collaboration site, this period covered 1978 to 1989, that is, the year of establishment to the completion of the R8/YY project on which the field study focused.
6. This process refers to quality circles adopted by engineers to solve problems at the end of each build phase.
7. CHA may be criticized for reducing data to binary values. Ragin (2008), within the QCA method, has addressed this concern by introducing the fuzzy set logic to measuring attributes in comparative method. These sets grant a certain degree of uncertainty for the variables where categories in between 1s and 0s can be incorporated into the analysis.
8. The lower-case letter denotes the absence of a condition.
9. A number of neo-institutionalists outside the 'varieties of capitalism' camp have emphasized the need to investigate the role of interest and agency in the enactment of institutional logic (for example, Johnson et al. 2000; Dacin et al. 2002).

REFERENCES

Amenta, E. and J.D. Poulsen (1996), 'Social politics in context: the institutional politics theory and social spending at the end of the new deal', *Social Forces*, **75** (1), 33–60.

Avdagic, S. (2010), 'When are concerted reforms feasible? Explaining the emergence of social pacts in Western Europe', *Comparative Political Studies*, **43** (5), 628–57.

Barger, B.B. (2007), 'Culture an overused term and international joint ventures: a review of the literature and a case study', *Journal of Organizational Culture, Communication, and Conflict*, **11** (2), 1–14.

Berg-Schlosser, D. (1998), 'Conditions of authoritarianism, fascism and democracy in inter-war Europe: a cross-sectional and longitudinal analysis', *International Journal of Comparative Sociology*, **39** (4), 335–77.

Berg-Schlosser, D., G. De Meur, B. Rihoux and C. Ragin (2009), 'Qualitative comparative analysis (QCA) as an approach', in Rihoux and Ragin (eds), pp. 1–18.

Cheng, J.L.C. (2007), 'Critical issues in international management research: an agenda for future advancement', *European Journal of International Management*, **1** (1/2), 23–38.

Child, J. (2000), 'Theorizing about organization cross-nationally', in J.L.C. Cheng and R.B. Peterson (eds), *Advances in International Comparative Management*, **13**, Stanford, CA: JAI Press, pp. 27–76.

Collier, R.B. (1999), *Paths toward Democracy: The Working Class and Elites in Western Europe and South America*, New York: Cambridge University Press.

Collier, R.B. and D. Collier (1991), *Shaping the Political Arena: Critical Junctures, Labour Movement and Regime Dynamics in Latin America*, Princeton, NJ: Princeton University Press.

Cress, D. and D. Snow (2000), 'The outcome of homeless mobilization: the influence of organization, disruption, political mediation, and framing', *American Journal of Sociology*, **105** (4), 1063–104.

Crouch, C. and M. Keune (2005), 'Changing dominant practice: making use of institutional diversity in Hungary and the United Kingdom', in W. Streeck and K. Thelen (eds), *Beyond Continuity: Institutional Change in Advanced Political Economies*, Oxford: Oxford University Press, pp. 83–102.

Dacin, M. Tina, J. Goodstein and W.R. Scott (2002), 'Institutional theory and institutional change: introduction to the special research forum', *Academy of Management Journal*, **45** (1), 45–57.

Danford, A. (1998), 'Work organization inside Japanese firms in South Wales: a break from Taylorism', in P. Thompson and C. Warhurst (eds), *Workplaces of the Future*, Basingstoke: Macmillan Business Press, pp. 40–64.

Dirks, D., M. Hemmer, J. Legewie, H. Meyer-Ohle and F. Waldenberger (2000), 'The Japanese employment system in transition', *International Business Review*, **9** (5), 525–53.

Dixon, M., V.J. Roscigno and R. Hodson (2004), 'Unions, solidarity, and striking', *Social Forces*, **83** (1), 3–33.

Djelic, M.-L. (1998), *Exporting the American Model: The Post-war Transformation of European Business*, Oxford: Oxford University Press.

Djelic, M.-L. and S. Quack (2003), *Globalization and Institutions: Redefining the Rules of the Economic Game*, Cheltenham, UK and Northampton, MA, USA: Edward Elgar.

Dore, R. and M. Sako (1997), *How the Japanese Learn to Work*, London: Routledge.

Eisenhardt, K.M. (1989), 'Building theories from case study research', *Academy of Management Review*, **14** (4), 532–50.

Elger, T. and C. Smith (1998), 'New town, new capital, new workplace? The employment relations of Japanese inward investors in a West Midlands new town', *Economy and Society*, **27** (4), 523–53.

Esping-Andersen, G. (1990), *The Three Worlds of Welfare Capitalism*, Princeton, NJ: Princeton University Press.

George, A.L. and A. Bennett (2005), *Case Studies and Theory Development in the Social Science*, Cambridge, MA: MIT Press.

Goertz, G. (2006), 'Assessing the trivialness, relevance, and relative importance of necessary or sufficient conditions in social science', *Studies in Comparative International Development*, **41** (2), 88–109.

Goldthorpe, J.H. (1997), 'Current issues in comparative macrosociology: a debate on methodological issues', *Comparative Social Research*, **16**, 1–26.

Huber, E. and J.D. Stephens (2001), *Development and the Crisis of the Welfare State: Parties and Policies in Global Markets*, Chicago, IL: University of Chicago Press.

Invest in Britain Bureau (1995), *Japanese Manufacturing Companies in the UK*, London: Department of Trade and Industry.

Jackson, G. and R. Deeg (2008), 'Comparing capitalisms: understanding institutional diversity and its implications for international business', *Journal of International Business Studies*, **39** (4), 540–61.

Johnson, G., S. Smith and B. Codling (2000), 'Microprocesses of institutional change in the context of privatization', *Academy of Management Review*, **25** (3), 572–80.

Jones, G. and T. Khanna (2006), 'Bringing history (back) into international business', *Journal of International Business Studies*, **37** (4), 453–68.

Jonoski, T. and A.M. Hicks (1994), *The Comparative Political Economy of the Welfare State*, Cambridge: Cambridge University Press.

Kogut, B. and C. Ragin (2006), 'Exploring complexity when diversity is limited: institutional complementarity in theories of rule of law and national systems revisited', *European Management Review*, **3** (1), 44–59.

Lane, C. (1996), 'The social constitution of supplier relations in Britain and Germany: an institutionalist analysis', in R. Whitley and P.H. Kristensen (eds), *The Changing European Firm: Limits to Convergence*, London: Routledge, pp. 271–304.

Lillrank, P. (1995), 'The transfer of management innovations from Japan', *Organization Studies*, **16** (6), 971–89.

Mahoney, J. (2004), 'Comparative-historical methodology', *Annual Review of Sociology*, **30**, 81–101.

Marx, A. (2006), 'Towards more robust model specification in QCA: results from a methodological experiment', working paper WP2006-43, www.compasss.org.

McMillan, C.J. (1996), *The Japanese Industrial System*, 3rd edn, Berlin: Walter de Gruyter.

Miles, M. and A.M. Huberman (1984), *Qualitative Data Analysis*, Beverly Hills, CA: Sage.

Mill, J.S. (1843 [1967]), *A System of Logic Ratiocinative and Inductive: Being a Connected View of the Principles of Evidence and the Methods of Scientific Investigation*, Toronto: University of Toronto Press.

Morris, J., J. Hassard and L. McCann (2008), 'The resilience of "institutionalized capitalism": managing managers under "shareholder capitalism" and "managerial capitalism"', *Human Relations*, **61**, 687–710.

Öz, Ö. (2004), 'Using boolean- and fuzzy-logic-based methods to analyze multiple case study evidence in management research', *Journal of Management Inquiry*, **13** (2), 166–79.

Ragin, C.C. (1987), *The Comparative Method: Moving Beyond Qualitative and Quantitative Strategies*, Berkeley, CA: University of California Press.

Ragin, C.C. (2005), 'Core versus tangential assumptions in comparative research', *Studies in Comparative International Development*, **40** (1), 33–8.

Ragin, C.C. (2008), *Redesigning Social Inquiry: Fuzzy Sets and Beyond*, Chicago, IL: University of Chicago Press.

Redding, G. (2005), 'The thick description and comparison of societal systems of capitalism', *Journal of International Business Studies*, **36** (2), 123–55.

Rihoux, B. (2003), 'Bridging the gap between the qualitative and quantitative worlds? A retrospective and prospective view on qualitative comparative analysis', *Field Methods*, **15** (4), 351–65.

Rihoux, B. and C.C. Ragin (eds) (2009), *Configurational Comparative Methods: Qualitative Comparative Analysis (QCA) and Related Techniques*, Thousand Oaks, CA: Sage.

Rihoux, B., C.C. Ragin, S. Yamasaki and D. Bol (2009), 'Conclusions: the way(s) ahead', in Rihoux and Ragin (eds), pp. 167–77.

Rueschemeyer, D., E.H. Stephens and J.D. Stephens (1992), *Capitalist Development and Democracy*, Cambridge: Polity.

Ruta, C.D. (2005), 'The application of change management theory to human resource portal implementation in subsidiaries of multinational corporations', *Human Resource Management*, **44** (1), 35–53.

Saka, A. (2003), *Cross-national Appropriation of Work Systems: Japanese Firms in the UK*, Cheltenham, UK and Northampton, MA, USA: Edward Elgar.

Salisbury Economic Development and Tourism Unit (1998), *Information Pack on Socio-economic Facts on Salisbury and South Wiltshire*, Salisbury: Salisbury District Council.

Selznick, P. (1957), *Leadership in Administration: A Sociological Interpretation*, New York: Harper & Row.

Skocpol, T. and M. Somers (1980), 'The uses of comparative history in macrosocial inquiry', *Comparative Studies in Society and History*, **22** (2), 174–97.

Strauss, A. and J. Corbin (1998), *Basics of Qualitative Research: Techniques and Procedures for Developing Grounded Theory*, Thousand Oaks, CA: Sage.

Szulanski, G. (1996), 'Exploring internal stickiness: impediments to the transfer of best practice within the firm', *Strategic Management Journal*, **17** (Winter Special Issue), 27–43.

Varone, F., B. Rihoux and A. Marx (2006), 'A new method for policy evaluation? Longstanding challenges and the possibilities of qualitative comparative analysis (QCA)', in Rihoux and H. Grimm (eds), *Innovative Comparative Methods for Policy Analysis*, New York: Springer, pp. 213–36.

Ventresca, M.J., D. Szyliowicz and M.T. Dacin (2003), 'Innovations in governance: global structuring and the field of public exchange-traded markets', in M.-L. Djelic and S. Quack (eds), *Globalization and Institutions: Redefining the Rules of the Economic Game*, Cheltenham, UK and Northampton, MA, USA: Edward Elgar, pp. 245–77.

Whitley, R. (1999), *Divergent Capitalisms: The Social Structuring and Change of Business Systems*, Oxford: Oxford University Press.

Yamasaki, S. (2003), 'Testing hypotheses with QCA: application to the nuclear phase-out policy in 9 OECD countries', paper presented at the European Consortium for Political Research (ECPR) General Conference, Marburg, Germany, 18–21 September.

Yamasaki, S. and B. Rihoux (2009), 'A commented review of applications', in Rihoux and Ragin (eds), pp. 123–45.

Yin, R.K. (2009), *Case Study Research: Design and Methods*, 4th edn, Thousand Oaks, CA: Sage.

PART V

Taking account of diverse contexts

21. Fleas on the backs of elephants: researching the multinational company

**Tony Edwards, Phil Almond and
Trevor Colling***

INTRODUCTION

Multinational companies (MNCs) are key players in the process of globalization. The United Nations estimates that there are close to 800,000 subsidiaries in the world belonging to MNCs which collectively are valued at close to US$12 trillion. The geographical spread of the investments made by MNCs has increased in recent years, with developing nations accounting for a growing proportion of the total (United Nations 2007). The growing size and spread of MNCs are factors in the growing recognition in the research community that we need innovative ways of shedding light on how such companies operate – and therein lies the very substantial challenge. So vast are many of these companies, and so multidimensional, that the experience is akin to that of a flea on the back of an elephant: even if you know what you are dealing with, it is difficult to see the whole picture, to keep track of its limbs or even its direction of travel. One way of carrying out such research is to establish an internationally coordinated project consisting of partners in multiple countries. Yet, the literature provides only a few examples of case studies that examine several research sites of the same firm in this way. This can be attributed to the challenges involved in such research, particularly the access and resources required. Nevertheless, the benefits of research of this nature are considerable.

In this chapter we address three particular issues concerning case studies of MNCs using multiple research sites. First, if the elephant has many different parts, how should the fleas be arranged around it? Or in other words, how can international research teams be organized when researching MNCs? We contrast approaches based on a controlling centre in which one part of the team obtains and distributes the funding and devises the research instrument, with those based on a federal approach in which the national research teams obtain their own resources and the research instrument is arrived at collaboratively. Second, once the organization of the research team is established, then consideration needs to be given to whom to interview and how to interpret what they say. In particular, we consider the challenges that are presented in attempting to address differences of interest between groups of actors in MNCs and how conducting case studies of MNCs can be sensitive to the specific issue of the multiple roles and identities that actors possess. Third, if managers are the conventional respondents in research on MNCs, what value is there in incorporating employee perspectives? Studying the work and orientation of employees may be akin to studying the detailed workings of each limb or organ on the elephant as opposed to simply glancing at each one, and doing so may generate an enhanced understanding of the entirety of the object in question. Accordingly, we investigate what interviews with non-managerial employees can tell us that those with managers or other senior actors alone cannot.

Throughout the chapter we make use of our experiences on a large project examining US-based MNCs in Europe (Almond and Ferner 2006). This project comprised four national teams – in Germany, Ireland, Spain and the UK – and focused on the ways that US MNCs manage their international workforces and the extent to which this reflects their American roots. The primary research tool in this project was interviews with a range of respondents and the project involved research in the same companies across borders. In one case this led to research being conducted in all four countries, the European HQ (which was in a different country) and the global HQ in the US. In other companies research was conducted in some but not all of the countries, either because access could not be secured or because the firms did not operate in all countries. In five of the case studies we were able to interview a range of employees in addition to managers and we refer to these as the core case studies (for details, see Almond and Ferner 2006). The wider project involved around 15 researchers working in concert over more than three years and we focus in this chapter mainly on our experiences as the 'British fleas'.

Our reflections on this project are supplemented with reference to the literature, particularly those studies that have attempted to shed light on the issue of employment relations in MNCs through fieldwork in multiple countries. We begin with some observations concerning the challenges in making comparisons within MNCs and proceed to tackle the issues of organizing multicountry studies, choice of respondents and the value in interviewing employees who are involved in shop-floor production work or service activities rather than just managers.

COMPARING THE INCOMPARABLE: THE NEVER-ENDING CHALLENGE OF COMPARATIVE RESEARCH

Perhaps the major challenge in comparative research, aside from its logistical and organizational difficulties, is separating out what it is that one is trying to compare, and what one is trying to hold constant in order to make sure that one is looking at the same thing in two or more countries. In organizational research, the simplest route is to compare organizations with similar task contingencies (size, technology, products and so on), as well as contingencies less closely related to the task itself (for example, nature of ownership and governance). Taking its prompt from contingency theory (see Hickson et al. 1971), which posits that firm structure and organization is shaped by such factors, early systematic comparative research such as the seminal 'societal effects' research programme (Maurice et al. 1986) sought to compare 'matched plants' in different societies in order to perceive how the social setting of business operations shaped how tasks were performed and how organizational actors perceived their identities and interests. In simple terms, one should compare a British petro-chemical plant employing 1,500 people using given technologies with, say, a French plant of similar characteristics. Differences in such issues as the organization of work teams, the relations among managers, supervisors and workers, the wage gaps between different groups of employees, and industrial relations were then put down to a 'societal effect', which frequently required recourse to the national socio-economic structure of capitalism and industrialization in order to be explained.

While this research programme yielded vital insights into cross-national differences in organization, holding contingencies constant is a less simple business than it might initially appear. Two examples illustrate this point. First, if we examine large-scale food retailers on either side of the English Channel, a British hypermarket might have a small delicatessen, a small butcher's stall, sometimes a small bakery, more rarely a fishmonger. These, though, employ a very much smaller proportion of the store's turnover, and workforce, than would be the case in a typical hypermarket in France or Spain, and the variety of products available is much less. This means that the aggregate task environment, in a store of the same size of chains competing in similar segments of the market, is different. How does the comparative organizational researcher deal with this? Do we try to find a French store that looks like a British store, even though, if we found one, it would probably be in a much lower position in terms of market segment, in order to permit an analysis based on matched establishments? Or should we attempt to match on the basis of market positioning, which will inevitably mean, in this case, that the task environments, even for relatively simple operations such as hypermarkets, will be non-identical? In the second case, we are implicitly recognizing that societal effects (the social structure of taste, the availability of craft skills and so on) intervene not only during, but prior to, the task environment itself.

The second example comes from the automobile industry, much researched in the field of human resource (HR) management. If an attempt at matching required, say, a comparison of mass market car factories that were not operations of foreign MNCs, within Europe a comparison could be made between Germany, France and Italy, but other large EU countries such as the UK and Spain lack such plants; both the last two have a substantial auto industry, but all the major plants are foreign owned (for reasons which themselves are related to the social organization of car production in these countries, as well as the history of national industrial policy). If we want to compare 'matched' British and French car plants, then, we immediately run into a problem. Either we ignore the national ownership of plants and assume the organizational environment of car production in Britain is 'British' even if the plant is German or Japanese owned, an option which is highly problematic, or we hold constant foreign ownership (for example, compare Toyota's British and French manufacturing operations). The latter is clearly of interest to students of international management, but once again illustrates the point that 'matching' plants or organizations across countries is fraught with difficulties.

This general problem of internationally comparative organizational research does not disappear when we look at the operations of individual MNCs; in fact, the problem is often worse. Again, while ideally we might want to look at how a given MNC does similar things in different host environments, as noted above an increasing number of MNCs have increased the extent to which national subsidiary operations take on specified roles. While access to local markets is sometimes dependent on local presence (Carrefour obviously needs to have hypermarkets in Spain in order to compete in the Spanish market), such replication of operations across countries, at least within trade blocs such as the EU, is becoming rather rarer than in the past. As trade barriers have diminished, MNCs have increasingly located particular operations in the most appropriate location. Quite aside from the movement of many operations to lower-cost countries in Eastern Europe and Asia, societal institutionalist theory (Whitley 1999; Hall and Soskice 2001) implies that different types of operations should be sited in different countries, because of the possibilities offered by different social systems of production. So, for example, organizations might locate high-end engineering facilities in a country such as Germany, where the workforce and collaborative infrastructure required is relatively readily available, but are unlikely to site customer service centres or relatively deskilled manufacturing operations in such countries. One of the companies involved in our own case study work (Almond and Ferner 2006), for example, partially ran information technology (IT) outsourcing operations for Denmark from the UK, because of restrictive regulations on night working in the former country.

Such differences in what MNCs' subsidiaries actually do in different countries can be a problem, a finding, or both, depending on the nature of research questions and how the research is configured. A research project examining the productive system of a given MNC, without specifying in advance the country operations to be examined, could, in principle, have these differences as its research problem. However, our own experience suggests that tracking the value chain of a given MNC of any size or complexity across the globe would be an extremely complicated business, and for a variety of reasons would run into enormous organizational and intellectual difficulties if the question of how international management relates to home- and host-country embeddedness were a significant part of the research problem. More commonly, international management research either treats the nature of host country operations very superficially, or, somewhat more satisfactorily, looks in detail at operations in one or more host countries which are specified in advance.

Our own research took the latter approach, examining the organization of human resources in US-owned MNCs in Germany, Ireland, Spain and the UK. This, though, meant that 'matching' was in most cases difficult or impossible. Despite the fact that our research focused mainly on very large MNCs, most did not replicate organizationally significant operations across each of these four countries. Of the manufacturing-based MNCs, none had significant operations in all four countries. Even very large firms such as 'ITco' (Almond et al. 2005), which combined a declining manufacturing business with software and IT services to businesses, had significantly different operations in the different countries examined: the established manufacturing business was still significant in Germany, and to a lesser extent Spain; Ireland combined some newer greenfield manufacturing operations with customer service operations; and the UK operation had moved very strongly into the outsourcing section of the business, as well as being a centre for the coordination of European management. In such a situation, one has to be cautious about comparing, say, the industrial relations policies of one country's manufacturing operations with another country's business outsourcing operations, as the social identity of the organizational members themselves, as well as the structures within which they operate, is likely to be different. This does not mean that nothing can be said about international (HR) management if national operations serve different functions. As we hope our research shows, how actors within MNCs work with, through or against host-country systems and traditions of organization, and how actors in host-country operations accept and/or challenge higher-level strategies and policies, are endemic processes in all MNCs. How researchers might establish projects that are capable of getting at these phenomena is considered in the next section.

CONSTRUCTING AND ORGANIZING THE RESEARCH

In a classic article on the nature of the multinational company published four decades ago, Howard Perlmutter (1969) established three types of MNCs which relate to the assumptions that shape the basic orientation and management style of the company. These can be applied not only to MNCs themselves but also to the research teams that study them; in this section we use Perlmutter's typology to highlight the various ways of organizing research of this sort.

The ethnocentric firm is one in which there is a common approach based on the norms of the country in which the multinational originated. MNCs with this orientation adopt a centralized approach to managing their international operations and key positions in the governance of the firm are filled by nationals of the country of origin. In principle, an ethnocentric style has the advantages of achieving consistency across borders, which is important in serving global customers, and of there being an unambiguous understanding of who is in control. In the context of researching the multinational, an ethnocentric model consists of the research design being developed by one national team with the assumptions that underpin this design reflecting the research norms in that country. Thus the focus and substance of the project reflect the ways of doing things in the country in which the research project was first developed, which govern both what is studied and how it is studied. In implementing the design, an ethnocentric research project can either send members of the team out to the various countries in which fieldwork is to be done or it can reach agreement with individuals or teams in the countries concerned which join the project on terms set by the originator. Rather like the multinational itself, the main advantage of this research design is consistency across borders; a key criterion against which comparative studies are often judged is whether the process of research was sufficiently standardized to mean that like is being compared with like. An ethnocentric research design also ensures that there is no confusion concerning the governance of the project.

A strongly ethnocentric research design is quite common in quantitative studies (see Salmi, Ch. 22 in this volume on this point). With the advent of web-based surveys, it is quite feasible to develop and administer a questionnaire in one country and apply it in others without even visiting the countries concerned. While this may appear to create new opportunities for comparative analysis, it also carries with it the danger that such research will be insensitive to the peculiarities of the various national systems being studied. In qualitative studies, however, a purely ethnocentric approach is less common, arguably because the research process requires a significant local presence; sole reliance on sending members of the original research team will come up against linguistic and cultural barriers and this team may lack the contacts necessary to gain access. There are some studies with an ethnocentric dimension, however. One of the earliest empirical projects examining US MNCs in Europe was carried out by an American academic with the motivation for the project being driven by the assumption that American norms would create hostility to forms of worker representation in their European operations (DeVos 1981).

The polycentric firm is based on devolution of responsibility to national subsidiary companies. This involves a loose federation of national units that are bound together by common ownership but have relatively little to do with one another on operational issues. A polycentric approach has the advantage of local responsiveness in the sense that it allows the company to go with the grain of the system in question. For researching the multinational, a polycentric design takes the form of each set of national researchers raising their own resources and having considerable autonomy to pursue issues of interest in their context. Thus it can comprise a general research question, such as what is distinctive about MNCs, but with each national team encouraged to explore this in ways that they see fit. Thus there will be much variation between countries in the precise focus of the research and in the ways in which the subsidiaries of MNCs are studied. The advantage of such an approach is that issues of great importance in one country that would not be appreciated by an ethnocentric design can emerge during the course of the research and be fully understood. In other words, it allows the researchers to get to grips with the nature of the operations located in a given country and the character of 'host-country' effects within this country.

A pure polycentric approach is rare in comparative research. While the MNC itself may operate quite successfully this way, with national units selling into their respective national markets and providing a financial return to the centre, research projects on MNCs must have a degree of consistency if they are to be able to engage in meaningful comparisons. A strong focus on the national context of the subsidiaries of MNCs is evident in those single-country studies that look at the multinational company from the 'bottom up', as is the case in a range of studies of Japanese MNCs in Britain (for example, Webb and Palmer 1998; Elger and Smith 2005), but these should not be thought of as genuinely polycentric because their focus was on only one country.

The geocentric firm is one in which there is a common approach across the firm but, in contrast to the ethnocentric firm, this emerges from collaboration between different parts of the firm rather than being imposed by managers from one country. Perlmutter (1969) argued that MNCs would only gradually move towards this organizational form, referring to it as the 'tortuous evolution' of the multinational firm, but also stressed that it had the potential to deliver both a degree of consistency across borders and also the ability to make the most of the diversity of practice that the firm has access to in different countries. For research projects, the geocentric approach has some similar advantages to those that may accrue to firms. Most notably, it ensures that a degree of coherence is arrived at across the international team, meaning that similar phenomena are compared across countries. Moreover, the way that this is arrived at through shared knowledge, discussion and compromise leads to the resulting commonalities reflecting the expertise and knowledge of those across the team, rather than simply the perspectives of those at the HQ. The dispersal of distinctive roles across the team also ensures that national teams are able to study some distinct aspect of MNCs in the environment concerned, thereby providing a degree of local responsiveness. Thus a truly geocentric research project has the potential to deliver a strong degree of coherence, the scope for the sharing of knowledge and the tailoring of the research agenda to national specificities.

Arguably, the case for a geocentric research design is strengthened by contemporary developments in the nature of MNCs, as argued in the previous section. A range of sources of evidence point towards the emergence of distinct roles for individual operating units within internationally integrated processes of production or service provision. In some cases this leads to a national operating unit being granted a formal 'mandate' (Birkinshaw 2000) from the HQ to carry out a particular activity. More generally, Dicken (2003) has argued that technological innovations have permitted many MNCs to pursue strategies involving 'complex integration in which different parts of a firm's operations are reconfigured and relocated according to the relative advantages of alternative locations' (p. 248). It is reasonable to argue that an ethnocentric research design is not well placed to appreciate the character of these locational advantages; equally, a polycentric design would not capture the internationally integrated nature of these processes. A geocentric design, on the other hand, is likely to be much more effective in understanding both local specificities and the ways in which MNCs integrate their operations across borders.

There are some multicountry studies of MNCs that have a geocentric element in their research design. One of these is the study of ABB by Bélanger et al. (1999), a key element of which was the dispersal across countries of key roles in the project at a very early stage. This avoided the danger of any one national team dominating the development of the project, yet the agreement on the core issues to be examined ensured a degree of comparability. A second example is Kristensen and Zeitlin's (2005) study of the British multinational APV, which consisted of detailed, longitudinal research in initially the American and Danish, and subsequently the British, operations over a 10-year period. The story of this case is one of fortune in that Kristensen, a Dane, and Zeitlin, an American, discovered that they were each carrying out independent research into the same company in their respective countries and the case study evolved from there. In this sense, the collaboration emerged and there was no controlling centre.

How did these considerations inform the construction of our own study of US MNCs? Our starting point was that it was designed in such a way that the dangers of ethnocentrism could not arise. This was the case for two reasons. The first was that the study was the result of the collaborative effort of four national research teams, each of which took on the responsibility for the fieldwork in its own country, ensuring that the significance of local institutions and practices was appreciated. The second reason was that the international team did not have a US partner that might have assumed a dominant position given the substance of the research, meaning that we could not fall into the trap of seeing US MNCs solely or mainly through American eyes. Rather, the team did the fieldwork in the US through a series of visits during the course of the project. This carried with it the quite different danger of the nature of 'Americanness' not being properly understood. This danger was minimized by the pre-existing research links that many members of the team had with the US and by others spending substantial periods of time based there during the project.

The design also sought to avoid the dangers of each national team going its own way, as would be the case in a polycentric model. The principal way in which we did so was by arriving at a common research design at the beginning of the project which all of the partners signed up to at the outset, which was arrived at after considerable discussion and negotiation. This involved a core set of issues to be covered and a reliance on the semi-structured interview as the primary research tool. Nevertheless, a virtue was made of a degree of decentralized responsibility for carrying out the research. For instance, the core issues covered did not exclude others also featuring where they were of particular interest in one national context, such as how US MNCs deal with works councils in Germany. Moreover, the research design was based on national experts examining the issue of how 'Americanness' was felt in different countries.

The project had a strong geocentric element, of which there were several key aspects. One was that each team raised its own resources and so entered the network from a position of some strength, while each had primary responsibility for its own country and team members were of course experts in that country. Related to this, the absence of a US partner to the research team meant that all of the national teams were in the same position in that they were examining the American system from afar. Thus there was a degree of comparability in the roles of each partner, yet each held expertise of value to the project as a whole. In addition, the coordination that was necessary came through occasional meetings of the whole international team, more frequent bilateral meetings between two partners and some cross-interviewing in which members of different national teams joined together to jointly conduct interviews in those cases where the same firm was studied in different countries.

Despite the advantages of a geocentric research design, there are also major challenges in adopting one. What are the conditions that make a geocentric approach feasible? Essentially there are two main ones. The first is for the international team not to be constructed around a dominating national centre. Funding is one aspect of this; where one team has been awarded a grant which it then allocates to other countries, this inevitably means that the central team calls the shots to a considerable extent. In contrast, a geocentric approach sits more easily with a situation in which each team brings its own resources, or at least its members are co-applicants for a grant, since this allows them to enter the international team from a position of influence. The second condition is that there are mechanisms that bind the international team together, helping to ensure that each national team does not go off in its own direction. Our own experience in this respect was that regular full meetings of the international team need to be scheduled and costed at the outset, while other forms of coordination such as *ad hoc* bilateral meetings and joint interviewing also aid each team to be cognisant of the progress and approach of the others.

RESEARCHING ACTORS, INTERESTS AND IDENTITY IN MNCs: MULTIPLE IDENTITIES, MULTIPLE INTERESTS

Alongside the organizational issues dealt with above, research into MNCs has to deal with the following question: who speaks for (different parts of) the organization, and should consequently be targeted in the research?

While this question is present in all organizational case study research, the questions of scale implicit in our title make it perhaps especially difficult to resolve in the MNC; we argue that this is because of the greater multiplicity of identities that actors within the MNC carry with them. Identities to be considered, as will be shown, are both organizational and extra-organizational in nature. There is no 'one best way' of resolving this question, as the most important levels of research focus depend on the nature of research questions. Within the broad field of labour management, for example, it is arguable that research into the formulation of HR strategies has little need to take systematic account of employee perspectives; however, where it is important to know something about the implementation of those policies data on employee experiences and responses may well become critical. The interest in taking account of the perspectives of (non-managerial) employees is considered in some detail in the next section. For now, the argument is that despite (or perhaps because of) the fact there is no simple answer to the question of 'who speaks for the MNC', careful consideration of it both in initial research design and through the process of research itself are essential to the validity and triangulation of data gathered in case studies within MNCs.

Researching MNCs through the home/host prism carries with it an ontological assumption that the identities of the actors with which one is concerned are at least partly derived from their (national) social system of production. So, US-owned MNCs are likely to do certain things because of their Americanness, Japanese firms because of their embeddedness in the Japanese business system and so on (Whitley 1999), but being 'American' or 'Japanese' abroad is a challenge, because of international differences in normative, cognitive and regulatory environments.

While this problem is sometimes stated in different terms to the above, for example, through the use of the term 'national culture', that actors in different countries within the same MNC have somewhat different identities, is the core assumption without which the entire field of international management loses most of its distinctiveness. The question remains, how do we access these identities in our research? Who, access permitting, should we be talking to? And how do we know that these identities are national cultural–societal?

The first point to make is that actors (individuals within an MNC) do not have one simple identity. We know that we carry with us a number of identities to different extents (for example, gender, class, religion, ethnicity, political beliefs, membership of occupational communities as well as our 'national social' identity), all of which might impact on how we react to given managerial practices. In the MNC, we also need to recognize that our organizational loyalties are complex for reasons to do with organizational structure. Taking the 'matrix' metaphor of organizational design, an organizational member of an MNC may be said to carry a 'matrix identity'. In other words, the interest-affecting identities of, for example, a senior (British) HR manager in the British operations of Ford may include: Ford Inc.; Ford Europe; Ford UK; the division of Ford he/she represents; Ford's global HR function; and Ford's UK HR function, as well as some of the extra-organizational identities referred to above. Of course, firms try to 'manage culture'; our own research showed that practices such as international assignments and access to global internal labour market systems, were, at least for senior managers, influential in the diffusion of 'global' (American) management culture. But this process is rarely absolute; at the most obvious level, it is in the interests of the overwhelming majority of British managers (and, of course, workers) that the British operations of their MNC remain active, even where the corporation might have other ideas.

Matrix identities mean that, if case study researchers want to examine the transfer of managerial practices and policies in MNCs, they have to seek to understand the identities and interests of a wide range of actors. The logic of institutionalist frameworks is that horizontal movement is significant. In other words, if we want to understand how the US business system affects the HR operations of a US firm in Germany, it would be useful not only to elicit information on how respondents with HR roles interpret 'Americanness' and their reaction to it, but also to seek the perspectives of those in roles widely seen as affecting how work and employment are organized outside HR itself. For example, in our research we sought the perspectives of UK finance managers and operations managers. While this is sometimes difficult in terms of access (finance managers may not immediately see the connection between their role and HR), where possible further critical knowledge of the matrix of identities within the subsidiary can be gained.

As well as this 'horizontal' movement across different parts of the multinational there is also a need for 'vertical' movement up or down subsidiary hierarchies. This goes beyond the triangulation of facts (although this too is important, it is often the case that the performance management system, for example, looks 'global' to the national HQ manager but distinctly local to shop-floor supervisors). If we are to assume that all organizational members have at least some agency or ability to strategize (Crozier and Friedberg 1980), then how those in different organizational positions within the subsidiary define (consciously or otherwise) their interests is of prime importance to research. At the very least, this means that research needs to attempt to gain access to organizational members in a wide variety of hierarchical positions. Thus it is to the specific issue of studying non-managerial workers and their representatives to which we turn in the next section.

WHAT ABOUT THE WORKERS? THE ROLE OF STUDYING NON-MANAGERIAL EMPLOYEES IN MNCs

Thus far we have reviewed the operational and ontological challenges faced by researchers seeking to understand the operation of MNCs. Important questions of coordination across national contexts and of sensitivity to different (multiple) identities add to the scale of the research task suggested in our title. What we have not considered so far, however, is the advantages to be gained from going beyond using managers to speak for parts of the multinational and in this section we address the specific issue of worker perspectives and the value of seeking to explore them in multinational contexts. They provide, we argue, important fine-grained data, often casting new light on developing lines of enquiry, and real insights into the lived experience of work in these organizations. In circumstances where the flea-researcher finds it hard to see the elephantine limbs all at once, gathering employee data at least allows access to the bloodstream.

For many active researchers in this area, these arguments will be far from new or original. Debates between broadly quantitative and qualitative approaches have raged between organizational researchers for decades, and there are countless authoritative statements of the importance of building ethnographic understandings of organizational life, drawing in data not just about the incidence of management systems but how work roles are developed and experienced:

> It is to the workplace that one must look to consider what happens in practice: how the structures of law and agreements combine with workers' and managers' own goals to create a workplace regime that governs how work is actually performed. (Edwards et al. 1994, p. 4)

Approaches of this kind are especially necessary when researchers try to identify contextual factors and how they influence behaviour and decision making within complex organizations (Bryman 1992). Beynon (1973), responsible for one of the seminal close-hand studies of work in an MNC, has noted the 'political' character of research in large organizations; their capacity to influence the process and contest the outcomes makes it important to gather a complete picture from a range of actors (Beynon 1988). Researchers from an industrial relations tradition are inherently sensitive to issues of this kind; the idea that organizational events will be driven by contending interests and subject to quite different interpretations is in the marrow of most of us:

> Industrial relations theory starts from an assumption that an enduring conflict of interest exists between workers and employers in employment relationships . . . From this perspective, the key task of industrial relations theory and research is to contribute to an understanding of how conflicting interests can be resolved periodically and how the parties can expand the frontier of joint-problem solving. (Kochan 1998, p. 37)

Arguably, this methodological imperative, to engage with a full range of actors, should be particularly compelling in MNCs, since they are large organizations often wielding significant power over the communities and workers with whom they engage. Certainly, important contributions to the literature have taken account of worker perspectives and those of their representatives, alongside those provided by managers. Our understanding of behaviour within subsidiaries has been informed by rich workplace studies (for example, Bélanger et al. 1999); research into consultation arrangements has drawn on data from employee representatives and non-participant observation (for example, Marginson et al. 2004); and thorough understanding of innovations in work organization has required in-depth understanding of worker experience (for example, Danford 1998; Woywode 2002; Doeringer, et al. 2003).

But the case for approaches of this kind can no longer be presumed; increasingly it has to be stated. In part, of course, there are pragmatic considerations of the kind mentioned above: if your interest in MNCs focuses on areas uninfluenced by employee concerns or experiences, there is little reason to accommodate them in your data gathering. Arguably, this justifies the limited appearance of worker data in the now voluminous literature on expatriate managers, for example. Surely it is simply a management issue and requires only management inputs? The problem, of course, is that in contexts where managers palpably are the most potent and powerful actors, almost every research issue can be constructed in this way.

There has been a strong tendency in recent years for business research to become management research, without any of the paradigmatic assumptions just referred to. Potentially, the recent interest in institutional theory adds to this dynamic. A central concern in research of this kind has been to identify transnational environmental influences on MNCs and their interpretation within the firm. Managers are central to this process and can often provide the central focus for research. Exclusive reliance on management data has provided the foundation for influential analysis of control systems across subsidiaries (Harzing and Sorge 2003) and the connections between employee relations strategies and firm performance (Tüselmann et al. 2007). Revealing and insightful as work of this kind can be, the dangers of simplifying complex and contested processes are obvious. As Kochan notes (1998, p. 38),

> Much organisational theory sees organisations as essentially co-operative systems or takes a top-down managerial perspective in framing research problems. One consequence of this perspective is that it also denies or at best ignores the legitimacy of institutionalised or collective challenges to managerial authority.

Our research was designed as far as possible to avoid pitfalls of this kind. As a minimum, the views of employee representatives were sought in our case studies wherever formal systems of employee participation existed (unionized or not). In a sample of cases, we also developed in-depth interviews with groups of employees. These data provided at least four dimensions to our understanding of the firms; three of them deepened our understanding of key themes in ways we expected or hoped, one of them was unanticipated and often prompted new lines of inquiry.

First, employee data provided invaluable contextual information, extending our understanding of what plants actually did. This was particularly useful in service contexts, where the product or production process was not easily identifiable. Employees in 'ITCo', for example, explained to us precisely the consultancy services they offered to clients, how project teams were constructed, and their experience of management systems in 'virtual environments', where line managers could often be located many miles away. Similarly, employees in 'Eng Servs' were able to explain the interaction of engineering disciplines in project teams and, critically, the use of national engineering standards in international projects. In this way, employee data revealed the practical aspects of how policies were developed and implemented in highly variable contexts.

Second, employee views offered often arresting perspectives on American influences over subsidiaries and important measures of the 'depth' of central controls. There emerged a colourful array of indicators of 'Americanness', from superficial features of the firm to detailed accounts of management style and behaviour. Often our attention was drawn to American flags flying at the front of offices, to corporate mission statements, and to briefing material originating from the US. Occasionally, surface similarities had deeper underlying significance, such as the layout of US and UK subsidiaries connoting transnationally standardized production systems. Employee data often provided important indications of the 'depth' of central controls, measured, for example, in the extent to which performance imperatives were communicated to workforces and understood by them. Cost pressures were ubiquitous and productivity comparisons between plants were made regularly in some UK subsidiaries. One set of employees was able to reflect on the forceful 'hire and fire' approach they had experienced in the handling of a recent bout of redundancies, and contrast it with more conventional approaches experienced in other employment. Another strong indicator perceived by employees was procedural standardization, or 'buzzwords' as it was often termed. Company 'operating systems' were to the fore in several plants, influencing every detail of what individual employees were able to do. Employees transferred from a British company to ITCo, for example, reflected on the impact of centralized computer-driven administrative systems upon their work and sense of identity. Failure to submit a range of routine reports resulted in automated messages to the employee, informing them that they were 'delinquent'. British employees found this feature alien to their experience of work and contrasted it strongly with management style in previous employers:

> They work on threats and absolutes. [Previous employer] is consensus, unless 5,000 people have spoken about it . . . they can't do anything. ITCo just say, 'you're doing that and if you don't you will be reprimanded'. DJ Delinquent! My mate, when we moved in, just said, 'my name is going to be DJ Delinquent!'. Delinquency to me is like a small child. Like, 'you are bad' is better. You are delinquent, you are a small child that doesn't know what they should be doing. Amend your behaviour!

Third, again as expected, employee data often highlighted tensions within management systems and direct contestation of them at the workplace level. For example, overt expression of American management style often met a frosty response, particularly in long-established British subsidiaries. American-style training accompanying the launch of teamworking and diversity programmes was ridiculed and counterproductive effects were reported. Hostility occasionally became more explicit. During the final year of the research, ballots for industrial action were won in manufacturing sites owned by two of our core case studies. In one instance, strikes were averted only after promises to review the role of team leaders within the management structure. Employee experiences of instances like these illustrate precisely the intersections between host- and home-country influences in MNCs.

Finally, and most unexpectedly, employee data often cast new and important light on management data and what might often be construed as management issues, such as control systems. In one case, an automotive manufacturing site had recently reorganized the production line and introduced teamworking. These developments seemed important, in a project looking at host- and home-country influences on employment practice, and we expected employee data to tell us about the development and implementation of the processes.

Many of the employee interviews illuminated and extended aspects of the data we had collected previously from managers, but during one encounter we seemed to run into a brick wall of mutual incomprehension. One former team leader seized the opportunity to tell us about the difficulties his team had experienced with radiator hoses. These were too long for the product they were producing, he complained, and his team had to cut them to size. Since this wasted time and materials, they had logged the problem as part of the continuing improvement process. He demonstrated to us, through reference to the team's logbook, when the issue was raised and the responses received, culminating in a visit to the shop-floor in the corporation's analogous facility in America:

> So we sent somebody over from here and said, 'right, while you're there, have a look'. So they went out to see the gentleman on the shop-floor. Yeah they're having no problem; all they're doing over there is shoving the hoses down, which eliminates 116 mm of hose! Can you see where I'm coming from?

We certainly did not. The significance of the events was evident enough: the trail left by the issue through the team's log was several months long and ended abruptly with a single entry: the words, 'TOTAL SURRENDER' entered in large block capitals and highlighted with purple marker pen. But what exactly did this tell us about our research themes? There were some obvious lessons about the limits to worker autonomy in contexts like these but were his concerns any more than that, a disgruntled employee wanting to settle a score with his managers? His passion obliged us to reflect and probe further. It emerged subsequently that he was highlighting the complexity of change in management systems in these large organizations. The general trend towards subsidiary autonomy, which had permitted the introduction of teamworking by British managers, was an uneven process. Managers had indicated previously the retention of engineering design and control in America for some products; this incident indicated starkly the implications for subsidiary initiatives. Teams in the UK attempting to highlight quality control issues ran up against the priorities of American engineers. Given the costs involved in altering production and parts specifications for UK and US sites, they were reluctant to do so unless the problems were demonstrably affecting production in both sites. Careful explanation by production workers helped us to understand more fully that management control systems are multifaceted; that they can develop in different and contradictory ways; and that innovations in one can be affected by another. Much of this was implicit in our management data, but only discussion with employees brought out explicitly the full force of the points.

CONCLUSION

In this chapter we have made several arguments: that examining the multinational company means that researchers have to grapple with the challenges of 'comparing the incomparable'; that geocentric research designs have many advantages but are difficult to execute in practice; that an approach using key informants has much to commend it but is complicated by the multiple identities that actors possess; and that interviewing employees adds considerable depth to our understanding of the realities of life in multinationals. These challenges are connected, of course; for example, an ethnocentric research design entails assumptions about the possible contribution of the various nodes of the research team, conditioning how flexible the team as a whole is to what is being compared across countries.

We illustrated these arguments with reference to our own experience in a multicountry research project. While this had much strength, it had its limitations too of course. Notably, while the choice of case study firms was governed by a rationale of selecting companies that represented different parts of the American business system, this choice was constrained by considerations of access. We were able to cover firms in a range of sectors, to contrast publicly listed with family-owned firms and to examine both large and small multinationals, but as in any such project we could only research those companies where a knock on the door generated an invitation to enter. Similarly, within each firm we had varying rationales for seeking access to particular sites, but these preferences were not always realized. A second set of limitations relates to the geographical coverage of the companies concerned. The four countries in which we carried out research varied in important respects, particularly in the strength of employee representation and patterns of labour market regulation, but of course our findings are confined to these parts of Europe and do not provide an Asian or African perspective, for example. Given that many of the firms we examined were very large indeed, in some cases operating in more than 50 countries, this is a major consideration in interpreting our findings.

Indeed, the contrast between the size of such MNCs and the limited resources at the disposal of researchers highlights the pertinence of the metaphor of 'fleas on the back of elephants'; as academics trying to understand the workings of multinationals we can only begin to appreciate the nature of the firms we are studying. Coupled with the considerations of comparing the incomparable, the difficulties in adopting a geocentric research design, unravelling multiple identities and of achieving depth of understanding through a multinational, this suggests that a healthy dose of humility in interpreting how such firms operate is an important aspect of good research in this area.

NOTE

* As mentioned in the text, the project involved a large number of people. In the UK, besides the three authors of the chapter, the research team consisted of Anthony Ferner, Peter Butler, Ian Clark, Len Holden and Michael Muller-Camen. The British arm of the project was funded by the Economic and Social Research Council (award number R000238500). In Ireland the team members were David Collings, Paddy Gunnigle and Michael Morley. In Spain the research team consisted of Javier Quintanilla, Lourdes Susaeta and Marta Portillo. Hartmut Waechter, Rene Peters, Anne Tempel and Michael Muller-Camen conducted the research in Germany. We are grateful to all of them.

REFERENCES

Almond, P., T. Edwards, T. Colling, A. Ferner, P. Gunnigle, M. Muller, J. Quintanilla and H. Waechter (2005), 'Unravelling home and host country effects: an investigation of the HR policies of an American multinational in four European countries', *Industrial Relations: A Journal of Economy and Society*, **44** (2), 276–306.

Almond, P. and A. Ferner (2006), *American Multinationals in Europe: Managing Employment Relations Across National Borders*, Oxford: Oxford University Press.

Bélanger, J., C. Berggren, T. Bjorkman and C. Kohler (1999), *Being Local Worldwide: ABB and the Challenge of Global Management*, Ithaca, NY: Cornell University Press.

Beynon, H. (1973), *Working for Ford*, Harmondsworth: Penguin.

Beynon, H. (1988), 'Regulating research: politics and decision-making in industrial organisations', in A. Bryman (ed.), *Doing Research in Organisations*, London: Routledge, pp. 21–33.

Birkinshaw, J. (2000), *Entrepreneurship in the Global Firm: Enterprise and Renewal*, London: Sage.

Bryman, A. (1992), *Research Methods and Organisation Studies*, London: Routledge.

Crozier, M. and D. Friedberg (eds) (1980), *Actors and Systems: The Politics of Collective Action*, Chicago, IL: University of Chicago Press.

Danford, A. (1998), 'Work organisation inside Japanese firms in South Wales: a break from Taylorism?', in P. Thompson and C. Warhurst (eds), *Workplaces of the Future*, London: Macmillan, pp. 25–39.

DeVos, T. (1981), *US Multinationals and Worker Participation in Management: The American Experience in the European Community*, London: Aldwych.

Dicken, P. (2003), *Global Shift: Reshaping the Global Economic Map in the 21st Century*, London: Sage.

Doeringer, P., E. Lorenz and D. Terkla (2003), 'The adoption and diffusion of high performance management: lessons from Japanese multinationals in the West', *Cambridge Journal of Economics*, **27** (2), 265–86.

Edwards, P.K., J. Bélanger and L. Haiven (1994), *Workplace Industrial Relations and the Global Challenge*, Ithaca, NY: ILR Press.

Elger, T. and C. Smith (2005), *Assembling Work*, Oxford: Oxford University Press.

Hall, P. and D. Soskice (eds) (2001), *Varieties of Capitalism: The Institutional Foundations of Comparative Advantage*, Oxford: Oxford University Press.

Harzing, A. and A. Sorge (2003), 'The relative impact of country of origin and universal contingencies on internationalisation strategies and corporate control in multinational companies: worldwide and European perspectives', *Organisation Studies*, **24** (2), 187–214.

Hickson, D., C. Hinings, C. Lee, R. Schneck and J. Pennings (1971), 'A strategic contingencies theory of intraorganizational power', *Administrative Science Quarterly*, **16** (2), 216–29.

Kochan, T. (1998), 'What is distinctive about industrial relations research?', in K. Whitfield and G. Strauss (eds), *Researching the World of Work: Strategies and Methods in Studying Industrial Relations*, Ithaca, NY: Cornell University Press, pp. 31–45.

Kristensen, P. and J. Zeitlin (2005), *Local Players in Global Games: The Strategic Constitution of a Multinational Corporation*, Oxford: Oxford University Press.

Marginson, P., M. Hall, A. Hoffman and T. Muller (2004), 'The impact of European works councils on management decision making in UK and US based multinationals: a case study comparison', *British Journal of Industrial Relations*, **42** (2), 209–233.

Maurice, M., F. Sellier and J. Silvestre (1986), *The Social Foundations of Industrial Power*, Cambridge: Cambridge University Press.

Perlmutter, H. (1969), 'The tortuous evolution of the multinational corporation', *Columbia Journal of World Business*, **4** (1), 9–18.

Tüselmann, H., F. McDonald, A. Heise, M. Allen and S. Voronkova (2007), *Employee Relations in Foreign Owned Subsidiaries*, Basingstoke: Palgrave.

United Nations (2007), *World Investment Report*, New York: United Nations.

Webb, M. and G. Palmer (1998), 'Evading surveillance and making time: an ethnographic view of the Japanese factory floor in Britain', *British Journal of Industrial Relations*, **36** (4), 611–27.

Whitley, R. (1999), *Divergent Capitalisms: The Social Structuring and Change of Business Systems*, Oxford: Oxford University Press.

Woywode, M. (2002), 'Global management concepts and local adaptations: working groups in the French and German car manufacturing industry', *Organization Studies*, **23** (4), 497–524.

22. International research teams and collective case studies: an abductive approach

Asta Salmi

INTRODUCTION

International research collaboration is widely advocated as a way of conducting research in the area of international business. It is often regarded as a 'quick fix' to the problem of accessing local data and contextual knowledge. Yet few scholars discuss their experiences of international teams in conducting case studies or ponder how teamwork is suited to case analysis. But these issues are worth raising, as there are no guidelines for conducting case studies collectively, let alone across borders. The iterative nature of a case study may well contradict the coordination needs of teamwork, meaning that case teams may not make use of all the potential opportunities for cooperation.

The aim of this chapter is to reflect on the implications of having an international team as opposed to a single investigator carry out and analyse a case study. My key argument here is that the diversified resources of an international team ought to be used not only to reach different international contexts, but even more importantly to conduct case *analysis* that is culturally and contextually sensitive. In particular, I shall refer to the 'abductive' approach to case studies. This approach builds on the inevitable interaction of theory and method, and on the back-and-forth character of the research process (Ragin 1992; Van Maanen et al. 2007), thus acknowledging an evolving framework and an evolving case (Dubois and Gadde 2002). This (alternative) view to case studies has been gaining momentum in management studies (Dubois and Gibbert 2010) and presents new challenges for teams conducting case studies in international business too.

The chapter is organized as follows. The next section illustrates how the existing literature on international research collaboration tends to concentrate on quantitative projects and rarely discusses teamwork in case studies. Furthermore, relatively linear research processes are assumed. This perspective is challenged by those case analysts – and the advocates of the abductive approach in particular – who call for more flexible processes. The third section therefore discusses the abductive approach and the potential implications of flexibility and emergence for case analysis in a team. Then, I draw on my own experiences to shed light on the research processes for international collaborative case study projects. The discussion section points to areas that would inform the way collective case studies are conducted in the future. The chapter ends by suggesting that case teams should pay more attention to the role of a common platform for analysis.

PRIOR LITERATURE ON RESEARCH COLLABORATION

Numerous articles discuss how best to conduct research in teams. Most of the discussion assumes a quantitative research project, but nonetheless, these normative and practical accounts provide guidance on how research teams are typically seen to work. The literature so far has paid most attention to issues of team constellation and team processes, but has given little consideration to the analysis phase in the research process.

Turning first to team constellation, the focus has been on how the make-up of the team influences project success (Nason and Pillutla 1998; Segalla 1998; Teagarden 1998). Diversity has attracted a particular interest, and in general, it is suggested that heterogeneity is needed to execute a complicated research task successfully (Nason and Pillutla 1998). In international marketing research, Kumar (2000) suggests the inclusion of researchers from different cultural backgrounds, so that the team as a whole can consider all the different facets of the research problem. Discussions on team constellation usually also cover sources of team diversity other than culture, such as language (Usunier 2011), career, status, communication and commitment of the researchers. Publication policies and reporting are discussed, often in connection with the career stage and thus the motivation and skills of different researchers in the team (Milliman and Von Glinow 1998; Teagarden 1998; Peterson 2001). Scholars have also looked at how institutional background and varying research views influence teamwork. Increasingly, the effect of different research paradigms and cognitive referential systems is pondered, noting the need for open discussion of different paradigms (Milliman and Von Glinow 1998; Sauquet and Jacobs 1998; Turati et al. 1998).

Another stream of the extant literature looks at the processes of team research: modelling the process of cooperation (Teagarden et al. 1995) or suggesting a life-cycle model, which is a relatively linear process of research (Bournois and Chevalier 1998). Furthermore, the literature discusses coordination of research projects (Turati et al. 1998; Geringer and Frayne 2001; Peterson 2001). Often, these papers suggest the need for clear leadership by one or few researchers – 'project champions' – to coordinate the process (Teagarden 1998; Geringer and Frayne 2001). The team leader is also seen as responsible for synthesizing the teamwork (Stake 2005). Kumar (2000), for instance, suggests that the researcher who is familiar with the relevant culture take the lead.

Despite all these insights into the dynamics of international research collaboration, I would argue that two important gaps remain. The first is the lack of attention paid to the analysis phase of the research process. This can be seen in the model of research cooperation outlined by Teagarden et al. (1995), which is widely cited and thus provides a reference point for how the team is usually seen to work. While this model covers different stages of the research endeavour (that is, inputs, interactions and outcomes, with a strong focus on project management), it does not provide much guidance on the analysis phase. Interpretation is basically seen to follow 'reliable and valid data gathering', although the authors note that the process moves back and forth between the different research stages as learning occurs (Teagarden et al. 1995, p. 1281). Furthermore, the diversity of team composition (that is, level of knowledge, skills, characteristics and resources) is seen to affect 'accurate interpretation', but the authors do not discuss how this interpretation is jointly carried out. In general, the writings so far seem to reflect a process in which the analysis takes place towards the end of the joint research project, and is relatively simple to carry out.

The second gap is that methodological texts on research teams largely assume that collaboration concerns a *quantitative* project. Nor is there any guidance on collective studies in the methodological literature on case studies (for exceptions, see Segalla 1998; Easterby-Smith and Malina 1999; Salmi 2010). Rather, methodological texts (implicitly) assume that a single analyst is conducting the case study. The assumption of a sole researcher perhaps stems from the stress placed on deep understanding and interpretation found in the literature on qualitative case studies. A case study is viewed as a 'personal contract [that] is drawn between researcher and phenomenon' (Stake 2005, p. 449). Nevertheless, the input of other researchers is acknowledged in passing. For example, Stake (p. 453) refers to 'teaming' in the context of data gathering for a large case study. Dubois and Gadde (2002, p. 558) note that the evolving case should be made 'a platform for discussions' with other researchers, and Stake (2005, p. 453) suggests that the project champion's case synthesis should be commented upon by team members, informants and 'selected sceptical friends'.

This chapter addresses these gaps and bridges insights from the methodological literature on international collaborative research and qualitative case studies. The next section focuses on the abductive approach and shows how it can be affected by having a team working on (international) case studies. I then turn to three examples of collective case studies from my own research experience.

THE CHALLENGES OF ABDUCTION IN TEAMWORK

Before proceeding any further, one should pause to consider what kind of collective case study is being undertaken. Case researchers have increasingly started to question the positivistic assumption of a linear research process (for example, Dubois and Gibbert 2010; Piekkari et al. 2010). The abductive approach can be seen as an alternative view on case analysis that stresses emergence and flexible processes as strengths of good case studies (Dubois and Gadde 2002; Dubois and Araujo 2007). The approach has attracted recent interest, but has historical roots: Charles Sanders Peirce (cited in Van Maanen et al. 2007) argued in 1903 that discovery rests primarily on abductive reasoning. While the abductive approach has wide-ranging implications for case research generally, authors have not yet addressed the role of teamwork.

Given the different approaches to case studies and to the criteria for good studies (Piekkari et al. 2010), it is important that the research team considers early on what its members mean by a case study. Thus, the team should agree on the general research design and the approach to project dynamics (concerning, for example, redirections and evolving frameworks). For successful collaboration, these choices need to be made explicit. Indeed, Dubois and Araujo (2007, p. 179) note that 'researchers selecting methods without due attention to their implicit assumptions and coherence with theoretical aims risk incoherent conclusions or falling into the trap of brute empiricism'. This chapter is targeted to those research teams that adopt the abductive approach; an issue which to date has received little attention in methodological texts. Accordingly, I now discuss the research processes, case selection and analysis, as well as their implications for teamwork.

Research Process

The abductive approach is based on redirections in the research process. Rather than relying on deduction or induction, the abductive logic stresses going back and forth between theoretical framework, data sources and analysis; in other words, the 'matching' of these three elements (Dubois and Gadde 2002, p. 554). These notions stress emergence in case studies: it is important to let empirical reality interact with conceptual ideas in the analysis, to be open to new issues and to let the case process develop. According to Peirce, abduction is 'a path of critical reasoning in which conjectures follow surprises' (Van Maanen et al. 2007, p. 1149). Therefore, this approach sees flexibility as a key strength in case analysis (Dubois and Araujo 2007). However, this does not mean a directionless study. Dubois and Gadde (2002) note that in the abductive approach neither a loose (for example, Stake 2005) nor a tight (Yin 2009) framework is appropriate. The former brings too little discipline while the latter is too rigid. What they argue is the need for a framework from the start, but this framework should be allowed to further evolve. The evolving framework and the evolving case thus become the cornerstones of a case study.

These aspects of emergence and flexibility pose a challenge to any researcher, but particularly to a research team. On the one hand, a case study should be allowed to evolve in a way that cannot be controlled or prescribed; on the other, some control and coordination of teamwork is needed to ensure feasible cooperation. An international dimension brings further challenges to the balancing act: for example, a multicultural/multinational research team may call for additional coordination efforts, while the challenge of collecting data in contexts not familiar with academic research – such as Eastern Europe (Clark and Michailova 2004) – may require even more flexibility and often additional time.

It may indeed be challenging for a team to make abduction work: it does not suffice merely to bring the (end) results to the common table, but during the process the team should be ready for intensive discussions, remain sensitive to emerging issues and readily adopt changes in the process. The suggestion by Dubois and Gadde (2002, p. 558) to go for a 'tight and evolving' framework for the case study therefore seems to suit teamwork well. If the research is initially guided by a tight framework (that is, well-specified issues of shared interest), there is a better chance of not merely collecting data about the different national contexts and foreign research sites, but of analysing them with a focus. Simultaneously, the evolving case study ensures that the emerging (empirical) observations and (analytical) findings that researchers in different sites achieve are also accounted for. Indeed, if these diverse outcomes of fieldwork are brought together during the analysis phase of the group, the wide knowledge base and diversity of the team may be most fruitfully used.

Case Selection

Case selection is a complex and critical issue in any study. According to Dubois and Araujo (2007, p. 179), it is the most important methodological decision to be made, and yet 'the relevance of a case is not necessarily known prior to the study'. Given the redirections in the case process, 'the task of the analyst is to progressively construct the context and boundaries of the phenomena under investigation, as theory interacts with methodological decisions and empirical observations' (Dubois and Araujo 2007, p. 171). The process of 'casing'; that is, questioning what the case is a case about (Ragin 1992), takes place right until the very end of the study.

Having a team working on the case may affect case selection and 'casing' (Ragin 1992) in several ways. Dubois and Araujo (2004, p. 210) note that: 'The boundary around what constitutes a case evolves in response to both practical contingencies affecting the research process and the dialogue between theory and empirical evidence'. A (multinational) team is bound to affect both the practical contingencies and the dialogue. A particular risk is that team members select cases based on the convenience of their respective nationalities and ease of access, rather than considering other more theoretical criteria, which derive from the emergent understanding of the case. Despite the criticality of case selection, case researchers 'often overlook the justification of why a case was selected and why it deserves the attention of the reader' (Dubois and Araujo 2007, p. 179). For a team it is critical to define the case selection(s), because this also explicates the reasons for the collaborative effort.

Analytical Processes

Most of the potential for team innovation lies in the collective matching process, provided that the different backgrounds and knowledge bases of the team members are allowed to interact. This also applies equally to, for instance, contract researchers who have been used for reaching local contexts during fieldwork (Easterby-Smith and Malina 1999). To provide a deep understanding of complex qualitative data, it is important to bring in all members of the team. Furthermore, in order to use the potential of teams to the full, there must be enough 'scope to compare, challenge and synthesize "insider" and "outsider" perspectives' (Marschan-Piekkari and Welch 2004, p. 13). One needs a reflexive dialogue, which requires 'space in which to exchange expectations, assumptions, and feelings' (Easterby-Smith and Malina 1999, p. 85).

Furthermore, time is required both for reflection and reconsideration of one's opinion, and to change mindsets (Lunnan and Barth 2003).

Heterogeneous teams often struggle with the challenges of coordination and communication, and some members may become frustrated by the long processes involved. One should, however, remember that it is indeed the various perspectives, iterations and rethinking that make collaborative study valuable and its results unique. When working jointly on an emerging case, it seems particularly important to bring the empirical findings into the group discussions early on and not leave teamwork to the end of the case process. The initial stories (Ghauri 2004) collected from the field should be shared within the group, thus putting them immediately under the analytical gaze of several observers. These discussions should be carried out using the empirical language of the field rather than imposing theoretical language too early (Dubois and Gadde 2002). Still, the casing and the theoretical framing of the case study are not necessarily easy: Dubois and Gadde note that interaction with other researchers may even be a source of confusion.

To summarize the implications of abduction and matching in case analysis by an (international) team, there seems to be a particular need for creating a platform for joint reflection. Only then are the diversified resources of a team used not only to reach different contexts, but also – and in particular – to produce an analysis that is contextually and culturally sensitive.

CONTRASTING EXPERIENCES OF COLLECTIVE CASE STUDIES

In this section I draw on my own experiences of participating in case collaborations. Based on these experiences, there are two types of collective case studies: shared and independent (see Edwards et al., Ch. 21 in this volume for a similar discussion). In the former, the team focuses on the same case(s), while in the latter the team adopts a case approach, but the team members conduct their own studies relatively independently. My examples in this section consist of one independent multiple case study and two shared cases. These are summarized in Table 22.1. All examples come from the network tradition of business markets, in which international business relationships are a popular topic and research is often carried out in teams (Salmi 2010). My examples concern cooperation among Nordic researchers in relatively small and homogeneous teams. The working language in collaboration and reporting was English, while the interviewees (managers) were usually addressed in their mother tongue.

Table 22.1 first presents the generic dimensions (team composition, team process) that are addressed in the existing literature, and then the

Table 22.1   Comparing the collective case studies

Project	Networks in transition	M&A in networks	Managing project ending
Type of case study	Independent cases	Shared case	Shared case
Team size (nations represented)	11 (3 FI, 7 SWE, 1 DK)	3 (1 FI, 1 SWE, 1 FI/SWE*)	2 (1 FI, 1 FI/SWE*)
Heterogeneity	Heterogeneous	Homogeneous	Homogeneous
Earlier cooperation	No	Yes	Yes
Time from initial idea to the key output	5 years	5 years	3 years for the joint work (10 years for my colleague)
Team process and coordination	Two team leaders, inner and outer group of team members, some meetings	Self-organizing team, regular meetings & emailing	Self-organizing (micro) team, intensive interactions (phone, email, face to face)
Case selection	Carried out individually (independently) by group members	Carried out jointly within the group	Case available; joint decision to focus on this case for a new purpose
Research design/ process	Initially a tight design, then loosening (as the initial aim for a joint interview guide was abandoned)	Initially a loose design which evolved as the empirical case developed over time	Material and case available, joint decision to focus on certain points and let others 'be silent'
Matching process between theory and data	1. concept: network change & transition 2. empirical cases of foreign market entry under transition 3. new concept: learning 4. more analytical work on the cases and new cases added	1. concept and empirical case developing simultaneously 2. scope extended (from acquisition targets and immediate relations to the larger networks/ network perceptions).	1. concept to show the effects of network changes to managers 2. suitable empirical case available 3. analysis of the case and existing literature (on projects) 4. iterative writing

Table 22.1   (continued)

Project	Networks in transition	M&A in networks	Managing project ending
		Interview targets were added in the process 3. network change/ horizon discussed conceptually and empirically in iterations	5. focus: managerial challenges in ending project management
Analysis by the team	Case narratives presented and commented in the team Case combination and comparison carried out by the project champions	Interview transcripts jointly reflected upon to produce the case study	Sharing the material and discussing the initial case narrative, then joint analysis and iterative writing of the case
Output	A book with 11 cases for analysts and managers	Scientific articles (and conference papers)	A book with one integrated case for managers

Note: * A Finn living in Sweden.

dimensions that are particularly relevant to case research – case selection, process and analysis – which are also an attempt to bring into play the emergent and flexible nature of case research. It should be said that our teams gave little explicit consideration to (the choices of) the research paths to be followed. The discussion in this section is thus based on my *ex post* reflection on what types of processes were present, and to what extent abductive logic was adopted.

My examples all followed different dynamics with regard to the research processes. For the shared cases, several iterations and redirections took place, and the highly integrated teams felt comfortable with intensive interactions. One case study evolved according to the real-time developments around the empirical business case, while the other was analysed (for this purpose) only afterwards, when most data had been collected and analysed by my colleague for the initial case study. For both, raw data were discussed by the group and the reported results were much affected, indeed strengthened in depth and insightfulness, by the iterations and by the teams devoting plenty of time to joint reflections. The independent case example followed a more linear path and even a deductive logic, with an initial aim of achieving a relatively tight framework. Even in this example, new directions were taken in the process, especially with regard to the issues (concepts) that were to be analysed in each of the cases. Thus, emergence was evident in all three studies (discussed in detail later). Abductive logic was used more extensively in the projects with shared cases. Next, I provide a brief overview of each individual project, from their design to the analysis and final output.

Project No. 1: Networks in Transition

This example of a multiple case study (see Table 22.1) concerns a 5-year Nordic project focusing on Eastern European transition and foreign market entry (reported in Törnroos and Nieminen 1999). The initial research group was formed in 1993 in connection with an International Management Development Association conference, and the results of the cooperation were published in a book in 1999. The key rationale for collaboration was the joint interest by several scholars in Denmark, Finland and Sweden in analysing the ongoing transition process and Eastern European countries as potential target markets for Nordic companies. The leading authors, two Finnish researchers, initiated the project and gradually involved others, so that the book has 11 contributors in total. Nine empirical case studies are presented, and in addition, six chapters discuss the concepts of networks and learning, present the transitional business context, describe the methods and summarize the analysis with a case comparison. This project group was relatively large and involved researchers in different career stages (professors, postdoctoral researchers and doctoral students).

Research design and process
In the initiation phase, the group met in different constellations and discussions revolved around the issue of how to apply the (industrial) network approach to the analysis of transition and foreign market entry. Later, the issue of learning was emphasized, showing that some abduction – redirecting the theoretical focus from networks – took place. We decided that each case study would investigate two key issues: business relationships and learning. The researchers were given a free hand in case selection; some used material they had already collected, while others conducted new case studies for this project.

The project initiators invited scholars whom they knew to have similar research interests and/or who had already worked with some companies (cases) to analyse the transition process. In the early stages of cooperation, there was some integration of the group and joint reflection about the focus of the study. The idea was to conduct case studies for comparison, and for about a year discussions centred on developing interview questions for the project. However, while some scholars worked intensively on the issues listed, not all members were keen on forcing their research into this formula, and the original idea of a common interview guide for all data collection was abandoned. The group had grown and become heterogeneous, and the members had very different case data to hand. The draft interview guide still provided the basis for analysis in some, but not in all, of the cases (Søderberg and Vaara 2003 also report deviation from an interview guide). Accordingly, in their data collection, some of the researchers took the liberty to deviate from the guide as this was seen as necessary and rewarding for conducting successful interviews. These examples show how skilful researchers may adapt to different situations and still contribute towards the common goal in a joint study. Indeed, adaptations are needed in research interviews (Wilkinson and Young 2004), and particularly in international business, where interviewees in different contexts may need special treatment.

Analysis and output
The nature of our cooperation changed over time: the initial phase involved a smaller, inner group and was characterized by enthusiasm and intensive discussions. This was followed by less frequent meetings, the gradual dispersion of the original team and the introduction of some new members. Some of the individual case reports were developed during the process and show the influence of the (initial) teamwork, while those added in a later phase remained somewhat as outliers from the original idea. Nevertheless, the group ended with concrete results thanks to the project champions, without whom the project would have been 'one among many other international projects that are discussed but never achieved' (Håkansson 1982, p. 37).

This project involved researchers who were all alert to the transition process and, thanks to the diversity of the team, our discussions were intensive and provided new insights into transition developments. While the individual cases (and the theoretical chapter drafts) were presented to the group and briefly commented upon, the analysis was not carried out jointly. No background information (for example, interview transcripts) was shared, as we discussed only the key outcomes that individual researcher(s) had reached. We thus discussed our results solely at the general level of learning in networks in transition. Therefore, the case comparison also plays a minor role in the book and the key contribution is provided by the independent cases.

Our motivations to join the cooperation were different, but we all targeted the book as the key goal and outlet of the independent case studies. The aim was to provide a timely analysis of the (then new) phenomenon of the transition process and of the experiences of different companies entering the Eastern European market. Personally, I was actively involved in the project almost from the beginning, participating in the discussions and also in the development of the joint interview guide. I produced one (novel) case study for the book (Salmi 1999), but did not participate in the final comparison of the cases. The two project champions took an active role in the publication process, and were responsible for the summarizing analysis and case comparison, thus synthesizing the project.

Project No. 2: M&A in Networks

This case analysis (reported in Anderson et al. 2001; Salmi et al. 2001) is an offshoot of a larger research project, begun in 1995, examining networks in the Nordic graphics industry. Here we focused on the effects of an international acquisition on a network over a period of five years (see Table 22.1).

Research design and process

Research cooperation in our team had started among peers – initially doctoral students, then academics in their early career – all investigating business networks. Having a common interest in the dynamics of networks (Halinen et al. 1999), we decided to add empirical cooperation to our joint conceptual work. The case approach was a natural choice, because we had all conducted prior case research and felt it was needed to understand the holism prevailing in networks.

In the course of discussing the general topic of dynamics at one meeting, the idea of looking at M&As (mergers and acquisitions) as causing potential disruptions in network relationships emerged. One researcher raised the issue of M&As, while another was familiar with a Swedish company that had been going through several M&As. Shortly afterwards, a Finnish company announced an acquisition that would also affect the Swedish company. Being alerted to the conceptual issue (M&As' effect on network dynamics), our Finnish–Swedish team seized the opportunity to follow real-time developments around the M&As of a number of companies in the international (Nordic) context. Thus, we soon set out working on a shared case study. We adopted a longitudinal approach and conducted interviews in Finland, Sweden and Norway during 1998–2001. In total, 13 managers from seven companies were interviewed.

Analysis and output

As the case analysis was conducted over time, we could follow and reflect on the dynamics in real time, as well as make iterations in our research design. In particular, when following the developments, we used a snowballing technique in approaching new, connected companies. The key informants were approached four times over the years, adding up to 18 interviews in total. In this way, we were able to deepen and question the initial findings from the interviews. With regard to analysis, the cooperation and discussions within the group were intensive: we brought to meetings several viewpoints and local understanding for the group to reflect upon. We shared the interview transcripts and notes; everyone could understand the English and Swedish material, while the contents of the Finnish material were given more time during discussions in order to transfer the meanings to the whole group (see also Welch and Piekkari 2006).

Our research setting allowed us to look at relationship developments over time. We started with a focus on the immediate effects of the acquisition and on the managerially intended results of the deal, but the case developments led us to understand the spread of change in an international network more extensively and also to see the unanticipated effects. An important emergent finding of our case study therefore was to show how difficult it is for individual network members to see the more distant parts of the network and to perceive developments other than in the direct relationships. Accordingly, in the process of casing (Ragin 1992), we took a broader view of the network, by way of posing new research questions and involving more interviewees.

It was essential for our study that we obtained information from different contexts and network actors. We needed good access over time, but also the time and space in group meetings to develop our understanding of the case. Many factors contributed to the success of the case analysis: first, the team was relatively small (comprising three, and two more in the related projects); second, the members knew each other well and shared a similar status, which led to open discussions about the case; and third, we had access to different sites and could address the respondents in their own language. We were also active in writing (for example, conference papers) in different constellations, thus building up understanding of the case from different angles. The key outputs of the project were journal articles. A new challenge emerged towards the end of the project; as the team members all took up other responsibilities, it became increasingly difficult to find time for this project. Consequently, our plans to compile a book on the topic of 'M&As in Networks', for which other researchers had been invited and additional cases were to be included, did not materialize.

Project No. 3: Managing Project Ending

As a follow-up to the previous case, we continued Finnish–Swedish cooperation and aimed, in particular, to turn our academic understanding of network dynamics into managerial lessons (Table 22.1). My colleague Virpi Havila (a Finn living in Sweden, see Table 22.1) had collected rich material for a case on the termination of production of commercial aircraft in Sweden. This was an 'ending' project successfully carried out by a Swedish company, Saab Aircraft AB, and to us the case material illustrated a success story of how a company can handle a challenging situation by renegotiating contracts with its suppliers. We decided to use these data to discuss the network context of ending projects, together with the consequent implications for project management, and to write a managerial book on project ending (Havila and Salmi 2009). My interest in the project was based on my work on network dynamics, as well as earlier learnings from project managers.

Research design and process

This case analysis was conducted in a micro team, a dyad of two researchers, but had its background in our joint experiences of working in the M&A team. The decision to initiate the project was based on the availability of case material that could be used to illustrate a managerial point that we felt had been neglected in earlier project management literature: the challenges found in project ending. Given our existing, rich empirical data we had several options as to where to focus and how to build our argument. Thus, the process of casing here meant narrowing down the conceptual lenses, focusing on certain aspects (that would be new and relevant for project managers in particular), while paying less attention to other aspects. Our joint reflection, together with some additional reading and data gathering, was needed to produce the case we have in the final book.

The process of analysing the data and of writing the book was highly iterative. For two years we were in regular contact via telephone, email and face-to-face meetings. I familiarized myself with the case material (including the interview notes) and initial case narrative, and we both looked at a wide variety of secondary sources. My colleague had conducted 13 interviews in different countries, and we subsequently interviewed two of the company representatives. For some aspects in our study (concerning different actors' viewpoints), we would have liked to conduct repeat interviews, but the respondents were no longer reachable. From this perspective, this example shows the value of bringing the initial findings under discussion into the team, when one still has the opportunity to go back to the data sources.

Analysis and output

It took time to familiarize myself with the case, and this project showed me how difficult it is to 'embrace' a case (Stake 2005, p. 455) if one has not been involved in the data collection. On the other hand, my 'outsider' views opened new windows onto the material and our discussions brought new perspectives to the rich data. For instance, we started with the view-point of a project manager, and then – as a result of reflecting on the wider implications of the holistic network view – extended this to the roles of the ending project manager and the top managers responsible for company strategy. It was as a result of the case analysis, combined with our previous understanding of network management concepts, that we uncovered the critical role of these two managerial levels to the ending of projects of this kind. Accordingly, the original interest in understanding what was happening in the immediate 'ending' relationships was thus directed to the key tasks of managers in different positions and also, to the broader networks. This example thus shows an emerging framework, because some of our initial research questions changed over time.

Taking turns during the writing process was necessary to absorb the data thoroughly and make analytical iterations. Initially we tried to divide the writing of individual chapters among ourselves, but soon noted that this was a fruitless task; in order to produce coherent and joint analysis we had to proceed from the beginning to the end. So one wrote the first draft and then the other revised it; the individual chapters took 3–5 iterations before the first version of the manuscript was ready. Next, we asked for comments from experts, and took their advice into consideration before writing the final version. The key target and outcome of our cooperation is the book published in 2009, which is very different from the initial case analysis in 2003 that my colleague had produced. We have used the text for teaching and executive education, but in addition, continued writing on the topic, using new conceptual ideas relating to, for instance, risk management.

DISCUSSION: COLLECTION OF CASES OR COLLECTIVE CASES?

This chapter started by indicating the lack of attention given to the (methodological) requirements and opportunities that teamwork may bring to case analysis. By providing an 'insider's view' of international research projects and investigating the reality of case analysis in teams, I have aimed to show the challenges and the potential of case studies and, in particular, of the abductive approach. In this penultimate section, I discuss two things that seem to emerge as critically important for research teams to consider. First, I address the question of working with shared or independent cases. Second, I look at the interplay between teamwork and analytical processes (emergence) in case studies.

Case studies often result in rich data. When scholars present the strengths of heterogeneous research teams, they assume that the rich data are actually subjected to the analysis and further work of the team. When this happens, there is the potential for in-depth discussions and different interpretations. The necessary condition, however, seems to be that the material is shared and the team becomes involved in framework development. Two of my examples show intensive reflections on the data and analysis, while in the first example (with multiple cases) we did not, for instance, see each other's interview notes or transcripts. In order to embrace the cases, extensive sharing of information is essential. For example, Søderberg and Vaara (2003) report that their research team had intensive discussions, in which researchers who were familiar with different countries contributed to the interpretation of the findings. This was possible since the team was working on the same internationally operating organization; in other words, a shared case.

A team may work with a single case or with multiple cases. Thus, the team may share either the *collective case* (potentially with embedded cases by different researchers at different sites) or engage in the *collection of cases*, where the cases are conducted separately and only their combination or comparison is jointly worked on. Both approaches to conducting case analysis are feasible, but they lead to different results and provide different bases for using abduction. In my experience, the latter approach is more common – many of the collaborative case studies are indeed collections of independent cases organized around a common topic. Often, the most trivial features of collaboration (such as access to different research sites) are the main motivation for the joint effort, and (too) often joint decision making concerns only the practical, operational aspects of research. The risk then is that researchers are satisfied with adding descriptions rather than analysis: the team follows the naive path of collecting a wide empirical database, without necessarily conducting collective analysis. Forming a joint understanding of the case(s) calls for true collaboration by all members: empirical findings and new developments need to be constantly shared within the team. Thus, by bringing the issues and the analysis to the team, the cases may be produced collectively.

Joint analysis seems easier to achieve when conducting a single, shared case. But the group benefits from joint abduction in a multiple case study too, if it reflects on the nature of the 'collection'; in other words, what can be achieved by a specific combination of cases. Given the twists and turns present in case research processes (also seen in my examples), there is a need to reconsider the selection of and contributions of the independent cases at different points of the research process – reflecting on such questions as: do the initial case selections match what the group wants to study, even if the research question is changing? How about the selection of additional cases and the sequencing and ordering of cases? Should the cases be approached in a different way? How do team members learn from the case studies along the way?

Abductive logic stresses joint effort, particularly with regard to the analytical framework. Concepts, which constitute both input and output in an abductive study, can give rise to a multitude of meanings (Dubois and Gadde 2002), which need to be accounted for. In the area of international business, the different meanings of concepts and their potential to vary depending on context have increasingly been recognized (Geringer and Frayne, 2001; Faria and Wensley 2002; Meyer 2007); and therefore, teamwork in abductive analysis indeed offers special potential for future theory development in the field.

If well executed and reported, a case may be used in several ways, as shown in my examples. For instance, the project ending case could be used for analysing the ending of different inter-cultural supplier relationships or of supply risk, while the managerial book focused on the effects of project ending on managers. In the process of analysing the Nordic M&As, our attention turned from immediate relations to broader networks and the network horizons of the actors. To arrive at these results, it was necessary to have access to several international actors in the network (via the team members), and to build a deep understanding of this case. Rich data therefore enhance the potential to use the cases in different projects – depending on the issue under study (Stake 2005), and on the evolving frameworks used. However, researchers seem to be poor at 'reusing' case studies, despite the intensive and long hours of work they have taken to produce.

The question of sharing the cases relates to the features of the group and its ways of working together. My examples show that it is easy to bring the ideas and findings under joint discussion in a small and homogeneous research team. It is certainly difficult to conduct analysis in a large group; in other words, to reach 'embraceable' cases in large numbers. Team heterogeneity brings in new ideas, but may make the achievement of joint understanding really challenging. A collective case study means a high need for coordination, joint problem solving, as well as mutual adjustment, which implies behavioural integration (Nason and Pillutla 1998). Looking again at my examples, integration was clearly highest in the two shared, single cases. In the multiple-case project, in contrast, research tasks were conducted separately, with less interdependence, but with a more powerful role for the team champions. In the former cases the team was integrated like 'ingredients in a melting pot', while the latter resembled 'a tossed salad', to use Bachman's (2006) analysis of teams working on a complicated task. Both kinds of teams can produce valuable case studies, but the end results are bound to be different. The key question is whether abductive analysis is carried out within the team, or by individual researchers. Even in my 'project ending case', a major part of the abductive analysis had been conducted by my colleague, as I joined in only later, when we started to use the case for a new purpose.

The process of abduction is largely hidden from view (Van Maanen et al. 2007). Teams, as case analysts in general, often fail to report their analytical paths, which, however, would be needed in order to convince others of the relevance and theoretical contributions of the study (Dubois and Araujo 2007). It is common (and visible in my examples too) that scholars carefully document the data sources, interviews and timing of research, even group meetings, but do not report the actual analysis. It would seem to be exceptionally valuable for research teams to report the analytical processes openly, as I have attempted to do in this chapter; to recount what was done jointly within the team, and what was left for individual analysts.

CONCLUSION

The manifold challenges of collective case analysis seem to boil down to the issue of a shared platform. To use collaboration fruitfully, the team should acknowledge this platform and also actively work towards building it up. The common platform for analysis may be found at the case level (shared case) or at the level of a case collection; both are feasible choices for teamwork, but lead to different research processes. My example of a team working on independent cases seems to be a typical example of international collaborative research, in which the case studies are not in fact turned into a common platform for discussion.

Indeed, given the increasing interest in the abductive approach, there seems to be a need for more careful consideration about what is shared in research teams. Thus, the key contribution of this chapter has been to bridge the topics of international teams and abduction. I have offered insight into independent versus shared cases as platforms for abductive case studies, as well as some of the implications for international business scholars.

To date, researchers have been relatively poor at explicating the reasons for collaborative international case studies: teams seem to be used to avoid the problems that a single researcher may have in trying to grasp different national contexts and research sites. This chapter shows that a team should not be satisfied with merely building the practical infrastructure for collaboration, but needs to go further to form a shared platform for collective analysis. This would mean joint matching processes; in other words, working together on one or several cases, but consciously making the analysis a group task, by sharing the empirical findings, discussing the changing framework and evolving case, and working together for research reporting.

I have proposed that abduction and joint matching may be used more and in better ways in collective cases, and this would particularly benefit case analysis in international business. This approach means, however, that the team needs to consider the common platform explicitly and what kinds of issues are brought there. This leads to the practical question: is there enough scope and time for collective analysis? Indeed, all the case studies reported here involved several years of more or less intensive cooperation – thus timewise, a joint case study is not a quick fix. Essentially, the team needs to be explicit and unanimous about the adopted case approach, in order to make more-informed choices regarding the research.

Although tackling these challenges may not be easy, it is certainly worth the joint effort – there is no doubt that using the community features of research teams for analysis will lead to better-informed and innovative case studies in international business. It seems to me that real-life case processes are 'messier' than reported in the methodological literature. Indeed, in practice research teams often follow the iterative and emergent processes of abductive case studies. The aim of this chapter has therefore been to explicate these processes and challenges, and thus to contribute to better collaborative case research in the field of international business.

REFERENCES

Anderson, H., V. Havila and A. Salmi (2001), 'Can you buy a business relationship? On the importance of customer and supplier relationships in acquisitions', *Industrial Marketing Management*, **30** (7), 575–86.

Bachman, A.S. (2006), 'Melting pot or tossed salad? Implications for designing effective multicultural workgroups', *Management International Review*, **46** (6), 721–47.

Bournois, B. and F. Chevalier (1998), 'Doing research with foreign colleagues: a project-life cycle approach', *Journal of Managerial Psychology*, **13** (3–4), 206–13.

Clark, E. and S. Michailova (eds) (2004), *Fieldwork in Transforming Societies: Understanding Methodology from Experience*, Basingstoke: Palgrave Macmillan.

Dubois, A. and L. Araujo (2004), 'Research methods in industrial marketing studies', in H. Håkansson, D. Harrison and A. Waluszewski (eds), *Rethinking Marketing: Developing a New Understanding of Markets*, Chichester: Wiley, pp. 207–27.

Dubois, A. and L. Araujo (2007), 'Case research in purchasing and supply management: opportunities and challenges', *Journal of Purchasing and Supply Management*, **13** (3), 170–81.

Dubois, A. and L.-E. Gadde (2002), 'Systematic combining: an abductive approach to case research', *Journal of Business Research*, **55** (7), 553–60.

Dubois, A. and M. Gibbert (2010), 'From complexity to transparency: managing the interplay between theory, method and empirical phenomena in *IMM* case studies', *Industrial Marketing Management*, **39** (1), 40–48.

Easterby-Smith, M. and D. Malina (1999), 'Cross-cultural collaborative research: toward reflexivity', *Academy of Management Journal*, **42** (1), 76–86.

Faria, A. and R. Wensley (2002), 'In search of "interfirm management" in supply chains: recognizing contradictions of language and power by listening', *Journal of Business Research*, **55**, 603–10.

Geringer, J.M. and C.A. Frayne (2001), 'Collaborative research: turning potential frustrations into rewarding opportunities', in B. Toyne, Z.L. Martinez and R.A. Menger (eds), *International Business Scholarship*, Westport, CT: Quorum, pp. 117–34.

Ghauri, P. (2004), 'Designing and conducting case studies in international business research', in R. Marschan-Piekkari and C. Welch (eds), *Handbook of Qualitative Research Methods for International Business*, Cheltenham, UK and Northampton, MA, USA: Edward Elgar, pp. 109–24.

Håkansson, H. (1982), 'Methodology', in Håkansson (ed.), *International Marketing and Purchasing of Industrial Goods: An Interaction Approach*, Chichester: John Wiley, pp. 28–56.

Halinen, A., A. Salmi and V. Havila (1999), 'From dyadic change to changing business networks. An analytical framework', *Journal of Management Studies*, **36** (6), 779–94.

Havila, V. and A. Salmi (2009), *Managing Project Ending*, Routledge Advances in Management and Business Studies, Oxford: Routledge.

Kumar, V. (2000), *International Marketing Research*, Englewood Cliffs, NJ: Prentice-Hall.

Lunnan, R. and T. Barth (2003), 'Managing the exploration vs. exploitation dilemma in transnational "bridging teams"', *Journal of World Business*, **38** (2), 110–26.

Marschan-Piekkari, R. and C. Welch (2004), 'Qualitative research methods in international business: the state of the art', in R. Marschan-Piekkari and C. Welch (eds), *Handbook of Qualitative Research Methods for International Business*, Cheltenham, UK and Northampton, MA, USA: Edward Elgar, pp. 5–24.

Meyer, K. (2007), 'Contextualizing organizational learning: Lyles and Salk in the context of their research', *Journal of International Business Studies*, **38** (1), 27–37.

Milliman, J. and M.A. Von Glinow (1998), 'Research and publishing issues in large scale cross-national studies', *Journal of Managerial Psychology*, **13** (3–4), 137–42.

Nason, S.W. and M.M. Pillutla (1998), 'Towards a model of international research teams', *Journal of Managerial Psychology*, **13** (3–4), 156–66.

Peterson, M.F. (2001), 'International collaboration in organizational behavior research', *Journal of Organizational Behavior*, **22** (1), 59–81.

Piekkari, R., E. Plakoyiannaki and C. Welch (2010), '"Good" case research in industrial marketing: insights from research practice', *Industrial Marketing Management*, **39** (1), 109–17.

Ragin, C. (1992), '"Casing" and the process of social inquiry', in C.C. Ragin and H.S. Becker (eds), *What is a Case Study? Exploring the Foundations of Social Inquiry*, Cambridge: Cambridge University Press, pp. 217–26.

Salmi, A. (1999), 'Computer business on the Estonian market: the case of Mikrolog', in Törnroos and Nieminen (eds), pp. 109–29.

Salmi, A. (2010), 'International research teams as analysts of industrial business networks', *Industrial Marketing Management*, **39** (1), 40–48.

Salmi, A., V. Havila and H. Anderson (2001), 'Acquisitions and network horizons: a case study in the Nordic graphics industry', *Nordiske Organisasjonsstudier*, **3** (4), 61–83.

Sauquet, A. and G. Jacobs (1998), 'Can we learn from Herodotus?', *Journal of Managerial Psychology*, **13** (3–4), 167–77.

Segalla, M. (1998), 'Factors for the success or failure of international teams: the special case of international research projects', *Journal of Managerial Psychology*, **13** (3–4), 133–6.

Søderberg, A.-M. and E. Vaara (2003), 'Theoretical and methodological considerations', in Søderberg and Vaara (eds), *Merging Across Borders: People, Cultures and Politics*, Copenhagen: Copenhagen Business School Press, pp. 19–48.

Stake, R.E. (2005), 'Qualitative case studies', in N.K. Denzin and Y.S. Lincoln (eds), *The Sage Handbook of Qualitative Research*, 3rd edn, Thousand Oaks, CA: Sage, pp. 443–66.

Teagarden, M.B. (1998), 'Unbundling the intellectual joint venture process: the case of multinational, multifunctional interdisciplinary research consortia', *Journal of Managerial Psychology*, **13** (3–4), 178–87.

Teagarden, M.B., M.A. von Glinow, D.E. Bowen, C. Frayne, S. Nason, Y.P. Huo, J. Milliman, M.E. Arius, M.C. Butler, J.M. Geringer, N.-H. Kim, H. Scullion, K.B. Lowe and E.A. Drost (1995), 'Toward a theory of comparative management research: an ideographic case study of the best international human resources management project', *Academy of Management Journal*, **38** (5), 1261–87.

Törnroos, J.-Å. and Nieminen, J. (eds) (1999), *Business Entry in Eastern Europe: A Network and Learning Approach with Case Studies*, Helsinki: Kikimora Publications.

Turati, C., A. Usai and R. Ravagnani (1998), 'Antecedents of coordination in academic international project research', *Journal of Managerial Psychology*, **13** (3–4), 188–98.

Usunier, J.-C. (2011), 'Language as a resource to assess cross-cultural equivalence in quantitative management research', *Journal of World Business*, **46** (3), forthcoming.

Van Maanen, J., J. Sorensen and T.R. Mitchell (2007), 'The interplay between theory and method', *Academy of Management Review*, **32** (4), 1145–54.

Welch, C. and R. Piekkari (2006), 'Crossing language boundaries: qualitative interviewing in international business', *Management International Review*, **46** (4), 417–37.

Wilkinson, I. and L. Young (2004), 'Improvisation and adaptation in international business research interviews', in R. Marschan-Piekkari and C. Welch (eds), *Handbook of Qualitative Research Methods for International Business*, Cheltenham, UK and Northampton, MA, USA: Edward Elgar, pp. 207–23.

Yin, R.K. (2009), *Case Study Research: Design and Methods*, 4th edn, Thousand Oaks, CA: Sage.

23. How to use ethnographical case studies to decipher national cultures

Philippe d'Iribarne

INTRODUCTION

Empirical research using attitude scales, dominated by Hofstede's work (1980 [2001]), enjoys an almost hegemonic status in the field of cross-cultural management. An exhaustive literature review of this field (Boyacigiller et al. 2004) refers only to large-scale quantitative studies, making the use of such methods appear self-evident (Sackmann and Phillips 2004). This assumption is particularly pronounced in English-language research.[1] By contrast, the bulk of research using an interpretative approach focuses on the analysis of specific organizational cultures. In principle this approach could be applied to all forms of culture, including national cultures (Alvesson 2002). Yet with regard to national cultures, the aim of interpretative research at the organizational level is not to highlight the supposedly persistent characteristics of certain cultures. It is rather a matter of analysing how, within a given organization, the interaction of people from different societies and with different habits drives the emergence of a local culture, understood as a common way of doing things (Brannen and Salk 2000; Sackmann and Phillips 2004). The challenge is then to decipher what represents national culture and what is uniquely local.

Consequently, Schein's complaint (1996, p. 229) seems particularly justified: 'I believe our failure to take culture seriously enough stems from our methods of inquiry, which put a greater premium on abstractions that can be measured than on careful ethnographic or clinical observation of organizational phenomena'. The reasons behind this situation are no doubt complex. Here, the difficulties an observer is likely to face should be mentioned:

Ideas are more difficult to handle scientifically than the economic, political, and social relations among individuals and groups which those ideas inform. And this is all the more true when the ideas involved are . . . the half-formed, taken-for-granted, indifferently systematized notions that guide the ordinary activities of ordinary men in every day life. (Geertz 1973, p. 362)

More significantly, a fundamental question arises: how can observations made in a specific case be transformed into evidence of the society's culture as a whole? It might be appropriate to proceed with an ethnographic approach when dealing with relatively homogeneous societies (Lévi-Strauss 1958). But does this still hold true when referring to a modern society in which there is great diversity of values, of sensemaking and of behaviours? Does it even make sense to speak about national cultures, when referring to such societies? In fact, doesn't this dilemma inevitably lead us to revise thoroughly our conception of what a culture is?

My colleagues and I at the Gestion et Société (Management and Society) research centre have been tackling these issues by conducting numerous case studies, to date carried out in about 50 countries across every continent. This ongoing research aims to build up progressively an inventory of how organizations function within national cultures. The initial research compared three plants belonging, or having belonged until recently, to the same industrial group and respectively located in the USA, the Netherlands and France (d'Iribarne 1989). Subsequently, investigations were conducted into two types of cases: situations where management tools are used in another cultural context than the one in which they were originally conceived, and situations involving the functioning of multicultural organizations (d'Iribarne et al. 1998; d'Iribarne 2003, 2006a; Segal 2009). Moreover, we have examined the role culture plays when translating a text into different languages (d'Iribarne 2009b). In conducting our research, we met with numerous challenges, both theoretical and methodological, that arise when one attempts to delimit or define what a common culture can be within a modern society (Dupuis 2004). Only after a great amount of searching has it finally seemed possible to overcome these difficulties (d'Iribarne 2008). This chapter is based on what we have learned along the way.

The generic term 'case studies' covers a large number of purposes (Butler 1997). The manner in which such studies should be carried out depends considerably on the research objectives. In this chapter, we only focus on case studies whose specific aim is to decipher national cultures. The next section will be devoted to specifying what is to be understood by national culture within modern societies. The third section will concern the data-gathering phase, in which the clues that are spotted and brought to the surface enable the observer to track down specificities of the culture under study. The fourth section will be about making the transition from a collection of indications or clues to an overall understanding. The penultimate section will deal with distinguishing between what (when examining a single case) belongs to the general characteristics of a national culture, as opposed to what is only local (corporate culture, professional culture and so on). The final section concludes.

NATIONAL CULTURES AND IDEALIZED VISIONS OF COEXISTENCE

The idea of shared meaning is at the heart of interpretative approaches to culture. Culture is seen as constituted by 'the entire collection of shared meanings dramatized within a society or some other social unit' (Wuthnow 1987, p. 120). However such a formulation makes it difficult to conceive that there can be shared cultures within modern societies at all. This is because, first, meaning is not only received but also produced; and, second, society is divided into distinct social groups.

A major intellectual trend has emphasized the important role of actors in sensemaking (Garfinkel 1967). In a postmodern context the constant negotiation of significance is highlighted. Hence for Staber (2006, p. 192), expressing a widely shared point of view: '[c]ulture-based understandings are not a static, pre-existing condition that can be seen as exerting a simple causal influence on action. They are themselves fundamentally constructed phenomena that arise and are sustained or adjusted through social interaction'. But, if everything is constantly being renegotiated, this can only be done at a local level and it is hard to see what can be sustained on a large scale (Søderberg and Holden 2002).

Besides, within a society, rival definitions of reality coexist, even if there are also dominant definitions (Berger and Luckmann 1966; Douglas 1986). The attention drawn to this diversity has led to an interest in connections between culture and the sense of belonging to a particular social group rather than to a society as a whole. E.P. Thomson (1963) asserts that: 'Culture is . . . the very material of our daily lives, the bricks and mortar of our most commonplace understandings, feelings and responses' (quoted in Alexander and Seidman 1990, p. 183). But he sees culture as connected to class: 'The direct experiences of production are worked through and over in the praxis of different cultural discourses' (p. 184). From this perspective, the idea of a national culture has to be rejected, and can even be accused of hiding domination behind a mask of unity (Alvesson 2002).

However, when one puts together data about a single country – whether related to the way people living there attribute meaning to their working lives, the way its philosophers consider how society should be organized, or even the law that regulates workplace relations – one finds some 'family resemblance' (Wittgenstein 1953) between all these dimensions. In fact, even those attributing differing, or even contradictory, meanings to a particular reality are largely using the same categories to do so. One is dealing with a shared mental universe. The social sciences do not have adequate tools to define or delimit such a universe. The current idea of culture, as it is understood by anthropologists, appears intimately linked to notions of community, customs and ancestral practices, the latter superstitiously and faithfully followed. But when it comes to so-called 'modern' societies, we should let our attention be drawn elsewhere. One could hint at old sociological notions, such as 'spirit of a nation' (Montesquieu 1748) or even 'national character' (Weber 1905 [1958]), which draw out the existence of a certain unity and continuity within societies that are simultaneously divided and changing. Nevertheless, these notions seem too vague to be satisfying. In contemporary writings, various metaphors have been used, such as 'grammar' (Roy 2007) or the 'inner folds of thought' (Jullien 2000). Still, one cannot be totally satisfied with these either.

For our part, we have not actually come across shared ways of reacting and responding to situations in those societies where we have conducted our investigations. Therefore, we have not been able to use conceptions of culture borrowed from the literature available on the subject, since they are too closely linked to the idea of community (*Gemeinschaft*) to be applicable to heterogeneous groups. Several fruitless efforts were made before we reached a coherent interpretation of what we had found out. In the end, what emerged, after much reflection on what we had observed, was that a shared framework of meaning can be found within the same society (d'Iribarne 2008). What is striking is the existence of a certain vision of what constitutes the proper way of living together: how people manage to reach a *modus vivendi* in spite of more or less conflicting or contradictory desires – a conception of an acceptable way of getting along. It is by referring to that vision that actors can attribute meaning to what they experience. At this initial stage of analysis, it is already possible to obtain a deep understanding of what differentiates organizational forms in various societies. But this alone does not provide an understanding of the strength of the actors' attachment to a particular way of living together. To understand that part, one has to go much further. The existence within a given society of a fundamental fear that its members, both individually and collectively, seek to alleviate through actions and through words, appears to play a decisive role.

Each society's idealized image of coexistence – whether in accordance with everyday life or very distant from it – is unremittingly present in the background for those who are evoking their experiences, whether positive or negative. That vision does not directly determine practices, which can deviate considerably from it. However, considerable, more or less success-ful, efforts are produced to configure daily reality using this vision as a reference point. This does not mean that actors are conscious of it or are able to explain it clearly. It remains a kind of implicit evidence. It is left to the researcher to make out its contours. As the investigation proceeds, new areas are explored and the observations of various spheres in social life are brought together, these differentiated visions of an ideal manner of coexisting gradually begin to take shape for the observer.

Let us take the case of the USA (d'Iribarne 2008). Life in society in general, and in the workplace in particular, is conceived, in its ideal form, as contractual relations. The need to delimit clearly each individual's responsibilities is obvious to everyone. Every individual should be judged according to the way in which he/she attains a certain number of precise objectives that have been clearly defined in advance, objectives he/she is committed to fulfil. According to this ideal construct, subordinates are bound to their superior by a form of contract analogous to an agreement between a supplier and his/her customer. As the objectives are being fixed, the terms of the contract must be defined, specifying the product the subordinate is committed to deliver, the time period, and the means of delivery. This contractual conception can also be found in the relations between an 'order' and a 'customer' or, in unionized companies, between the company and the union.

This approach has no doubt been spread around the globe by manage-ment theories, but it is not regarded everywhere as a model. The ideal construct prevailing in France is clearly of a different nature (d'Iribarne 2006a). Every individual's activity is determined by the specific position he/she holds in society, by the customs and practices associated with this position, by what is considered 'normal' for someone holding this posi-tion, and by how this position can be ranked in comparison to others that may be more or less 'noble'. When the French speak about their working life, whether they are workers, managers, corporate employees, civil serv-ants or professionals, referring to the specific position that one occupies within a society and to what one 'is', is omnipresent, even if the words used vary according to each individual's activities.

It is difficult to share the same institutions, the same laws and the same forms of government without sharing the same ideal of what a society should be. Although people act quite differently from one another, they have something in common which corresponds to these above-mentioned visions of an ideal manner of living together. Moreover, experience shows that this same vision prevails within a given society when people try to set up a way to coexist, irrespective of the size of the entity one is dealing with. This is particularly true of people working together.

Founding Fears

Everywhere, humans are prey to a vast number of fears which they strive to assuage (d'Iribarne 2008, 2009a, 2009c). But what counts as the most terrifying fears are not the same everywhere. Each society has its own peril, perceived as singularly terrible and accompanied by 'paths to salvation' that permit people to avert this fear. For instance, American society permanently attributes great significance to the fear of being at the mercy of someone else; this fear can be averted as long as one controls one's destiny in a manner similar to the way an owner controls his/her estate or property. In French society, the fundamental fear is to be driven to bend, through fear or interest, before someone who might either harm you or shower you with favours. This could lead you to appear, in your own view or in that of another, as acting in a petty manner (*bassement*). You can escape this only if you are treated with the consideration due to your rank, or if you fight to be treated with dignity.

These fears, which mark all social existence, are particularly present in the life of organizations. Many events taking place in their midst (receiving an order from a hierarchical superior, having one's work evaluated, awarded or sanctioned, responding to an order made by a customer and so on) are likely to revive these fears. And everywhere, actors try to set up methods of functioning that allow them to avert or mitigate the main fear that marks their society. Simultaneously, they try to provide consoling interpretations of what they are experiencing.[2]

In the USA, organizational existence tends to be highly structured, both in terms of language and of practice, so as to avert the most feared image of having to depend on the will of someone else. The importance given to contractual relations allows society to obtain this result. Indeed, in a society governed by such relations, nobody can force anything on you except that to which you have already consented by signing the contract that binds you. In so far as consent is given freely, the fear of not mastering one's own destiny is assuaged. Similarly, in France, reference to a *métier*,[3] to an *homme de métier* (a professional) and to how exalted this *métier* is, with all the representations and practices – including the rights and duties – that come with it, plays a decisive role in assuaging the fear of finding oneself in a position considered as servile. Relations with authority and customers tend to be organized and spoken of in such a way that it becomes possible, to a great extent, to associate them with positive images.

To describe a culture that can be called national is to bring all these elements to light: on the one hand, the ideal representations of social life to which, in practice, reality can conform more or less strictly; on the other hand, the fears that these visions conceal; and in addition, the connections between everyday working life and these representations. These are the elements we shall be referring to in the following sections when we speak of national culture.

OMNIPRESENT CLUES

Nature of Investigation

Experience shows that the above-mentioned features of a national culture persistently structure the discourse, whether written or spoken, of those whose minds it has shaped. In order to gather traces of these elements, all that is required is a collection of interviews with those working in an organization. The proper method for doing this is not to pose direct questions about culture, since the underlying explanation for the interviewee's reaction is generally the last thing he/she is able to explain. Instead, people are requested to speak freely in their own terms about their work, preoccupations, challenges and how they overcome them. These accounts are impregnated with clues to the culture. One finds in their conversations multiple clues of the implicit vision against which they judge things surrounding them. Similarly, one finds expressions revealing both the fears that haunt those expressing them, and the ways used to assuage them. Traces of these elements can also be found in the written documents produced within the organizations themselves (annual reports, corporate guidelines and communication).

For these elements to be perceived, one does not need to consider particular types of situations such as critical incidents. One only has to ask those being interrogated to speak about their work in general. Discussion can be narrowed down by asking more questions about a specific subject: such as delegation and control processes, the setting up of a computer system, quality approaches, the corporate code of ethics, policies towards relations with customers and so on. At this stage of the investigation, the most important thing is to be open to each individual's preoccupations and to the way in which they are expressed. Moreover, the reference points enabling people to make sense of the world are the same whether they tell the truth or not. Therefore, when attempting to bring these references to light, it is not necessary to try to reconstruct the very actions and sentiments that lie behind people's words. Finally, evidence characterizing a culture appears repeatedly in the corpus (of interviews and so on) produced by people of a particular culture. This is why, when one is interested in a given culture, listening to a large set of interviews is not necessarily useful; a limited number will suffice. After 20 interviews or so, one quickly reaches saturation point (Bertaux and Kohli 1984). What is difficult in this kind of research is not the interview phase; rather, it is the subsequent analysis and handling of the interviews.

For this type of investigation, the categories that structure the discourse (the 'outer form') are more pertinent than what the interviewees are seeking to get across ('the content'). It is therefore extremely important that this outer form be well preserved, without the interviewer's immediate translation into his/her own categories (Dumont 1997, p. 33). This form should be carefully preserved through a literal transcription of the text, which implies that interviews must be recorded.

In order to find out what is pertinent in the collected materials, a comparative approach is essential. In fact, no clues will stand out unless there is something with which to contrast them. This is particularly true when analysing one's own culture. Without a comparision, one runs the risk of not finding anything worthy of attention in the materials that have been assembled, since everything seems to be going the way it should. Varied and fruitful ways of generating such contrasts exist. One can, for example, compare situations that are as identical as possible, in two or more different countries (for example, factories carrying out the same function and belonging to the same company but located in different countries). One can also analyse the disruption caused when members of an organization are confronted with foreign ways of working, whether this confrontation results from direct contact with the change agents, or indirectly from importing these foreign practices, for example, from headquarters to a subsidiary of a multinational corporation. A comparative element can also result from the contrast between the interviewee's and the observer's cultures, which leads the latter to notice words and practices that look strange in comparison to what he/she deems 'natural'. Another reference point can be provided by management theories. One can notice differences between what one observes and what one is led to expect from the literature. Often, several of these means of comparison coexist within a single case study.

Generally speaking, once one has detected a way of deciphering what is unique to one culture, this particularity can easily be detected in any interview or written material. The salient question that we are now going to look at is how to bring these references to light when one does not yet know what they could actually be. Here we are dealing with a classic hermeneutic circle (Gadamer 1960 [1996]). The clues that have been assembled can only take on their full meaning when they fall into place in the overall picture, and this big picture is in turn built up from these clues. The results are only convincing when several features, which at first glance seem ill-assorted or disparate, begin to take shape in a way that is felt to be coherent and makes sense. Before arriving at this coherence, one may have to grope around laboriously and at length (d'Iribarne et al. 1998). The general method here would be to gather the first clues of what one wishes to bring to light and to build up a tentative global picture based on these clues. Subsequently one continues to look for clues, this time with the insight provided by the initial global picture, going back and forth between these two steps, which are closely connected even though analytically distinct.

The Gathering of Clues

In interviews and written documents gathered during fieldwork, numerous clues to the culture can be found. For instance, words that appear distinctive when compared to those heard elsewhere draw one's attention. What is significant is not how often they appear, but the fact that, according to a foreigner, they are used 'out of context'; in other words, in situations where it does not appear 'normal' to use them.

In the Mexican subsidiary of an international group (d'Iribarne 2003), for example, words such as *ayudar* and *apoyar* (to help, support) were used in the most varied of contexts, irrespective of the relative positions of the interviewees (peer to peer, superior to subordinate, company to surrounding communities and so on) or of the exact nature of their relations (counsel, rescue or first aid, execution of subordinate tasks, payment). We had never (and have not since) encountered anything equivalent in any other geographic region. Such clues reveal a vision of society in which help given and received plays a major role. Furthermore, the clues led to the discovery of the central fear that marks Mexican society, that of not being capable of making one's dreams come true on one's own. Such a fear nurtures the desire to work together in a way that helps overcome this very fear.

We could take as another example the principles enacted by a large multinational group for which there are two versions, one in French and one in English. These two versions are supposed to have exactly the same content. Let us observe two short passages (among the many that could reveal similar observations) about relations between customers and the company:

'*provide* the construction industry' / '*offrir* au secteur de la construction'; '*delivering* the . . . products . . .' / '*proposer* les produits . . .'.

Linguistically, nothing would stop the French from using the words *fournir* and *livrer*[4] – the exact translations of 'provide' and 'delivering', respectively. Yet the difference is worth highlighting. The words 'provide' and 'delivering' illustrate, in a manner that conforms to managerial ortho-doxy, the meaning of commercial relations between the ordering party (the customer) and the provider (the company), who are both interested in the transaction. By contrast, the word *offrir* sounds strange since there is no doubt that the company will charge the client for its services. One is con-fronted here with a way of dressing up reality. In isolation, this clue could not lead to any particular conclusion about anything. Yet, when associ-ated with other elements, it paves the way for overall comprehension. The words *offrir* and *proposer* give the impression of a gratuity which shelters the French from their fundamental fear of submitting themselves to the demands of the other (in this case the customer's) to satisfy petty interests.

The reference points one is trying to bring to the fore can also emerge from a series of stories that, although using different words, refers to the same kind of relations between actors. In a French factory (d'Iribarne 1989, p. 27) several interviewees used expressions which connected what they had to do at work with the essence of their *métier*: 'A supervisor for me should . . .', 'for them this seems normal; for us, as manufacturers, we do not like to . . .', 'this is part of my function as a technician', 'I carry out my role as usual'. These expressions, once they were noticed (which took a great deal of time), played a significant role in putting us on the trail of how French people conceive the way an organization should function, attributing considerable significance to each *métier*, to its traditions, its status, the duties attached to it – to everything that sums up the honour of a *métier*.

Through both the words and the expressions used, as well as through the stories or plots in which these words appear, one can begin to trace the chain of associations for making sense of social reality. When moving from one culture to the other, the same reality is interpreted through a different chain of associations and oppositions. Hence, for instance, hier-archical relations inspired by a paternalistic model will be read according to a system of very different associations and oppositions in European cultures (where they are marked by the opposition between paternalistic versus democratic) as compared to those of Maghreb countries (where they are marked by the opposition between son and slave) (Zghal 1994).

At the same time, various practices draw attention due to their strange-ness; in other words, what is surprising compared to what is obvious in the observer's culture or because of their non-conformity to current theories about how a company should function. For instance, in an Indian factory, three workers in charge of carrying out successive phases of the same operation (to remove the melted aluminium in a pot) do not coordinate their actions: the first one does not take into account the consequences of the way he performs his tasks on the quality of the results obtained by his colleagues, and the second one has the same attitude towards the third person. Moreover, their managers do not know how to improve the situation. Or, in an American company, seniority, which plays a central role in managing hourly workers, is defined in such detail that it comes as a surprise to a foreign observer: one clause in a contract between a company and a union not only specifies how decisions related to those hired on the same day should be made (they are arranged in alphabetical order), but also stipulates what should be done in case one of these employees changed his/her name between the date he/she joined and the date on which the contract comes into force (his/her former name would count) (d'Iribarne 1989). The surprise felt by a non-American observer leads him/her to wonder what lies behind these practices; that is, what makes them meaningful to actors. This provides clues of the society's ideals and fears.

FROM A COLLECTION OF CLUES TO THE CONSTRUCTION OF A GENERAL IMAGE

By analysing speech and observing practices, a collection of clues of an underlying culture is gathered. But formulating a structured and coherent representation of a culture from this assortment of clues still remains to be done. It consists of searching for the link between the interviewee's actions and the web of meaning found in what he/she says. The process is carried out for each person who is interrogated, and then extended to a much larger scale.

A Progressive Ordering of Ideas

A necessary (although not sufficient) step consists of forming conjectures that lead to an overall hypothetical interpretation of all the clues assembled. This abductive process (Peirce 1934–48; Eco 1992; Czarniawska 1999) is similar to that of trying to solve a criminal investigation from a series of clues. The quality of the results will largely depend on the pertinence of the conjecture. The next step consists of verifying whether all the clues tie in well with the initial hypothesis. If they do not, new conjectures will need to be formed.

As has been shown, of all the clues assembled the actors' words play a prominent part. However, according to the hermeneutic circle mentioned above, the precise meaning of a word (for example, friend, trust) or expression cannot be fully understood in isolation from the broader cultural context. This is all the more important since different cultures are susceptible to attributing different meanings to the same word, even when using the 'same' language. This is true, for example, of the French word *partenaire*; for a French national, it evokes relations that are very different from what the word represents in regions that, although French speaking, are marked by their own culture. From a French national's point of view, a good 'partner' is one who, striving to excel inventively and intelligently according to the norms of his/her *métier*, is interested in the expectations of the person with whom he/she is cooperating and provides that person with something better than a standard product. For French-speaking Martiniquans, a *partenaire* is rather a person/entity you build ties with in such a way that you help him or her unconditionally when he/she is in need (d'Iribarne 2006b).

To know what precise meaning to attribute to a word or expression in a certain universe of meaning, one should pay attention to the stories or anecdotes in which these expressions are used. These very stories and anecdotes provide clues as to what precisely the words mean in that given context: a word only takes on its real meaning when considered in context. At the same time, the association of a word (honour, equal) with a collection of stories allows us to understand what they have in common. There is a complementarity between the paradigmatic – the models, the metaphors – and the syntagmatic – the stories and the plots (Czarniawska 1999).

Arranging the collected data leads to a rough image whose specificities still need to be refined. Paying attention to ways of acting, attitudes and words that, although they had at first appeared satisfactory, are at odds with the as-yet-too-rough construct is an essential step in the analysis. For instance, one should be attentive to the ways in which hierarchical superiors impose their views in cultures where equality is placed at the forefront; and conversely, to whether an individual does more or less what he/she wants to do, in a context where at first glance, deference to authority is the rule. At this stage, one's attention is drawn to how the culture under study gives meaning to such 'contradictory' attitudes; one tries to understand the interpretative frame within which these attitudes appear coherent and perfectly rational; such as in Morocco, where an affirmation of equality is consistent with affection towards a 'paternalistic' hierarchical superior (d'Iribarne 2003).

The discordance between what appears logically connected (or logically incompatible) in different cultures plays an essential role in the misunderstandings that inevitably occur in intercultural relations. A great deal of vigilance is required to avoid building up an imaginary vision of foreign cultures by presuming that they go by the same logic as the ethnographer's culture. To avoid misinterpretation, one must have developed an understanding not only of the singularities in other cultures, but also in one's own.

Difficulties in Finding a Language to Describe a Culture

Describing one culture in the language of another (whether in a totally different language or in the 'same' language used in another cultural context) can be a formidable task. There is always a considerable risk – especially when progressing from a phenomenological analysis (reference is often made to 'thick description'; Geertz 1973) to a more synthetic presentation – that one may mask what does not in another culture directly correspond to one's own.

To explain what another culture is, one is led to use descriptive tools which have meaning both for the author and for the reader. Since forms of social life are under observation, the images or categories that are used by the researcher can either be universal or reputed to be universal, such as community, market, slavery and so on, or concrete forms that the reader is familiar with or understands (the caste system in India, court society under Louis XIV, African *palabra* and so on). Such is the available stock of images and associated words used in order to make sense of empirical data. However, one is occasionally faced with a difficulty: the words that are used render the realities observed only badly or feebly.

When Geertz (1973, p. 402), referring to Bali, tries to express how inappropriate behaviour is experienced there, he asserts that the word 'shame', the only one available in English, is misleading. That word, far from corresponding to a category with a universal scope, corresponds to quite a different sentiment from the one he wished to portray. The Balinese word '*lek*' does exist, but it does not speak directly to someone who has no intimate knowledge of Balinese life. In order to overcome this difficulty, Geertz uses the French term '*faux pas*'. This presupposes that the reader, probably a well-read American, has in mind a certain image of French court society and the sentiments that inhabit such a world. Moreover, for this image to make sense to readers, one must assume that they have lived through situations in their own society that have some connection with those experienced in French court society, even if these situations are not common enough for them to be described by specific words. Moreover, one must take for granted that readers are in a position to link up what they have experienced with the image used by the author. One cannot be sure that all Geertz's readers are in a position to grasp fully what he tried to elucidate.

Such difficulties can arise when one tries, in one's own culture, to account for realities considered to be incongruous with the society's official representations. France may be an example of such an extreme situation. It is a democratic society governed according to republican law, and yet it rests upon a combination of two opposites: on the one hand *bon plaisir* (or 'will'); on the other, the association of the ethics of a *métier* and 'allegiance' to a hierarchical superior whose ability to bring perspective to, and rise above, all situations cannot be questioned. The latter can only be seen as originating in 'feudal' relations that do not fit in with current republican views. That is how Michel Crozier (1963, p. 340) sees it when he presents the success of the bureaucratic system as dependent 'on the anarchical and feudal society that it struggles with but on which it leans'. How can this be accounted for? To convey what is observed one is forced to use words – such as allegiance, honour, fidelity, nobility, to fall from rank and so on – which at first glance describe realities that do not exist in contemporary France. A substantial amount of work is to be done before the link between what these words point to and the realities one is trying to account for is made obvious. Here again, readers may well be unequally equipped to grasp precisely what all this is about.

Extending from the Case Study Data

A case analysis always begins with work on the gathered material, without worrying, at first, about how to connect it with pre-existing views of the society under study. However, the fact that one has some other knowledge of this society than that revealed by the case study, can be useful as one proceeds with the analysis.

The clues about the ideal vision of a society can be difficult to interpret as well as to spot. Having a pattern that bestows meaning on the clues can help to make them out in the jumble of collected material. One is faced with such a situation when the traditional forms previously in force in a society have been so thoroughly eradicated from its apparently 'modern' vision that they assume a veiled appearance in discourse. Thus, in a France that considers herself as modern, it is difficult to openly affirm that the conception people have of their professional duty is closely linked to the position they occupy in a company, and in particular to how high this position ranks on a scale of 'nobility'. The image Montesquieu (1748) depicted of the honour-bound France he observed enables one to understand the subtleties of the republican reinterpretation of the *Ancien Régime*.

Even when the ideal vision of society is sufficiently visible for it to be brought to light without the benefit of a historical pattern, this pattern can nonetheless be useful to test the scope of what has been established. For example, as we were analysing the functioning of a factory located in the Netherlands, we managed to understand the underlying logic without prior consultation of any analyses of the Dutch political system. Later, our discovery of a strict homology between the ideal image of life in society we had elicited from our materials and the classic representation of this system (Lijphart 1968) confirmed that we had managed to bring to light the general characteristics of a Dutch way of living in society.

Furthermore, the bringing together of materials stemming from very diverse epochs and very different contexts multiplies the chances of revealing clues about what is specific to a culture. This background reading helps to recognize these characteristics where they only appear in a veiled manner. Thus, *The Federalist* (Hamilton et al. 1787–88) provides particularly revealing evidence of the American mindset and of the fundamental fear at its heart. In the brief central text concerning the structure of institutions of the Union (no. 51), the feeling of peril brought out by words such as 'insecure', 'insecurity', 'danger' and 'attack' is omnipresent. Faced with this danger, the will to protect oneself is ever present. One must defend oneself ('defense', 'self-defense', precautions, guarded against, resist, counteract, protect) by appropriate means (armed, sentinel). One must arrive at a situation where one is secure (preservation, safe, security, secure). What then is feared? What sheds light is that the word 'encroachment' keeps recurring ('encroachments of the others', dangerous encroachments), affirming the will to 'resist' this encroachment. According to Webster's dictionary, 'encroach' means 'to trespass or intrude (*on* or *upon* the rights, property, etc. of another)'. It is with this intrusion that the ideas of dependence, oppression and submission (dependence, oppress, submit) are associated and this is what one must protect oneself from. The setting up of a system of checks and balances is seen as a privileged means of defence: 'the constant aim is to divide and arrange the several offices in such a manner as that each may be a check on the other – that the private interest of every individual may be a sentinel over the public rights' (*Federalist*, no. 51). We are in a universe where each person is threatened by the actions of others and where it is fundamental to 'preserve' what is important to him/her. What stands out is this: being submitted to another's will is *the* feared experience; and forming an organization that permits citizens to control their destiny is the way to avert this fear.

Each case analysis brings to light the culture of the society under study and is also susceptible to lead to a widening of the questions asked about other cultures. Behaviours that surprise the observer simultaneously prompt him/her to wonder what underpins them in that society and what it is that makes their occurrence unthinkable elsewhere. The further one looks into the diversity of solutions deployed to overcome the difficulties of social life, the better one understands how contingent they are to each society.

As we were studying a case in Cameroon, we were struck by the means used by sub-Saharan African cultures to stop the cycle of suspicions raised about other people's intentions and to break the never-ending chain of interpretations and accusations. From a European point of view, these means – for example, calling a seer reputed to be capable of detecting hidden intentions – can look strange (Henry 2007). This observation put us in a better position to understand, in European societies, the deference towards institutions or procedures reputed to be legitimate (the expert who is judged competent, the majority vote and so on), which similarly plays the role of preventing the cycle of interpretation and suspicion that entails such disastrous consequences.

On the whole, each case study contributes its part in gradually advancing towards a more global understanding of the diversity of the world. Just as they apply to the materials gathered for each case analysis, the hermeneutic circle principles apply at the case study collection level. Each case finds its full scope in the entire collection of case studies and in the understanding of the diversity of cultures. And this understanding is in turn fed by the information provided by each new case.

HOW DOES ONE DISTINGUISH NATIONAL FROM LOCAL?

Some people have questioned the legitimacy of the move from local or individual features, such as what is perceived in a case study, to something more general. Thus, for Wuthnow (1987, p. 48):

> Phenomenology stresses description of the rich meanings held by specific individuals or in specific situations; yet these meanings are not only complex but idiosyncratic and continuously in flux. Having discovered all the meanings a set of symbols conveys to an individual today, one cannot be certain that the same meanings will still be present tomorrow.

What allows us to move from a few interviews to a culture considered in its entirety is the extreme coherence of the data: normally, during a case study, the ideal ways of living and working together, as well as the fears that play a central role in the society being studied, can be observed in every interview.[5] When exceptionally, this is not the case, we are clearly dealing with multicultural societies containing very distinct populations.

When performing ethnographic studies, the question arises as to how particulars that are really shared in a country can be distinguished from those that by contrast are only specific to a small locality (a company or a plant). From experience, we can provide three responses to this concern. First, the diversity of the people within a small-sized entity such as an industrial establishment should not be underestimated, and what was common to them does not only reflect something specific to that group. For instance, we conducted an investigation in an aluminium plant located in a small town in Maryland (d'Iribarne 1989). There we met a great variety of people. Some had worked in a sister plant of the West Coast. Many had rather complex professional and geographic itineraries. We spoke to engineers, workers, managers, trade union members, white, black, young and not so young people. Most were men, though there were a few women. What was common to them could not therefore have originated from the singularities of a particular group of people. It appeared that what they shared could be found in American society more generally; it was because they all belonged to that society that they had (despite all their differences) something in common.

It is true, and this is the second point, that one sometimes has to deal with a company with a very particular culture, which introduces something that interviewees have in common besides the fact that they all belong to the same country. This was the case, for instance, in the investigations we conducted in Mexico and Morocco (d'Iribarne 2003). However, it was not difficult to distinguish the particularities of the company from the characteristics of the country in general. In both cases, the majority of those we met had not pursued their career in the same company. In addition, some (sometimes the same) individuals had known the company at a time when it functioned in a very different manner. They constantly brought to light the way in which what we observed in their company was exceptional. Moreover, one could clearly detect two very different layers of meaning in what they said: at the one level, mostly unconscious reference points for judging situations and events (the representations they had of the proper way one should live and work together or their underlying fears); at the second level, descriptions of ways of functioning which they obviously perceived as original. The Mexican construct of a community of equals who help each other undoubtedly belonged to the first genre. The same went for the Moroccan image of a community united by a rule preached by a hierarchical superior who is simultaneously strong and humble before the law. The precise description of the functioning of such a company, such a department, the behaviour of such and such an individual undoubtedly belonged to the second genre. The third point, the fact that we could match up the field observations with data from other field studies, provides us with an extra safeguard. Similarly, one can attempt to see if conceptions of social life match up with the country's political institutions. If one encounters in a modern American factory conceptions analogous to those found in the *Federalist*, or in Locke (1690), it will be difficult to see this as happening by chance.

All in all, the risks of seriously confusing what concerns a culture in its entirety with what is distinctly local are slim. Moreover, the reception to one's findings is revealing of the latter's scope. Thus the picture given in *La Logique de l'honneur* (d'Iribarne 1989) of the functioning of French companies is founded on the observation of a singular factory located in a secluded valley in the Alps. Nevertheless, the numerous comments it aroused in French organizations and elsewhere confirmed its adequacy: 'I would have thought it was my plant, my hospital, my organization that was being described'. In countries where we have analysed several cases – particularly France, where dozens of cases were studied – the image of a national culture we arrived at on the basis of a first study was not challenged or questioned by later research. While this construct could no doubt be enriched and fine-tuned, the principal traits of the French national culture would not be called into question. Moreover, the progress is attributable just as much to evolution in our own thinking as to what we learned from new case studies. The multiplication of cases did, however, play an irreplaceable role in understanding the diversity of the concrete functioning of organizations that are compatible with the same national culture (Segal 2009).

CONCLUSION

In the current state of 'cultural studies', case studies tend only to be used for relatively local cultures, such as organizations or parts of organizations. The analysis of national cultures is mostly left to research that uses attitude scales. Although there is widespread recognition that a few coefficients alone cannot account for a satisfactory analysis of a culture, such opinions have led to only a very slow modification of the status quo. The application of an interpretative approach based on case studies provides a viable alternative to quantitative approaches. It makes it possible to highlight visions of an ideal way of living and working together, as well as the fears everyone tries to assuage that are unique to each society. Clues of these visions and fears can be found in the overall discourse of actors belonging to the same society and in the writings they produce. By following a hermeneutic approach, one can gradually proceed from these clues to a global comprehension of each culture and to what differentiates it from other cultures.

ACKNOWLEDGEMENT

Translated from the French by Maya Putois, Fanny Salignac and Geneviève Felten.

NOTES

1. Thus, in the revised edition of *Culture's Consequences*, Hofstede (1980 [2001]) examines the link between his approach and idiographic and qualitative approaches. In this context, he only refers to French qualitative research.
2. These phenomena can be compared to Barley's (1983) finding that a corpse in a mortuary is metaphorically associated with someone being asleep. This presupposes a deliberate staging aimed at establishing the greatest possible resemblance between the two. The difference is that in the case of the corpse it is only make-believe, whereas in the case of organizations it is only partly illusory. The other part is about finding organizational structures that bear a real resemblance to what constitutes a reference point in the society being studied.
3. One's professional role or field of expertise. In France people commonly perceive their work in a manner similar to the way in which professionals (such as lawyers and doctors) in the US do (Translator's note).
4. In some cases, the particularities of a culture appear in the existence of words that are so specific they become untranslatable. But generally, they result from choices among various possibilities and stand out as different from uses elsewhere. What is at stake here is not so much the way in which a language categorizes reality but rather the way in which a particular community uses this language to represent reality. Two different communities can use the same language to describe the same situation in very different terms (conversely, two communities using a different language could use practically equivalent words in both languages to describe the same situation).
5. To counter any doubts this assertion may give rise to, let us keep in mind the role played by the Rosetta Stone for the intelligibility of Egyptian hieroglyphics: despite the small sample of writing, scholars were able to bring to light very general characteristics of Egyptian writing.

REFERENCES

Alexander, J.C. and S. Seidman (1990), *Culture and Society: Contemporary Debates*, Cambridge: Cambridge University Press.
Alvesson, M. (2002), *Understanding Organizational Culture*, London: Sage.
Barley, S.R. (1983), 'Semiotics and the study of occupational and organizational cultures', *Administrative Science Quarterly*, **28** (3), 393–413.
Berger, P. and T. Luckmann (1966), *The Social Construction of Reality*, New York: Doubleday.
Bertaux, D. and M. Kohli (1984), 'The life story approach: a continental view', *Annual Review of Sociology*, **10**, 215–37.
Boyacigiller, N.A., M.J. Kleinberg, M.E. Phillips and S.A. Sackmann (2004), 'Conceptualizing culture: elucidating the streams of research in international cross-cultural management', in B.J. Punnett and O. Shenkar (eds), *Handbook for*

International Management Research, Ann Arbor, MI: University of Michigan Press, pp. 99–167.

Brannen, M.Y. and J. Salk (2000), 'Partnering across borders: negotiating organizational culture in a German–Japanese joint venture', *Human Relations*, **53** (4), 451–87.

Butler, R. (1997), 'Stories and experiments in social inquiry', *Organization Studies*, **18** (6), 927–48.

Crozier, M. (1963), *Le Phénomène bureaucratique* [The Bureaucratic Phenomenon], Paris: Seuil.

Czarniawska, B. (1999), *Writing Management: Organization Theory as a Literary Genre*, Oxford: Oxford University Press.

d'Iribarne, P. (1989), *La Logique de l'honneur* [The Logic of Honour], Paris: Seuil.

d'Iribarne, P. with A. Henry (2003), *Le Tiers monde qui réussit* [Successful Companies in the Developing World: Managing in Synergy with Cultures], Paris: Odile Jacob.

d'Iribarne, P. (2006a), *L'Étrangeté française* [The French Oddity], Paris: Seuil.

d'Iribarne, P. (2006b), 'L'AFD et ses partenaires: la dimension culturelle' ['The French Development Agency (AFD) and its partners: the cultural dimension'], AFD, document de travail no. 23.

d'Iribarne, P. (2008), *Penser la diversité du monde* [Thinking the World's Diversity], Paris: Seuil.

d'Iribarne, P. (2009a), 'Conceptualising national cultures: an anthropological perspective', *European Journal of International Management*, **3** (2), 167–75.

d'Iribarne, P. (2009b), 'Entre français et anglais: une entreprise se met en scène' ['Between French and English: the staging of a company'], *Langage & Société*, **129**, 101–18.

d'Iribarne, P. (2009c), 'National cultures and organizations in search of a theory: an interpretative approach', *International Journal of Cross Cultural Management*, **9** (3), 309–21.

d'Iribarne, P., A. Henry, J.-P. Segal, S. Chevrier and T. Globokar (1998), *Cultures et Mondialisation* [Cultures and Globalization], Paris: Seuil.

Douglas, M. (1986), *How Institutions Think*, Syracuse, NY: Syracuse University Press.

Dumont, L. (1997), *Groupes de filiation et pratiques de mariage: introduction à deux théories d'anthropologie sociale* [An Introduction to Two Theories of Social Anthropology: Descent Groups and Marriage Alliance], Paris: Gallimard.

Dupuis, J.-P. (2004), 'Problèmes de cohérence théorique chez Philippe d'Iribarne: une voie de sortie' ['Theoretical inconsistencies in Philippe d'Iribarne's works: a way out of the impasse'], *Management International*, **8** (3), 21–30.

Eco, U. (1992), *Les limites de l'interprétation* [The Limits of Interpretation], Paris: Grasset.

Gadamer, H.-G. (1960 [1996]), *Vérité et méthode: les grandes lignes d'une herméneutique philosophique* [Truth and Method: The Outline of a Philosophical Hermeneutics], Paris: Seuil.

Garfinkel, H. (1967), *Studies in Ethnomethodology*, Englewood Cliffs, NJ: Prentice-Hall.

Geertz, C. (1973), *The Interpretation of Culture*, New York: Basic Books.

Hamilton, A., J. Madison and J. Jay (1787–88 [1992]), *The Federalist or, The New Constitution*, London: Everyman.

Henry, H. (2007), 'Revolution by procedures in Cameroon', in P. d'Iribarne with

A. Henry, *Successful Companies in the Developing World: Managing in Synergy with Cultures*, Paris: Agence Française de Développement.

Hofstede, G. (1980 [2001]), *Culture's Consequences*, London: Sage.

Jullien, F. with T. Marchaisse (2000), *Penser d'un dehors (la Chine): Entretiens d'Extrême-Occident* [Thinking from Outside (China): Interviews from the 'Far-West'], Paris: Seuil.

Lévi-Strauss, C. (1958), *Anthropologie structurale* [Structural Anthropology], Paris: Plon.

Lijphart, A. (1968), *The Politics of Accommodation, Pluralism and Democracy in the Netherlands*, Berkeley, CA: University of California Press.

Locke, J. (1690 [1960]), *Two Treatises of Government*, edited by Peter Laslett, Cambridge: Cambridge University Press.

Montesquieu, C. (1748 [1964]), *De l'Esprit des lois* [The Spirit of the Laws], in *Œuvres complètes* [Complete Works], Paris: Seuil.

Peirce, C.S. (1934–48), *Collected Papers*, 4 vols, Cambridge, MA: Harvard University Press.

Roy, O. (2007), *Le Croissant et le chaos* [The Crescent and Chaos], Paris: Hachette littérature.

Sackmann, S.A. and M.E. Phillips (2004), 'Contextual influences on culture research; shifting assumptions for new workplace realities', *International Journal of Cross Cultural Management*, **4** (3), 370–90.

Schein, E.H. (1996), 'Culture: the missing concept in organization studies', *Administrative Science Quarterly*, **41** (2), 229–40.

Segal, J.-P. (2009), *Efficaces, ensemble: un défi français* [Effective, Together: A French Challenge], Paris: Seuil.

Søderberg, A.-M. and N. Holden (2002), 'Rethinking cross cultural management in a globalizing business world', *International Journal of Cross Cultural Management*, **2** (1), 103–21.

Staber, U. (2006), 'Social capital processes in cross cultural management', *International Journal of Cross Cultural Management*, **6** (2), 189–203.

Thomson, E.P. (1963), *The Making of the Working Class*, New York: Vintage.

Weber, M. (1905 [1958]), *The Protestant Ethic and the Spirit of Capitalism*, New York: Scribner's Press.

Wittgenstein, L. (1953 [2001]), *Philosophical Investigations*, Oxford: Blackwell.

Wuthnow, R. (1987), *Meaning and Moral Order*, Berkeley, CA: University of California Press.

Zghal, R. (1994), *La Culture de la dignité et le flou de l'organisation: culture et comportement organisationnel* [The Culture of Dignity and the Blurring of Organization: Culture and Organizational Behaviour], Tunis: Centre d'études, de recherche et de publications.

24. Doing case studies in China: two perspectives

Hui Tan and Matti Nojonen

PERSPECTIVE NO. 1: THE CHINESE RESEARCHER NOW LIVING ABROAD

Hui Tan

INTRODUCTION

In the past three decades, how the Chinese conduct their business and management has been a topic attracting much fascination (Stening and Zhang 2007). However, management research on China has largely been shaped by Western institutions. An analysis of research on Chinese organization and management in leading international journals showed that 80 per cent of the authors of the most-cited papers were from the USA, Canada or the UK (Li and Tsui 2002). My perspective on China is different as I have developed into a boundary spanner between the Chinese and Western worlds, having been born in China, but trained in the UK.

When conducting management research in China, most researchers choose quantitative rather than qualitative methods (Tsui 2004). This is a reflection of the fact that most research on China consists of 'testing' theories instead of theory building. This is understandable as China is a great testing ground to establish the applicability of mainstream Western theories (Roy et al. 2001). However, due to China's distinctiveness, more research of an exploratory nature is needed to understand the characteristics of management in China, thus theory-building research based on qualitative methodology, including case studies, is expected to be more frequent than theory-testing ones (although theories can also be tested with case studies derived from well-researched contexts) (Meyer 2006; Tsui 2006). This is not only very useful in learning about management and business practices in China, but also important in understanding other emerging economies.

The other reason why quantitative methods have dominated management research on China can be attributed to a general lack of understanding, at least on the part of foreign researchers, of how to conduct case studies in this unfamiliar environment. While China is an exciting but challenging place to conduct case studies, how to conduct quality case studies remains a black box to most researchers (Eckhardt 2004). There have been a small number of papers based on case studies published in Western journals (for example, Yan and Gray 1994; Walder 1995; Sonobe et al. 2002; Tan and Litschert 2006). They have contributed to our thinking about and understanding of case research in the Chinese environment. However, these papers are scattered in different outlets for management research, leaving very few clues on how to properly conduct case studies in this distinctive market.

I have conducted case studies in China for more than 10 years. It started with my doctoral dissertation which was based on case studies of four 'foreign-invested' firms in two industries: Motorola China and Shanghai Bell in the telecommunications industry, and Shanghai VW and Beijing Jeep in the automobile industry (Tan 2000). In recent years, I have also conducted case studies on state-owned enterprises (SOEs) (Buckley et al. 2005). My latest round of case research took place in the spring of 2009 when I visited a number of the largest automotive manufacturers in China. Methodologically, I follow Eisenhardt (1989) and Yin (2009) in the design and execution of case studies.

I did not start as a case study researcher. Indeed, I was very dismissive of case studies and instead was a fanatic of quantitative methodology until I was exposed to the full doctoral methodology training at the School of Management at the University of Bath, in which case-based methods were compared with other methods on an equal basis. As the topic of my PhD thesis was on the 'what' and 'how' of knowledge transfer from the headquarters of foreign-invested firms to their Chinese subsidiaries (Tan 2000), case research methodology provided the appropriate means to tap into an unknown area with robust quality assurance and integrity. Moreover, it would have been impossible to collect meaningful data through the use of surveys in this national context. This is due to the weakness in theoretical constructs in what was then a new topic area and the poor reception towards foreign-sponsored questionnaire surveys by Chinese firms.

As a Chinese growing up on the mainland and speaking Mandarin Chinese, I do not face cultural or language difficulties in communicating with people from this area. On the other hand, it is probably true that I do not have a specific 'home region' as I do not speak a Chinese dialect, which can sometimes bind people even more closely. While there have been some amazing memories, I also experienced the challenges of doing case studies in a fast-changing country such as China. These will be shared in the following sections.

CASE SELECTION: A MATTER OF RELATIONSHIPS

A frequent criticism of the case study is that companies are chosen based on convenience instead of strict selection based on data availability and methodology (Yin 2009). Convenience sampling is sometimes unavoidable when conducting case studies in China, and there is widespread agreement on the difficulties of gaining access to case companies (Eckhardt 2004). The public in the West in general is appreciative of research and often provides access to researchers. However, it is a different story in China where research is traditionally viewed more as a governmental activity. The case study approach is a very common form of policy research orchestrated by the research arms of the government or the Communist Party. Companies are not willing to offer research access for fear of leaking unhelpful information to the public unless this is requested from governmental offices. The perception towards research requests from those based overseas, in particular the West, is one of vigilance and even suspicion (Shenkar 1994).

On the other hand, I have noticed that there is a difference in attitudes towards case research between local companies and foreign-invested firms. While local firms are not keen to be the subject of research by foreigners, as described above, foreign-invested firms are more open and cooperative. This can be seen partly as a result of the transfer of corporate culture from the foreign headquarters to its China subsidiary. My own experience indicates that foreign-invested firms are more responsive to requests for research access, including data provision and meeting arrangements. For example, when I conducted a case study into the telecommunications manufacturing industry in China in the late 1990s, I contacted 19 foreign subsidiaries in China which met the selection criterion of a minimum of five years' production experience in the host country. Positive responses were received from seven of the above firms after two months and two rounds of chasing. Two firms were eliminated because they were unable to provide access within the time schedule of the field research. Following pilot fieldwork of the five remaining firms, Shanghai Bell and Motorola (China) were selected as comparable case study firms, being large final assemblers in the chosen industry (Buckley et al. 2003).

There are two ways of opening access to case companies in the context of China. First, a direct approach. This means writing to prospective case companies, normally to their head office in the West first in the case of an international joint venture (IJV) or wholly owned subsidiary, or to their Chinese headquarters in the case of SOEs. If a foreign researcher succeeds in convincing the host of the positive benefits arising from the proposed research, a formal agreement for allowing access is often issued by the CEO's Office, and sometimes by the Public Relations Department. In an extreme case, it can be the Propaganda Department of the Party branch of the company concerned. When I wanted to carry out a case study in some top-tier foreign-invested firms in the telecommunications industry, I just contacted their general manager with a full explanation of my research purpose and its impact. Within one week, two companies replied, allowing me to follow these leads. My experience suggests that foreign-invested firms are more receptive to research requests from academics, although it has to be recognized that even in an IJV situation it is likely to be very difficult for foreign academics to conduct interviews in the Chinese partner firm if it is an SOE (Nojonen 2004). It would be most efficient and effective to break the gridlock by establishing a link first with the Western headquarters before approaching their Chinese subsidiaries.

An alternative strategy for gaining access is through personal networks, or *guanxi* (Xin and Pearce 1996). As China is a society characterized by relationships, it often makes more sense to tap into personal networks to obtain support. Personal contacts offered by a friend inside the host company can be the catalyst for more and repeated access, thus removing some of the difficult procedures of negotiation. I have been able to gain access to some of the largest foreign-invested firms in China, and more than half of them were gained through personal contacts. Of course, the potential downside is that the use of personal networks can distort case selection and restrict the choice of interviewees; it is a fine line between exploiting *guanxi* and being trapped by it. Therefore, I adopted a twin-track strategy in my case study of Shanghai Bell: I contacted the headquarters of its foreign partner directly, but, to be on the safe side, also contacted a middle manager through a friend of mine. This middle manager eventually helped me to interview more managers in similar positions, in addition to providing some inside knowledge of the firm over time. His contribution complemented those leads I obtained through the official route by directly contacting its foreign parent. As the manager of a new subsidiary of Shanghai Bell, which itself was a joint venture between Alcatel Bell and its Chinese parent (the then Ministry of Post and Telecommunications of the Chinese government), he provided me with considerable inside knowledge. I was also able to identify the second leg of knowledge transfer from Shanghai Bell to this new subsidiary after the initial knowledge transfer from Alcatel Bell to Shanghai Bell. This resulted in a new model of knowledge transfer (Buckley et al. 2003).

While this path may not seemingly be open to a foreign researcher without these personal contacts, it is possible to liaise with Chinese academics who in turn may provide their own networks for the purposes of the study. It is thus very important to have an insider involved in a China-related project. Sometimes a foreign researcher has to prepare for the likelihood of no route (no access) being available at all: in China it is very difficult, if not impossible, for foreign researchers to gain access to SOEs and if they do, candid responses will not be given (Nojonen 2004). When this happens, it would be better to go back to the drawing board to see if any changes can be made to the research design, or at the very least, try other SOEs that are potentially accessible and receptive.

CAPTURING DIVERSITY IN INTERVIEWEE SELECTION

When conducting business and management case studies in China, interviewees normally include managers (foreign versus local, senior versus junior, male versus female) as well as shop-floor workers, managers and shop-floor workers of other firms (for example, competitors, suppliers, customers), and government officials. It makes a lot of sense to differentiate interviewees of any firm into senior and non-senior managers given their contrasting styles in interviews. Senior managers, either of multinational enterprises investing in China, or of SOEs, are usually chief executives, vice presidents, or partners in service firms, who have had vast experience of international operations and possess important information about a firm's organizational as well as operational processes. Therefore, these interviewees may appear as prestigious, knowledgeable, experienced and very formal when meeting foreign researchers. Their physical appearance and manner can also work in their favour. Their responses to any questions raised by the interviewer may be skilfully organized to present a different picture from the one the interviewer is seeking.

In contrast, middle managers are less confident, more cautious, and rarely totally open. For example, some interviewees can deliberately lie because the question raised is too sensitive, or the interviewee does not want to give a socially undesirable answer, or he/she simply misunderstands or misinterprets the question. Apart from language issues, lack of confidence and risk avoidance are the main reasons behind such behaviour. That is why it is quite common to have group interviews instead of one-on-one interviews at this level when the interviewer is a foreigner. This can apply to both foreign-invested firms and SOEs.

When comparing employees working for SOEs to those of foreign-owned companies in China, it is surprising to see that the former are generally more relaxed, less protective and less arrogant. This might be the result of different employment relationships with their respective companies. SOEs are still operating with the assumption of lifetime employment for employees. Their staff are very aware of the technological and management advantages enjoyed by the foreign-invested counterparts. Those employed by such companies are bound by strict company rules and corporate culture. They have to fulfil their roles to maintain long-term employment. On the other hand, senior managers of the above two types of companies are very similar to each other: open, direct, confident and proud.

It is notable that there is also a difference in attitudes towards case studies based on age. Traditionally, China did not have a culture of collaborating with researchers from the West (Shenkar 1994). Instead, there is still a mindset among many people even today that it would create unnecessary trouble if you say too much to a foreign researcher. In comparison with older generations who suffered from such experiences of contact with foreigners during China's cultural revolution, younger people are more open and willing to participate in foreign-sponsored research. Given this, it would be ideal to have a balance of both young/junior and old/senior in the investigation. However, one has to be prepared for refusals from those 'older' generations. Even if they agree to participate, such interviewees should be categorized as special because their answers are most likely to be well thought through to avoid any possibility of repercussion.

In my own experience of doing a case study on Shanghai VW, I was surprised that the answers from different age groups in response to the same questions could be so different. For example, when asked about the corporate culture transferred from VW headquarters to its subsidiary in Shanghai, most young interviewees were dismissive of traditional Chinese culture and full of support for the 'German way', expressing the wish that the more German corporate culture was introduced to Shanghai VW, the better. On the other hand, every older employee emphasized the importance of mixing German corporate culture with the Chinese national and regional cultures in the subsidiary – 'otherwise it would not work here' (one interviewee). On this very point, I was struck by the cautious and balanced tone from the older employees, and chased them for more explanation. One manager simply said to me: 'You can never forget the influence of the Party when talking about any corporate culture in this country'.

LANGUAGE DIFFERENCES IN THE INTERVIEWING PROCESS

My observation during interviews in China is that many managers, regardless of whether they work for foreign-invested or state-owned firms, have a good command of English and can communicate with foreign researchers directly without translators (although this is probably not so true for smaller and domestically focused firms). However, foreign language competence deteriorates rapidly when going lower down the organizational hierarchy. Indeed, most shop-floor employees, including those in foreign-owned firms, can barely communicate in English. Foreign researchers have to rely on a translator when interviewing them. I have accompanied my British colleagues to conduct interviews in China over the years. It was always easier for them to communicate with senior managers or government officials with or without interpreters, but communication shifted into a low gear when interviewing shop-floor employees, with an interpreter (sometimes myself) acting as bridge to enable any sensible exchange (on the use of interpreters, see Welch and Piekkari 2006). Simply put, English competence can vary hugely within the same organization in China.

When conducting case studies in China, an interviewer who has an accent can cause serious misunderstanding. This is quite common given that nearly every Chinese has no exposure to the 'world of Englishes' when learning the language. The majority of Chinese actually learn English speaking and listening from CDs recorded with pure mainstream British or American English. For the lucky few who have been taught by foreign teachers, these teachers are scrutinized first and foremost on their dictionary-style pronunciation. Those interviewers with a strong accent will certainly experience communication problems when interacting with Chinese interviewees. The best advice here is to use a Chinese interpreter with a background in the English language to moderate the negative impact of various accents. When an interpreter is needed, it is preferable to keep a complete record in order to have an opportunity of back translation of all the data collected.

DATA ANALYSIS AND RESEARCH OUTCOMES

Given the lack of transparency and openness in Chinese society, researchers need to pay great attention to the quality of the data and its interpretation. My solution was to conduct interviews, where possible, at the headquarters of the Western partner, and carefully compare their replies with those from subsidiaries on the same question. This is a strategy termed 'unit triangulation' (Marschan-Piekkari et al. 2004, p. 254). These interviews were revelatory in that they were likely to be in sharp contrast to the responses received from the IJV operation in China. For example, when I interviewed managers in Shanghai Bell regarding the role of the Chinese Communist Party in the management of IJV operations, one Chinese manager replied: 'The Party does not play a significant role here in this firm except by providing an enabling environment internally and effective communication with Chinese parent externally'. For the same question, Belgian managers at the headquarters of the foreign parent commented:

> The Chinese Communist Party's involvement in business operation is unbelievably extensive, especially in respect of management localization. Some of the very promising local staff cannot be promoted to the right positions due to the fact that they are not Communist Party members. Belgian managers don't have a say in selecting Chinese managers. Even when they made suggestions, the Chinese partner did not listen to their advice.

Interpreting data in context is essential to resolve conflicting findings. Therefore, contextual validity (correctly 'incorporating the context in describing, understanding, and theorizing about phenomena within it', see Tsui 2006, p. 2) is worth emphasizing when doing data analysis in China. The seemingly obvious conclusions may not be the right ones when viewed in context. For example, when analysing localization in the Chinese automotive industry, researchers would notice that in the 1990s the local content rate by value stalled or even decreased (Tan 2000), which could give the impression that the Chinese government strategy of promoting localization failed. This was against the background that the Chinese government made a hefty investment following its 1994 national automotive industrial policy, and local firms made great inroads in technical and production capacity. As a result, local content by number of components was raised year after year. In truth, the reduction in local content rate by value was caused by the devaluation of the local currency Renminbi against the US dollar during that time, resulting in the value of key components through imports, such as engines, increasing, hence a higher proportion of these imported components in the total value of a finished product. While the Chinese automotive industry has experienced explosive growth in the past few years, it is the investment and upgrading of technical capacity in the 1990s that laid the foundations for such unprecedented growth. Thus, a foreign researcher would misjudge this issue if the data analysis did not take the local context into account.

Authorities on case research methodology (for example, Yin 2009) advise that other data than interviews should be considered to present a better picture of the emerging management issues pursued, such as company reports, internal documents, annual yearbooks published by the relevant industry/ministry/province, and government research reports. But a note of caution here is that this information is not always objective – sometimes it can be tricky. For example, press reports and annual yearbooks can be marketing channels in China. Additional work has to be carried out to squeeze out those self-promotional elements while taking the remaining information as issues for further inquiry or validating them through triangulation. Among these types of data, of particular value are company internal reports and government research reports. The former are produced (either in-house or by external consultants) for managers making strategic or operational decisions, and therefore have to be based on timely data. The latter, on the other hand, are reports by the research arm of governmental agencies (either provincial or ministry lines of administration). In China, such researchers can, through government channels, gain access to anyone in a firm they wish, including top management teams, therefore these reports often contain insights not seen elsewhere. This applies equally to foreign-invested enterprises as it is in their own interests to maintain rapport with the government in this transition economy (Tan and Litschert 2006). Another beauty of such reports is their objectivity and comparisons between firms of the same industry or in the same locality. The difficulty for foreign researchers here is to gain access to these reports. Apart from libraries in Chinese universities, these reports are mostly likely to be available in the Chinese Academy of Social Science (and its provincial counterparts) or various research institutes at national and provincial levels.

While standard methodological texts advocate respondent validation or member checking (Lietz et al. 2006), initiating and maintaining any post-interview interaction with Chinese interviewees is problematic. Many local interviewees are happy to provide any support and give their views when you are on-site, but it would not be easy to continue such a relationship when the foreign researcher is gone. Further requests for clarification and information are normally addressed incompletely at best or not taken seriously at all. This can frustrate foreign researchers as it is vital to have such post-interview interaction for quality and consistency. The reason for this lack of cooperation can be attributed to the fact that Chinese people think that they have done their bit by having granted an interview in the first place. They would be resistant to further 'greedy' requests unless asked by a good friend or boss, or if such requests were accompanied by personal benefits. A clear agreement should be reached during the interview that further interaction is anticipated so the interviewees are prepared for such requests.

Different expectations concerning the end point of the case study process exists between the West and China. While it is common practice in the West to expect a report or a published paper at the end of a research project, Chinese hosts (especially those from SOEs) are more fascinated by the propaganda effects arising from case studies. They are keen to present a positive picture of the issues involved and expect the interviewer to follow the same style of flowery descriptions. This often poses a challenge to the foreign researcher. Anyone in this position should be prepared to press the interviewees for a more balanced picture and be ready to dig for more truthful data through repetitive queries and clarifications. Sometimes this approach can endanger the rapport between the two parties when the divergence of expectations between the parties escalates. Foreign researchers may need to prepare the host with respect to the purpose of the research and its publication, and to guarantee confidentiality. Such informal and formal interactions can be used to adjust the expectations prior to the interview.

Another important issue associated with case research in China is generalization. Tsui (2004) identifies three types of management knowledge: context free, context bounded and context specific. The first type, context free, can be understood as universal knowledge which can be applied regardless of context; the context-bounded type consists of that management knowledge partially applicable in all contexts, while context-specific knowledge is thought to be applicable only in one context. This indicates that some findings from case studies are never to be generalized due to their context specificity. Tsui concludes that findings from theory-building research have been too context specific to extend them out of the Chinese environment. Having said that, she adds that generalizability of the findings from a China-based case study should not be judged as an integral part of the contribution of such research. As long as valid findings have been developed, case research in China is a useful addition to global management knowledge (White 2002; Meyer 2006). Personally, I have never placed generalizability at the core of my research. This, however, does not prohibit me from developing propositions which can potentially be generalized outside China. The model of the two-leg knowledge transfer from foreign parent to the new venture owned by its Chinese subsidiary (Buckley et al. 2003) is an example in point.

Conducting case research in China is challenging even for an overseas Chinese like myself. Having grown up in China but trained in the West, I have felt that there are always two sets of rules opposing and fighting each other inside me. While I can adopt the 'Chinese way' of doing case studies by easily gaining access to firms and interviewees through *guanxi*, I have to step back and review each action in light of the rules of doing proper case studies proposed by Eisenhardt (1989) and Yin (2009). I had to abandon those data collected from cases where the practice could not withstand the rigours expected by the 'bibles' of case methodology. Therefore, to be able to produce publishable output in international journals, it is imperative to guard the quality and integrity of case studies in China throughout the entire research process. I have suggested that this involves selecting cases based on research and methodological merit instead of convenience, gaining access to interviewees through *guanxi* but not being trapped by it, avoiding bias in interviews caused by cultural misunderstanding and language differences, and analysing data based on the specific Chinese cultural context.

PERSPECTIVE NO. 2: A CONFESSIONAL TALE BY A WESTERN RESEARCHER

Matti Nojonen

INTRODUCTION

In the following sections I shall describe a foreigner's perspective and experience of doing fieldwork in different parts of China and within different Chinese organizations over the last 15 years or so. I am Finnish, and I shall elaborate, based on my own personal experience, how fieldwork has changed, what new forces have emerged and what has remained the same in conditioning the fieldwork experience in a rapidly developing China.

I began my Chinese journey by studying Chinese language and culture both in China and in Sweden. I obtained my Master's degree in Sinology from Stockholm University and moved to Shanghai in 1996 to conduct a mixed-method study involving case studies and a questionnaire for my thesis on Chinese business ethics among MBA students in Shanghai, Beijing and Taibei. This became an almost three-year-long odyssey, a journey during which I had to completely change my research topic and methodology. This radical change came about because the local university did not provide approval for my research, and as a solution, I conducted my fieldwork without official permission – rather than conducting an officially sanctioned case study. This experience gave me a good taste of how the non-transparent regulations can, in a rather arbitrary fashion, hamper academic research in China.

REGULATORY FRAMEWORK CONDITIONING FIELDWORK

A host of regulations exists that guide not only the foreign research conducted in China, but also that conducted by local researchers. There has been no improvement in the regulatory system conditioning fieldwork during the 15 years between the mid-1990s and 2010. Indeed, I shall illustrate that, despite the increasing opening and tangible development of China, the regulatory framework conditioning the work of foreign journalists and researchers has become much tighter in recent years, and more alarmingly we, the foreign scholars studying China, are sacrificing our academic integrity at the altar of increasing Chinese might.

The regulation which forbade my original research was based on a non-transparent 'internal regulation' (*neibu guiding*). This regulation was created in the mid-1990s, but was not publicly available at the time, to restrict foreigners from conducting 'uncontrolled' research in Chinese society or organizations. Indeed, there are a number of rules, regulations, laws and policies that control quantitative and qualitative research by foreigners in Chinese societies and organizations. Foreign researchers are directly subject to Chinese regulations on foreign affairs (*waishi jilü*) and to 'internal regulations', both of which also control foreign research in China. *Waishi jilü* regulations are partly arbitrary by nature and the internal regulations lack transparency. However, two general lines of enforcement can be detected (Nojonen 2004).

One set of rules conditions and restricts independent foreign-conducted quantitative research. These rules forbid all research conducted by foreigners and require foreigners to submit their quantitative research proposals to the National Statistical Bureau (NSB) or to those research centres and state universities that have the necessary NSB approval. Research institutes that have gained NSB authorization are also obliged to evaluate the political correctness of the research proposal. The evaluation of the political sensitivity of a project is complicated because the criteria change according to the prevailing political winds or are determined by internal political factional fights (Nojonen 2004).

A second set of regulations regarding qualitative research is even more ambiguous, plagued with non-transparency and complexity (Nojonen 2004). Often foreign researchers study foreign organizations in China, such as IJVs or wholly foreign owned subsidiaries. To my understanding there have never been any reports showing that the Chinese authorities would have restricted access to these organizations. On the contrary, despite the official regulations, the authorities allow and even openly support foreign research that is conducted in such organizations. Consequently, foreign researchers have a distorted understanding of the actual regulatory framework within which they do fieldwork, and more generally will obtain a biased picture of the institutional environment in which most Chinese people live (Nojonen 2004).

On the other hand, foreign scholars intending to carry out a qualitative field study in Chinese-run organizations and local societies are subject to a completely different regulatory system and treatment. The first required step is to name a 'host institute' in China, usually a university or a think-tank, whose responsibility it is to check the political correctness of the research. The host institute is also required to appoint a supervising person to the project and will usually also supply an assistant who will help to carry out interviews and if needed, act as translator.

The regulatory framework of these non-transparent internal regulations (*neibu guiding*) guiding qualitative research remains unclear, but is shaped by vague notions of 'state secrets' and political, economic or cultural sensitivity (Fang 1999; Nojonen 2004). These 'state secrets', which represent the most arbitrary type of regulation, have a central role in defining fieldwork practices and are subject to wide interpretation. Information provided by the official state-run media, covering central and regional TV and radio broadcasts, all newspapers, and most magazines and journals, can, in a surreal way, become a state secret if Western or local scholars or journalists attempt to access it (Fang 1999). In Nojonen (2004, p. 159), I quote a foreign ministry spokesman, Tang Guoqing, who argued at a news briefing for foreign correspondents that '[t]he law on [state] secrets has clear stipulations'. However, when asked to provide an example, Tang continued, 'Clearly, I cannot answer on this occasion. The specifics cannot be told because they are state secrets'.

In addition to this arbitrary regulatory system, there are two additional factors of great importance that constitute particular challenges for successful fieldwork. The first is the rather short history of social science research in China. Despite the fact that Chinese universities carry out an increasing amount of fieldwork, ordinary people are not yet accustomed to being interviewed, particularly by foreign researchers. The second reason is the 'culture of fear'. This term refers, on the one hand, to China's tumultuous political history where all forms of social and human conduct could be subjected to harsh political rectification campaigns (that is, campaigns that are aimed at 'rectifying' individual or collective behaviour). On the other hand, the term refers to the genesis of low trust, which is based on the traditional division of insiders and outsiders (*nei-wai you bie*, there is a difference between those who are insiders and those who are outsiders). This cultural structure refers to a tradition where individuals tend to trust people of the same kinship and locality and distrust strangers from outside their immediate social circle. This is naturally a challenge for the researchers who carry out interviews in such societies (Fukuyama 1996).

Furthermore, the control apparatus reacts to the political swings between periods of 'rectification' and relaxation, the most recent being the tightening of control prior to the Beijing Olympics. The current regime of Hu Jintao has not relaxed these controls since then; on the contrary, Beijing has tightened the regulatory framework controlling the work of journalists (and researchers) in the country. General Secretary Aidan White of the International Federation of Journalists (IFJ) referred to 'the steady stream of official bans as well as new rules in 2009 which make it virtually impossible for local journalists who work in traditional or online media to receive the accreditation they need in order to conduct their profession' (IFEX 2010). The IFJ report details 62 bans issued from January to November 2009, among hundreds of regulations issued by central and provincial authorities in the previous year (IFJ Report 2010, pp. 9–12).

Despite the existence of these regulations they are not necessarily followed or monitored – local officials at all levels of administration can, in a surrealist manner, bend the central government laws or party regulations if they find it appropriate or if it yields them certain benefits. In doing this, it is not uncommon for the local administration to legitimize their action by paraphrasing a famous Chinese expression 'Those above have their policies, we below have our counter-means'.

It is common for business scholars, either consciously or unconsciously, to *de-politicize* China by coming under the spell of the fast-growing economy. They regularly explain their findings with reference to certain elements of traditional Chinese culture or particular institutional norms or practices. However, the price of this de-politicization is blindness to the political texture that generates an 'increasingly fractured society', in the words of Qinghua Sociologist Professor Sun Liping (Sun 2003). The recognition of and sensitivity towards this political texture would provide a much richer understanding of Chinese society. Business scholars seem to ignore the basic rule – in China, politics are in command and the world's biggest one-party regime is particularly keen to control all aspects of information processing – restricting journalists' and researchers' fieldwork, and controlling the research questions, analysis and dissemination. It is likely that this reality first became apparent to a wider audience when one of the most important information providers of our era – Google – found this out the hard way and threatened to withdraw from China in January 2010 (Jacobs and Helft 2010).

What is particularly alarming today is that the actual 'China-hands' who are familiar with Chinese politics are also conditioning their research and findings. This becomes evident in the '2009 Report to Congress of the US–China Economic and Security Review Commission' (USCC 2009), which details the emerging phenomenon of self-censorship among political scientists, China specialists and economists working on China. The report illustrates how the country utilizes both coercive and incentivizing means in dealing with foreign scholars doing work on China. This policy is systematic and part of China's foreign policy strategy to improve its international image. As the leading official of the country's propaganda system, Li Changchun (also a member of the Standing Committee of the Politburo), stated on national TV:

> Enhancing our communication capacity domestically and internationally is of direct consequence to our nation's international influence and international position, of direct consequence to the raising of our nation's cultural soft power, and of direct consequence to the function and role of our nation's media within the international public opinion structure. (Bandurski 2009, n.p.)

This policy is carried out, on the one hand, by rewarding 'friendly' scholars with access to career-enhancing fieldwork experiences, interviews and documents, while on the other, punishing non-friendly researchers by restricting their access to the field or even denying them visas (USCC 2009). Hence, Beijing has an increasingly decisive role over the career trajectory of foreign scholars.

This image strategy is generating self-censorship among foreign scholars (USCC 2009). The '2009 Report to Congress' included a number of statements from foreign scholars on this emerging pattern of self-censorship. Illustrative was the fact that many of these scholars preferred to remain anonymous. One such academic economist stated, 'Academics who study China . . . habitually please the Chinese Communist Party, sometimes consciously, and often unconsciously . . . [T]he incentives for academics all go one way: one does not upset the Party' (USCC 2009, p. 298). Dr Terill, who works at one of the leading China centres in the world, the John K. Fairbank Center for Chinese Studies at Harvard University, stated bluntly:

> Self-censorship, which is a daily necessity for journalists in China, also occurs in diluted form among American editors, academics, and others dealing with China. Folk worry about their next visa, their access to a sensitive area like Xinjiang for research, or take a Beijing point of view because of the largesse available for their projects from the Chinese side. (USCC 2009, p. 299)

UNAUTHORIZED FIELDWORK IN THE 1990s IN CHINESE ENTERPRISES

My original research back in 1996 was forbidden by the Chinese authorities. They could not cite the non-transparent internal regulation, but rather encouraged me either to allow their appointed assistant to conduct the questionnaire survey of my original research plan, or to drop it and conduct a study in one joint venture in Pudong district, Shanghai. As the first proposal was out of the question and the latter – the officially approved field study – was not interesting enough, I decided not to apply for any further permission for my research and quietly carried out ethnographic research on an issue that was gaining wider interest among foreign researchers: networking (*guanxi*) in Chinese business. Eventually I managed to conduct 84 informative interviews in three different cities. The usual interview language was Mandarin Chinese, but I used English if the interviewee so preferred.

Under unauthorized circumstances, imagination and flexibility in fieldwork are essential, particularly when the topic of research is somewhat sensitive. The unauthorized nature of my research had a direct impact on a number of issues (for more details, see Nojonen 2004). It affected the sample, as in China it was virtually impossible to, say, pick up the Yellow Pages and start to call around as a foreign researcher hoping to gain access to companies in a particular industry to do interviews on a sensitive topic such as *guanxi*. The only solution was to proceed through networking; first asking local friends and utilizing their networks. The next step was to ask informative interviewees to become intermediaries and to introduce me to their network. It was classic snowballing, but occasionally the snowball hit a rock and I had to begin to roll a new snowball again.

In building the network I grasped all available opportunities; I talked to people at airports, entered into discussion with co-passengers on planes and trains and actively engaged with people in local communities. Chinese people are very talkative and making initial contact with them was very easy. It was also easy to obtain their general opinions about *guanxi*. However, when I suggested a formal interview to discuss the subject I was greeted with polite refusal or sometimes with suspicion: 'are you a journalist?' In Qingdao, where there are fewer foreigners, some potential interviewees even asked: 'are you a spy?' Indeed, I also faced similar questions during a number of interviews.

Based on my experience, there is no 'particular Chinese way' of gaining access to networks. It is conditioned by universal factors, such as finding a common interest or worldview through socializing and mingling with people. However, as soon as this kind of connection was established and a

certain degree of trust emerged, I could ask for the favour of being introduced to a contact's friends. The common 'Chinese pattern' of extending
networks was through dining; for the Chinese it is a usual and natural
platform where people are introduced to each other.

Unauthorized interviewing also affected me personally as I was aware
of my precarious position – conducting fieldwork without official approval
could mean, in the worst-case scenario, expulsion from China. As Yang
(1994) describes, conducting an unauthorized study under an arbitrary
control apparatus affects the researcher, the research process and pro-
longs the fieldwork. From the researcher's point of view it provides one
important element – it gives the researcher a small taste of living under the
'culture of fear'.

All my interviewees were working in Chinese companies or for the state
sector and had had little or in most cases no experience of talking to a foreigner. In retrospect, the interviewees certainly did not possess any critical
information that could have threatened the society or state. Nevertheless,
the minimal exposure to foreign contacts and social research formed a
fertile ground for the culture of fear and low trust. This setting had practical consequences that materialized in the fear of being tape-recorded
during the interview. I climbed a steep learning curve in the interviewing
process. It was learning by doing, coloured with challenges, learning from
mistakes and luck.

During this process, a certain generic pattern of interviewing emerged.
First was the warm-up stage during which I gave a short presentation of
myself and the purpose of the study, and affirmed the confidentiality of
the research. Gift-giving was also an important part of this stage of the
interview. I usually gave a small gift (typically wooden artefacts from my
home region of Finnish Lapland) during the first minutes of the encounter.
The gift-giving was a symbolic gesture with which I attempted to bridge
the gap between the interviewee and myself by accompanying the gift with
a small personal story behind the gift. With this symbolic gesture and
story I wished to generate a common base of intimacy, and by revealing
something personal about myself I aspired to create an element of trust
in the interview process. These gestures were followed by normal warm-
up questions on the background of the interviewees. In the early stage of
my research I followed a strict script, but eventually I recognized that the
most fruitful way of gaining data was to be flexible, innovative and self-
reflective in adjusting and improvising my own roles and reactions during
the interview. My opening role was that of 'student of China', at which
point I raised the more generic questions of the interviewees' daily work,
how *guanxi* practices affected them in their daily work, and so forth. I
would also make use of this role later in the interview to pose follow-up

questions, along the lines of, 'You mentioned this, but as a foreigner I do not really understand what you meant by it'. This kind of iterative, not too hasty approach proved to be very fruitful in interviewing Chinese respondents about the potentially sensitive issue of *guanxi*.

At a certain stage of the interview I eventually and gradually exposed my knowledge of the *guanxi* issue – moving into the role of 'savant' – by asking more detailed questions, using certain *guanxi*-related expressions or elaborated *guanxi*-related cases I had collected from previous interviews. If the interviewee had began to trust me, he/she usually grasped this opportunity and began to talk in more detail about the issue. At this stage we both became full discussants and I could relinquish my previous roles. I learned that drawing was a particularly effective method of gaining information and breaking the normative and strict physical construction of having the interviewee and interviewer sitting upright, facing each other. On many occasions the interviewee took the pen from my hand and began to analyse the case in great detail, seemingly having completely forgotten the issue of personal sensitivities.

I also had to learn the sensitivities surrounding note-taking; in particular, when to stop making notes. This is what Goffman calls (2002, p. 152) 'faking off-phase note taking', referring to a deliberate practice of not making notes when the interviewee exposes some personally sensitive information. In addition, this skill is important when socializing with the interviewee after the official interview. According to my experience, in studying sensitive issues such as *guanxi* the potentially most informative discussions are after the official interview during dinner, karaoke or over a pint of beer. Making notes during this kind of situation could have potentially destroyed the relaxed and friendly atmosphere. Because of this I sometimes had to utilize the 'toilet anthropologist' method and make some notes in the restroom during long banquets.

FIELDWORK IN TWENTY-FIRST CENTURY CHINESE THINK-TANKS

In this section I shall describe my fieldwork experience in my new role working as a programme director at the Finnish Institute of International Affairs (FIIA) and compare this experience with my fieldwork experience in the 1990s. I also altered my research topic from *guanxi* to Sino–US relationships from a politico-economic perspective and Chinese strategic behaviour and thinking. The differences in fieldwork experiences are striking.

My institutional setting is dramatically different today compared to the mid-1990s when I was a postgraduate student in China. By law FIIA is an independent research institute under the auspices of the Finnish parliament. In the Chinese context, the FIIA's governmental connection has proved to be a double-edged sword. Chinese scholars, officials and ordinary citizens believe that we represent the official view of Finland or can provide some insights into European Union (EU) policies. For the Chinese it is perfectly normal to assume that our research topics are dictated by the Finnish government or are at least in the interest of some policy direction taken by internal decision-making circles. This belief is hard to change, since in China all research institutes belong to the government and produce policy papers and analysis for the government. There is a strong patron–client relationship between the central government and research institutes, whereas the FIIA is a non-partisan research institute with no policy line.

If in the 1990s I occasionally had to make a considerable effort to convince some of my Chinese counterparts that I was not a journalist or a spy, I now have to spend quite a lot of time in convincing some of them that my opinions have nothing to do with the official policy of Finland or the EU. For the Chinese, having parliament supporting an *independent* think-tank is an alien institutional arrangement. The benefit of working in a think-tank under the umbrella of parliament opens a lot of doors in China; however, I believe that this is not a particularly Chinese phenomenon, because the same logic appears to work in other countries as well. Gaining access through these doors provides me with an opportunity to meet and work with the most brilliant and educated minds in China. This is an additional structural difference compared to my previous experience in the 1990s when I was primarily working with not so theoretically oriented, but extremely streetwise Chinese entrepreneurs or lower-level officials. In addition, the whole atmosphere is different as I do not have to struggle to obtain access to these institutions – it is business as usual and there are no indications of 'unfriendly' institutional elements involved.

Despite the fact that the atmosphere is friendly and non-hostile, it is not without challenges. The institutional setting of these organizations, being close to the Chinese decision makers, forms a somewhat competitive environment. Specifically, most of the prestigious research institutes with ample resources from all corners of the world are keen to work with these institutes. The criteria of competition are not only determined by the proposed research agendas, but are also based on *realpolitik* factors where the gravity of power talks. In this game the players from other major powers have an upper hand in comparison to institutions that come from smaller countries. The foreign institutes are also facing a new situation in which they can no longer simply persuade their Chinese counterparts to work with them by bringing in money or other forms of benefits, because most of these Chinese institutes already have very good funding, and research centres are even providing lucrative deals for foreign researchers to work for them.

Networking is also different. First, I utilize my institutional background to gain access to circles of power – and I do not necessarily need to use intermediaries to gain access. Second, referring to third parties in order to generate common ground is not necessary. However, if I do work through third parties my current experience differs from the traditional pattern. Namely, in Chinese networking it is common to generate familiarity between parties by referring to a third party known to both. I assume that the reason for this changed behaviour is the intense competition and the nature of the industry, where people frequently meet in conferences and know each other's products (articles and books), thus eroding these kinds of 'name-dropping' methods. On the contrary, what counts is your personal history; who has been your supervisor and with whom you have been working.

Based on my retrospective analysis of my own behaviour among Chinese specialists, I recognize that the social construction of personal professional identity and respect demands a different 'role-play' from the one I experienced during my fieldwork on *guanxi*. I recognize that I am not resorting to the roles I utilized when working at the street level in the 1990s. Also, the exposure to foreign cultures is radically different. Most of the staff working in these institutes have taken one or two degrees in the most prestigious universities of the world. Consequently the traditional cultural challenge of building social trust between insiders and outsiders is no longer evident. In fact, based on my observation of the international exchanges occurring in these institutes, I assume that the personal and collective institutional inter-cultural experience can in most cases surpass our foreign counterparts' inter-cultural experiences. Hence, for these Chinese scholars meetings and cooperation with foreigners are not flavoured with exotic expectations or conditioned with a sense of mistrust. Indeed, in many cases foreigners have their heads full of stereotypical ideas of how the Chinese should behave, while the Chinese in these central research centres have at least some insight into the cultural differences in Western and Asian countries.

Wining and dining also has a different role in these organizations. Usually during the first meetings lunch or dinner is arranged in some nice restaurants, but once the actual work has begun the food can be ordered in lunch-boxes from street-corner restaurants and eaten in the office. There is no extravagant show of lavish dinners involved. During social gatherings I have had no experience of intimate questions being posed to me nor has my level of Chinese (either reading or spoken) been tested, as was sometimes the case in the 1990s.

In the fieldwork literature, the notion of a 'culture of fear' is frequently mentioned. However, working now with the Chinese specialists who are most likely to possess information that could be of a critical nature for the whole system, it is paradoxical to note that I have not yet sensed or witnessed anything even slightly resembling 'the culture of fear' described in the literature or what I experienced earlier. On the contrary, based on my understanding there are no political taboos that cannot be discussed and argued with the specialists. Naturally the degree of trust and circumstances in which politically sensitive issues are discussed condition the tone of the Chinese answers. It goes without saying that if a Chinese scholar advocated a different political system for China in front of a wider public, he or she would be punished by being sacked from work and would most likely face a prison sentence.

We need to understand that the Chinese system does not have a single voice or monolithic view. Chinese scholars can disagree and are disagreeing with central government policies. This is always like skating on thin ice, requiring scholars to take into consideration the prevailing political attitudes and the topic under discussion. Scholars who have the strong backing of someone high up in the system can talk more freely, but even for them certain topics remain taboo, like questioning the unity of the country or the position of the party. It is a paradoxical situation where the central government expects and even demands from these specialists critical reports on China, but these reports cannot be too critical.

However, opinions delivered to wider audiences on even sensitive issues vary in their tone, not to mention the contrast with statements delivered in more private circumstances. In addition to personal differences of opinion, institutions have different political stances that should be noted when collecting data in China. Certain institutions (such as the Chinese Institute of International Studies) are famous for their conservative policy lines, while other institutes or university departments are more open and within the system could be regarded as radical. However, it is notable that a neo-conservative trend is currently emerging, flavoured with criticism of Western hegemony. In general, scholars in Shanghai state that they are much more strictly monitored than their colleagues in Beijing.

CONCLUSION

Doing fieldwork in China is one of the most rewarding and exciting phases of research, involving many gatekeepers, pitfalls, tangible and non-tangible obstacles, regulations and positive surprises. As I have detailed in this 'confessional tale', I have conducted fieldwork in two different institutional environments during the past 15 years. These fieldwork journeys have provided me with radically different experiences. The first experience was within Chinese organizations and enterprises during the latter part of the 1990s – although I decided not to go down the route of an officially approved case study. The lack of official support and unauthorized nature of my fieldwork in a hostile institutional environment meant that I was plagued with a culture of fear that considerably prolonged my data gathering. The second fieldwork experience has been carried out in Chinese research institutes and think-tanks in the twenty-first century. During this fieldwork journey my institutional setting has been dramatically different from that in the 1990s. The natural conclusion of this is that institutional background plays an important role in gaining access to the field.

Hence, based on these two different fieldwork experiences, we as scholars should be careful in labelling our isolated fieldwork experiences as representative of the whole of China. Are we not too easily generalizing our findings to represent all of China? I am certain that the street-corner sociologist will still face the culture of fear and other revelations in interviewing, while researchers entering multinational Chinese enterprises might face a completely different environment. We should take seriously the Chinese sociologist's warning of a 'fracturing Chinese society' in which a number of parallel realities have emerged that do not form a pluralist society, but rather a fragmenting one (Sun 2003). Characteristic of the fracturing society, according to Sun, is that different realities are institutionalized in China: the neo-feudal structures in the countryside and the emergence of market or exploitative capitalism, Communist Party jargon as the dominant language of control and Hong Kong soap operas exist side by side, but are not able to communicate with each other.

China is changing fast and these changes are on the one hand helping our fieldwork, while others are creating novel and serious challenges for our work. During my 15 years of working in China, the country has opened up and modernized dramatically. Living, moving around and talking to ordinary people is like everywhere abroad. Also, access to certain information has become dramatically easier, for example, access to public information, such as acquiring library cards and internet archives of newspapers and journals. The Chinese government is also actively supporting foreign researchers' access to foreign-run organizations. As most foreign business scholars carry out their fieldwork in foreign enterprises, organizations or in successful Chinese companies, they are tempted to depoliticize China in trying to understand its success.

Despite these positive structural changes, the regulatory structure for controlling foreign-conducted fieldwork in China has been tightening. There are a number of new laws, regulations and stipulations controlling free and independent access to the field. Very few foreign researchers are aware of this, as they mostly work inside IJVs or foreign-run organizations in China. From Beijing's point of view, controlling fieldwork has so far proved to be a successful part of China's national-level 'soft power', or more precisely image strategy. First, Beijing has been systematically restricting access of foreign scholars, knowing full well that foreign researchers and the global audience are keen to deepen their understanding of the country that is altering the global power constellation. The Beijing government's next step has been to reward friendly and to punish critical scholars, which has reportedly caused self-censorship among foreign scholars desiring to gain access to career-enhancing data. To put it bluntly, China is utilizing individual researchers' desires of personal career advancement and hunger for access to the rapidly developing China for Beijing's own power-political objectives. The cost of this process is immeasurable – the integrity of independent and critical academic thinking.

There is one generic collective myth that Westerners still believe in, whether consciously or unconsciously, and we need to be aware of it. Westerners seem to assume that as China becomes more open and more modern it will increasingly resemble Western societies and at an individual level their value base will become more 'Western'. In fact, if we observe the foreign scholars studying China, we can see that there is a danger of the opposite happening – they are on the verge of becoming more Chinese as they are voluntarily sacrificing their academic integrity in order to please Beijing.

So how to conduct successful fieldwork in China? Based on my experience there is no magic potion. I could not have replicated the successful patterns of my own fieldwork practices as the structural, cultural and individual conditions differed so dramatically and next time I enter the field it will once again be a different ball-game. As the famous Chinese strategist, Sunzi, states on the impossibility of copying success: 'You can never repeat the battles you have won'. The only way is to be flexible, innovative, self-critical and take nothing for granted.

REFERENCES

Bandurski, D. (2009), 'Li Changchun on the media and China's global influence', *China Media Project*, available at: http://cmp.hku.hk/2009/01/19/1457 (accessed 15 January 2010).

Buckley, P.J., J. Clegg and H. Tan (2003), 'The art of knowledge transfer: second-ary and reverse transfer in China's telecommunications manufacturing indus-try', *Management International Review*, **43** (2), 67–93.

Buckley, P.J., J. Clegg and H. Tan (2005), 'Organizational change in a Chinese state-owned enterprise: Sinotrans in the 1990s', *Management International Review*, **45** (2), 147–72.

Eckhardt, G.M. (2004), 'The role of culture in conducting trustworthy and credible qualitative business research in China', in R. Marschan-Piekkari and C. Welch (eds), *Handbook of Qualitative Research Methods for International Business*, Cheltenham, UK and Northampton, MA, USA: Edward Elgar, pp. 402–20.

Eisenhardt, K.M. (1989), 'Building theories from case study research', *Academy of Management Review*, **14** (4), 532–50.

Fang, T. (1999), *Chinese Business Negotiating Style*, London: Sage.

Fukuyama, F. (1996), *Trust: Human Nature and the Reconstitution of Social Order*, New York: Simon & Schuster.

Goffman, E. (2002), 'On fieldwork', in D. Weinber (ed.), *Qualitative Research Methods*, Oxford: Blackwell, pp. 148–53.

International Freedom of Expression eXchange (IFEX) (2010), 'IFJ report lists China's secret bans on media reporting', available at: http://www.ifex.org/china/2010/02/01/secret_bans/ (accessed 8 October 2010).

International Federation of Journalists (IFJ) (2010), 'China clings to control: press freedom in 2009', available at: http://www.ifex.org/china/2010/02/01/china_clings_to_control.pdf (accessed 8 October 2010).

Jacobs, A. and M. Helft (2010), 'Google, citing attack, threatens to exit China', available at: http://www.nytimes.com/2010/01/13/world/asia/13beijing.html (accessed 12 January 2010).

Li, J. and A. Tsui (2002), 'A citation analysis of management and organisa-tion research in the Chinese context: 1984–1999', *Asia Pacific Journal of Management*, **19** (1), 87–107.

Lietz, C.A., C.L. Langer and R. Furman (2006), 'Establishing trustworthiness in qualitative research in social work: implications from a study regarding spiritu-ality', *Qualitative Social Work*, **5** (4), 441–58.

Marschan-Piekkari, R., C. Welch, H. Penttinen and M. Tahvanainen (2004), 'Interviewing in the multinational corporation: challenges of the organisa-tional context', in R. Marschan-Piekkari and C. Welch (eds), *Handbook of Qualitative Research Methods for International Business*, Cheltenham, UK and Northampton, MA, USA: Edward Elgar, pp. 244–63.

Meyer, K. (2006), 'Asian management research needs more self-confidence', *Asia Pacific Journal of Management*, **23** (2), 119–37.

Nojonen, M. (2004), 'Fieldwork in a low-trust (post) communist society', in E. Clark and S. Michailova (eds), *Fieldwork in Transforming Societies: Understanding Methodology from Experience*, Basingstoke: Palgrave Macmillan, pp. 157–76.

Roy, A., P.G.P. Walters and S.T.K. Luk (2001), 'Chinese puzzles and paradoxes: conducting business research in China', *Journal of Business Research*, **52** (2), 203–10.

Shenkar, O. (1994), 'The People's Republic of China: raising the bamboo screen through international management research', *International Studies of Management and Organization*, **24** (1–2), 9–34.

Sonobe, T., D. Hu and K. Otsuka (2002), 'Process of cluster formation in China: a case study of a garment town', *Journal of Development Studies*, **39** (1), 118–39.

Stening, B.W. and M.Y. Zhang (2007), 'Methodological challenges when conducting management research in China', *International Journal of Cross Cultural Management*, **7** (1), 121–42.

Sun, L. (2003), 'Women zai kaishi miandui yige duanlie de shehui' ['Are we beginning to confront a fractured society?'], available at: http://www.sociology.cass.cn/pws/sunliping/grwj_sunliping/t20031008_1192.htm (accessed 6 October 2010).

Tan, H. (2000), 'Multinational corporations' knowledge transfer in China: a multiple-case investigation of two industries', PhD thesis, University of Bath.

Tan, J. and R.J. Litschert (2006), 'Environment–strategy relationship and its performance implications: an empirical study of the Chinese electronics industry', *Strategic Management Journal*, **15** (1), 1–20.

Tsui, A.S. (2004), 'Contributing to global management knowledge: a case for high quality indigenous research', *Asia Pacific Journal of Management*, **21** (4), 491–513.

Tsui, A. (2006), 'Editorial: contextualization in Chinese management research', *Management and Organization Review*, **2** (1), 1–13.

US–China Economic and Security Review Commission (USCC) (2009), '2009 Report to Congress of the US–China Economic and Security Review Commission', available at: http://www.uscc.gov/annual_report/2009/annual_report_full_09.pdf (accessed 4 January 2010).

Walder, A.G. (1995), 'Local governments as industrial firms: an organizational analysis of China's transitional economy', *American Journal of Sociology*, **101** (2), 263–301.

Welch, C. and R. Piekkari (2006), 'Crossing language boundaries: qualitative interviewing in international business', *Management International Review*, **46** (4), 417–37.

White, S. (2002), 'Rigor and relevance in Asian management research: where are we and where can we go?', *Asia Pacific Journal of Management*, **19**, 287–352.

Xin, K. and J. Pearce (1996), 'Guanxi: connections as substitutes for formal institutional support', *Academy of Management Journal*, **39** (6), 1641–58.

Yan, A. and B. Gray (1994), 'Bargaining power, management control, and performance in United States–China joint ventures: a comparative case study', *Academy of Management Journal*, **37** (6), 1478–517.

Yang, M. (1994), *Gifts, Favors and Banquets: The Art of Social Relationships in China*, Ithaca, NY and London: Cornell University Press.

Yin, R.K. (2009), *Case Study Research: Design and Methods*, 4th edn, Thousand Oaks, CA: Sage.

25. Conducting processual studies in transition economies: reflections on a case study

Martin Johanson

INTRODUCTION: IN SEARCH OF A CASE

Picture the following scenario: early one morning a rather new doctoral student drove to an airport close to Stockholm. The spring had just begun to blossom and everyone was beginning to dream about the forthcoming summer. The student took off for Kaliningrad from Bromma airport with some colleagues in a small four-seater aircraft. After touching down on the island of Gotland in the middle of the Baltic Sea for refuelling, they arrived in rainy Kaliningrad. It was 1995 and the transition to a market economy in Russia had been ongoing for some years, but Kaliningrad, squeezed between Poland and Belarus, was still virgin land for Westerners.

The Swedish International Development Cooperation Agency (SIDA) had decided to support several Swedish consultants in their attempts to reconstruct a handful of former state-owned but recently privatized Russian firms in the Kaliningrad district. The administration in the district had chosen the firms that were to take part in the project, and the doctoral student was commissioned to visit three firms located in Kaliningrad to collect data and prepare a brief report on each of them. This information was to be the basis for the next step in the consulting project. The doctoral student also nurtured hopes that one of these three firms would be interested in participating in his dissertation. The firms were Kvarts, Fakel and Mikrodvigatel. The first two were based in the city of Kaliningrad, whereas Mikrodvigatel was located in Gusev, a town a few hours' drive from Kaliningrad.

Kvarts, which comprised a large number of different types of operation, was the first to be studied. The doctoral student spent one-and-a-half days walking around the firm with the 'shadow' he had been allocated. Everyone met the student with suspicion, but since the managing director had given his approval they all had to speak with him. Kvarts had one predominant customer during the Soviet era – the Soviet defence ministry – but after the collapse of the Soviet empire it had lost the major part of its sales. Kvarts's two most important business areas had been the production of computers and coatings, but due to the greatly decreased volume of military orders, two previously 'inessential' parts of the business – the production of wood packages for computers and the firm's construction department – had since become critical to Kvarts's existence. A newly opened retail shop, which in principle sold everything from food to stationery, was also an important source of income. Above all, Kvarts was extremely diversified: kindergartens, hotels, holiday camps and *kolkhozes* (collective farms) could all be found under the Kvarts umbrella.

The next day the doctoral student and his shadow went to Gusev, where representatives from Mikrodvigatel welcomed him with a table groaning with vodka bottles and ham sandwiches. The firm produced electronic micro motors and had only two types of customer: the military and sewing machine manufacturers. The firm, which had about two to three thousand employees, was in a miserable condition and the staff worked only two or three days per week. The buildings, which were in a state of extreme disrepair, had been erected by the Germans before the Second World War when the region was still part of eastern Prussia, where Königsberg, renamed Kaliningrad after the war, was the capital. During the last few years, sales had decreased by 60 to 70 per cent. On the day of the visit, the firm was closed but about 10 people had come to the factory exclusively to meet with the doctoral student. With the help of large quantities of vodka and sandwiches, an atmosphere of trust and openness emerged. At a level of detail too technically complicated even for the doctoral student, the managing director described how the firm's motors were used in Soviet submarines, and talked about some of the gigantic projects the firm had planned in order to survive. Among other things, he had plans to build an international airport on one of the firm's sites. A few hours later and still a little tipsy, the doctoral student fell backwards into the car and took solace in the fact that Gusev was a place he did not have to go to again in his lifetime.

On the third day, he was driven to Fakel, the pride of Kaliningrad. Fakel actually supplied only the defence and space industry, and after a few minutes of discussion with the manager of the foreign trade department, the doctoral student realized that it would be impossible to obtain any kind of useful information. The manager's stock answer to almost all questions was 'I can unfortunately not tell you that', and the student never got close to the firm's operations (and, in fact, never got beyond the plastic-coated fabric sofa in Fakel's plain entrance). Even though – after perhaps the one hundredth 'I can unfortunately not tell you that' – the manager suddenly suggested that they go out and have a look at the firm, the student was ultimately led to the parking lot. Once there, the manager briefly began to tell the student about the firm's departments, and then took him with a firm hand around the walls surrounding the plant. They plodded through muddy fields around the fortress while talking about what lay behind the high, anonymous walls of the building. Long before his excursion was finished – it did not take long, despite the mud – the student realized that neither his research nor the project's ideas about reconstruction had any future at Fakel. The next day, the group returned home to Sweden over a windy Baltic Sea.

RESEARCH CONTEXT

The student was myself; I remember this trip to Kaliningrad, which took place in spring 1995, as one of the low points in my quest to conduct doctoral research in Russia. To me, the experience typifies the challenges of doing research in a country that has not thrown off its culture of secrecy. Unfortunately, I did not leave the frustration in Kaliningrad; combined with a growing feeling of desperation, it followed me for over a year. My search for a case study took place in Russia at a time when the country was undergoing an extensive and difficult transition from a planned to a market economy. The purpose of this chapter is to share some of the experiences gained from conducting processual studies in this type of economy. The fact is that a 'normal' market in today's global economy is not one characterized by stability and maturity – it is not industrialized and does not have mature institutions in place. Instead, today's typical market is characterized by turmoil, institutional changes, transition from a planned system to some kind of market system, and extensive social and political transformation that is often characterized by a transition from dictatorship to an emergent democratic system. These economies and markets are important, as they represent a large portion of the global economy. While countries like Brazil, Russia, India and China are undeniably transition economies and emerging markets, almost all of Central and Eastern Europe, the remaining 14 former republics of the Soviet Union, as well as several other countries in Africa, Asia and Latin America also fall into this category.

Given this, one can easily argue that these markets are undergoing a complex process that consists of not just a beginning and an end, but also a long period of interrelated sequences and phases. This means that, if we want to increase our understanding of what is happening in these economies and markets, we need a method for capturing this complex process, or at least some aspects of it. Transition implies institutional changes, but also social, cultural and economic changes that do not take place overnight; it is rather an extended process of intertwined events, people, decisions and actions that takes place over time. In this chapter, I aim to reflect on the methodological approach I have developed, in the hope that it may suit (or at least inform) other studies of transition economies and emerging markets. Perhaps those who follow in my footsteps will be better equipped and can avoid my mistakes.

THE SEARCH CONTINUES

My search for suitable case companies actually started before my trip to Kaliningrad. I had already conducted my first interview in June 1990, and subsequently interviewed 10 representatives of Swedish firms that had formed joint ventures in the Soviet Union. I formally commenced my PhD in spring 1991, but interrupted my studies soon thereafter to take up the position of vice-consul at the Consulate General of Sweden in St Petersburg. I served at the consulate from August 1991 to October 1993, and was responsible for covering economic and political developments, as well as monitoring Swedish aid in the region. As an illustration of how dynamic and turbulent this period was, both my arrival and departure were accompanied by failed *coups d'état.*

My responsibilities at the consulate frequently put me in the company of politicians, journalists and businesspeople. From these experiences, a conviction gradually evolved that it would be possible to commercialize the knowledge and the contacts I had acquired. Together with two partners, I founded a consulting firm in St Petersburg, with Swedish firms and organizations forming the majority of our customer base. From January 1994 to April 1996 I visited about 100 Russian firms and met, interviewed and spoke with at least double that number of Russian businesspeople working on various projects. At the time, I believed that these experiences gave me a unique platform for conducting empirical studies in an economy undergoing an interesting transition.

The trip to Kaliningrad in 1995 was undertaken in connection with a project financed by the European Bank for Reconstruction and Development (EBRD). The Swedish Management Institute (IFL) ran the project together with the consultancy firm Interconsult, and initially had two counterparts in Kaliningrad and Karelia: KIBS and KarelNOK, respectively. These were small and newly founded organizations, with the aim of training representatives from the industry in those regions. The intention was to transfer IFL's knowledge of management training to small and medium-sized firms, thereby achieving two goals: training employees in various industries within the regions, and contributing to the development of KIBS and KarelNOK as institutions. My participation in the project was somewhat sporadic until autumn 1996, when Interconsult left the project and SIDA replaced EBRD as the financiers. The project expanded to eventually include six additional regions.

The reason for describing this project at some length is that I made numerous attempts to turn firms related to it into case studies for my PhD research. All of these attempts failed. In April 1996, I went to St Petersburg to interview two firms. With the help of a structured interview guide, the first two interviews were conducted with the managing director and the head of the purchasing department at Ulitsa Sofii. The interviews were a catastrophe, and provided me with nothing beyond the lessons learned from the experience itself. First, the interview guide was too complicated – the number of questions had to be reduced and the guide had to be less detailed. Second, my behaviour had to change. I could not start by bombarding the interviewee with questions about details of customers, suppliers, volumes, investments, products and so on. Rather, I had to build up a pleasant atmosphere in which I could gradually encourage the interviewees to share their experiences and opinions.

After revising the interview guide, on the following day I met the managing director for Interbusiness, which was intended to be the second case in the study. The interview guide and my behaviour had changed, producing good results; the managing director even gave me a contact in an additional firm, Luga UPP. During the interview with Interbusiness, the quantitative questions were mingled with qualitative ones. The first 10 to 20 minutes were crucial for establishing an atmosphere of trust and comfort. Moreover, I realized that silence had to be used more extensively as an interview tool, as it stimulated the interviewees to speak.

From St Petersburg I went to Petrozavodsk, where a contact was waiting for me. The aim was to use the revised questionnaire and undertake interviews with representatives from three firms: DOK, NPO-Tsentr and Scorpio. The results were mixed: the interviews with DOK representatives produced excellent results, while Scorpio's representative never even came to the meeting. My Russian contact then managed to persuade the managing director and marketing director of the local liquor and vodka factory to participate in the project. Early on, however, it was evident that it was not a traditional interview, but rather a more general conversation about the business climate, which meant that the factory was removed from the list of possible participants. In the interview at NPO-Tsentr, the managing director and owner avoided several questions, and I suspected that it would be difficult to undertake further interviews with the company.

Before I left Petrozavodsk, my local contact found Scorpio's managing director and we were able to complete an interview of high quality; while we only partially followed the interview guide, the interviewee did his best to be open and tell us as much as possible.

In May 1996, a professor at St Petersburg State University arranged two interviews. Together with one of her doctoral students, I interviewed the marketing director at the brewery Baltika, a Finnish–Russian–Swedish joint venture. As my focus was on firms without foreign capital and management, this did not conform to my framework. However, I decided to be pragmatic and the interview was successful, although the interviewee did not have the required quantitative data. Another interview had been arranged for the following morning at ORS, the purchasing firm that supplied the Russian railway's trains and stations with food, beverages, newspapers and other sundries. Interestingly, the largest supplier to ORS was Baltika. The interview with the representative of ORS was good, but unfortunately, further cooperation with the professor came to nothing after she moved to Moscow.

I returned to Petrozavodsk in November 1996 to complete further interviews at DOK, NPO-Tsentr and Scorpio. At this time, a major difference was that IFL's training programme had since finished, with the result that NPO-Tsentr immediately declined further interviews. DOK and Scorpio, however, welcomed us and we also undertook an interview with the founder and owner of an additional firm, MVduet. The interview was of good quality, but my Petrozavodsk contact left the city shortly thereafter. Once the IFL project wound up the following year I was informed that further interviews would not be possible.

A CASE FINDS A RESEARCHER

Fortunately, by this stage another prospect had firmed up. In the spring of 1995, just before the trip to Kaliningrad, a Swedish firm called Accurat contacted me. Accurat had just established contacts with the printing house Tipografiya in the city of Novgorod. An ambition to create a joint venture had gradually emerged, and Accurat was interested in utilizing my skills as a consultant in the project they were running. Thus a new phase of my PhD quest began. In September 1996, Tipografiya was within a year of celebrating its 220th anniversary. It had for a long time been located in the central area of the city of Novgorod, situated about 200 kilometres from St Petersburg and 500 kilometres from Moscow – generally considered a geographically advantageous position. Over the last 10 years, the Novgorod district has experienced relatively positive economic development compared to almost the whole of the rest of Russia. In 1992 the region ranked low in terms of investment potential (63rd out of 89 districts), but by 1997 had moved up to sixth place after seeing significant success in attracting foreign capital. That year, the Novgorod region had attracted 2.5 per cent of Russia's total foreign capital investment, and since it represented only 0.5 per cent of the total Russian population, Novgorod ranked second in terms of per capita investment. The region also encouraged small business development and tried to attract domestic capital, but without the same striking results. Nevertheless, during the 1990s the Novogorod district experienced positive economic development compared to other parts of Russia (Ruble and Popson 1998).

While I was actually seeking more than one case for this study, after a search lasting several years and interviews with a total of 14 firms, I was left with Tipografiya. This long process of case selection did have some benefits. The formal interviews and many discussions with company representatives deepened my knowledge of the Russian transition to a market economy. I also gained valuable experience in the art of interviewing in Russia, where interviewees were not used to participating in interviews, and were often unwilling to do so. All too often, the risks attached to doing any given interview were seen to outweigh any potential rewards.

It is difficult to find firms in Russia that are actually interested in participating in research, but even when a firm has been found, problems continue. One such problem is the difficulty of gaining access to interviewees, an essential element in empirical studies. Access refers to the possibility of meeting with and interviewing people who have information that is of value to the study. There were no major problems with access at Tipografiya; the problems were that the interviewees did not want to, could not, or did not dare provide access to the required information. Long questions and short answers (often combined with bad temper) characterize a poor interview, and this was something that also occurred at Tipografiya. A key part of processual studies is being able to follow the subject over time – that is, having constant access to the interviewee and information – which is made more challenging in such a rapidly changing environment. In several cases (such as with Baltika, DOK, Interbusiness, Luga UPP, MVduet, ORS and Scorpio) the reason for not completing more interviews was the lack of opportunity for repeated access – interviewees and information were not available on more than one or two occasions.

I played the dual role of consultant and researcher while I was involved with Tipografiya. Accurat (not Tipografiya) needed and financed my role in the consulting project. Since the aim was not to change or influence Tipografiya's operations, I was not engaged in action research. I was not commissioned to perform that task, nor was it a task I set for myself. Instead, I had two other responsibilities. The first was to analyse Tipografiya from a broad perspective, to inform Accurat, and to write reports based on these analyses. Specific emphasis was placed on understanding Tipografiya's marketing and purchasing operations. My second role was as a kind of cultural interpreter, and Accurat often consulted me before important decisions were made concerning difficult problems. On some occasions I even translated and interpreted. All other activities I undertook were aimed at the collection of data for my dissertation. Tipografiya and its management knew of my dual role and were informed that all data would be used for two purposes: a consultancy report and a dissertation. In addition, each interviewee was informed about my role at the initial interview. Tipografiya had already provided its verbal approval in September 1996.

The purpose of the original contact made between Accurat and Tipografiya, which occurred during a trade exhibition in Finland, was to transfer knowledge and expertise through training, and then to extend this by forming a joint venture. My personal impression is that Tipografiya, beyond the stated purpose of the partnership, also tried to achieve one more objective within the framework of the project – namely to find, through Accurat, a new printing press that could be financed by non-Russian financiers. Accurat also entertained hopes of finding a new export market. It is worth emphasizing that only by participating in the project as a consultant was I given the opportunity to collect such a quantity of data; one could even say that without the project there would have been no dissertation. However, my work on the project was not regulated by any formal contract and the tasks were not specified in any kind of documents.

The firm that turned out to be my case study, Tipografiya, corresponds quite well with two of the requirements usually believed to be suitable for a case study: the unique and significant subject, and the revelatory case study (Yin 2009). The case of Tipografiya represented a phenomenon which, at that time, had been sparsely studied but was still of such importance that it deserved to be studied. Moreover, Tipografiya represented an opportunity to observe and understand a previously inaccessible subject.

THE UNIT OF ANALYSIS IN TRANSITION

Rather than representing the end of the process, identifying a case was just the beginning; my next step was to define the unit of analysis. This is never definitive for a case study, but is something that the researcher defines recurrently, meaning that a unit of analysis is always preliminary. It is the unit of analysis that, in the end, becomes the case. While the unit of analysis can be a firm, a department, a person, a market, a product, or a technology, since my focus was on understanding the process a critical step of the study was to identify the unit of analysis in its process of change. This could be done in two ways. One was to let the unit emerge: patterns and similarities in the collected data allow the researcher to see boundaries that could make up the unit of analysis. As the researcher follows the unit of analysis over time, some things change while other things remain the same. Another way of defining the unit of analysis, which I ultimately adopted, is to let theory determine the unit of analysis, which could be done by departing from one or more key concepts in an existing model or theory. I decided to apply a network perspective, partly because I worked in an environment where this perspective dominated, and partly because existing studies on the Russian and the Soviet economy tended to be empirically weak but relatively strong when it came to the crucial role of relationships and networks. By making this decision I could keep the theoretical instrument constant, which, in the context of a processual study in a turbulent economy, is beneficial to the researcher.

Since I chose to follow change over time, the unit of analysis was put into a process. One method for defining a process is to view it as a sequence of individual and collective events, actions and activities that develop over time in a specific context (Van de Ven 1992; Pettigrew 1997). Thus, the term 'process' does not necessarily mean that everything is changing: inertia, stability and things being constant over time are as much ingredients of a process as are dynamism, change and modifications. One process can be linear, directional, cumulative and irreversible, while another can be non-linear, radical and transformational. While it is clear that both time and history are of crucial importance, the result of the process and the process itself are of interest. Thus, a process takes place over time, but does so in the context in which it is embedded. This makes both the context – in terms of structure, environment, organization or, as in my case, a business network – and the process key. As such, once I had found Tipografiya, I had to define the context that would be in focus and how I should study it; that is, I had to identify the unit of analysis in the context of change.

As I was looking for categories, my aim was not to produce a case history or a narrative, but rather a case study that could help me understand the process and be able to compare the nature of three types of networks: planned networks, transition networks and market networks. These aims correspond with Pettigrew's ideas (1997) about the advantages of a case study, which reach beyond the limits of a case history in three aspects: (i) the researcher seeks patterns in the process and tries to compare case A with case B; (ii) the researcher tries to find the underlying

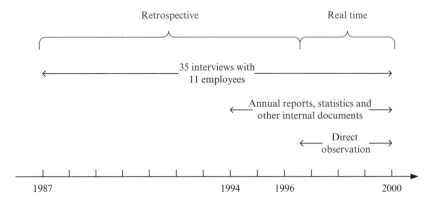

Figure 25.1   Data collection from 1987 to 2000

mechanisms that create patterns in the process; and (iii) the main factor
that turns a case history into a case study is that the exploratory inductive
search for patterns goes hand in hand with more deductive verification.

The aim of my research project was to explain the links between context
and results in this process and how and why they developed. If one aims
to understand a process over time, the data collected must represent the
period as much as possible, which means that the researcher can either retrospectively collect data about what happened during the process, or try to
collect data in real time as the process happens. Finally, one can combine
these two approaches, which ultimately became my own approach (Figure
25.1). I conducted interviews, used documentary sources and made direct
observations in real time from 1996 to 2000. The period before this (that
is, between 1994 and 1996) was studied in retrospect through interviews
and documentary sources, while data prior to 1994 could only be collected
via interviews.

One of the most striking effects that time has on people is the quest to
turn the uncertain into the certain. Although the future is clearly unknow-
able, people make forecasts based on guesses and beliefs, which guide their
behaviour and strategies. At the same time, people try to make things that
have already happened comprehensible, and do this by establishing logical
chains of events. The processual researcher must manage this tension
between the past, present and future; this is the reason why processual
studies have a function to fulfil, and is necessary if one seeks to understand
how phenomena evolve over time. The tension between the unpredictable
future and the already interpreted, established and categorized past is the
processual study's core, and the more the processual researcher is able to
study process in real time, the more he/she is able to capture this tension.

A processual study that follows the unit of analysis in time is stronger than a processual study that is retrospective in character, as it is better equipped to capture the tension and entails a smaller likelihood for *ex post* rationalization, simplifications and linear reasoning. A processual analysis is needed if one seeks to understand the process, not only in terms of what takes place over a specific period, but also in terms of the dynamic that exists in the tension between the past, present and future.

This is exactly what makes everything that takes place in a transition economy so difficult to analyse and understand, but also makes the process itself tricky to plan and the results problematic to predict. The unit of analysis I had decided to define was the firm, Tipografiya, and its relationships with its most important customers and suppliers. The unit of analysis, therefore, was an inter-firm network with a focal firm. A network is not reality, but a theoretical concept; however, I needed grounding in theory to identify it in reality. Moreover, I had to follow the process as it was changing. I did this by taking three steps.

Step 1: Quantitative Mapping of the Firm's Network

The purpose of the initial interviews at the majority of the firms interviewed was to map the network structure within which Tipografiya had operated during recent years. The structure was quantitatively mapped using a structured questionnaire. Step 1 allowed me to identify Tipografiya's most important relationships. A secondary purpose of this step was to study Tipografiya's organization: its formal structure, ownership, financial status, the number of employees that worked there, and their tasks and authority.

Step 2: The Qualitative Mapping of the Firm's Network

As this was a case study based on qualitative data, after the first step I had to populate the network with real information. I also gathered information on the resources used in the relationships. Tipografiya's relationships with its customers and suppliers were the objects and I was looking for data concerning different types of activities such as manufacturing, warehousing, investments, payment, communication and transportation. During this step I used a static approach and was not explicitly interested in how and why the relationships changed, but rather in how they were working at that time. The aim was to draw a picture of how Tipografiya operated and related to its customers and suppliers. Open-ended questions were mixed with more concrete and specific questions. Examples of these open-ended questions included: 'Tell me more about it', 'How?', 'What do you mean by that?', 'Last time, you mentioned . . . could you tell me more

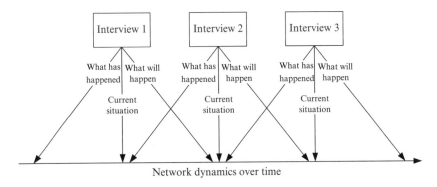

Figure 25.2 Interview strategy to capture the dynamics of the network

about that?' Once Steps 1 and 2 were complete, it was time to go forwards and backwards in time.

Step 3: Investigation of Dynamics and Change in the Firm's Network

The aim of Step 3 was to grasp the dynamics of the network. In this step, I focused on both change and stability, with the main purpose being to identify the driving forces in these processes. As this is the main component of the processual study I conducted, this also took the most time. This step consisted of two approaches. The first covered the period from 1985 to 1996 and was studied in retrospect. In this respect, the most difficult part of this approach was stimulating the interviewees to remember information and details while simultaneously trying to avoid influencing them. The second approach also aimed to capture the dynamics of the network, but as this could be done in real time, by conducting interviews over time, and through visual observation over time, it had a somewhat different character.

Each interview during this step aimed to cover the past, present and future situations in the network, and began with a set of questions about how the interviewees perceived the current state (see Interview 2 in Figure 25.2). The second set of questions concerned how the interviewee perceived what had happened in the network since the previous interview – a kind of historical 'flashback'. Finally, the third set of questions concerned the future of the network, as I strived to get a picture of what would happen in the network, what problems and opportunities the interviewee anticipated, and how he or she expected to act in response.

By consistently applying this strategy to each interview, I was able to collect data on how the interviewees experienced the process, since the first and second set of questions could later be compared and analysed in relation to what the interviewee predicted about the future during previous interviews. Through this process, I patched together the data that were collected, including where each interview overlapped with other interviews, and in the end had an empirical picture of the unit of analysis in change.

SOME CONSIDERATIONS WHEN DESIGNING A PROCESSUAL STUDY

Interplay was a key concept that guided my case study project. Interplay can take place in three different ways: between theory and empirical data, between two or more cases, and between different data sources. While I did not incorporate the interplay of two or more cases, as I shall now explain, the other two forms of interplay were important to my project.

Interplay between Theory and Empirical Data

Interplay between theory and empirical data is not a linear research process in which one starts with either theory or data and, once finished with one, continues with the other. This approach differs from both the traditional inductive and deductive methods. Going back and forth from theory to data creates the interplay, the continuous comparisons and combinations of the two, which is a critical activity. Confrontation between theory and data is frequent and mutual (Dubois and Gadde 2002), and the research process is not made up of two distinct phases. I decided to apply a network approach to my firm and its business partners, but once this decision was made the whole process became a continuous interplay. For instance, each time I thought I had observed something that I could not put under any theoretical concept, I went back to the literature and tried to find pieces of conceptual thinking that fit what I had observed. In my case, this meant that the network approach was increasingly complemented by other theories, such as organizational learning and entrepreneurship.

However, existing theories could not offer sufficient intellectual support. I therefore had to partially develop concepts specifically for this study that required more data collection than already existing concepts – since the new concepts had to be approached from various angles and be sufficiently deep and sophisticated. As such, the main focus of the latter interviews was on collecting data that could confirm these new concepts, and data that could help build theoretical arguments for their existence and function. In this analytical interplay, the most important instruments were a pair of scissors and a highlighter, as I cut the interview transcripts into pieces and assembled quotes that consisted of both old and new concepts.

Interplay between Data Sources

Perhaps the most critical characteristic of processual data is its rich-ness, and combining different approaches to data collection provides the researcher with the possibility of achieving this richness of data. Within the boundaries of the unit of analysis, there is an advantage in collecting a vast volume of data, since it makes it more likely that the data will be heterogeneous. Different data sources help the researcher do this; indeed, both Eisenhardt (1989) and Yin (2009) argue for the use of several data sources. Deeper, wider and richer material makes observations more reliable, particularly if several sources provide similar evidence. It is also likely that one data source helps the researcher collect data and make observations that could not have happened using another data source. Moreover, as learning and discovering previously unknown phenomena is an important element in the process, it is not only legitimate to vary and add methods during the process of data collection – it is necessary if the researcher is to reach a better understanding of the studied phenomenon.

Three methods were used in the Tipografiya study: direct observa-tions, documentation and interviews, although the last was dominant. In reality, using direct observations never constituted a conscious method for data collection. However, during my time at Tipografiya, I had complete freedom to walk around, to study the building and equipment, and to have short conversations with the employees. As such, there is no doubt that the direct observations influenced the data collection. It was, however, some-thing that emerged gradually, rather than a conscious choice of method. The excursions mainly took place on two occasions, in September 1996 and August 1999. I did not take notes or keep records during my walk around the firm, but the observations were filed as memories and impres-sions. For example, one thing that struck me during these visits was the age of the equipment and how dirty and worn the premises were. While unstructured and opportunistic, observations such as these were impor-tant for strengthening conclusions reached from my interviews.

One of the most striking observations was how the second floor (where the relief printing shop was and where the composition for relief printing took place), which had been the most intensively active area in September 1996, was almost devoid of people in August 1999. Moreover, computer-ized typesetting had extended its territory significantly since 1996. Other observations included various deficits, such as the lack of a common-room for employees, the absence of regular meetings and a formal process for communicating information to employees, and limited contacts between different departments.

Although analysis of documentary sources was not the predominant method, some documents were important for my work. As opposed to direct observation, using documentary sources was a conscious strategy. Scott (1990) identifies four criteria for assessing documents, and these are taken as a point of departure for the following discussion about the documents used in this study. Two types of documents were used. The first type was different kinds of statistics mainly intended for internal use at Tipografiya, and these documents were used most extensively. I was sometimes given photocopies of the originals; other times I received typewritten copies of the statistics I needed. The second type of documents consisted of photocopies of Tipografiya's annual reports, which were only used as background material.

Scott's first assessment criterion is authenticity, which refers to the genuineness of the document – whether the document is actually what it purports to be. In the case of the statistics, two of the interviewees provided them to me. Scott mentions soundness as a component of the document's authenticity, referring to the documents not having been corrupted or damaged, or being incomplete in some way. Authorship is the other important component of the concept of authenticity. In this case, authenticity was confirmed by the fact that these were internal documents compiled by members of Tipografiya's staff for use by the firm.

Scott discussed credibility as the second criterion, and it has two main components. The first is sincerity, and Scott indicates that particular attention should be paid to material interests and incentives. Uncertainty prevails around the sincerity of the documents I used because of the way that statistics in many Russian firms were typically produced at the time. During the era of economic planning, Russian firms strived to produce statistics that fulfilled the instructions of central planning authorities, even though such reports did not reflect reality. Without suspecting Tipografiya of wrongdoing, I believe that Russian firms today are struggling to portray their firms in their annual reports in a similar way – only this time it is done to lower their tax burdens. The second component mentioned by Scott is accuracy. The authors of these documents were directly involved in their production and had several years of experience working with these kinds of documents. Moreover, most of them were also involved in the events and processes which were featured in the documents. My impression is that these individuals were both accurate and trustworthy. An important point to be made here is that the documents were not prepared just for me but partly because they were required by the authorities, and partly because they were used to inform management decisions. This was an important observation for me, since the purpose of this study was not to analyse statistics, but rather to analyse and understand the firm's behaviour.

Scott's third criterion is representativeness (survival and availability). With two exceptions, I received all of the documents that I required. I was interested in gaining access to quantitative data from the periods both before and after 1992. During the first interview in September 1996, I had already been told that all statistics older than three years had been viewed as obsolete and therefore destroyed. Consequently, I would only have access to statistics from 1993 onwards. The second setback came a little later when I was informed that it was too difficult to prepare statistics about what I called 'other customers'. I could not get any information about these customers for the period after 1996.

Scott divides the meaning of documents – his fourth criterion – into two parts: one literal and one interpretative. As the documents only contained figures, it is difficult to question their literal meaning. I did not actively and formally interpret the documents. They were not coded, but formed a background and a point of departure for the interviews (which I did interpret). Ultimately, the 35 interviews I conducted with Tipografiya employees constituted the major data source. I now turn to this process.

Conversation Strategies in Transition Economies

Spontaneous and semi-structured interviews with people directly or indirectly involved in the process helps achieve data richness, since the richness comes from people's willingness to share experience and opinions – which is more likely to occur when the interviewee trusts the interviewer. Such interviews often take the form of a conversation (Kvale 1997), which tends to result in qualitative data. While the aim was not to quantify objective data at Tipografiya, it is important to underline that conversations did not exclude quantitative data. The goal of my study was to arrive at spontaneous descriptions about the unit of analysis with the aim of interpreting the meaning of the described phenomena, which means that they were neither completely open and unstructured conversations, and nor did they strictly follow a structure specified in advance (Kvale 1997).

At a minimum, before each conversation I tried to have an idea about a tentative unit of analysis and a set of subjects that the conversation should cover. The more conversations that were conducted, the less tentative and more defined the unit of analysis became, and the more specific the subjects were. Thus, the conversations contained topics and subjects rather than conventional questions, and were not only descriptive in nature, but also aimed at encouraging interviewees to share their stories spontaneously

(Kvale 1997). However, one has to underline that this type of conversation had a focus and a subject, which I have already discussed. The interviews at Tipografiya mostly resulted in words rather than figures, and their focus was on specifics. As such, I tried to encourage the interviewees to describe specific situations and courses of events in their world.

An interview either has an exploratory purpose or aims to test a hypothesis (Kvale 1997). The present study had exploratory aims, and as such I was open to unexpected answers and explanations. Kvale established six quality criteria for an interview. First, it should be spontaneous, rich and specific. Second, it should be characterized by short questions and long answers. Third, the interviewer should follow up and clarify the meaning of the answers during the interview. Fourth, the interviewer should form and, fifth, verify these interpretations during the interview. Finally, the interview should be 'self-communicating', in that it should stand on its own as a story worth reading.

Based on these criteria, there were two reasons for my difficulties in conducting the interviews. Most significantly, all of my interviewees tended to answer my questions directly rather than tell me stories as a result of my questions. This forced me to be more active and made it more difficult to fulfil Kvale's first two criteria. This may have been due to the interviewees' lack of experience with or exposure to interviews, or perhaps their unwillingness to provide me with information. After all, there was nothing to gain from telling a rich and open story. The difficulty in satisfying the remaining four criteria rested with me. The fact that all the interviews were conducted in Russian precluded the qualities described in the first and second criteria, along with the clarification of the meaning of the answers, interpretation, and verification of the interpretation during the interviews as required by the third, fourth and fifth criteria.

In hindsight, I believe that the quality of the interviews in the form of conversations was a result of a combination of experience, craftsmanship and luck. These features are always important, but especially in these contexts. In general, there are four tactics concerning the structuring of a conversation that I would consider make up craftsmanship in this context:

1. *Building trust, then collecting data* Interviewees from transition economies usually lack experience in being interviewed and show a general level of distrust towards people who are unknown to them or with whom they do not have any direct or indirect social connections. Moreover, most people are also afraid to share information and experiences, as they do not know how it will be used. The quality and the quantity of data collected during a conversation are almost completely dependent on the researcher's ability to demonstrate that

he or she is trustworthy. Therefore the researcher has a lot to gain by initially focusing on building trust rather than obtaining answers to questions.

2. *Moving from the general and non-personal to the personal and specific* Usually people prefer to talk about themselves through discussions about how others think and behave. It is therefore an advantage to begin an interview by talking about other people – what do other people think about specific phenomena and how do they behave? Answers to these types of questions help the researcher and interviewee develop mutual trust and build a platform for the rest of the conversation.

3. *Moving from listening to asking* A conversation is better when the researcher is more silent and allows the interviewee to tell his or her story. However, the interviewee always has an agenda and specific objectives for the conversation. While it is better if the interviewee spontaneously realizes the researcher's intentions and objectives of the conversation, this is seldom the case. Instead, the researcher has to help the interviewee understand the goals of the conversation; this is achieved by gradually asking questions more actively. This means that the researcher's two most important virtues are the ability to ask few, but good questions and, when not asking questions, the ability to remain silent.

4. *From non-sensitive to sensitive* As already indicated, suspicion characterizes the beginning of most conversations with strangers. People are sometimes afraid or simply shy, which makes them reluctant to talk about sensitive things. However, since the interviewee may perceive many of the subjects the researcher is interested in as sensitive, the researcher must manage this conflict. Reducing suspicion is directly related to the degree of mutual trust; as trust gradually emerges the researcher can gradually ask increasingly sensitive questions.

SOME FINAL OBSERVATIONS AND CONCLUDING REMARKS

While all of this suggests that I undertook a very systematic, deliberate and conscious research process, it is only in hindsight that I now understand what I did. As I was doing it, I was sailing on a sea of uncertainty, and was just trying to hold onto the mast. This uncertainty was partly a result of the context, and partly a consequence of my theoretical and empirical ambitions.

The challenges of context have been highlighted in this chapter and did, of course, influence the possibility of fulfilling my goal of conducting a processual study. The Russian context affected not just the findings, but also the way the study was conducted. As I noted at the beginning of this chapter, I had significant problems gaining access, which forced me to be both open and flexible about the firm I could study, as well as what data sources could be used. Finding a case could be seen as a trial-and-error process in which, in the end, the case came to me once I was invited to work as a consultant at Tipografiya. Otherwise, this process was mostly dominated by errors and failures, and finding a case did not mean that my problems were over.

Rather, the uncertainty increased as I began to collect data. Some of the documents I needed had been destroyed, while the reliability of others could be (and had to be) questioned. Although I would never have been able to build a study based solely on these documents, when they were combined with the other data sources they made an important contribution to the whole set of collected data. They strengthened my observations during interviews and provided me with a lot of knowledge, making me feel safer. Having been there and having observed the people, having drunk tea and vodka with them, as well as having discussed political developments, made me feel more comfortable with what I later wrote about Tipografiya in various books and papers.

A specific problem was conducting interviews. This had several causes. First, most interviewees were unused to sharing information in general, particularly information that could be considered somewhat sensitive. This meant that most interviews were characterized by suspicion and therefore an unwillingness to answer questions. However, when the suspicion had been removed, a 'what's in it for me' atmosphere appeared instead. However, the general manager of Tipografiya helped manage the most difficult interview situations – he literally ordered his employees to participate in the interviews. A related problem was, of course, the language barrier, since the interviewees and I were from a different country and had a different mother tongue. These barriers were exacerbated by the fact that so many words, terms and concepts that I took for granted had different meanings in the interviewees' world – they had lived their whole lives in a planned economy and were raised with a different set of words and logic. While I was aware of this given my background as a diplomat and consultant, misunderstandings were common and I often had to spend a lot of time during the interviews explaining what I meant or what the words I used meant.

Finally, the problems with access and with the interviews were accompanied by a rapid change of not just the research object, but also the context in which I was supposed to be doing my job, as well as in the whole of Russian society. This concerned the people at Tipografiya, particularly the impact of this transition on their relationships to other firms and organizations, to laws and rules, and other factors. It also led to practical problems, such as with visas, passports, hotels, telephone communication, or transport; these problems cannot be underestimated as it made everything more time-consuming than I had expected.

On the other side of the uncertainty coin were my ambitions to conduct a processual study in this research context. I knew in advance that this was risky but I tried to handle this by being rigid in some aspects (for instance, in the choice of the theoretical framework) and being flexible and open in others (such as for things that happened during the process). This was combined with my ambition to perform the study during the period when the transition from a planned economy to a market economy was taking place. I was completely convinced that we were going through a unique process that would never be repeated. I had practised this approach in another study (for example, Johanson and Johanson 2006), but had now refined the research design. However, since I was interested in things that happened before I could begin to collect data, I could not do it in real time but only in retrospect.

I had the ambition of collecting a vast amount of data for two reasons. First, I thought that if I had a lot of data I would be able to use it for purposes other than my dissertation. Second, I was always interested in being able to tell a story, a narrative, or a fairytale about the transition to a planned economy. This ambition required richness of data; in this respect, I believed that I partially failed – ultimately, there was a lot of data, but not a sufficiently vast amount. However, while this project could be viewed as a failure as, in my eyes, I did not collect enough data, to a large extent it has transformed into a success: I defended my doctoral thesis and wrote several articles based on the study. But, today, many years after having started it, I am more than happy to leave it behind me and instead pursue new studies.

REFERENCES

Dubois, A. and L.E. Gadde (2002), 'Systematic combining: an abductive approach to case research', *Journal of Business Research*, **55** (7), 553–60.

Eisenhardt, K.M. (1989), 'Building theories from case study research', *Academy of Management Review*, **14** (4), 532–50.

Johanson, M. and J. Johanson (2006), 'Turbulence, discovery and foreign market entry: a longitudinal study of an entry into the Russian market', *Management International Review*, **46** (2), 179–205.

Kvale, S. (1997), *Den Kvalitativa Forskningsintervjun* [The Qualitative Research Interview], Lund: Studentlitteratur.

Pettigrew, A.M. (1997), 'What is a processual analysis?', *Scandinavian Journal of Management*, **13** (4), 337–48.

Ruble, B.A. and N. Popson (1998), 'The Westernization of a Russian province: the case of Novgorod', *Post-Soviet Geography and Economics*, **39** (8), 433–46.

Scott, J. (1990), *A Matter of Record*, Cambridge: Polity and Basil Blackwell.

Van de Ven, A.H. (1992), 'Suggestions for studying strategy processes: a research note', *Strategic Management Journal*, **13** (Summer), 169–88.

Yin, R.K. (2009), *Case Study Research: Design and Methods*, 4th edn, Thousand Oaks, CA: Sage.

Index